THE

William E. "Bill" Davidson Family

To Beverley my dear and lovely cousin. I have fond memories of your dad and you kids.

Donald H. Davidson
4-25-09

Cover: William E. "Bill" Davidson at his 100th birthday celebration.

Design by BookSurge

Printed in the United States of America

ISBN: 1-4392-1614-2
ISBN-13: 9781439216149

Visit www.booksurge.com to order additional copies.

The William E. "Bill" Davidson Family

The Life and Times of a Centenarian and His Family

Donald G. Davidson

ACKNOWLEDGMENTS

My many thanks go to several people who without their contributions I would never have been able to write this book. Betty Ramey, John Wallace Davidson's great granddaughter, provided information she had researched and collected over the years about our early family history. My Dad for his many and varied accounts and stories of his life. My Mom for leaving her writings about herself and her ancestors. My brothers, Bill and Sam, for taking the time to relate their experiences to me, and Sam's wife, Rowena, for providing written accounts of their lives. My brother Bob's children, Steve and Paula, for providing written accounts of Bob's life experiences. My sister, Ann, for providing written accounts of her life experiences some of which were narratives written by her husband, Fred. I am also grateful to Ann for proof reading my manuscript and making many suggestions most of which are incorporated herein. I'm also grateful to my cousin, Rose Edna French for providing the Clarke Family information, and to an Internet friend, Mary Stuart, for providing the Wainwright Family information. And, finally my wife, Pat, for being tolerant and supportive of my endeavor to write this book.

TABLE OF CONTENTS

INTRODUCTION

I have been interested in family genealogy and history for years. My interest was first piqued the summer of 1953 when I stayed with my Aunt Mary and Uncle Jim Dunahoo and Grandma and Grandpa Davidson in Kansas City. Grandpa was dying with cancer and needed close care. I worked nights so I could be with Grandma and Grandpa during the day while Jim and Mary were at work.

During those many hours I spent with Grandpa he talked a lot about many things including the family. He knew he was dying more than I realized. I listened to his many rambling reminiscences of family and events in his life, but I did not pay close attention or make notes.

Grandpa died that summer in August at age eighty. After the funeral I returned to school at Oklahoma A&M in Stillwater, Oklahoma. I busied myself with my studies, but haunting questions kept surfacing especially in my spare moments of relaxation and reflection. I tried to remember the details of Grandpa's stories, but mostly to no avail. From time to time I began to jot down what I could remember. I began to realize I knew very little about my ancestors. I also soon learned my siblings and cousins knew even less than I did.

After a while I began to ask questions of my other grandparents, my parents, my aunts, and my uncles. I bought a good reel-to-reel tape recorder. It was a lot of money for the day. The technology was primitive compared with today's technology. It was portable but very bulky and heavy weighing about forty-five pounds. I made a few tape recordings of interviews with various family members, but recording tapes were costly. I had very little money. The recorder was so bulky and heavy it was difficult to set up for a proper interview, and I wasn't very experienced as an interviewer. I still have some of the tapes which, if possible, I intend to convert some day to a more modern medium such as compact disk.

Years later after mother died I bought a video camcorder. I felt the same loss of family history as I did when Grandpa Davidson died. I flew to Phoenix and spent several days with Aunt Marge, mother's next younger sister, and video taped interviews with her. I later made videotapes of some of the Jones Family Reunions, and some really neat videos of Aunt Jewel, another of mother's sisters.

In the meantime I also got into family genealogy and attended several seminars. My initial approach was to just record pertinent genealogical information. I began to collect old letters, scraps of diaries, old newspaper clippings, old documents, etc. I attended Jones and Clarke Family Reunions and made notes. I accumulated a large amount of unorganized material and information.

About ten years ago I began to correspond with Betty Ramey, Dad's first cousin in California. Betty worked on Davidson history and genealogy for many years. She and I collaborated on the compilation of a John Wallace Davidson genealogical and history profile which was put in loose-leaf notebooks and sent to the genealogy libraries in Camden, Tennessee, and Hardy, Arkansas.

When Dad turned a hundred years of age, my wife, Pat, and I with help from my brother, Sam, and his wife, Rowena, organized and threw one fine party for him. To honor the occasion I did a history on Dad's life with a few old photographs. I gave copies to Dad, each of his five children, and to his grandchildren that attended the evening family dinner.

There came a time a few years ago when I said that if I ever intended to organize and present this information in a readable form for posterity I had better get off the dime and do it because I was beginning to see my own mortality looming on the distant horizon. Thus, began my effort to write this book.

There are two characteristics I have that need to be told before going forth with this effort to give a better insight and understanding into my psychic and reasons for this undertaking.

First, I have always been a vivid dreamer. Even as a child I had vivid dreams. I remember that sometimes I had bad dreams, but don't remember ever having horrible nightmares like some children. I usually dream in great detail. Other times my dreams are vague. I almost always dream in full color unless it is twilight, dusk or darkness. The grass is green, the water in the lake is blue, the rose in the garden is red. Sometimes it is twilight or night time in my dreams and the colors are either muted or tones of gray. I was thirty years old before I learned most people do not dream in color. I was astonished. What a shame!

Second, I have a good memory of actual events in my life. My earliest remembrance is when I was about three years old. I remember many events before I was six years old as well as numerous other events later in life.

My very earliest memory was February 1932 when I was three years and two months of age. I was staying with my Grandmother and Grandfather Roller. They lived on a farm along the banks of Panther Creek at the foot of The Table Hills in western Garvin County in Oklahoma. I remember the event but not the specific date. I remember the date only because years later my grandmother told me. I spent a lot of my childhood summers with my grandparents where I roamed the banks of Panther Creek and the breaks of The Table Hills.

I don't remember recent events quite so well. I remember things like the family phone number (5-5913) when I was five years old, or the phone number (WI3-3664) when I was a teenager. I remember the phone number (430-0146) when my wife and I lived years later at Bartonville.

I'm not as good with names and faces as with events. I remember names and faces but sometimes have trouble getting the right name to the right face. I remember the names of almost all my teachers from kindergarten through college.

I remember family occasions and other events throughout my life. I usually remember these with a great deal of detail. My brothers and sister think I'm a little weird, but they sometimes call me when they want to know who was where and when and doing what.

Well into adulthood I developed a keen interest in history and family genealogy. I am the self-appointed family historian and over the years have accumulated considerable information about our family. I finally decided to organize it and put it in a book.

I asked each of my siblings to write whatever they would like for me to include in a chapter on them. I never realized how difficult it would be to beg, plead, and cajole to get them to provide enough information to give a reasonable account of their lives. But, I finally prevailed after many long phone conversations, exchanges of correspondence, and written descriptive accounts of events.

This history is as comprehensive and inclusive as I could make it within reasonable time constraints and limited resources. I've worked on it off and on the past twenty years. There came a time when I had to say this is it and wrap it up. I've tried to be as factual and accurate as possible with several plausible scenarios about our early ancestry.

I know for certain that John Wallace Davidson is our ancestor. I am certain John and Mary Wallace Davidson are his parents. However, it is not known for certain who John's parents or Mary's parents are. There seems to be a likely Davidson sire lurking at every twist and turn in the genealogical forest. Therein lies the great mystery and much speculation.

This is a work of genealogy as well as family history. I don't expect most people will read this book from cover to cover. They will probably read only the parts that interest them the most. There are instances where the reader will find duplications of certain events that are described from the perspective of several different people. Also, some of the genealogical data will appear repeated in the various family descriptions.

What is lacking in professionalism is compensated by spirit. This has been a labor of love. I hope you and others enjoy reading about my family, The William E. "Bill" Davidson Family.

Donald G. Davidson

2008

CHAPTER I

THE ANCIENT DAVIDSON HISTORY

Our family name, Davidson, has its roots in the early 1300's. Donald Dubh of Inverhaven, was the third son of Robert Comyn and the grandson of John Comyn, known as the Red Comyn, who was killed by Robert the Bruce in the year 1306 in Dumfries. Donald married the daughter of Angus, the sixth chief of the MacKintoshes. The Davidson family name comes from their son, Dhai Dhu, or David Dubh of Inverhaven. By 1308, Robert the Bruce had completely destroyed the Comyn or Cummings and caused the name Comyn to be proscribed around 1320. Because of this, the descendants of Dhai Dhu changed their name and became known as Clan Dhai, or MacDhais or Davidson.

Although Davidson sounds like an English name, it is in fact derived from the Gaelic "MacDhaibhidh," The Clan Dhai was one of the earliest to become associated with the confederation of the Clan Chattan. This association almost proved to be the end of the Davidsons.

In the late 13th Century the Camerons invaded Arkaig which was Clan Chattan land. In 1370 a group of Camerons were returning from a raid into Badenoch, when they were met by a force of MacKintoshes, MacPhersons and Davidsons. This became known as the Battle of Inverhaven. Prior to engaging the enemy a dispute broke out between the MacPhersons and the Davidsons regarding the right to command and military precedence. This was not an unusual occurrence in the Highlands where clans were accustomed to claim the honor of certain positions on the field of battle. When the MacKintoshes supported the Davidsons' position the MacPhersons withdrew from the field while in sight of the enemy. The Camerons exploited the chaos and the Davidsons suffered badly in the battle. The MacPhersons did eventually take the field and routed the Camerons. Even though the Clan Dhai had lost their Chief, Lachlan Davidson, and his seven good sons in the clan battle, the MacPhersons were accorded credit for the victory. The outcome of this battle was a bitter feud between Clan Chattan and the Camerons that would last until 1666.

In ancient times the Davidsons controlled the lovely picturesque valley of Glen Truim. Their stronghold was at Inverhavan in Badenoch near the mouth of Truirn Water where it emptied into the Spey above Craig Dhu. In the aftermath of the Battle of Inverhaven the Chief of Clan Davidson along with many of his followers migrated north and settled in Cormarty where the Chief's property became known as Davidston. In the 18th Century Davidston was sold and the Davidson Chief bought the estate called Tulloch in Ross-shire. This branch which became the leading line of the family became known as the Davidsons of Tulloch. Tulloch Castle, a keep built in 1466 near Dingwall, Ross-shire, became the family seat through the marriage of Alexander Davidson to its heiress, Miss Bayne of Tulloch. This Chief was the hereditary Keeper of the Royal Castle of Dingwall, and his descendants continued to reside at Tulloch.

Some of the Davidsons remained in Chattan and the Davidsons of Cantray in Nairnshire and Inverness are their representatives. Another major branch of the family is the Inchmarlo with Dess.

By the 16th Century the name Davidson had spread from Aberdeen to Ayr. There was a family of Davidsons at Samuelston in the Borders and the name Davidson can be found along with the Elliots and Turnbulls as wild and unruly clans. Duncan Davidson, Lord Lieutenant of Ross-shire, was a favorite of Queen

Victoria whom he used to call upon regularly when she visited Balmoral.

During the 1715 and 1745 uprisings the Clan Davidson largely fought on the Jacobite side and suffered because of it. During this time the chief of the MacKintoshes was an officer in the Black Watch and fought on the government side. This, however, did not stop his wife, a Farquharson, from raising the Clan Chattan Confederation in his absence. She selected the MacGillivray of Dunmaglas as commander and he led the Clans, including the Davidson Clan of Clan Chattan to victory in the Battle of Falkirk in 1746.

The Davidson Coat of Arms are Argent, on a fes Azure between a dexter hand couped accompanied by two pheons in chief and a pheon in base Gules, a buck lodged Or. Above the shield is placed a helmet befitting his degree with a Mantling Azure doubled Argent and on a Wreath of his liveries is set for a Crest a stag's head erased Proper and in an Escrol over the same the motto SAPIENTER IS SINCERE (Wisely if Sincerely). It means "in whatever you do or say act with sincerity if you can't always act in wisdom."

Considering the Davidsons are all descended from the Black/Red Comyns, and if one was to rehash history the Comyns excuse would have been that they acted with sincerity to back the wrong side for the Crown of Scotland even though it was not wise since Bruce won and the only surviving decedent of the Black/Red Comyns was forced to give up the name, and seek refuge with his only friend, Chief of MacKintosh, Donald Dubh, grandson of the Black Comyn. The first Davidson must have had a sense of humor if he was the one who coined the motto.

The Presbyterian Scots, including the Davidsons, were transplanted by the British Crown to Ulster Plantation on the soil of the Catholic Irish. There they professed and maintained the superior status of conquerors; but their sincere affection for Erin and its traditions is evident from their willingness to join St. Patrick societies in order to perpetuate Irish memories after they arrived in the American Colonies. Nevertheless, the term "Scot-Irish" is, in a sense, a misnomer. It refers more accurately to the geographic rather than the ethnographic origin of the breed. Marriage between the Scots and Irish appears to have been the exception rather than the rule.

England's effort to bind Catholic Ireland more closely to herself by colonizing the northern counties with Protestants brought into Ulster many an alien element. The largest group was the Calvinist Scots; but the Anglican English were considerable and there were, in addition, Puritan English, French Huguenots and other foreigners who professed no faith at all.

Whatever their religious complexion, the Ulstermen were robust colonists. The Naboth's vineyard which they cultivated flourished. Indeed, it was their assiduous industry which eventually brought about their wholesale exodus, for the canny instincts and close economy of the Scots soon produced an export trade in wool, and later flax, that upset the British monopoly. This was more than England had bargained for and Parliament quickly imposed duties that stifled Ireland's contacts with outside markets. Many of the Scots were tenants on estates of English court favorites, and as their leases expired the rents were raised. The low living standards of the native Irish enabled them to underbid and oust the Scot lessees. In addition to these delusions and snares, the Calvinists had also to bear the onus of paying tithes for the support of the established Episcopal Church and were subject to disabilities and restrictions laid upon dissenters by the English penal laws.

In the early 1700's there was little to induce the destitute or devout Calvinist Scots to remain in Ireland. The Scot-Irish deserted the Emerald Isle by the thousands early in the eighteenth century. The fact that 1740 and 1741 were famine years in Ireland is not without significance. It is estimated that more than one half of the Presbyterians in Ulster came to America before the Revolution. By 1775 they constituted about one sixth of the population of the revolting colonies.

There is no final answer to the question as to whether the primary impulse for the Scots to emigrate was religious or economic. The force of motivation differed with individuals. For those with strong established Calvinist congregations in the New World, the scales weigh in favor of worship. Nothing on the frontier enforced religious observance. The obstacles against it were formidable. Even the most forgiving of Presbyterians, however, had difficulty forgetting the ruin of the woolens industry and exorbitant land rents imposed by the British. The emigrants carried with them a heritage of hatred that was vented in grape and buckshot when the Redcoats invaded their American Canaan in the Revolution.

The Davidsons were devout Calvinist Presbyterians. They brought their strong religious convictions with them to the New World. Their fatalistic belief made them worthy warriors in the cause of the American Revolution.

CHAPTER 2

THE EARLY DAVIDSON HISTORY

It is not certain who our early Davidson ancestors were or when they arrived in the Colonies. It is believed they probably arrived around 1725. The Davidsons had a penchant for certain given names which they regularly used profusely. Names like: John, William, George, James, Abraham, Samuel, Mary, Ann, and Elizabeth. It is difficult, if not impossible, to trace a certain given name of a specific individual Davidson beyond the year 1800.

Also, the early Davidsons resided mostly in Virginia and North Carolina, and later in Tennessee and Alabama. During the Civil War many of the courthouses in the South were burned by the Union armies. Many of the documents and records were destroyed by fire. That further complicates searches for early ancestors who resided in the South prior to the Civil War.

> Years ago I attended a genealogy seminar in Dallas. The featured speaker was a professional genealogist. She was introduced as an expert on Virginia and North Carolina families. At the outset of her session she announced in no uncertain terms that she "never does Davidsons or Powells." That piqued my interest.
>
> At the first break I buttonholed her with my Davidson nametag plainly showing. I asked why she refused to research Davidsons. At first she was evasive but I persisted. She finally said, "Because they are so difficult." I wasn't about to take

that for a final answer. I asked, "What do you mean they are so difficult?" She finally said, "They are too close. Too close genetically and too close-mouthed. They are well known for keeping the Ten Commandments and anything else they can lay their hands on." I later learned there also was an old saying among the Scots, "Never kill a Davidson because you will then have to kill his wife."

JAMES DAVIDSON

According to the family folklore, it is thought our first ancestor to come to The Colonies was James Davidson. He was a native of Scotland who came to North America with his family and settled near the Susquehanna River in Pennsylvania. He claimed to be one of the first Davidsons to come to America.

It is believed James Davidson had a son named John born about 1730 in Pennsylvania but moved to and lived in Virginia. He lived in that part of Virginia that came to be known as Wythe County and later (1799) Tazewell County along the Clinch River in what is now the extreme southwest part of Virginia. That part of Virginia in 1730 to 1790 was the outer fringes of the frontier. Indians still largely inhabited that part of Virginia.[1]

GEORGE WASHINGTON

In 1753 the French seized and imprisoned some English surveyors and traders of the Ohio Company in the wilderness between the upper waters of the Alleghany River and Lake Erie. The French regarded the English as intruders and deployed about twelve hundred French soldiers to erect forts in the area.

---

1 (An interesting sidelight to the Davidson history is the Roller Family [Johannes Roller, born about 1725; married Anna Ocher, born about 1730] lived in the same general area of the Clinch River. In 1925 William E. Davidson. (1901 - 2005) married Mary P. Roller (1905 - 1988).

Robert Dinwiddie, a member of the Ohio Company and governor of Virginia, received instructions from England to repel the French by force of arms, if necessary. Dinwiddie determined to first send a letter of remonstrance to M. de St. Pierre, the French commander. He selected young George Washington for this important mission.

Washington then was a little more than twenty-one years old. He was of an excellent and honorable family, whose roots lay far back in English history. As a public surveyor and skillful hunter he had traversed the forests of Virginia far in the direction of the Ohio. At the time England claimed Virginia lay west all the way to the Mississippi River.

OLD JOHN DAVIDSON

Washington left Williamsburg, the Virginia capitol, on the thirty-first day of October 1753. He was joined by John Davidson as Indian interpreter, Jacob Van Braam, a Hollander by birth, acquainted with the French language, and a Mr. Gist as guide.

Is this John Davidson the Old John Davidson of Wythe County, Virginia, killed in 1793 by Indians? After the Revolution that part of Virginia along the Clinch River became Wythe County and was located in the far western part of the state as it is configured today. In 1753 it was a virtual wilderness. If this John Davidson born in 1730 is the son of James Davidson then he would have been 23 years old in 1753, about the same age as George Washington when he accompanied him on this mission. John Davidson was 63 years old in 1793 when killed by Indians.

The Davidson name was not unfamiliar to George Washington. Lieutenant Colonel William Lee Davidson of North Carolina served with him at Valley Forge and sat as president of a court-martial there. December 19, 1778 Washington sent orders for Lieutenant Colonel Davidson, who was stationed near Smith's Clove, New York, to march immediately to Philadelphia by way of Trenton.

A little over two years later on February 1, 1781, then Brigadier-General William Lee Davidson was killed opposing Cornwallis at the Battle of Cowan's Ford on the Catawba River in North Carolina.[1]

There surely must have been a close affinity of the Davidsons with George Washington. Almost every Davidson Family for the next several generations after the Revolution named a son, usually the first one, George Washington Davidson.

The book, A History of Southwest Virginia 1746 to 1870, by Lewis P. Summers, page 426 states:

> October 1, 1789 Indians captured the Wiley Family on the headwaters of the Clinch River. During the same year, John Davidson, who lived on the headwaters of the Clinch River was waylaid and killed by a band of Indians while feeding his horse at a cabin. The Indians were accompanied by a white man who robbed Davidson's saddlebags of their contents.

The following from a manuscript, "Indian Atrocities along the Clinch, Powell and Holston Rivers," pages 241-242, by Emory L. Hamilton states:

> Pendleton, in his History of Tazewell County, page 235, quoting from Bickley's History of Tazewell County, 1853 said that sometime in 1789 or 1790, John Davidson, a man advanced in years, was killed by Indians on Clinch River, half a mile above the present town of North Tazewell. Mr. Davidson had been on a business trip to Rockingham County, Virginia, and was returning home when the murder was committed.
>
> The circumstances connected with the tragedy were afterwards made known by white people who had been in captivity, and who were told by the Indians, when they were prisoners, how, and why, Mr. Davidson was killed. He had

1 (See the book, "Piedmont Partisan-The Life and Times of Brigadier-General William Lee Davidson" by Chalmers Gaston Davidson, Davidson College, Davidson, North Carolina, ©1951.)

> stopped at a deserted cabin to feed his horses, and while thus occupied was shot to death.
>
> The Indians also said a white renegade was with them when the deed was done. It seems the crime was a double one, as the Indians and their companion found a considerable amount of specie in the saddlebags of the old man which was stolen by the murderers. Bickley says: "A few days after, his son, Colonel Davidson, became uneasy on account of his absence, and raising a small company went in search of him. Luckily, when they got to the cabin they found a hatband which, being of peculiar structure, was recognized as that worn by Mr. Davidson. After considerable search, his body was found stripped of clothing, and somewhat disfigured by birds. As the Indians had too long been gone to be overtaken, Mr. Davidson was taken home and buried."

Both Pendleton and Bickley are in error on their date of the killing of John Davidson. A letter written by Daniel Trigg, to the Governor of Virginia, under date of April 10, 1793, writes:

> Since the 20th of March they (Indians) have been constantly hovering over this part of our frontiers. John Davidson murdered by them, and a number of horses stolen from Wolf Creek, Bluestone and Island Creek, for and will all which they have escaped, with impunity, except the party entrusted with the care of conveying away the horses from Island Creek, who have been pursued, the horses retaken, together with the arms and blankets of three warriors, who were killed and scalped by the justly incensed followers at the mouth of Little Cole.

The number of Indians concerned in the murder of Davidson, at the Laurel Fork of Wolf Creek, was judged about twelve, who carried off a number of horses from the neighborhood, and passed with them in daylight through the heart of the Bluestone settlement. From the above letter it can be safely assumed that John Davidson was killed at some time between the 20th of March and the 10th of April 1793. Also it seems unlikely that Davidson could have been missing as long as Bickley says, since the Indians passed through the Bluestone settlement with stolen horses in open daylight. Surely the whole countryside must have been alerted and Trigg says in his letter that the Indians had been hovering over the frontier since March 20th which conveys the knowledge that the settlers were aware of their presence.

Judge Johnson in his "History of the New River Settlements" says that John Davidson was called Cooper Davidson, being thusly labeled because by trade he was a cooper.

Nevertheless, it is interesting to read the will of John Davidson (exactly as written) as follows from "Early Adventurors of the Western Waters - Probated Will of John Davidson, Sr.-Vol. III, Part I, by Kegley, page 205."

> In the name of god Amen, july 1791. I John Davidson of Wythe County and state of Virginia being very sick and weak in body but in and of perfect mind and memory thans be given unto god calling unto mind the mortality of my body and knowing that it is appontef or all me one to die do make and ordain this my last will and testament that is to say principally and firs of all I give and recommend my sole unto the hand of almighty god that gave it and my body I recommend to the earth to be buried in decent Christian burial at the discretion of my executors nothing doubting but at the general resurrectiion I shall receive the same again by the mighty power of god and a touching such world by estate wherewith it hath pleased god to bles me in this life I give and devise & dispose of the same in the Following menner and from first I give and bequeath to my sons Andrew John and George Davidson my land at the mouth of absolam wels counting 400 hundred akers to be devided betwixt them as follows George Corner to stand at the meadow and run ther a long the old line to the corner at the pounding Mill brench and then to the creek to be the line from that throught and the remainder part of said land to be divided betixt andr/and/John in quantity and quantity likewise I bequeath a tract of myne lying on the brushey Fork known by the nam of the quekers Cabans to John Burk Likewise I

bequeth to my dought Betse a track of myne lying of the head waters of Lortons lick creek likewise I do bequeath to Marthew my beloved wife the plantation on which I now reside which I bought of my son William Davidson to be for her seport if shee thinks proper to keep house upon it if not to disspose of the same to George Peery or John Bele for or at its value and to take his mentanens out of the same land likewise I do bequeth my tow sons John & George my still and my wife the thirds of the profits maid by hir hile shee lives Likewise I bequeth to my sons Wm & Joseph Davidson one Englis Crown Starling apees to George Preery Lo Brown and John Belle to eatch of them I bequeath one Crown Starling to be leved out of my astat and I dow hair by utterly disallow revoke and disavowel all and every other other former testaments will Legancies bequest and executors by me in any wise before naimed will and bequethed Ratifying and confirming this and no other to be my last will and testament in witness whereof I have hair unto set my hand and seal this 22 day of July in the year of our Lord 1791

(signed) John Davidson

Signed Sealed published pronounced and declared by the sd John Davidson as his last will and testament in the presents of us who in his presents and the presence of each other have hair unto subcribed our names.

(signed) Robert Wallace
(signed) David Wallace

At a Court held for the County of Wythe on Tuesday the 3rd day of June 1795, this the last will & testament of John Davidson Dec'd was exhibited in Court & proven by the oaths of Robert Wallace & David Wallace the witnesses thereto and ordered to be recorded. Teste: Samuel Crockett, D.C.[1]

---

1 (At the time it was not unusual that it was two years after the fact before wills were probated. The courts met only once a year and then for only a few days to a few weeks depending on the number of items on the docket.)

If this John Davidson is the son of James then he would have been 63 years old when murdered by the Indians. Certainly a man of advanced age for the times.

Robert and David Wallace must have been neighbors and certainly true and trusted friends of John Davidson for him to entrust them as witnesses to his last will and testament. Since Tazewell County records of 1801 show that Mary Wallace was the owner of slaves it is reasonable to assume she may have been the daughter or granddaughter of either Robert or David Wallace.[1]

A History of the Bailey Family indicates that John Davidson and Richard Bailey, born 1735, in Lancaster, England, were close neighbors and friends. John Davidson signed as a witness to Richard Bailey's last will and testament in 1790. Richard Bailey had a son, John, born 1764, who married Nancy Davidson in 1783, daughter of John and Martha (spelled Marthew in John's will) Davidson with the notation that Indians murdered John Davidson 9 March 1799.

There is much speculation about the date of John Davidson's murder by Indians. It is certain it was sometime after 22 July 1791, date of his will, and before 3 June 1795, when his will was exhibited at Court for Wythe County to be proven.

The Annals of Tazewell County, Virginia, from 1800 to 1922 in two volumes, by John N. Harman, Sr., pages 172 and 174 states:

> January 1801 Court Term - William George and William Peery qualified as Coroners of the county under a commission of the Governor dated September 13, 1800: Ordered that the following persons be recommended to the Governor as fit and capable persons to be appointed to fill the following offices: Joseph Davidson to act as Colonel Commandant for the 112th Regiment; George Davidson to act as Captain of a Company of Light Infantry of the 1st Battalion, and John Davidson to act as Lieutenant in the 1st Battalion of said Regiment.

---

1 (In 1799 western Wythe County was divided to create Tazewell County.)

> This court proceeds to make up in their minutes an account of all expenses incurred by the Court under authority of the Law, in that case made and provided the following are claimants of the Court to wit: "The Clerk of this County for exofficio services for the years 1800 and 1801, the claims allowed last September Court: John Davidson $2 for one old wolf."[1]

JOHN DAVIDSON

Another likely possibility of our ancestry is another John Davidson, born 1730, also thought to be the son of James Davidson and a native of Pennsylvania. He moved to and lived in Virginia for a while, then moved to and settled in North Carolina. There he married Hannah Hughson, born 1730. They had the following children:

1. Abraham Davidson born 22 October 1755 in Guilford County, North Carolina, and died 1839 in Benton County, Tennessee. He was 21 years old in 1776 when the American Revolution began. He married Sarah Ellis. They had the following children: (1) Hudson, (2) John, born 1785, (3) Thomas, born 1787, (4) Ms. Davidson, born 1789, and (5) Abraham, born 1791.
2. Joseph Davidson born about 1757 in Halifax County, North Carolina, and died in 1820. He married Elizabeth, born 1768. They had the following children: (1) John, born 1785, (2) Thomas, born 1787, (3) Sarah, born 1789, (4) Jesse, (5) Abraham; (6) Ann, born 1793, and (7) Joseph, born 1795.
3. John Davidson, Jr., born about 1757 in Halifax County, North Carolina.

---

1 (This John Davidson may be the son, John, mentioned in the will of Old John Davidson, above, and may have married Mary Wallace.)

Microfilms made in the 1930's as a WPA project of Dickson County Court documents for January 30, 1807, in the Waverly, Tennessee, Genealogical Library show:

> Vol. II, p. 109 - Dickson County Court Minutes ordered that Abraham Davidson be appointed Overseer of the road leading from Charlotte toward Palmyra from Irwins Mill to the County line and that he have the following hands to wit, all at John Altons, all at James Woods, all at John Davidsons, all at Dennis Burnes, all at John Davidson, Junr., all at Jesse Jernigans, all at William Jernigans, and all at other hands living convenient thereto.
>
> Vol. II, p. 110 - Dickson County Court minutes Ordered that the following appointed in each Capt. Company as Valueors of property in this County, to wit: Capt. Burlon's company, Abraham Davidson, Joseph Brown, and George Mitchell.[1]

The 1820 Census for Humphreys County, Tennessee, (later partitioned to make Benton County) shows Abraham Davidson in a household with: "one male under age 10, one male age 16 to 26, one male age 26 to 45, and one male over 45." The Census also shows the household had: "one female age 16 to 26, and one female over 45." Abraham was 65 years of age.

The Tennessee Pension Roll of 1835 for soldiers of the American Revolution shows that Abraham Davidson served as a Private and resided in Humphreys County, Tennessee. It shows his annual allowance was $60 and he had received a total of $180 since his pension started 12 September 1833 at age 79. He lived in Benton County, Tennessee when he died in 1838. Since he was age 79 in 1833 he was age 84 when he died.

---

1 (Dickson County was later partitioned to make Humphreys County. The Dickson County Courthouse was burned by Union troops during the Civil War. Many of the documents were destroyed. Some and parts of some were saved. The microfilms show burned half pages and burned edges on many of the documents.)

LUCINDA "LUCY" DAVIDSON

The true relationship of Lucy Davidson is not known for certain. In the 1820 Census she was 18 years old. This is known because the 1830 Census shows her age as 28. Therefore, she was born in 1802. She could be the "one female age 16 to 26" in the Abraham Davidson household in the1820 Census. If so, why was she living in the Abraham Davidson household? Could she be Abraham's daughter? Niece? Were John and Lucy brother and sister? There hasn't been any evidence found that this is true. If she was Abraham's daughter he was 47 years old when she was born in 1802. John was 17 years old when Lucy was born. Is Lucy John Wallace's sister? She was 12 years old when he was born in 1814. This is thought to be the more likely relationship.

It is known John Wallace Davidson was born 14 March 1814 and his parents were John and Mary (Wallace) Davidson. This means that if John, Jr., is his father, then John, Jr. was 57 years old when John Wallace Davidson was born. Not too likely. Abraham's son, John, was born in 1785. If he is the father of John Wallace Davidson, he would have been 29 years old when John Wallace was born. This is a more likely scenario.

We've done a lot of research trying to pin down with evidence who John Davidson and Mary Wallace actually are, where they came from and what happened to them. Also, the search continues to determine exactly who Lucinda "Lucy" (Davidson) Perkins is and why she took on the task to raise young John Wallace Davidson. Was he orphaned by the early death of his parents, John and Mary (Wallace) Davidson? Lucy was 22 years old in 1824 when she married Ephraim Perkins, an upstanding citizen of Benton County, and had three children by him.

The search continues on John Davidson and Mary Wallace Davidson. If it could definitely be determined exactly who they were, where they came from, and what happened to them it would point in the direction of their ancestors, and solve an entire passel of nagging questions begging for answers.

The Tazewell County tax records as recorded in the book, "Archives of the Pioneers of Tazewell County, Virginia," by Nettie Schreiner-Yantias, shows a John Davidson and a Mary Wallace as slaveholders in 1801. This places John Davidson and Mary Wallace in the same locale at the same time. Was John and Mary Wallace married in 1801? Lucy Davidson was born in 1802 in Virginia according to the 1850 Census of Benton County, Tennessee. Is Lucy the oldest child of this union? Is this John Davidson and Mary Wallace *our* John and Mary? Seems to be likely.

So, who *was* Lucy? Why did she take on the responsibility to raise young John Wallace Davidson? This is what is known about Lucinda "Lucy" Davidson. She was born 1802 in Virginia and married Ephraim Perkins, probably about 1824. He was one of the early settlers of Benton County, Tennessee. They lived on a large farm on Burnside Creek near Camden. Ephraim was a veteran of the War of 1812. He was a lawyer and politically active. He was very much involved in the formation of Benton County and the town of Camden. He was one of the County Magistrates when Benton County was formed in 1836, and was elected Chairman of the Benton County Court in 1843 and 1846. He was well acquainted with all of the legal aspects in the courts of Camden.

In the 1830 Census of Camden, Benton County, Tennessee, Ephraim Perkins is listed with: "One male age 0 to 5 years, one male age 10 to 15 years, one male age 30 to 40 years." The same census shows: "Two females age 0 to 5 years, one female age 5 to 10 years, one female age 20 to 30 years." Lucinda was 28 years old in 1830. The "one male age 10 to 15 years" most likely is young John Wallace Davidson since he was born in October 1814.

Lucy and Ephraim had three children age five or under according to the 1830 Census. It is probably safe to assume she and Ephraim married about 1824 and had their first child in 1825. Lucy would have been 22 years old in 1824. Young John Wallace was 10 years old in 1824. If young John Wallace is Lucy's son, then she would have been 12 years old when he was born. Not very likely. Assuming he is the "one male age 10 to 15 years" in the Perkins household in the 1830 Census, the unanswered question is: "Why did young John Wallace go to live with Lucy and Ephraim Perkins?"

In the 1850 Census of Camden, Benton County, Tennessee, Ephraim Perkins is shown as 55 years of age and that he was born in North Carolina. Therefore, he would have been born in 1795. His wife, Lucinda, is shown as 48 years of age and she was born in Virginia. Therefore, she would have been born in 1802. Their children are shown on the census as Rebecca age 21, Thomas age 18, Samuel age 16, Andrew age 15, and Lucinda Barrum age 7. In 1850 John Wallace Davidson was 36 years old.

Lucinda died in 1853 and Ephraim died in 1866. They are both buried in the Ephraim Perkins Cemetery located on a hill about three hundred yards directly behind the home of Lanier Vick at 1595 Flatwoods Road, north of Camden on property owned by Billy Mitchell. There are no markers in the cemetery. They were vandalized years ago. Known to be buried there are: "Ephraim Perkins, 1795–3 August 1866"; and "Perkins, Lucinda - wife of Ephraim Perkins 1802–1853." There are approximately ten unmarked graves in the cemetery.

BIOGRAPHICAL and HISTORICAL **MEMOIRS OF NORTHEAST ARKANSAS**

The Biographical and Historical Memoirs of Northeast Arkansas - Sharp County, page 739, published by The Goodspeed Publishing Co., 1889, states that John and Mary (Wallace) Davidson were innkeepers in Huntsville, Madison County, Alabama. John moved to the Mississippi Territory near what is now Huntsville, Madison County, Alabama, and married Mary Wallace, a beautiful young lady of Scottish ancestry. Her family were early settlers in that part of the Mississippi Territory that later became Alabama in 1819.

Their union was blessed with five children. They were: (1) Abraham, (2) Berry, (3) William, (4) Lucinda "Lucy," and (5) John Wallace born in 1814. Is this the Lucy that married Ephraim Perkins? If she was born in 1802 then she was 12 years old when John Wallace was born. Are Lucy and John Wallace brother and sister? It is reasonable to believe they are. The only one of the children we know the descendant history of is John Wallace Davidson.

Following is an excerpt from "The Biographical and Historical Memoirs of Northeast Arkansas - Sharp County," page 739, published by The Goodspeed Publishing Co., 1889. This excerpt is taken from the biographical sketch written by Sam H. Davidson, brother of William Mordecai Davidson. Speaking of his father, John Wallace Davidson, Sam H. Davidson wrote:

> His father, John Davidson, was born in Virginia or North Carolina during the latter half of the eighteenth century, removed to and was an inn-keeper in Huntsville, Ala., and died there in 1815. His mother was Mary Wallace, of Scottish ancestry, noted for her beauty and culture among the early settlers of North Alabama.
>
> The father of John Davidson was Abraham Davidson, a Pennsylvanian, a soldier of the Revolution, who settled In North Carolina, and afterward in Montgomery County, Tenn., and who died in Benton County, Tenn., in 1838.
>
> The father or grandfather of Abraham, James Davidson, was a native of Scotland, who with his family settled near the Susquehanna River, Pennsylvania, and claimed to be the first Davidson to settle in North America.

JOHN DAVIDSON and MARY WALLACE

There is reason to believe John Davidson may have lived in and died at Huntsville, Scott County, (formerly Claiborne County), Tennessee, and not Huntsville, Madison County, Alabama (formerly

Mississippi Territory). This is mostly because my sister, Ann (Davidson) Melton, and I have been to Huntsville, Alabama, several times searching county documents and genealogical records for John Davidson, Mary Wallace, and John Wallace Davidson with no results. There were no Davidsons or Wallaces recorded in the 1809 Census or the 1816 Census of Madison County.

There are microfilms in the Public Library in Waverly, Humphreys County, Tennessee, of court records which make mention of a John Davidson and a Lucy Davidson in the 1800 to 1815 time frame. Humphreys County is closer to Huntsville, Scott County, Tennessee, than to Huntsville, Alabama, which was then part of the Mississippi Territory. Alabama became a state in 1819.

There is a possibility John Davidson and Mary (Wallace) Davidson came from Tazewell County, Virginia, and moved to Huntsville, Tennessee, sometime after 1802 since Lucy was born in Virginia in 1802 according to the 1850 Census for Camden, Benton County, Tennessee. It may be possible they married in Virginia and relocated to Huntsville, Tennessee, sometime between 1802 and 1810 instead of the Mississippi Territory near what is now Huntsville, Alabama. It seems reasonable they migrated less than two hundred miles westward to Huntsville, Tennessee, rather than several hundred miles to Huntsville, Mississippi, later (1819) Alabama. However, the Clinch River flows southward through Tazewell County, Virginia, and into the Tennessee River which flows within a few miles of Huntsville, Alabama. That would be a fairly easy riverboat trip as opposed to two hundred miles overland in a wilderness.

A History of the Tennessee River states:

> Between 1805 and 1809 some wealthy and cultured slave owners came into the county in large numbers. They came from North Carolina, Virginia and Georgia. They came in flat-bottom boats and landed at Ditto Landing on the Tennessee River in Madison County. John Ditto was the first white settler in Madison County in 1804.

The Tennessee River flows west from Madison County and turns north and flows across Western Tennessee into Kentucky and thence the Ohio River. This can perhaps explain how the Davidsons came to be in Humphreys and Benton Counties in Tennessee. The river flows between these two counties. Again, it would be a fairly easy boat trip as opposed to going over land.

The following excerpts about the early history of Madison County, Mississippi Territory are taken from the "History of Old Madison County" by Thomas J. Taylor, Probate Judge, 1866, to his death in 1894, and from the "Early History of Huntsville" by General Edward C. Betts:

> The life of these pioneers was very primitive as they drew solely on the resources of the surrounding wilderness for their necessities and comfort. Their houses contained no iron, being constructed entirely of wood logs. The floors were covered with well packed dirt and only in very rare cases was the floor covered with puncheon, a broad flat piece of rough dressed timber.

By a proclamation of the Honorable Robert Williams, Governor of the Mississippi Territory, Old Madison County was created and established December 13, 1808, with a population of 5,000. It was not until February 27, 1809, that the laws relating to the judiciary and militia of this territory were immediately extended to the County of Madison.

On December 22, 1809, the Territorial Legislature created a commission to lay out the town (now Huntsville) and when laid out, was to be called and known by the name of Twickenham.

On March 2, 1819, the Territorial Constitutional Convention, by an act of the U.S. Congress, authorized the people of the Alabama Territory to hold a convention in Huntsville for the purpose of drafting a state constitution. The Convention assembled at Huntsville on the first Monday of July 1819.

The Convention unanimously voted for statehood and after two years as the Territory of Alabama, on December 14, 1819,

Alabama became the 22nd state admitted into the Untied States of America.

A Census was taken in January 1809 of Madison County (Alabama) Mississippi Territory. Another Census taken in 1816 showed Madison County had a population of 14,200. It is perplexing that not one Davidson or Wallace shows up in either Census. If they were in Madison County (Huntsville) during the period 1804 to 1820, why do they not show up on the Census of 1809 or 1816?

The information that John Davidson moved to Huntsville, Alabama, is taken from the Biographical and Historical Memoirs of Northeast Arkansas published in 1889 by The Goodspeed Publishing Company from an account written by his grandson, Samuel Houston Davidson.

In this biographical account of his life Samuel Houston Davidson states that his father, John Wallace Davidson was born 1814 in Huntsville, Alabama, and died in October 1870. An actual on site observation of John Wallace Davidson's headstone in the Evening Shade Cemetery reveals the actual date he died is October 12, 1869.

Samuel Houston Davidson also could have been mistaken about his grandfather being from Huntsville, Alabama, instead of Huntsville, Tennessee. Or, a Goodspeed copywriter could have misinterpreted or misread Samuel's handwriting and listed it as Alabama instead of Tennessee. Actually, there was no Alabama in 1815 when John Davidson supposedly died. It was then a part of the Mississippi Territory.

John Wallace Davidson is known for certain to be *our* ancestor. It is well established his father was John Davidson and his mother was Mary Wallace. It is thought Lucinda "Lucy" (Davidson) Perkins was either John's sister or his daughter. If his daughter then she is John Wallace Davidson's older sister. Beyond this very little is known for certain about our Davidson ancestors. Following leads on John Wallace Davidson's parents is like running down rabbit trails with a new briar patch at every twist and turn. We have yet to conclusively determine whom John's father actually is.

It is not known what happened to John Davidson and Mary (Wallace) Davidson. Things are never quite certain in the realm of early day genealogy. Dates are often elusive, misleading and misconstrued. Facts are often speculative or wishful thinking. That having been said there is reason to think the early Davidson ancestry may be one of the following:

A. The Virginia Connection:
James Davidson (unknown) - unknown
Old John Davidson (1730-1793) - Martha unknown
John Davidson (circa 1756) - unknown
John Davidson (1785-1815) - Mary Wallace
John Wallace Davidson (1814-1869) - Susan L. Prance

B. The North Carolina Connection:
James Davidson (unknown) - unknown
John Davidson (1730- unknown) - Hannah Hughson
Abraham Davidson (1755-1838) - Sarah Ellis
John Davidson (1785-1815) - Mary Wallace
John Wallace Davidson (1814-1869) - Susan L. Prance

The only one we know the history of for sure is John Wallace Davidson. He was a respected citizen of Camden, Tennessee, and was a well known and active figure in the politics and courts of Benton County. There is a wealth of information about him in the genealogy section of the Camden Library as well as the records at the courthouse. Sadly, there is nothing we've been able to find that gives any positive clues about his parents, John Davidson and Mary (Wallace) Davidson. It gives cause to wonder whatever happened to them and why there is not so much as even a dim trail to follow. Lucy is our only clue but she too fades away into the oblivion of the genealogical briar patch. The search continues.

CHAPTER 3

JOHN WALLACE DAVIDSON

JOHN WALLACE DAVIDSON was the son of John Davidson and Mary (Wallace) Davidson. He was born at Huntsville, Madison County, Alabama, 14 March 1814. John Wallace Davidson married Susan Lyons Prance in 1836 in Humphreys County, Tennessee. She was born in 1818 in Montgomery County, Tennessee. She was the daughter of John Prance and Mary (Cooper) Prance. John Prance was of French-Irish descent. He died in Montgomery County, Tennessee. Mary Cooper was of Irish descent. She was born in Montgomery County, Tennessee, and died in McCracken County, Kentucky.

John Wallace and Susan had nine children. They were: (1) Mary Ann, (2) George Washington, (3) Lucinda "Lucy" Margaret, (4) Leathy Malissa "Lee", (5) William Mordecai "Bill", (6) Samuel Houston "Sam", (7) Martha W., (8) Harrison John "Jack", and (9) Thomas Jefferson "Jeff."[1]

---

1 (The above information is from "The 'Biographical and Historical Memoirs of Northeast Arkansas - Sharp County", page 739, published by The Goodspeed Publishing Co., 1889, written by Sam H. Davidson, brother of William Mordecai Davidson.. There is reason to believe John Davidson and Mary [Wallace] Davidson lived at Huntsville, Tennessee, instead of Huntsville, Alabama when John Wallace was born. See the previous chapter, "The Early History.")

John Davidson, father of John Wallace Davidson, died at Huntsville in 1815. The cause of death and place of burial are unknown. The date and place of Mary Wallace Davidson's death is not known. It is assumed their deaths were unexpected and sudden.

There are no known facts about young John Wallace's childhood. Sometime after the death of his parents he was sent to live with Lucy (Davidson) Perkins and her husband, Ephraim Perkins, on Burnside Creek near Camden, Benton County, Tennessee. It is thought Lucy was John Wallace's older sister. She was twelve years old when John Wallace was born.

John Wallace Davidson was a Benton County magistrate in 1836. He was chairman of the Benton County Court for the year 1848. He was Circuit Court Clerk for Benton County in 1848 through 1852. While he served in these positions he studied and practiced law in Camden until 1865. He was a member of the Tennessee Legislature, representing Benton and Humphreys Counties, in the House of Representatives from 1859 through 1861. He was a member of the Tennessee Legislature on the 7th of May 1861 with Governor Isham Harris presiding when they passed an ordinance of secession and an alliance with the Confederate States of America.[1]

For many years John Wallace was a faithful Mason. He was a member of the Methodist Church from 1865 until his death.

The aftermath of the Civil War and Reconstruction wrecked havoc on and totally devastated many Southern families. The John Wallace Davidson Family was no exception. Three of John Wallace Davidson's sons served in the Confederate Army. The 14th Amendment was written and passed (without the Southern white vote) to specifically punish persons who served in the Confederate military or served the Confederate government in any capacity. They were disenfranchised from voting or holding any public office until they were officially paroled by the Federal government.

1 (Isham Harris' mother's name was Lucy Davidson.)

That was a long tedious process taking five to ten years in most instances. Many of the Southern families simply pulled up stakes and moved west to put the past behind them and start a new life. The John Wallace Davidson Family was one of many such families fleeing the aftermath of the war.

In 1865 John Wallace and Susan with their children moved to Graves County, Kentucky. Not being satisfied there, they moved to Jackson, Cape Girardeau County, Missouri. Their stay there was short. In 1866 they moved to Randolph County, Arkansas, and in 1867 to Doniphan, Ripley County, Missouri. Then in 1869 hearing of a new county seat in Sharp County, Arkansas, they moved one more time to Evening Shade. This was the final move for several members of the family. John Wallace died a few months later.

Sons, Bill, Sam, Jack and Jeff followed in the footsteps of their father and took up the practice of law in Sharp County. Bill and Sam were elected and served as state representatives for Sharp County at the Capitol in Little Rock. Jeff served many years as the County Clerk for Sharp County. He had a very good hand for penmanship. Examples of his handwriting can be seen in the many old county documents now in the new courthouse at Ash Flat.

John Wallace Davidson died October 12, 1869, in Evening Shade, Arkansas. The cause of death was liver disease. He was buried in the Sharp Cemetery (now the Evening Shade Cemetery). His headstone is broken. When the pieces are fit together the engraved words are:

John W Davidson
Husband of
Susan L Davidson
Born
Mar 14, 1814
Died
Oct 12, 1869

The 1870 Census for Sharp County, Arkansas, shows Susan L. Davidson is a widow living with her sons William, Samuel, Jackson and Jefferson. In the 1880 Census for Sharp County her sons are all married and she is shown living with her youngest son, Jefferson, and his family in Evening Shade.

Susan was a member of the Methodist Church in Evening Shade. She was a faithful Methodist for more than forty years. According to the records in the History of the United Methodist Church at Evening Shade, Susan L. Davidson died May 11, 1896. It is assumed she is buried in the Evening Shade Cemetery though several searches of the cemetery have failed to find a headstone for her.

Four articles appeared in the Sharp County Record newspaper of May 15, 1896, as follows:

> We regret to chronicle the death of "Grandma" Davidson, who departed this life Monday, after an illness of several weeks. She was 78 years old, and leaves several sons and daughters, and a host of friends to mourn her loss. The bereaved family has the heart-felt sympathy of everyone.
>
> H. J. Davidson, of Hardy, attended the burial of his mother at this place Tuesday.
>
> G. W. Davidson and sister, Mrs. Gordon, left for their home at Batesville Wednesday morning, after spending a week with relatives, and attending the burial of their mother Tuesday.
>
> Prof. Metcalf dismissed school Tuesday so that his pupils might attend the burial of "Grandma" Davidson (Susan Lyons [Prance] Davidson).

Many sources of information were searched and reviewed to try to determine which John Davidson actually is John Wallace Davidson's father, but the results are somewhat speculative. For instance there was a John Davidson who served in a Tennessee Volunteer unit during the War of 1812. It is easy to speculate that since *our* John died in 1815 he may have died from wounds received during that war. But, there is no evidence found so far to prove this John is *our* John. There are numerous such instances in which it can be reasoned and speculated that a certain John Davidson is *our* John, but none are conclusive.

There is some evidence that indicates John Wallace's brothers, Abraham, Berry and William, also moved from Alabama to Tennessee to live after the death of their parents. At least they can be placed in Western Tennessee after 1815. Whether they came from Huntsville, Alabama, or Huntsville, Tennessee, is still speculative.

CHAPTER 4

WILLIAM MORDECAI DAVIDSON

WILLIAM MORDECAI "Bill" DAVIDSON, the fifth born child, son of John Wallace and Susan Lyons (Prance) Davidson, was born 22 February 1844 at Camden, Benton County, Tennessee. He married Mary Elizabeth "Mollie" Wainwright 27 July 1870 at Evening Shade, Sharp County, Arkansas, with the Rev. John W. Campbell officiating. They had six sons: (1) John Walter, (2) Samuel Mordecai "Mord", (3) George Osborn, (4) Frederick "Fred" Roscoe Edgar, (5) Virgil Lee, and (6) Cyrus Byers.

William Mordecai Davidson disappeared 28 February 1883.[1] Remains which were discovered 1 March 1884 on Pennington's Bar in the Arkansas River twenty miles below Little Rock were identified as those of William Mordecai Davidson. He was buried 25 March 1884 in Lots of the Masonic Grand Lodge No. 17, South Cypress, near the extreme southwest corner of Mount Holly Cemetery, Little Rock, Pulaski County, Arkansas, in an unmarked grave.[2]

---

1 (See newspaper accounts herein from the Arkansas Gazette.)

2 (An appropriate headstone was erected at William Mordecai Davidson's gravesite in 1998 by his grandson W. E. Davidson; great grandsons W. L. Davidson, R. J. Davidson, D. G. Davidson, and S. M. Davidson II; and great-great grandsons S. M. Davidson III, C. E. Davidson, and G. S. Davidson.)

MARY ELIZABETH "Mollie" WAINWRIGHT, daughter of Samuel Wainwright and Helen (Thompson) Wainwright, was born 25 February 1852 in Mississippi. She did not remarry after the death of her husband. She died 11 June 1903 near Hardy, Sharp County, Arkansas. She was buried 12 June 1903 in Sharp Cemetery, now Evening Shade Cemetery, Evening Shade, Sharp County, Arkansas.

SAMUEL WAINWRIGHT, son of William E. Wainwright and Nancy B. Turner, was born 29 November 1818, in Madison County, Alabama. He died 29 October 1898, Sharp County, Arkansas. He married Martha Helen Tompson in 1849 at Jonesboro, Craighead County, Arkansas. She was born in 1829 in Alabama, and died 1856 at Elgin, Jackson County, Arkansas.

WILLIAM E. WAINWRIGHT was born 12 December 1785 in Dinwiddie County, Virginia (near Petersburgh). He died 25 July 1855 in Evening Shade, Sharp County, Arkansas. He married Nancy B. Turner on 3 January 1815 in Lincoln County, Tennessee. She was born 11 May 1799 near Lynchburg, Lynchburg County, Virginia. She died in 1864.

William Mordecai Davidson was a Confederate soldier in the Civil War. At age 17 he enlisted as a private in the 2nd C Company, 5th Regiment, Tennessee Infantry, on 20 May 1861 at Paris, Henry County, Tennessee. He was promoted to 1st Lieutenant 17 December 1861. He served as aide-de-camp to General Patton Anderson, Brigadier-General, C.S. Army, Commanding the Second Brigade, Ruggles Division, Second Army Corps, Army of the Mississippi, at the Battle of Pittsburg Landing, also known as Shiloh, in Tennessee. General Anderson mentions Lieutenant Davidson's name twice in his official report, and commends him by his full name, "Lieut. William M. Davidson."

Following are excerpts from General Anderson's official report, recorded in A.O.R., Series 1, Volume X/1 (S #10) No. 173:

> Again the lines of the enemy gave way, but a battery to our front and left now disclosed itself in heavy fire upon our center

> and right. About this time each command in the brigade lost several gallant officers and many not less gallant men. I dispatched an aide (Lieutenant Davidson) to the rear to order up a battery, and withdrew the infantry a short distance to better shelter. The artillery gained a favorable position in a few minutes (perhaps before Lieutenant Davidson had had time to deliver my order) and promptly opened fire upon its antagonist.
>
> A hurried reconnaissance revealed a point from which the enemy could be more advantageously assailed. Lieutenant Davidson, of my staff, was dispatched to General Ruggles, not far off, with a request that he would send up a few pieces of artillery to a position indicated, whence a vigorous fire, I felt confident, would soon silence the battery, which was the main obstacle to our onward movement.
>
> Lieut. William M. Davidson, aide-de-camp, was constantly by my side, except when absent by my orders, all of which he delivered with promptitude and intelligence. While engaged in this and passing from one portion of the field to another he made many narrow escapes, having frequently to pass under most galling fire to reach his point of destination.

Following is a story that is part of the family folklore. The truth of it can not be vouched for because there is no known official account of the incident:

> Young Lieutenant Davidson was dashing on horseback carrying orders from one field commander to another during the heat of battle. He had to take a circumventing route to avoid Union troops. However, he was detected by a small detachment of Union cavalry that took up a hot pursuit. William spurred his horse and rode frantically over hill and through the woods. He rode to the barn of a house whose occupants were known to be sympathetic to the Confederacy. He dismounted, slapped his horse on the backside and sent him running into the woods. William made a mad dash to the back door of the house. The rather large matronly lady of the house let him in. He asked if there was someplace where he could hide. They looked out a

> window and saw a detachment of Union troops riding up the front driveway. There was precious little time to hide William. The lady beckoned him to her side next to the front door. She grabbed him by the head of the hair, jerked him down, pushed him under her full hoop skirt, and commanded, "Don't move!" She stood next to the door and let the Union officer and some of his troops in. They searched the house. Others searched the barn and grounds while all this time she stood next to the door. Satisfied that the Confederate soldier was not there the Unionists left. A little later William scoured the woods and found his horse. He mounted and continued to his destination though slightly delayed.

Following is a list of the battles in which the Tennessee 5th Regiment participated. It is not known if William Mordecai participated in all these battles. However, it is factually known he was at Shiloh and it is reasonable to believe he participated in some, if not all, of these battles:

- Island #10 (4/6-7/1862)
- Shiloh (4/6-7/1862)
- Corrinth Campaign (Apr.-Jun. 1862)
- Bridge Creek,MS (5/28/1862
- Richamond, KY (8/29-30/1862)
- Perryville (10/8/1862)
- Murfreesboro (12/31/1861) (1/3/1863)
- Tullahoma Campaign (June 1863)
- Chickamauga (9/19-20/1863)
- Chattanooga Siege (Sept. - Nov. 1863)
- Atlanta Campaign (May - Sept. 1864)
- New Hope Church (5/25 - 6/4/1864)
- Kennesaw Mountain (6/27/1864)
- Peach Tree Creek (7/20/1864)
- Atlanta (7/22/1864)
- Jonesboro (8/31 - 9/1/1864)

- Franklin (11/30/1864)
- Nashville (12/15 - 16/1864)
- Carolinas Campaign (Feb. - Apr. 1865)
- Bentonville (3/19 - 21/1865)
- Surrendered at Smithfield, NC on April 9, 1865

Lieutenant William M. Davidson, CSA - 1861

After the war William Mordecai moved to Evening Shade, Sharp County, Arkansas, with his father, mother, and other family members. During their move they lived for a short time at Doniphan, Ripley County, Missouri. William Mordecai had been studying law with his father for several years, and he was admitted to the bar at Doniphan, Missouri. He immediately entered the practice of law after coming to Evening Shade.

He was a successful lawyer and in 1879 he formed a law partnership with Rufus King Arnold, a very successful young lawyer who had moved to Evening Shade from Kentucky. Rufus, like William Mordecai, was a Confederate veteran of the Civil War.

Rufus was named after his grandmother, Catherine (King) Arnold, and her brother, William Rufus King, who was Vice-President of the United States, but who died shortly after being appointed. Rufus met an untimely and tragic death November 19, 1914, the murder victim of unknown bandits. He is buried in the Sharp Cemetery.

In 1882 William Mordecai became a candidate for the Arkansas Legislature. Following is one of his campaign pieces run August 24, 1882, in The Sharp County Record, Evening Shade, Arkansas:

> Fellow Citizens: I am a candidate for the Legislature. I am in favor of immigration, but none at our expense. I believe in morality and religion and think the way to advance them is to educate the masses.
>
> The road and estray law needs amendments. I am opposed to class legislation; favor regulating freights and passage on railroads, and think they ought to bear their equal part of the burden of taxation.
>
> I am in favor of a uniform system of assessment and taxation, and of economizing the tax books. I favor the holding of all defaulting officers to a strict accountability for all losses and deficits. I oppose free passes and, if elected, will take none. I

think jurors before Justices should receive pay for their time lost. The next general assembly will re-district the state for congressional purposes; and, if elected, I will contend for a fair division of territory, and will guard our time of holding our circuit courts.

I will not waste your time in idleness. I have been living in this county going on fourteen years, and have been a student of law all this time; I have seen the evils of much legislation and think I know how to take advantage of it. The constitution is the law makers keystone, and ours has been violated many times in legislation, in my opinion, since its adoption.

And now, fellow citizens, if you will elect me, I will legislate for you, and not for monopolies, rings, cliques and corporations, and will conduct myself in such a manner as that you will have no cause to express regrets.

I am yours, respectfully,
W. M. Davidson

William Mordecai won the election by a flattering majority vote. He served in the House of Representatives in Little Rock as the representative for Sharp County until his untimely death.

Following are newspaper accounts of his life and death in Little Rock:

A SAD ENDING[1]

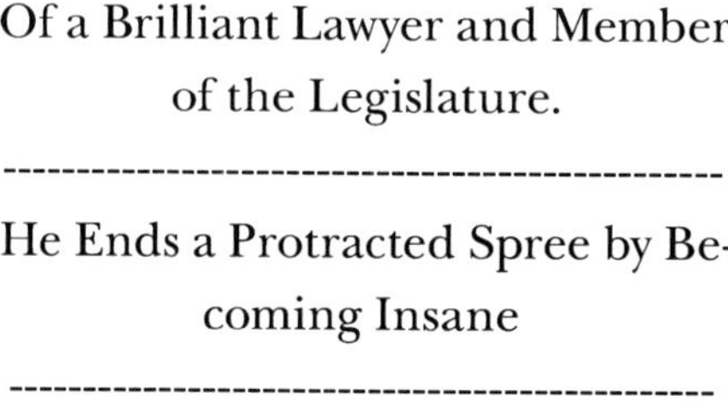

Of a Brilliant Lawyer and Member
of the Legislature.

He Ends a Protracted Spree by Becoming Insane

---

1 (Arkansas History Commission, One Capital Mall, Little Rock, AR., Newspaper Collection, Arkansas Gazette, March 1, 1883, Little Rock, Arkansas)

And Hurling Himself into the River–
Action of the House–Work of
Friends–Statements, Etc.

It is sad to chronicle death at any time, but when it comes with horrible details it is doubly so. This morning we announced the death by drowning of Hon. W. M. Davidson, of Sharp county, member of the Lower House of the General Assembly. But few of our citizens knew him, for the reason that his visits to Little Rock were few and far between.

HE MET HIS DEATH

probably about 3 o'clock yesterday morning, and his body is now eddying and tossed about in the depths of the swollen and muddy Arkansas.

The deceased who was elected representative by a flattering majority took his seat at the convening of the legislature, occupying a desk on the east of the house with Representative Davidson, of Izard county. He was gladly welcomed by those who knew him, and many who knew his brother, Hon. S. H. Davidson, also of Sharp County, sought him out and wished him well. During his younger days and, in fact, until a few years since, he had been a heavy drinker. However, realizing at last that he was throwing his life away, he made a general reformation, and for many months prior to coming to Little Rock not a drop of intoxicating liquor had passed his lips. He was respected, honored and beloved. His ambition was high, and those who knew him best and were aware of his ability as a lawyer and honor and integrity as a gentleman placed no gauge upon his ambition. He was a most eloquent speaker, and gifted with a logical and winning manner. He

William Mordecai Davidson - 1882

ADDRESSED THE HOUSE ONLY ONCE OR TWICE but when he spoke, everybody listened. But to go back a little: On reaching Little Rock, after successfully fighting through the first week with its attendant excitements and temptations, he was lured by friends into the haunts of his old enemy, and fell an easy victim. His friends generally, and members of the legislature especially, hurried to his aid and were unremitting in their attentions. Every effort was made to restore him to his right mind, but all in vain. The old conqueror–a disease beyond his power to combat–had him in its grasp, and he abandoned himself utterly. "Poor Davidson", his friends would sigh, as they met him on the street, and, one on each side, would by persuasion and force take him to the Grand Central, where he boarded, only, however, a few hours later to see him on the street or in the state house yard. Tuesday he was wild and desperate, and

FAILED TO RECOGNIZE

those he knew. That night the clerks of the house worked on their journals, and about 2 o'clock in the morning (yesterday), Richard Daniels, a colored man, and one of the janitors of the house found him wandering aimlessly around the yard. He took him by the arm, and finally got him into the house and up by the fireplace. There the colored man made a pallet and placed a pillow under his head. Other matters then required his attention, and half an hour later, hearing pistol shots he cast a quick glance at the spot where he had left the deceased, saw he was gone and hastened downstairs, fearing he had shot himself. He arrived just in time to see him run down toward the railroad, west and in rear of the state house. Almost at that instant he heard

A SPLASH IN THE RIVER

and cries for help. Daniels was interviewed yesterday by a reporter of THE GAZETTE, with the following result:

"How was Davidson acting when you saw him?"

"Like a crazy man. I saw him riding his cane like a boy ten years old."

"Did you talk to him?"

"Yes; he told me he was afraid someone intended to kill him, but he was 'fixed', clasping his hand upon his revolver."

"How many shots did you hear?"

"Three."

Hon. J. F. Rives, of White County, who was at the state house Tuesday night, made the following statement to THE GAZETTE reporter:

"About 2:30 a.m. two shots were heard, then a third, and immediately someone jumped from the back portico of the capitol and ran to the northwest corner of the yard. Soon afterwards the cries of someone in distress were heard in the direction of the river. In a few moments the cry 'Oh, God,' was followed by

"HE IS GONE."

Men in a boat were seen with lanterns eagerly searching along the prow and sides of the vessel. A search was made at 7 o'clock near the corner of the enclosure above mentioned, and the tracks of a man were discovered on the outside, as if he had fallen against the embankment."

The deceased leaves a wife and four children. He was 39 years of age, a native of Tennessee, had been a resident of Arkansas for sixteen years, was a member of the Methodist Church, and a resident of Evening Shade, the county seat of Sharp County.

HIS REMAINS

are clad in a dark suit of clothes, white shirt and underclothing. In the pocket of his pants is a roll of money, supposed to be about $30; in his vest pocket a two and one-half ounce key-winding coin silver watch, also a three strand wire link gold vest chain, and gold keystone charm. On one of his fingers is a cameo and pearl ring.

In the house yesterday great regret was expressed at the sad death of the member. A full report in relation thereto will be found in the legislative proceedings.

# # #

THE DEAD LEGISLATOR[1]

Interviewing One of His Friends and the Result Thereof

The Killing of Holloway–Employment of Guards to Watch for the Body

---

"I'll tell you," said a member of the house yesterday to a reporter of THE GAZETTE, "when Davidson, as we all called him, was himself, no nicer man could be found in our state. During the past year or two he had taken higher rank than ever before among members of the bar, and was classed as one of the rising men of north Arkansas."

"In what condition did he leave his family?"

"A wife and four children are left almost destitute. They depended on his practice."

"Was he a successful lawyer?"

""Yes, and of late unusually so; he was always eloquent, and when 'fired up' he became impassioned and no jury could withstand his appeals."

"It is said he killed two men during his life. Do you know the facts?"

"No, I think, however, he killed only one–Holloway. This was at Clover Bend, and during reconstruction. If I remember correctly, it was due to political differences. He was the friend of every man when he was himself, and one truer to his friends never lived."

"Has word of his death been sent to his widow?"

"Yes, and it probably reached her yesterday. A telegram was sent to Batesville, with orders to forward by special messenger to Eve-

---

1 (Arkansas History Commission, One Capital Mall, Little Rock, AR., Newspaper Collection, Arkansas Gazette, March 3, 1883, Little Rock, Arksnasas)

ning Shade. We look for Sam Davidson, his brother, on tomorrow's train."

Yesterday the House of Representatives by resolution ordered the employment of three guards to be stationed at different points along the river for the purpose of recovering the body should it come to the surface.

IDENTIFIED[1]

It seems almost without doubt that the dead body found on Pennington's bar, described in yesterday's GAZETTE, was that of Hon. Wm. M. Davidson, of Evening Shade, Sharp county. He was a member of the legislature of 1881, and committed suicide by jumping in the river. His body was never recovered. He was a member of the Royal Arch Masons, Rural chapter No. 50, which was the inscription on the Mark Master's key or fob, and his initials were on the watch discovered on the dead man.

# # #

MUST BE DAVIDSON[2]

The following letter was received from Hon. Geo.Thornburgh, of Powhatan, yesterday:

To the Editor of The Gazette:

The dead body of a drowned man, found twenty miles below Little Rock, and reported in THE GAZETTE of the 1st, is certainly that of Wm. M. Davidson, who was supposed to have drowned himself at Little Rock in February, 1883, while he was a member

---

1 (Arkansas History Commission, One Capital Mall, Little Rock, AR., Newspaper Collection, Arkansas Gazette, March 2, 1884, Little Rock, Arkansas)

2 (Arkansas History Commission, One Capital Mall, Little Rock, AR., Newspaper Collection, Arkansas Gazette, March 5, 1884, Little Rock, Arkansas)

of the legislature, from Sharp County. His initials were W.M.D. and Rural Chapter, R.A.M., is located at Evening Shade, where he lived.

Yours, etc., GEO. THORNBURGH

###

HON. W. M. DAVIDSON[1]

> Yesterday morning the remains of Hon. W. M. Davidson of Sharp County were laid to their last resting place in Mount Holly Cemetery. The sad fate with which he met, and the strange discovery of his bleached skeleton on the sands at Pennington bar, are remembered by every body. He was a Mason, and was buried in the lots of the Grand Lodge. Governor Berry, State Treasurer Woodruff, Secretary of State Frolich, Hon. A. J. McGinnis, of Sharp County, and others were present at the cemetery, and the Rev. T. C. Tuper read the beautiful Episcopal service. The flag over the state house was placed at half-mast during the day, in respect to the memory of one of the state's brightest and most unfortunate sons.

The coin silver pocket watch found on the remains of William Mordecai is still in the Davidson Family. It was passed down from generation to generation and is now in the possession of great grandson Donald G. Davidson having been passed to him by grand daughter Elizabeth V. "Betty" (Davidson) Ramey. The gold watch fob recovered the same time as the watch was stolen several years ago from the person who had it at the time.

The Family never completely accepted the conclusion that William Mordecai committed suicide. How is it a man commits sui-

1 (Arkansas History Commission, One Capital Mall, Little Rock, AR., Newspaper Collection, Arkansas Gazette, March 26, 1884, Little Rock, Arkansas)

cide by shooting himself three times and then throws himself into a river?

There is reason to believe it could have been a revenge killing by Holloway's family. William Mordecai killed Holloway in an altercation in a dispute over the manner in which penalties were handled under the Reconstruction regulations. William Mordecai was exonerated by reason of self-defense. The Holloway family members refused to accept that verdict and vowed revenge.

Life was not easy for Mary and her family after William Mordecai died. She was left with very little resource and five sons, the oldest only eleven years old and the youngest three months old. The boys received very little education.

The fourth son, Frederick "Fred" told his children what life was like when he did go to school. He said he would take a cornbread and molasses sandwich to school for lunch. And, when he was ready to eat his lunch the ants had already been there and eaten the molasses.

All the sons had to quit school and go to work at an early age to help support the family. About 1884 Mary was awarded a contract to carry the U.S. Mail from Hardy (which was on the railroad) to Evening Shade and other nearby towns. The older boys carried the mail on muleback.

Fred often told his children about carrying the mail on mule back when he was eleven years old. Samuel Mordecai "Mord" also told his grandchildren about carrying the mail on muleback when he was a youngster.

However, with all the hardship and hard work, the sons of William Mordecai and Mary endured their childhoods. Throughout their lives they were men of good character, honest, honorable, good husbands and loving fathers. William Mordecai and Mary would be proud of them.

Sometime shortly before 1900 Mary and her sons moved to a farm near Hardy, Arkansas. They lived there when the 1900

Census was taken. Mary had been sick with asthma for several years. One day in June 1903 she was very sick. She asked Fred to stay home with her while the other boys went to work on the farm. She died that day while alone with Fred.

Her sons took her to Evening Shade for burial in the Sharp Cemetery, now known as the Evening Shade Cemetery, about half a mile southeast from Evening Shade proper. She is in an unmarked grave. Several searches have been made in the cemetery. So far, we have been unable to locate her grave.

CHAPTER 5

SAMUEL MORDECAI DAVIDSON

SAMUEL MORDECAI "Mord" DAVIDSON, the second born child, son of William Mordecai and Mary Elizabeth "Mollie" (Wainwright) Davidson, was born 9 February 1873 at Evening Shade, Sharp County, Arkansas. He married Meta Pauline Clarke 2 January 1901 at Hardy, Sharp County, Arkansas. Mord and Meta had two children: (1) William "Willie" Edmund, born 10 November 1901; and (2) Mary Arabella, born 29 September 1903.

Meta's parents were Edmund Stillman Clarke (1852-1930) and Arabella Taylor (Champlain) Clarke (1852-1934). Edmund Stillman Clarke's parents were Paul Roger Clarke (1802-1877) and Polly Barton (Rogers) Clarke (1800-1869). Arabella Taylor Champlain's parents were Charles Champlain (1824-1903) and Hannah Maria (Taylor) Champlain (1829- ?). She was part Narragansett Indian.

Mord's father, William Mordecai Davidson, died at Little Rock, Arkansas, in 1883, when Mord was ten years old.

Mord died 29 August 1953 at Kansas City, Wyandotte County, Kansas. He was buried 31 August 1953 in Memorial Park Cemetery, Section 12, Lot 114, Space 6, Edmond, Oklahoma County, Oklahoma. His wife, Meta, died 6 July 1970 at Kansas City, Wyandotte County, Kansas, and is buried next to her husband in

Memorial Park Cemetery, in Space 5, Edmond, Oklahoma County, Oklahoma.

Following is an obituary in the Kansas City newspaper. The newspaper was faded brown when found January 23, 1999, taped to the inside cover of an old journal kept by his son, William E. Davidson, of Brenham, Texas. There was no date on the notice:

> SAMUEL M. DAVIDSON, 80, of 1504 North Thirtieth, died this morning at the home. He was a retired farmer. Mr. Davidson had been a resident here eight years. He was a member of the Methodist Church in Lexington, Okla.
>
> Surviving are his wife, Mrs. Meta Davidson of the home; a daughter, Mrs. Mary Dunahoo, of the home; a son, William E. Davidson, Oklahoma City, Okla.; two brothers, Fred Davidson, Sacramento, Calif., and Cyrus B. Davidson, Rogers, Arkansas., and eight grandchildren and eleven great-grandchildren.
>
> Services will be held Monday in Oklahoma City. Burial will be in that city also. The body will lie in state after 5 o'clock this afternoon at the Porter & Sons funeral Home.

Mord appears in the 1880 Census living with his father and mother at Evening Shade. After the death of his father Mord and his brothers carried the U.S. Mail by muleback between Hardy and Evening Shade to help support the family. He joined the United Methodist Church in Evening Shade in September 1892. He moved to Hardy sometime later with his mother and three of his brothers. He appears in the 1900 Census with his mother and brothers at Hardy, Arkansas.

After marriage in 1901 Mord and Meta lived on Meta's 160-acre farm located in Section 17, T19N, R6W, on Big Otter Creek adjacent to and north of the original Clarke homestead near Hardy, Arkansas. Meta homesteaded this place a few years before their marriage. Meta's father and brother, Norman, helped Mord and Meta build a house on the farm.

Their first child, William Edmund, was born at the Clarke homestead near Cedar Spring as was their daughter, Mary Arabella.

Mord cleared the land, cut ties, split rails, and farmed the cleared land for the next few years.

Mord, for most of his life, had a kind of restless wanderlust about him. He seemed to be always longing and searching for some intangible thing, thus he was more often than not a rolling stone that never gathered much moss

For whatever reasons, Mord and Meta in January 1908 packed all their belongings and loaded them with their two children into a covered wagon, hitched a team of mules and headed for western Oklahoma. John Collins, a relative, had a farm on Salt Fork of Red River near Sayre, Oklahoma.

Mord and family stayed a short time with John Collins until they located a farm at Welk's Corner eight miles north of Sayre owned by Mr. Welk who also owned a store and cotton gin. Mord made a share crop arrangement with Mr. Welk to plant cotton on his farm for a share of the proceeds from the crop. A thunderstorm with large hailstones destroyed the crop in June.

Mord once again loaded his family and belongings into the wagon and headed for Oklahoma City to seek work. There they located on a fifty-five acre farm located about a mile west of St. Mary's Academy on SW 29th Street. The Voltz brothers owned the farm. They also owned a major plumbing company.

Mord planted a corn crop and worked around Oklahoma City doing odd jobs. His son, Willie, said Mord made a good corn crop on the Voltz place because he remembers a Mexican man coming to get corn shucks for making tamales.

Willie and Mary attended Lee elementary school located near SW 29th and South Walker Streets.

Mord and family sometime in 1909 moved from the Voltz Farm to a house at 429 West Washington Street in Oklahoma City.

Mord used his wagon and team of mules to haul brick, sand and gravel during the early day construction boom in Oklahoma City. Many of these materials were used for the construction of some of the Oklahoma City schools, including Willard Elementary at NW 2nd and Blackwelder Streets. Many of the bricks were laid to make the brick streets in downtown Oklahoma City.

A Negro man named Kenny slept over the barn and worked for Mord loading and unloading the materials on the wagon, and sometimes driving the team. Willie and Mary attended Washington Elementary School.

Mord again in October 1911 loaded his family and belongings into the covered wagon and headed for Texas. When they got to Red River near Idabell, Mord went down and looked at the river. He decided not to cross into Texas. They turned east and went into Arkansas to DeQueen. They didn't stay there long. They shortly returned to southeast Oklahoma in McCurtin County.

They meandered around and through eastern Oklahoma the next two years. Mord worked timber, worked as a day laborer, made railroad ties, worked at sawmills, and worked the hay fields. Mord, Meta and the children picked cotton, gathered potatoes, and picked apples. Anything to make a little money.

When the winter of 1913 arrived, Mord and family were at Wagoner, Oklahoma. Mord became sick and was "raving mad with fever," as told by Willie. Meta drove the team and wagon with Mord and children to her parent's home near Hardy, Arkansas. There, Mord recuperated and regained his health.

Mord, Meta and children moved back into the house on Meta's farm next to her parents' farm. Meta rented a small apartment in Hardy for $2 a month so Willie and Mary could go to school. For whatever reason, that arrangement lasted only a few weeks. Mord worked cutting timber and making railroad ties.

In January 1914 Mord again loaded his family and Meta's parents, Edmund and Arabella Clarke, in a covered wagon and headed west through northern Arkansas for Oklahoma. They departed early in the morning and that evening they camped on a hill about ten miles west. After nightfall Mord looked east and saw the reflection in the sky of a large fire over the distant horizon. He commented there must be a big fire back to the east. Months later they learned it was their house on Meta's farm that burned to the ground that night. They never knew what caused the fire.

Willie told of a traveling visitor from Texas to their campfire one evening near Eureka Springs in the heart of the Ozark Mountains. The Texan had a small suitcase with a short piece of rope hanging out. Meta asked if he was a cowboy. He answered, "No. Why do you ask?" Meta pointed to the rope and asked, "Then why do you carry a rope with you?" The man said, "I use it to tie myself to a tree when I sleep so I won't roll down these hills."

Mord, Meta, the two children and Meta's parents arrived at McGuire late in February 1914. It was a small community east of Noble, Oklahoma. Mord's brother, Cyrus and his wife, Emma, lived at McGuire. They stayed with Cyrus and Emma about two weeks while Mord looked for a farm to rent. Willie remembers helping Cyrus cut willow trees and burning them. He also remembers that Emma and Mrs. Clarke did not get along very well.

Mord and family with the Clarkes soon moved onto the Gray Place southeast of Noble. Willie remembers that soon afterwards they took his grandparents, the Clarkes, to the train station in Noble to catch the train back home to Arkansas. Mr. Clarke did not like the sandy prairie lands and red soil tainted rivers of Oklahoma. He preferred the hills, rocks, tall trees and clear water streams of northern Arkansas. Willie and Mary attended Alamo school while they lived on the Gray place.

Mord share cropped the Gray Place and made good corn and cotton crops in 1914. However, in 1915 the crops were hailed out and they had to move. They moved in January of 1916 to a fifty-five acre farm known as the Smith Place. It was on the east bank of the South Canadian River southwest of Noble. Willie remembers the old house and barn were "like the Leaning Tower of Pisa." Willie and Mary attended Canada school.

Mord planted twenty acres of cotton and thirty acres of corn. That fall he made ten bales of cotton and harvested about sixteen hundred bushels of corn. The soil was a good sandy loam and the rains that year came at just the right times.

In January 1917 Mord and family moved to the Boggs Place southeast of Noble, Oklahoma. It was a hundred and sixty acres of upland with twenty acres of pasture and the rest in cultivation. It did not have much of a house or barn. It was owned by Frank Boggs, the sheriff of Cleveland County. Mord had a share crop arrangement with the sheriff. Willie and Mary went to Canada school. Mord made good crops in the years 1917, 1918, and 1919. He got good prices for his crops.

In the winter of 1919 Mord and family moved to the Kline Place near Willow View northeast of Lexington, Oklahoma. This was the year Mord's brother, Fred, and his wife, Nora, and family moved to McGuire, Oklahoma. By this time Willie was no longer going to grade school. He took the County Educational Equivalency Exam and received a certificate that entitled him to attend high school.

Samuel M. and Meta Davidson with children Mary Arabella and William Edmund - 1908

In 1920 Willie planted thirty acres of cotton. By fall the price of cotton was so low it would cost more to pick it than it would sell for at market. He left it in the field and left home to go to high school at Oklahoma Central State Teachers College in Edmond, Oklahoma. This same year Mord's brother, Cyrus, had twenty bales of cotton and could not sell it. So, he and his family packed up and moved to California.

Mord and Meta continued to live on the Kline Place during the years 1919 through 1925. Mord become well acquainted with John Abernathy who owned a wholesale grocery business in Purcell, Oklahoma, just across the river from Lexington. John was the son of J. L. Abernathy of Evening Shade, Arkansas, who relocated to Purcell in Indian Territory sometime prior to 1898.

Mord had several teams of good mules. He and John decided to become business partners and go into the roadbed building business. John was the financial mainstay for the partnership. Mord provided the mule teams, equipment, and laborers.

In 1925 they bid and received a contract from the State of Oklahoma to build two and a half miles of roadbed for Highway #77 between Nobel and Lexington. By this time Willie had finished school at Edmond. He was working on a dragline for the General Construction Company dredging Little River. The company soon after went defunct and Willie came home to work for his father on the roadbed construction job. He was plowboy, straw boss, and powder monkey blowing out tree stumps with dynamite.

When the Noble roadbed construction job was completed Mord bid and received a contract on a four mile roadbed construction job on Highway #270 between Holdenville and Wewoka, Oklahoma.

In the meantime Willie married Mary Pauline Roller. He and his new bride lived with Mord and Meta in a tent at the construction site while Willie continued to work for his father. Willie's wife worked helping Meta prepare and serve meals for the work crews. This arrangement didn't last long. Willie and wife soon moved to Oklahoma City to make a life of their own.

In 1927 Mord bid and received a contract for a roadbed construction job from the State of Arkansas near Forrest City. This job was a disaster for two reasons. First, Mord greatly under bid the job not realizing the amount of fill dirt required to be hauled long distances to lay down a roadbed through some of the swampy areas. Second, his partner, John L. Abernathy, was in serious financial difficulty. Mord and Meta returned to Oklahoma City practically penniless.

John L. Abernathy was a partner in the retail grocery firm of Abernathy & Sneed; Abernathy & Hoggard; and the Purcell Wholesale Grocery. He organized the Abernathy Oil and White Daisy Oil companies that operated in Purcell; also the Troy Granite Gravel Company which did a large road gravel business with headquarters in Purcell. His death on 9 September 1931 resulted from an accident at his office while loading a gun.[1]

By 1928 Mord and Meta lived on North Francis Street in Oklahoma City. Mord worked for a while as a laborer at a pickle factory on North Broadway. He later worked as a flagman for the Rock Island Railroad flagging at North Harvey and Second Streets. Meta worked at the NuWay Laundry at North Western and Sixth Streets with Jewel Roller, Pauline's younger sister.

Sometime during 1930 Mord and Meta moved back to Arkansas. This time they located on the upper Herron Place west of Hardy. It was situated near a steep rocky bluff across Cow Ford on the west bank of South Fork River next to Raccoon Springs.

Sometime in the past the Herron Family had been good friends of the Davidsons at Evening Shade. A kind lady fondly known by all as Aunt Kate Herron rented the farm to Mord at a very reasonable rate.

It is not known what happened to the farm owned by Meta when Mord and Meta first married. It was located only about a mile from the Herron Place on Little Otter Creek. It is assumed that at some time of great financial need the farm was sold.

---

1 (Mord's son, Willie, said Abernathy was in serious financial difficulty before the Crash of 1929 which also contributed to the failure of their partnership. Willie said Abernathy's death was not an accident. It was a suicide.)

Today, the Herron Place and Meta's farm are part of what is known as Cherokee Village, a large retirement and recreational community. The golf course occupies most of what was the Herron place. Today a person can stand at the approximate location of the house, look across the fairways toward the river and see the steep bluff on the other side across old Cow Ford. Raccoon Springs was modified into a holding pool and is a source of water supply for Cherokee Village, a resort development of several hundred homes.

In the early days Raccoon Springs was a rushing torrent of crystal clear cold almost knee-deep water rushing from its source in the hillside, down a gentle slope, over a roaring waterfalls, and then underground to flow into the river beneath the surface. Today, only a trickle of the water reaches the river. Most of it is siphoned out by two large pumps for the resort water supply.

Mord and Meta lived on the Herron Place at Cow Ford until the fall of 1942. Mord tilled the soil, kept a few cows and raised hogs. The house was a small two room wooden frame house. It had a front porch that extended the full length of the house. Meta cooked on a wood burning cookstove. A wood burning stove was in the other room for heat in the winters. They did not have electricity. They used kerosene lamps and lanterns. There was a crude wood picket fence around the front yard.

The source for household water was a spring down the hill about fifty yards toward the creek. Mord shaped it out and made an enclosed spring box. Meta also floated buckets of milk and butter in the spring water during the warm months to keep them cool. Meta loved flowers and plants. She had many different kinds of plants in the yard and hanging baskets from the eaves of the porch. She had a small lemon tree in a large tub she kept in the house during the cold winter months. She moved it outside in the warmth of spring and summer. She prized the few lemons she was able to harvest each year from that little tree.

Meta also loved birds. She did all the various things to attract them around the house. For several years a pair of wrens nested in her kitchen and raised their young. She went to considerable effort to accommodate and protect the family of wrens, even making the cat stay outside.

Meta also liked to fish. It was not unusual to find her with her hook and line in the current of the river catching a "mess of fish" for supper.

At this time during the 1930's only four of the six Davidson brothers were still alive. Virgil Lee died in 1882. George Osburne died in 1908. Walter lived at Thayer, Missouri. Fred and Cyrus lived in California.

Meta's youngest brother, Edmund, and his family of ten children lived on the original Clarke farm. It was about two miles from where Mord and Meta lived on the Herron Place at Cow Ford. It is believed that Meta probably felt more at home there than all the other places they previously lived after they first left Arkansas.

Willie and his family of five children visited his father and mother in 1932, 1934 and 1936 while they lived on the Herron Place. Mary and her family of three children would sometimes visit her parents at Cow Ford on South Fork River.

In 1942 Willie and his family lived on a farm southwest of Moore, Oklahoma. They lived there several years. Willie worked in Oklahoma City. He and the boys worked the farm. They managed to have several fairly good crops and accumulated a good team of mules, a few farm implements, and several good milk cows.

Sometime in the summer of 1942 Mord and Willie decided to go together in a farming partnership. They rented the Cochran Farm on Strawberry River about three miles north of Evening Shade, Arkansas. The Cochrans were related to the Herrons. It was through dear Aunt Kate they were able to rent the Cochran Place.

In November after the crops were harvested, Willie and family moved from Moore to the house on the south side of the river on the Cochran Farm. They made two trips in a 1937 Ford truck from Oklahoma to Arkansas. One to move the mules and cows. The other was to move the implements and household goods.

The house on Strawberry River was an old two room wooden frame with a lean-to kitchen and dining room on the back. Each of the two rooms had a stone fireplace. At one time there had been a 'dog-trot' between the two rooms. It had long ago been enclosed and made into a small room and storage area. A plank front porch ran the full length of the house.

The barn was across the road from the house. It was a conventional type barn of fairly good construction. In fact, the barn was still standing in the year 2004 in good shape. The house had long since deteriorated to nothingness. Today a new modern paved highway runs directly over the place where the old house was.

Mord and Meta again packed their belongings and moved to the house on the north side of Strawberry River on the Cochran Farm. Willie and the boys helped move the livestock, farm implements, and household goods from the Herron Place on South Fork River to the Cochran Farm on Strawberry River. The house was an old two room wood frame with a lean-to kitchen on the back and a small front porch. It sat on a small rocky hill about a quarter of a mile from the river ford crossing.

The Cochran Place was one thousand and eighty-three acres of mostly hilly upland covered with timber and rocks. However, it had three bottoms along the river. One was behind the barn and consisted of about sixty acres. Another was across the river from the sixty acres. It consisted of about forty acres. The Big Bottom was on the same side of the river as the barn but because of a big bluff and the way the river flowed, it was necessary to cross the river twice to get to it. It was about a quarter of a mile wide and half a mile long. It consisted of about three hundred acres of good bottomland soil. They subleased the north part of the Big Bottom to a neighbor, Mr. Kunkel.

Mord and Willie pooled their resources and purchased an old Farmall F-20 tractor with steel lug wheels and some farm implements. With Mord's and Willie's mules they had six spans of mules plus Old Bill. He was a tall lanky contrary mule that couldn't be teamed with another mule, but he was stout as an ox and twice as stubborn as a mule. He was used only on single hitch jobs.

Mord, Willie and the boys did the spring plowing and planted corn in the sixty-acre bottom north of the barn, cotton in the Big Bottom, and hay in the small bottom. Mord and Willie gambeled all their resources on one good crop. The country was mobilizing for World War II and prices for farm commodities were good. But, Lady Fortune did not smile upon them.

They were flooded out, not once, but twice. The cotton was just planted and started to germinate when the first flood came. It destroyed the entire crop. The water receded in a few days. The tractor had been left in the field and was almost buried out of sight. It had to be dug out and overhauled. Everyone turned to and re-planted the crops.

The cotton was about three inches tall when the second flood came. It was much worse than the first one. It came in July. It was unheard of to flood in July. The floodwaters came to the back of the barn. It covered the fields for the better part of a week. When the waters finally receded, large sandbars had washed over the fields. The crops were destroyed.

It was a total disaster for Mord and Willie. It was much too late to even think of trying to put in another crop, even if they had the money to do it. They tried to salvage a little by cutting and baling hay. They had totally expended their resources and had no recourse but to give it up. They sold what little hay they had harvested, sold the cows, the mules and the farm implements that could be salvaged.

In the fall of 1943 Willie and family returned to Oklahoma City where they owned a small house. Willie could get work at his former place of employment as a dockworker at Joe Hodges, a motor freight line company. Mord and Meta moved to the lower Herron Place below Johnson Bend on South Fork River near where Otter Creek flows into the river near Hardy. This arrangement lasted a few short years.

Sometime in 1947 Mord and Meta again packed their belongings and moved to Kansas City, Kansas, to live with their daughter, Mary, and her husband, Jim Dunahoo. They lived in a small apartment in the basement.

Mord first worked for a contractor that contracted with the Southern Pacific Railroad to clean out the burn boxes on steam locomotives. They had to inspect for repairs and restart fires in the burn boxes. It was dirty, grimy and hard physical labor, and Mord was no young man. After about a year he gave that up and went to work for a major produce wholesaler and retailer in Kansas City. He handled crates of produce and made fruit and vegetable displays on the retail counters. He worked there until the spring of 1953 when it was discovered he had throat and lung cancer.

Mord never used tobacco. He never used alcohol. The only thing that could have caused his throat and lung cancer was the coal dust he breathed while cleaning and servicing the burn boxes on the steam locomotives. The only protection the workers wore were kerchiefs covering their mouths and noses.

Mord suffered through the late spring and summer of 1953 with failing health. Meta had her hands full trying to care for Mord. She was not a young woman. The physical and emotional stress was almost overwhelming.

Mary was employed at Singer Sewing Machine Company. Jim was employed with the Rock Island Railroad in the Armourdale Yards. Mary and Jim worked days. Mord and Meta's grandson, Don, also worked for the Rock Island Railroad out of El Reno, Oklahoma, as a brakeman. With Jim's influence and effort Don transferred to the Armourdale Yards as a switchman so he could live with Mary and Jim to help Meta care for Mord.

Don worked from midnight to seven o'clock in the morning. He got home about eight o'clock shortly after Mary and Jim left for work. He was there during the day to help Meta with Mord. Don took Mord to his doctor appointments, and stayed with him during his treatments. Don read books, magazines, newspapers, and the sports pages to him. Mord in his youth played baseball and was always interested in the results of baseball games. He knew the batting averages and pitching statistics of certain players.

Mary got home from work about four-thirty o'clock in the afternoon. Don would go to bed and sleep until eleven o'clock. Then he would get up and be on the job in the Armourdale Yards at midnight. This arrangement lasted until a few days before Mord died.

Death did not come easily. Mord suffered immensely. He died 29 August 1953 at Mary and Jim's home in Kansas City. He was eighty years old.

Life was not easy for Meta. She had practically no resource. Yet she was always smiling, loving and pleasant. She was not one to dwell on the unfortunate events in her life. Most of her remaining years she traveled from family member to family member to live a few days, weeks, or months, until she felt she had worn her welcome thin. She visited her Grandson, Don, and his wife in Brownsville, Texas, and went deep-sea fishing and visited Mexico. Several years later in 1958 she visited a few months with Don, his wife, Pat, and their baby son, Greg, in Oklahoma City.

Meta died July 6, 1970. She was ninety-three years old.

CHAPTER 6

META PAULINE CLARKE

META PAULINE CLARKE, first born child, daughter of Edmund Stillman (1852-1930) and Arabella Taylor (Champlain) Clarke (1852-1934), was born 1 May 1877 at Westerly, Washington County, Rhode Island. She died 6 July 1970 at Kansas City, Wyandotte County, Kansas, and is buried next to her husband in Memorial Park Cemetery, in Space 5, Edmond, Oklahoma County, Oklahoma.

She married Samuel Mordecai "Mord" Davidson 2 January 1901 at the home of her parent's three miles southwest of Hardy, Sharp County, Arkansas, by Esquire H. D. Dark. Meta and Mord had two children: (1) William Edmund, born 10 November 1901; and (2) Mary Arabella, born 29 September 1903.

Edmund Stillman Clarke was the son of Paul Roger Clarke (1802-1877) and Polly Barton (Rogers) Clarke (1800-1869). He was born 23 June 1852 at Little Genesee, New York. He died 27 July 1930 at Hardy, Sharp County, Arkansas. He married Arabella Taylor Champlain, the daughter of Charles Champlain (1824-1903) and Hannah Maria (Taylor) Champlain (1829) on 12 August 1876. She was born 2 August 1852 at Bradford, Connecticut. She died 2 July 1934 at Hardy, Sharp County, Arkansas. Edmund and Arabella are buried in the Highland Cemetery a few miles south of Hardy, Arkansas.[1]

1 (See Appendix 5 for the Clarke Eleven Generations Chart.)

The Clarkes lived at Westerly, Rhode Island, located on Pawcatuck Sound in the very southwest part of the state. Fishing was a mainstay of the Westerly economy. It also served as a port of call for transoceanic cargo sailing ships.

Some of the Clarkes were seafaring people during the age of the three-mast clipper sailing ships. They traveled to many foreign ports and among the islands of the West Indies where they often acquired large conch shells.

A small hole was bored in the large end of the shell. This enabled a person to blow through the hole causing a large horn-like sound. Each shell had its own unique sound. These shells were used as fog horns on the ships. They also were used to summon the workers to the house for meals, or other reasons, much like dinner bells were used on many early day farms.

Meta's grandson, Don Davidson, has one of the Clarke conch shells. Meta told him, "It was kept at the front door and used to summon the menfolks from the docks to the house." The shell is very old and bleached from being outside a number of years when in possession of Meta's son, "Willie" (Bill). Don learned how to blow it when a boy and can make a few different tones with it.

When Meta was five years old her family moved from Westerly, Rhode Island, to Farina, Illinois. They traveled part of the way by mule-drawn canalboat, by train through Canada, sailing on a boat across Lake Erie, and by train to Farina. It is not known why they re-located from Westerly to Farina.

The Edmund Stillman Clarke Family relocated from Farina, Illinois, to Hardy, Arkansas in 1897. Edmund Clarke had a successful slaughter business in Farina. They lived in a very nice house as evidenced by old photographs. It is unknown why Edmund decided to sell his business and house and relocate from Farina to Arkansas. They traveled by covered wagon with another family, the Metcalfs.

Meta was twenty years old at the time and well educated for a young lady of the times. She kept a daily diary of the trip.[1]

Following is a letter written November 7, 1968, by Meta to her son, Bill, and his wife, Pauline, when Meta lived in Kansas City, Kansas, with her daughter, Mary, and her husband, Jim Dunahoo. The letter was transcribed June 25, 1999, by her grandson, Don Davidson. No attempt was made to correct grammar or misspelled words:

> Dear William & Pauline:
>
> I will try to scratch you a few lines. I may have to hunt a different pencil. It seems like this one won't do much good.
>
> Here today has been bright and sunshiny. Jim and Mary has been off most of the day. They had a borrowed book which I wanted to read.
>
> I don't see good out of my eyes and don't read long or steady. The book was wrote by a doctor I had met, but did not know well. Thomas A. Dooley, M.D. The story was the Night They Burned the Mountain. He wrote it to his mother and to Dwight Davis.
>
> It was in or around about Aug. or Sept 1958 or 1959 I had met the Dr., but did not know him well. Some of his writing I did not know, but some was as I remembered them. I liked the Dr. He could be and, could be funny at times, but when it came to business he was there and strick. As a friend he was there in some things. We didn't always agree.
>
> Mary is getting ready. She and Mary Belle is giving a big dinner Friday. Will have a house running over full and a big dinner. Yes, they will let me nosey around them for most are good friends of mine, or were before I took sick.
>
> I have wrote this at so many different times it will take more than a California lawyer to read it, but it's full of love to over flowing. Worlds of love from Mother. øøøø. If you ever get it waded through. Love.

---

1 (See Appendix 2 for a transcription.)

I have messed these up so folded them seperate. Maybe can make them out and get a little good. If not, chuck them in the fire. They will make (kindlin) fire to cook your supper.

Anyway, Mother loves her Son, William.

I hope you can make this out. You may have to be a lawyer, but anyway is full of love from your Mother.

CHAPTER 7

WILLIAM EDMUND DAVIDSON

WILLIAM EDMUND "Bill" DAVIDSON, first born child, son of Samuel Mordecai "Mord" and Meta Pauline (Clarke) Davidson, was born 10 November 1901 near Hardy, Sharp County, Arkansas. His sister, Mary Arabella, was born 29 September 1903 near Hardy.

Bill (also known as "Willie" by his mother and father) married Mary Pauline Roller 8 May 1925 in Pauls Valley, Garvin County, Oklahoma. Pauline was born 1 March 1905, the daughter and second child born to Dillmus Elias Roller and Arlie Luvida (Jones) Roller.

Bill and Pauline had five children: (1) William Lee, born 3 March 1926; (2) Bobby Joe, born 11 May 1927; (3) Donald Jean, born 7 December 1928; (4) Meta Luvida born 1 July 1931; and (5) Samuel Marvin born 20 January 1933.

Bill Davidson died 7 December 2005 at the Gazebo Convalescent Center in Brenham, Washington County, Texas. His wife, Mary Pauline, died 25 December 1988 at home in Brenham. She is buried in Section 12, Lot 114, Space 2 at Memorial Park Cemetery, 13400 North Kelly Street, Oklahoma City, Oklahoma County, Oklahoma 73131. Bill is buried in Space 1 next to Mary Pauline.

When Bill was born Mord and Meta lived on Meta's homestead, a 160-acre farm in Section 17, T19N, R6W. It was on Big Otter

Creek adjacent to and north of the original Clarke homestead near Hardy, Arkansas. Meta homesteaded this place before she married Mord. Meta's father and brother, Norman, helped Mord and Meta build a house on the farm. Bill was born at the Clarke home near Cedar Spring close to Little Otter Creek.

In January 1908 Mord and Meta packed their belongings and loaded them with their two children, Bill and Mary, into a covered wagon. They hitched a team of mules and headed for western Oklahoma.

This is a story Bill told during this time about the first automobile he saw:

> We were traveling by mule-drawn wagon from Arkansas to Western Oklahoma. We stopped in Muskogee and Dad went into a store to buy some supplies. Mary and I were playing around the wagon. Across the street we saw what looked like a buggy without shafts. We went over to look at it. A man wearing a long coat and a cap with goggles came out and got something from the floor of the buggy. He walked around to the front and started winding it up, or at least that is what we thought. All of a sudden it made a loud bang and then a loud noise. It scared us and we ran for the wagon. We watched the buggy go down the street in a cloud of dust. We couldn't understand what was making it go.
>
> That was my first time to see a car. It didn't have a steering wheel. It was guided by a hand lever.

John Collins, a relative, had a farm on Salt Fork of Red River near Sayre, Oklahoma. Mord and family stayed a short time with John until they located a farm at Welk's Corner eight miles north of Sayre owned by a Mr. Welk. He also owned a store and cotton gin.

Mord had a share crop arrangement with Mr. Welk to plant cotton on his farm for a share of the proceeds from the crop. The cotton crop was hailed out in June. Mord again loaded his family and belongings into the wagon and headed for Oklahoma City to seek work.

Bill told the following:

> Somewhere between the Welk farm and Oklahoma City we camped for the night. When we woke up the next morning the mules were gone. We could not understand how it was the mules got loose. Dad set out to track them so he could catch them and bring them back to the campsite. He left Mother, my sister, and me alone on the prairie with only the wagon.
>
> Late that afternoon a man on horseback stopped at the campsite. He asked Mother for something to eat. We didn't have much but she served him what little we had. He asked why we were alone in the middle of the prairie with only a wagon and no man around. Mother told him the mules got loose and Dad had gone to look for them. The man said he was a federal marshal and he thought he knew what happened. He said he would get the mules and rode off.
>
> The next afternoon Dad returned with the mules. It turned out the marshal knew about a man in the vicinity known to take things that did not belong to him, including mules and horses. I don't really know exactly what happened but apparently the marshal found Dad and took him to the man's place where Dad identified his mules. I don't know what happened to the man.

At Oklahoma City Mord located on a 55-acre farm about a mile west of Saint Mary's Academy on SW 29th Street owned by the Voltz brothers. They also owned a major plumbing company. Mord planted a corn crop and worked in and about Oklahoma City doing odd jobs. Bill remembered that his father made a good corn crop on the Voltz farm because he remembered a Mexican man coming to get corn shucks to make tamales. Bill and Mary attended Lee Elementary School located at the southeast corner of SW 29th and South Walker Streets.

Sometime in 1909 Mord moved the family from the Voltz farm to a house at 429 West Washington Street in Oklahoma City. Mord used his wagon and team of mules to haul brick, sand and gravel during the early day construction boom in Oklahoma City.

Bill and Mary attended Washington Elementary School. Bill was acquainted with a boy his age whose father was the janitor at the school. Saturdays Bill and his friend helped the father at the school. He let them slide down the enclosed curving fire escape from the second floor to the ground outside.

Bill was also acquainted with the King boys whose father owned King's Laundry on South Walker Street. Saturdays when the laundry was closed Bill and the King boys roller skated inside the laundry building among the washers and dryers. The floor was smooth concrete and it was great fun to skate around and through the building.

Bill's father took him to the Selz Brothers Flowtow Show at Delmar Garden on south Western Avenue. Delmar Garden was on the north bank of the North Canadian River. The Selz Brothers Flowtow Show was a two-ring circus under a big tent. It was there Bill first saw an elephant. It was also about this time that Bill's father took him to Delmar Garden to see Buffalo Bill Cody's Wild West Show. Bill shook hands with Buffalo Bill as he walked around the arena shaking hands with all the youngsters.

This is a story during this time Bill told about seeing an airship:

> My sister, Mary, and I one day in 1909 slipped away from the house at 429 West Washington in Oklahoma City and went to Delmar Garden where there was a show and carnival going on. We saw a big tent so we pulled the side up some to see inside. There was some kind of a machine in there. Didn't know what it was. Looked like a big long bag with a little house under it.
>
> About then a big man grabbed us and said in a gruff voice, "What you kids doing?" We were scared. Couldn't run. He had

> a hold of us. He says, "Scared?" I said, "Uh, huh." He says, "Do you know what I am going to do?" I said, "No, please don't hurt us." He said, "We're going in there and let you see that thing." I was still scared and Mary began to whimper. But, he said, "Don't be afraid. I'll take care of you."
>
> He took us inside and let us climb up in the little house and look it all over. He said, "This is an airship, and it goes way up in the sky and flies." He took us outside and said, "You kids better get on back home, but always be careful about crawling under tents." I guess we thanked him by the way we looked. He told us, "Bye-bye" and we took off for home.

Bill's family led a nomadic life from October 1911 until February 1914. They lived in a covered wagon as his father traveled from place to place in Eastern Oklahoma and Western Arkansas looking for work at any kind of jobs he could find. Bill and his sister did not attend school during this time.

Something about this period in Bill's life was bothersome to him. In his later years he told over and over that:

> I don't know why Dad suddenly pulled up and left Oklahoma City. He had a team of mules and a wagon. He was doing good hauling building materials around Oklahoma City. Mary and I were in school and we lived in a house. Dad joined the Teamsters Union.
>
> I was only ten years old but I remember there were problems with the Teamsters getting unionized and recognized by the contractors. There were a lot of disputes about work rules and payment. One day a man was killed in a melee with unionists. We left Oklahoma City the next day. I've often wondered if Dad had any thing to do with that.

In 1913 Mord became very ill. Meta with the two children drove the mules and wagon to Hardy, Arkansas, to the home of her parents. It was there that Mord recovered. In 1914 Mord and Meta once again loaded their belongings in the covered wagon with Bill and Mary and moved back to Oklahoma. Only this time they located on a farm near Noble, Oklahoma.

This is a story Bill told about that time in his life when they lived on the Gray Place southeast of Noble:

> I was fourteen years old and we lived on the Gray place northeast of Lexington. On Sunday mornings before church I would walk about a mile to the Methodist Church. I would get a fire started in the stove to warm the building, dust off the pews and chairs, arrange the hymn books, and make sure everything would be ready for the Sunday service.
>
> One day an itinerant traveler showed up riding a jenny with his few personal belongings in saddlebags across the jenny's backside. He always dangled a carrot or some other goodie on a stick out in front of the jenny to make her go. He hung around the community and was soon working at odd jobs. We soon learned his name was Benjie. He was a good worker and always very helpful. A neighbor let him stay in a little shack way over on the back part of the farm. He built a small stall for the jenny to stay in.
>
> Benjie was friendly and likeable. He appeared to be about thirty-five years old. He seemed to be knowledgeable about a lot of things. He was also handy with his hands making things and repairing them. Everyone liked Benjie, but knew very little about him. He was very closemouthed about his past or where he came from.
>
> One Sunday morning when I arrived at the church, Benjie was there. He had already started the fire and done the other little chores to get ready for church. Benjie never stayed for the church service. The next several Sundays when I went to the church Benjie had already been there and done what needed to be done. So, I quit going to the church early on Sunday mornings.
>
> Then, one Sunday when we arrived for the regular church service there was no fire in the stove and nothing had been done to get ready for the church service. Benjie had not been there. A few days passed and no one had seen Benjie. Some of the men went over to where he lived in his little shack. The

> jenny was in her stall with the saddle and bridle hanging nearby, but no Benjie. A few of his personal belongings appeared to be missing, but no sign of Benjie. For the next several days we all hunted everywhere for Benjie. We searched fields, old abandoned buildings, the forest, gullies and ditches, but no sign of Benjie.
>
> Some of the neighbors cared for the jenny, and for the next few months we occasionally would go out and search for Benjie. We never found him. There was much speculation as to what happened to Benjie. No one ever knew. He vanished as suddenly as he appeared. I've often wondered what happened to Benjie.

The first two days in January 1916, Mord moved the family to a fifty-five acre farm known as the Smith Place on the east bank of the South Canadian River southwest of Noble. Bill remembers the old house and barn were "like the Leaning Tower of Pisa." Bill and Mary attended Canada school. Mord planted twenty acres of cotton and thirty acres of corn. That fall he made ten bales of cotton and harvested about sixteen hundred bushels of corn. The soil was a good sandy loam and the rains that year came just at the right times.

This is an account Bill told about moving to the Smith Place:

> We had to leave the farm where we had lived for two years. Dad had rented another farm about seven miles away. The day was warm and the snow and ice were breaking up. It was so foggy that you could only see about three hundred yards. Dad was driving one team pulling a wagon and Mom was driving another team pulling the other wagon. As the mules walked their feet would break through the ice. It made terrible walking for them, and the wagons were hard to pull. It was bad for us because we were all walking to take as much load off the mules as possible.
>
> Before we got to the other place we came to a creek. The creek was running almost bank full from the melting snow and ice. We all got on one of the wagons to cross. When we got

> right into the stream the wagon lurched to one side. The creek was swift and what should happen but the tongue to the wagon broke. That meant you could not guide the wagon. Dad told Mom and Mary to take the other team and wagon and go on to the house. He and I would put another tongue in the wagon.
>
> Dad took the axe and cut down a small tree growing on the bank. He cut and shaped the tree and bored a hole where the pole could be placed and a long pin put through it. Dad got in the creek and we had a hard time holding the pole so we could fasten it to the wagon, but dad finally got it done. We sure did have a time getting the mules back into the creek. They didn't want to go into the water. Dad finally got them hooked to the wagon and out it went, and on to the house. Everyone was wet and cold.

January 1917 Mord and family moved to the Boggs Place southeast of Noble, Oklahoma. It was a hundred and sixty acres of upland with twenty acres of pasture. The rest was under cultivation. It did not have much of a house or barn. It was owned by Frank Boggs, the sheriff for Cleveland County. The years 1917 through 1919 were good years, and Mord got good prices for his crops. Bill and Mary went to Canada school.

In 1918 and 1919 Bill was a teenager. He worked part time for a man in Noble known as "Peg Leg" Davis. He actually had a peg leg. He owned a McCormack farm equipment dealership and a small hardware business. He sold various kinds of farm implements including binders, cultivators, and planters that were shipped to him in large wooden crates.

When Peg Leg received a shipment for a local farmer he would get in his Model-T Ford truck and go get Bill. They would load the equipment on the truck still in the crate and haul it to the farmer's field. There they uncrated the equipment and assembled it. Bill helped assemble about thirty binders during this time. They sometimes would go to farmers' fields or barn lots to repair various kinds of implements. Peg Leg paid Bill twenty-five cents an hour.

The winter of 1919 Mord bought the Kline Place near Willow View northeast of Lexington, Oklahoma. This was the year Mord's brother, Fred, and his wife, Nora, and their family moved to McGuire, Oklahoma. By this time Bill was no longer going to grade school. He took the County Educational Equivalency Exam and received a certificate that entitled him to attend high school. Bill was eighteen years of age.

This is about the time Bill started to date local girls. One such girl was Susy Garner who lived a half mile south of the Kline Place. He didn't date her very many times. Bill said, "All she wanted to do was talk about a former boy friend, so I quit going with her." He also dated May Umphree and Buela Ewing. They usually walked the several miles to dances or parties at different homes in the community. Bill's sister, Mary, dated the Arnold boys, Leonard Jones, Leonard Ewing, and Albert, a school teacher at Willow View.

Bill thinks it was Albert who encouraged Mary to go to high school at Edmond to further her education. It was through her acquaintance with Leonard Jones that Mary later met Jim Dunahoo who eventually became her husband. Jim lived in Oklahoma City. He and Leonard Jones were friends. Jim would come to Lexington to visit Leonard and thus he eventually met Mary. Jim and Mary were married 17 January 1925.

The spring of 1920 Mord let Bill plant thirty acres of cotton on the Kline Place. This is a story Bill told of an event that occurred during that time:

> When I was nineteen years old I went to the schoolhouse where they were giving what they called a literary meeting. Children reciting poetry and doing plays by acting. People came in buggies, wagons, on horseback, and walking. While everyone was busy watching what was going on in the building, some boys put a horseshoe under the saddle of the horse that one of the men rode to the schoolhouse.

> Everything was all right until the man got on his horse. Then all hell broke loose. The horse went bucking all over the schoolyard, and bucked him off. Was he mad. The horse ran off, but another man got on his horse and caught it. The man was madder when he found what made the horse buck. After he stopped cussing he said, "I'll kill the blankety-blankety boy that put that under my saddle." Word soon got out that he was riding around to all the boys in the community questioning them, and he was carrying a gun.
>
> I was plowing cotton with a riding cultivator one day when he rode up to the end of the row I was plowing. He commenced asking me about the ruckus at the schoolhouse. Some of the boys had told me he got real nasty about it and threatened them. Well, I told him I was inside the schoolhouse and didn't know a thing about it. He pulled his rifle out of the saddle holster, so I reached in my toolbox and pulled out my old blunderbuss. I couldn't hit the side of a barn with it, but he didn't know that. The gun was a .38 on a .45 frame and kicked like a mule. I laid it across my lap and looked at him. I said, "You know how you came in here so you better leave the same way." I don't know what he thought, but he turned and rode away without saying a word. Boy, was I glad.
>
> I decided I better get in some practice with my blunderbuss. So, one evening a neighbor boy and I went out in the pasture and picked a big cottonwood tree to shoot at. I pulled the old pistol out and was going to throw down on the tree. Well, when I raised it up to throw down, it went off and I blowed a large hole in the brim of my hat. Some marksman I was. So much for my Wild West actions.

By the fall of 1920 the price of cotton was so low it would cost more to pick it than it would bring at market. So, Bill left it in the field and left home to go to high school at Oklahoma Central State Teachers College in Edmond, Oklahoma. That same year Mord's brother, Cyrus, had twenty bales of cotton and couldn't sell it. So, he and his family packed up and went to California.

This is Bill's account while he was in school at Edmond:

> When I was going to school at Central State Teachers College in Edmond, I worked for several different families doing housework and yard work, washing dishes, windows, floors, and beating rugs.
>
> You hung the rugs over a clothesline. Sometimes eight-foot by ten-foot rugs. They sure were hard to handle. The beater was about four feet long made out of heavy wire, a wood handle, and a big wire paddle. You beat the rugs for about an hour to get the dirt out of them. They didn't have electric vacuum cleaners. I did this for twenty-five cents an hour.
>
> I did all the housework for one of the families. It was a job. They had three small children and I don't think she ever did one bit of housework. I did the house and yards for three teachers from the college. Four wash days a week—no washing machine, just a wash board and tub.

On occasional weekends when Bill went home to visit his parents he rode the train from Edmond to Noble, and then walked the several miles to their house. Here is a story Bill told about the time he was at Edmond:

> I was staying with a family in Edmond while I was going to school. There was a boy in the family about thirteen years old. His name was Bob. We were near the public school one day and found a baseball lying in the gutter. We picked it up and took it home with us. We would play catch with it bare handed. He wanted a glove to play catch so his mother gave him some money to buy one. We went to the store and got a nice glove for him.
>
> There were some boys in town who were stealing things. They had been in this man's store and "copped" a few things. One day we were in the store and Bob had his glove with him. The merchant accused Bob of stealing it. We said, "No, he did not steal it", but when we got home the police were there and was Bob's mother mad. I asked her, "What's the matter?" She

> said, "Bob storied to me. He took the glove instead of paying for it." I said, "They are wrong." She said, "Bob does not have a receipt." I said, "Yes, but I do", and went and got it. I showed her where the storekeeper had written a receipt and even wrote the glove number on the receipt and marked it "Paid in Full."
>
> Man! Did some police and a storekeeper ever have to eat crow! The storekeeper had to give her another glove, a new baseball, and a bat to get her to hush up. She also made the storekeeper give her a receipt for them.

Bill became acquainted with another young man, Paul, who was a singer and interested in religion. Paul was a little older than Bill. He was a teacher and came to Edmond to further his education. On Sundays they would walk four or five miles west of town to a small country church. They would lead the singing and conduct part of the church service. One time Bill was asked to preach the Sunday sermon, which he did. Bill thinks the church was Pentecostal.

Bill worked at a local bakery called Perfect Systems making breads and pies in return for his board–no other pay. The oven was like a large barrel about six feet in diameter with gas burners underneath. The barrel had multiple tiers where bread, pies, and other pastries were placed for baking. The tiers rotated inside the barrel oven.

Bill worked from ten o'clock at night until six o'clock the next morning. He had to be in class at eight o'clock. As a result he more often than not would nod off in class. One day Bill was napping in class. The professor severely chastised him, and said, "If you weren't spending so much time staying out all night with the girls you might be able to stay awake in class." Bill told the professor that he worked all night at a bakery. The professor didn't believe him. Bill suggested that if he didn't believe him that he should drop by the bakery at three o'clock some morning.

A few days later, sure enough, the professor knocked on the back door of the bakery at three in the morning. Bill invited him in and they had a piece of pie and a cup of coffee. That day in class the professor apologized to Bill.

A short time later Bill was fired from his bakery job for drinking two cokes. Bill considered his board at least included cokes as well as staples. The owner, an ex-Navy man named Young, didn't see it that way. So, they had a parting of the ways. Bill went to work at Morrison's Cafe. It had six tables and a counter that would seat twelve people.

It was at Oklahoma Central State College where Bill and Pauline met in 1923. Actually, Pauline became aware of Bill before he knew her. They were students in the same civics class taught by Mrs. Nash. One Monday morning as a pop quiz, Mrs. Nash asked the students to stand before the class and tell some important event they had read in the Sunday newspaper.

When it was Pauline's turn to recite she stood up and struggled trying to think of something of importance. She finally stammered out a few words about the Teapot Dome scandal. The teacher said, "You get a 'C' for that." In those days teachers were not so much constrained as to what they said to their students.

When it was Bill's turn to recite he stood up and bashfully dug his toe into the floor, hung his head and said, "I read the funny papers." Mrs. Nash said, "True confession is good for the soul." She gave Bill an 'A' for being truthful. Pauline was furious at the smart aleck and angrily muttered to her desk mate, "Teacher's pet!"

It was a short time later when Bill met Pauline. He was working at Morrison's Cafe on Broadway Street in Edmond. He was cook, dishwasher, and sometimes waiter, cashier, and part-time baby-sitter for the two Morrison children. For this he got board and room in a small storage room in the back of the cafe which he shared with an occasional rat or two.

Mrs. Morrison sometimes left Bill alone at the cafe with the two children while she went elsewhere. The kids gave him fits. A young woman, Bertha Johnson, was a part time waitress at the cafe. She and Bill became acquainted.

As it was, Bertha and Pauline were friends. Bertha came from the same area west of Pauls Valley where Pauline did. One day Pauline came to Morrison's Cafe to see Bertha. It was then and there that she more or less officially met Bill, though she already knew who he was. It was the first time Bill really become aware of Pauline, though he had seen her in class.

Shortly thereafter they began to date. Late one afternoon Bill and Pauline went walking west of Edmond. They walked hand in hand alongside a large field of wheat. The wind was gently blowing the waves of grain. The sun was a large orange ball just setting on the western horizon.

They stopped to take in the beauty of the moment. Pauline said in a most romantic mood, "Oh, what a beautiful sight. The sun setting in all its glory over the waves of grain make me think of an ocean. What does the sun make you think of?" Bill studied a few moments and replied, "A big ball of cheese." So much for Pauline's romantic mood.

The Belle Isle Lake and Park near North 50th Street and Western Avenue was a few miles south of Edmond. It was a favorite spot for young lovers. There was a small amusement park and a row boat concession for romantic boat rides on the lake.

One day Pauline had a date with another boy. She and her date took a boat out onto the lake. Bill was there that day and he watched the two from shore with a little envy in his heart. Pauline's date didn't know how to row a boat so Pauline did all the rowing. Later when Bill confronted Pauline about her date she said she would never go out again with a man that couldn't row a boat.

It was about this time Bill first became acquainted with Jim Dunahoo. Jim lived with his parents in Packing Town, an area in Southwest Oklahoma City. Jim had become acquainted with Leonard Jones, a friend of Bill's. Leonard lived near Bill's parents north of Lexington. Jim had a Model-T Ford and he let Bill drive it one day. That was the first time he ever drove an automobile. Through his friendship with Bill and Leonard Jones, Jim met Bill's sister, Mary. They were soon dating, and Jim later became Bill's brother-in-law.

Bill completed high school in the spring of 1924. He went with Mr. Morrison to Slick City, a little oil boomtown near Seminole, Oklahoma. Mr. Morrison had the intention to open a cafe in Slick City for the rough and tumble oil field workers. Bill was to be his cook.

Mr. Morrison had a Model-T Ford and they drove to Slick City arriving late one evening. They slept overnight in the car. The next day they ate breakfast at the only eating establishment in town. It was housed in a large tent with board sides about three feet high. The sides of the tent were rolled up several feet above the boards. Inside were large plank boards laid across barrels for tables. Seating was heavy plank boards on wooden kegs resting on the dirt floor. A large wood-burning cookstove was at the back. It was definitely a temporary arrangement. After breakfast they looked around Slick City for a desirable location for a cafe.

The next day Mr. Morrison and Bill talked with the man who owned the eating establishment. He offered to hire Bill as his cook. Mr. Morrison said, "I thought you had a cook." The man replied, "Yes, I did yesterday, but this morning he made a bad batch of biscuits and got shot dead."

Bill turned that thought over in his mind a few seconds and decided Slick City was not for him. If the cook was going to get shot over a pan of bad biscuits Bill had no intention of being a cook in Slick City. He went to Norman where he met Mr. Edwards with General Engineering. He hired Bill to work for him. Mr. Morrison went to Seminole and opened a boarding house.

The fall of 1924 found Bill working as a 'grease monkey' for General Engineering. They operated a dragline dredging and straightening Pond Creek eight miles east of Lexington. As 'grease monkey' Bill did a variety of jobs. He kept all the machinery fueled, oiled and greased. He filled and maintained the acetylene lights.

He helped move and reposition the pontoons and he dynamited stumps when needed. He was paid three dollars a day and board.

When he first went to work on the dragline the company had him quartered with an old lady eighty years old who rented out rooms in her home. She about drove Bill crazy because all she would talk about was how and why her late husband hung himself from the peach tree on the north side of the house. This lasted only a few weeks. The company soon provided a large crew tent for the dragline workers and contracted with local farm women to provide meals.

The dragline operated twenty-four hours a day. Bill worked the shift from midnight to eight o'clock in the morning. In November it turned very cold. One cold day a bunch of hogs got into the crew tent. They turned the place into a shambles and knocked over the heating stove. Bill and the other crewmen were so tired and so cold when they came off their shift they didn't straighten up the mess. They just layed down and slept with the hogs because they were warm.

On weekends when Bill had time off from his dragline job he would ride with Mr. Clark, the dragline operator, to Edmond to see Pauline. Mr. Clark lived near Edmond and would travel there to visit his wife and family. But, Bill would stay so late on Sunday evenings with Pauline that he couldn't ride back with Mr. Clark.

Bill would catch the last departing interurban trolley from Edmond. That put him in Norman at one o'clock in the morning. He would buy a nickel hamburger at a nearby hamburger stand and walk from Norman to Pond Creek munching his hamburger. He arrived there at an early morning hour. He would sleep during the day and be ready to go to work at midnight.

Bill's parents lived on the Kline Place during the years 1919 through 1925. Mord became well acquainted with John Abernathy who owned a wholesale grocery business in Purcell, Oklahoma, across the river from Lexington. Mord had several teams of good mules. He and John decided to become business partners and go into the roadbed construction business.

In 1924 they bid and got a contract with the State of Oklahoma to build two and a half miles of roadbed for U.S. Highway No. 77 south of Noble. Bill had finished his schooling at Edmond and had been working on the dragline. General Engineering Company ceased to operate. Bill came home to work for his father as plow-boy, straw boss, and powder monkey blowing out tree stumps.

When the Noble roadbed construction job was completed early in 1925 Mord bid and received a contract for a four mile roadbed construction job on U.S. Highway 270 between Holdenville and Wewoka.

Bill lived with his parents in a tent and worked for his dad on the construction job. Pauline was still in school at Edmond. On a weekend visit to Edmond Bill proposed to Pauline. Bill returned to Holdenville. He and Pauline exchanged letters and agreed to meet May 8th and be married.

Bill and Pauline were married May 8, 1925, by a justice of the peace in Pauls Valley, Oklahoma. They traveled the eighteen miles from Pauls Valley to the Roller home place on Panther Creek. There for the first time, Bill met Pauline's parents, Mr. and Mrs. D. E. Roller. Their marriage was a complete surprise to Bill's new in-laws. Mary and Jim Dunahoo had married the previous January 17th.

This is Bill's account of his and Pauline's wedding day:

> I was working for Dad on the Holdenville roadbed construction job and we lived in a tent at the site. Pauline and I had exchanged letters and agreed to meet on May 8th and get married. After work the day before, I left about seven o'clock in the evening with only thirteen dollars in my pocket to walk to Wewoka and catch a train to Oklahoma City.
>
> I soon met up with a man who was having trouble with his Model-T Ford. He was cussing and raving at the car because it wouldn't start. It was obvious he had been drinking too much.

I told him I'd take a look at it and see if I could fix it. The fuel sediment bowl was full of sediments. He had been using casinghead gas. I cleaned the bowl and the fuel line. The car started.

He told me he would take me to Wewoka, but he first needed to check on some oil wells. He was a pumper. We drove all over the countryside to a dozen or so oil wells. Every time he stopped to check a well he would take another drink. He was getting pretty tipsy and I was getting concerned. We finally got to Wewoka about 2:00 a.m. and only about five minutes before the train arrived. I had just enough time to buy a ticket and board the train.

When I got to Oklahoma City I hung around the depot until after 8:00 a.m. I then went to the office of General Engineering on North Harvey to collect twenty-five dollars they owed me for some cottonwood logs I sold to them to use as pontoons over on Buckhead Creek. The guy at first told me he didn't have the money. I got a little mad and told him I wasn't leaving until I had my money. He said he would write me a check. I told him that was okay, but he was going to go to the bank with me to cash it.

After I got my money I called Jim Dunahoo. He and Mary were married and living in Oklahoma City. Jim had a Model-T Ford. He came and took me to a jewelry store in the Hightower Building. I bought a wedding ring for twelve dollars. Jim took me to the depot and I bought a ticket for one dollar on the noon southbound Santa Fe train for Pauls Valley that Pauline was to be on. I walked through the passenger cars until I found her.

In Pauls Valley we went to the courthouse to get a marriage license and then to the Justice of the Peace. He was down by the gin cutting weeds. The clerk sent someone to get him and he came to his office and married us. He charged me three dollars. The clerk and another man were our witnesses.

We planned to catch the train from Pauls Valley to Maysville, but it had left by the time we got there. I paid two dollars to ride the bus from Pauls Valley to Maysville. It was a hearse with folding chairs. Pauline's dad was to meet her in Maysville with a wagon and team of horses. When she wasn't on the train he thought she wasn't coming, so he left for home without her.

In Maysville I hired a man for two dollars to take us to the Roller home on Panther Creek. He took us within two miles. We walked the rest of the way.

Everyone was surprised to see Pauline and even more surprised to see me, her new husband. My new father-in-law just said, "Humph, she's yours now. You take care of her." We spent the night there and it rained all night. I slept on the floor. Pauline's Uncle Robert was there in his Model-T Ford.

The next day we rode with him to his house four miles south and two miles west of Maysville. The roads were muddy and we came to a big ditch. He went to a nearby farm house and got two big planks. He laid them over the ditch and drove the car across. Rush Creek was flooding and we drove through the water over hubcap deep.

We spent the night with Uncle Robert and his family. That evening Uncle Robert wanted to play checkers with me. Pauline whispered in my ear that he would beat me unmercifully. I beat him six straight games.

The next day Uncle Robert took us to Maysville where we caught the train to Pauls Valley. There we caught the Santa Fe northbound to Oklahoma City. I gave Pauline ten dollars and she went on to Edmond to finish the school year. I caught the train to Wewoka and went back to work with Dad. I had one dollar left in my pocket.

When Pauline finished the school year later that month, she went to live with Bill and his parents in a tent at the construction site between Holdenville and Wewoka. Bill continued to work for his dad. Pauline helped Meta prepare and serve meals for the work crews. This arrangement didn't last long. Bill and Pauline soon moved to Oklahoma City to make their own life.

In September 1925 Bill and Pauline moved to 1900 NW 28th Street in Oklahoma City. Bill had three hundred dollars in back wages for working with his dad. They rented a very small three-room house with only a 'monkey-stove' in it. Pauline's father gave them a cotton mattress. They had no chairs or table. They used wooden boxes that Jim Dunahoo got from a local store.

William Edmund Davidson - 1924

That same month Bill enrolled at Hill's Business College on West Main Street in Oklahoma City. He took a business course of bookkeeping, business math and grammar. After four months of study a man from Lexington, John Robinson, came to Hill's

College looking for a ticket seller for the Oklahoma Railway Company. Though John did not previously know Bill he hired him because he was from near Lexington. Bill worked the shift from two o'clock in the afternoon to midnight.

Bill's sister, Mary, and her husband, Jim, lived in a small house on NW 30th Street near where Bill and Pauline lived. Jim worked at Choctaw Mills at SW 2nd and Western Avenue 'coopering' railroad boxcars used to transport flour. The railroad cars were fully lined with a heavy paper secured to the sides, top and bottom with wood laths. Then they were filled with flour. After the boxcars were used, the paper and laths had to be removed and new installed before flour could be loaded. The used laths were scrap.

When Bill got out of school he went to where Jim worked. When Jim got off work they gathered large bundles of laths and carried them on their backs three miles to Jim and Mary's house. Jim used the laths to build a chicken pen. They did this almost every workday for several months.

Jim built his chicken pen, raised some chickens, and gave Bill and Pauline fresh eggs. Jim and Mary also had a garden and gave them produce. They were a big help to Bill and Pauline in the early days of their life together.

After a few months Bill and Pauline moved to another place which was a small hut on the back of a lot behind the house at 1909 NW 28th Street. Bill described it as a "chicken hut" converted to living quarters. It was very primitive compared with today's standards. It had no running water and an outhouse toilet. It was here their first child, William Lee, was born 3 March 1926.

Bill dug a basement by hand for the landlord who lived in the house at the front. He had to crawl in through a crawl space opening, dig and haul the dirt out the opening. The landlord paid him twenty-five cents an hour.

Bill also worked part time for Mr. Edwards who he knew from General Engineering. After the demise of General Engineering

Mr. Edwards went into the house building business. Bill worked for him sawing boards and nailing them together to make fence panels.

Bill had a steady job as Ticket Seller making sixty dollars a month. Early in 1927 he and Pauline moved to a small three-room house at 3204 NW 13th Street. Leonard Jones, the friend from Lexington, moved them in his old truck. The house was a small white wooden frame house near the back of the lot. It had a large front yard. Bill and Pauline made a garden in the front and had vegetables for the family table. It was here their second child, Bobby Joe, (Robert) was born 11 May 1927, and their third child, Donald Jean (Gene), was born 7 December 1928.

In 1929 Bill was promoted to Assistant Ticket Agent with a salary of ninety dollars a month. In October the stock market crashed but had little effect on Bill and Pauline. Bill had a good steady job.

Bill's parents, Mord and Meta, lived in Oklahoma City. Mord worked at various construction jobs. He helped build a beautiful stone wall and entrance to a new cemetery, Memorial Park, north of Oklahoma City and south of Edmond. At the time he said he wanted to be buried there.

In 1930 Bill and Pauline bought a house at 2709 NW 40th Street near the Oklahoma Railway Company interurban line from Oklahoma City to El Reno. The interurbans were large electric passenger trolleys. This house was also a wood frame house, but larger than the previous one. It had indoor plumbing (septic) with hot and cold running water supplied by a private water company from a local well. It had a living room, dining room, kitchen, two bedrooms, a screened back porch, and a covered front porch. There was a detached garage and a chicken house. They had a telephone. The number was 5-5913.

There was half an acre of land with the house. They had a large garden, kept chickens, and milked a cow. Bill's mother loaned them the money to buy a milk cow that was half Jersey and half Guernsey. She was a good milk producer. She was called Bossy.

That same year they bought a 1928 green Chevrolet sedan with solid metal wheels. It had six cylinders and 46 horsepower. Bill and Pauline would occasionally get a neighbor teenager, Maureen McCaskell, to baby-sit the children while they had an evening out. Maureen had flaming red hair and ample freckles. She was good with the children, even when she was on crutches with a broken leg.

During 1930 Mord and Meta once again moved back to Arkansas. This time they located on the upper Herron Place west of Hardy. It was near a steep rocky bluff across Cow Ford on the west bank of South Fork River and next to Raccoon Spring. Sometime in the past the Herron Family had been good friends with the Davidsons at Evening Shade. A lady fondly known by all as Aunt Kate Herron leased the farm to Mord at a very reasonable rate.

In 1930 a man named McGuire worked with Bill at Oklahoma Railway. He knew a man (whose name Bill could not recall) that touted himself as the inventor of a new and improved pump used to clean out oil wells. McGuire convinced Bill and Smitty, a streetcar conductor, to invest in the venture to manufacture and sell the pumps.

Thus, the Red Devil Pump Company was formed. McGuire was president, Smitty was a vice-president, the inventor was a vice-president, and Bill was secretary-treasurer because he was good with figures and had experience with bookkeeping. In essence, Bill actually ran the company. He hired a machinist in Okmulgee to make ten pumps. The pumps were 3.9 inches in diameter to run into 4.0 inch casing. They were 20 feet long. The pump had a special unique type of plunger and release mechanism.

Bill hired an out of work production superintendent to sell the Red Devil pumps. He sold six at $1,250 each. Bill had four more made. He paid $100 to a patent attorney to secure a patent on the pump. Bill kept all the records and financial accounts for the company. He rented out two of the pumps for $125 a day.

They ran a pump in the Alva #1 in the East Capital Hill Field and one in the Harold Davis #1 near Southeast 29th Street. They lost the pump in the Davis well. It was during the prohibition era and Bill knew of a kid that hung around the terminal and sold bootleg liquor. Bill paid him five dollars for a gallon of bootleg whiskey and gave it to an old production man he knew to get him to fish the pump out of the well. He retrieved the pump on the first try. One time they were running the clean-out pump in the Alva #1 and pulled up the 'shot-can' from the adjacent well.

Bill and Pauline lived at the 40th Street address when their fourth child, Meta Luvida (Ann), was born 1 July 1931 at Wesley Hospital in Oklahoma City. Bill took Pauline to the hospital and then went to work. During his lunch hour he came to the hospital to be with Pauline. Much to his surprise when he walked into the room Pauline was about to deliver. Bill and a young nurse's aide delivered the baby before the nurses or doctor could get there.

Though the nation was in a serious depression, things were not too bad for Bill and Pauline. Bill had a good steady job. They raised vegetables in a large garden and canned some for later use. They had a milk cow, raised chickens and had fresh eggs. They occasionally butchered a calf or a hog they raised for fresh meat.

Bill once brought home a large metal drum. He intended to cut out the top and use it for scalding a hog he planned to butcher. He cautioned the boys that the drum had been used to store denatured alcohol and to leave it alone.

Bobby Joe wanted to see what denatured alcohol looked like. He removed the bung and looked in, but it was dark. He couldn't see anything. So, he struck a match and held it up to the bunghole to look in. Before he could get his eye over the hole the residual vapors of alcohol in the drum exploded and severely burned his forehead. Luckily he didn't have his eye over the hole, or he may have been blinded in that eye.

William Edmund and Mary Pauline Davidson - 1925

Bill made a big kite about five feet tall. He and the boys would fly it on nice windy days. One day they had about two thousand feet of string out when a small bi-wing airplane flew through the string and broke it. Bill and the two older boys jumped in the car and spent the next several hours looking for the kite. They finally found it, but it was badly damaged.

The three boys attended school at Sequoyah Elementary at 2400 NW 36th Street. They walked under the interurban trestle on Turkey Creek and crossed 39th Street which was part of old U.S. Highway 66. They cut across Log Cabin Park to the school. Log Cabin Park was not a park in the usual sense. It was a series of several small log cabins to rent overnight to travelers. Such places were called "motor parks." The term "motel" had not yet been coined.

There was a large open field west of Log Cabin Park near the busy intersection of May Avenue and NW 39th Street. Various traveling entertainment enterprises would set up large tents in the field to attract customers. Some were traveling exhibits of various kinds, some were dog and pony shows, some were wild animal shows, but the most popular at the time were the 'Dance-a-Thon' shows. These were contests on a temporary dance floor under a large tent. Couples danced to a small band until they dropped from exhaustion. The last couple dancing won the contest and prize money. There would also be entertaining specialty dance contests in which the contestants could win extra prize money. People would actually pay to watch these contests. Bill sometimes got free promotional passes to these shows and took the boys to see them.

In 1932 John Robinson, the Ticket Agent, quit Oklahoma Railway Company to go to work for a candy company. Bill was promoted from Assistant Ticket Agent to Ticket Agent with a salary of one hundred and fifty dollars a month. His office was near the northeast corner of the downtown streetcar terminal pavilion. His duties included overseeing the sale of streetcar tickets and tokens. They also included the management of a small newsstand selling a variety of newspapers and magazines, as well as, cigarettes, cigars, chewing gum, candy and other small merchandise items. Lester

Winters, Johnny Hightower, Louie Stalken and Johnny Sasser worked for him.

Johnny Sasser was interested in the new phenomenon known as radio. He was good at making and repairing them. He put together two transceivers that were small, portable and battery powered. To test them he talked Bill into taking one and going to the bridge on South Western across the North Canadian River while Johnny stayed in his apartment about a mile away. They transmitted and received voice transmissions–the beginning of the 'walkie talkie' era.

A police cruiser came along and the officer saw Bill standing on the bridge talking into a hand held device. He stopped and asked Bill what he was doing. When Bill explained the officer became very interested and asked a lot of questions. He obviously saw its possibilities in police work.

The streetcar terminal was a busy hub of downtown Oklahoma City activity. Streetcars and interurbans were the main mode of transportation from the 1920's into the late 1940's for Oklahoma City and surrounding areas. The terminal was located at Grand Avenue between Hudson and Harvey Streets. It was a large covered pavilion over numerous streetcar tracks. It was a major transfer hub for most of the various streetcar lines.

The west side of the terminal consisted mostly of the freight and interurban part of the business. The east side was where the Ticket Agent's office was located and where agents sold streetcar tickets and tokens. There was a multitude of various small retail business shops all along the east side concourse selling all manner of things like hot dogs, hamburgers, popcorn, peanuts, candy, novelties, tobacco products, etc.

Punch cards were very popular and most of the retail businesses had several kinds. For a penny, nickel, or dime a punch patrons could win various items of merchandise. There was an arcade (or mall as they are called today) extending east from the terminal concourse to Harvey Street. There was a barbershop, florist, antique store (owned by the Turk sisters), costume jewelry, State Theater and other small business on the arcade.

In 1932 Bill, Pauline and the four children visited Bill's father and mother while they lived on the Herron Place near Hardy. They traveled by train on railroad passes that Bill was able to get as a benefit of his employment with the Oklahoma Railway Company. They rode the Rock Island from Oklahoma City to Memphis, then the Frisco from Memphis to Hardy.

Their fifth child, Samuel Marvin, was born 20 January 1933 at Wesley Hospital while they lived at the 40th Street address. Mother and child were brought home from the hospital in a tan and white ambulance with orange wheels. Pauline had major surgery, a hysterectomy, while in the hospital. She was in no condition to care for a new baby and four other rambunctious kids. Pauline's teenage sister, Beatrice Roller, came to live with Bill and Pauline to help care for the children. The years she was there she attended Classen High School where she graduated.

In 1933 President Roosevelt by executive order established the National Recovery Administration (NRA known as the "Blue Eagle") under the National Industrial Recovery Act as part of his New Deal Program. The NRA prepared and enforced codes of fair competition for businesses and industries. Roosevelt abolished the NRA in 1935 after the Supreme Court ruled the recovery act unconstitutional. But the damage had been done for Bill and many other workers whose wages were reduced drastically under the provisions of the NRA.

The summer of 1933 Bill and Pauline at different times visited Bill's Uncle Cyrus and Aunt Emma Davidson in Oxnard, California. As an employee of a railway company Bill was able to obtain railroad passes for the vacation trips. It was their first times to visit California and see palm trees, citrus groves, and the ocean. Pauline's sister, Hazel, stayed with and cared for the children while Pauline was gone.

The summer of 1934 Bill, Pauline and children again traveled by train on vacation to visit his parents near Hardy. They would usually visit Pauline's parents on occasional weekends and holidays since it was only a two-hour trip by car to the Roller's farm home.

The Red Devil Pump Company had been active since 1930 and was on the verge of breaking into a financially sound business. Then in 1934 things fell apart. Bill learned that the man who was the inventor had unknown to the others sold the patent rights for the pump to the Mid-Continent Oil Tool Company. In the meantime the patent attorney Bill hired had not yet secured a patent. Thus, the Red Devil Pump Company expired and Bill chalked it up to life's experience.

In October 1934 Pauline was driving the '28 Chevy north on May Avenue south of 10th Street. It was after dark. All the children were in the car. As she approached the Rock Island railroad grade crossing she slowed down. An employee of Baash-Ross Tool Company driving a company car plowed into the left rear of the Chevy knocking it over a steep embankment. The Chevy rolled over onto the right side and then hung up on a large tree stump. Otherwise, it would have rolled into water at the bottom of the embankment.

Bill settled with Baash-Ross Tool Company for $1,250. He traded the wrecked Chevy plus $50 to Jim Robinson, brother to John Robinson from Lexington, for a 1929 Windsor automobile. It was a four-door sedan with a flathead straight-eight cylinder engine, wooden spoke wheels, hydraulic brakes (a new innovation for the day), and a travel trunk on the back. It was a 'running jessie' and could easily and quickly accelerate to 60 mph. There were very few of these cars made. The company was organized in 1928, manufactured a few cars in 1929, and went bankrupt with the Crash in October of 1929.

The summer of 1935 Oklahoma's two most famous sons, Will Rogers and Wiley Post, were killed in an airplane crash in Alaska.

They lay in state in the rotunda of the state capitol building as Oklahoma mourned their deaths. Pauline and the children stood in their front yard and watched hundreds of small airplanes fly over the capitol building dropping huge bouquets of flowers.

Under the NRA act in December 1935 Bill's salary was cut from $150 a month to $90 a month. That was a huge reduction and caused financial difficulties for Bill and Pauline. They were unable to make the mortgage payments on the house at NW 40th Street. Kruger Investment Company foreclosed on the property in January 1936.

Bill used part of the settlement from Baash-Ross Tool Company to purchase a modest four room wood frame house at 3608 NW 13th Street on a 50 x 150-foot city lot. He paid $900 cash and financed the balance on a note co-signed by Pauline's sister, Hazel.

The house was on a dirt street and it was muddy when it rained. The house had a living room, dining room, kitchen and one bedroom. It did not have indoor plumbing. An outhouse served that purpose. It did have running water provided by the city utility. It also had an unattached garage. Bill built a small shed on the back for Bossy, the milk cow.

The four older children attended Linwood Elementary School on 16th Street. The family attended the Linwood Methodist Church with Rev. R. J. Palmer, pastor, at NW 17th and Drexel Streets, from 1934 through 1937.

In the summer of 1936 Bill and Pauline with the children and Pauline's father, Dillmus E. Roller, traveled in the 1929 Windsor from Oklahoma City to Ava, Missouri, to visit the old Roller home place and some of Mr. Roller's relatives. They then went to Hardy, Arkansas, to visit Bill's parents.

This was always great fun for the children. South Fork River ran along the east side of the farm only a hundred and fifty yards from the house. The Clarke cousins lived only a mile up the rocky bluff and over the hill to Cedar Spring. Raccoon Spring was nearby. Everyone played in the spring water, swam in the river, fished, and boated. There were hills, rocks and deep woods to explore.

June 19, 1936, Joe Louis and Max Schmeling met in a boxing match. Schmeling won by a knockout. Bill had a one-dollar bet on Schmeling with Mr. Yarbrough, the next door neighbor. Bill and family listened to the fight on an old RCA box radio. When Louis was counted out in the 12th round, Bill ran out the front door, jumped off the porch, dashed across the driveway, jumped a three foot high white picket fence, ran onto Mr. Yarbrough's front porch knocking at the door to collect his one dollar bet. In the return bout June 22, 1938, Louis knocked out Schmeling in two minutes and four seconds of the first round.

Bill was fired in December 1936 from his job as Ticket Agent at Oklahoma Railway Company. It had to do with a labor dispute between management and the workers trying to organize a labor union. Since the unconstitutional NRA drastically cut his salary forty per cent Bill considered he was one of the workers, not management. Thus he participated in the unionization activities. Management considered him a part of management and fired him for his union associations. This was catastrophic for a provider with a wife and five small children and no job or other source of income at the height of the Great Depression when jobs were scarce and difficult to come by.

Bill secured employment in February 1937 with the Meadow Gold Dairy as a route deliveryman. His take home pay was six to eight dollars a week. The Meadow Gold Dairy plant was located at NW Fourth Street and Western Avenue. The horse barn was nearby. Claud Roller, Pauline's uncle, worked there. He harnessed the horses and hitched them to the milk wagons. Bill's route was on NW 18th and 19th Streets from Indiana Street to Portland Avenue, a distance of two and a half miles. He delivered milk, butter, cream, eggs, chocolate milk, and orange juice to household customers from a horse drawn wagon.

Potatoes were penny a pound. Bacon was fifteen cents for two pounds. Bread was ten cents a loaf. Haircuts were fifteen cents. Though prices were low a salary of six to eight dollars a week was barely subsistence living for a family of seven.

The spring of 1937 another of Roosevelt's New Deal work programs (WPA) constructed a sewer line behind the house at 3608 NW 13th Street. Bill paid a neighbor, Mr. Allred, a carpenter, to remodel the bedroom into an indoor bathroom and a closet, and to build a wood frame lean-to on the back with two bedrooms and a closet in between.

By the fall of 1937 Bill and Pauline had exhausted what money remained from the settlement with Baash-Ross Tool Company and what little they had in the way of savings. They needed a place where they could raise a garden for food, keep the cow for milk and raise chickens for eggs and meat.

In November 1937 they moved to a forty-acre place south of Oklahoma City and three miles northwest of Moore. It was known as The Johnson Place. The house was on the southwest corner. Today there is a Mazzio's Pizza shop on that corner at the intersection of SW 104th Street and South Western Avenue in Oklahoma City.

The Johnson Place had a small two-room wood frame house set on concrete blocks. Bill and Mr. Johnson used scrap lumber to build a lean-to porch on the back. That was where Billy, Bobby Joe, and Gene slept. Meta Lu slept in a closet, and the youngest boy, Marvin, slept in the room with Bill and Pauline. The other room served as the kitchen and dining room.

The house had no running water or indoor plumbing. Water was hauled in ten-gallon milk cans from a deep well at the Nu-Way Laundry in Oklahoma City. Also, water was toted in five-gallon buckets from a water well at a cemetery about a quarter of a mile away. There was no electricity. Kerosene lamps were used for lighting. Pauline had a three-burner kerosene stove for cooking. A small pot-bellied stove was used for heating the kitchen. The other room and the lean-to had no heat. Bathing was in a 'No. 8' wash tub. Pauline and children did the washing on a rub board.

The children went to school at Moore. They rode in a flatbed truck modified to be a school bus. The driver was "Tiny" Spencer, a local farmer. The family attended the Moore Methodist Church, Rev. W. T. Pugh, pastor, in Moore from 1938 until November 1942.

Bill still worked at the milk route job with Meadow Gold. He got up at 3:30 a.m. each work day and drove the old Windsor to Oklahoma City, ran his milk route, and returned home late that afternoon.

Mr. Johnson, the landlord, hauled scrap lumber to the place. Bill and the boys helped him build a barn. This was in lieu of paying rent. They also built a chicken house and a shed for Bossy.

The spring of 1938 Bill bought a horse named "Ribbon." She was used to plow and cultivate a garden. Pauline and the children planted the seeds, tilled the soil, and gathered the vegetables. Pauline had an old pressure cooker and she canned as much of the harvest as she could for the coming winter. Bossy was milked twice a day and provided milk and butter. Chickens were raised for fresh eggs.

Hospital bills accumulated. Chickens were raised, slaughtered, plucked, dressed, packed in tubs of ice and taken to the hospital as barter to pay the bills. This was a weekly ritual for most of the summer of 1938.

Bill made a large 2x10 by 12-foot board with twelve wire hooks supported by two wooden posts at each end. The chickens were snared with a long wire hook, hung on the board, and their throats slit. After bleeding they were plucked, gutted, cleaned, dressed, packed in a tub of ice and taken to the hospital.

One nice day in the summer of 1938 several neighborhood boys who were Gene's friends came by the house. They wanted Gene to go play with them. Pauline told them Gene had chores to do and could not go. Bill and a neighbor were cleaning out an old dug well to see if it could be made to draw water for the cow, horse and chickens.

About half an hour later one of the boys came running breathlessly to the house. He told Pauline they were swimming in a nearby pond and one of the boys was about to drown. Pauline sent Gene running to tell Bill. She went out to the highway and flagged down the first motorist to come by. She asked him to stop at the first place he could and call for emergency help.

Bill and the neighbor ran as fast as they could to the pond about two hundred yards away. The boy was nowhere to be seen. The other boys pointed to where he was last seen in the water. Bill and the neighbor dove in. After a few minutes they found the boy on the bottom of the pond in about eight feet of water. They pulled him out and tried artificial respiration to no avail. When the fire department arrived it was too late to save the boy, Arbrey Lee Davis, one of Gene's classmates.

The spring of 1939 Bill hired a neighbor, Mr. Lagali, who had a tractor and planter, to plow about two acres and plant cotton. The boys used a one-horse double shovel to cultivate the cotton. They chopped and hoed it. In the fall they picked it. Bill made about twenty dollars from the cotton crop.

They also raised a large garden and continued to barter fresh dressed chickens to pay hospital bills. Bobby Joe went outside after dark, tripped, fell into a wash tub and broke his left arm. Shortly afterwards Gene fell about four feet backwards off a stack of scrap lumber and completely dislocated the two lower bones from the upper bone in his left elbow. His arm was a pitiful sight and very painful. Bill rushed him to the hospital in Oklahoma City where the doctor and a nurse set his elbow. It was very painful. He carried it in a sling for the next several weeks.

Bill and Pauline continued to raise chickens to help pay hospital bills. They bought baby chicks at weekly intervals and raised them to fryers. Each Saturday when Bill was off from his job they slaughtered, plucked, cleaned, and dressed several dozen chickens. Bill iced them down in a tub and took them to the hospital as payment.

Davidson children with Great Great Aunt Eve Bunyard - 1936
L. to R. Gene, Marvin, Bobby Joe, William, Meta Lu

In the meantime Bill changed jobs. He went to work for Consolidated Motor Freight as a dockhand loading and unloading trailers at a freight dock. It was a deal where a worker showed up and if they needed him, he punched-in on the timeclock and worked until not needed. Then he punched-out and waited until needed again. The work was irregular and more physical but Bill made from twelve to fifteen dollars a week. This was more than he made delivering milk.

The fall of 1939 Bill and Pauline moved to the Turk Place, two miles south of the Johnson Place. The Turk sisters of Oklahoma City owned the farm. They had an antique store in the arcade next to the Oklahoma Railway streetcar terminal. Mr. Collins of Moore had the farm leased from the sisters. He sub-leased the house, barn and pasture to Bill at a very reasonable rate just to have someone living on the place.

The house set on the southwest corner of what is now SW 149th Street and South Western Avenue in Moore. The house was a white wood pitched roof frame. It had two small bedrooms in the attic. Downstairs were a living room, dining room, kitchen, pantry, and a bedroom. It had a large front porch and a back porch. The house did not have running water or indoor plumbing. There was, however, a waterwell and a windmill. No more hauling water for household use. There was a reasonably good barn and a chicken coop.

By now Old Bossy had produced two heifer calves which were now milk cows with their own calves. Ribbon, the horse, was still used to plow and cultivate a garden. They also had chickens and a few turkeys. Thankfully, the hospital bills were all paid. No more killing and dressing chickens, except for the family table. The children attended school in Moore. Mr. J. C. Fishburn, a neighbor, was the school bus driver.

Mr. Collins planted cotton, corn and oats. Bill had an agreement with Mr. Collins for him and the boys to hoe the cotton and corn for a part of the oats crop. Mr. Collins also let Bill clear a few acres of weeds and plant kafricorn. Mr. Collins used his tractor to plow the ground. Bill used Ribbon and a double shovel plow to lay out the rows and a one-row planter to plant the seed. Henry Janko, a neighbor who did custom grain thrashing, was hired by Mr. Collins to thrash the oat crop in June. His thrashing machine blew a large haystack west of the barn. Bill got two hundred bushels of oats.

Pauline and the children had a traumatic experience in June of 1940. Bill was at work. It was late afternoon. It was obvious bad weather was coming from the west. The clouds were dark and threatening. The boys did the chores earlier than usual as it was getting dark. The wind blew, the lightening flashes were brilliant, and claps of thunder were loud. It definitely was going to be a stormy evening.

Pauline did not light a fire in the cook stove. She served a cold supper of leftovers. She lighted a kerosene lamp and set it on the table for light. She finished the prayer and the children had just started to eat when it slammed into the house. The entire house shook. Plaster fell from the ceiling and walls. Pauline quickly blew out the lamp. It was too late to even think about going to a storm cellar. She quickly herded the children into a small closet under the stairway to the attic. There they huddled and Pauline prayed while a tornado swept over them.

Tornados do strange and unusual things. There was only minor damage to the house except it ripped the back porch apart. The barn and the chicken house sustained major damage. Most of the chickens were killed. Those not killed were without feathers and soon died. The other animals were okay except for cuts and bruises.

Tree limbs were twisted and broken. The new straw stack west of the barn was scattered everywhere. Straws were matted into a field wire fence so thick and tight a person could not thrust a fist through it. Thousands of straws were driven through the limbs of trees.

Actually, the straws are not driven through the limbs, it just looks that way. What happens is the twisting and pulling action of the tornado on the tree limbs causes them to split a little. With thousands of straws swirling through the air at a high velocity they become clogged in the split openings in the limbs. When the tornado moves on what's left of the tree limbs return to a near normal position. They pinch down on the straws in the splits and trap them there. Thus, it appears they were driven through the limbs.

Later in the summer of 1940 was also a traumatic time for the boys. Bossy was getting old. She had difficulties calving that spring. She had a nice heifer calf out of Mr. Gamble's Jersey bull. They named the calf Chang. Bill and Pauline decided to take Bossy to market after she weaned her calf. It was a sad day for the boys when they loaded up Bossy in a trailer and took her to market. She was a good gentle cow. The boys had grown fond of her. She was an easy milker. They learned on her how to milk a cow by hand.

Bill and Pauline moved once again in the fall of 1940–this time to the Sullivan Place a mile east and a quarter mile south of the Turk

Place. It was located on what is now Santa Fe Avenue a quarter of a mile south of 149th Street in Moore. The Sullivan Place had a hundred and sixty acres with forty acres of pasture and the rest in cultivation.

The Sullivan Place at Moore - 1941

The house had a living room and bedroom downstairs, and a large room for dining in one end and a kitchen in the other end. Upstairs were two bedrooms, one large and one small. The boys slept in the large room. Bill and Pauline slept in the small room. The daughter slept on a day-bed in the only downstairs bedroom. There was a small back porch and a rickety storage room attached to the side. It also had a small covered front porch with six large cedar trees in front. The house did not have electricity or indoor plumbing. Kerosene lamps were used. An outhouse served the other purpose. Water for the house was carried from the well with a windmill. A large wood burning stove in the living room provided heat.

The Sullivan Place had a very good barn with milking stanchions in the south part, horse stalls in the north part and two granaries in between with access to one from the east end and access to the other from the west end. It had a large hayloft overhead. There was a waterwell with a windmill and a large stock tank for watering the livestock. There was a rickety shed used as a garage, a shop and part of it for storage. There was a small hut for chickens.

By this time Bill and family had accumulated several good milk cows which the boys milked twice a day. One of the cows was Chang that was a cow Bossy had raised. She was gentle and had Bossy's disposition. Bill bought a Guernsey cow which the boys named Chow. She was a kicker. She would kick at anyone who got anywhere close to her. Milking her was a challenge even with stanchion and hobbles. The boys built a special stall and stanchion for her. Once in the stall and the boards put in place she was unable to lift her foot to kick.

The milk was carried to the house and run through a hand turned centrifugal cream separator. The cream was sold or used for household use. The skimmed milk was mixed with bran shorts and fed to the hogs. Bill had bought a sow and she had sixteen piglets and raised twelve.

A neighbor had a large pecan tree he wanted removed. Bill agreed to saw it down and cut it up for firewood. Part of the deal was to also dig out the stump and level the ground. Bill and the boys worked on this project over several weekends.

Clouds of war loomed over Europe and Asia. Prices for commodities, livestock and farm produce were higher than they had been in years. Bill was working regular at Joe Hodges Motor Freight in Oklahoma City. Pauline and the boys were doing the day to day things to run the farm.

Bill borrowed three hundred dollars at the bank in Moore and bought a team of mules named Pete and Jack. A neighbor, Henry Janko, co-signed the note at the bank. Part of the deal with Henry was to sublet sixty acres to him so he could plant oats, which he did.

The first night the mules were at their new home they managed to open a gate and get out. They ran away looking for their old home. Late in the night they got onto Highway #74 about two miles away. They were just over a small rise in the highway. A car came over the hill at a high speed. The driver frantically applied his brakes but still hit the mules. One rolled onto the hood of the car and then fell off. The mules were frightened and ran through a barbed wire fence into a field. When Bill finally got them home they were badly injured, especially Pete. He stayed in his stall several weeks. The boys doctored, fed and watered him nursing him back to health. After two months he was eased into a harness and hooked up with Jack.

One day a stray mixed breed female dog came to the house. She was pitifully under fed and very hungry. The boys put out food for her and she found a home. They called her "Lady." The Rupe family lived on the farm across the road. They had a beautiful full blood Collie male dog. It wasn't long before Lady had a litter of eight half Collie pups. Soon half grown dogs were running all around the place. Attempts were made to give them away to good homes. They gave one to Pauline's mother on Panther Creek. The boys kept one of the male dogs. They named him "Laddie."

One day Gene and Laddie were walking through a field across the road from a neighbor's barn, but not on the neighbor's property. The neighbor was a crotchety old man and had accused the dogs of chasing his sheep. Gene heard a gun shot, but didn't think anything about it. It was not uncommon to hear gun shots in the country. Laddie was in front of Gene about thirty yards when he heard a second shot. He heard Laddie yelp and saw him suddenly spin around. Gene first thought Laddie was bitten by a snake, but then realized he had been shot. Gene and Laddie ran to the house.

The small caliber bullet entered Laddie's chest just behind his front left leg. It exited the other side barely missing his heart. The boys doctored and nursed him back to health.

Laddie became a very good stock dog. On command he would round up the cows and bring them to the barn if he could see where they were. So, it was not unusual to hold him up to where he could see or get him up in the barn loft so he could see where the cows were. He would jump down, run get the cows and bring them to the corral at the barn.

December 7, 1941, the Japanese attacked Pearl Harbor. The "Day of Infamy" and the nation was at war with the Japanese in the Pacific and the Germans in Europe. Prices went up and shortages prevailed. That Sunday evening Gene was at the Price's, the closest neighbors, listening to a radio program with his friend, Willis. A commentator broke in and announced the attack on Pearl Harbor. Later when Gene got home he told the rest of the family about the attack. No one believed him. They thought he was joking around. Bill and Pauline did not have a radio so it was the next day before they learned Gene was not joking.

Bill continued to work in Oklahoma City during 1942 and work the farm along with the boys. They planted several acres of corn, about thirty acres of cotton, and about ten acres of kafricorn. Henry Janko planted sixty acres of oats. The weather was favorable to the crops and the harvests were good. They had several good crops and had accumulated a good team of mules, a few farm implements, several good milk cows, and some pigs. Ribbon, the trusty old horse, died suddenly during a severe lightning and thunderstorm. It appeared she was struck by lightning while standing in the pasture. William and Bobby Joe bought lambs and raised them as their FFA projects to show at the county fair. Bill let Gene raise some piglets as his 4-H project to show at the county fair.

By this time Bill and family were fairly well situated in the rural community surrounding Moore. Though they had moved several times, the children had been attending school in the Moore Consolidated School District five years, longer than any time in their lives at any other school. They were well assimilated into the educational system, had many friends and participated in school activities. They rode School Bus Route #4 to school. Mr. Fishburn was the driver.

Bill and family were regular members of the Moore Methodist Church. Bill was recognized as an honest and respectable man in the community. The boys were considered to be good solid workers. When they could be spared from the farm they worked for other farmers earning money to help pay their way.

The summer of 1942, after much discussion, Bill and his father decided to go together in a farming partnership and rent the Cochran Farm on Strawberry River about three miles north of Evening Shade, Arkansas. The Cochrans were related to the Herrons. It was through Aunt Kate Herron they were able to rent the farm. Bill's parents lived on the Herron Place at Cow Ford near Hardy until December 1942.

Bill bought a 1933 Chevrolet sedan in the summer of 1942. The old 1929 Windsor was worn out and dispatched to the scrap pile to aid the war effort. That September Bill bought a used two and a half ton 1937 Ford V8 truck with dual rear wheels from a neighbor, Mr. Price. Bill made a large cattle frame on the back of the truck. He also made a small trailer to tow behind the Chevy. Then once again began the process of preparing to move.

After the crops were harvested in November 1942, Bill and family moved to Evening Shade, Arkansas. They made two trips from Oklahoma to Arkansas. One to move the mules, cows, sow hog, and Laddie. Bill took William and a friend, Junior Janko, with him to move the livestock from Moore to Mord's farm near Hardy. William stayed with Mord and Meta. Bill and Junior came back to Moore to move the implements and household goods. Pauline, Bobby Joe, Meta Lu (Ann) and Marvin (Sam) traveled in the Chevy pulling the trailer. Bill and Gene traveled in the Ford truck which was heavily loaded, and not without incident.

Near Afton, Oklahoma, a rear dual tire blew out. Pauline in the Chevy with the other children went on to Hardy. Bill left Gene with the truck and hitchhiked to Afton. He found a man that had a used tire to fit the wheel. Tires were rationed during the war and difficult to get. They changed the tire and were soon on their way.

Near Halltown, Missouri, the truck was pulling hard and could barely go. Bill drove into a mechanic's garage in Halltown. The left rear wheel bearing was burned out. It took three days to fix it. Bill and Gene slept in the truck.

The first night a blue norther blew in with wind and snow. They were chilled to the bone by morning and for the next two mornings. The cafe across the street opened at six o'clock each morning. It was a wonderful and warming sight to see each morning when the lights turned on. It was here Gene wrapped his bitterly cold fingers around a hot cup and drank his first coffee. They got to Evening Shade two days later and spent the night with Aunt Kate Herron.

Arrangements were made with Aunt Kate to temporarily move into a house she owned two miles southwest of town. The tenants on the Cochran Farm did not have to vacate until the last day of the year. During December Bill and the boys cut and split stove wood for Aunt Kate as payment for house rent. Early January 1943 Bill and family moved into the house on the Cochran Farm.

The Cochran house on Strawberry River was an old two room wood frame house. The two rooms had a stone fireplace in each end for heating. At one time there was a 'dog-trot' between the two rooms, but it long ago was enclosed and made into a small room and storage area. A plank front porch ran the full length of the house.

A lean-to of plank construction with no space for insulation had been added to the back. It served as a combination kitchen and dining room. The planks long before had been papered with several layers of newspapers to help keep out the cold. An old round oak table served the family for meals. Each had their individual place at the table which was situated such that directly over Bill's head was a worn newspaper banner headline. It read: "Cunningham Sets Mile Record 4:4.4." The paper was worn so only the year "1938" showed in the dateline.

A large garden was west of the house as was a chicken house. The barn was across the road from the house. It was a conventional looking barn of fairly good construction. A passageway ran the full length through the middle with a hay loft overhead. Both sides were enclosed granaries and storage areas. Sheds were constructed on both sides. There was a large corral and several smaller holding pens. The barn still stands today in good shape, but the house has long since deteriorated to nothingness. A modern paved highway now runs over the site.

Bill's parents packed their belongings and moved to the house north of Strawberry River on the Cochran Place. Bill and the boys helped move the livestock, farm implements, and household goods from the Herron Place to the Cochran Place. The house was an old two room wood frame with a lean-to kitchen on the back and a small front porch. It set on a small rocky hill about a quarter of a mile from the ford crossing of the river.

The Cochran Place was a thousand and eighty-three acres of mostly hilly upland covered with timber and rocks. However, there were three bottoms along the river. One was about sixty acres behind and north of the barn. Another was forty acres across the river opposite the sixty acres. The Big Bottom was on the same side of the river as the barn, but because of a large rocky bluff and the way the river flowed, it was necessary to cross the river twice to get to it. The Big Bottom was about a quarter of a mile wide and a little over half a mile long. It was about three hundred and eighty acres of good bottomland soil. Bill and his father subleased the north part of the Big Bottom to a neighbor, Mr. Kunkel.

The children attended school in Evening Shade. The family attended the United Methodist Church in Evening Shade from December 1942 until September 1943. Bill's great-grandmother, grandparents and father attended this same church the latter part of the 1800's.

Bill and his father pooled their resources and purchased a used Farmall F-20 tractor with steel lug wheels and some farm implements. With Mord's mules and Bill's team they had three spans of mules plus "Old Bill." He was a tall lanky contrary mule that could not be teamed with another mule. But, he was stout as an ox and twice as stubborn as a mule. He was used for jobs that required only a single hitch.

The boys milked the cows twice a day by hand. The morning milk was run through a separator and the cream flowed into five-gallon milk cans. The cans full of cream were set beside the road. The milk truck came by early each morning, picked up the full cans and set off the empties. The cans of cream were taken to a creamery in Batesville. There it was used to make butter and cheese. This was a source of a modest weekly income when the check came from the creamery. The milk from the evening milking was used for the household, and the surplus mixed with feed and fed to the hogs.

Bill, his father, and the boys did the spring plowing. They planted corn in the sixty-acre bottom north of the barn, cotton in the Big Bottom, and cut hay in the small bottom. Bill and his father gambled all their resources on one good crop. The nation was at war and prices for farm commodities were good. But, "Lady Fortune" did not smile favorably on them.

They were flooded, not once, but twice. The cotton and corn was barely planted and starting to germinate when the first flood came. It destroyed the entire crop. The water receded in a few days. The tractor had been left in the field and was almost buried out of sight. It had to be dug out and overhauled.

Everyone got busy and re-planted. The cotton and corn were several inches tall when the second flood came. This one was much worse than the first. It came in July. That was practically unheard of so late in the season. The floodwaters came to the back of the barn and covered the fields for a week.

When the waters finally receded, large sandbars were washed over the fields. The second flood was a total disaster for Bill and his father. It was much too late in the season to even try to plant another crop, even if they had the money to do it. They tried to recover some by cutting and stacking hay. They had totally expended their resources and had no recourse but to give up.

They sold what little hay they harvested, sold the cows, the mules, the tractor, and the farm implements that could be salvaged. It was a dreadfully low point for Bill and Pauline. Laddie took up residence at a Boy Scout camp located on South Fork River. When Bill's cousin, Joe Clarke, returned from World War II he became the camp manager and kept Laddie. He became a favorite pet at the camp and lived there the rest of his life.

Everything had gone so badly the boys were so disheartened by all the work and the failures that they wanted to leave Arkansas for good. Late August Bob (Bobby Joe) took the old truck as a parting token for his labors and went to Missouri to haul hay and work at a dairy. Gene left to go to school in Thayer, Missouri, and work at the YMCA for his room and board. William stayed a few weeks longer and helped cut and stack hay. He hitchhiked to Moore where he stayed with the Morrow family.

The Morrows were friends from the earlier days at Moore. Mrs. Morrow, a widow with five children, was post mistress at Moore. She also had a janitorial contract with the school. William worked for his room and board sweeping floors at the post office and the school.

After a few weeks at Thayer things were not working out for Gene with his custodians, an elderly couple, at the YMCA. They bought a train ticket for Gene to go back to Hardy and thence to Evening Shade on a bus. No way was Gene going back to Evening Shade. He got up very early that morning and left. He hitchhiked from Thayer to Oklahoma City where he went to work at the YMCA as a clean up and janitorial worker for Louie Stalken. Louie was the manager of the steam room, athletic and recreational areas of the YMCA facility. Louie had worked for Bill when he was Ticket Agent at the Oklahoma Railway Company. Gene lived the next several weeks with Louie at the Travelers Hotel on North Robinson Street.

Pauline returned by bus to Oklahoma City in September 1943. She and Bill still owned the small house at 3608 NW 13th Street. She had to do what was necessary to get the renters to vacate the house so she and Bill could move in. Pauline obtained employment at a restaurant located on NE 23rd Street to earn some money to help relocate the family back to Oklahoma City. She temporarily roomed with a fellow worker.

A few weeks later Bill with Meta Lu (Ann) and Marvin (Sam) returned to Oklahoma City in a pickup truck driven by Bill's Uncle Cyrus Davidson. A few weeks later Mord and a man he hired with a truck arrived in Oklahoma City with the few household goods Bill and Pauline had left, including an old upright piano that was Pauline's one luxury item.

Bill went back to work as a dockhand at Joe Hodges, his former place of employment. He joined the Teamsters Union, Local No. 886. In the meantime they were unable to move into their house until the renters moved out. Rent controls were in effect during the war. It wasn't a simple matter of just asking them to vacate the house. There was a bureaucracy to deal with.

Alvin and Wilma Teel, friends from Moore, let Bill and Pauline store their meager household goods in their garage. Alvin was a fellow worker at Joe Hodges. Bill and Pauline with Meta Lu (Ann) and Marvin (Sam) lived with the Teels until November. Gene reunited with the family in October.

Bill and Pauline were finally able to move into their house in November 1943. Marvin (Sam) attended school at Linwood Elementary. Meta Lu (Ann) and Gene attended Taft Junior High School. Bob returned and attended Classen High School. William continued to live at Moore and attended school there. He went to work at the Moore Messenger newspaper for a small wage and a place to live.

Bill and Pauline rejoined the Linwood Methodist Church January 5, 1944, at NW 17th Street and Drexel Boulevard. Rev. Donald F. Harrell was the pastor. Meta Lu (Ann) joined the Linwood Methodist Church April 2, 1944. The three older boys did not rejoin.

By early spring 1944 all but William had rejoined the family in Oklahoma City after the traumatic experiences from the move to Evening Shade. All the family except Marvin (Sam), the youngest, were working to earn money to regain some financial stability. Bill worked at Joe Hodges. Pauline was working at a local restaurant. William worked at the newspaper in Moore and went to school there. Bob and Gene worked at the Union Bus Station at 4th and Walker as baggage checkers and handlers. Meta Lu (Ann) worked at Veazey's Drug Store at the soda fountain.

Bill's parents continued to live on the Cochran Place until summer of 1944. They first moved to a place near Highland. A few months later they moved to the lower Herron Place below Johnson Bend on South Fork River near where Otter Creek flows into South Fork River west of Hardy. They moved to Kansas City, Kansas, in 1947 to live with their daughter, Mary Arabella, and her husband, Jim Dunahoo.

William was drafted into the U.S. Navy March of 1944 and sent to San Diego for basic training. During a leave home he married Mary Elizabeth Grisham, a neighborhood girl.

When Gene started the ninth-grade in junior high school at Taft he began to use his first name, Donald, and went by "Don." Meta Lu (Ann) attended Taft Junior High School. That summer Don worked at Joe Hodges with Bill as a dockhand loading and unloading long-haul trailers.

Don attended Classen High School that fall in the tenth-grade. He played football on the B-Team and later fourth string on the varsity championship team with Bob. Meta Lu still attended Taft and Marvin attended Linwood Elementary.

At the start of 1945 it was still full mobilization for the war effort. All the family was working at various jobs. Bill continued to work at Joe Hodges. Pauline worked at a factory sewing tents for the army. Don worked the graveyard shift at a war plant as a jig rigger and later as spot welder making bomb racks.

That summer Don helped his Uncle Henry, Pauline's brother, farm the Roller place on Panther Creek in Garvin County. Hostilities ended August 1945. That fall Don attended Classen and played football on the varsity team that won the conference, but lost in the championship playoffs. Meta Lu attended Taft Junior High School. Marvin attended Linwood Elementary School.

At the start of 1946 Bill still worked at Joe Hodges with Alvin Teel, Chester Williams, John Fitzgerald and Bobby Willard. Bill was a member in good standing of the Teamsters Union Local No. 886 in Oklahoma City. William was in the Navy serving in the Pacific. Bob had been drafted into the Army Air Corps. In March Don was inducted into the Army and processed at Camp Chaffee near Fort Smith, Arkansas. He was assigned to Fort Belvoir, Virginia, for basic training. He was later assigned to the Corps of Engineers Yuma Test Branch about thirty miles north of Yuma, Arizona, on the Colorado River just below the Imperial Dam. He later served thirty months occupation duty in Japan with the Army Paratroopers.

July 1946 World War II was officially declared ended. That fall Meta Lu (Ann) attended Central High School. She legally changed her name to "Ann." Marvin attended Taft Junior High School. Pauline worked at Boulevard Cafeteria at 10th and Walker.

During 1950 Bill and Pauline still lived at 3608 NW 13th Street. William was out of the Navy, married to Mary Elizabeth Grisham, and had a son, Johnny Lee. Don was out of the Army, married to Patricia Paschall, a neighborhood girl, and enrolled at Oklahoma

A&M College. Ann was married to Fred Melton, a neighborhood boy. Marvin (Sam) was in the Navy and had started using his first name, Samuel, and went by "Sam." During July 1950 Sam was home on leave. The entire family gathered at Will Rogers Park for a family picnic.

Bill and Pauline owned and operated a twenty-seat cafe during 1952 and 1953. It was in the Voss Building on Washington Street across from Joe Hodges. They served breakfast and lunch only. William worked for them as their cook. Pauline managed the cafe and handled the cash register. Bill worked at Joe Hodges.

Early in 1953 Bill and Pauline moved from 3608 NW 13th Street to 3223 NW 11th Street. They attended St. Johns Methodist Church. Bill was a deacon.

For the next several years Bill and Pauline cared for and raised two of their grandchildren, Paula and Steve. Bob's wife, Dorothy, left the children with Pauline for the day, but never returned. It was later learned she ran away with another man to California. Bob divorced Dorothy and lived at home with Bill and Pauline the next several years.

In June 1953 Bill got the sad news his father had cancer. Mord and Meta were living with their daughter, Mary, and son-in-law, Jim, in Kansas City. Don worked as a brakeman on the Rock Island Railroad out of El Reno. Jim worked for years on the Rock Island. He managed to get Don transferred as a switchman in the Armourdale Yards in Kansas City so he could live with him and Mary to help Meta care for Mord.

Mary worked for Singer Sewing Machine Company. She and Jim worked days. Don worked the graveyard shift from midnight to eight o'clock in the morning. He helped Meta with Mord during the day and took him to his doctor appointments. Mary and Jim were home by six o'clock to help Meta in the evening and at night. Don slept from six o'clock until eleven. Then he got up and went to work at midnight. Mord passed away August 29th. He was buried in Memorial Park Cemetery, Edmond, Oklahoma. He helped build the cemetery stone fence and entrance in 1929.

By 1953 Sam was out of the Navy and married to Martha Rowena Vance. He met her at Melton's Drugstore at 14th Street and Portland Avenue. All four boys served in the U.S. Armed Forces. Sam served on several destroyers and was injured when a gun mount exploded while firing at the coast of North Korea. The children were all married and making lives for themselves.

Bill and Pauline sold the cafe in 1954. Pauline worked at Street's, an upscale ladies ready-to-wear clothing store in downtown Oklahoma City. Street's later opened a store in Shepard's Mall in North Oklahoma City. Pauline transferred to work at the new store. She thoroughly enjoyed helping ladies, especially the younger ones, try on and select fine dresses and clothing that she had never been able to have for herself. Bill worked at Joe Hodges and was an active Teamsters member. Don graduated from Oklahoma A&M and went to work for a major oil company in Texas.

The next several years the family occasionally gathered at Bills and Pauline's house for family get-togethers. There was always much discussion about a variety of things and a lot of spirited conversation. William and Bob always argued about which car, Ford or Chevrolet, was the best. Don, the always-irreverent third born little brother, would insist Plymouth was the best just to be antagonistic, not that he really believed it. Nothing he loved better than to 'egg' his two older brothers into going at each other. Bill almost always remained aloof to all the harangue. He would much rather tell tall tales to the grandkids. After a few years these family get-togethers became less and less frequent as some of the children's careers and lives took them to other states to work and live.

Bill, Pauline and Meta, Bill's mother, traveled to Brownsville, Texas, in the summer of 1955 to visit Don and his wife, Pat. Bill and Pauline flew on Mexicana Airline from Brownsville to Monterrey, Mexico. This was their first time to fly. They spent a few days sightseeing in Monterrey and then took a return flight to Brownsville.

Don and Pat took Bill, Pauline and Meta deep-sea fishing in the Gulf of Mexico. Don and Pat with their friends, Leonard and Doris Holland and Tom and Janice Hill, rented a forty-two foot cabin cruiser for the day. Captain Williams took them out thirty-two miles offshore. They trolled with three lines out. They caught king mackerel, ling, and bonito, a kind of tuna. They weighed from fifteen to twenty-five pounds each. Bill had never caught such large fish. It took a lot of effort to reel in one. They caught a total of twenty-seven. Meta sure wanted to land one of those fish. It took a lot to convince her that it was too much for an eighty-year old woman.

In 1960 the Teamsters became involved in a labor dispute over seniority rights and work rules with the local motor freight companies. Bill no longer worked at Joe Hodges. Another company had bought them. He worked at Braswell-Hall. The Teamsters struck some of the local motor freight companies including Braswell-Hall. Bill was on strike.

Bill and Pauline flew to Salt Lake City in the summer of 1963 to visit Don and Pat. They took several sightseeing trips around Salt Lake City and into the mountains of Utah. They visited Pauline's sister, Beatrice, who lived at Price, Utah.

Bill walked the picket line until 1965 when he suddenly collapsed and was rushed to the hospital. He suffered a major stroke and was hospitalized at St. Anthony's hospital in Oklahoma City under the care of Dr. Warner for six weeks. He was discharged and went through a lengthy rehabilitation at home to regain muscular use.

Pauline was constantly at Bill's side and worked diligently with him during this long rehabilitation. It was several years before he was completely recovered. In the meantime he retired and started drawing his Teamsters pension. The road to recovery was long and tedious, but by 1968 he was pretty much back to normal. Bill's mother, Meta, suffered several small strokes during the 1960's.

Early in 1969 Bill and Pauline went to a place near El Centro, California, in the Imperial Valley for several months. Carl Self, a friend from Pauline's childhood, was in the real estate business in California. He came into a citrus orchard through some kind of real estate deal.

The orchard had been neglected for several years. It needed someone to take charge and get it into shape so Carl could sell it. Bill and Pauline agreed to take on that responsibility. They lived in a house trailer on the property. They hired laborers to do the clean up work and take care of the orchard to get it back into good condition. They learned a lot about living in the desert, irrigation, and citrus grove management and production.

Late in 1969 Bill and Pauline moved from 3223 NW 11th Street to an acreage on the south side of Shawnee Lake ten miles west of Shawnee, Oklahoma. They owned ten acres and started a Christmas tree farm. They planted five acres of pine tree seedlings. They kept a large garden. They attended Bethel Methodist Church.

William E. Davidson Family - 1952
Front L. to R. Ann, Pauline, William E.
Back L. to R. Don, Bill, Bob, Sam

Several years later at Christmas time they advertised in the local newspapers for people to bring their children to select and cut their own Christmas trees. Bill and Pauline enjoyed very much helping the young people pick out their trees and cut them down.

Bill's mother, Meta, suffered a stroke 6 July 1970 and passed away. She was ninety-three years old. She was buried next to Mord at Memorial Park Cemetery at Edmond, Oklahoma.

Bill and Pauline celebrated their 50th Wedding Anniversary 9 May 1975. They rented a large room at the Holiday Inn in Shawnee. They had a ceremony and repeated their wedding vows. They had a catered sit down dinner served for the guests. A professional photographer took color photos for an album and of the several family groups. Pauline liked to write poetry. She assembled some of her poems and published them in a booklet, "Whispering Leaves", to commemorate the occasion.

Afterwards, they had a reception at their home west of Shawnee. Bill's sister, Mary, and her husband, Jim Dunahoo, attended. Pauline's sisters and brothers-in-law that attended were: Jewel and Tom Gardner, Blanche (Gardenhire) and Larry Stewart, and Dixie and Ed Huffman. Pauline's sister Hazel Roller and her brother Henry Roller also attended.

Bill and Pauline took a trip to Europe in November 1975. They landed at Gatwick Airport south of London and visited Ann and Fred who lived in Bristol, England, at the time. They went sightseeing in Southern England and Wales where they visited Chepstow Castle. They went to Scotland where they toured Tulloch Castle and Dingwall Castle, the hereditary castle of the Clan Davidson. They traveled to Belgium and Germany where they visited with Don Stevenson, grandson of a neighbor and childhood friend of Gene (Don) when they lived at Moore. Don Stevenson lived in Germany and had a business interest there. He took Bill and Pauline touring many interesting places in Germany and Austria.

Bill and Pauline moved from Shawnee to Brenham, Texas., in July 1978. There they joined the United Methodist Church. They made many new friends. They had a large lot and each year Bill and Pauline planted, cultivated, and harvested the fruits of a well-kept garden. They often gave produce to friends and surrounding neighbors.

They celebrated their 60th Wedding Anniversary in May 1985 at the United Methodist Church. Many friends and relatives attended. They thoroughly enjoyed the next ten years together cultivating their garden, caring for the flowers and plants, and remodeling part of the house.

Pauline always wanted to be a writer. She spent a lot of time writing about religion and life. Bill liked to read and work cross-word puzzles.

William E. Davidson Family - 1956
L. to R. Sam, William E., Bill, Pauline, Ann, Don

Early in December 1988 Pauline was hospitalized at The Trinity Medical Center in Brenham with a heart condition. She was released after a few days and returned home.

Early Christmas morning of 1988 the local EMS rushed her to the hospital. Bill called Don and Pat, in Bartonville, Texas, about two o'clock in the morning. They rushed to Brenham and arrived at the hospital about eight o'clock only to find Pauline had been discharged and sent home. Later that afternoon about four-fifteen o'clock Pauline died at home in her own bed. She always said that was where she wanted to die, "at home in my own bed."

Pauline was religiously devout. She wanted so very much to do so many good things for so many people. This was a compelling influence in her life. Others often misunderstood the things she did because she did not possess the delicate communication skills and finesse commensurate with her desire and zeal to do good for others. Yet, she never asked anything of others for herself and she never wanted to be a burden to anyone. She was a very independent person and very strong willed in that way.

She truly picked her place and time to die. She died quietly and peacefully in her own bed in Bill's arms without pain or suffering. She went quietly and quickly with head held high and in her own way asking nothing from anyone. She brought life to her children and she went on ahead like a good mother to prepare the way for the rest of those whom she loves so dearly.

Two funerals were held for Pauline–one in Brenham and one in Oklahoma City for relatives and friends. She was buried 31 December 1988, at Memorial Park Cemetery, Edmond, Oklahoma, in the same lot with Bill's father and mother.

Bill continued to live alone at the home in Brenham. In November, 1991, when he was ninety years old, his sons, Don and Sam, and their wives, Pat and Rowena, planned and held a large birthday celebration at the United Methodist Church recreation center in Brenham. It was thought this might be the last birthday celebration for Bill. Many relatives and friends attended. Pauline's sisters

Jewel, Blanche, and Dixie attended. Many photos were taken and a video made of the event.

November 1996 Don, Pat, Sam and Rowena again planned and held a ninety-fifth birthday celebration for Bill at Don and Pat's home near Brenham. It was thought this would probably be the last birthday celebration for Bill, so Don, Pat, Sam and Rowena went all out to make it an eventful birthday. Again, many relatives and friends attended. A friend flew William and Mary from Liberal, Kansas, so they could attend. Bob and Bonnie, and Ann and Fred attended. Many photos were taken and a video made to record the event.

November 10, 1998, Bill's friends held a ninety-eighth birthday celebration dinner for him at the K&G Restaurant in Brenham. The following Saturday evening the family held a birthday celebration for him at the same restaurant.

In June 2001 Bill traveled with his daughter, Ann, and her husband, Fred, to the Clarke Family Reunion at Rose Edna (Clarke) French's home near Hardy, Arkansas, only a few miles from where Bill was born. Rose Edna is Bill's first cousin. Bill traveled home to Brenham with Don and his wife, Pat. Bill made the trip very nicely and without incident. He enjoyed very much meeting and visiting with his Clarke cousins.

By September 2001 Bill lived alone in Brenham at the home he shared with Pauline all those precious years. He was ninety-nine years old and continued to enjoy reasonably good health considering his age. His mind stayed keen and very alert. He busied himself reading, working crossword puzzles, watching TV, and visiting with friends. He occasionally attended church at the United Methodist Church. He sometimes attended the Methodist Men's Club and met with a group of seniors known as "Keenagers". He sometimes attended Saint Pauls Lutheran Church in Brenham with friends.

Bill's son, Don, and his wife, Pat, planned and handled all the arrangements for a one hundredth birthday party for him Saturday, 10 November 2001 at St. Peters Episcopal Church Parish Hall in Brenham. Some of Bill's children and grandchildren helped defray the expenses. Various family members pitched in the last day or two and helped. Many friends and family attended.

Trumpets sounded and a long red carpet was rolled out by two of Bill's great grandsons, Casey and Daryl Davidson, as all sang "For He is a Jolly Good Fellow." He sat in a king's chair as Sue Johnson sang personal songs. The choir from the Methodist church sang for him. Certificates of Recognition from President Bush, Governor Perry, Congressman Brady, State Representative Lois Kolkhorst and State Senator Steve Ogden were presented. County Judge Dorothy Morgan issued a Proclamation commemorating his 100th birthday. Family members told stories and anecdotes about his life. Photos were taken and a video made by Greg, his grandson, to record the event. Don was the master of ceremonies.

Bill lived alone until 5 September 2002, when Don took him to Trinity Medical Center with an angina attack. He was in the hospital several days. September 9th he was released from the hospital and checked himself into the Gazebo Convalescent Center. Sally Boehm, a social worker at the hospital, convinced him that he needed to be in a nursing home. Bill signed a legal document at Trinity Medical Center giving Don and Ann medical power of attorney. Ann handled his trust as the executrix and Don handled his financial affairs. Bill was not too happy at Gazebo. After a few days he commented, "There's nobody here but old people."

Paula, Bill's granddaughter, and her husband, Gary Lynch, agreed to live with Bill at home and care for him for the same amount he was paying to stay at Gazebo. He came home 31 October 2002. This arrangement was satisfactory until Bill had a serious angina attack 25 February 2004 that went into atrial fibrillation. Bill slumped unconscious at the breakfast table. Gary summoned the EMS. Bill had no vital signs when EMS arrived and was not responding to their efforts, but they were able to revive him and transported him to the Trinity Medical Center. Don stayed with him until he was released to go home that evening.

The angina attack anxiety and other factors prompted Paula and Gary to discontinue their service caring for Bill. Paula and Gary took him to Gazebo 12 March 2004. That is where he lived until he passed away December 7th 2005. He gave some of his household goods to family and friends. The rest was sold at an estate sale. The home Bill and Pauline knew for so many years in Brenham was put up for sale. Don coordinated the remodeling and Ann handled the sale.

Bill lived the rest of his days at Gazebo. He watched television and played dominos and bingo. Up until the last few months Bill played six bingo cards at a time. He won a quarter for each bingo. He won so often the other clients complained so that Bill was allowed to play only three cards at a time. He kept a daily diary though his penmanship was getting weak and shaky. A few friends sometimes came to visit, though his friends had mostly passed away. Other than Don and Ann the rest of the family seldom came to visit. Don handled his financial matters and ran errands to take care of things he needed. Ann was trustee for his trust fund.

An interesting sidelight to Bill's life is he said he had been declared dead five times, yet much to everyone's surprise, he came back alive.

Pauline and William E. Davidson - 1978

First, he was born at his grandparents' house. They thought he was stillborn. His parents and grandparents were discussing where to bury him when his mother noticed him take a breath.

Second, when he was three years old his father was carrying some timbers to the other side of a creek. His father told him to hold onto his pants leg as he waded across the creek. When he got to the other side Bill was nowhere to be seen. His father frantically looked downstream only to find Bill at the bottom of a pool of water. His father carried his limp body over his shoulder to the house. His parents thought he was dead and were discussing where to bury him, when again his mother noticed him take a breath.

Third, when he was seven years old a mule kicked him in the head. Bill's father carried his limp body to the house. His parents were discussing what to do when again his mother noticed him take a breath.

Fourth, when he was sixty-two years old he had a massive stroke and was transported to the hospital where he was pronounced dead. A few minutes later a nurse noticed him wiggle his toe.

Fifth, when he was a hundred and two years old he had a heart attack at the breakfast table. His granddaughter called 911. When the EMS team arrived he had no vital signs. They worked with him a few minutes and he was not responding. Paula thought he was dead. Then he came around and the EMS technicians noticed he took a breath. They transported him to the hospital. He recovered and lived another two years.

Bill died at 1:35 a.m. December 7th 2005, Don's birthday. The nurse at Gazebo called Don at 1:40 a.m. Bill had been failing noticeably the past several months. About six months ago he began to have severe pain in the left side of his neck, jaw and head. Several different pain medicines were tried to find one that would give him relief. None seemed to work very well.

The day before Bill's 104th birthday Don took him to Dr. Maraist, a neurologist in College Station that specialized in pain management. He gave Bill a cortisone shot in the left side of his neck and a prescription to start taking a few days later. The cortisone shot gave him good relief for only about twenty-four hours.

They had a small celebration at Gazebo for Bill on his 104th birthday. Bill's friends, Leo and Mariann Strom, Josephine Helm, Ruth Peters, Evelyn Lueckemeyer, Alice Hein, several of the Gazebo residents, and Don attended. Ann came later after the party. Bill felt fairly well.

The next several days Bill had a few reasonably good days and some bad days. He was perfectly lucid, alert, and talkative. The morning of November 21st he fell hitting his head on the floor. Gazebo called Don and he rushed over. Bill was on his bed limp and lifeless like. The nurse said his vital signs were weak.

This is an email Don sent November 22nd to all the family:

> A note to let you all know about Dad.
>
> He has deteriorated markedly the past few days. He has excruciating pain in his head, jaw, and neck. He mumbles and is incoherent most of the time. He has trouble recognizing me even though I see him at least once and sometimes two and three times a day. He keeps his eyes closed. He hallucinates at times. When a little water or milk trickles down his chin he thinks he is drowning. He won't eat. This evening I had to help the Gazebo aid almost force feed him some chicken noodle soup, a small amount of ice cream, and about a third of a small glass of milk. At times he says he is dying. He says over and over, "It hurts. It hurts. It hurts." It is heart wrenching to be at his bedside at a time like this.
>
> Last month I insisted an MRI be done on Dad's head and neck. The doctors said the results showed his brain to be normal–no tumors, water on the brain, etc. It showed he had severe arthritis in his neck. I think this is where the pain comes from. I think the nerves that come out of the spinal column in the neck area to the head are inflamed or under some kind of pressure or irritation from the arthritis. I haven't been able to convince the doctors I am right.
>
> November 9th I took Dad to a neurologist in Bryan. He referred Dad to another doctor (neurologist). I took him to the second doctor November 15th. He gave Dad a shot of cortisone in the neck. It relieved the pain for about 24 hours. Then it resumed. November 21st we started a regimen of Tegretol twice a day. It is a very strong medicine. Today the doctor doubled the dosage. He is still in severe pain. The past two

months Dad has been on a number of strong pain medicines like Hydrocodone, Vicidin, Ultram, and Neurotrin. None have brought him relief.

I don't think Dad is going to be with us much longer unless he experiences a dramatic turnaround in the next few days. However, he has fooled us before. He is one tough old guy.

Sorry I can't send good news. Have a Happy Thanksgiving.

This is a fax Don sent December 4th to Dr. Maraist:

I am William E. Davidson's son. I have a Medical Power of Attorney from Dad on file at the Trinity Medical Center.

William E. "Bill" Davidson's 100th birthday party - 2001
L. to R. Bill, Don (kneeling), Sam, Ann, Bob

I am very concerned about the sudden dramatic change in Dad's condition. Prior to November 20th he was lucid, alert, talkative and able to feed himself and go to the bathroom without assistance. The only serious problem was the persistent excruciating pain in the left side of his neck and head, and pain in his left jaw.

> Dad and I visited your office November 15th. You gave him a cortisone shot in the left side of his neck. It lasted about twenty-four hours during which he was virtually pain free. You prescribed Tegretol (100 mg) twice a day to start November 20th if the pain had not subsided. That regimen was started. The next day (November 21st) I called you because Dad was in excruciating pain. You faxed the Gazebo to double the dosage which they did starting November 21st.
>
> Something sudden and dramatic happened November 21st. Dad fell and hit the left side of his head on the floor causing an abrasion near his eye with a nasty looking blackeye. I first thought he had a stroke because he was limp as an old rag, could not or would not speak, and could not or would not open his eyes. He was totally non-responsive. His vital signs (as taken by the Gazebo nursing staff) were weak. Consequently, I called you and you instructed the Gazebo staff to reduce his Tegretol dosage back to 100 mg twice a day. I called you a few days later and you instructed the Gazebo staff to reduce the Tegretol dosage to 50 mg three times a day. They now give him that dosage at 9:00 a.m., 1:00 p.m., and 5:00 p.m. daily.
>
> As of today Dad will barely eat or drink. He sometimes nods his head for "yes" or "no." I have to really coax him to say my name. I ask him if his head hurts and he shakes his head "No." I am very concerned, especially since there was such a sudden and dramatic change in his condition.
>
> Do you think he may have had a stroke? Is there some way to test for that? Do you think the Tegretol could have had such a sudden and dramatic effect on him? Do you think it advisable to gradually wean him from the Tegretol and see if his condition improves? If so what other medication do you advise?

Don thinks Bill had a stroke and fell. He was never quite right after the fall. He had to be really coaxed to open his eyes and look at anyone. He could not talk, just made sounds. He would not, or more likely could not, eat or drink. He could not swallow food or liquid. Don and the nursing aids would try to force him to swallow, but he couldn't. He had very little use of his arms and legs.

Bill's daughter, Ann, visited him about this same time. She tells that as she was leaving she kissed him and told him she loved him. She said he managed to weakly whisper, "I love you."

Bill died at 1:35 a.m. December 7th 2005 at Gazebo.

What follows is Don's account of events following Bill's demise:

> We had a funeral at Brenham Memorial Chapel December 9th in Brenham, Texas. The afternoon of December 11th we had a wake at the Smith and Kernke Funeral Home in Oklahoma City. The morning of December 12th we had a funeral service at Memorial Park Cemetery in the mausoleum conducted by my son, Greg, and Dad's grandson, Steve Davidson. Greg is an ordained Presbyterian minister and Steve is an ordained minister in his church. Burial was that day next to Mom and with Dad's parents, Mord and Meta Davidson.
>
> The past year I came to know my father in a way I had never known him. I went to see him almost every day and sometimes two or three times in a single day. Nice days I would push him outside in his wheelchair around the Gazebo grounds. We would talk about a lot of things. We would sometimes stop and watch the traffic zipping along on Highway #290 in front of Gazebo. We would speculate about the different vehicles and where they were going. One day a pickup went by pulling a fishing boat. Dad said, "Well, we know where he is going."
>
> Dad loved to tell stories. He was a great storyteller. He loved to spin a good yarn. Years ago he told some people of an incident for which I had personal knowledge. Later I told Dad, "That wasn't exactly the way it was. You embellished it somewhat." Dad looked me square in the eye and said, "Son, if a story is worth telling it is worth embellishing."
>
> He often told stories to kids at the Brenham elementary schools, the library or when a teacher brought kids to Gazebo. He had an entire litany of stories about his dog, Spot. I asked him one day if he ever really had a dog named Spot. He said, "No. He was just an imaginary dog."

I sat in on some of Dad's story telling sessions with school kids. One of his many stories was about a bear he met one day in the woods near his house when he was a kid. He told how he played peek-a-boo behind trees and bushes with the bear. He told how he would play hide-and-seek with the bear. He told how he played tag with the bear. He would chase the bear and sometime the bear would chase him. He told of going out the next day to play with the bear, but it was gone. He never saw it again.

There always was an element of truth to Dad's stories, but with considerable embellishment and outright omission. What he did not tell the kids was that when he was a kid traveling medicine shows were commonplace. They were horse drawn and often had a trained performing bear as an attraction to draw a crowd to sell the various tonics and salves for aches and pains. The bears were accustomed to people, usually very old, almost toothless, and declawed. This particular bear escaped one night from a traveling medicine show nearby. Dad actually played with the bear the next day in the woods. And, of course the medicine man went looking for his bear. When he found it he took it back to the show wagon. Dad never saw the bear again. The kids loved it!

The people at Gazebo, staff and clients, liked Dad. Even family members that came to visit other clients got to know Dad and liked him. He was a willing conversationalist and told them stories. Everyone marveled at his advanced years and often asked him the secret of his long life.

The program director, a young woman, at Gazebo tried to conduct sitting physical exercise classes for the elderly clients, but not too successfully. Dad and one or two others attended her classes. One day Dad volunteered to conduct the classes. She agreed but was skeptical. After a few sessions twelve to fifteen people began to attend. They felt intimidated that a man over a hundred years of age was conducting the classes and thought they should at least make an effort.

One day the program director suggested that Dad make some changes in his routines and the times. Dad told her, "I volunteered to do this. If you are going to tell me what to do and when to do it you will have to pay me." That ended that. She let Dad run the classes his way.

I began to see a different personality in Dad than the one he had around our family. There were too many old memories of bad times in the family. Other people never knew about that "baggage" Dad carried, so he was much more relaxed and gregarious with others. He had a friendliness and openness with a dash of wit I had never experienced when I was with him around others at Gazebo. I think this is what attracted Mom to him when they were so young. He came to accept me more as his good friend than as his son from the past. Thus, we came to have a close camaraderie I had never before had with him. He was always thoughtful of me and always appreciative for what I did for him. He always without fail thanked me when I took my leave.

So, Dad, I'm glad I had the opportunity to get to know you in a way I think was your true self unencumbered by the bad times. I wish others in the family could have known you as I came to know you. I truly miss you. I pray you are with Mom and at peace.

CHAPTER 8

MARY PAULINE ROLLER

MARY PAULINE ROLLER, second child and first daughter of Dillmus Elias "Dill" and Arlie Luvida (Jones) Roller, was born 1 March 1905 near Antioch, Indian Territory (I.T.), in what is now Garvin County, Oklahoma. Pauline married William Edmund "Bill" Davidson 8 May 1925 in Pauls Valley, Garvin County, Oklahoma. They had five children: (1) William Lee born 3 March 1926; (2) Bobby Joe born 11 May 1927; (3) Donald Jean born 7 December 1928; (4) Meta Luvida born 1 July 1931; and (5) Samuel Marvin born 20 January 1933.

Dillmus "Dill" Elisa Roller, son of Henry Harrison Roller and Mary Ann (Osborn) Roller, was born 15 October 1877 at Ava, Douglas County, Missouri. He married Arlie Luvida Jones, daughter of Cornelous Coats "Trick" and Sarah Lugaine (Jones) Jones, 10 February 1901 at Johnsonville, McClain County, I.T., now Oklahoma. Dill died 28 December 1965 at Maysville, Garvin County, Oklahoma. Arlie died 14 October 1961 at Maysville, Garvin County, Oklahoma. They are buried side-by-side at Antioch Cemetery, Garvin County, Oklahoma.

Mary Pauline had two brothers and seven younger sisters. Her older brother was Loyce Elmer born 5 April 1903. Her sisters were: Margaret "Marge" Ellen born 7 December 1906; Hazel Pearl born 26 October 1908; Cora Jewel born 8 May 1911; Edna Blanche born 22 May 1913; Emma "Bea" Beatrice born 5 May 1915; Naomi "Dixie"

Elizabeth born 22 October 1920; and Elsie Alice born 31 October 1923. Her brother, Henry Cornelous was born 17 June 1917.

Dill Roller's parents were Henry Harrison Roller (1848-1915) and Mary Ann (Osborn) Roller (1851-1935). Henry Harrison Roller's parents were Dillmus Elias Roller (1812-1887) and Elizabeth (Paine) Roller (1817-1882). Dillmus Elias Roller's parents were Jacob Roller (1766-1860) and Eve (Zirkle) Roller (1774-1858). Jacob Roller's parents were Johannes Roller (1725-1816) and Anna (Ocher) Roller (1730-1786).[1]

Mary Ann Osborn's parents were Etcyl Osborn (1815-1886) and Cyntha (Nelson) Osborn (1817-1848)

Arlie (Jones) Roller's parents were Cornelous Coats "Trick" Jones (1843-1929) and Sarah Lugaine (Jones) Jones (1848-1897). Cornelous did not like his name and went by "C.C." or "Trick" Jones most of his life. His parents were Wiley E. Jones (1804-1885) and Elizabeth H. (Talley)[2] Jones (1805-1877). Lugaine Jones' parents were Rev. James Madison Jones (1819-1892) a part Cherokee and Matilda (Cook) Jones, a Cherokee. It is believed that James Madison Jones was of illegitimate birth.

Nothing is known about our Cherokee heritage except they came to Indian Territory from what is now Georgia on the Trail of Tears and Sarah Luganie was born somewhere in Northern Arkansas. Matilda's father, John Randall Cook, was half Scot and half Cherokee. His wife was full Cherokee. Their daughter, Matilda, was three-fourths Cherokee. She married James Madison Jones. He was half Cherokee. His mother was full Cherokee. His father was unknown, except according to family folklore it is thought he was one of the Federal troops that escorted the Cherokees on the

---

1 (See Appendix 6, Roller Six Generations Chart)

2 (There has been a long-standing family controversy as to the correct surname. Some say it is Butterworth, while others say Talley. Arlie [Jones] Roller told Don, her grandson, years ago that it is Talley. This is given more credence by the fact one of the children [Zachariah] has the middle name of Talley.)

Trail of Tears from Georgia to Indian Territory. He claimed his name was "James Madison Jones", so that was what she named her child. Its ironic that James Madison, the fourth president of the United States, died in 1836 about this same time.

Pauline's parents, Dill and Arlie, lived most of their married life on the banks of Panther Creek in the shadow of the Table Hills[1] in what is now western Garvin County, Oklahoma, a few miles southwest of the community of Antioch. They were married 10 February 1901 at Johnsonville (which no longer exists) in Indian Territory (in what is now McClain County, Oklahoma). They first lived in a house which Dill and his brothers built near Alex, Oklahoma. That is where their oldest child, Loyce, was born.

Pauline's father was a farmer. Her mother was part Cherokee. They lived at three different locations along Panther Creek. The last place was a 120-acre farm Dill bought about a mile south of the earlier location.

Following is a transcript taken from typed and handwritten papers written by Pauline as an account of her life, philosophy and beliefs as well as her family history. She started this years ago but never finished it before she died December 25, 1988. The original sheets were given to her son, Don, by his father in July, 1998.

There were numerous typographical, grammatical and spelling errors that were corrected. Parts were edited to make it more comprehensible, but the context was not altered.

A ROLLER/JONES FAMILY HISTORY

Historians dress up the events of our history until we have to dig for the undesirable aspects that make daily news as it is happening. This possibly is best for youth that have to study it.

1 (The Table Hills are geologic plateau escarpments several hundred feet high.)

But, when they arrive at maturity and have to take the reins of government in their own hands, they need to know the true facts in order to know what to expect and learn how to best cope with the pitfalls of state and nation.

I'm thinking of a president and a governor whose political lives were ruined by crooked deals. In the literature of my school days, books like Thereau's "Walden" and William Cullen Bryan's "Thanotopsis" and "To A Waterfowl" were expounded and none of the pitfalls and erring ways of our leaders were brought to the foreground.

Only time can tell if revealing all the wiles of men is better for our great society or will the people just come to accept graft as a part of life.

It seems that outwitting the law always has been considered smart. I've heard my mother tell about two of her brothers-in-law trapping quail in Territorial days. It seems they were allowed just so many birds. If the law caught them with more than the law permitted they would be jailed. That happened to these two men, and they were being taken to jail. They were traveling in a spring wagon to reach the jail. The men were riding in the back of the wagon where the birds were cached in crates. Although they were handcuffed, one of the men managed to raise the trap door. Since it was dark by this time, the birds quietly slipped out of the trapdoor and fluttered to the ground without being detected. When the officers got to the judge they had no evidence so had to let the men go. That was a small incident, but they felt elated.

There were also men of God who were concerned about the morals of mankind. I've heard much about the old circuit riders of Territorial days. One of my great-grandfathers filled such a capacity in Texas soon after the close of the Civil War.

This great-grandfather was christened James Madison Jones and was married to Matilda Cook, a Cherokee. Their daughter, my grandmother, Lugaine Jones, was born on the Trail of Tears after the Cherokees arrived in what is now Northern Arkansas. How it is they reached Texas is a story I never heard. They may have been running from the Civil War conflict.

Another of my great-grandparents was also named Jones. He was Wiley E. Jones, born February 15, 1804. He died November 29, 1885. His wife, Elizabeth H. (Talley) Jones was born May 12, 1805. She died March 14, 1877. They are buried in the Jones Cemetery about five miles south of Eagan, Johnson County, Texas. Their children were: Calvert (1828); Lafayette W. (1830-1883); Jack Hall (1832-1920); Elizabeth H. Tennessee (1836-1867); Wiley Sumner (1839-1907); Zachariah Talley "Zeke" (1841-1931); Cornelous Coats "Trick" (1843-1929); Eudocia M. (1846); William (1849); and Robert A. (1851).

They first lived in Sumner County, Tennessee. About 1840 they moved to a farm near Conyerville, Henry County, Tennessee, near the Kentucky stateline. They farmed a plantation there with slaves. They also owned and ran a grain mill a Conyerville.[1]

When this wise old sage saw the storm clouds of the Civil War gathering, he sold all his holdings, loaded his family in wagons and headed for Texas in wagon-train fashion.[2] My grandfather, Cornelous Coats Jones, and his older brother, Zeke, took on the job of driving their livestock through by herding and grazing them

---

1 (This mill was located at what came to be known as Jones Mill, a very small village in far north Henry County, Tennessee, very near the state line.)

2 (They apparently arrived in what is now Johnson County sometime after July 1854 and settled near what is today known as Egan, Texas. The Registrations of Deeds in Henry County, Tennessee, shows that on September 8, 1853, Wiley E. Jones conveyed 50 acres to E. A. Atchison for the sum of one thousand and twenty dollars such deed recorded July 1, 1854, pages 178 and 179. A Texas Land Grant granted 320 acres on the waters of the North Fork of Chambers Creek to Wiley E. Jones, filed November 1, 1859, and recorded December 15, 1859, signed by H. R. Rummels, Governor, and recorded in Book A, Vol. 19, No. 87, Johnson County, Cleburne, Texas. This grant is today known as the Wiley E. Jones Survey for legal descriptive purposes.)

on open land all the way from Tennessee to Texas. They had no sooner completed their task than the Civil War began.

C. C., or "Trick" as he was nicknamed, and his brother Zeke, returned to the South to aid in the war against the North leaving their parents and older married brothers and several younger siblings whose names are listed above.[1]

Many were the tragic stories told by Grandfather Trick Jones. One story was of him contracting a fever of some sort and of being given a discharge and sent on his way to avoid contaminating the rest of the army. He traveled for days, part of the time semi-conscious. He finally arrived home but his mother was afraid they would all die from the fever, so he was housed in a small building by himself and given his old Negro mammy to look after him. She nursed him back to health. He was no sooner well than he headed right back into the war where he stayed by his brother's side until the end of the war.[2]

When they were told they would have to surrender their horses to the North, the Jones boys along with some others slipped away in the hours of darkness and headed for Texas–this time on the run. By the time they reached Texas the Federal troops were hot on their trail. Their next destination was Mexico. I have heard

---

1 (The military records for C. C. Jones show he was mustered in to the Confederate Army, 12th Cavalry, Texas, at Camp Hebert near Hempstead, Texas, October 28, 1861, as a Private, age 19, by W. J. Neal. C. C. Jones traveled 260 miles to rendezvous, his horse, named Maco Mano, was valued at $140, and his personal equipment valued at $15. He acquired the nickname "Trick" as a result of several escapades during the war where he tricked his captors and escaped. At first he was called "The Trickster" which later just became "Trick." The horse's name probably was a derivative of "Macho Mano" meaning strong hand in Spanish.)

2 (The military record for C. C. Jones, 4th Cpl., Co. C, 12th Regiment Texas Cavalry, shows he was Present on the Company Muster Roll for the period September 1 to December 31, 1863. at Hempstead, Texas, by Lt. Sparks, last paid August 31, 1863, by Capt. Terrell.)

grandfather tell of almost starving of thirst as they crossed the plains.

I don't know what route they took to Mexico. I have studied the map of Texas and it seems to me there were rivers near enough to each that a day's journey from one to the other even on horseback would be possible. Of course, if they went via a western route and entered Mexico in the Big Bend country, or even farther west around El Paso, that would have been a different story. This is a more likely scenario.

However they went I've heard grandfather tell of being so very thirsty. They were veering to the right as they went but his horse kept trying to go left. They wanted to go right for some reason. After they were returning from this journey grandfather followed his horse and found a huge lake of water. Thereafter he followed his horse instead of guiding him. He loved this horse almost as much as life.

As they journeyed on this safari they finally came to a huge gorge which looked as if there would be water in the bottom. So, they climbed down into it and indeed found water. Grandfather said he carried a hat full of water to his horse before he drank any for himself. They remained there to drink water and refresh their horses for several days before journeying on to Mexico.

Right after the Civil War a disturbance arose between the United States and Mexico. The United States government did not want any Americans down there stirring up strife.[1]

After the Southern men returned from Mexico, my grandfather took a job as an Indian fighter guarding the cattle drives that went north to Dodge City. They had many skirmishes with Indians. I've heard grandfather tell how he thought he may have given Geronimo the scar that he carried to the grave.

---

1 (They later obtained official Federal paroles to return to the United States with their guns, horses, and saddles.)

They were on a cattle drive and the scouts were trying to draw the Indians away from the cattle by bantering them into following them so the cattle wouldn't be scattered on the plains. A terrible looking chief in war paint came dashing up to grandfather with a lariat to rope him.

As the chief raced alongside grandfather he was so certain he had his man that he raced right up beside his prey. Just as he threw the lariat circle grandfather raised in his stirrups, bent over his saddle horn, and laid his head against the neck of his steed. The loop slipped harmlessly over grandfather's shoulder.

In the meantime, grandfather had jerked his sword from its scabbard. He made a vicious back slash at the chief's head not waiting to see if his blade had taken its toll. The Indians dropped back and in a few moments were seen loping off in the direction from which they had appeared.[1]

Another story I have heard grandfather tell was about a West Texas village that was fearful of an Indian attack, so the men all banded together and went out to meet the onslaught. The doctor was the only man left in the village. The following morning the doctor's wife awoke bright and early. She told her husband of a terrible dream she had in the night. All of the men except one had been killed and he was near death. She told him exactly where this battle had taken place and that this man was lying under a mesquite bush. She dreamed she walked out there carrying a pitcher of water and gave him a drink.

Later in the day when they had heard nothing of the men, she finally persuaded the doctor to take her to the place. There lay all

---

1 (The Indian probably wanted Trick's horse. A continuing part of the story as told by his daughter, Arlie, is that when Trick sat back up in his saddle he looked around to see where the Indian was. He didn't see him. Then he saw the Indian's horse gallop out of a deep gulch. At first Trick thought he had knocked the Indian from his horse, but taking a second look he saw the Indian clinging to the underneath side of his horse as it galloped over a ridge and out of sight.)

the men dead and scalped except for one who insisted the doctor's wife came to him in the middle of the night with a drink of water when he was dying of thirst.

It seems rather ironic that C. C. Trick Jones would marry a half Indian when he had spent so much time fighting them. Luganie was the daughter of a Methodist circuit rider. Luganie's mother was Cherokee.[1]

This grandfather, C. C. Jones, was born into a home of slave owners. He never really learned how to work and manage a home or family without a helping hand from someone. Neither did my mother know how to keep house as my grandmother had moved from one district to another as the daughter of a Methodist circuit rider. When she married C. C. Trick Jones they were a pitiful pair to begin life on the prairies of Texas south of what is now Fort Worth.[2]

---

1 (C. C. Jones married Sarah Luganie Jones who is believed to be three-fourths Cherokee. She was the daughter of James Madison Jones whose mother, Matilda Cook, was Cherokee, an Eastern Indian. Trick spent his time fighting Plains Indians.)

2 (The severe hardships endured by the Cherokees in their trek from their eastern native lands to the foreigh lands of Arkansas, Oklahoma, and Texas are well documented. This grandmother, Sarah Luganie Jones, was born somewhere in Northern Arkansas during the forced relocation of the Cherokees in 1838 to about 1849 from their homelands in parts of Georgia and Alabama. This was known as The Trail of Tears. These people had to be very resourceful just to have survived.
The hardships endured by the men of the Texas 12th Cavalry [Trick's unit} during the Civil War are utterly unbelievable as documened by diaies, letters, and detailed accounts written by the soldiers. They had to be hardy and resourceful just to survive the entire ordeal of war with the lack of food, clothing, medical care, etc., not to mention engaging the enemy in battle. Also, a man who not only served well during the struggle, but also spent several years as a cattle herd guard, mostly as an Indian fighter, would be savvy and resourceful in the ways of life on the Texas prairie in 1868.)

Another great-grandfather was Etcyl Osborne[1] who lived in Georgia at the time of the Civil War. He was a Baptist minister and against slavery. This made him very unpopular. He had two sons that were drafted into the Confederate Army. Their names were Mack and George. I can remember admiring their pictures when I was a small child. They were very stately gentlemen.

Although they were in the Confederate Army, the first opportunity they got they surrendered to the North. They were suspected of being spies for the South and were kept in prison for some time. Finally, assigned to the medical corps, they learned to be doctors and that was their profession the remainder of their lives. John, a younger brother, was also drafted into the Southern army and defected to the North.

The father, Etcyl Osborne, was so unpopular in Georgia that he had to disappear for the duration of the war. That left the mother, Cyntha Nelson Osborne, three girls, one of whom was my grandmother, Mary Ann Osborne, and a small boy I have known only as Uncle Cobb. The girls were drafted into the cotton mills to weave cloth to make uniforms for the Southern soldiers. My grandmother told of working in the mills while shells were exploding outside.

I have studied great-grandmother Osborne's picture and imagined what it must have been like to live alone with a small boy and three young girls in an unfriendly atmosphere with a war raging outside, and not even knowing where any of the men of the family were. She must have been a brave woman to stay in the house in an area where men were fighting and dying while she had no one to depend on to protect them. But, I suppose all people in that area lived rugged lives when we realize that the United States was only eighty-nine years old at the end of the Civil War. We had fought

---

1 (Mary Pauline spelled Osborne throughout with an "e" at the end. A photograph of Etcyl's burial headstone spells Osborn without the "e" at the end.)

the War of 1812 and were continually fighting skirmishes with the French to the north and Mexico to the south.

I often wonder how we can call ourselves a peaceful nation when we have fought the Spanish American War, World War I, World War II, the Korean War, and Vietnam in this Century, and we still have one-fifth of the Century to go. It is my opinion that any country that instigates a war is an ignorant bunch of renegades or a bunch of greedy thieves that will gamble with men's lives against a dollar.

If a nation of men and women are intelligent and filled with empathy for their fellow men, they will find ways of surmounting problems of any country with which they are drawn to do business. The above statement does not mean that I am against our country. We have one of the greatest constitutions of this world. But, how we do need some brave, honest, upright, intelligent people to set examples for the rest of the world. We could be the greatest nation that has ever been established. But, it is up to us as individuals to work to make it so.

I wish I knew how the Osbornes escaped from Georgia. It seems I heard grandmother tell of escaping in the middle of the night. All this time the mother and girls knew nothing of what had happened to or where the men were. It seems I have heard that grandfather wrote to them using grandmother's brother's name. He got together a wagon and team, and on a certain night he slipped into town, loaded them and all their belongings. Daybreak found them well on their way toward the Mason-Dixon Line.

They began to inquire about the men who had defected to the North. I don't know how they got in contact with George and Mack, but John, if I remember correctly, had been shipped to a concentration camp in Illinois. He was finally released and they all got together in the little town of Ava, Missouri. That is where they spent the remainder of their lives, except John, Cobb, and two of the girls who moved on to Indian Territory with their families.

I have photographs of the tombstones of my great-grandparents, the Osbornes and the Rollers, taken in a country cemetery. I believe the name is The Jackson Cemetery, near Ava, Missouri. These are the inscriptions taken from the photographs:

Elias Roller Born Sept. 12, 1812 Died March 3, 1882	Elizabeth Pain Roller Wife of Elias Roller Born May 10, 1817 Died December 19, 1882
Etcyl Osborne (dates obscured)	Cyntha Nelson Osborne Wife of Etcyl Osborne Born May 16, 1817 Died February 24, 1884

This is a poem I wrote after my first visit to that little town in 1936.

MEMORIES MEMORIES

I found a little inland town
Where no rattling trains go by,
No clanging streetcars screech over streets,
Nor skyscrapers dot the sky.

No hit and run drivers roam their streets.
No robbers make raids by night.
No glaring midway lights their streets,
But the moon is shining bright.

No First Lady stops to visit their town,
Probably knows not that it exists.
But, oh! The peaceful tranquility
Our First Lady has missed.

No newspaper loudly acclaims
The town's most worthy citizens.
But, everyone knows what everyone does
And praises are handed down.

Kind deeds and acts of mercy for man
That man has done for man
For generations past to the present
Have lived again and again.

A rising sun with the song of a bird,
A friendly home in a grove on a hill,
A tall pine tree in a country graveyard
Are memories that linger still.

I know very little about the Roller Family. Great Aunt Eve (Roller) Bunyard told me in 1936 that they came from Rogersville, Tennessee. I later met a Roller in Ava, Missouri, who told me some of Aunt Eve's and my grandfather Henry H. Roller's brothers remained in Virginia. After consulting a map, I found Rogersville to be very near the Virginia line. So, it is possible that some had married and lived in that state.[1]

As I stated previously, Mary Ann Osborne married Henry H. Roller. They were one set of my grandparents. They reared ten children, eight of whom were boys.

The two youngest boys were like older brothers to me. My own brother didn't like his younger sister tagging along with him when he went to parties and square dances. But my two uncles, Don and

---

1 (Rogersville is in northeast Tennessee about thirty miles south of the Virginia border. The early Roller family settled about 1750 on a tributary of the Clinch River in southwest Virginia. There are still many Rollers living in the area. Jacob [1767-1861] and Eve (Zirkle) [1774-1858] Roller were the grandparents of Henry H. Roller. They are buried on a steep hilltop near Clinchport, Virginia.)

Claude, were more mature and quite often took me places, or if they found me in the wrong crowd often rescued me and set me straight on whom I should be out with.

My grandmother having been reared in a Baptist minister's family was quite staid in her beliefs, and having been handed eight boys to rear in Indian Territory days was quite frustrated at the antics of the environment her children became involved with. I remember one time I was staying with them, and the youngest boy, Claude, sat down in the kitchen while fastening his supporters to his fancy silk sox. Grandmother eyed the sox and supporters with a sort of disdain and said, "Hummm, some get up you are using for those fancy sox." Claude said, "Yeah, Ma. Girls wear a supporter that goes plum around their waist." "See", said grandmother, "I'd like to know how you would know about that."[1]

The South Canadian River was the territorial line between Indian and Oklahoma Territories. When it was at flood stage it was a death trap to both man and beast. No bridge in those days had spanned this mile wide expanse of drifting sands and shifting water currents which have now been tamed to some degree by a few dams which partially control the flood waters. When this river is at low ebb it looks more like a massive sandbar with a narrow ribbon of water meandering to and fro as it seeks it way to the sea.

My husband, Bill Davidson, lived near this river when a young lad, and he tells of seeing a three foot wall of water rolling down that sandbar with a cloud of sand and leaves rushing ahead of it like a mighty roaring wind.

Alcoholic beverages were not allowed in Indian Territory. Anyone wishing to so indulge had to cross that treacherous river to

---

1 (She was a feisty little old woman. After her husband died she lived with my grandpa and grandma Roller. I often visited my grandparents on Panther Creek. One day when I was about five or six years old I sassed the "old woman." She promptly threw a dipper of water in my face.)

get into Oklahoma Territory to buy whiskey. Lexington at that time was a border town. It was to this point that most whiskey was shipped and from there found its way across the river and into many lives of both Indians and early day settlers alike. At this writing a building still stands in Lexington that has what looks like portholes. I have been told this building housed the old Porthole Saloon in Territorial days.

My mother's mother was Cherokee. They came to Indian Territory from down Texas way. My mother, Arlie Luvida (Jones) Roller, was born 27 February 1881 in Parker County, Texas, while my father's family drifted out of the Ozarks and onto the Oklahoma plains, crossed that treacherous river and settled in the same community near my mother's family. My mother told this story years ago:

> When I was ten years old my dad packed all our belongings in a covered wagon and we left our home near Egan, Texas, and headed for Indian Territory. My mother was part Cherokee and she had a 'headright' that entitled her to claim her right for land in Indian Territory. This was the attraction for my dad–to own land.
>
> We traveled several days and then crossed the Red River into Indian Territory. We camped near the old Washington Ranch that was located several miles west of what is now Marietta to rest the horses and stock. My dad worked several weeks for the Washington Ranch. My sisters and I made a playhouse in some of the trees near our campsite where we played with our few toys and rag dolls.
>
> One day my dad said for us to load up in the covered wagon because we were moving further into Indian Territory. We hastily gathered all our things, put them in the wagon and left the campsite by mid morning.
>
> After we traveled five or six miles I remembered I had forgotten and left my ragdoll in our play house in the trees. I begged dad to turn around so we could go back and get it, but he was not about to do that. It was too great of a trek to go. It would take too much time and effort. I was tearful about

> the loss of my doll, but my sister and I talked about it and we decided that maybe an Indian would find it and take it for his little girl to have and play with.

After my parents began dating my father, Dillmus, asked permission to take Arlie, my mother, to a Woodsman of the World dance in Lexington. After much cautioning on how he must care for her he was given the honor. Men in those days were held responsible body and soul for the welfare of the women whom they escorted. Dill, short for Dillmus, had borrowed his brother's spirited team of horses and shiny new buggy for the ten-mile journey.

They arrived safely to the dance, but noticed there was more water in the river than usual. Dances in pioneer days were mainly square dances, not like we see today on television, but boys in cowboy boots or stodgy shoes. Very few neckties were worn. Even some shirttails were flapping as they swung their ladies and do-si-doed.

The dance was reaching a lively point when Dill came over and warned Arlie that they had better leave in order to get back across the river because some late arrivals had said, "She is rising fast."

They made a quick departure and headed for the river. A full moon had risen which was casting enough light on the water to make it visible. Dill scanned the darkened waters for a moment or so then warned Arlie that it was dangerous to attempt a crossing. "I've got to get back! Pa will kill me if I am out past midnight", exclaimed Arlie.

Dill, with many forebodings, jumped from the buggy and with a strong rope in hand began to tie the buggy bed to the frame and axles so it would not float away when they reached deep water. A mile of water so deep that the horses would be swimming part of the time wasn't an enticing thought. But the longer he waited the deeper the water rose around the feet of the horses.

So, jumping into the buggy with a "Giddy up" to the team they started on an experience they would long remember. Dill turned to Arlie and admonished her to climb into the seat, kneel and hold tight to the side and top of the buggy as water would presently be coming into the floor of the buggy. He braced his feet, one on either side of the buggy bed. He wound the left rein around his left hand, and with the other around his right hand, began urging the team steadily onward. He gradually pulled them to the right to keep them from drifting downstream.

Higher and higher the water rose until it filled the bed of the buggy, and now it seemed to be floating. The horses were swimming, not in slow easy strokes, but in lurches and lunges that sometimes seemed it would capsize the buggy. Then, after what seemed like ages, the horses were stumbling along in water too deep to wade and too shallow to swim, when Whamo! A huge tree trunk hit the upstream horse causing him to loose his footing. Dill yelled, "Oh, God, Arlie! If that breaks the buggy tongue we are sunk!" He simultaneously jerked the rein of that horse which raised the heads of both horses enough so the log floated under the buggy tongue and between the other horse's front and back legs, and again they were pawing and snorting to get to the other bank. In all the excitement they had missed the crossing and didn't quite know where they were.

Dill scanned the shoreline in the semi-darkness and finally decided they were above the crossing. So, they began easing along looking for a place to try to pull out of the water. They were afraid to stop for fear quicksand would get them. They soon came to a bank that looked as if it was cleared of underbrush enough to permit them to rise onto good old terra firma once more.

Dill shoved the reins into Arlie's hands demanding, "Hold these reins tight! Here, take this whip and lay it to 'em! I'm getting out to push."

Before Arlie realized what was happening, she was in the buggy alone grasping the reins tight and lashing those poor horses like a muleskinner. Up the bank they lurched with Dill lifting, pushing and sometimes holding on for dear life.

Now they were once more safe and to give the horses a chance to get their wind, they just sat there. Dill dripping wet and Arlie so tousled and bedraggled and still trembling with fright that neither of them had a thing to say. They had enough excitement to last them for quite some time.

We have so modernized life for youth today that they have to go in search of excitement. Whereas, the pioneer youth lived with it daily whether it was fording swollen rivers, taming wild broncos, going for a buffalo hunt, or catching a wild runaway team. Pioneer life was a character building experience that made men of the boys or broke them, sometime physically, other times morally.

Outlaws moved into territories where there was less law and order. Some came to reform and get a new start in life. Others were just laying low until another opportunity to make a haul presented itself. I've heard my grandfather speak of the Dalton Gang, Belle Starr and the James Boys.

My mother told of living near a family with several young people. The mother seemed to manage for them. The father drifted in and out. When he was away the children always said he was away working. One time he was in jail waiting to be returned somewhere for trial. He asked for permission to write to his family and to send his wife an extra sheet of paper to send him an answer. Such items were scarce in territorial days. What he actually did was write a note with a pen dipped in alcohol instead of ink on the blank sheet of paper. Now, I don't know if this actually works, but the story goes that his wife knew to hold this paper up to the lamplight so she could read the writing.

He told her to bring his horse to a certain place and leave him tied. Also, bring a bedroll, some clean clothes, especially socks, roll all this in the bed roll, tie it securely to his saddle and come to the one window in his cell which was above the office of the federal officers. There she would find a long yarn string, unraveled from his home knitted sock with his knife tied to it to weight it to the ground. (He had already learned what these western prairie winds could do to upset plans.) She was to tie one end of his lariat to the twine, stick his knife in the front and leave as fast as she could to make a safe get away.

All this she did alone which took her most of the night as they lived a half days journey from the federal jail. Of course, she saddled her husband's horse and led him while riding another. This story could have inspired the old song, "Riding Old Paint Leading Old Bald." The object was to get his rope through the window, secure it inside then slide down the rope to freedom. There were no bars on jail windows in Territorial days. He then took the knife, cut his rope loose minus twenty feet, and away to the wild blue yonder he loped. I think this man may have inspired the song, "Don't Fence Me In." The wife told this story to my grandmother, who being Indian, knew how to keep secrets. Many years after this family had moved away in the darkness of night the story was handed down to me.

There was a federal officer named John Swain that roamed Indian Territory chasing outlaws and trying to keep bootleggers away from the Indians. He was a crack shot, but some outlaws lived by their guns, too. He had an outlaw pinned down in one of our prairie gulches, but the outlaw also had Swain pinned down. They were shooting it out in a late afternoon battle when John exposed himself a little too much and the outlaw got in a fatal shot. John knew this, so he raised up, took dead aim and fired. They both dropped back dead.

John's wife, Sue Swain, had him buried at Wayne or Paoli. I'm not sure which place. She also sent a picture of John back east and had a replica of him made into a statue. She placed it at his grave as a marker, but outlaws and other renegades continued to shoot at it. They just couldn't let him rest in pease. Sue finally took it to her home. None of my family ever seemed to know what happened to it or her.[1]

---

1 (The Guthrie Representative newspaper, October 4, 1894: Deputies Matt Cook and John Swain came to Purcell last Tuesday with two whiskey peddlers named Lee Masters and James Julien, whom they caught

I know very little about my parent's courtship, only that they were married February 10, 1901 about ten o'clock at night in a snowstorm at my mother's family home.

My mother's mother from whom I get my Cherokee heritage had departed this life when mother was only sixteen. Mother was twenty and father twenty-three when they married. She had an older sister, Viola, who I believe was ten years mother's senior that had held the family together and made a home for all. So, she planned the wedding, including making my mother's wedding dress. They had made arrangements for a minister to be there at a certain hour. They had invited all the neighbors and relatives in for the wedding. Wedding cake and all, I don't remember who made the wedding cake, but it was certainly home made. The hour came and no minister. Six o'clock and still no minister. They finally ate the wedding dinner, cake and all. The minister finally arrived at ten o'clock that evening.

The minister said a child had died in a community farther away and he had been called upon to conduct the funeral. There were no such things as telephones in those days. He figured the young people waiting to get married could wait just a little longer. He thought it was important that he take care of the funeral first. Some of the guests had given up and gone home. The ones that did stay spent the night sleeping on the floors or feather beds and hay straw beds. Some took turns keeping the fireplace roaring. There was lots of timber in those day, and free for the cutting. It was a very cold night and they had a roaring fire outside in front

---

at Tom Ike's Crossing on the Canadian, about fifteen miles southeast of town. They had a wagon and team and had just crossed over from the Oklahoma Territory side, where they had been to Lexington and stocked up with a plentiful stock of alcohol which they had in jugs and were prepared with coloring, canteens, funnels, etc., a regular peddler outfit, all of which was captured by the marshalls and bear unmistakable evidence of their intentions. The canteens were made to slip on a belt and buckle around the body, being somewhat new and novel. They were tried before Commissioner Gates and set to jail in default of $500 each.)

of the house. The preacher stood between Arlie and Dill and the fire. His back was plenty warm, but Arlie and Dill were chilled to their bones.

There were no such events as honeymoons for pioneer people. They did have shavarees or chavarees. Webster calls that a loud and noisy serenade for newlyweds. I don't recall mother ever telling if they were chivareed or not. In a snowstorm I doubt if they braved the weather. Back in those days they did such things as ride the bride on a rail and duck the groom in a river.

The first year mom and dad were married they lived with dad's parents. Thus, began the first instructions for my mother on how to become a wifely housekeeper. My grandmother having been reared in the fastidious South and though not a slave owner family (you recall their experiences of the Civil War as the daughter of a Baptist minister) some of the Southern traditions had rubbed off on the family.

Housekeeping was still carried on by my grandmother though in a real pioneer setting. She could make a pioneer shack or log house look like a mansion. Walls may have been papered with newspapers or canvas that was similar to unbleached muslin if they were wealthy enough to buy it. I remember a roll of heavy paper similar to what is used today between walls that are not insulated. It was a dull pink or pale blue (instead of black), and was tacked to walls with tacks that were punched through a silvercolored tin the size of our halfdollars.

A few years ago we were roaming through the woods on some rangeland owned by one of our sons and we came across an old pioneer shack that was covered with those tacks. But, we had nothing to pry them off with, not even a pocketknife. They would be valuable now as relics of the past

I remember going to grandmothers and seeing a common pine table with a white skirt around it with a white cloth spread over the top. There were books and papers stacked beneath on a shelf and antique dishes on the top. One that I remember was a white milk glass butter dish with a hen sitting over the top for the lid. A large mirror was hanging on the wall at the back of the table. I can still picture that mirror with everything reflected in it from the table. A kerosene lamp sat in the middle of the scene.

There were always jellies from wild plums and home baked loaves of bread. Sometimes we arrived while the bread was still hot, and how good it was! Mother would say, "Now don't ruin that loaf while its hot", but grandmother would always say, "They are hungry after walking all that way", which was a mile or more.

With all the above examples for my mother, she began to learn some from what she was seeing. I've heard mother tell that in her girlhood home no supper dishes were washed until the following morning. When she and dad moved into their own house, after supper she stacked the dirty dishes in a dishpan. Dad said, "No, Arlie, we wash the dishes now. Pour the hot water from the teakettle over them and wash. I'll dry them for you." From that day on the kitchen duties were not finished until dishes were washed and put away.

My mother began copying from grandmother. I remember some wall paper company that dad had talked with gave him some old sample wallpaper books. He and mother papered one whole inside wall with those samples. I'm sure it looked like a hen with a flock of mixed breed chickens. It was difficult to find two sheets 30"x30" of the same pattern and never two the same color. The outside walls were canvassed. It was also held on the walls with those same round things the size of halfdollars. The ceilings were also covered with canvas tacked to the ceiling joists. Very few pioneer houses had solid ceilings. But, how bright and happy the white canvas walls were with all those beautiful pieces of sample wallpaper decorating the inside walls. We kids didn't look at the wall as a whole. We picked out each piece and tried to decide which wall was the most beautiful.

We lived in several different houses from pine to warped cottonwood lumber. None were beautiful, but they were homes and our father's mother played her part in making them so. She never worked outside the home, but she worked as best she could to care for her home and always cared for and welcomed her grandchildren.

My mother became the same type of grandmother to her grandchildren only she became even closer to them than did my grandmother to us.

The second year of marriage my father worked with a crew to build part of the Santa Fe Railroad. It had its origin in Kansas or near Bartlesville, Oklahoma. I don't know the exact place but it ended at Lindsay, Oklahoma. While dad worked on the railroad mother boarded the crew that worked with my dad.

My older brother, Loyce, had made his arrival by then and dad's brother, Walter, came to live with them and go to school. After school he came home and cared for the baby while mother cooked for the railroad work crew. I've heard mother tell how Loyce cried and cried so much of the time, and Uncle Walter would jump behind the door with him in his arms and say, "Listen, listen! Wild cats." Wild cats were the first words Loyce spoke as a baby.

After their part of the railroad was finished, dad took the money they had saved from the year of work and bought a team and farming equipment. He and his parents and family moved to an area east of Pauls Valley that is now the county seat for Garvin County. Mom and dad rented Indian land. I don't know what land his parents rented, but a place near by. They lived there one year and dad followed the railroad almost to its end. I believe mother's family had also moved to this vicinity.[1]

---

1 (I recall the summer of 1949, shortly after I was discharged from the army, I went with my grandparents and Uncle Loyce to show me where their early life began together. I recall that a few miles northwest of what is now Alex, Oklahoma we came to a cornfield. Much to grandpa and

They lived there one year then my father's younger brother, Robert, came to live with them and they moved farther inland onto a creek known as Rush Creek. What my father lacked in good judgment was filled with beauty on that notorious Rush Creek which isn't as notorious now as then. It is a creek that has its source on the north side of the Table Top Hills that range back into Grady and Stephens Counties and extend their range well into Garvin County. This Rush Creek is so named, I presume, because the waters come rushing out of those hills and find their way into the Washita River just on the south side of Pauls Valley.[1]

Many times when the headwaters on the Washita collided with the headwaters on Rush Creek, Pauls Valley received the brunt of the waters. Stores were flooded and homes in the lowlands were inundated. Even the courthouse has had to move some of their valuable papers to second floor landings.

After spending one year on Rush Creek Dad pushed inland still another six to eight miles across Rush Creek and onto Panther Creek, a tributary to Rush Creek. This is where I was born in 1905. Dad continued to live in that area fifty-five years on the same creek but about three miles further upstream near the foot of the Table Top Hills.

I visited that same little piece of God's Green Earth in 1981. It has changed ever so much, but given time and a little help from nature it may reclaim the same beauty it had when I first saw it.

My earliest impressions were received right there and I have many times congratulated my dad for having an eye for beauty if nothing else. For to me that was truly a beautiful place. Wild redbuds lined both sides of the creek. Tall cottonwoods lifted their branches to the heavens with sturdy oaks and spreading elms filling the spaces in between. What we lacked in comforts was cer-

---

grandma's surprise the house grandpa and his brothers built, and in which Loyce was born, was still standing. It had been added on to but the basic structure was still there and in fairly good condition.)

1 (The creek is named after a man with the name Rush.)

tainly filled with natural beauty. Every kind and color of bird that nested in Indian Territory was on that creek—bluebirds, wild canaries, natural cardinals, and another red bird that we see only in the Rockies now along with cocky jays, and saucy robins. Rabbits and squirrels were our daily wild pets. They ran when we pitched them corn to eat, but if we got quite and still Mr. Squirrel soon came sniffing out of hiding, and when he got near his prize food we would jump and watch him take off again, sometimes grabbing some of his food as he went. If we got real still after placing a handful of corn for Mr. Squirrel, he would sit and take the grains in his paws and quite efficiently eat all the heart from each kernel.

All the pastureland at that time was open range and many were the brands that roamed the hills and dales. One cattleman that we knew was Deat Brown. He branded his cattle with a large "D". Many of my older brother's play hours were spent pretending he was Deat Brown rounding up his cattle. He would get on his stickhorse and come dashing up to the front gate, stop in front and begin calling "Hello" and the longer he called the louder he got until my mother would go to the door. He would call out, "I'm Deat Brown. Have you seen any of my cattle on this range this week?" Then mom would tell him how many she had seen and what area they were grazing, and when she saw them last. Off he would dash with his stickhorse pitching blue circles with him.

Our little cabin in the wilds of Indian Territory with all its beauties also had many fears. Many kinds of fur bearing animals, a few mink, opossums, raccoons, wolves, prairie coyotes, an occasional panther and wild bulls roamed the prairies.

I think the worst blood curdling fear of my early life was to hear a herd of cattle gathering around spilled blood. I don't know what triggers it, but when one is attracted to it then here came the whole herd. They put their nose to the ground and formed a circle each fighting to get its nose to the spot, and with all the bellowing, bawling, and screaming put into one sound. It makes a sound that no one wants to hear.

My dad and uncle had butchered a young beef in the fall and unthinkingly butchered it on the open range. Many times I was awakened in the middle of the night to this distracting noise. My heart would pound and my blood would run cold. I'd cover my head and crawl as far down in the bed as possible. That didn't take away all the noise, but I felt more secure anyway.

In 1905 I made my appearance on this tributary to Rush Creek. It is still called Panther Creek and is to a certain extent returning to its original existence. The land was cut up into 160-acre farms and farmed to death for about 30 to 40 years. By then erosion of wind and rain had ruined it for farming. Much of it was never terraced which made huge gullies and washes that we never dreamed of. For instance, the old farm dad bought has recently washed out a huge gully that partly uncovered a prehistoric animal with tusks like an elephant.

We lived in this same cabin in 1908, the year that all old timers know as "the wet year." Panther Creek overflowed as often as twice daily that year. Dad and Uncle Robert had built an extra box room near the log cabin with a hallway between with rocks for a floor. Our abode was just across the road from the creek and many times I've seen the water come up and cover that roadway.

Sometimes when feeding time came, the creek was at flood stage and the cows and pigs were across the creek from the house and barns. When the men began calling them at feed time the stock would all come running to cross the creek, but the water would stop them momentarily. The cows would walk up and down the banks and survey the situation, then cautiously ease themselves into the water and slowly go deeper and deeper until their heads were all that were sticking out, then slowly swim to the other bank.

Not so with the pigs. They ran up and down the bank squealing and finally with a woof! woof! woof! into the water they went with a big splash. They would go out of sight and sometimes come up against a high bluff that they couldn't struggle up. So down the creek they would go until they reached a sloping bank where they could struggle up, shake off the water and run for the feeding pen. Some would be so winded they would lie down for a while to get their breath, then take off for the feeding pen.

I had a humorous experience that wasn't so humorous at the time but is quite comical now. My grandkids get a bang out of it yet. We had an unframed picture of a barnyard scene with a house and barn in the background. There were white horses and a flock of beautiful white geese in the foreground. I had never seen tame geese and I often stood and admired that picture, especially the geese. When my baby sister was about six months old my mother took my brother, baby sister, and me to Pauls Valley to have our pictures made. I kept asking if the picture would have a goose on it. I was disappointed because it just had us kids on it.

A woman who lived farther up Panther Creek owned a large flock of geese. The creek got up once and some of them floated farther down stream than usual. Some came down too far. When the stream got too low for them to swim back they became disoriented.

Mother and her sister who was visiting permitted her children and us to go across the creek into a pasture where wild flowers were blooming. We were having a great time gathering flowers when we heard the most awful scream we had ever heard. My brother grabbed Cousin Ruth and me around the neck. We were screaming louder than the noise. Sam who was a little older took off toward the house screaming, "Good God! Panther! Good God! Panther!" every time his feet hit the ground. Mother and auntie just knew a wild bull or some other wild animal had some of us down. But, when they couldn't see or hear anything they were about ready to spank all of us. But, later that afternoon we were playing near the house when this beautiful white gander came into the yard. We were all admiring it, and called our mothers to come see the beautiful bird. But, suddenly it flapped its wide wings and let out that awful scream. Sam said, "That's that damn thing we heard." It all but sent us into another panic. I couldn't feature my great beautiful white bird making such a terrible noise.

When we stop to consider, life is very much like that. All the beauty isn't bound up in any one thing or person. The peacock is a beautiful sight to behold, but oh my! Such an ugly voice. The parrot has beautiful plumage, but such ugly head and feet. The nightingale is a homely bird, but has a melodious voice.

So it is with life. We all have some ugly things in our lives, but we also have some beautiful thoughts, smiles, and memories like golden sunsets and fishponds with lovely lily pads. The first robins of spring, rain on the roof, and the first flowers of spring, the first snowfall of winter and sweet childish faces to kiss good night at bedtime.

My grandfather was deaf. He couldn't hear the mocking bird sing, nor the strains of melodious music. He could enjoy lovely flowers, pictures and scenery, but the noise of the grandkids didn't bother him at all. The trouble with most of us is we take beauty for granted. We don't create lovely friendships. Many years ago we started out for a beautiful autumn drive in the sunshine. On our way we drove by a cheap picture show. People were lined up waiting to get inside to spend two hours of fantasy when there was real life and beauty and warm sunshine beckoning them to come outside and enjoy the natural beauty.

Sometimes nature can play some mean tricks on everyone. We first moved into this cabin abode which was used as a living and bedroom. The kitchen and eating-place was about seventy-five feet away. It was dug back into a bank and partially walled with logs. Mother had set up a cot in one corner for me to lie on while she worked.

One morning when it was raining and all the creeks were flooded, brother and I were lying on the cot. Brother Loyce let out a scream. A long centipede had all its feelers buried up and down his spine. Mother said dad and Uncle Robert almost pounded him soft getting the thing off of him. They just knew he would die, but what could they do? It was miles to a doctor, no telephones, and the creeks were flooded until not even a horsebacker could get through, and for sure not with a child in his arms.

So, there they sat watching expecting Loyce to fall over any moment. I'm sure my mother was crying. Possibly dad was applying turpentine as poltices that would draw out the poison. Loyce never showed any ill effects, but I'm sure that was when pressure was put on dad to build another room. I don't know who paid for the lumber (we were renting, you know), but I'm sure dad and Uncle Robert furnished the labor.

In the early winter of 1906 on December 7th, a beautiful baby sister came to be my playmate. She had all the beauty of both families and none of their flaws. At age 75 she still has the most perfect features of all eight of us girls.[1] The following Christmas my father's family arrived from southeast Texas where they had gone to prove up on land, but the swamps, mosquitoes, chills and malaria had driven them off the land. There were four teenage boys in the family and they thought I was something to behold. "A little girl in the family at last."

I was small for my less than three years, and when one of the boys bought a pair of boots I crawled into the cardboard box and they pushed me all over the house and yard. When Christmas came, the older boy bought me the loveliest set of china dishes with gorgeous flowers painted on them. The next boy bought me a beautiful doll with real hair, a head made of exquisite wax with rosy cheeks, red lips, and the bluest glass eyes. It also had a body made of kid leather with arms and feet of china. I don't know what my parents bought for me, but I was on cloud nine with my dishes and doll.

I'm sure I had no training on how to care for a doll so gorgeous, and before spring arrived the head had come loose from

1 (This sister is Margaret. She died 1 January 2001 at age 94 years in Phoenix, Arizona.)

the body. So, I persuaded my mother's cousin, Ida Jones, a teenage girl, to sew the head back to the body. While she was sitting by the fireplace preparing to sew the two parts together, she dropped the head on the rock hearth and broke it. I flew at that girl with all the fury a three-year-old could muster, kicking, hitting, pulling her hair, and screaming with all my might. Mother finally had to take me in hand and apply some of her force to calm me down. I still had my beloved dishes. I thought they were the most beautiful possession I had and I wanted more and more of them.

Come spring when my parents were preparing to plant potatoes, they explained that each piece they planted would come up and grow making lots of potatoes. Well, I wanted more dishes, so unbeknown to them I dropped a cup here, a plate there, and they were covered to make more and more dishes. That reminds me of the goose that laid the "Golden Eggs."

The fall of 1908 brings another vivid memory of another baby sister. Mother's cousin was hurrying us off to the neighbor's and I was poking along as a three-year-old can. I looked back and saw the doctor coming across the creek in his buggy. I wanted to go back and see who was coming to see us. Cousin Lugani said that's the old sewing machine salesman. He is just bringing your mother's new sewing machine. All day I wanted to go home to see our new sewing machine. When we were finally permitted to return home, we were ushered in to see the new baby. I said, "But I want to see the new sewing machine." This same cousin who escorted us to and from the neighbor's died before Christmas that year. That was my first experience with death.

The next few years I'm sure were the most difficult years my father ever faced from a financial position. He had a good start in livestock, but he had made the mistake of investing in horses instead of cattle. He had one of the most beautiful teams of pure white mares I have ever seen. They must have been from the Clydesdale strain, at least they were built like them, but there was not a blemish to mar their color. Their manes and tails were also pure white. Their names were Lucy and Anny. Mom said they could belong to my younger sister and me. So Margie took Lucy and I claimed Anny.

Anny took sick and I awoke one morning to find her dead. The men were preparing to drag her off to be devoured by coyotes and wild dogs. When they tied her hind legs to the back of the wagon and started dragging her off, I screamed. To see her poor head bumping along the rough ground, I just knew it was hurting her. I went up on a little hill back of our house and watched them drag my beloved Anny out of sight. No one had ever explained to me about death. So, I cried and cried. When my father came back he came up and got me, took me to the house, washed my face and put me to bed. After a sleep I felt better, but the hurt was still there.

The Graham Family farmed the upper side of our place and when they moved away in the winter of 1908, Dad rented the whole place. We moved into the upper house that had some barns, but I can't say it was a more comfortable house. It was up where the north winds could strike us full force in winter and no shade trees for summer, but mother and father both worked hard.

There was a family of six to cook and wash for. The washing was all done by hand on a washboard. Water was drawn from a well and heated in one of those big black iron kettles that people prize so today as antiques. I have never had a desire to own one. They mean too many hours of hard labor to me. There were fires to keep burning to heat the water to wash in and then more water to draw from the well to boil the clothes. More cold water to pour over the clothes when taken from the boiling water. If any dirt was left in anything, some more washing on the scrub board, then put through rinse water before hanging on a barbed wire fence to dry. There were always two or three and sometimes four pots of clothes to boil.

Dad never thought of a clothesline and clothespins, and mother being of Indian descent always left things like that up to dad. (My husband after we were married bought and strung the first clothesline my mother ever owned.) I can see till yet three sides of our garden fence draped with various clothes, sheets, pillow cases, blankets, towels, tea towels, panties and bloomers, men's overalls, shirts, girl's slips, dresses, and all the odd pieces that make up a household. By the time I was married our family had grown to twelve (ten children), but all of us were never living at home at once by then.

Of course, there was ironing to do–not with electric irons, but with flat irons of various models. First, the old flat irons that we set on the cookstove with a roaring fire to keep them hot. Sheets were folded and placed on the dining table as beds. Sometimes two of us girls were ironing from either side of the table. It took a whole morning for two of us to get that all done. In the meantime, dinner (our noon meal) was cooking. Ham with brown beans and cornbread was a standard meal.

I'm not too sympathetic with all the heart breaking stories of hardships of the ghetto people and Third World peoples (except the ones in war torn areas) when I look back at the way we survived in the early 20th Century.

I became very ill in the fall of 1910. Things were still going downhill. Dad had lost some more livestock, including a colt I claimed. We called her Black Bess. She was a beauty with a star in her face just below her eyes and again I lost out. I had begun to adjust to losses in life. I was a big girl, so I thought–all of five and a half years by then.

The doctor finally had to be called in when home remedies didn't make the fever go away. After the doctor examined me and asked a few questions, he fixed me some medicine. He then turned to dad and said, "Dill, I'd like to talk with you outside." After the doctor drove away dad came in and by the look on his face mom knew it was bad news. She said, "What did the doctor say?" Dad got that fighting expression on his face, cleared his throat, and in a clear voice said, "Typhoid!" I'm sure mother went into the far end of the kitchen, or slipped outside and cried.

All of the nearby relatives and some not so nearby assisted in caring for me. My grandmother was one of my favorites. She brought food I didn't want, but tried to eat. My mother's sister who always came to the rescue came from 20 miles away and left her family to help me through the crisis. The boys of dad's family that I've spoken of before pitched in and helped dad finish picking cotton. They were young men by then and I was always admiring their fancy jewelry, imitations I'm sure.

One day grandmother came in and said, "Is there anything I could bring you that you would like to have?" I said I would like to have one of the uncles' pretty pins. I know she had reference to food for me to eat. She said, "I'll see", and bade me goodbye for that day. I don't know if she came back the next day or a week later. My mind was tattered from semi-conscious to consciousness as the days drug on. But, when grandmother returned I don't know what else she brought, but there was always home churned butter, buttermilk and various other foods showing up when she came. But, she came in and said, "Now, Pauline, I don't know who this belonged to, but this is the only pin I could find", and she held out to me a stick pin that was worn in men's ties in those days. It looked like yellow gold. It was what was called a friendship pin in those days, and was shaped like the swastika that was adopted by Germany as their emblem in 1935. It was also known as a good luck pin. Maybe that is why I survived. But, survive I did and God has been looking over and guiding me ever since.

There were several incidents in connection with my illness I must mention. This was in late autumn before the weather was cold enough to butcher fresh meat and keep it without spoiling. Hence, chicken was about the only fresh meat there was. I got so tired of chicken I refused to eat it.

One night the old mother cat came in with a quail she caught for the kittens. Dad grabbed it away from her, pulled its head off and began cleaning it. Mother gutted it while dad got a sharp stick, raked hot coals into the hearth of the heating stove and began broiling it. As the juice dripped onto the coals the aroma filled the whole room. To this day I can not think of any aroma that was so appealing. I don't remember how it tasted.

I asked my younger sister recently if she could remember that incident and if she resented it that the quail was given to me. She said, "Yes, I remember, and I didn't resent it although I was less than four years old. I realized you were sick and we learned to do without for you because we wanted you to get well."

Another plus for grandmother was that she told mother to boil our drinking water. We had a dug well that was walled with rocks. Rats would get under the flooring at the top of the well. Some would fall into the water and drown. Mother thought that was so horrible that we started drinking water from a stock pond. I'm sure that is where I picked up the typhoid germ.

All in all, I survived and have had a very healthy life. The only other thing I remember about that year was at Christmas. I don't remember what we got for presents except that my older brother, Loyce, got a little red wagon. We went to grandmother's house for dinner. The family was walking, but baby, my second sister, and I were riding. I was still too weak to walk very far. So, dad and brother were taking turns pulling us in his little red wagon. It was about a mile and a half to grandmothers.

Our fourth baby girl was born the following spring. The year 1911 also ushered in the toughest year we ever experienced. Just as 1908 had been referred to as "the wet year", 1911 was "the dry year." I remember how hot and dry it was. The ponds dried up and the well failed until it barely furnished water to drink. Dad and a neighbor went together and dug a well in the bed of Panther Creek that ran along the lower edge of both farms. They would take turns watering at the well.

Our father, like most renter farmers, borrowed from the bank to make a crop and pay it off in the fall. But, that year no farmer could begin to pay all his notes that fall. When the bank started pressing dad for money he sold all his livestock to pay off the bank notes. We had Old Lucy and a balky mare called Mag that no one would buy. Our cows were gone. We had one sow left. She and the two mares almost starved before grass came out the next spring.

We ate oatmeal without milk for breakfast, beans and cornbread for dinner, biscuits and sorghum molasses without butter for supper. It was a real treat if grandmother got enough milk ahead to send us some milk or butter or eggs. We had a few hens that survived by eating droppings from the two mares. But, of course, there were no eggs. They ranged the pastures searching for grass and weed seeds. Dad found a general store that promised him the bare necessities of food and clothing–flour, sugar, corn meal, oatmeal, and some coffee, and occasionally a piece of salt pork and a box of snuff for mother. I still have mother's old snuff box to remind me of those days.

We had an early spring in 1912, and our grass was good since we had no grazing on it all winter. Dad's brother, Robert, had extra cows, but no pasture left since they had grazed it all through the winter. So, he let us have some cows to milk for the grazing. So, by March we were getting milk to drink and was that ever a treat. When I think of kids today and what they would consider a treat, I can't worry very much for them when we are spending millions on third world people and welfare programs. There were no such things in 1911-1912.

Dad couldn't even borrow money to start a crop in 1912. It was one of those bank moratorium years when the banks had borrowed all they could and had no more to lend. The banks told dad they simply had no money. He would be the first to get it if they had it. Since we were in the broomcorn belt and that was the earliest crop to mature, dad got enough seed to plant from our general store.

Years later when I had a family of small children, dad was spending a night with us in Oklahoma City. I said, "Dad, it seems to me that 1911 was the worst year we ever went through." He got a long look on his face and said, "Yes, that was a booger!" But, he brightened immediately and said, "Yes, but we really made it in '12. We made twelve tons of broomcorn and I got $100 a ton for it. I hadn't borrowed money to live on so all we owed was our grocery man and the harvest crew! I had all our corn crop and a little cotton extra."

So far this has sounded like a grim life. Some of it was grim, but there were days when we had fun. My younger sister, Marge, and I were laughing recently about a game we used to play that we more or less made up. It was "The Last One on Wood is a Mad Dog."

We had a neighbor who owned a Jersey bull that was a holy terror for all of us. Their pasture fence came very near our house. When he was on a rampage we all stayed near our own back door. So, we changed our game to "The Last One on Wood is Mr. Hardeman's Old Bull." Our older brother was the "bull." He caught one of the younger kids and had her down pawing, bellowing, and mauling her to death. Marge seemed to think that he was the real bull and was really killing our little sister. There was a piece of broken crockery near her piece of wood. So, she jumped off her base, grabbed the broken crockery, and threw it with all her might at brother as she yelled, "Hi there!" It landed squarely on his head and really got his attention. He came up screaming and yelling for mama. Poor mother, I don't know how she lived through all the squabbles we kids created.

Marge declares to this day that she really felt that he was that real bull. It took so little to entertain us in those days. We played house with broken pieces of dishes and corncob dolls. Once when Dolly Parton was telling about their corncob dolls I knew exactly what she was talking about. We would cut cute faces from Sears Catalogs and paste them on our dolls. It didn't matter if one was lost or torn up, we just got busy and made more.

It was quite an excursion for mother to take all of us a half-mile to the creek to hunt wild greens in the spring. We also found sand rock in that same area to scrub our kitchen floor. We pounded it up and used it like we use commercial cleanser today. There wasn't such a thing as linoleum for kitchen floors. When greasy spots fell on the floor it soaked into the wood and nothing but lye soap and sand rock with a lot of elbow grease got it up. But, how those boards did shine when they were washed, rinsed and dried which took most of an afternoon on a sunny day.

Machinery for harvesting was another exciting time at our house. We lived in the broomcorn belt and at one time Lindsay, Oklahoma was known as the largest broomcorn market in the world.

The very first broomcorn seeder that thrashed our corn was powered by a horse drawn bullwheel. It had a circular platform ten or twelve feet across. Beneath it was a mechanism attached to the seeder that turned the rollers of the seeder. It had long teeth that looked like long spike nails driven into it. These teeth stripped the seed from the broomcorn head before it was baled and shipped to the broom factories.

Horses walked in a wide circle to make the energy to turn the machinery that powered the bullwheel. That, I'm sure, is where our high powered engines get the tag "400 H.P." Even lawnmowers have 3 H.P. After the bullwheel powered machines came the steam engines. They moved five to ten miles per hour over all sorts of bad roads, but the lightweight bridges could not hold up under their weight. So, they had to go several miles around sometimes to get to a farm.

The old steam engine had plenty of power, but it was slow moving on roads, and their steam whistles let you know several miles away they would be arriving. It was really exciting for us kids to climb up on that engine and pull that whistle. It took wood or coal to heat the water that generated the steam. I talked with a younger sister the other night and she said that old Waukeshau steam engine scared her almost to death, and to this day she is afraid of machinery. She didn't ever learn to drive a car.

The horse-drawn equipment was finished by 1913. That is when the steam-powered engine came into our area. Remember,

Oklahoma was only six years old in 1913. Our school equipment and way of life was quite ancient at that time. No roads were even graveled, but we caught onto modernization fast. In 1914 the great First World War started in Europe. Prices for farm produce began to rise and farm equipment started to improve.

In 1915 my father put most of his land into grain. My uncle bought a binder to get the grain cut, but it turned out to be one of those wet years and the binder bogged down in the fields. Much of the grain fell down and the binder couldn't pick it up. It rained all summer and into the fall. It would have been a good year for corn, but not small grain. I can't remember what was done with the grain as it was thrashed. We had no graineries. They must have hauled it twelve miles to a railroad and put it into railroad cars to be shipped.

I can't remember very much about farming that year (1915) as my mother was ill most of the time. Although I was only ten years old, I did most of the housework before and after mother recovered enough from having another baby girl to care for. Mother was plagued with gallstones and that was one of her worst years. The idea of surgery was unheard of in our area. It was a hundred miles to Oklahoma City which had very little in hospital equipment, and the only way to get there would be by lumber wagon and train.

After the steam engine came the gasoline engine. It was drawn by horses. All the power went into the bull wheel. This engine was drawn by horses and had to have wheels set down in holes dug into the ground to hold the engine in place while it was pulling the seeder to thrash the seed from broomcorn.

My grandfather, my father's father, died October 17, 1915. It rained all summer and into the fall. The night that grandfather died it came the most terrible rain and storm. The roads and bridges were washed out and fences had to be torn down to get the wagons to the cemetery. But it was a clear day and we had a beautiful autumn.

We kids went to grandmother's and stayed to pick cotton for the two boys left single to care for grandmother. We had very little cotton that year as dad had gone too heavy on small grain. I can't even remember the time we started to school that year. World War I started in Europe in 1914. The war years took all the young men of the community and left boys. My older brother and father had to register for the draft.

These war years caused a lot of changes which included land rental. Dad had never rented any way except thirds and fourths, a third of feed crops and a fourth of cotton and other money crops. When his landlord demanded $250 cash rent for the farm, dad refused. She had not demanded this in time to give him the legal time for farmers to move which was before the first of the year. So, we stayed there through 1916. Incidentally, dad had a good crop year and paid more crop-rent than if he had of paid cash rent. However, he had received the legal notice to vacate. So, we had to move.

Dad looked and looked but could not find a crop rent place. Finally he heard of a place about fifteen miles away where the owner wanted a year off for him and his family. So, dad agreed to buy his livestock if he would rent the farm for crop rent. They finally agreed on a price and we were ready to move. But, we had lived on this same farm all my life. I was eleven years old by then and had never lived anywhere else. It was a traumatic move for us older children.

There were days of moving feed. One day they had loaded the wagons the night before to be ready to roll by sun up, but one driver never showed up. So, dad finally said, "Pauline, I guess you will have to drive this other wagon." I was excited because I had never driven a wagon off the farm.

My first problem was when I approached a long slope entering Rush Creek bottom. I was atop a double deck wagon of corn. Dad said, "Put on your brake." I put it on as far as I could which wasn't tight enough, and I didn't know how to tighten the reins to make the team hold back. So, down the slope we went. Dad could just see the team slamming the wagon tongue into the rear end of his wagon, busting the end out of his wagon and spilling half of his load. So, he crawled to the back of his wagon and began beating at my team with is old felt hat. This forced them to hold back. Dad was really perturbed with me because I hadn't put on my brake tight enough. He just didn't realize I wasn't that strong and that my legs were not long enough to push it down with my feet. That was my first mistake.

I tried to stay real close to dad for fear of the traffic in the little town of Maysville that was only farm wagons and a few cars, buggies and horsebackers. But, I knew I wasn't an experienced driver. When we reached the farm we had to turn into a very narrow lane which meant we had to circle far to the right in order to drive straight into the lane. That I was unable to anticipate, and again dad let me make the mistake before telling me. So, I drove straight into the garden corner post and broke it. This embarrassed me to no end for there were children and adults that saw me do it.

We all caught the measles that winter, including mother. Of course, dad had them years before, but again he had to do all the chores and wait on sick kids, as well as on mother who was pregnant again. I was always in fear of mother dying with gallstones or some other ailment. I couldn't think of anything worse than a family being left motherless. If I had only realized it, we would have fared far worse if we had lost our father. Years later I realized that father had almost lost his life with tuberculoses, but he kept going and finally whipped it. Years later when x-rays were taken it showed that he had deep scars on his lungs as a result of that bout with tuberculoses.

Before we were completely well from the measles we all took whooping cough which was a mild case for most of us. We had always lived in prairie upland and now we were living on lowland to a tributary of the Washita River and we got chills.

In the meantime in 1917 a little baby boy came to live in our home. There had been six girls born into our family and now a baby brother. Dad was still having trouble adjusting to cash rent farming. He had always farmed on the thirds and fourths, a third of feed crops and a fourth of cotton and other money crops. So, he was trying to find a farm to rent again. He made quite a good year on this farm he had rented by buying the livestock from the owner. He had resold some of the teams at a profit and still had more cattle and horses than when we left the old hill country farm.

Dad finally found a 120-acre farm for sale that he could afford to buy, but it was right back to the hill country again on the same old Panther Creek, but closer to the hills this time. Dad had come from the Missouri hills and I guess the level valley farms just weren't a part of his "cup of tea." Again we moved into a log house and not a very comfortable one at that. A log cabin about eighteen feet square with a lean-to on the north side that served for kitchen and dining room.

They show pictures on television now of how terrible people live without running water or indoor toilets, and I say to myself, "So what!" We lived through that era right here in the good old USA and there were no food stamps, no welfare, and no aid of any kind. What we got was by the labor of own two hands.

We cleared this land, rented extra land, farmed corn, cotton, broomcorn, and various kinds of hay. In less than ten years we had a new six room house, still not modern, but a place that we could feel proud to invite our friends into. Years later it took the R.E.A. to bring electricity into these remote areas.

Two more baby girls were born into our family making ten children in all. There were trying times during the flu epidemic after World War I when many families lost loved ones. Naomi, the one younger than our baby brother, had flu along with the rest of us. Then she came down with pneumonia. We were afraid she was going to die. But, she survived that only to get whooping cough and again pneumonia before she was a year old. She finally pulled through that. Remember, there were no miracle drugs then.

My brother, Loyce, and I finished the eighth grade and passed the county examination to enter high school. We hear so much about Third World economies and federal aid for this and that, but there were no such things in those days. We got by on our own. A man's word was as good as cash. So, when I started to high school, dad took me to the bank and let me borrow $100 for a semester in school. There was no tuition. We had a five-dollar entrance fee that admitted us to all games. It was a state school where high school and college were both taught in the same buildings and by the same teachers. We had no "fandangled" teachers then. The Three R's plus penmanship, history and grammar was our daily "cup of tea."[1]

Yes, I came into the "new world" in a hurry when my father loaded my trunk into a lumber wagon, and with our country school teacher drove us twelve miles to the train station. There we caught the train for Edmond, Oklahoma. I saw my first streetcar that day, and was introduced to my first modern bathroom. But, we learned fast in modern methods as well as classroom knowledge. After one semester in high school we could take a county exam and get a third class certificate to teach school. I taught school two years at Parks School in Garvin County.

Oklahoma was a new state. I was only fourteen years old when I started teaching. But, I grew up fast, also politicians along with other things. Alfalfa Bill Murray was an uncouth unkempt sort of man, but he knew citizens rights and called out the state militia on more than one occasion to enforce what he believed to be citizens' state rights. He was instrumental in forming the state constitution. One provision was that no foreigners were permitted to own land in Oklahoma. I am not certain that provision is still on the statutes.

---

1 (Oklahoma Central State Teachers College at Edmond, Oklahoma.)

At least one governor was impeached and another one was sent to prison on some fraudulent issue. I studied Oklahoma history but much of it has slipped my memory.

In 1925 I married an Arkansas boy who like myself had come to Edmond to get an education. Neither of us realized the problems that were in store for us.

William Edmund and Mary Pauline Davidson - 1953

Over the years Pauline and and her sister, Marge, became close and often exchanged letters and phone calls. Marge never quite accepted religion the way Pauline did, but they respected each other's viewpoint. To celebrate and honor Pauline's eightieth birthday Marge wrote a poem, "The Boat Sails On." Over the years it since became the hallmark of the Roller Family tradition. It was read at the eightieth birthday celebration for each. A symbolic boat paddle was made and handed down to each until Elsie, the last of the siblings. She gave it to her nephew, Don, Pauline's son. He gave it to Jewel's daughter, Norma, to keep it in the Roller Family.

The poem:

FROM THE YESTERDAYS
THROUGH THE TOMORROWS
THE BOAT SAILS ON

They blazed many trails;
And They built a good boat,
Knowing the time soon would come
When They would set it a-float.

So their crewmen were trained
To be honest and strong;
And the banner They chose
Said, "The Boat Sails On."

The mast They built
Stands tall and strong.
It must sail the High Seas
When the nights grow long.

It must serve through the dark nights
When hope was very low;
And reflect the first rays of sunrise
To its crewmen below.

Then They let down the anchor
And said, "We will let the boat be–
The next generation will
Take her out to sea."

The Captain they trained
Was steady and strong;
Decisions were made
So it didn't take long.

He put out to sea
Without hesitation,
Knowing each crewman aboard
Had it's own destination.

And, His confidence didn't falter,
When hope was remote.
He knew not a crewman aboard
Would desert the Old Boat.

As each one must serve;
So, each must depart;
And, the next to take over
Must man the Old Ark.

The next Captain stepped aboard
With a pain in Her Heart;
It was time to take courage
And preserve the Old Ark.

She approached her station,
Brushed a tear from Her eye;
She turned to Her crew
And the crew stood by.

She looked to the mast
Standing tall and strong;
And, the banner it flew
Said, "The Boat Sails On."

Heading into storms
Where sailing gets rough,
Demanding the oars,
But, the crewmen grew tough.

Being tossed this way or whether
They would hold it together.
On to the time when the
Last crewman is gone.

But the Old Boat won't sink,
It can go it alone,
Though her decks may grow silent,
It won't be for long.

With sails stayed to the sunset,
The Boat sails on.
To a place beyond sunsets,
Into the great unknown.

There will be other generations
To sail the Boat on and on.

"And Cap, when you hit Port, don't forget
To swagger as you walk down the street.
You have manned a Great Boat
With a crew that is hard to beat."

Eighty years is a long, long, journey.

–Margaret Roller Weldon
1984

Pauline had two brothers and seven sisters. All, except one, married and had children. The third girl, Hazel, never married. She was a devoted teacher. Of all of Don's aunts he knew Jewel, the fourth one, the best. She and Don were soul mates. After adulthood Don was never around his Aunt Hazel very much. He often wondered why she never married, but never asked.

At a Jones Family Reunion on the Cimarron River in North Central Oklahoma Don visited with his Aunt Elsie from Arizona. She told him she had a story Jewel wrote about Hazel. Don asked her to send him a copy which she did. It is a very touching account of a part of Hazel's life he had never known. The story follows:

OF LOVE AND SERVICE
or
"FROM YOU KNOW WHO"

The chain clinks along the flagpole as Old Glory nears the top. A slight breeze unfurls the flag as the sun breaks the horizon. Another Memorial Day is beginning in this little rural cemetery.

As I stroll through the markers memories come flooding back; memories that will be lost when my generation has gone to join those already here–memories of gallantry, bravery, beauty, and love.

It's hard to tell when they fell in love, although it was a time when falling in love and getting married needed no coaching or lecturing. They neither seemed to fit that mold. Hazel and Roy, though both under twenty, were among the older of the unmarried group. They seemed to accept a responsibility to keep us younger ones in line. This they did without seeming too straightlaced.

The Black Bloomers, a girl's basketball team, benefited both from Hazel's talents as a player and a peacemaker. She had a way to exert authority and calm a fight without anyone realizing that his or her cause had been neither won nor lost.

Roy saved many a Saturday night square dance from becoming a knock-down-drag-out free-for-all. If there was too much white lightning smuggled in and a fight was brewing, Roy could always persuade the fiddlers to get the music going and the dancers back on the floor.

It seemed a natural thing for Hazel and Roy to walk home together as those in authority always seemed to stand together. I always thought of it as just being convenient for them, never in romantic terms. Even though they did seem to dance together a lot, there were no outward signs of romance. The one night that I saw Roy kiss Hazel I was shocked. Here they were, the two who were too old and too tight-laced, acting like the rest of us. Then Roy backed away and said, "Race you to the gate." This seemed to take away the romance of the moment and I didn't relate to any possibility of a love relationship.

In 1925 the self-imposed responsibility that Roy had assumed became much more so. His parents were killed in a freak accident. He was left with two younger sisters, a brother, grandmother, and the family farm to run. Any thoughts of marriage that Roy and Hazel may have had were pushed aside.

Hazel left for college and Roy busied himself with the planting and harvesting of the crops. A full year soon passed and Hazel was home from school. A community pie supper to be followed by a dance was planned to raise funds for the little rural cemetery as Memorial Day was soon approaching. Burial sites in the cemetery were never sold. The only money for the cemetery was collected through charitable events and donations.

At the supper Roy bought Hazel's pie. They paired off to catch up on the recent happenings in their lives. As others finished and milled around to visit Roy and Hazel continued their private chat. Later when the music began Roy offered his hand and led Hazel to the center of the dance floor. There they danced until only a few couples were left on the floor. Then they walked home hand-in-hand.

That summer as Roy's work on the farm continued Hazel worked at home with the younger kids and fieldwork. It was soon broomcorn harvesting time and Roy needing money got a job running a broomcorn seeder. This meant twelve to fifteen-hour workdays as rain could ruin a crop if it was not cut, seeded, and stored all in the same day. Roy would move the seeder from farm to farm working each farmer's crop.

After several long days the seeder broke down. It was clogged with dirt and seeds. In a hurry to get it back in working condition, Roy tore into the engine using gasoline as a cleaner.

No one really knows what happened, but the gasoline exploded and Roy was engulfed in flames. He threw himself to the ground and rolled out the flames. His clothes were charred into his flesh and dirt covered his burns.

He was carried to his home where he was attended to by his grandmother and sisters. The country doctor was called but there was little they could do other than try to ease his pain.

When we heard what had happened, Hazel asked me to bake a cake and go with her to take to the family. When we arrived friends and family had gathered. The house was small and many sat around in the yard. I remained outside while Hazel took the cake and went into the house. She sat almost an hour at Roy's bedside.

I looked up as she stepped through the door. The expression of grief she wore has remained vivid in my memory. She walked past us as if we were not there and went straight to our old truck. Once inside she bowed her head over the steering wheel and gave way to great trembling sobs. I was surprised at her open expression of grief and didn't know what to say or do. After a while she turned her grief inside and only low almost silent sobs remained.

I finally asked, "What's the matter?" She looked out into nowhere and replied, "I'll never see him again." Only then did I know the extent of their love.

The next day Roy was buried in the little cemetery for which he had helped raise funds. The graveside service was short with only a few words, a song, and a prayer.

Family and friends passed by the casket including Hazel. She could not suppress her grief entirely and folks could not hide their surprise at her show of emotions. No one realized the extent of the relationship between Hazel and Roy so no one stepped forward to comfort her.

Hazel threw herself into work more than ever. She was the first to volunteer for any job that needed to be done. She found work where there was really none to do.

A revival was announced and a brush arbor built. On the second night Hazel made her confession of faith and dedicated her life to service.

From then on Hazel never attended the dances or engaged in the younger peoples' social activities. Instead, she turned to her books and the study of the Bible. She never talked with me about Roy, and I not knowing what to say never mentioned him either.

That fall Hazel returned to school. She had dedicated herself to a service and it was teaching. She gave up basketball as she thought her time was better served at study. She gained weight with the inactivity and knew her peers considered her a country hick. I heard her say she really didn't care what they thought because she could show them all with her grades–and she did.

The following year on Memorial Day our family went to the cemetery as we had always done in the past. As we were finishing our work on the family plot I looked up to see Hazel with a small handful of wild flowers making her way to Roy's grave. It was marked by only a small wooden cross. She stood there a moment and I could see her lips move as if she was talking to him. Then she laid the flowers on his grave and turned back to us.

In 1927 Hazel graduated and began her teaching career. Although the school was small she was back among the rural people she so wanted to help. Her duties not only included teaching but also the upkeep of the schoolhouse. Any repairs she took care of herself. The winter months were often very cold but she always had a fire built and the classroom warm by the time her students arrived.

Her talents were soon recognized and she gained a reputation as an excellent teacher.

The Great Depression hit hard and many of Hazel's students could not afford pencils and paper. She always managed to have supplies for any of her students who were in need.

The years passed and Hazel's services to her students and community left little time for a personal life. Reflecting back, I believe that was the way she wanted it. If the subject of men or marriage was ever brought up she would always have an answer. I once heard her asked if she was a man-hater. Her reply was, "Of course not. I have the most wonderful man in the world for a father." Then the inevitable question was asked, "Did Roy's death have anything to do with you not marrying?" She shrugged her shoulders and said, "Well, we did have plans but they probably wouldn't have materialized anyway." I noticed a hint of moisture veil her eyes, but it was completely unnoticed by the others.

During World War II Hazel was relentless in her service. She helped raise money for War Bonds and the USO. Gasoline was rationed and any trip to town she made she either took along friends and family or ran errands for them.

After the war she felt she still had a duty to fulfill. We were all surprised but not shocked when she announced she was going to Japan to teach the children of the soldiers stationed there.

On her return everyone could see the years were adding up and like the story of Evangeline, "each had taken from her youth and beauty."

That year she didn't wait for Memorial Day. She went to the cemetery a few days after her return. There she found Roy's grave overgrown and the little wooden cross missing. Roy's family had moved away and no one had worked his grave since she left. She ordered a small headstone and asked me to accompany her while it was being placed.

After the workers left she stood there for a moment and as she bent to place a small bouquet of flowers, I saw her lips move. In a barely audible voice I heard her say, "These are from you know who."

Swiftly the time was passing. During the Korean and Viet Nam wars she did all she could to ease the pain and loneliness of families whose loved ones were in the service. Many of her nephews and former students were called to serve. They were all her sons.

When she retired she built the home she had always dreamed of. Stones she collected from around the world were mortared into the fireplace. She planted trees and flowers and welcomed all who visited.

As her health began to fail she began to put her affairs in order. She had all her legal work finished and instructions about all of her possessions. She made regular trips to the cemetery, but if she had any special instructions where she was to be buried she never made that known.

She died like she lived most of her life–alone. We found her with her boots on which was just the way she had always said she wanted to go. She never wanted to be a burden to any one.

We laid her to rest in the family plot of the cemetery as no one was sure about her wishes. I would have liked for her to be placed alongside Roy, but others thought it wouldn't be proper. Maybe not, but I felt they were lovers and should have been laid side-by-side.

When I place flowers on Hazel's grave I always remove a single posy and make my way across the dew covered grass to Roy's grave. As I stand there I can almost see them once again walking hand-in-hand, and hear Roy challenge Hazel, "Race you to the gate." As I lay the posy on his grave I whisper, "These are from you know who."–Jewel (Roller) Gardner (Hazel's little sister)

Don wrote this account January 1989 after his mother, Mary Pauline Davidson, died Christmas Day, 1988:

> The phone rang at 2:15 a.m. It was Dad. The paramedics had just left to take Mom to the Hospital. She had awaken Dad at about 2:00 a.m. gasping for breath and he couldn't get her

awake. The paramedics said she had a very weak pulse. They gave her some oxygen. It caused her to rally. She was awake when they took her to the hospital. I told Dad that Pat and I would get ready and be there as soon as we could.

We quickly got dressed. Pat hastily packed an overnight bag in case we had to stay over with Dad while Mom was in the hospital. We had called Mom and Dad Saturday evening and told them we would spend a few hours Christmas Day with them–that we would not stay overnight since Mom was still recuperating from her stay in the hospital earlier in the month.

We had planned to get up at 5:00 a.m. Christmas Morning and drive to Brenham, spend a few hours with Mom and Dad, and drive back home late Christmas Day evening. When we called Saturday evening (Christmas Eve) Dad said Greg had called and he and Donna would like to come to Brenham Christmas Day and spend a few hours sharing Christmas with them.

Pat and I left for Brenham at 3:30 a.m. We arrived at the Bohne Hospital at 7:45 a.m. After a few minutes the nurse told us they had sent Mom home. We stayed a few minutes longer and talked with the doctor who treated Mom in the emergency room. He said there was nothing different about her condition except she had 210/90 blood pressure and a slow heart beat rate of about 42. The doctor said he talked with Dr. Landgraff (Mom's personal physician) and he said her usual heart beat rate has been low for years.

We left the hospital about 8:15 a.m. and drove the few blocks to Moms and Dad's house. Dad saw us drive into the backyard and greeted us at the door. He said Mom was asleep and she was feeling better since he brought her home from the hospital. We told Dad we came by the hospital and they told us they had sent Mom home.

We visited a while with Dad and he updated us on Mom's condition. Pat re-programmed Dad's phone to get the correct number for Dr. Landgraff at the clinic. When she lifted the receiver the life-line device in Mom's room sounded a short, but very audible tone. Dad said it did that every time someone picked up the phone receiver. Then Pat auto-dialed the number to be sure it was right and the tone sounded again.

Since those tones sounded I figured they must have awakened Mom. In a few minutes I tiptoed down the hallway to peek in on her. She heard me coming and had turned her head to where she was looking at the doorway when I stuck my head around the corner. She said, "Come on in. I'm awake. I want to visit with you." I bent down and kissed her and she kissed me. I wished her a Merry Christmas.

I stood by her bedside and we visited a few minutes—just small talk about how she was feeling, and about our trip down, and our conversation with the doctor at the hospital. I apologized for the life-line tone waking her and said for her to get some rest. About then Dad and Pat came into the bedroom. Pat greeted Mom and wished her a Merry Christmas. Pat asked Mom how she was doing and we talked about water buildup in her legs. I checked her feet for any signs of fluid buildup. Found none. Mom said she was okay, and that she needed to get up and go to the bathroom. Dad helped her to the bathroom and I joined Pat in the living room.

In a few minutes I went to the back part of the house and as I came by the bathroom the door was open. Mom was standing at the lavatory brushing her false teeth and putting them in. I stopped a few seconds and watched her to see how her coordination was. I went on into the living room and joined Dad and Pat.

In a few minutes Mom joined us. She had combed her hair and she looked nice in her red robe. She sat on the sofa in the living room and we visited. Dad asked Mom if she wanted to eat breakfast. She said she would like some oatmeal. Dad and Pat fixed the oatmeal and some toast for the rest of us. I helped Mom to the dining table and Dad held her chair for her. She asked for a glass of fruit juice that she had left over from the day before. I got it out of the refrigerator and set it on the table for her. When we were all seated we all joined hands and Dad said the Blessing I have heard him give so many times: "Father, we thank you for this day and its many blessings, we ask you to bless and keep our friends and loved ones. We ask you to bless this food as we take its nourishment to our bodies. We ask all this in Jesus' name. Amen."

Mom ate most of her bowl of oatmeal with brown sugar and cream. She drank most of the fruit juice. We talked about Mom's low sodium diet, the various foods and their sodium content. We looked at some of the cereal boxes of her favorite cereals and read the sodium content to see which ones she could eat and which ones to avoid.

The phone rang and Dad answered. It was Sam. He talked briefly with Dad and then asked to speak with Mom. I helped her turn a chair to the phone and get seated. Sam wished her a Merry Christmas and they visited a few minutes. I talked briefly with Sam before we hung up.

Mom said she was a little tired and that she was going to go in the bedroom and rest a little while. Dad, Pat and I sat in the living room and visited. Two or three times I got up and tiptoed to the bedroom door and peeked in to see how Mom was doing. She was sleeping and breathing very gently.

About eleven o'clock Greg and Donna arrived from Austin. We sat around the living room talking and telling them about Mom's condition. I guess all the talking woke Mom because she came in to the living room wearing her red robe, and said she had to get in on all this conversation since most of it was about her.

For the next two hours we all had a rousing good time talking and reminiscing about when Mom and Dad first met and their early life together. Mom told about how angry she was with Dad one day in their civic class they had together at Edmond. The teacher had a surprise pop quiz on Monday morning. Each student had to get up before the class and tell about something they had read in the newspaper over the weekend. While the other students were telling about what they had read, Mom said she was racking her brain to think of something really significant she could tell about. She said when it came her turn she told, as best she could with a lot of stuttering and stammering, something about the Teapot Dome scandal in Wyoming. She said she thought she got a 'C' grade. When it came Dad's turn Mom said he got up in front of the class, hung his head, dug his toe into the floor and said, "Well, I read the funny papers." Mom said the teacher said, "Confession is good for the soul. You get an A." Mom said she was really angry that Dad got an 'A' for just reading the funny papers.

Dad told about how he worked nights in the bakery to earn his way through school and how one day the teacher caught him napping in the class. The teacher chastised him and said if he wasn't so interested in "campusology" and staying out late at night with the girls, maybe he could stay awake in class. Dad told the teacher that he worked from midnight to eight o'clock each morning at the bakery and then came to class, but said he didn't much think the teacher believed him. The next morning at 3:00 a.m. there was a knock at the back door to the bakery. When Dad answered it was the teacher. Dad invited him in and they visited about half an hour while Dad worked. They had some pie and coffee, then he left. The next day in class the teacher apologized to Dad and said anyone that wanted an education that much could sleep in his class any time he needed to.

Mom told about one evening she and Dad went walking west of town in the countryside. She told how the wind was gently blowing and the grain was swaying in the breeze. She said she was feeling so romantic and the orange sun was setting on the horizon over the swaying grain and it looked just like a sunset over the ocean. She said to Dad in the most romantic manner she could say it, "What does that big orange sun look like to you?" Mom said Dad kind of studied it a few seconds and said, "A big hunk of cheese." Mom said that just totally ruined her romantic moment.

We all had a big laugh and Dad said, "Can you imagine someone wanting to marry a guy that thought the setting sun looked like a big hunk of cheese?" Greg said, "Yeah, I guess she just wanted some ham to go with her cheese." Then we all had another big laugh.

We talked about when Mom and Dad first got married and how they lived in a tent on the road construction site near Wewoka, and how Dad worked with the road construction crews and on the dragline, and how Mom helped cook for the crew workers. Dad told about when he was working on the dragline that the crew lived in a tent with a wood burning stove for heat. He said that one cold wintery day they returned to their tent after dark. A bunch of hogs had gotten into the tent and knocked the stove down and generally made a shambles of the place. Dad said they were all so tired and cold that they just bedded down with the hogs for the night for warmth. We all had a good laugh on that one.

During all this Mom was very alert and talkative. She always liked being in on a good conversation. Her mind was very active and she related several good stories. There was only one time when I thought for just a few moments she got a far off pensive look in her eyes like she was a million miles away. She snapped out of it very quickly and continued to join in the conversation.

About 2:00 p.m. we said we needed to go so Mom could rest and regain her strength. We each bid her a fond farewell and kissed her good-bye as she sat on the living room sofa. I told her I loved her and to take good care of herself and to get plenty of rest. Then we left.

Outside we had a brief conversation with Dad. We told him to be sure and call us if he needed anything. We told him we would call when we got home.

Dad said there was a pretty rose in the garden that he wanted to cut and take to Mom because she loved roses so much. I walked to the rose bush with Dad. He cut and trimmed the rose. Dad walked to the car with us. He gave us a big hug and told us he loved us. We told him we loved him and to take good care of Mom. As we backed out into the street Dad stood there forlorn holding the rose and waving good-bye.

When we got home the telephone was ringing as we walked through the door. It was Greg. He was calling from Austin to tell us Dad called him and said Mom had died about 4:15 p.m. Christmas Day.

What I remember most about Mom is she wanted so very much to do so many good things for so many people. This was a compelling influence in her life, and the things she did were often misunderstood by others because she did not possess

> the delicate communications skills and finesse commensurate with her desire and zeal to do good for others. Yet, she never asked anything of others for herself and she never wanted to be a burden to anyone. She was a very independent person and very strong willed in that respect.
>
> I truly believe she picked her place and time to die. She died Christmas Day, 1988, quietly and peacefully in her own bed without pain or suffering. She went quietly and quickly with head held high and in her own way asking nothing from anyone.
>
> She brought us life and she has now gone ahead like a good mother to prepare the way for the rest of us whom she loves so dearly.

For whatever Pauline was, she was the mover, the shaker, the motivator–she was the one that made things happen. A lot of people didn't like the things she did and the things that she made happen, but she was not one to sit still and watch the world go by. Her mind was never idle. She was constantly thinking, planning, preparing, and doing–right up to the day she died. She was the motivating force that urged, no insisted, that Sam and Don plan and organize the Davidson Family Reunion the spring of 1988.

She knew her life on this earth was nearing an end, and she wanted so much to see positive steps taken to bond and preserve The Family. Her last written words were to tell Sam and Don that she was giving them the responsibility and duty to care for their Dad and to carry on and preserve the family unity.

CHAPTER 9

CORNELOUS COATS "Trick" JONES

CORNELOUS COATS "Trick" JONES, fourth born child, son of Wiley E. and Elizabeth H. (Talley) Jones, was born April 14, 1843, in Henry County, Tennessee. He died February 12, 1929, at Alex, Grady County, Oklahoma. He is buried in the Paoli City Cemetery, Paoli, Garvin County, Oklahoma, next to his wife, Sarah Luganie Jones. Cornelous married Sarah Luganie Jones, daughter of James Madison Jones and Matilda (Cook) Jones, January 2, 1868, at Alvarado, Johnson County, Texas. Luganie died April 21, 1897, and is buried in the Paoli City Cemetery, Paoli, Garvin County, Oklahoma. Cornelous and Luganie had eleven children. They were: Eudocia Mabel (1868, died in infancy), Lee Wightman (1870-1957), Martha Viola (1871-1960), Mary Ruth (1873, died in childhood), James Elmo (1874, died in childhood), Otis Hartswell (1876-1929), Charles Cornelous (1878, died in childhood), Arlie Luvida (1881-1965), Lula Alice (1883), Emmett Bascum (1886-1972) and Elizabeth Esthel (1890).

Cornelous was a veteran of the Civil War. He served in the Confederate 12th Cavalry of Texas, mustered in as a Private at age nineteen in Capt. Wm. J. Neal's Company, 4th Regiment Texas Volunteers, at Camp Hebert near Hempstead, Texas, Oct. 28, 1861, by W. J. Neal, for a period of twelve months. Miles traveled to rendezvous: 260. Valuation of horse: $140. Value of equipment: $15. Horse's name: Maco Mano.

This company subsequently became Company C, 12th Regiment, Texas Cavalry. The 12th was also known as the 4th and as Parsons' Regiment, Texas Cavalry. It was mustered into the service of the Confederate States October 28, 1861, for a period of 12 months, and re-organized May 1862. In the field it was also known as the Dragoons and Mounted Volunteers. Cornelous was 4th Corporal, Company C, 12th Regiment, Texas Cavalry, and appears on the Company Muster Roll for September 1 to December 31, 1863, dated December 19, 1864, enlisted October 28, 1861, Hempstead. Texas, by Lieutenant Sparks for a period of 3 years, last paid by Captain Terrell, to August 31, 1863, present.[1]

Cornelous Coats did not like his name and preferred to be officially known only by his initials, "C. C." He was better known by his nickname Trick, or the combination of "C. C. Trick." He was a lance corporal in Company C, Parson's 12th Texas Cavalry, during "The War for Southern Independence" more commonly known as The Civil War. Company C was known as The Slashers. Part of the time he served as a scout which means he was a point man that scouted out the territory ahead to determine where the enemy was and its strength.

Cornelous rode his personal horse 260 miles to rendezvous at Camp Hebert near Hempstead, Texas, in October 1861. His horse was named Maco Mano (a derivative of Spanish "mucho mano" meaning "good hand.") Trick rode Maco Mano all during the war, and afterwards when he was a drover and guard on long cattle drives from Texas to the railheads in Kansas, and during some close scrapes with Indians on those drives. Trick liked Maco Mano very much and in his later years often got teary eyed when talking about his Maco Mano.

---

1 (SOURCE: From copy made in te R. & P. Office, War Department, August 1903, of an original record borrowed from Mr. W.H. Getzenhauer, Waxahachi, Ellis County, Texas.)

Cornelous got his nickname Trick while in the military service of the Confederate States of America. The following was told years ago by his daughter, Arlie Luvida (Jones) Roller, Don's grandmother, and recorded as best as he could remember:

> My Dad's name was C. C. Jones, but he'd rather be called Trick which is a nickname he got during the Civil War. Sometimes he was a scout and had to go ahead to see where the enemy was and how many there were. He sometimes got too close and would almost get caught, but would pull some kind of trick to get away. After several of these close calls he came to be know by the other men as The Tricker. After a time it was shortened to just Trick.
>
> He was also known as The White-Headed Kid. Years after the war was over he had a chance meeting with an older man who was a guest at a dinner. During the conversation about the war the old man said something about the White-Headed Kid. Dad told him, "That was me." The old man said, "Then you are Trick." Dad said, "Yes, I am Trick, but who are you?" The old man wouldn't tell Dad who he was. He said he had done some things in his life that he was not proud of and he did not want his family to know about them, but that before he died he would tell Dad who he was. About a year later a rider came to Dad and told him the old man had consumption and was on his deathbed. He asked for Trick to come see him. So, Dad left right away to go see the old man, but he didn't get there in time. The old man died before he got there. Dad never knew who the old man really was, and for the rest of his life he was troubled about whom the old man was as he often pondered about the mystery.

Cornelous never officially surrendered to the Federal Army after the Civil War. He and thirteen others made their way to Mexico rather than surrender. After a period of negotiation with the Federal authorities, it was agreed they would be paroled and could return to the United States and could keep their guns and horses.

He worked for a while as a "drover" and a guard. He made several cattle drives from South Texas across Indian Territory into Kansas. Afterwards he came home and settled near what is now Egan, Johnson County, Texas, a small community about twenty miles south of Fort Worth.

Luganie's parents were James Madison Jones and Matilda (Cook) Jones. James Madison Jones was of illegitimate birth and a half-breed of Cherokee descent. He was a Methodist Circuit Rider preaching the gospel to several communities south and southeast of Fort Worth, including the community of Egan. Matilda Cook was born in Northern Arkansas on the Trail of Tears, the daughter of John Randall Cook. He was Scot and half Cherokee. He died on the Trail of Tears from Alabama to Indian Territory. John Randall Cook's wife is unknown, but it is thought she was a full blood Cherokee.

Cornelous died February 12, 1929 and Luganie died April 21, 1897. They are buried in the Paoli City Cemetery, Garvin County, Oklahoma, side by side located in the southeast section of the northeast quadrant about thirty-two paces due east of a large pair of cedar trees in the southwest section of the northeast quadrant. The inscriptions on their headstones are:

MRS. LUGANIE JONES
WIFE OF
C. C. JONES
BORN SEPT. 10, 1848
DIED APRIL 21, 1897

GRANDFATHER
C. C. JONES
APR. 14, 1843
FEB. 12, 1929
CONFEDERATE VETERAN

Following is a presentation Don gave March 21, 1995, at a meeting of the Sons of Confederate Veterans, Stonewall Jackson Camp #901, Denton, Texas, about C. C. Trick Jones, 4th Corporal, Company C, Parson's 12th Texas Cavalry Regiment, CSA:

I recently became interested in learning more about the Civil War, because my great grandfather participated in that war. My interest was sparked by my research in family genealogy for my wife and me. While researching the genealogy I learned that my great grandfather served in the Civil War. I did not start my research early enough. Family members who could provide a great deal of information are no longer living. A lot of old letters and documents were not saved, and those that were have been destroyed by fire.

My great grandfather, Corneilous Coats Jones (he preferred C. C. Jones) served in Company C of the 12th Texas Cavalry Regiment, also known as Parson's Texas Cavalry Brigade. I knew very little about my great grandfather's service to the Confederacy. Several years ago I obtained a copy of his military record. All I knew about him was in his military record, U.S. Census records I have researched, and family stories.

Shortly after I became a member of this Camp, Gary Sweet recommended a book to me entitled "Campaigning with Parson's Texas Cavalry Brigade" which I read. Not being a student of the Civil War I asked members of this camp about things in the book I did not understand.

In one of these inquiring sessions with Gary Sweet and Bruce Cunningham it was suggested that I research what I could on my ancestor and give a presentation to our Camp on what I found as part of a future program. Gary loaned me a book entitled "The Ragged Rebel–A Common Soldier in Parson's Texas Cavalry."

I read both books and I'm going to tell you what little I know about my great grandfather, C. C. Jones, and his service in the Texas 12th Cavalry and after. Also, I will relate to you some of the things I found interesting and enlightening from the books.

The book, "Campaigning with Parson's 12th Cavalry," is a compilation of letters and a personal journal written by Henry Orr while in the service of the Confederacy. The Introduction to the book states: "If Henry Orr, a young farmer in Ellis County, Texas, in 1861, had not had a sense of history and some literary ambitions, a significant addition to the history of the Confederate Trans-Mississippi Department would have been lost. He inspired his sister, Mary, to preserve his journal and the correspondence of the four brothers who fought during the whole war for Texas and the Confederacy." I enjoyed this book because the person who put it together presented the journal and letters exactly as written, with misspelled words, misuse of grammar, etc. with very little annotation and explanation.

The book, "The Ragged Rebel," is a biography of David C. Nance from a place called Heath Branch in Ellis County. The book is liberally annotated and was very interesting and informative with some very unusual happenings to this young man. Though this book is very good and provides a great deal of insight, it nevertheless is a scholarly biography, and a lot of the author's perspective creeps into the narratives.

The various counties comprising the Texas 12th Cavalry had different designations. They were:

- The Hill County Volunteers - Company A
- The Freestone County Rangers - Company B
- The Johnson County Slashers - Company C
- The Bastrop County Rawhides - Company D
- The Ellis County Grays - Company E
- The Ellis County Eutaw Blues - Company F
- The Kaufman County Guards - Company G
- The Ellis County Rangers - Company H
- The Williamson County Bowies - Company I
- The Limestone Mounted Rifles - Company K.

My great grandfather was from Johnson County and was in Company C, also known as the Slashers. When anything is mentioned in the books about The Slashers, I assume that my great grandfather must have been involved. I was told by two of his granddaughters that he never talked about his war experiences. One granddaughter told me that he kept his personal things in a trunk, including his papers, letters, documents, enlistments, discharges, etc. This would have been great, except his trunk was kept by a granddaughter whose house burned forty years ago destroying the trunk and its contents.

Like many Texans, C. C. Jones was born in Tennessee near a place known as Jones Mill in Henry County near the Kentucky border. In 1850 his father, Wiley E. Jones, moved the family from Tennessee to what is now Johnson County near the community of Egan. In January 1852 Wiley E. Jones, acquired a land grant from the State of Texas and to this day the grant is known as the Wiley E. Jones Survey. Wiley Jones was a rancher and did some small amount of farming. Young C. C. Jones grew up at home in the saddle and was very familiar with the firearms of the day.

I know very little about his life experiences until he was mustered in at age 19 as a Private, in Capt. Wm. J. Neal's Company, 4th Regiment Texas Volunteers, at Camp Hebert near Hempstead on October 28, 1861, by Capt. Wm. J. Neal. His record shows he traveled 260 miles to rendezvous, his horse was valued at $140, his equipment was valued at $15, and his horse's name was Maco Mano. His record shows a company muster roll for: "C. C. Jones, 4 Cpl., Co. C, 12th Regiment Texas Cavalry for Sept. 1 to Dec. 31, 1863, dated Dec. 19, 1864; enlisted Oct. 28, 1861 at Hemp. Tex by Lt. Sparks for 3 yrs., last paid by Capt. Terrell on Aug. 31, 1863."

The rest of what I know about C. C. Jones is mostly family folk lore related to me by several of his still living granddaughters. He lived to the age of eighty-six. He died October, 1929. When I was very young my mother took me to visit her grandfather the summer before he died. I was too young to remember the visit.

Since C. C. Jones never talked about his war time experiences, I'll extrapolate from the two books. On Monday, July 7, 1862, he probably was near Brownsville, Arkansas, at Parson's Cache River encampment when a skirmish line encountered a Federal advance guard. A three-hour battle ensued, which was pretty much a standoff between the two opposing forces. I assume C. C. Jones was involved because Captain William J. Neal, commander of the Slashers (Company C), was killed. Henry Orr also mentions that "Dave Nance was wounded in three or four places then taken prisoner, but finally gave the enemy the dodge and got away."

Soon after he entered the military service in September, 1861, Henry Orr started a journal in which he made almost daily entries for about nine months. He noted routine camp events, the weather, rumors, illnesses and deaths among the troops. Sometimes at greater length, he described his feelings about the war. The following introduction to his journal was written shortly after he first went to camp:

"The storms were gathering dark over the land; we had dissolved our connection with the Federal government and declared ourselves no longer under Northern domination but a free and independent people. This enraged our northern foe, and they declared they would bring us back unto the Union by suppression and subjugation, for the ties connecting us could not be dissolved. This was proclaimed by the authorities of the Federal government and by fanatics and the press throughout Lincolndom, and an approaching storm was clearly manifest. Hostilities soon commenced on the shores of Carolina. War now became inevitable; the gallant sons of the South, with the principles that glowed so brightly in the hearts and lives of their Revolutionary sires, began to lay aside their domestic pursuits and prepare themselves to go forth to battle for their rights–homes and firesides–and drive the invader from our soil. Companies were organized to prepare for the conflict. Old men and young, the farmer and mechanic, the minister and the clerk, indeed all classes began to enlist in their country's defense."

I noted that nowhere in Henry Orr's writings did he ever mention "slavery." The Orr Family and the Nance Family from Ellis County were not slave holders. The Wiley E. Jones Family of Johnson County brought an elderly slave woman (Mammy) with them from Tennessee to Texas. No where in Henry Orr's statement giving the reasons for going to war does he mention slavery. Contrary to what I was taught and what is still taught in our schools, it is evident these young men did not go to war to keep slavery. If they had been approached with the prospect of going to war for the purpose of keeping slavery, they would have declined the prospect. I also noted the few times Henry Orr wrote about encounters with people of African descent, he always referred to them as "Negros" and always spelled the word with a capital "N."

In a letter dated August 21, 1862, Henry Orr wrote: "On Sabbath morning, August 3rd, three hundred of our regiment and forty of Johnson's Spy Company attacked about 200 of Col. Edward Daniel's lst Regiment, Wisconsin Cavalry, on the east bank of L'Anguille River fifteen miles below the military crossing at Hughes Ferry about good day on the morning of the 3rd and killed about forty, wounded forty-three (their own report), and took sixty-three prisoners. They had a good many Negros with them; about 40 of them were killed and 120 captured; also about 150 horses and 200 mules; thirteen wagons, and over 200 guns, a good many pistols, and a great deal of ammunition. Our loss was two killed and nine wounded, one of whom has since died. We attacked them on two sides. They fought bravely for a few moments, thinking we were Missouri troops. But they couldn't stand against Texas."

I noticed the Texans were especially fond of their horses and went to great lengths to see they were fed and cared for. They fancied themselves as "cavalry" and took pride in that fact. Henry Orr's horse was named Jeff. C. C. Jones' horse was named Maco Mano. Both horses survived the war. C. C. Jones had his horse a number of years after the war and in his elderly years always spoke very affectionately and sometimes a little tearfully about his Maco Mano. Henry Orr often wrote about casualties among the horses as well as among the troops. A few days after the battle at Cache River he wrote a lengthy letter home telling about the battle and asking his father to tell Lieutenant Payne that Muggins was killed in the battle. Muggins was Lieutenant Payne's horse. He was home in Ellis County recovering from injuries. In another letter Henry Orr wrote: "We have a pleasant encampment one and one-half miles east of Cotton Plant village. We get plenty of corn for our horses. Dixie (Robert Orr's horse) has got over his founder. Jeff's (Henry's horse) foot is about well, and they are looking tolerable well."

In a letter from Camp Burford, Arkansas, dated November 4, 1862, Henry Orr wrote: "We have been cooking some this evening and preparing to start on a scout in the morning. It will be composed of 25 men from the Slashers, Blues, and our company, aggregate seventy-five; will be gone some five days. From what I have lately heard, I think we are going about Batesville, though don't know for what purpose." I assume C. C. Jones may well have been a part of this scouting party. Henry Orr wrote in a later letter that on Wednesday morning November 14, 1862, they started on an expected scout ". . . Wednesday night two miles below Claredon. Thursday morning turned east towards Trenton. Traveled about twenty miles by two o'clock when rather unexpectedly our advance guard and the enemy found themselves close together. The Fed advance fired at ours hurting no one; our boys getting a fair view of the Blue Jackets, about 1,500 strong, thought best to give back. So our little band of Blues, Slashers, and Rangers of eighty-odd dodged into the bushes. They discharged one "big gun," formed line of battle, and marched that way awhile, but we kept out of reach. We passed round and down to Spring and Big Creek within about twelve miles of Helena. The Yanks moved on towards Clarendon, then turned northward and went to Moro and divided there, one division going the Spring Creek road, the one we were on, to Helena, the other via LaGrange and down the St. Francis River. They fired at some of our pickets on the way but without effect. They had a flanking party on each river, so we did not think proper to 'bushwhack' them as we could not do so advantageously. In the evening (Saturday) Captain Lusk of Carter's Regiment came to us and said he had received a request from Sanders for us all to join him at LaGrange, and we would bushwhack the Feds there. In a few moments we were in our saddles and on the way to LaGrange as fast as our war steeds could carry us. After a seven-mile heat, we found ourselves near the village. Their pickets fired on us and got for town. We formed a line of battle, and Captain Lusk and Haley were considering the propriety of charging them in town, when Lieutenant Bowman of Lusk's scout (of eighty men) ordered a charge, then Lusk's squadron proper spurred and raised the yell. We followed in hot pursuit. They charged up the lane and fired on the Feds and wheeled and came back a-kiting, hollowing for all hands to retreat. So but few of our squadron got a shot. The Feds sent their singing missiles at us as we got away, wounding several of Lusk's men, but fortunately no one was killed. They turned loose their battery on us, but no one was seriously hurt by it. Their powder and grapeshot must have been mixed, for it fell around and rolled off the horses like hail—hit some but only bruised a little. There were about 100 of them. They shelled the woods, but we all came out straight. We traveled about six miles and camped. The Feds left the next morning."

May 9, 1863, Henry Orr wrote from Silver Lake, Arkansas, that: "Colonel Dobbins and a portion of his regiment had a little fracas with the enemy down towards Helena last week. Killed upwards of twenty and took thirty-three prisoners without loosing a man. Lieutenant Haley and twenty Slashers start down there on a scout this morning." In a letter several weeks later Henry Orr wrote: "We have all drawn the regular cavalry sabre. Colonel Parsons has appointed Harper Goodloe drillmaster. He performs admirably, Parsons having drilled him for the above purpose. The boys are all learning fast. 'Red' Williams tells us the time is coming when it will be necessary for us to be proficient in sabre exercises." It would be several years after the war when C. C. Jones would have occasion to make good use of his sabre in an encounter with Indians.

As the war entered the summer of 1863 shortages and hardships were taking a toll. Horses were at a premium, and rumors abounded. Henry Orr wrote home: "Whenever the war closes, the government will be compelled to repudiate her debts, for our country cannot pay the interest on it then. I would advise you to pay off all you owe with Confederate money, for it may depreciate in value Saturday." Again, he later wrote home: "I am sorry to learn that Confederate money is depreciating in Texas, that there is such a spirit of speculation, and that the people are becoming greatly discouraged at the prospect of the war. I fear that speculation and want of confidence in our government will yet ruin us. I have ever believed that if our people are united and have the interest and welfare of the country in view that success will crown our efforts."

In June, 1863, Henry Orr wrote: "The 1st Squadron (Weir's and Kizer's) have been armed with Enfield rifles. I wish they would arm the regiment that way and let us go on the Mississippi River to harass the transports."

May 14, 1864, from near Keatchie, Louisiana, Henry Orr in a letter to his sister wrote: "Had I opportunity I could write a little volume of interesting incidents connected with our first month's life in the valley of Red River, but one event crowds fast upon the heels of another that they appear stale or out of date in a week from the time they transpired. The enemy came out in force on the 5th and drove our brigade several miles, retreated that night, but came out again Saturday and drove them back again a few miles farther than on Thursday. I have not ascertained the loss. William Price was killed. Some five or six of the company were wounded. Lieutenant Hall of Company C was killed and Lieutenant Haley wounded." I assume C. C. Jones was engaged in this skirmish since he was assigned to Company C (the Slashers).

By July 1864 troop commands were in disarray, supplies and ammunition in short supply, and rumors were numerous. The most frequent rumor was that Parson's brigade would be dismounted to fight as foot soldiers. The Texans had considerable disdain for the notion of being dismounted. On July 10, 1864 from Bayou Rapids, Louisana, Henry Orr wrote: "Again we have reached the valley of Red River. Struck camp eight miles above McNutt's Hill. Day after tomorrow we move upon Cane River. Madam Rumor now says that we are going to Lanesport, but judging from our late experience there is no telling where we will turn up next. We have been traveling for five to eight miles per day, but our horses have not minded as the grass in the fine timber is coarse and tough. Another like trip would dismount us all. Rumor says the notorious conduct of the 12th has been reported to Shreveport Headquarters and that we may be dismounted, but they will hardly do it."

In a postscript to this letter he wrote: "Morning of the 11th. A dispatch from Colonel Parsons last evening which states that none of the veteran troops would be dismounted, which settles that question."

Henry Orr wrote his last letter April 7, 1865, from Wallace's Prairie, Grimes County, Texas, as follows: "We are encamped in a thicket of timber with a high rolling plain extending far out northward, eastward, and westward, presenting a fine field for the practice of 'Hardee' and 'Phillip St. George Cooke', the books we study; also pasturage for our horses. Jeff has recovered from his founder and seems to relish the prairie grass very highly. We are well supplied with meal and soon will get some beef which will be relished as we desire a change. It has not fallen to our lot to get any smooth bread yet; would relish some highly. There is a prospect of our returning to Hempstead; hope we may as I prefer active life to being cooped up in the brigade. There has been a thorough organization of our corps and several changes. Our brigade is the fourth and junior one in the division. Parsons assumed command yesterday."

Parsons Brigade moved from Grimes County sometime after April 7th, and was at Hempstead, Texas, when news of General Lee's surrender reached the Trans-Mississippi Department late in April. The scene at Hempstead was described by a man named Blessington as follows: "The soldiers were gathered in groups everywhere, discussing the approaching surrender. Curses, deep and bitter, fell from lips not accustomed to use of such language; while numbers, both officers and men, swore fearful oaths never to surrender. The depth of feeling exhibited by compressed lips, pale faces, and blazing eyes, told a fearful story of how bitter was the hopeless surrender of the cause for which they had fought, toiled, suffered for long years. The humiliation was unbearable."

A. M. Dechman, a member of Parsons Brigade, wrote in 1883 that: "On May 23rd, 1865, our distinguished Brigade Commander Colonel W. H. Parsons called the Brigade as soldiers together, and as we felt for the last time, then with a touching and saddened address to his gallant Brigade announced the end of this great and unequal struggle, bidding us to retain our arms and horses and to return to our homes, to be as faithful there in upholding our rights as we had been in the field of battle. Our ranks broken, we wended our sad and weary way to our homes."

Henry Orr reached home on May 24, 1865. Shortly thereafter, he wrote the following final entry in his journal: "At home again. Blessed word! Were no regrets associated with the return, unbounded would be my gladness. Ah! Deeply do I deplore the circumstances under which I come–not as my soul yearned to come, under the genial rays of the sun of Independence and the soul-inspiring anthems of Liberty–but after the demise of all my bright hopes for Southern nationality–after the Southern sun had sunk behind a portentous cloud to rise perhaps no more forever–when gloom, thick and appalling, sat upon our countenances and sank deep into our hearts. Oh! Saddening reflection and humiliating to every true Southern that our efforts, all our sacrifices have proved abortive, and that we must look for mercy to an enemy whose vile and atrocious deeds of cruelty and inhumanity have transcended those of the most barbarous nations of the heathen times. Can we forget the past? Can former friendship be restored? Time must note the potency of mutation in its rapid revolutions. Heaven grant that better things are in store for us than the present promises and that our future may not be altogether void of sunbeams."

I am certain these same sentiments were shared by all of the men of the 12th Texas Cavalry Brigade, including my Great Grandfather, C. C. Jones. These are not the words of racial bigots as the so-called "politically correct scholars" would have us all believe about the Confederate soldiers and the cause for which they fought. These were young men fighting for the same cause their Revolutionary forefathers fought for, freedom. Freedom from an intrusive and tyrannical government. We would do well today to emulate their efforts in a peaceful way to preserve that freedom. All three of these young men, Henry Orr, Dave Nance, and C. C. Jones were deeply religious and thoughtful men. They endured hardships we can't even imagine to defend a cause near and dear to their hearts, and which we must endeavor to preserve.

Family folklore has it that C. C. Jones and thirteen other members of his unit never surrendered to the Federals. They kept their horses, saddles and guns and fled to Mexico. After a few years they negotiated a return to the United States and were paroled. C. C. Jones and some of his companions rounded up a herd of wild longhorn cattle in south Texas and drove them north across Texas, Indian Territory (now Oklahoma), and to market in Kansas.

C. C. Jones made several longhorn cattle drives as a drover and guard. On a return trip to south Texas he and his companions were set upon by a band of Indians intent on stealing their horses. In the melee that followed C. C. Jones was hotly pursued by an Indian twirling a lariat to snare and pull him from his horse. Just as the Indian dropped the lariat loop, C. C. Jones leaned low in his saddle such that the lariat slide over his back. The Indian was not deterred and spurred his horse closer to try to knock C. C. Jones from his horse with a small club. Just as the Indian struck out with the club, C. C. Jones drew his old cavalry sabre and struck the Indian squarely across the face. C. C. Jones first thought he had knocked the Indian from his horse, but he saw the Indian clinging to the under side as the horse disappeared into a small ravine. Thus ended the pursuit.

Years later many photographs were displayed of the Indian Chief, Geronimo, showing a large scar on his face. In later years C. C. Jones often wondered if he was the one who put that scar on Geronimo's face.

After a few years C. C. Jones quit driving longhorn cattle and returned to his father's ranch in Johnson County. Shortly thereafter he married an Indian woman of Cherokee ancestry. They drove some cattle to Indian Territory (now Oklahoma) to claim land for her head right and to start a ranch. A lawyer's office in Tahlequah (the Cherokee capital) conveniently burned destroying all her documents. The lawyer became land wealthy, and C. C. Jones and his wife became "sooners."

C. C. Jones was a rancher and farmer in what is now south central Oklahoma. He and his wife, Luganie, had eleven children. My grandmother was the eighth child. Luganie died in 1897. C. C. Jones never remarried. He lived at various times with his several children in his later years. He spent many hours in quite solitude in the shade of a favorite pecan tree. He never talked about his war time experiences, but my aunts tell me he was a very philosophical and religious man frequently calling on his lifetime experiences when giving grandfatherly advice to his granddaughters. He was a respected elder in the community. He died October 1929 at age 86 and is buried at Paoli, Oklahoma. His headstone reads: "C. C. JONES APR 14, 1843 - FEB 12, 1929, CONFEDERATE VETERAN".

"The Civil War is not ended: I question whether any serious civil war ever does end". — T. S. Eliot

Following is a typed transcription of a letter to C. C. Trick Jones written November 30, 1927, by Alice Jones, daughter of Trick's nephew Jack Jones:

Egan, Tex.
Nov. 30, 1927

Mr. C. C. Jones
Alex, Okla.

Dear Uncle.

Guess you thing (*think*) we have quit you. I'll admit we have neglected you shamefully, but seems like it just can't be helped. This leaves us all up and doing fine.

Got all our crops gathered, sold and spent. Didn't make very good, but things could be worse.

Today is one of the windiest days I ever saw. We are awfully dry down here.

Wish you could come to see us some time soon. We haven't yet got hold of that man that had uncle Zeek's address. Guess it was all a mistake.

Saw Lee McClure the other day and she is as fat as she can be. Uncle Trick, we still love you if it has been a long time since we told you so.

Well, another old man has passed on to the great beyond and that is Old Grandpa Booth (Preacher).

Jack has started to clean off the old Jones Grave Yard again. He will sprout it off then burn it off. It sure does need to be worked off. He fixed up the fence.

Well, Uncle Trick, as news is scarce I'll close for this time ans (*answer*) soon and I'll do better next time.

Love to all
Jack, Alice and Evelyn

The Jones Family Cemetery is located on the Gentry farm in the Wiley Jones Survey in Johnson County about six miles south of the small town of Egan, Texas, on a gravel road. Egan is located on FR-917 where it crosses the Santa Fe railroad tracks approximately five miles west of the intersection of FR-917 and I-35 about twenty-five miles south of Fort Worth. The cemetery is situated on a small tree covered hill about one hundred and fifty yards east of the gravel road.

For years the cemetery was in a very badly run down condition. Cattle were permitted to roam the cemetery for a number of years, and many of the headstones were knocked over, dislocated, and broken. Many of the large old cedar trees were cut down for commercial purposes.

In recent years Ms. Doris Lanfear of Cleburne founded the Johnson County Cemetery Association with the purpose to restore and maintain all the old cemeteries in Johnson County using jail inmates for labor. The Jones Family Cemetery has been fenced and restored by the association. Access is through the Gentry farmyard. Ask for permission to visit the cemetery. Texas law specifies that a person cannot be denied access to a cemetery even though you have to cross private property.

Following is a transcription of a letter from C. C. Trick Jones to his daughter, Arlie (Jones) Roller, my grandmother. The original letter was found tucked inside the pages of an old and terribly damaged Bible that belonged to Arlie. It was handwritten in pencil on yellowing and fading paper. Don took the liberty to correct misspelled words and correct grammar in the interest of making it more readable and still retain the flavor and meaning.

Oct. 8, 1928
Lindsay, Okla., Route 1

> Dear Arlie and Kiddies:
>
> I got home alright. Had good luck all the way till I got home. Met Walter and Bill in Bradly and they brought me home. I opened my grip and it was stuffed full of baby clothes, but don't you tell old Pady about it. She will be laughing all over the place. I did not get the woman nor the babies, but I went back next morning and got my grip and the people in Bradly sure had the laugh on me, so no one was hurt and all things now are right.
>
> After I got home I felt like a young man one day. I was walking around and over the field when all at once I turned blind, had a fit and down I came, and if I had not been able to get up I guess I would have been lying there yet because the place where I fell in they never would of found me till the buzzards found me.
>
> I commenced taking a trough of liver medicine. I believe I was the biliors (bilious) human I ever saw. I am up now and feeling fine. My little Kiddies liked to have had fits and they are not done wallering over me yet. I haven't seen any of the folks yet. Only Walter and Bill.
>
> Everything (everyone) that is big enough to pull a lock of cotton out of the boll is in the field. I don't believe there will be a bale of cotton in the fields in this country 30 days from

now. Emmett will finish picking this week. He will have 2 bales. His late cotton did not make anything. The weevils got it all. His broomcorn did not make hardly anything. The rest of his crop is good.

Now, I will bid you good night and go to bed and dream of streets lined with "Babys and fountains of Cheery Nobles."

Good morning. Everybody is well and in the field. My bean farm is putting on another fine crop and you will not get a bean if you do not come after them for I am not going to send them to you. Ha, ha. I will eat them and think of you when I am eating them. That will make you feel good. I will send you dizpies (?) last letter.

Tell Pady I never heard from the letter she wrote for me to the eye glasses company at Chicago.

Well, yesterday I got a box out of my mail box. It had been broken open, but I don't think any thing had been taken out. They sent me one of the best eye testers I ever saw and when I get my glasses if they are as good magnifiers as the tester. . . [1]

Following is a transcription of the original land grant to Wiley E. Jones, C. C. Trick Jones' father, by the State of Texas as recorded at the Johnson County Courthouse in Cleburne, Texas.[2]

No. 87. Preemption Vol. 19

In the name of the State of Texas

To all to whom these presents shall come known, Ye I, H. R. Runnels, Governor of the State aforesaid, by virtue of the power vested in me by law and in accordance with the laws of said State in such case made and provided, do by these presents Grant to Wiley E. Jones his heirs or assigns forever, Three Hundred and Twenty acres of land situated and described as follows, In Johnson County in the Lower Cross Timbers on the Waters of

---

1 (This is at the end of page 4. The rest of the letter is missing.)

2 (The courthouse has since burned. The original document may have been destroyed.)

the North Fork of Chambers Creek about 8-1/2 miles N. 75° E. of Buchanan by virtue of preemption Certificate No. 11 issued by the Clerk of the County Court of Johnson County by order of said Court on the 2nd day of February 1857 Beginning on the East line of a Third of a League surveyed for Wm. McClure 490 varos North of his S.E. Corner at a stake from which a Post Oak 15 in. in dia. bears N. 57-1/2' W. 80 varos. Thence N. 60 E. with the South line of Geo. S. McIntosh--assignee of S. M. Williams Survey, 1200 varos to a stake from which a Post Oak 10 in. dia. brs. S. 67-1/2 E. 5 varos another 11 in. dia. brs. N. 30 E. 7 varos. Thence East 509 varos to a stake in Glover's West line from which a Black Jack 5 in. dia. brs. S. 88-1/2 E. 2 varos and a post 20 in. dia. bears N. 79° W. 3 varos. Thence South with said Glover's West line 1368 varos to a stake from which a post 13 in. dia. brs. S. 25-1/2 W. 18 varos another 12 in. dia. brs. N. 33 E. 10 varos. Thence West 1548 varos to a stake from which a Post Oak 18 in. dia. brs. S. 20 E. 5 varos another 10 in. dia. brs. S. 75 W. 5 varos. Thence North 768 varos to the place of beginning. Hereby relinquishing to him, the said Wiley E. Jones and his heirs or assigns, forever all the rights and title in and to said Land heretofore held and possessed by the said State, and I do hereby issue this Letter Patent for the same.

In testimony whereof I have caused the seal of the State to be affixed as well as the seal of the General Land Office.

Done at the City of Austin on the Seventh day of June In the Year of Our Lord One Thousand Eight Hundred and fifty-nine.

Francis M. White — H. R. Runnels
Commissioner of the Gl. Ld. Office — Governor
Filed for Record Nov. 1st 1859 at 9 O'clock A.M.
Recorded Dec. 15th 1859 at 4 O'clock P.M.
Jas. H. Tosbett, Clerk

Following is the obituary for C. C. Trick Jones published in The Lindsay News, February 15, 1929, Lindsay, Garvin County, Oklahoma

AGED MAN PASSES
C.C. JONES LIVED NEAR LINDSAY 41 YEARS
HAD COLORFUL CAREER

C. C. Trick Jones passed away Tuesday, February 12, 1929, at the home of his son, Emmett, on Route 1 northwest of Lindsay, aged 85 years, 9 months, and 28 days; his death was hastened by an attack of influenza. The funeral was held Wednesday, interment being in the Paoli Cemetery.

The deceased is survived by seven children, vis: Wight Jones, Blanchard; Mrs. Eugene True and Mrs. Walter True, Alex; Mrs. D. E. Roller, Maysville; Emmett Jones, Lindsay; Mrs. Mat Smith, Norman; and Mrs. C. B. Fry, California. All were at his bedside when the end came, save Mrs. Fry. Four children of Mr. and Mrs. Jones died in infancy.

Mr. Jones was born in Tennessee and moved to Texas at the age of 12. He entered the Civil War at the age of 17, as a member of the 12th Texas Brigade, 12th Command, under General Parsons. Following the war Mr. Jones served for two years as a member of the Wild Irish Scouts under Captain Keenan. He crossed the plains of Texas under the leadership of Joe Bell and had some exciting experiences in fighting Indians who were under the command of Geronimo, etc. We hope in the near future to publish some of this history.

Mr. Jones and family came to this vicinity 41 years ago, and made their home here the remainder of their days. Mrs. Jones died at Purdy in 1893.[1]

---

1 (Her headstone indicates she died in 1897.)

CHAPTER 10

WILLIAM LEE DAVIDSON

WILLIAM LEE "Bill" DAVIDSON, first child, son of William Edmund Davidson and Mary Pauline (Roller) Davidson, was born 3 March 1926 at 1905 NW 28th Street, Oklahoma City, Oklahoma County, Oklahoma.[1]

William married Mary Elizabeth Grisham 20 June 1944 in her parent's home at 3608 NW 14th Street, Oklahoma City, Oklahoma County, Oklahoma. She was born 18 December 1929 at 602 West Oklahoma Street, Enid, Garfield County, Oklahoma. Her parents were Homer Elvin Grisham and Villa Virginia (Wofford) Grisham.

Mary died Saturday, September 23, 2006, at the hospital in Liberal, Seward County, Kansas. She is buried at Restlawn Cemetery in Seward County next to their son, Joseph Allen.

William and Mary have four children. They are:

(1) Johnny Lee Davidson born 19 May 1947 in Oklahoma City, Oklahoma County, Oklahoma, m. Margaret Rosemary Brewer, 29 June 1985 in Swaffhan, Norfork, England. She was born in Southport, Lancshire, England. They have one daughter, Isabella Elizabeth Faye, b. 8 September 1985 in Bury, St. Edwards, Suffolk, England.

---

1 (William Lee went by "William" until he entered the military service during WW II. He went by "Bill" after he came home from the navy.)

(2) Jimmy Lynn Davidson born 31 July 1950 in Oklahoma City, Oklahoma County, Oklahoma, m. Ruth Elaine Fredrick, 20 December 1969. She was born 8 October 1952 in Liberal, Kansas. They have two children: Brandie Dawn born 26 April 1973 in Liberal, Kansas; and Joshua Dean born 3 June 1975 in Liberal, Kansas. Jimmy married Pat Crittenden. No issue.

(3) Joseph Allen Davidson born 11 June 1953 in Oklahoma City, Oklahoma County, Oklahoma, died 2 August 1996 in Amarillo, Potter County, Texas, buried at Restlawn Cemetery, Liberal, Seward County, Kansas. No issue.

(4) Deborah Jean Davidson born 4 October 1954 in Oklahoma City, Oklahoma County, Oklahoma. m. Don Horton. They have one child, Angela Marie, born 19 February 1974. Deborah m. Kevin Holt. They have one child, Julian Carl, born 14 June 1977. Deborah m. Randy Schmitzer. No issue.

According to Williams's father the house where he was born was not much of a house. It was more like a chicken hut converted to living quarters without running water. William's mother and father were a young couple with very little resource.

William's father soon got a job with the Oklahoma Railway Company. He with his wife and new son moved to 3204 NW 13th street where two younger brothers were born. This house was actually a garage converted to living quarters, but an improvement over the "chicken hut" house.

William's father's job situation improved and the family moved to 2709 NW 40th Street. William said:

> The place on 40th street was about two acres. We raised chickens, kept a cow and had a large garden. We also raised grapes.

> I remember one year Mom made grape juice and sealed it in canning jars. She buried the jars in saw dust and wood shavings so the juice would not freeze in the winter. When she opened the first jar several months later the juice had turned to wine. She was really surprised. We children did not get any of the grapejuice.
>
> One summer my brother, Bob, and I decided to pick some grapes and eat them. Our Uncle Loyce was visiting. We put the grape seeds in the fuel tank of his car so mother would not know we were eating the grapes. His fuel line later became clogged. When he unclogged it he found grape seeds. He was not happy with his nephews.

When William was about seven years old his father brought home a pair of kid boxing gloves. William and his brother, Bobby Joe, put them on, but did they box each other? No, they pummeled little brother, Gene.

When William was about eight years old the family went to a big Easter egg hunt near Edmond. He found the golden Easter egg and won a five- dollar bill for the prize.

The Great Depression years were 1930 to 1940. In 1936 William's father lost his job at the Oklahoma Railway Company. Jobs were scarce. Money was tight. The mortgage on the house at 40th Street came due. There was not enough money to make the payment. The mortgage company foreclosed.

William's mother was in an automobile accident hit by an employee of Baash-Ross Tool Company who ran into the back of the car. William's father used the settlement money to buy a house at 3608 NW 13th Street.

The family did not live there very long. It was soon obvious that making the payments and keeping food on the table over extended the income. The decision was made to rent the house and move to an acreage in the country where they could raise a garden, keep a cow, and have chickens.

In November 1937 when William was eleven years old the family moved to the Johnson Place near Moore, Oklahoma. The children rode the school bus to Moore to attend classes. William's father worked for Meadow Gold Dairy as a retail milk deliveryman in Oklahoma City.

> We rode an old school bus to school. It was actually a farm truck. When school started Tiny Spencer, a local farmer, took the truck body off and bolted the bus body to the truck. It had bench seats along each side-wall. Down the middle was a bench the boys had to straddle. There was no heater.
>
> My brother, Bobby Joe, and I pulled a small garden plow while Mom guided it so we could till the soil to plant a garden. We also pulled the plow to cultivate around the plants. The garden provided food for the table and Mom canned the rest for the winter.

When William was about twelve years old he wanted to make some money. He saved what he could and when he had enough money he responded to an ad from the back of a farm magazine.

They sent him a small hand operated potato slicer and some cellophane bags. Bill was to provide the potatoes, peel them, cut thin slices with the slicer, deep fry them, package them in the cellophane bags, and sell "Potato Chips" to stores and others. The slicer never worked as advertised. Bill didn't make any money.

The family moved from the Johnson Place to the Turk Place two miles south. They lived there about two years and then moved to the Sullivan Place a mile east and a quarter mile south.

It was here that William began to work part time for a neighbor farmer who also did custom farming. William broke his wrist while cranking a tractor. It kicked back causing the crank handle to strike his left wrist.

When I was thirteen years old I hired out to work for Henry Janko. He hired me to shock bundles of grain. He had a daughter about three years younger than me. She brought a jug of water to the field so I had water to drink. I didn't know how to shock the bundles. She showed me. She also showed me how to hide the water jug under a shock to keep it cool, and to lay a bundle on the ground next to it to know where the water was kept.

I made enough money working for Henry to buy a young Southdown ewe as my FFA project. I groomed and worked with her to perfection. I showed her at the Cleveland County fair and won a blue ribbon for first place. Later at the state fair I came home with a red ribbon for second place in the FFA Division. In the adult division the competition was too keen. I competed against adults and got second place in the Open Division.

Dad bought a team of mules, Pete and Jack. We used them on the farm. I did most of the plowing with a walking turning plow. It took me three full twelve-hour days to plow forty acres.

We planted cotton and corn, raised chickens, and milked three cows. My Southdown ewe had two lambs and I got a goat to protect the sheep.

We went to school at Moore. I was enrolled in the FFA program which had a boxing team. I was on the team. I was knocked out one time.

After working for Henry a couple of years he put me in charge of the tractor and thrashing machine. We went to work at five o'clock in the morning. My job was to set the tractor, and belt it to the thrasher. It was my duty to see that the tractor and thrasher was properly lubricated at all times. I had to add fuel to the tractor while it was running. I had to be very careful. I took care of all the equipment while Henry went looking for more jobs.

> At home I chopped cotton, cultivated corn, took care of my sheep, milked the cows, and helped with the livestock when I was not working for Henry.

In November 1943 the family moved to Evening Shade, Arkansas. William and Junior Janko (Henry's son) went with William's father to haul the mules and cows to Grandpa Davidson's place near Hardy. William stayed with them while his dad and Junior came back to Moore to get the rest of the family and household goods.

William and his brothers and sister went to school in Evening Shade. It was much smaller than the school at Moore, and somewhat backward comparatively speaking.

> We arrived in time to take the end of semester tests. We had already taken the tests at Moore. We took the tests and the three students with the highest test scores were from Moore, Oklahoma.
>
> The principal called an assembly of the entire school from the seventh through twelfth grades. He told the Evening Shade students about our high grades and how dumb they were. This made some of the students mad at us. It was fight from there on. I was called into the principal's office and given a good talking to about fighting and that it would not be tolerated. I was called a "hoodlum" right there in the office.
>
> To make things worse I wrote an essay that graded tops in the class. The teacher worked with me to perfect it to enter in the county contest. I won first in the county and it was entered in the state contest where I won second. It was written up in the local newspaper which did not help my popularity.

The U.S. Corps of Engineers hired William to take a twice daily reading of the Strawberry River flow gauge on the side of the bridge north of the house. He recorded it on a form and mailed to the office in Little Rock. He was paid twenty dollars a month.

> One day I was gauging the river when the circuit preacher came along. He stopped and asked if I would preach at the little church over the mountain at Qualls. I told him to talk to Dad. I started preaching. It was mostly me reading the Bible and one of the Qualls girls leading the singing. I still have the old songbook put away as a keepsake.

William and his brothers worked the farm with their dad and grandpa. They plowed the fields and planted the crops. Cotton was the main cash crop. Unfortunately, the first planting was flooded when the river banks overflowed the fields. This destroyed the crops. When it was dry enough they replanted only to be ruined by a second flood. It was too late in the season to attempt a third planting even if they had the money.

> We planted cotton and corn. The crops came up looking really good. We milked the cows and sold the cream to the milk truck that picked it up daily in five-gallon cans. The creamery in Batesville paid each month by check.
>
> One day I was cultivating corn in the bottom behind the barn. That evening when I quit I left the tractor in the bottom where I quit cultivating. Early the next morning I heard a swooshing noise. I opened the door and looked outside to see what it was. The bottom was flooded. I could not see the tractor or the crops. The tractor was totally under water. I was disappointed. No crops and the tractor was ruined.
>
> Dad and I got the tractor out when the river went down. We parked it behind the house on the high side of the hill. Dad and I cleaned the tractor up. Dad bought new pistons and cylinder assemblies. It was like new when we finished it.

> Later after the bottoms dried out we planted a second crop. It too looked real good but not for long. A second flood ruined the crops again. This time the tractor was behind the house.

William's brother, Gene, went to Thayer, Missouri, to go to high school. His brother, Bob, took the farm truck and went to Missouri to work at a diary. William stayed on the farm and helped his dad and grandpa cut and bale hay to sell. It was the only meager cash realized from all the expense and work.

> I left August 22nd to go back to Moore. Mom gave me a pillowcase to put my clothes in. I told Mom and Dad good-bye. Dad said, "I'm sorry I have no money to give you." I said, "Dad, fifty cents is all I have, but I'll make it." I started walking and hitchhiking to Moore.
>
> A lady stopped and gave me a ride. It was a 1938 Ford coupe. She asked if I could drive. I told her I could. She let me drive for a while then said she was tired and wanted to sleep. She said to wake her when we got to West Plains, Missouri. That was where she lived.
>
> The next ride I got was a Sunflower gasoline tanker truck. He asked me if I could drive a semi-trailer truck. I had the audacity to tell him I could. I drove for a while and he said to wake him when we got to Tulsa. He gave me five dollars and said to buy a bus ticket to Oklahoma City.
>
> When I got to Oklahoma City I had enough money to buy a train ticket to Moore. There I went to the postmistress, Mrs. Morrow. She was a lady I knew.

William lived with the Morrow family in Moore. She was a divorcee with three girls and a boy to raise. They were neighbors when William's family lived on the Johnson Place at Moore. She was post mistress and had a contract for janitorial work at the

Moore School. He earned his keep by helping with the janitorial work.

> I stayed with the Morrow family until November. The next oldest daughter's name was Dorothy. Saturdays Dorothy and I worked all day cleaning the school building. We swept, mopped, dusted, and cleaned windows. It took all day.
>
> One Saturday Mrs. Morrow told her oldest daughter, Barbara, to clean the house, do dishes, feed the small children, and have supper fixed. When Mrs. Morrow, Dorothy, and I got home Barbara had done nothing. It made me angry and I told off Barbara in no uncertain terms. Mrs. Morrow told me I was not her father and that it was best if I left. I took my pillowcase and meager belongings and was gone.
>
> I walked to town and saw the door was open to the weekly town newspaper, The Moore Messenger. I asked the man if he needed help. He asked if I could run a printing press. I told him I couldn't but I sure could learn. He asked where I lived. I told him I didn't have a place to live. I told him what happened to our family in Arkansas. He gave me a small room in back of the shop.
>
> It had a small pot-bellied coal burning stove. I used it for heat and to cook on top. There was a cot for me to sleep on. He went home and got a blanket for me. This was the middle of November. I went to school every day and ran the printing press at night. I was paid five dollars a week.
>
> I also got work cleaning the local drug store at night. I earned enough to buy food and have a little extra to spend.

In the meantime William's parents moved back to Oklahoma City with his sister, Meta Lu (Ann), and youngest brother, Marvin (Sam). They lived at their old address, 3608 NW 13th Street. Later, Gene (Don), and Bob joined them. They went to school in Oklahoma City. Bill continued to go to school at Moore.

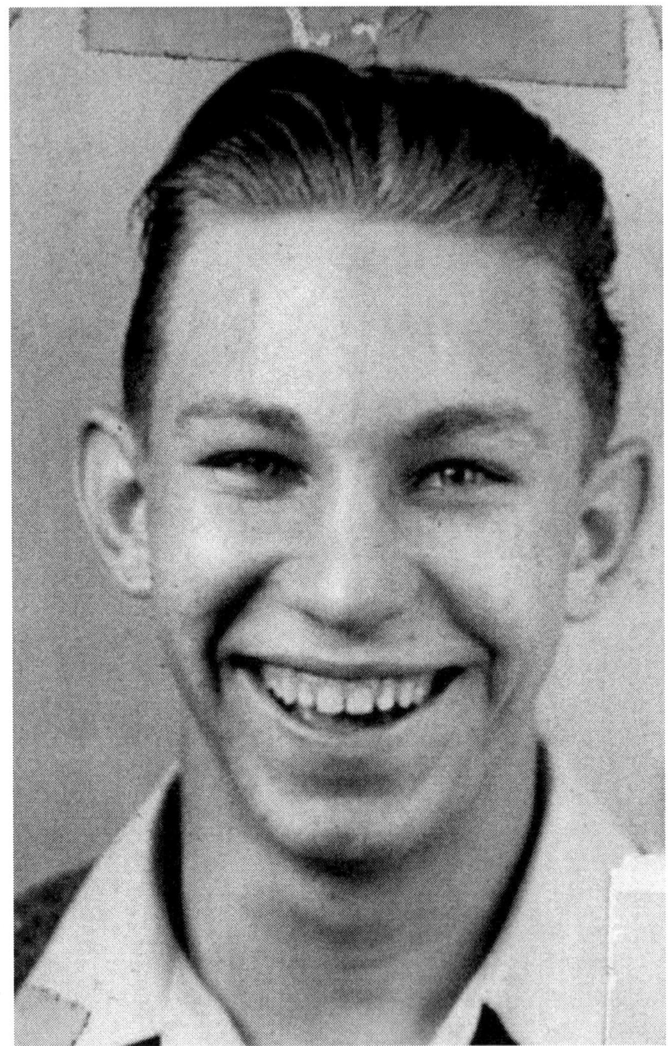

William Lee Davidson - age 17

On a visit to see his folks William met a young girl, Mary Elizabeth Grisham, on a blind date. She lived at 3608 NW 14th Street. A romance blossomed and they were soon seriously dating.

Early one weekend in February I had a little money left over to go rollerskating. I had learned that Mom and Dad with the rest of the family were living at our old house in Oklahoma City.

I went to see them. I asked my brother, Bob, to go skating with me. He said, "No. I have a date with a girl after church. She has a little busy-body sister you can take for a date." [1] We met them after church. Bob took his date and left. I saw this little girl he called the "little busy-body." I said to myself, "What a beauty. This is my girl forever." We sat on the street curb talking until her folks came home. Her name was Mary. I had to hustle to catch the interurban back to Moore.

I dated her the next three weekends. Then on March third my family celebrated my eighteenth birthday. Mary was there to help celebrate.

World War II was still in full force in 1944 when William turned eighteen. He was drafted before he graduated from high school. William went to Hardy to visit his Grandma and Grandpa Davidson. Then, he reported for induction into the Navy and basic training.

I wanted to see my Grandpa and Grandma Davidson before I had to report to the service. I hitchhiked to Evening Shade and spent four days with them. I then hitchhiked back to Moore. I got all my things together and told everybody good-bye.

I went to Oklahoma City where my folks lived. On April 8th I reported for induction. I wanted to be assigned to the Army Air Corps. When they asked what branch of service I wanted I told them Air Corps. The Navy man setting there said, "You look like a Navy man to me." So, I had to go to the Navy.

They gave us two weeks to get our affairs in order. They gave us each a sealed packet and said to report to the train station with packet in hand. I dated Mary till I had to report. Mother, Mary and I reported to the train station at nine thirty o'clock that morning. At eleven o'clock we said our good-byes. I got on the train and three days later arrived in San Diego, California.[2]

---

1 (She actually was a niece. Bob was dating her aunt, but he assumed they were sisters because the aunt lived with them.)

2 (In the Navy William began to go by the name "Bill.")

Bill took boot training at the Naval Base at San Diego. It was up at four o'clock every morning, formation, physical training, close order drill, gas mask drill, and gunnery training. After five weeks they were given a one- week pass.

Bill returned to Oklahoma City. He and Mary were married June 20, 1944, at her parent's home by the Portland Avenue Baptist Church minister, Rev. Sewell. In a few days Bill returned to San Diego and completed basic and advanced training.

Bill was sent to Camp Bradford near Norfolk, Virginia, for beach landing training. He was assigned to Amphibious Landing Division 1056. He trained to make beachhead landings off LST's. They are flat bottom ships with bow doors that open and ramp down to unload army tanks. December 1, 1944, Bill was assigned to LST-982 that had participated in the D-Day landing on Normandy Beach. It suffered considerable damage. It was back in Norfolk for repair and retrofit. This is where Bill was assigned to the ship.

The shakedown cruise for LST-982 was to haul a load of aviation fuel in 55-gallon drums to Iceland. On the return trip the ship stopped at Davisville, R.I., to take on the pontoons. From there it sailed through Panama Canal and up the California coast to Long Beach. The crew was due one week of leave.

Bill took his leave and arranged to meet Mary in Phoenix. The day Mary arrived he got telegraph orders to return immediately to the ship. He hitchhiked from Phoenix to Los Angles.

> I called Mary and told her to meet me in Phoenix at my Aunt Elsie's house. The day I arrived Aunt Elsie received telegraphed orders for me to return to the ship immediately. Mary was on the train that I was supposed to get on to go back to Long Beach. I spent the night with Mary. Six o'clock the next morning I kissed her good-bye and hitchhiked to Los Angeles.

In Los Angeles a chauffeur driven limousine stopped and picked Bill up. The man asked where he was going. Bill said. "Long Beach." On the way the man asked Bill if knew who he was. Bill said, "No." The man said he was Howard Hughes.

Bill had no idea who Howard Hughes was. He was just a kid from Oklahoma and had never heard of Howard Hughes. He had no idea what Howard Hughes looked like. All Bill knew was the man said he was Howard Hughes.

When they arrived at dockside in Long Beach LST-982 was gone. It had sailed. Bill said, "Oh, boy! I guess I'm AWOL." The man said maybe not and went to talk to the Executive Officer in charge. He told the man LST-982 had sailed for Port Hueneme north of Long Beach.

The chauffeur drove them to a nearby office complex. The man got out and told the chauffeur to drive Bill to Port Hueneme near Oxnard. In about an hour they arrived at the dock in Port Hueneme. The chauffeur let Bill out and drove away.

As Bill walked up the gangplank the Petty Officer in charge told him he was AWOL. He asked Bill who it was that brought him there in that limousine. Bill acted tough and said, "Howard Hughes." The Petty Officer didn't believe him, but was impressed with the fact a limousine had brought him to the ship. He let Bill on board and did not report him AWOL.

Bill went below to his bunk and slept two hours when the alert sounded to get underway out to sea. They were under way about two hours when a leak was discovered in the salt water cooler that cooled fresh water for Engine Number Two.

They changed course and went to Seattle, Washington, for repairs. Two days later they left for Hawaii.

> In Hawaii I bought Mary a pair of shoes. I had bought her a pair in Panama. Shoes were rationed in the States. Mary needed shoes but had no shoe stamps. Shoes were not rationed

in Panama and Hawaii. We sailed from Hawaii. We did not know where we were going.

Later we arrived at Johnson Island where we unloaded aviation fuel. The island was just big enough for airplanes to land and take off. There was a small building for a barracks, a small mess hall, a fueling station and a repair hanger. A ship was sunk about a mile from the beach. It was sunk by the Japs when they tried to destroy the island which was a fueling and repair stop for patrol planes in the Philippines area.

From Johnson Island LST-982 participated in the landing at Okinawa. Bill did not want to relive the experience by telling about it. From Okinawa they went on sea patrol. While on patrol they encountered a typhoon. It battered the ship for almost two days. They then made landings in the Philippines, Negros, and Cebu. They sailed to Palau Island for three days rest. Then they started training for a landing in Tokyo Bay.

We became part of the flotilla being assembled to make the pending invasion of Japan. There were ships everywhere as far as I could see. Battleships, aircraft carriers, cruisers, destroyers, landing ships, PT-boats, etc. After a few days the sea turned bad. We feared a typhoon. Our worst fears were realized. It lasted two days. Our sister ship lost the bow doors and had to go into dry dock.

A few weeks later we were ordered to sail a due southeast course and ordered not to look back. However, we did look back, but could not figure out what we saw. Later, we learned on the radio that we saw the atomic bomb cloud over Japan.

I passed my exam for promotion that was over due. The next day I was awarded my new Petty Officer stripes. Three weeks later we were ordered to Tuvalu-Nui Island a part of the Truk Atoll in Oceanesia to take Japanese POW soldiers to Tokyo.

We crossed the equator and date line at the same time. All the crew got "Shell Back" certificates. We were now real seafaring sailors. When we sailed back to the Philippines I had enough points to go home. I got off LST-982 and onto a banana boat with about a hundred other sailors and sailed for home.

I was processed at the Norman Naval Base. Just before I was discharged the Navy made me an offer. They said if I would sign up they would give me a 30-day leave and an additional stripe, which would make me a Second Class Petty Officer. I respectfully declined and took my discharge.

When Bill was discharged from the Navy he came home to Oklahoma City to be with Mary. In the meantime Mary had graduated from Central High School. They stayed with her parents a short time until they got a place of their own in the southeast part of Oklahoma City. It wasn't much. It could best be characterized as a glorified chicken house. It had been cleaned up, painted, and had electricity. They carried water for household use. They bathed in a galvanized tub using water heated on the stove. They used an outhouse.

Later, Bill and Mary bought a house with a VA-loan in Dell City southeast of Oklahoma City. Their son, Johnny Lee, was born May 19, 1947, and their son Jimmy Lynn was born July 31, 1950 while they lived there.

Bill took on-the-job-training with Otis Elevator Company and worked for them installing and repairing elevators. He changed jobs and went to work for Greenlease-Moore in Oklahoma City as a parts man. Later he worked for the Cadillac Motor Division through a Cadillac distributor for Oklahoma City handling warranty service.

Cadillac sent Bill and Mary to the factory in Detroit. Bill went through their school for warranty customer relations. Mary went through the parts department management school. They returned to Oklahoma City and worked for the Oklahoma City Cadillac distributor another two years.

In the meantime their son, Joseph Allen, was born June 11, 1953, and their daughter, Deborah Jean, was born October 4, 1954.

Cadillac offered Bill an opportunity that involved a move to Liberal, Kansas, to work warranties with the Doll Cadillac dealership with the understanding he would be transferred to the Kansas City office when he got the dealership back in the black. Bill went to Liberal in January, 1959. Mary and the children moved there in July the same year.

Bill worked with Cadillac nine years at the Doll dealership. Mary worked in the parts department part of the time. Bill got the warranty operation in the black the second year. Cadillac never made good on their part of the deal. So, Bill quit. He worked two years with American Motors before they went out of business. He then leased a Mobil service station for two years. The property owner would not renew the lease so he had to give that up.

Bill went to work for Freightliner Trucks, the dealer for White and Autocar heavy-duty trucks. A number of years ago he completed a course in electrical training at Oklahoma City University. More recently he had forty hours of vocational technical schooling in automotive electrical systems. He was the electrical technician for Freightliner. He rebuilt starters and alternators, and repaired truck and automobile electrical systems. He worked fifteen years at Freightliner. One day the owner died. His daughter took over. She made a lot of changes and fired all the old mechanics. Subsequently, she ran the business into bankruptcy.

As far back as 1963 Bill began repairing and rebuilding starters, generators and alternators as a part-time sideline. When he left Freightliners Trucking in 1980 he started his own business, B and M Rebuilders, and devoted full time to his business rebuilding starters, generators, alternators, and electrical systems on RV's.

Bill and Mary were active in their church and for several years made annual treks to Mexico for relief work at church orphanages.

In 1992 the lady who was manager of the school bus drivers for the Liberal School District asked Bill to become a driver. He has been driving a school bus ever since. He also does electrical work on the school buses and repairs starters and alternators while also operating his B and M Rebuilders business.

Bill and Mary's son, Johnny Lee, served in the Air Force during the Viet Nam era and after twenty years service retired from the Air Force. He lives in Liberal with his wife, Margaret, and their daughter, Isabell.

Bill and Mary's son, Jimmy Lynn, drives eighteen-wheeler tanker trucks for Phillips. He lives in Fritch, Texas, with his second wife, Pat. Jimmy's children by his first wife, Ruth, are Brandi Dawn born 26 April 1973; and Joshua Dean born 3 June 1975.

Bill and Mary's daughter, Deborah Jean "Debbie", and her husband, Randy Schmitzer, live in Turpin, Oklahoma. They have no children. Debbie is a pharmaceutical technician at Wal-Mart in Liberal. She has two children from previous marriages. They are Angela Marie Horton born 19 February 1974; and Julian Carl Holt born 14 June 1977.

Bill and Mary's son, Joseph Allen was a cook in several leading restaurants. He died August 2, 1996, and is buried in Restlawn Cemetery at Liberal.

Bill and Mary celebrated their 62nd Wedding Anniversary June 20, 2006 in Liberal.

In addition to running his repair and rebuilding business and driving a school bus Bill sometimes writes poetry for fun and relaxation. Here is a poem he wrote about school bus drivers:

I LOVE MY JOB! I DO LOVE MY JOB!

I love my job. I love the pay!
I love it more and more each day.
I love my boss, she is the best!
I love her boss, and all the rest
For I know we all do our very best.

I love my route and its destination.
I even hate spring break for vacation.
I love my diesel bus, it's bright yellow.
I love the soft seats for each gal and fellow.
It gets me greasy and sometimes breaks down
With no warning to make me frown.

I think my job is swell,
There's nothing I like so well.
I love to work with my peers,
I love to hear their leers and jeers.

I'm happy to be here.
I'm full of cheer.
I'm the happiest school bus driver
In all these lands.
I'll wave good-bye
With my cuffed hands
Cause I even love those friendly men
In their clean white coats.
Those friendly men with arm totes
Who came today
To take me away.

Bill also has strong religious convictions. Here is a poem he wrote about his beliefs:

LIVE IN HIM

God said He would send His Son
Salvation would be won,
Christ was born in Bethlehem
So that man would live again,
Thirty years he walked the land

To all in need He lent His hand,
On the hard wood of the Cross
He suffered and died for us,
On the third day He did rise
Now he lives no more to die,
Now we too can live anew
Live in Him need all we do.

Bill turned eighty years of age on March 3, 2006. His daughter, Debbie, and her husband, Randy, planned and held a surprise birthday party for him Saturday, March 4th at their home in Turpin, Oklahoma, ten miles south of Liberal. Attending were:

- William "Bill" Lee and Mary Elizabeth (Grisham) Davidson
- Donald Gene and Patricia "Pat" Sue (Paschall) Davidson
- Samuel Marvin and Martha Rowena (Vance) Davidson
- Johnny Lee and Margaret Rosemary (Brewer) Davidson and daughter Isabelle Elizabeth Faye
- Jimmy Lynn and Patricia "Pat" (Crittenden) Davidson
- Brandie Dawn (Davidson) Reynolds and children Kathrine Rachelle, Felicity Nicole, Sydney Deanna, and Mattie-Belle Elaine
- Debroah Jean (Davidson) and Randy Schmitzer
- Virginia Hysell (Mary's niece) and friend, Kirk Pinkerton
- Heather (Vaughn) and Mike Smith and children Gabe, Shepard, and Melody (Heather is Ann [Davidson] Melton's granddaughter)
- Miranda and James Grimes and children Clarissa, Raceton, and Natalie (Miranda is Pat's [Jim's wife] daughter by a previous marriage.)
- David and Virginia Hall (friends)
- Brandon Hall (friend)
- Vernon and Jean Reieger (friends)

Bill's wife, Mary Elizabeth, died September 23, 2006, at Liberal, Seward County, Kansas. She is buried at Restlawn Cemetery next to their son, Joseph Allen. The funeral service was held at the Christian Life Center Church in Liberal with the Reverend Ken Willard officiating. The casket bearers were: Don Nash, Bobby Adams, Kelly Sherrill, Alvin Sherrill, Scott Bromlow, and Dee Reynolds.

Following is Mary's obituary as it appeared in the Liberal Southwest Daily Times, page 2, Sunday, September 24, 2006:

In Loving Memory
Mary Elizabeth Davidson

Mary Elizabeth Davidson, 77, departed this world to be with the Lord on Saturday September 23, 2006 at Southwest Medical Center in Liberal, Kan.

She was born December 18, 1929, to Homer E. and Villa (Woffard) Grisham at Enid, Okla.

She married William L. Davidson June 20, 1944, at Oklahoma City, Okla. He survives.

She graduated from Central High School in 1947 and attended Hills Business College in Oklahoma City.

She was a bookkeeper for a local warehouse, a nurse's aide for Liberal Good Samaritan Center and a bus aide for USD 480 for the last 10 years.

She was a 15-year member of the Rebecca Lodge in Del City, Okla., and Liberal.

She was a member of Christian Life Center in Liberal.

She is survived by two sons, Johnny L. Davidson and wife Margaret, of Liberal and Jimmy L. Davidson and wife, Patricia, of Fritch, Texas; one daughter, Debbie (Davidson) Schmitzer and husband, Randy, of Turpin, Okla.; one sister, Beverly Denwalt and husband, Linn, of El Reno, Okla.; nine grandchildren, Brandie Reynolds, Josh Davidson, Miranda Grimes, Julian Holt, Shane Hammerschmidt, Angela Whitley, Thomas Schmitzer, Heather McMillan and Isabell Davidson; 19 great-grandchildren; and many friends.

She was preceded in death by her parents and one son, Joseph Davidson.

During the service for Mary the Reverend Ken Willard read the following which were written by Mary's daughter, Debbie, and her son, Jimmy:

I remember Mom teaching me (through her own experience) that you can do all things through Christ with his strength.

I was in the Sixth Grade and we were just arriving to church. At that time we attended Evangical United Brethren. At that time my Mom was a chain smoker (smoking like a chimney on a ten below winter night).

We pulled up in the parking lot. She put out her cigarette and said, "With God's strength that will be my last." Silently I was singing my hallelujah praises. To that day, my Mother never picked up another cigarette.

My point is my mother was a woman of strength. She never complained about how she felt. God can give us all strength and comfort through anything we give to him to take care of.

God bless to my Dad, Brothers and their families, and all of our friends. We will miss our Mother dearly. – Debbie

---

I remember when I was young I used to go snake hunting. I was at the Cimarron River bridge with a friend when we found a den of blue racer snakes. I put about twenty snakes in a tow sack and took them home.

Not wanting to leave the snakes outside I took them upstairs, twisted the top, but not tying it off thinking they would stay in the sack and I would take them outside the next day and turn them loose.

Those snakes had a different idea and they worked their way out of that tow sack and decided they would make their self at home in my bedroom.

My Mom not knowing those snakes were on the beds and on the floor went upstairs to take some of my laundry and put it away when to her surprise there were twenty or so snakes in my room checking things out. I had just got home when I heard my Mom scream. Not knowing my Mom could move so fast I realized she could move fast enough that she could make her shoes smoke.

In the end I realized the real meaning that you can laugh and cry at the same time cause I laughed, then I cried. –Jim.

Reverend Willard said their church always had a time when anyone could say or read a message to the congregation. He said Mary sometimes always read this same story about the old violin written by Myra Brooks Welch:

The Touch of the Master's Hand

'Twas battered and scarred, and the auctioneer thought it scarcely worth his while to waste much time on the old violin, but held it up with a smile: "What am I bid, good folks," he cried, "Who'll start the bidding for me? A dollar, a dollar; then two. Only two? Two dollars, and who'll make it three? Three dollars, once; three dollars twice; going for three." But no, from the room, far back, a gray-haired man came forward and picked up the bow. Then, wiping the dust from the old violin, and tightening the loose strings, he played a melody pure and sweet as caroling angels sing.

The music ceased, and the auctioneer, with a voice that was quiet and low, said, "What am I bid for the old violin?" And, he held it up with the bow. "A thousand dollars, and who'll make it two? Two thousand. And, who'll make it three? Three thousand, once, three thousand twice, and going and gone", said he. The people cheered, but some of them cried, "We do not quite understand what changed it's worth." Swift came the reply: "The touch of a master's hand."

And many a man with life out of tune, and battered and scarred with sin is auctioned cheap to the thoughtless crowd, much like the old violin, a mess of pottage, a glass of wine, a game, and he travels on. He is "going once and going twice." He's going and almost gone, but the Master comes, and the foolish crowd never can quite understand the worth of a soul and change that's wrought by the touch of the Master's hand.

CHAPTER II

ROBERT JOE DAVIDSON

ROBERT JOE "Bob" DAVIDSON,[1] second child, son of William Edmund Davidson and Mary Pauline (Roller) Davidson, was born 11 May 1927 at 3204 NW 13th Street, Oklahoma City, Oklahoma County, Oklahoma.

He married Dorothy Jean White 25 October 1946 at Olivet Baptist Church, Oklahoma City, Oklahoma County, Oklahoma. Dorothy was born 24 November 1928. They had two children:

(1) Paula Jean, born 3 August 1950 in Oklahoma City, Oklahoma County, Oklahoma. Paula married John Luther Ford 14 February 1970. They have two children: John Jason, born 24 May 1973; and Nicole Jean, born 22 April 1980. Paula married Gary A. Lynch 28 December 1994. Paula retired from Southwestern Bell Telephone Company. She and Gary have since divorced. No issue.

(2) Steven Joe, born 3 November 1951 in Oklahoma City, Oklahoma County, Oklahoma. He married Sheila Gallant, a British subject he met at Gulfport, Mississippi, in 1977. Sheila had two children from a previous marriage. Steve and Sheila had a daughter, Stefanie born 3 June 1972. Steve married Terri Gilbreath in

---

1 (Robert Joe's given name was "Bobby Joe." He went by that name until the family moved to Arkansas. He then began to go by "Bob" and later made his official name "Robert Joe.")

1977. They have a son, Scott Joseph, born 15 September 1977. Steve married Janet Jessalie Redman in 1980. They have two daughters: Sarah Jessalie, born in 1982; and Shannon Joy, born in 1985. Steve owns and operates a computer software company in Oklahoma City.

Bob and Dorothy were divorced in 1952. Dorothy died 6 December 1977. She is buried at Memorial Park Cemetery, Oklahoma City. Oklahoma.

Bob married Bonnie Mae (Craddock) Fleshman 17 September 1959 at Wickline Methodist Church in Midwest City, Oklahoma. Bonnie had two children from previous marriages. They are Karen Ann Dodson born 26 February 1950 and David Eldon Fleshman born 18 May 1954. Bob adopted David and he took the Davidson surname. No issue.

Bob died 24 June 2007. He is buried at Antioch Cemetery, Garvin County, Oklahoma.

When Bobby Joe was two years old the family moved from 3204 NW 13th Street to 2709 NW 40th Street in far north Oklahoma City. Bobby Joe and his brothers, William and Gene, attended Sequoyah Grade School on NW 36th Street.

The house at 2709 was situated on a small acreage. Bobby Joe's parents raised a garden and kept chickens. Bobby Joe and his brothers helped work the garden and care for the chickens. They also had room for a cow which they kept to provide fresh milk for the family.

Bobby Joe's dad got a young pig to fatten for slaughter. He built a pen and the boys helped feed and care for it. When it came near the time to slaughter the pig Bobby Joe's dad brought home a metal 55-gallon drum. He intended to cut the top out and use it to scald the pig. He cautioned the boys not to fool around with the drum because it had "contained denatured alcohol and was dangerous."

Bobby Joe just had to see what "denatured alcohol" looked like. He opened the bung lid and looked in. It was dark and he couldn't see anything. He sneaked some matches from the kitchen and took to the drum. He struck a match over the bung opening and started to look in when "BAM!!" The match ignited the fumes from the alcohol. Bobby Joe had barely gotten his forehead over the opening but not his eyes. It severely burned his forehead, but fortunately his eyes were not affected. A lesson learned the hard way.

Bobby Joe was big for his age and had large hands. He quickly learned to milk Old Bossy, the cow. It became his daily chore to milk her. His older brother, William, and younger brother, Gene, got the chore of feeding Old Bossy and cleaning her pen. They kind of resented this because they thought Bobby Joe had the easier task.

When the family moved to 3608 NW 13th Bobby Joe, his brothers and sister went to Linwood Elementary School on NW 16th Street. They walked the several blocks to and from school crossing a fairly large area between the Grand Boulevard right-of-way and the railroad track right-of-way. A small creek ran through the area with numerous grassy areas between 16th and 12th Streets.

After the morning milking and on the way to school it was Bobby Joe's and William's responsibility to lead Old Bossy to one of the grassy areas along the creek and stake her with a long rope so she could graze on the grass. On returning from school in the afternoon they led Old Bossy back to her stall behind the garage where Bobby Joe milked her.

Bobby Joe and his two brothers often spent part of their summers on the farm with their Grandpa and Grandma Roller. A cousin, Royce Weldon, who lived in Nevada, also often spent summers with Grandpa and Grandma Roller. One such summer, typical of boys, they were all playing "King of the Mountain" on the haystack in Grandpa's haylot. Of course, the object was to push everyone else off the top of the hay stack and proclaim yourself, "King of the Mountain."

Gene, being the youngest and smallest, was quickly dispatched to the bottom of the haystack. Brother William pushed Bobby Joe off. Royce pushed William off. He landed at the bottom hitting his arm on Bobby Joe's head. It broke William's arm. Forever after Bobby Joe was known as the "Hard-Headed One."

William was taken to the country doctor in Elmore City. He returned with his arm splinted with wood from the sides of a cigar box. They made cigar boxes in those days out of substantial wood ideal for making splints for kids when they broke their arms.

When Bobby Joe was in the fifth grade they moved from Oklahoma City to the Johnson Place near Moore, Oklahoma. it was a small forty-acre farm with room for a large garden, chickens, and Old Bossy with her heifer calf. Bobby Joe's daily chores included milking Old Bossy twice a day to provide milk and butter for the family. Bobby Joe and William also helped their mother plant and cultivate a garden to provide produce for the family. Bobby Joe and William pulled a small garden plow while their mother guided it.

Bobby Joe, his brothers, and sister went to school in Moore. They rode a school bus driven by a local farmer, "Tiny" Spencer. The bus was a farm flatbed truck that he converted to a school bus during the school year. For some reason Tiny called William "Pete." He called Bobby Joe, "Repeat." He called Gene, "Triple Pete," and Marvin "Little Pete."

Bobby Joe and William were in the same class because William was held back one year in the First Grade. Bobby Joe made good grades and was always quick with numbers. He always had his homework finished in a matter of fifteen or twenty minutes. He would then go to sleep sitting at the table while William labored for an hour or more to finish the same assignment. When William and Gene finished their homework it often was great sport for them to pull some ornery prank on Bobby Joe, like give him a "hot-foot", or splash water in his face, or hide his homework, etc., anything to antagonize him. This usually resulted in a ruckus with the boys' mother having to intercede to restore order.

The house on the Johnson Place was a two-room house with a lean-to on the back where Bobby Joe and his two brothers slept. It did not have inside plumbing or running water. There were no indoor toilet facilities. An outhouse served that purpose. Bobby Joe and his brothers carried household water a quarter of a mile in five-gallon buckets from a neighbor's well.

One dark night Bobby Joe was making his way to the outhouse. Unseen was a large metal wash tub near the pathway. He tripped and fell into the tub. He hit his arm on the side of the tub breaking it. About the same time Bobby Joe's younger brother, Gene, severely dislocated his left elbow. William had to milk and care for Old Bossy until Bobby Joe's arm healed.

Hospital bills accumulated because of Bobby Joe's broken arm, Gene's dislocated elbow, and other various medical problems. Bobby Joe's dad made a barter deal with the hospital to pay the bill by providing fresh dressed chickens for the hospital kitchen. Every Saturday for the next several months Bobby Joe, his dad, William, and Gene caught, slaughtered, plucked and dressed several dozen fryer size chickens. They iced them down in a large tub and Bobby Joe's dad took them to the hospital.

The landlord at the Johnson Place wanted to build a barn. He hauled a lot of scrap lumber and stacked it west of the house. He struck a deal with Bobby Joe's dad to help build the barn in return for rent. Bobby Joe and William helped their dad build the barn. It was here that Bobby Joe first learned the principles of carpentry.

Bobby Joe's dad bought a mare horse, a one-horse plow and a double shovel. They named the horse "Ribbon." Bobby Joe and William no longer had to pull a plow. They not only plowed and cultivated the garden with Ribbon, but also planted and cultivated several acres of cotton with Ribbon pulling the one-horse plow.

The family moved from the Johnson Place to the Turk Place. It was an improvement over the Johnson Place. It was a much larger house, but still no indoor running water or toilet facilities.

By now Old Bossy had given birth to several heifer calves. The chore for milking the cows was now shared by William. Bobby Joe with his larger hands and longer experience could milk two cows while William milked one. Little brother, Gene, could barely squeeze a teet. Bobby Joe would shoo Gene out of the barn and make him do some demeaning task, or something equally antagonizing. Gene came to believe Bob's main purpose in life was to antagonize him.

The cousin, Royce Weldon, was a few months younger than Bobby Joe. He lived in Nevada, but came to Oklahoma every summer to visit with Grandpa and Grandma Roller on the farm on Panther Creek at the foot of The Table Hills. Bobby Joe and his brothers also spent part of their summers visiting their Grandpa and Grandma Roller.

Henry was an uncle. He was the youngest brother of Bobby Joe's mother. He was about five years older than Bobby Joe. He took great delight in pitting Bobby Joe and Royce against one another in some kind of contest that usually ended up in a fist fight.

Royce was not quite as big as Bobby Joe but he was scrappy and could hold his own against him. Gene was delighted to see them mix it up because Bobby Joe sometimes came out on the short end.

One hot summer afternoon Henry baited Bobby Joe and Royce into a foot race to capture a quarter from under his hat. The first one to the hat was to run his hand under the hat and get the quarter. What Bobby Joe didn't know was Royce was in on the scam with Henry. Royce was to run shoulder to shoulder the entire distance, but at the very last moment let Bobby Joe win and run his hand under the hat.

Henry drew a line in the dirt and paced off about thirty yards. He gently set his hat over a fresh pile of cow manure. He came back to the starting point and said, "Get ready. Go!" The race was on. Royce stayed right with Bobby Joe until the last moment. Bobby Joe lunged at the hat ramming his hand underneath to get the quarter.

Instead he came up with cow manure all over his hand. Henry, Royce and little brother, Gene, had a hoot of a laugh. But Bobby Joe had the last laugh. He jumped in the middle of Henry's hat squashing it into the cow manure. Then he picked it up, threw it in a nearby stock tank, and ran to beat the dickens. If Henry could have caught Bobby Joe he would have "killed" him.

Bobby Joe was usually fairly smart about things, but he did a really dumb thing when he pulled down his pants in a patch of poison ivy to take a "crap." Needless to say he broke out and swelled up in places we don't even want to mention, including his arms and legs. He was one sick "puppy" for quite a long time and got to lay up in the bed in the downstairs bedroom where his mother and father usually slept.

Bobby Joe barely recovered from his episode with poison ivy when he was diagnosed with rheumatic fever. Again he was laid up for quite a long time in the downstairs bedroom. Brothers William and Gene had to take up the slack and do all the chores of milking and caring for the cows, feeding the pigs, feeding the chickens, etc. For a long time after recovery Bobby Joe would plead, "But I had rheumatic fever" when he didn't want to do a particular unpleasant chore or task leaving William and/or Gene to do it.

At school in Moore Bobby Joe was in the Future Farmers of America (FFA) program. Marvin Anderson was the FFA teacher.

One of the things they did was sponsor a boxing team ostensibly to teach sportsmanship, but mainly to raise a little money for the program. Bobby Joe along with his older brother, William, joined the boxing team.

The first boxing match of the year was with the FFA boxing team from Noble High School. It was talked around school that Noble had a really good boxer in Bobby Joe's weight class. He was a senior and had several years experience under his belt. Bobby Joe was a freshman and a novice.

Younger brother, Gene, just knew Bobby Joe was going to get his butt whipped. He gladly paid his fifteen cents to see it. There were several bouts prior to Bobby Joe's. The fighters mostly danced around throwing a punch here and there. Nothing to get excited about. Each bout went the full three rounds and the referee had to award the victory based on his judgment of who landed the most offensive punches.

When Bobby Joe's bout came up his opponent entered the ring cool and confident wearing a very nice royal purple robe and gleaming golden trunks trimmed in purple. He had a smart pair of black lace-up boxing shoes. He did a few little warmup jigs and a little shadow boxing routine in his corner. He definitely was a formidable foe.

Bobby Joe entered the ring without a robe and wearing a pair of cut-offs and well-worn old tennis shoes. He stood apprehensively and awkwardly in his corner of the ring. From all appearances it was a credible mismatch.

The referee called them to the center of the ring and gave them their instructions. They returned to their corners. The bell rang for the first round. Bobby Joe charged straight across the ring like a raging bull. He met his opponent about two-thirds of the way across the ring with arms flailing like a windmill in a windstorm. His opponent vainly tried to assume a boxer's stance to counter-punch, but the "windmill" just kept turning and coming at him keeping him completely off balance.

Bobby Joe pursued his opponent all over the ring with arms flailing, landing only a few punches, but enough to keep his opponent constantly back-pedalling on the defensive. Near the end of the round Bobby Joe landed a solid blow to the head that staggered his opponent. A few seconds later he landed a blow to the nose that splattered blood all over. The referee stepped in and stopped the fight. He awarded the victory to Bobby Joe on a technical.

Little brother, Gene, was slightly disappointed Bobby Joe didn't get his butt whipped, but at the same time he was a little bit proud of the way his big brother battled a "superior" opponent into submission. The next day at school Gene's Seventh Grade teacher, Mrs. Bridgewater, commented, "Bobby Joe was the only one that wanted to fight last night."

Bobby Joe had two Hampshire sheep for his FFA fair project. He spent a lot of time grooming, training and caring for his sheep. He won a blue ribbon on them at the county fair. He took them to the Fort Worth Livestock Show but did not place there.

The Dingler Twins, Meryl and Beryl, were identical twins. They were cute and no one could tell them apart. They thought it was great fun to fool people as to which one was which. Bobby Joe dated the Dingler Twins. He often didn't know if he was out with Meryl or Beryl. But, true to form, he had the ultimate solution. He dated both at the same time. Little brother, Gene, spied him at a movie theater in Norman with his left arm draped around one of the twins and his right arm draped around the other one. They cuddled next to him, as Gene Autry sat astraddle his horse, Champion, strumming his guitar while crooning, "South of the Border, Down Mexico Way."

Bobby Joe played football at Moore until the family moved to Evening Shade, Arkansas, in November 1943. The school in Evening Shade was very small and did not have a football team. The school had a gymnasium and a basketball team, but he was not a basketball player. They had an intramural volleyball program.

Mr. Cherry was the Vocational Agriculture teacher. Bobby Joe took Vocational Agriculture, but they did not have a FFA boxing program. Mr. Watson was the principle. His wife, Mrs. Watson, taught English. The Watson's son, Ray Bob, taught math, coached the basketball team, and ran the intramural sports program which was volleyball. At Evening Shade Bobby Joe began going by the name "Bob" only.

Bob was in the Tenth Grade at Evening Shade. The school was not only smaller but was also academically behind the school at Moore. Thus, Bob and his brothers were scholastically head and shoulders above their fellow classmates. Discipline was also more of a problem than at Moore.

Bob soon found a sweet little girl for his steady girl friend. Her name was Verneil Qualls. Following are two notes written in class by Verneil to Bob. They give a glimpse of insight into the experiences Bob and his brothers, William and Gene, experienced at Evening Shade:

> Dearest Bob,
>
> As you and I have both said before you're a hard business man. Imagine me offering you one yankee dime and you wanting three. ha. However, if you win the game and Ray Bob on the other team, I'll give you three. You'll have to win though, remember. What a captain you'll make. ha.
>
> You missed all the fun having to go to class this period. Miss Sullivan and Pug Kunkel got in a fuss. Miss Sullivan slapped Pug, then he slapped her. She brought him in to Mr. Watson and he got a paddling. It was fun while it lasted.
>
> And, speaking of fun, Mrs. Watson is about to put A. C. and Porter on the stage for laughing. She said where there was so much smoke there was bound to be a little fire.
>
> Mr. Cherry and the boys are working on the stage this period, so it's no wonder this letter is in such a mess.
>
> I'll bet Mr. and Mrs. Watson wondered why I didn't get in one place and stay there the first of this period. I went in Mrs. Watson's room to sharpen my pencil, then sat in your seat long

enough to get your letter, then moved up here by Jean, and next period I'll have to move to your seat again to put this letter in your book.

I believe someone put a bug in Mr. Watson's ear about you giving me letters as I go to literature class. If he doesn't send us at the same time in the morning I'll know that is what happened. There isn't a thing he can do about us using your book for a mailbox though, unless he makes me stay at my seat, and that's next to impossible.

Something else has happened. Those little Lassiter boys have been sent in here to stand on the stage. Mrs. Watson is having a hard time making them study, because every time she turns her back they turn around and make faces at us. This must be everybody's day to get in trouble. T.J. Carter is sitting over here singing "Be Honest With Me." If the old lady hears him it will be too bad. That's the sweetest serenade I've had in ages.

I'm not going to the Bottoms this weekend and Jean is going to spend the weekend with me. Say you won't be doing a thing the last period. How about writing me a letter? T.J. is singing the Marine Hymn now.

Well, I'll be seeing you tonight if you don't stand me up.

Lots of love,
Verneil

P.S. Mrs. Watson is about to put me on the stage now. There goes my A on deportment. L.V.Q.

P.S. No. 2. Boy, didn't Mr. Watson give this school a bawling out at noon. I wonder what he thinks has been happening in those class rooms.

Dearest Bob,

I don't have much time to write but I'll try to write a little. I've been working on the curtain on the stage. I've sewed until my fingers are so sore I just barely can move them. I really have had a time. I'll tell you more later.

Gene has some pictures at school I really would like to see. If he leaves them in his desk during bookkeeping class I'm going to see them.

William told me this morning that there was three cents due on my special delivery letter, but when he saw how anxious I was to see it he let me have it any way. If you ask me, there are some advantages to being broke. Or, to having good credit. ha.

I got to see the pictures after all. The old man went up on the stage to see how play practice was coming along, and Gene threw them to me. The only catch to the whole thing was that he almost hit Eudean Taylor in the head with them. They were good but I never could tell who was on the bridge.

Mr. Watson has figured up our grades, and Erline Wolfe is valedictorian, and Geraldine Graddy is salutorian. Jewel Dean Stroud thinks she has been cheated out of one of the two places and she intends to bring her report cards up here and see if she can have the record changed. As I expected I was away down the line. Not that I cared. I had a lot rather be class poet as valedictorian, and that's what I am.

William and Jewel Dean are really that way about each other judging by the way they sit around together.

This being a windy day, I wore that dress I wore last night, and the same thing happened that happened the last time I wore it, the only difference being that the eleventh and twelfth grade agriculture class was on hand to view the scenery. You can imagine how red my face got.

That was some letter you wrote this morning. It was better than none, but it wasn't half long enough.

I was mistaken about where Aunt Rosetta and Uncle Eather were going tomorrow. It is somewhere in Missouri instead of Stuttgart, and they may not be back at all Wednesday night.

I must have been fibbing when I said this wouldn't be a very long letter. I didn't know this period was going to be so long.

Claudia was just trying to scare you when she said she saw us Sunday. She was at home, and she didn't even know anything about it except what I told her.

I was glad to hear that Clyde didn't get his bluff in on you yesterday. After all, one of us needs to have some nerve. ha.

We got our diplomas in this morning. They aren't half as big as I wanted. As hard as I've worked the last four years, I think I ought to get one as big as I can carry. ha.

Aunt Rosetta didn't go to bed after I did get in early. I went to bed and went to sleep. And she was still sitting there reading. She said if she had known Uncle Eather would stand out there and talk half the night she wouldn't have minded so bad.

Pauline Arnold is going to stay with me tonight, and we are going to come to play practice tonight so I'll get to see the play twice I guess.

I should get a letter from Mother and Junie today. I haven't heard from Mother in about a week and it's been ages since I've heard from Junie. Honestly, I believe she's died and someone forgot to invite me to the funeral.

I asked Mr. Watson today what he would do if I played hooky and went boat riding, and he said he'd say "Goody." I think I'll try it sometime. You can't imagine how friendly he was with Claudia and I. Claudia said that him being in love with her would be the only thing that would account for him asking so many questions about the family.

Well, I must close and give this letter to Claudia to give to William to give to you.

Lots of Love,

Verneil

P.S. I watched the truck go out of town last night. I'll bet you wouldn't watch me that long. — L.V.Q.

Things did not go well for Bob's family in Arkansas. After two major floods the crops were totally devastated and it was too late to even try to replant. Bob's dad and his brothers had worked long and hard to make a crop. Now it was all for naught. Besides, Bob's dad and grandfather had exhausted their financial wherewithal. They gambled their scant resources on the success of that one crop.

Bob took the old Ford truck and went to Missouri to haul hay and work at a dairy. That didn't last long. The old truck soon was in a state of disrepair. Bob did not have the money to repair it. In the meantime his parents relocated back to Oklahoma City and Bob soon rejoined them.

Bob enrolled at Classen High School as a junior and went out for football under Coach Leo Higbie. The following year Bob was a senior and a member of the Classen football team that won the State Championship when they defeated Tulsa Central. Some of Bob's team mates were: Jim Hill, Gerald Lovell, Tom Balaney, Charles Shaw, Leroy Bergman, Woody Burkett, Jim Owens, George McKean, and Ronald Jackson.

The following was taken from an article in "The New Classen Life" published by the Classen High School Alumni Association, Inc., Vol. XX, No. 78, Spring Issue, p. 16. The article is entitled "Win, Place, or Show, Bob Davidson Loves his Horses," by Kathryn Yowell Baker '48:

> During the years when Bob Davidson '45 was about three to twelve years old, he spent the summers with his maternal grandparents on a large farm in western Garvin County at the foothills of The Table Mountains on Panther Creek. When he was just a young child, his grandparents let him ride horseback to the mailbox about half a mile from the house. It was at that time that he developed a love of horses which has led to his successful career as a breeder and racer of thoroughbreds.
>
> Bob was born in Oklahoma City, the second of five children. He can best be remembered at Classen as a member of the football team which won the first official state championship in the fall of 1944. His brothers, Don '50, and Sam '53, also played football for the Comets.
>
> Bob says that his most exciting and memorable moment at Classen was winning the football state championship. Higbie was his favorite teacher, and his favorite subjects were business math (taught by Higbie) and plane geometry. "I have used plane geometry all my life, in business and elsewhere," he stressed.

Robert Joe Davidson - age 17

When Bob was not playing football he worked at the Union Bus Station at Grand and Walker Streets in Oklahoma City with his brother, Don. They checked baggage, prepared manifests, loaded and unloaded baggage on the buses.

Shortly after Bob graduated from Classen in the spring of 1945 he was drafted into the Army Air Corps (Serial No. 38781916). He served at Scott Field fifteen miles east of St. Louis and later at Langley Field near Hampton, Virginia. He was discharged October 23, 1946. He married Dorothy Jean White October 25, 1946 at the Olivet Baptist Church in Oklahoma City. Dorothy was a young lady he knew and dated at Classen. William E. "Bill" and Ruth Landers attended the wedding.[1]

Bob and Dorothy lived on North Independence Street a few blocks north of NW 23rd Street when Paula was born August 1950. They lived in southwest Oklahoma City when Steven was born November 1951.

In 1950 Bob was an insurance salesman and a member of the Salesmen's Club in Oklahoma City. He enlisted his brother, Don, to participate in a patriotic Fourth of July extravaganza at Taft Stadium. The Salesmen's Club provided volunteer performers. In 1951 Bob had his own television and electrical repair shop on North Classen Boulevard at about 19h Street. His brother, Bill, bought a television set from him. In 1952 Bob worked as a furniture salesman at the Big Red Warehouse on West Main Street in Oklahoma City. His brother, Don, and his wife, Pat, bought a red easy chair from him.

Summer of 1952 Dorothy took Paula and Steve to Bob's mother to keep for the day. Dorothy never returned. When Bob arrived home from work that day all the furniture was gone. Only Bob's and the children's things remained. It was learned much later that Dorothy left with another man and went to California.

Bob and his two children, Paula and Steve, moved in with Bob's parents at 3223 NW 11th Street. For the next several years they lived there. Bob divorced Dorothy in February 1953. He received custody of the two children. During the next few years, Bob worked at several jobs, primarily selling insurance. He was in and out of businesses with several people. Paula attended elementary school at Linwood. Bob was pretty much foot-loose and fancy-free

1 (Ruth is Bob's mother's first cousin.)

during this time. He bought a yellow Ford convertible and later a speedboat and took up water skiing.

The summer of 1955 Bob and his brother, Sam, went to Brownsville, Texas, in the yellow convertible to visit their brother, Don, and his wife, Pat. They went to the beach on South Padre Island[1] and visited Matamoros, Mexico, several times.

In June 1959 Bob wandered into Sears, Roebuck & Company to kill some time between appointments. As he wandered down one aisle, a nice looking young lady wearing a sign, "Miss Polaroid," asked to take his picture. They talked about mutual interests and wound up going out for coffee. This led to dating, romance, and marriage. Bob called the former Bonnie Mae Craddock his "Mail-order bride from Sears & Roebuck."

Bob and Bonnie were married 17 September 1959 at Wickline Methodist Church in Midwest City, Oklahoma. Bonnie had two children, Karen Ann Dodson and David Eldon Fleshman, by previous marriages. Bob and Bonnie bought a home at 700 East Towery in Midwest City. The children settled into school at Steed Elementary. Bob and Bonnie became active in the children's school life, PTA, Cub Scouts, etc. Bob continued to sell insurance as an independent broker for Medley Insurance Company in Oklahoma City. Bonnie worked at Oklahoma City Mortgage and was a representative modeling for Polaroid Camera Company. Later she sold Sarah Coventry jewelry and was one of the early pioneers of "in home" sales for costume jewelry.

Steve and David joined the Cub Scouts and played organized YMCA baseball. Paula and Karen were active in the Bluebirds and Camp Fire Girls. The home on Towery Street had a large backyard and became the locale for the neighborhood baseball diamond.

Bob and Bonnie thought the best way to bond the children was to move to the country. In the spring of 1962 they began to look

1 (At the time South Padre Island was undeveloped and was open beach, except for a small state park at the southern most point of the island.)

for a farm to purchase. Bob sold his insurance business and he and Bonnie went to an auction in Lubbock, Texas. They bought forty head of Black Angus cattle. They leased eighty acres on the edge of Forest Park near Oklahoma City and moved the cattle there. Bob went to work for Jones Truck Lines in Oklahoma City as office manager. They tended the cattle evenings and weekends.

In 1963 Bob and Bonnie bought a forty-acre farm five miles east of Guthrie, Oklahoma, and moved the children and cattle there. The house was very small for a family of two adults and four children. Steve recalled that he and David had bunk beds. They could sit on the edge of the bed against one wall and open their dresser drawers against the opposite wall.

Steve and David attended a small rural school through the sixth grade at Meridian, Oklahoma, six miles from the farm. It had an enrollment of eighteen pupils. Paula and Karen rode the bus to high school in Guthrie. The school at Meridian was very unlike Steed Elementary in Midwest City that had an enrollment of over three hundred pupils. One day Steve and David came to school with their skate boards and rode them around in the gym during recess. The Meridian boys had never seen skateboards. The next day they showed up with roller skates nailed to the bottom of short two by six boards.

Meridian was the center of community activities for the local rural families. Steve recalled the box supper auctions to raise money for community activities. Bidders would vie to pay two or three dollars for a box supper hopefully donated by a pretty girl that you could meet and share the contents. Since the boxes were unmarked Steve said he invariably ended up with a box made by a local farmer's older wife.

At this point Bob learned that Bonnie had always wanted to own a horse. He came home from work one day, and she had bought a beautiful steel grey. Before long, every member of the family had their own horse. This was the beginning of their horse business. They became involved in such events as the Junior Rodeo and the annual 89ers Day Parade. The children became involved in Future Farmers of America. They raised calves to show at the county and state fairs. They had chickens, pigs, and Black Angus cattle.

Paula and Karen were responsible for cleaning out the chicken house and gathering eggs. Paula recalled that she had a Black Angus heifer. She named it Ellie Mae after the girl in the Beverly Hillbillies television program. She bottle fed the heifer, cared for her and showed her at the county fair. Paula's Uncle Don went to the fair grounds to see the heifer. Paula became very upset when she learned that Ellie Mae had to be sold for slaughter or breeding.

In 1967 Bob and Bonnie moved into town in Guthrie. It was a large four thousand square feet two story house built in the tradition of Frank Lloyd Wright by the man that built the Masonic Temple in Guthrie. Bob continued to work at Jones Truck Line.

The spring of 1968 Paula and Karen graduated from Guthrie High School. That summer they moved out of the family house to live on their own.

In 1968 Bob and his brother, Sam, formed a partnership to build in ground swimming pools. Sam had already been in the business several years. The partnership lasted only a couple of years.

Early in 1969 Bob and Bonnie moved to a ten-acre place in Forest Park, a Township northeast of Oklahoma City. That July they had a big Fourth of July celebration and picnic for many of the family members at their house. Bob's parents were there as were his brother, Don, and his wife, Pat, and son, Greg. Bob's brother, Sam, and his wife, Rowena, and their two boys, Marc and Chuck, were also there. Steve and David were there as were Paula and Karen with their husbands. Bob's sister, Ann, her husband, Fred, and their son, Bonny, had recently arrived from England and also attended.

Steve graduated in 1970 from Midwest City High School and entered the U.S. Navy SeaBees that September.

In 1970 Bob and Sam went their separate ways in the pool building business. Each maintained their separate companies.

During this time Bob and Bonnie owned and operated a gift shop, "Black Gold," at Crossroads Shopping Mall in southeast Oklahoma City.

Early in 1978 Bob and Bonnie sold their business interests and purchased a one hundred and twenty-six acre alfalfa farm near Chandler, Oklahoma. For a while they raised and raced quarter horses, but soon discovered that few quarter horse owners were making any money. Bob started raising thoroughbreds by trading three quarter horses for a thoroughbred. By the fall of 1979 he and Bonnie were having some success racing their thoroughbreds at Louisiana Downs and Delta Downs in Louisiana.

In 1980 they sold the Chandler farm and moved to Doyline, Louisiana ten miles east of Shreveport, home of Louisiana Downs. They purchased a hundred-acre tract of land and moved the horses from Chandler to Doyline. They continued their breeding program for thoroughbred horses and at one time had as many as fifty-two.

In 1982 the bottom fell out of the oil business and the collapse of Penn Square Bank greatly affected the horse industry. As a result Bob and Bonnie sold most of their horses at large losses and sold the farm at Doyline. They purchased a mobile home and moved it onto a large horse-training center near Benton, Louisiana. They managed the facility for the owner. They kept a few of their horses and began training horses for others.

In 1984 Bob and Bonnie moved to Lexington, Oklahoma, on a small parcel of land. They brought eight horses with them and began to rebuild their stable of thoroughbreds. Bonnie bought a small antique store in Lexington and Bob began to drive a cross-country eighteen-wheeler truck. Bonnie trained and took care of their horses as well as those for several other owners. After a while Bob quit driving a truck and joined her training the horses.

Later they moved to a mobile home near Spencer, Oklahoma, but kept their horses at Celestial Acres, a stable and training center in far south Oklahoma City west of Moore. In June 1990, Bob took four horses to the Woodlands, a new track in Kansas City, Kansas. He won only five races in the next three months but was on the board in thirty-eight of forty-four starts.

Shortly thereafter Bob began driving a city bus in Oklahoma City. In 1991 he and Bonnie purchased a house in southwest Oklahoma City. About this time Bonnie was diagnosed with breast cancer. After surgery, chemotherapy, and radiation treatments she was pronounced cancer free and has remained so as of 2007.

In December 2005 Bob was in Houston at the Sam Houston Racetrack with several horses. About noontime December 6th he paid a surprise visit to the Gazebo Convalescent Center in Brenham, Texas, to visit his father who had a stroke two weeks earlier. Bob's brother, Don, was there caring for their father who could not speak nor recognize anyone. Bob stayed a couple of hours and returned to Houston. The next day his father died. Bob came back to Brenham to attend the funeral on December 9th. Bob and Bonnie also attended the funeral in Oklahoma City.

In March 2006 Bob and his son, David, were in Houston with several horses racing them at Sam Houston Race Park. On the morning of March 2nd at the track Bob suddenly collapsed with a massive stroke. The EMS was called and they rushed him to Memorial Herman Memorial City Hospital. He was paralyzed on his right side unable to move his arm or leg. He was unable to speak or swallow. He had eye movement and seemed to recognize people. A few weeks later he was moved to a hospital in Oklahoma City and later to South Park Convalescent Care Center, 5912 South Ross, in Oklahoma City.

Bonnie sold their house in Oklahoma City and bought a double-wide house trailer in a trailer park in Tulsa to be near her daughter Karen. Her son, David, lives with Bonnie and helps train and run several thoroughbreds at Oklahoma tracks. In December 2006 Bonnie had Bob moved to a convalescent care center in Catoosa, Oklahoma, near Tulsa. He was there only a few months.

According to Equieline.com from 1982 to 2006 Bob and Bonnie participated in six hundred and ten Black Type Races. They had forty-four wins, fifty places (2nd), and sixty shows (3rd) with a total track earnings of $315,202.

Bob died June 24, 2007, at 5:03 p.m. at St. Francis Hospital in Tulsa, Oklahoma. Funeral services were held June 28, 2007, at Matthews Funeral Home Chapel in Edmond, Oklahoma, with Pastor Esten Leonard officiating. He was buried at Antioch Cemetery, Antioch, Garvin County, Oklahoma, with a military and flag ceremony for his service in the Army Air Corps during World War II. The Reverend Bruce McCray conducted the graveside ceremony.

OBITUARY

Robert Joe (Bob) Davidson peacefully passed away June 24, 2007, at St. Francis Hospital in Tulsa, OK with family at his side after a lengthy illness. One of five children, Bob was born May 11, 1927 in Oklahoma City to parents, Bill and Pauline Davidson. He was married September 17, 1959 to Bonnie Fleshman. Prior to his death, Bob was a popular winning thoroughbred horse trainer in Oklahoma City, Tulsa, and several other states. He is preceded in death by both parents and one great-grandson. He is survived by his wife, Bonnie, of nearly 48 years; children, Paula Lynch and Steve Davidson of Oklahoma City, Karen Williams and David Davidson of Tulsa, OK; 12 grandchildren; 11 great-grandchildren; brothers Donald Davidson of Brenham, TX, Samuel Davidson of Norman, OK, William Davidson of Liberal, KS; and sister, Ann Melton of Flatonia, TX. He leaves behind countless friends and colleagues. The funeral will be held at 1:00 p.m. on Thursday, June 28, 2007 at Matthews Funeral Home in Edmond, OK and followed by a burial at 3:30 p.m. at Antioch, OK. The family has requested donations to the Remington Park RTCA Chaplain's Fund, in lieu of flowers. Services are under the direction of the Matthews Funeral Home, Edmond, OK.

CHAPTER 12

DONALD GENE DAVIDSON

The Childhood Years

DONALD GENE "Don" DAVIDSON,[1] third child, son of William Edmund "Bill" and Mary Pauline (Roller) Davidson, was born 7 December 1928 at Oklahoma City, Oklahoma County, Oklahoma. He married Patricia Sue "Pat" Paschall 1 June 1950 at the First Baptist Church in Ardmore, Carter County, Oklahoma. Pat was born 6 January 1932 at Oklahoma City, Oklahoma County, Oklahoma. Pat's parents were John Bertrum Paschall and Mable (Patrick) Paschall. They were married 18 August 1928 in Norman, Cleveland County, Oklahoma.

John Bertram Paschall was born 27 February 1908 in Henry County, Tennessee. He died 11 February 1977 at Marietta, Love County, Oklahoma, and is buried in the Marietta City Cemetery. His parents were Pleasant "Pled" Wade Paschall (1882-1921) and Estella (Crowder) Paschall (1888- 1923). Pled Wade's parents were John Dill (1833-1898) and Malinda Jane (Nantes) Paschall (1845-1912). John Dill served the Confederacy as Captain of 'K' Company, 46th Tennessee Infantry Regiment.

Mable (Patrick) Paschall was born 21 August 1909 in Oklahoma City, Oklahoma. She died 11 February 1975 at Marietta,

1 (NOTE: Don's name on the birth announcement was Donald Jean. He went by Gene most of his childhood. He started going by Don when he entered junior high school.)

Love County, Oklahoma, and is buried in the Marietta City Cemetery. Her parents were Edward Arthur Patrick (1885-1976) and Susie Charlotte (Watters) Patrick (1889-1968). They are buried at Rest Haven Memory Gardens Cemetery in south Oklahoma City. Edward Arthur's parents were Jesse (1860-1947) and Susanna (Wilder) Patrick (1862-1900). Jesse is buried at Rose Hill Cemetery, Oklahoma City. Susana is buried at Laurel Cemetery, Pine Knot, Kentucky. Susie Charlotte's parents were Henry James (1853-unk) and Cynthia Jane (Hayes) Watters (1855-1910).

Don and Pat have one child. Gregory "Greg" Scott Davidson. He was born 27 December 1957 in the Deaconess Hospital at Oklahoma City, Oklahoma. Greg married Donna Elva Garcia 20 March 1982 in Austin, Travis County, Texas. Donna was born 3 February 1960 in Mission, Hidalgo County, Texas. They have one child (adopted), Mary Grace Davidson born 16 October 2001. Donna's parents are Ignacio Garcia, Jr. (1932-1973), and Josefina (Garza) Garcia (1932). Her grandparents are Ignacio and Francisca (Rodriguez) Garcia; and Julian and Isabel (Bazan) Garza.

Gene's parents, Bill and Pauline, lived in a small non-descript white frame house at 3204 NW 13th Street, Oklahoma City, Oklahoma, when he was born. It set on the back part of a city lot. It actually was a garage converted for bare essential living. It was one room with no inside facilities. Pauline cooked on a small oil burner stove.

It was an unusually cold December when Gene came into the world, and the winter continued to be colder than normal. Pauline had already birthed two boys, but Gene's was an unusually difficult birth. The old family doctor for Pauline's family was summoned, but arrived too late to assist.

The doctor completed the state-required form showing "Davidson male" in the space for Name of Child. He entered "Mary Jones" in the space for the mother's name. Jones was the maiden surname of Paulinc's mother. For whatever unknown reason, Gene's parents named him "Donald Jean." This was not without its problems. An official birth certificate was not obtained at the time.

Pauline already had two youngsters in diapers and now a new baby that was sickly from the first day. Things did not get much better. 'Baby Jean' was constantly sick and this was worrisome for Pauline. So worrisome that at age eleven months she took him to a professional photography studio to have a portrait made because she thought he would not live to be a year old. She had photographs taken of the other two children on their first birthdays.

The family did not live at 3204 NW 13th very long. It was much too small and inconvenient for a growing family. Within the year Bill and Pauline moved to 2709 NW 40th Street in what then was far north Oklahoma City. It was a wood frame house, but much larger. It had a living room, dining room, two bedrooms, kitchen, bathroom, front porch, and a screened back porch. It had hot and cold running well water and inside plumbing connected to a septic tank.

The house set on half an acre on the south bank of a small creek. It had a detached one-car garage, chicken house, and a place to keep a cow. There was plenty of room for a garden.

Bill's mother loaned him the money to buy a cow. He bought a half Jersey half Guernsey milk cow with a calf. She was named Bossy. She was a gentle cow. Bill and Pauline planted and tilled a sizable garden. The family had plenty of fresh produce and milk. Bill made a large box in the garage and filled it with sawdust so canned goods could be buried in the sawdust to keep through the winters.

This is Gene's account of his very earliest memories when visiting his Grandfather and Grandmother Roller, at their farm on Panther Creek.

> My earliest memories were in February 1931 following my third birthday in December. I was at my Grandma Roller's

house on Panther Creek. I remember looking out the window and seeing thousands of large snowflakes floating down on the snow covered ground. Everything was laden with a heavy covering of fresh white snow. I also remember it was warm and cozy behind the huge wood burning cookstove Grandma used to prepare meals. She used corncobs and kerosene to start the fire each morning. I remember Grandma and me playing in the kindling box making a 'log cabin' of corncobs–some were white, some were red.

Days later when the snow was mostly melted Grandma wanted to get out of the house. She took me for a walk along the creek. She took some tallow to feed the birds. I remember we were down in the creek bed. I helped Grandma tie tallow to the limbs of bushes for the birds. I remember I saw a red bird and how it excited me.

Years later as a young adult I was reminiscing with Grandma. I told her about seeing the snow and building the corncob log cabin. I told her about seeing the red bird. She filled me in on the details. She told me it was the February following my third birthday. She told me about our walk in the creek bed. She said she had cabin fever after so much snow and the first nice day she took me for a walk. She told me she took some tallow and we tied it to the bushes for the birds. She told me the red bird I saw was a cardinal. She said I was so excited that, to use her words, "You popped your little hands together and held your breath."

Grandma's one pleasurable vice was snuff. She dipped Garretts from a brown jar with a peach tree twig for a swish. Many a time she sent me to one of the two peach trees on the north side of the house to cut her a twig. I sometimes had to run to the old country store about a mile south to buy her a jar of Garretts.

Also, one of my earliest memories is of my grandfather Roller when he came to visit. He brought a small box as a gift for his grandchildren. In it was an adorable little baby squirrel. We had a great time playing with it and feeding it raisins.

I went running through a swinging door into the kitchen to get more raisins. Unknown to me the baby squirrel came running behind me. The swinging door caught and crushed thc lifc out of it in a matter of seconds. I was heart broken. I cried and cried. I felt like I had killed it.

I have memories of only one of my great grandparents, Mary Ann (Osborn) Roller. I met my great grandfather, C.C. Jones, when I was only about a month old. Mother took me to visit him in January when he was in failing health. He died February 12, 1929.

I remember Great Grandma (Osborn) Roller because she lived with Grandpa and Grandma Roller. She was elderly and mostly sat in a chair on the porch. Two things I remember most about her. One day she threw a dipper of water in my face because I sassed her. The other was her funeral. She died April 5, 1935. I remember her casket was brought to the Antioch Cemetery on a flat bed truck. It was draped with a beautiful quilt. I remember how my cousin, Vida Roller, cried. She is three years older than I am.

Many of my very best childhood memories are with Grandma and Grandpa Roller on Panther Creek at the foot of The Table Hills. Those were some of the greatest days of my life.

Meta Luvida (Ann) and Marvin (Sam) were born while Bill and Pauline lived at NW 40th Street. Gene was five years old when Marvin was born. He remembers the day his mother came home from the hospital with baby Marvin.

It was a nice day for late January. I was playing in the front yard. I saw a tan ambulance trimmed in white with orange wheels come into our driveway. I watched as the attendants took Mom and Marvin on a stretcher into the house.

Mom"s sister, Beatrice, a young sixteen year old, was there to help Mom while she recuperated. I didn"t know then that Mom not only had a baby but also had a hysterectomy.

Aunt Bea stayed with us the next two years to help Mom and look after us kids. Though she was only a teenager and the three older boys were five, seven, and eight she gained an insightful perspective of each of the boys that many years later she artfully articulated that was realistically descriptive of them as adults.

There was a large front yard with plenty of room for the children to play. Summer evenings it was great fun to run all over the yard catching lightning bugs and putting them in glass jars to make a constant light.

On weekends when Bill wasn't otherwise occupied he sometimes played with the boys. One such occasion he made a huge kite. At least it seemed huge to the boys who were little kids.

> Dad made a huge kite and we had great fun flying it. We played out lots of string and sent paper messages up the string. One day a biplane flew through the string and broke it. The kite went spiraling away. Dad with my brothers, William and Bobby Joe, jumped in the car and went to look for it. They spent hours looking. They finally found it torn, tattered, and broken. They brought it home and Dad fixed it to fly again another day. Years later Dad told me the kite was actually a little over five feet tall.

Though the Crash of '29 had occurred and the Great Depression started, Bill had a fairly good job for the times. He worked for the Oklahoma Railway Company at the Streetcar Terminal on Grand Street between Hudson and Harvey Streets in downtown Oklahoma City. He was a ticket seller and sold streetcar tokens and bus tickets to the thousands of riders passing through the turnstiles.

Later he was promoted to Ticket Agent. He was responsible for several ticket sellers. He was also responsible for the operation of a small newsstand. They sold newspapers, magazines, candies, gum and tobacco products as well as streetcar tokens and tickets.

The Interurban riders and the Streetcar Terminal with all the hustle and bustle of hundreds of people coming and going, and all the shops and sidewalk vendors stirred an excitement in that little towhead kid, Gene. He remembers Leo Winters, Johnny Sasser, Louie Stalken and Johnny Hightower worked in the newsstand with Dad.

It was during the Great Depression. Bill occasionally was able to get show passes to various local events.

> Dad sometimes took me to the traveling tent shows erected on the vacant lots on the south side of 39th Street with vaudeville comedy acts and the Dance-A-Thons. These were contests where couples had marathon dances. The last couple dancing won the contest and the grand prize money. They also had comedy dance acts for which the dancers won lesser prize money It was inexpensive entertainment and great fun.

Occasionally when Bill and Pauline had an evening out without the children they got a neighborhood teenage girl, Maureen McCaskell, to baby sit. Maureen was about fifteen years old, had flaming red hair and was amply endowed with freckles. She had a broken leg. Her left leg was in a cast and she was on crutches. She was a lot of fun. Gene was amazed at how agile she was with her cast and crutches when playing with them.

There was a family owned grocery store two blocks west on May Avenue. It was not uncommon for Pauline to send one of the children to the store to buy items she needed for the household.

> One day Mom gave me some money with instructions to go to the store and buy oatmeal cereal. When I got to the store I saw a box of new cereal with the cartoon figures Crackle, Snap and Pop on the box. I was so enthralled with the figures that I bought the box of Kellog's Rice Crispies instead of the oatmeal.
>
> When I got home Mom was angry with me. She made me take the cereal back to the store and get the oatmeal. I cried all the way to the store.

Hide 'n seek was a game the neighborhood kids often played.

> One summer afternoon a bunch of us kids were playing hide 'n seek. It was great sport to find a place to hide where no one could find you. I found just such a place.

> A neighbor man kept rabbits. He had several hutches secluded in his backyard. One of the hutches was empty. I just knew I had found the right place where I could not be found. I unlatched the door, climbed in and pulled the door closed behind me not realizing the latch locked into place.
>
> As I had planned I could not be found. The other kids called out "Ollie, Ollie, all outs in free" over and over, but I never came in. I couldn't. The latch was locked. I couldn't open the door. The other kids gave up and went home for supper. I was still in the rabbit hutch. I began to worry. Then panic. It began to get dark. I couldn't get out. I cried.
>
> Soon I heard people out looking for me calling my name. None came close enough to hear me cry out. It was dark. I was fearful I would be there until I died. Panic. I cried and cried to no avail. I wailed until after what seemed an eternity a man, I don't remember who he was, came to the hutch and opened the door. I'm not sure, but I think I was sent to bed without supper.

Gene attended Sequoyah Elementary School on 36th Street. Mrs. McBrayer was his kindergarten teacher. Mrs. Endicott was his first grade teacher. This is when Gene had the first difficulty with his name, Jean.

> The first day of school Mrs. Endicott asked if any one could write their name. I raised my little hand because Mom had taught me to write J-e-a-n. Mrs. Endicott asked me to go to the blackboard and write my name. I very exactingly traced the letters J-e-a-n with chalk on the blackboard. Mrs. Endicott was skeptical but accepted my explanation that it was my name.
>
> It wasn't long though before the kids on the playground were teasing me about my sissy name and sent me crying more than once to Mrs. Endicott. She taught me to spell my name G-e-n-e. I went by Gene the next eight years. I began to use Don in the ninth grade at Taft Junior High School.

The Summer of 1935 Will Rogers and Wiley Post started on an around the world flight in a new experimental airplane–not the famous Winnie Mae Wiley Post flew to set high altitude and speed records. They crashed on takeoff near Point Barrow, Alaska, shortly after a refueling stop.

> I remember they brought Will Rogers and Wiley Post back to Oklahoma for burial. They lay in state in the rotunda of the Oklahoma State Capitol Building.
>
> I remember standing in our front yard looking toward the capitol. We watched as dozens of airplanes flew in a large circle passing over the capitol. They dropped huge bouquets of flowers as they passed over the capitol building.

Bill and Pauline had a 1928 Chevrolet sedan. On a November evening after dark Pauline was returning home with all five kids in the car. They were northbound on May Avenue south of 10th Street.

> When Mom approached the unprotected grade crossing for the Rock Island Railroad she slowed to look for oncoming trains. A car driven by an employee of Baash-Ross Tool Company suddenly crashed into the left rear of the Chevy and knocked it over an embankment.
>
> I was in the left rear seat. The impact knocked me over the back of the front seat and onto the floorboard. I had no idea what was happening. I was panic stricken.
>
> The car rolled over one and a half times. It lodged on a large tree stump else it would have rolled into water. Fortunately none of us kids were seriously hurt. Mom's back was hurt which caused her a lot of pain later in life.

After the accident Bill bought a 1929 four-door Windsor. It had wood spoke wheels and a flat-head straight-eight engine. It had hydraulic brakes with the master cylinder on the firewall under the hood, battery under the hood, and electric windshield wipers. All were ahead of their time innovations. It had a separate trunk attached to the back. It was a 'running jessie.'

In the summer of 1936 Bill, Pauline and the family with Pauline's father, Dill Roller, went on vacation to Ava, Missouri, and Hardy, Arkansas. They got in the Windsor and left for Ava where Dill had relatives he had not seen for a long time.

> We were traveling on U.S. Highway 62 in northern Arkansas. It was a gravel road in those days. We were 'ginning' right along in the Windsor when a man in a truck overtook us. He frantically waved at us to stop. He told us our trunk lid on the back was open and we were scattering clothing all along the road the last several miles. We thanked him and spent the next few hours back tracking about ten miles to gather up the clothes from alongside the road.
>
> We went to Ava for a few days and stayed with grandpa's relatives. I remember Mom visited an old Roller Family cemetery and someone made a photo of her with her father in the cemetery. I remember Mom made a photo of us kids with great great aunt Eve (Roller) Bunyard. She was ninety years old. I have the photo.
>
> We left Grandpa Roller at Ava and went on to Hardy to visit Grandma and Grandpa Davidson. Enroute we stopped at Yellville for dinner (noon day meal) at a local cafe. I left a ten-cent tip for the waitress. My parents berated me for wasting my money. I thought. "But it was my money which I had earned. Why did it matter so?"
>
> When we reached Hardy we drove several miles over a very rough country road to a high bluff overlooking South Fork River. We parked the car at the top of the bluff and walked down. It was steep and very rocky. When we reached the edge of the river at Cow Ford Grandma was at the other side. She heard the car and came down to the river to greet us.
>
> My brothers and I took off our shoes, rolled up our pant legs, and waded to the other side. It was great fun for kids–not so much for grown-ups.

At the height of the Great Depression in 1936 Bill lost his job at the Oklahoma Railway Company. He was caught up in Roosevelt's National Recovery Act (the NRA blue eagle) which the Supreme

Court declared illegal two years later. This was catastrophic for a man with a wife and five growing kids. With so many people out of work the prospect of a new job was practically nil. Bill was unable to make the mortgage payments and the mortgage company foreclosed.

Bill used some of the settlement money from Baash-Ross to buy a smaller older house at 3608 NW 13th Street. It had a living room, dining room, one bedroom, and kitchen. It had an outdoor toilet and a detached one-car garage.

Bill moved Old Bossy and made a lean-to shed for her at the back of the garage. He used scrap lumber. It was a daily chore for William and Bobby Joe to milk her and then lead her two blocks east to the creek between Grand Boulevard and the railroad tracks. There they picked a spot with grass and staked her with a long rope. After school they brought her back to the shed and milked her.

Gene was in the second grade when they moved. He transferred to Linwood Elementary School on 16th Street. Mrs. Kendell was his teacher. She was a kind grandmotherly woman. For whatever reason she took it on herself to spend extra time helping Gene learn to read. Did she detect a talent, or did she feel sorry for this little kid that couldn't read? Gene stayed after school every afternoon usually for an hour with Mrs. Kendell. She sat next to him as he read aloud to her. She had a shelf full of primer books.

Mrs. Givens was the librarian. She had an abundance of three dimensional stereographs and several stereoscopes which the kids loved to look through. She had been to Europe and many of them were from her travels. Miss Tally was the gym teacher.

Thirteenth Street was a dirt street when Bill and Pauline first moved there. It turned into a muddy mess when it rained.

> One summer day when it rained, my brothers and I made a dirt dam in the street in front of our house. We were having a

great time playing around that muddy water hole with some of the neighborhood kids, including Shorty Ridgeway.

Mr. Bannon lived across the street. He was an old man but was the famous Kid Bannon boxer in his youth. He didn't like Shorty. He called me over and gave me a nickel to push him into the muddy water. I earned the nickel, but Shorty never liked me after that.

The Joe Yarbrough family lived next door east. Joe and his wife were older than Bill and Pauline. Their son was in college at Oklahoma A&M studying aeronautical engineering. He was building a two-seater biplane in Joe's garage. Gene had great fun playing in the fuselage and pretending he was flying.

Joe Louis and Max Schmelling first met in a boxing match in 1935. Schmelling won by a knockout in the twelfth round.

Dad had a dollar bet with Joe Yarbrough. We listened to the fight on the old RCA radio we had. I don't remember how Dad bet, but he won. I remember he ran off the front porch, dashed across the driveway, jumped a three-foot high picket fence, ran onto Joe's front porch pounding on the front door to collect his dollar.

The return match was in June 1937. I was staying on the farm with Uncle Bryan and Aunt Blanche. Uncle Bryan was a gambler and had some serious money bet on the outcome.

The evening of the match Uncle Bryan came in a little early from the fields to listen to the fight on the battery radio. He had to take care of the mules then hurry to feed the hogs and milk the cows. It was fight time and he wasn't finished. He told me to go to the house and listen to the radio. At the end of each round I was to run back and tell him who won the round. Then run back and listen to the next round. "Okay, Uncle Bryan," and off to the house I ran.

I was back in less than three minutes. I breathlessly shouted, "Joe Louis won, Joe Louis won." Uncle Bryan didn't believe me. In fact he thought I was being a smart aleck kid playing games with him. He shouted at me, "Get back up there and listen to the radio and quit fooling around."

"But, Uncle Bryan. It's over. Joe Louis won." He still didn't believe me and threatened to spank me if I didn't get back to the house and listen to the radio. I began to whimper, "But, Uncle Bryan, it's over. Joe Louis knocked him out in the first round." He finally believed me. I think he had bet on Schmelling.

Uncle Bryan also had an especially good racehorse. Her name was Nell. He took her to local races and she won most of the time. In fact she won convincingly at the Anadarko Indian Exposition one year with Floyd Brookshere up.

The next year Uncle Bryan took me with them when he entered Nell in the race at the Anadarko Indian Exposition. Floyd was again the jockey. The only thing is Floyd got to drinking liquor big time with some of the others. When race time came he was skunk drunk. Uncle Bryan was angry with him but had no other choice than to boost him up.

In those days at country horse races they did not have starting gates. They drew a line in the dirt. A starter dropped a red flag when all the jockeys got their mounts to the line at the same time. A split second before the starter dropped the flag Floyd turned Nell around to get a better position at the starting line. The other horses were off and Nell was facing the wrong way. By the time Floyd got her headed the right way the other horses had a thirty-yard start. Floyd was barely able to stay on Nell. He flogged her for all he was worth, but she finished a dismal last. It was not pretty. Uncle Bryan was furious. I actually feared for Floyd's life.

The Roosevelt administration implemented the Work Projects Administration (WPA), a make work program to provide jobs. One of the many projects was to put in a sewer line down the alley for the houses on NW 13th Street. Before that we had outdoor toilet houses.

Bill used the rest of the settlement money from Baash-Ross to hire a neighbor carpenter, Mr. Alred, to convert the bedroom to a bathroom and closet, add two bedrooms and a closet to the back.

The family now had more sleeping room, hot and cold running water, and indoor plumbing.

After an attempt at selling life insurance and several other ill-fated jobs Bill finally landed a job as a milk route deliveryman with Meadow Gold Dairy. Pauline's uncle, Claud Roller, worked at the company barn. He cared for the horses, harnessed, and hitched them to the milk wagons. Bill loaded his wagon with bottles of milk, cream, chocolate milk and orange juice as well as cartons of butter and eggs. He iced it all down before he left to deliver his route.

Bill's horse was named Sonny. He was an old retired circus horse. Bill's route started at Indiana Street and extended west on 19th Street to Portland Avenue. Then back east on 18th Street to Indiana Street. A total distance of a little over four miles. He also serviced 17th and 16th Streets from Portland Avenue to Grand Boulevard, a distance of about a mile. Sonny knew the route so well he didn't even have to be reined. Bill could stop, deliver several houses, and then whistle. Sonny would come to him.

> I sometimes walked the few blocks to 16th and Portland and waited for Dad to come by with the horse drawn milk wagon. He serviced a little Mom 'n Pop grocery on the southeast corner.
>
> Though money was in short supply Dad almost always managed to find a nickel for me to have a small bottle (no cartons in those days) of chocolate milk. He let me ride in the wagon two or three blocks. Then I had to get off and walk home.

Times were not easy. Bill and Pauline had difficulties meeting their financial obligations. They decided to move to the country where they could better keep a cow, plant a garden, and raise chickens. They rented the house at 3608 NW 13th and moved to the Johnson Place on Highway 74 (Western Street) south of Oklahoma City and northwest of Moore.

The house was a small two room wood frame house located on forty acres with a small barn. It was heated with a pot-bellied stove. It did not have running water or indoor plumbing. Household water was hauled from town or carried from a well at the cemetery caretaker's house nearby. Pauline cooked on a three-burner kerosene stove. Gene had a very unpleasnt experience while they lived on the Johnson Place.

> My older brothers and I were at a neighbor's house just south of us. They had a problem with a skunk that had been getting into their chicken house. The neighbor's teenage boy earlier saw the skunk go under the chicken house. He and my two older brothers were trying to make the skunk run out so he could shoot it with a .22 caliber rifle.
>
> They stationed me on the other side of the chicken house to watch and see if the skunk came out. I stood back what I thought was a safe distance of about fifty feet. I had a sizable stick in hand watching for the skunk.
>
> All of sudden here came the skunk. Right at me. I shouted to the others. They raced around to my side to see the skunk running toward me. They shouted, "Hit it! Hit it!"
>
> The skunk apparently didn't see me as I stood there frozen. It came closer and closer. It was only about ten feet from me.
>
> "Hit it! Hit it!"
>
> Dumb me! I drew back my stick to whack it when it came close enough. My movement caused the skunk to see me as a danger. In a heart beat he came up on his front legs, aimed his tail at me, and let go.
>
> Wow! Did I ever get it–all over me. I stunk like a skunk. It was sickening. I heaved my guts up. No one wanted close to me. I went to the water trough and jumped in. Still I stunk. I rolled in the mud. Still I stunk. I went home. Mom made me go to the barn. She brought me some fresh clothes. I still stunk.
>
> I stayed at the barn for over a week. Mom brought food, lye soap and hot water. Several weeks passed before I was completely rid of the smell.

Gene, his brothers and sister attended the Moore Consolidated School in Moore, Oklahoma. Gene was in the third grade. His teacher was Miss Platt. They rode a school bus. The driver was Tiny Spencer, a local six feet four inches tall farmer. He used his farm truck for the bus. During school he removed the truck bed and set on his home made bus body. It had side seats and a straddle seat down the middle for the little boys to sit on.

It was in the third grade that Gene first met some classmates that became life long friends. Jack Dreessen, a long time prominent citizen of Moore and former bank president who now lives in Port Aransas, Texas. Richard Snook, a retired minister, that lives in Moore. Wilma (Snook) Thomas, retired from federal government service, lives near Sulphur, Oklahoma. Oleta (Jury) Tolen, retired from Tinker Air Force Base, and lives at Moore. Arbrey Lee Davis was a neighborhood boy and Gene's classmate. He drowned in a nearby farm pond.[1]

About this same time Gene had an accident that caused him great pain. He fell and totally dislocated his left elbow separating the larger upper bone from both the lower smaller bones.

Mr. Johnson, the landlord, hauled a lot of reclaimed lumber and stacked it west of the house. He used it to build a larger barn. Gene's Dad and his older brothers, William and Bobby Joe, helped with the construction in return for rent.

There were several stacks of lumber and piles of wood scraps scattered around. Some of the scrap was laths. These are pieces of wood 3/16 inches thick by 1-3/8 inches wide and four feet long used to hold plaster to the wall. They made excellent play swords.

> A neighbor friend, Don Stevenson, and I cut short cross pieces and nailed them to two laths. We were playing sword fighting. In the style of the renowned movie swordsman, Errol Flynn, I leaped onto a stack of lumber about two feet high. My

---

1 (This tragic accident is described in the CHAPTER on Gene's father.)

friend charged with his sword and I danced backwards–too far.

I fell backwards off the stack. I had my 'sword' in my right hand. I threw my left hand back to catch myself as I fell. I landed full force on my extended left arm snapping the elbow out of joint. My left elbow was completely dislocated. The pain was excruciating.

I was stunned. I looked at my left arm. I can still see it clearly. There was a huge bulge just below my shoulder and a gap underneath. I was in a panic. All I could think was my arm would have to be cut off. Dad drove me to the hospital. The doctor gave me a general anesthesia to set my arm.

Years later I have thought I had an 'out of body' experience during the time I was unconscious. I still vividly remember floating above looking down at myself on the operating table with the doctor, nurse, and Dad gathered around. I had a serene sense of ease and well being. Then I heard the doctor say with great urgency, "Oxygen. Give him more oxygen! More oxygen!" I came around feeling very dizzy and sick. I vomited.

I carried my arm in a sling about six weeks. It swelled to twice its normal size. It was very sore to the slightest touch.

The Gambles lived on the farm west of the Johnson Place. The Lagali family lived on the farm west of the Gambles. Vincent Lagali and Gene were friends though Vincent was a little older.

Vincent had a bicycle and he let me ride it. He bought a small crystal radio set and put it together. We took turns wearing the ear phones to listen to the radio. We palled around and did all the crazy things young boys do.

One day we ran across a rather large snake with a bulge in its middle. After we killed the snake we turned it over to see what the bulge was. It was a golf ball. It had worn a hole all the way through its belly. It must have thought the golf ball was an egg and swallowed it. That snake must have had a terrible bellyache.

The Gambles were neighbors. They had two sons, Arthur and George. Both were in high school. For some reason George, the youngest, took a liking to me.

On an April Fool's Day George and I sat on their back porch reading the Farmer's Almanac. It was a warm sunny day without a cloud in the sky. The almanac predicted snow for Oklahoma that week. We laughed and thought it must be an April Fool's joke. Four days later we had a ten- inch snowfall.

After we lived on the Johnson Place a few months Dad bought a mare horse. Her name was Ribbon. She was used to pull a small plow to till the soil for a garden and to cultivate a small patch of cotton and feed. We also rode her.

After two years on the Johnson Place Gene's Family moved two miles south to the Turk Place. It was a larger house with a large front porch and a back porch. It had a kitchen with pantry, dining room, living room, and a bedroom downstairs. It had two small bedrooms upstairs. It did not have indoor plumbing. However, it did have a well and a windmill. It had a reasonably good barn.

This house was a vast improvement over the house on the Johnson Place. It was much larger. We no longer had to hand carry water from a neighbor's well for drinking and household use. We had more room for the livestock, chickens, and turkeys. We also had space for a garden.

A wealthy doctor from Oklahoma City owned the farm across the road. Kelsey Davis was the caretaker. His daughter, Wanda, was in my class at Moore. The doctor was into dog racing. He had Greyhounds. A Sunday afternoon of sport was for him and some of his friends to bring their Greyhounds to the farm and race them. I'm certain they probably gambled on the outcomes.

They needed jackrabbits for the dogs to chase. The doctor said he would give us twenty-five cents for every live jackrabbit we could bring to him in a 'tow sack.' Dad showed my brothers and me how to make a box trap to snare live rabbits. We had several traps set around the farm. We caught only a few rabbits. My older brothers got the money.

While they lived on the Turk Place Gene, his mother and siblings had a traumatic experience from a tornado.[1]

Gene was in Mrs. Varndell's fourth grade class. It was there he first met Buford Young, his lifelong good friend. Mrs. Varndell was a very good no nonsense teacher. She emphasized reading, writing, and arithmetic. She encouraged her students to read and read well. She also made sure we learned to spell. Buford and Gene became very close friends.

> Buford's parents for whatever reason decided to hold him over in the fourth grade. His birthday is in October and he started school early, thus he was one of the younger kids in his class. My birthday is in December. I started a year behind Buford.
>
> When I started the fourth grade Mrs. Varndal already knew Buford was having a trouble with his reading. I was a good reader. I was fortunate to have a teacher in the second grade that took great pains to teach me to read well. My Grandmother Roller was an avid reader. She often read to me and helped me learn to be a good reader.
>
> One of the teaching techniques of the day was to pair up the better readers with the students who were having trouble with reading. Thus, by fate, Mrs. Varndal paired Buford and I together. Thus began a long and enduring friendship.
>
> Buford was my very best childhood friend. We were pals. We were buddies. We were together as often as we could be–in the classroom, on the schoolyard, or roaming the back dirt roads, creeks, and hillsides.
>
> When our playmates chose sides to play a game or sport on the playground, it was unthinkable among our peers that we would not be chosen to play on the same team. It was only when we had to go home for the night that we were apart. Even then I slept over at Buford's house as often as I could.
>
> Buford and I were almost opposites of one another. He was a lefty. I was right-handed. He was an only child. I was the third kid in a family of five children. I had three brothers,

1 (This is described in the CHAPTER on Gene's father.)

two older. Buford had none. Buford was a nice looking usually well groomed kid. I was a tow headed unkempt sort of kid. He was a tall, slender well portioned kid. I was a scraggly runt of a kid. Buford had that serene self-assurance that most only children have. I had a sense of fiery insecurity that drove me to take risks and do and say things that often got me in trouble. Buford seldom got into trouble. In other words, Buford was a nice kid. I was a brat for the most part. Unlike a lot of only children, Buford was not selfish. He was sharing. I tended to keep and hide what was mine for fear someone would take it away from me.

Buford had a bicycle. I had a horse. Buford wished he had a horse. I wished I had a bicycle. So, it was not an uncommon sight to see Buford on my horse, and me on Buford's bicycle going down some country road happy as two larks.

Buford and I lived at opposite sides of Moore. We were about as far apart as we could live and still be in the same school district. Buford lived about three miles northeast of Moore in a small urban like community of oil field houses provided by the oil company that employed Mr. Young. My family lived about three miles southwest of Moore on a rent farm in an old run down house. My Dad worked at a laboring job in Oklahoma City.

Times were tough for us. My Dad left home about 4:00 a.m. and drove to Oklahoma City to work. Sometimes he got home in the afternoon in time to help work the farm. Most times he didn't. He depended mostly on Mom, my older brothers and me to care for the animals and work the farm. Dad didn't always bring home a full paycheck. There was a lot of ranting and raving in our household. My parents had their problems with a lot of fussing, arguing and hard feelings. I lived in an environment best described as chaotic and combative with fierce competition.

I was at constant odds with my two older brothers, especially Bobby Joe. He delighted in subjecting me to all manner of torment. We fought a lot. Since he and William were older and bigger I was always on the short end of things. I took a lot of mental and physical abuse, and at every opportunity I schemed covert ways to get even.

But, when I was around Buford, especially when we were together alone, I didn't feel that I had to prove anything to him or his parents. They accepted me for what I was with no criticisms and treated me in a friendly and congenial manner. I had more of a tendency to emulate Buford's behavioral mannerisms when I was around him and his parents. We played well together always sharing with each other. I can't remember that Buford and I ever spoke a cross word with each other, or that his parents ever spoke a cross word to me.

I loved to stay over with Buford. He had a BB gun and we would go along the creek south of their house and shoot at all manner of things. Best of all Mrs. Young always fixed a real nice lunch for us to pack to school the next day.

Our school didn't have a cafeteria. We didn't even have a lunchroom. We sat at our desks and ate our lunches. My lunches from home usually consisted of a biscuit with a piece of fatback meat or something equally unsavory. The lunches from Mrs. Young's kitchen were something to behold. We always had a nice sandwich on white bread, a piece of fruit, usually an apple, and a sweet treat, like a cookie or a small piece of cake. I know there were other times when she packed a little something extra in Buford's lunches so he could share with me at school.

I was the brother Buford never had. Buford was the brother I wished I had. Buford lived a quiet peaceful home life. I lived an existence of chaos at our house. My parents had all kinds of difficulties–financial, social and emotional. Poverty, ranting and raving with occasional fighting prevailed in our household. My parents argued a lot, and sometimes came to blows. William and Bobby Joe fought a lot, and frequently took their frustrations out on me in a physical way.

Bobby Joe was not only older than me but was a big ox of a kid, and a bully. He teased and taunted me unmercifully. My parents either didn't know or didn't care, but more likely were too engrossed with their own problematic relationship and were unable to deal effectively with the situation.

Buford's dad had a good job for the times. They lived in a modest, but very nice house. As often as I was in their household I can't remember a cross word ever between Buford's parents. I remember only one time Mr. Young kind of lost his cool. It was at a cow that walked in front of his new 1939 Plymouth when we were traveling about sixty miles per hour on a highway in New Mexico.

I stayed over at Buford's house as often as our parents permitted. I can recall Buford staying over at our house only one time. I was embarrassed to have him stay over with me and my family. But my Grandmother Roller's house was another thing. Buford and I would spend two or three weeks each summer at Grandma's house. Grandpa was a farmer. They lived in the country about sixty miles from where we lived. Grandpa had mules, horses, cows and pigs. Grandma had chickens and turkeys. They lived way in the country on Panther Creek near The Table Hills .

Grandma was kind and loving. Grandpa was a hard working no nonsense guy. But he had lots of patience with Buford and me. He let us drive the teams of mules. He saddled the horses for each of us to ride. He let us work with a broomcorn thrashing crew for two days and paid us as though we were regular hands. I don't remember the exact amount, but it was something like about thirty cents an hour. It was after all the 1930's. It amounted to about three dollars apiece. We thought we had a lot of money.

The broomcorn seed flew everywhere and would get down the inside of our shirts and caused a stinging and itching sensation. At the end of the day we went to the creek, stripped off and swam in the water to soothe the stinging. Buford commented to me in our much later adult years that he still remembered how bad the broomcorn seed stung and made us itch.

We roamed the creeks catching crawfish. We swung on the grapevines and did all manner of things that ten, eleven, twelve year old boys do. We rode the horses over and around the mountain area and went exploring among the huge rocks and cliffs. We stopped at a neighbor's house one day. They had killed several large rattlesnakes that they laid out in front of the house. Buford and I examined them very cautiously, even though they were dead. It was a great time for two young boys.

One day Buford's parents came to visit Mom and Dad. They asked if it would be okay for me to accompany them on their vacation trip that summer. My folks agreed. I was elated. Mr. Young had recently purchased a new 1939 Plymouth. It was green as I recall. I had been out of state only a few times when we went to Arkansas to visit Dad's parents.

Buford and I had a great time on vacation. It was the most memorable highlight of my childhood. We traveled across Western Oklahoma, through the Texas Panhandle and into New Mexico. We stopped at several roadside curio shops common in New Mexico. One had a donkey that drank soda pop from a bottle. Buford and I must have given that donkey a belly ache from drinking so much soda pop. Mrs. Young took a photo of Buford and me feeding that old donkey soda pop.

We went to White City and Carlsbad Caverns. We arrived late in the afternoon. A little after sunset we went to the entrance of the cave and watched the bats swarm out to go foraging for nighttime insects.

The next day we went through the caverns. It was a magnificent sight to behold for a couple of wide-eyed kids. We did a lot of walking. At the end of the tour we had the choice to either ride an elevator 750 feet to the surface, or take an hour to walk out. Of course, Buford and I wanted to walk out. Mrs. Young rode the elevator. Mr. Young probably wished that Buford and I would ride the elevator, too, but he was very accommodating and walked out with us. The entrance to the caverns faces west and long before we got to the entrance we could see this long brilliant shaft of sunlight streaming into the darkness of the cavern.

The next day we drove to El Paso. We walked across the bridge to Ciudad Juarez. It was a big thing for Buford and me when we crossed over into Mexico. We could tell everyone at school we had been out of the United States.

We mostly just went sightseeing. We shopped in a few of the shops and bought trinket souvenirs. Buford and I wrote on picture post cards and mailed them to the United States to friends and family. Mrs. Young enjoyed the shopping and the low prices. I can't remember anything specific she bought, but we did carry some packages across the bridge with us when we came back into the United States.

We drove all the way across New Mexico from south to north. It was a long drive, but Buford and I found ways, with Mrs. Young's help, to entertain ourselves.

We crossed Raton Pass into Colorado and went to the Royal Gorge to see the world's highest swinging bridge. Buford and I walked across the bridge. Mrs. Young took a photo of us standing in the middle of the bridge.

Then we went to Colorado Springs where Mrs. Young had relatives. We stayed with them for several days. The lady's husband had died since we left Oklahoma. The funeral was the day before we arrived in Colorado Springs. It was a sad time, but everyone was intent on making sure we were made to feel welcome and at home.

We went to Manitou Springs. Buford and I tasted the effervescence of the mineral spring water and thought it tasted like soda pop. We visited an amusement park where Buford and I drove little midget gasoline powered cars on a small track.

We went to Cripple Creek and saw one of the silver ore trains hauling the ore to the smelter. We went to the Garden of the Gods and Buford and I tried to push over The Balanced Rock.

We drove to the top of Pike's Peak. It was a gravel road most of the way. When we got to the top Buford and I jumped out like two wild goats running around looking at this and that. Then, all of a sudden we pooped out and couldn't hardly get our breath. The high altitude lack of oxygen did a number on both of us and we got kind of sick. That really slowed us down. I remember how cautiously Mr. Young drove down. The road was twisting and very steep and narrow in many places.

From Colorado Springs we went to visit Mrs. Young's relatives in Western Kansas. I remember there was a boy about our age whom we played with. They lived in a white frame oil company house near a gas compressor station. I remember going into a nearby large building which had a very large engine that drove the compressors.

From there we went further east into Kansas and spent part of two days and one night visiting a relative. They lived in a small house only about fifty feet from the Santa Fe Railroad dual track mainline from Chicago to California. The steam locomotives and occasional diesels roared by almost every half-hour day and night. Buford and I sat near the tracks and waved at the train crewmen when they went by. Once in awhile one would blow the whistle just for us and that thrilled us.

From there we went to a farm somewhere near Emporia, Kansas. It was way out in the countryside. I seem to remember it was Mrs. Young's brother and his family. They also had a boy about our age whom we played with. An elderly woman also lived with them. I think she was Mrs. Young's mother, though I'm not sure. I remember she really scolded me one day. It had rained and the weather cleared off. Buford, the other kid, and I went bare foot wading in the water. We caught crawfish and generally just played in the mud.

We came to the house about supper time all muddy. Buford and the other kid were at the water hose cleaning up. I saw an earthen crock in the yard with about two gallons of water in it. I was standing in it washing my feet when the elderly lady saw me. She was very upset with me. She kept saying the water was for the car which didn't make sense to me. It kind of embarrassed me, and later it was mentioned at the supper table. Buford's uncle said not to worry. It was rainwater he used for battery water in the car.

We went to Cottonwood Falls. Buford and I played along the banks of the Cottonwood River. Someone had a small .22 rifle. We stood at the railing on an old bridge and took turns plunk shooting at turtles in the water below.

From there it was home to Oklahoma and return to my family. Of course, everyone was interested in hearing all about the trip and my adventures. I told all about it. I reveled in my little moment of notoriety within the family group. But all too soon life at home returned to normal.

Buford and I got to tell all the kids in our class at school that fall all about our trip and our adventures. It was great fun and an exciting time for two young boys. That vacation trip with Buford and his folks was the highlight of my childhood.

> I still remember it with fond memories. Our friendship was nothing but the best and greatest right through grade school and into the eighth grade.

Gene's home life was such that he often pursued other diversions to establish himself as a person and not a down trodden kid at the whims of his older brothers. This sometimes got him into trouble. One of these diversions was he played marbles–for keeps.

> I made it a point to be good at marbles. I spent hours by myself shooting and shooting in a ring drawn in the dirt. I spent some of my meager money for good marbles and spent a lot of time selecting some really good taws.
>
> I played marbles with the other boys at school. At first I cautiously entered into games of 'keepsies.' I soon saw that I was much better than my competition and though it was frowned on by the school administration I frequently played for 'keeps.' I accumulated quite an inventory of good marbles that I kept in a large jar at home. I never played 'keeps' with Buford.
>
> One day Bobby Dunlap got in a game with Danny McCroy and I. Danny and I cleaned Bobby out of all his marbles. That wasn't the end of it. He went crying to the teacher. Danny and I were sent to the principal's office. We had to give back Bobby's marbles. The principal confiscated ours. We were strongly rebuked and forbidden to ever again play marbles of any kind on the school grounds.
>
> Mom kept my jar of marbles for years and years. I wish I knew whatever happened to them. From time to time when going through some of Mom's things I found a few marbles here and there. To this day I can identify my marbles on sight.

Gene sought other means of solace. He often secluded himself in out of the way places and secretively under took other satisfying activities.

> I wanted a camera. There was no way I could come up with the money to buy one much less buy the film and pay for the

processing. So, I undertook to make my own camera. I used two cigar boxes and tape to make a light tight box. I made a swinging lid at the back for a place to hold film. I found a magnifying glass about the size of a half-dollar.

I went into the barn loft where it was semi dark and spent hours trying to focus an outside image on the back inside of the box (focal plane) to determine how long (focal length) to make the box. I finally settled on a distance of about eight inches. I used my oldest brother's pocketknife to cut a hole in the box end and wedged the magnifying glass (lens) into the hole for a tight fit. I cut a piece of cardboard from the back of a tablet. I cut a slit in the top of the box and behind the magnifying glass. I attached a clothes pin to the cardboard (shutter) so I could pull it up to let light in through the magnifying glass and push it down to shut light out. I was never able to buy film to try and see if my contraption (camera) actually would make a photograph.

One of the first things I bought after I finished my army basic training was a 35mm Argus C3 camera. I later developed a keen interest in photography. After I was an adult I made a box pinhole camera and actually made some photographs with it–just to prove I could.

Another thing I did was play phonograph records. Not quite the way you may think. When Uncle Jim and Aunt Mary moved from Oklahoma City to Kansas City they gave us an old used hand cranked phonograph player and some seventy-eight rpm records. The only problem was the spring mechanism was broken. I soon learned to hand turn the records at exactly seventy-eight rpm's. I played the records over and over. I remember some of the lyrics and tunes to this day.

Some of the titles were: The New River Train, Hand Me Down My Walking Cane, Barnacle Bill the Sailor and Jailhouse Blues. The Big Rock Candy Mountains was a popular song during the Great Depression. It was a song I knew and sang as a youngster. It is the opening theme song for the movie, "O Brother, Where Art Thou" with George Clooney. The lyrics are:

One evening as the sun went down,
And the jungle fire was burning,
Down the track came a hobo hiking,
And he said, "Boys, I'm not turning.
I'm headed for a land that's far away,
Beside the Crystal Fountains,
So, come with me, we'll go and see
The Big Rock Candy Mountains.

In the Big Rock Candy Mountains
There's a land that's fair and bright.
Where the handouts grow on bushes,
And you sleep out every night.
Where the boxcars all are empty
And the sun shines every day
On the birds and the bees
And on the cigarette trees.
The lemonade springs
Where the bluebird sings
In the Big Rock Candy Mountains.

In the Big Rock Candy Mountains
All the cops have wooden legs,
And the bulldogs all have rubber teeth
And the hens lay soft-boiled eggs.
The farmers' trees are full of fruit
And the barns are full of hay.

Oh, I'm gonna go
Where the rain and sleet don't fall
And the wind don't blow
And it do not snow
In the Big Rock Candy Mountains.

In the Big Rock Candy Mountains
You never change your socks,
And little streams of alcohol
Come trickling down the rocks.
The brakemen have to tip their hats

And the railroad bulls are blind.
There's a lake of stew
And of whiskey, too.
You can paddle all around 'em
In a big canoe
In the Big Rock Candy Mountains.

In the Big Rock Candy Mountains
The jails are made of tin
And you can walk right out again
As soon as you are in.
There ain't no shorthandle shovels,
No axes, saws, or picks.
I'm a going to stay
Where you sleep all day,
Where they hung the jerk
That invented work.

I'll see you all
This comin' fall
In the Big Rock Candy Mountains

One of the fun things we did during the school lunch hour was go to the train depot two blocks away. We watched the post master hang the outgoing mail pouch on the 'snare frame.' Then we waited to watch the twelve fifty-five northbound Santa Fe Flyer steam locomotive roar by as a mail pouch was tossed onto the depot platform and the metal arm on the mail car snatched the mail pouch on the fly. Then we ran like the dickens to be in class when the tardy bell rang.

One night I went into the downstairs bedroom at the Sullivan Place to look for something. I had a match to light a lamp in the room. In the dark I struck down the wall to light the match. I shrieked out in pain. Mother had stuck a needle in the wall next to her treadle sewing machine. That was the precise place where I struck down with the match. It drove the needle into the end of my index finger on my right hand and into the bone. It snapped off. It was painful.

> Dad took me to Dr. Reichert in Moore. He had a fluoroscope device. He knew how painful it was. He tried to be very delicate and careful, but every time he touched the broken needle with the probe I jerked and let out a yell. After a while Dad had all of it his patience could stand. He held me tight as he could and told the doctor to get it out of there. I yelled but it came out. To this day the end of that finger is sensitive. I shudder every time I think about it.
>
> In the summer months the open space between the First National Bank building and the drugstore was used as an outdoor movie theater. A man brought a 16mm projector and after dark showed movies on the back side of the Platt Lumber Company building which was painted white. It cost a nickel to see the movie. Years later my good friend, Jack Dreessen, was president of the First National Bank of Moore.

Miss Womack was Gene's sixth-grade teacher. He liked her very much. She was a great teacher. She encouraged reading and free-thinking. She was a stickler for reading, writing, arithmetic and speaking the English language. Her students spent hours learning to diagram sentences.

> She had forty-four students. One of her teaching techniques was in some small way to reward the entire class when we achieved certain levels of performance. This encouraged the better students to help the slower students to bring them up to par or better.
>
> Several times when the class did exceptionally well she rewarded us by taking us to a matinee movie. She would arrange for one of the school bus drivers to drive us to the Redskin Theater in south Oklahoma City, and have us back in time to catch our buses home.
>
> It was one of these outings that we saw "Destry Rides Again" with James Stewart and Marlene Dietrich. I think she may have had some kind of connection at the Redskin Theater to get us in free or at a greatly reduced group price.

Gene's parents were friends with Dwight and Ruth Davis. They met when Bill and Pauline were students at Oklahoma Central State Teachers College at Edmond, Oklahoma. Dwight became an English professor at the college. Dwight and Ruth had two children. The oldest was a girl about Gene's age and the other was a boy. Bill and Pauline sometimes would take the family to Edmond to visit.

> When Dad and Mom were visiting Dwight and Ruth the other kids were outside playing. I liked to hang around and listen to the adults talk, especially Dwight because he seemed to be so well informed about so many things.
>
> Once Dwight was expounding about the lack of beneficial quality of soldiers. He said only men with little or no ambition became soldiers. He said, "In fact, soldier is the only noun in the English language that is also used as a verb." That struck me as peculiar, because since we lived on a farm I knew that the noun 'farm' was also used as a verb. The noun 'milk' was used as a verb as 'milk' a cow. I further reasoned that I used a hoe to hoe cotton. I quietly wondered why an English professor would make such a statement.
>
> As I became a little older I began to challenge people of authority, i.e. my parents, teachers, preachers, etc., when they made unequivocal incredulous statements beyond the realm of factual reasonableness. This often got me into serious trouble.

Gene's family were members and attended the First Methodist Church in Moore. The Reverend W.T. Pugh was the pastor. He had a fabulous cursive script signature that Gene greatly admired.

The family also attended the occasional revival meetings conducted by various traveling evangelists. Gene had a life defining moment with one such evangelist.

> He was an old man with a full flowing head of gray hair. He had a booming voice that spoke with the authority of God. He was a "hell fire and brimstone" preacher.
>
> It was the last night of the revival. He demanded everyone come forward to re-dedicate their lives to Jesus else their

souls would be forever committed to the fiery furnaces of hell. Everyone, including all my family, except me, arose from the pews and went forward. As he pleadingly prayed for the salvation of their souls he suddenly noticed this lone little kid sitting in a pew of an otherwise totally empty sanctuary.

He prayed to the Lord to take my hand and lead me forward. I didn't budge. Still praying he walked down from the pulpit. He walked down the aisle praying and stopped at the pew where I sat. I didn't budge. He prayed for the Lord to take his hand and place it on my hand to lead me to my salvation, else "...this child of God will burn forever in the bowels of hell."

I thought, "How do you know I will burn in hell?" He kept praying as he swiftly grabbed me by the arm. I thought, "God didn't make you grab my arm, you made you grab my arm," as he jerked me to my feet to drag me to my "salvation." I twisted loose, ran down the aisle and out the back door. I walked home.

I caught 'hell' when my parents got home. I never returned, not without retribution, to church until well after I was an adult.

It's not that I'm a non-believer. I'm probably a stronger believer than most of the people who beat it to church every time the doors are open. I think 'church' is a man-made social institution with all the frailties thereof.

I believe with all my heart there is a Creator of all things–God, if you please. It's all too perfect to just happen. I also believe mortal man hasn't the faintest notion what God's purpose is. If He ever reveals it to us it will probably be so complex we can never understand it, or so simple we can never believe it.

Going to 'church' is not going to expunge me of all my sins. That's between God and me–no one else.

Sunday, December 7, 1941, the 'Day of Infamy.' The United States was attacked at Pearl Harbor by Japan and propelled into World War II. Everyone was asking, "Where's Pearl Harbor?" The next day President Roosevelt addressed a joint session of Congress and war was officially declared against Japan, Germany, and Italy.

Gene's family lived on the Sullivan Place southwest of Moore. They did not have electricity. They did not have a radio. A neighbor family, the Prices, had a battery radio. They also had a son, Willis, who was Gene's age. Gene often visited his friend in the evenings and listened to the radio.

> The Price Family lived a quarter of a mile north of us. They didn't have electricity, but Mr. Price rigged up a wind charger using a car generator. It was connected to a wet cell car battery. When the wind was blowing it charged the battery. They had a radio that connected to the battery.
>
> Willis and I were friends. I often went to his house in the evenings to listen to the radio. We listened to Fibber Magee and Molly, Amos'n Andy, Baby Snooks, Gildersleeve, Mystery Theater, Inner Sanctum, Lux Theater, Bob Hope and Jack Benny.
>
> It was early Sunday evening and we were all listening to the radio. I don't remember the program, but it seems like it was the Lux Theater. An announcer interrupted the program to announce the Japanese had bombed Pearl Harbor, but gave few details. Then the program resumed. We didn't know where Pearl Harbor was.
>
> I went home after the program and told my parents the Japanese bombed Pearl Harbor. They didn't believe me. They thought I was joking around. It was the next day before they knew I wasn't.

In the seventh-grade Gene was installed in the Junior Honor Society and was elected Student Council Representative by his classmates. He had a 'puppy love' infatuation with Eleanor Ann Jones, a nice girl with flaming red hair. Buford Young and Jack Dreessen were his two best friends.

Some of Gene's other classmates at Moore were Wanda Davis, Betty Fox, Stephen Box, Billy Dale Jones, Herman Butler, Margaret Knight, Bobby January, Letha Bruce, Stinson Orr, Geneva Janko, Hubert Tuefel, John Gumm, Danny McCroy, Nita Norton, Lida Belle Burrell, Marilou Sala, Norma Thompson, Billy Teasley,

Oleta Jury, Willis Price, Emma Jean Cunningham, Jane Story and Jerry Foster.

In November when Gene was in the eighth grade his famly moved from the Sullivan Place southwest of Moore to the Cochran Place three miles north of Evening Shade, Arkansas. Buford and Gene were no longer separated by just a few miles; they were separated by over two hundred miles. A wonderful childhood friendship came to an abrupt and sudden end.

> We had a couple of fairly good years financially on the farm at Moore. The country was coming out of the depression. World War II loomed ever larger. Dad took what little he had accumulated and we moved to Arkansas. He entered into a farming arrangement with his father.
>
> A few months after we moved to Arkansas Mr. Young got a promotion and transferred to another part of his company. Buford and his folks moved to Drumright, Oklahoma. Thus, a great childhood friendship came to an abrupt end. I'm not sure Buford nor his folks ever fully understood the significance of the impact they had on my life during those so critically formative years.
>
> I experienced compassion, patience, understanding and tolerance. I learned there was something more than fighting with my brothers and the bitter after feelings. Though I carried my sense of insecurity and need to constantly prove myself well into my adult life, I learned from Buford and his folks how to live and cope with it, and how to make it work for me and not against me.
>
> I served in the Army Paratroopers during my military service and that was partly to prove I was as good as the next person. But, I never felt I had to prove anything to Buford and his folks. They were a refuge of friendly kindness, thoughtfulness, and caring consideration. I shall be forever grateful. Thanks, Buford. You were a great friend. And, thanks Mr. and Mrs. Young. You were great people. I forever love you for it.

Something else that portrays some of Gene's early life is a treatise he started to honor his Aunt Jewel on her eightieth birthday celebration May 4, 1991 after he received a letter from her daughter, Norma Ivey. Much to his dismay he did not finish it until several years after she died. It gives a glimpse into some aspects and events in Gene's early life and his long and loving relationship with his Aunt Jewel. She was his mother's younger sister.

When I first received Norma's letter I thought long and hard trying to come up with something clever and witty that would express something of my affection and love for my Aunt Jewel. The longer I thought the more I became convinced that what I wanted to say was from the heart, and the heart doesn't have to be clever or witty to be expressive.

I decided to write in the first person because she already knew all the things I could possibly have to say. So, I wrote this for other people to read so they will have the pleasure of knowing Aunt Jewel as I knew her.

First, Aunt Jewel was a beautiful lady in every sense of the word. She was loving and caring. She was thoughtful and kind. She was generous and giving. She was fun-loving with a sense of humor. She was one fine cook. What great biscuits she could bake. I always knew I was in for a real treat when I sat down to her breakfast table and a heaping platter of her biscuits.

There were so many things I could relate, I hardly know where to start. When I was about eighteen months old mother and I took a train trip all the way from Oklahoma City to Dallas to visit Aunt Jewel, but I don't remember that trip.

There were the numerous summers I spent with Grandma and Grandpa Roller on Panther Creek and the many, many times I would go up on The Mountain to see Aunt Jewel. She and Uncle Tom lived in a little one-room house with a lean-to on the back that served as the kitchen.

As a kid I remember early one morning when Uncle Tom stood in the front door and shot a wolf southwest of the house about seventy yards away. The wolf jumped when shot and made claw marks on the large sandstone rock he was standing on. Over the years I would look at those claw marks and marvel at the strength of the wolf to have made such scratch marks on the rock.

Years later when I was an adult and the old house was long gone I returned with Uncle Tom and Robert, his son, one day to see if we could find the claw scratch marks in the rock. Time and erosion had long since erased them.

As a kid I also remember that Uncle Tom and Aunt Jewel had a large solid black dog. He was a magnificent animal and very smart. He was a no nonsense dog. His name was Dare, as in "I dare you to mess with me." In fact, I was a little scared of him. He would just sit or lay there and stare at you. He was very protective of Uncle Tom and his family. He didn't take very kindly to strangers. He would mind Uncle Tom and would obey several voice and hand commands.

Years later one day I said to Uncle Tom, "I'm going to say one word and I want you to tell me the first thing that comes to your mind." Uncle Tom said, "Okay." I said, "Dare." Without hesitation he said, "Best dog I ever had."

One of my most memorable visits with Aunt Jewel was the summer Norma was born. I spent most of that summer on The Mountain with her and my cousins, Jimmy and Robert. Norma was a tiny baby only two or three weeks old. Uncle Tom worked somewhere away from home. I'm not sure where.

Mother sent me down to The Mountain to help Aunt Jewel. Uncle Tom had a Model-A Ford coupe. It had rained heavily and the roads from Purcell to Panther Creek and up onto The Mountain were muddy and slick. We spent almost all night slogging and grinding through the mud finally arriving in the wee hours of the morning.

The next two months I fetched water from the well, split and brought in firewood for the cookstove, and helped Aunt Jewel however she needed help. One of my main duties was to entertain Jimmy and Robert to keep them out of her hair while she took care of Norma and did what household chores she was able to do.

One thing I had to do each morning was hustle up to the Gardner house about a quarter of a mile away and let Mrs. Gardner, Uncle Tom's mother, know that Aunt Jewel and Norma were okay. I don't know that she ever knew Mrs. Gardner had admonished me to do so.

I played games with Jimmy and Robert, read to them, and generally palled around with them. I recall one day we went down on the creek east of the house and I taught them to smoke dried grapevine. Our tongues and mouths were sore for several days.

One morning Aunt Jewel didn't feel like getting up and she asked me to fix oatmeal for the boys. I stoked up the fire in the cookstove and soon had a boiling pot of water. I dumped some oatmeal into the boiling water, but the fire was too hot and I didn't stir fast enough. I scorched the oatmeal.

The boys turned their noses up at the prospect of eating my oatmeal. They said, "It doesn't look like mama's." I told them their mama didn't know how to fix oatmeal and I would show them. I heaped sugar on the bowls of oatmeal, poured on a lot of cream, mixed it up and ate some to show them how good it was. I must have been convincing, because they ate it like it was good.

Years later when Jim was a naval aviator officer he, Laquetha and their girls visited my wife, Pat, and I in Huntsville, Alabama. They spent the night with us. The next morning Pat fixed oatmeal for breakfast. Laquetha remarked that she always had to scorch Jim's oatmeal a little because he liked it that way. I broke out in a big laugh. They all thought I was a little "tetched." I then told the story of the scorched oatmeal.

One day I would have beat Jimmy and Robert to within an inch of their life if I could have caught them. I slept outside on the west side of the house on an old iron frame metal spring bed with a few quilts to make a pad. I was gone most of that day down on Panther Creek to Grandma Roller's house (about three miles) to report to her how Aunt Jewel was getting along and to gather some things I needed to bring back.

We didn't have telephones, or electricity for that matter, so communication was to send someone (usually one of the children) to see the other person. While I was gone Jimmy and Robert took the quilts off my bed and dragged them through a sand-burr sticker patch. They then made my bed up very nicely for me.

It was late when I got back and I was tired. I laid down on my bed only to leap up shouting with pain. I had a miserable evening trying to pick all the stickers from the quilts on my bed.

In a few weeks Aunt Jewel was feeling much better and it was getting time for me to return home and get ready to start school that Fall. Uncle Tom took me home in his Model-A Ford.

Gene spent part of the next summer on Panther Creek with his Grandma and Grandpa Roller. He doesn't recall that he was on The Mountain that summer to see his Aunt Jewel, but he probably did because he remembers he worked broomcorn that year in a field just north of the Gardner home place on The Table Top.

Gene spent many summers during his childhood and early teens with his Grandpa and Grandma Roller on Panther Creek. These were some of his happiest days.

Grandma loved to read and listen to soap operas on the battery radio. When Grandpa went to town he usually went by the library and checked out a book or two for her to read. One summer she and I read "Gone with the Wind." She read a page out loud and then I read a page out loud. We would shell peas or snap beans and listen to Ma Perkins.

I had a small set of artist oil paints with a few brushes. She encouraged me to paint. She got some pieces of pebble cardboard for me to paint on. I painted several pictures. She admired them. I wish I still had them. I don't know what happened to them.

Grandma cooked on a huge wood burning Kalamazoo stove with an oven and a water reservoir for heating water. It was amazing. She could stoke the fire, shake that grate, adjust those dampers and maintain the heat at just the proper temperature for whatever she was cooking or baking.

She baked bread every few days. She rolled out the dough, kneaded it, placed it in pans and let it rise. Then she plopped them into the oven. The whole house smelled wonderful with the odor of fresh bread baking.

Sometimes she made doughnuts. You can't believe how good they were. She rolled the dough out with a huge wooden rolling pin. She used a doughnut cutter to deftly cut out the doughnuts flipping each in the air catching it on her other thumb. When she had a half dozen on her thumb she carefully dropped each into a boiling pot of lard. She turned them with a wooden ladle. She used a crooked wood stick to fish them out and place on a cloth to drain while she sprinkled sugar on them. They were wonderful.

I also remember hog killing time. Grandpa never slaughtered just a hog. It usually was three or four. The day of the killing was a full day. Everyone, including a few neighbors, worked from early morning till late evening. That was just to kill, scald, scrap, gut, quarter and hang to cool.

The next several days were just as busy. Rendering lard in a huge black pot over a fire in the yard and making chitlins. Grinding and making sausage. Cleaning and scraping intestines to use as cases for the sausage. Rubbing the slabs of bacon and hams with a mixture of brown sugar and salt getting them ready to hang in the smokehouse.

Grandpa was a hard working no nonsense guy. He was about six feet tall but I don't think he ever weighed over a hundred and fifty pounds. He had a ferocious appetite. His idea of a hearty breakfast was a bowl of oatmeal swimming in pure cream and brown sugar, four fried eggs, a big thick slice of ham, several large biscuits with butter, and two mugs of hot coffee.

Gene's family arrived in Evening Shade, Arkansas, in November 1942. They lived temporarily in a house two miles southwest of Evening Shade. In January they moved to the farm known as the Cochran Place three miles north of Evening Shade on Strawberry River. The children attended school in Evening Shade. The family attended the First Methodist Church in Evening Shade, except Gene. He refused to go to church. He had an unpleasant experience at the church in Moore.

Gene and his two older brothers made extra money cutting down hardwood trees, hand sawing short eighteen-inch logs, and splitting them to make firewood. They hauled the firewood in a mule drawn wagon to Evening Shade and sold the wood to town residents who still used wood for heating and wood burning cookstoves. They got seventy-five cents a rick stacked at the back door. A rick is four feet high by four feet long cut to cookstove length.

There were few money earning opportunities for teenage boys in and about Evening Shade. Thus, they had very little discretionary money to spend on the few things they wanted. William, Gene's oldest brother, bought a small radio. They all listened to it, but it was his radio and it was only with his permission. Gene's next older brother, Bob, saved enough to buy a nice pair of cowboy boots. He was proud of those boots.

> From age eight to age fourteen my family lived on several different farms. We were poor and we moved several times to farms where we could keep a few cows and chickens, have a garden, and plant some row crops.
>
> I had two older brothers, a younger sister, and a little brother. From about age twelve we each were expected to start becoming self-sufficient. Our parents provided meals such as they were and a place to sleep such as it was.
>
> We were expected to work on the farm and when we could to work for neighbors and earn our own money. We were expected to buy our own shoes and clothes with an occasional assist from the folks. We had to buy our own schoolbooks and supplies, and we were certainly expected to earn our own discretionary money for fun and extraneous things.
>
> My brother, Bob, is nineteen months older than I am. He was a big ox of a kid. I was a little skinny runt of a kid. Not only was he big, but he was a bully. He delighted in aggravating other kids, and me in particular. He teased and aggravated me to no end. He would hold my skinny little wrists in his big fist and with his other hand use a grass foxtail to tickle under

my nose, in my cars, and poke at my eyes. All I could do was scream epithets at him and try to kick him on the shins.

He managed to save enough money to buy a nice new pair of cowboy boots. He loved those boots. He brushed and spit polished them all the time. He wore them only on special occasions and on Saturdays in town. He would swagger around town Saturday afternoons in those precious boots. He was so proud of them.

Like all growing boys the day came when he could no longer get his big feet into his precious boots. I'm sure Mom cut a deal to pay him something for his boots so they could be handed down to me. I could never visualize him just voluntarily out of the kindness of his heart allowing me to wear his precious boots.

I could hardly wait to put them on and parade around in front of him showing off my new boots. He let me know in no uncertain language that those were still his boots. I was just getting to wear them. I delighted in wearing his boots knowing full well he was watching me most of the time.

Several days later I was at the barn in the cow lot. I thought Bob wasn't anywhere around. Like any thirteen year old kid would be so inclined, I started stomping "those precious boots" in cow manure piles all the while saying to myself, "There, take that!"

I stomped about four cow piles when suddenly I was hit with a flying tackle. Unseen by me, he had witnessed my grievous acts of retribution on his precious boots. He literally flew over the gate, tackled me to the ground, and forcibly pushed my face into a fresh pile of cow manure. He yelled at me, "Take that! That's how my boots feel." He made me take the boots off and clean them till they shined like a six-bit shoeshine. I hated those boots and never wore them again.

Adjustment to the new school at Evening Shade proved to be a trying challenge for Gene. At Moore he was a straight-A student, member of the Junior Honor Society, student council representative for his class, and well liked by his teachers and fellow students.

The change to Evening Shade was a cultural shock for Gene, but nothing he couldn't adjust to, or a least that was what he thought.

> In November 1942 we moved from Moore to Evening Shade, Arkansas. I changed schools in the middle of the semester. The school at Moore had almost five hundred students first through twelve grades. There were forty-four students in my eighth grade class. The school at Evening Shade had a few less than a hundred students first through twelve grades.
>
> The entire school infrastructure at Evening Shade consisted of the main building, a gym building, an old house converted for home economics, a metal building for vocational agricultural and the old original school building converted to serve hot lunches. The main building, the old house, and the gym were of stone construction. The main building had a large room with a raised floor in front that served as a stage, two individual classrooms at the back, and two classrooms at the opposite end for grades one through six. All the buildings except the gym were heated by wood burning stoves. The gym was not heated.
>
> Grades seven through twelve were in the large room. Each grade was arranged in a single row of desks. The seventh grade was on the right side, the twelfth grade was on the left side, and grades eight through eleven were in between. There were ten students in the seventh grade, thirteen in the eighth grade, nine in the ninth grade, eight in the tenth grade, seven in the eleventh grade, and six in the twelfth grade. The eighth grade class of thirteen students was the largest ever eighth grade class.
>
> The entire faculty was two elementary teachers and five high school teachers. Mr. Watson, the principal, taught history and kept the study hall in the large room. Mrs. Watson, his wife, taught English in one of the back classrooms. Their son, Ray Bob, taught math and coached the basketball team. Miss Sullivan taught home economics in the old house and social studies in one of the back classrooms. Mr. Cherry taught vocational agriculture.

The various classes rotated the use of the classrooms in the back for English, math, and social studies. When not in one of the back classrooms the students were at their desks in the appropriate row for their grade in the large room supervised by Mr. Watson. He also taught history in the large room.

I was in the eighth grade. My first day at school a mid-semester exam on American History was scheduled. Mr. Watson told me that since it was my first day in the class I didn't have to take the test. I told him we had been studying American History at my old school and I would go ahead and take the test. I scored a hundred. The next highest score was in the seventies.

The next day Mr. Watson took the occasion of an all school assembly to use me as an example to shame the entire school for their lack of scholarly performance. He said my performance was the level they should all achieve. He extolled my scholarly abilities as the best. He heaped praise on me which made me feel good about myself. Little did he or I know the problems he had just created for me. I immediately became that "new smart aleck know-it-all kid."

The remainder of the school year I was from time to time subjected to taunts and torments most of which erupted into fisticuffs on the schoolyard. I had to fight a number of the boys in that school. I was able to make a significant impression on most of them because though I was small I was a tough scrappy kid. After all, I had been fighting two older brothers all my life.

Mr. Watson and the teachers came to look on me as a disciplinary problem child with serious antisocial tendencies. It never occurred to them it wasn't me. It was an indictment of their teaching abilities. The frequent fights were always my fault. Of course my 'smart mouth' often exacerbated the situation. The confrontations almost always started with the exchange of harsh words. When I would reply, "I can't help it you're dumb" or "Its not my fault you can't add two plus two," the fists started flying. Sometimes older kids from the high school took me on which really caused me problems. I got beat up real good several times by kids four years older than me. Still it was always my fault.

> One day a particularly dumb fifteen-year old kid in the seventh grade decided it was his day to beat up on me. I stomped the devil out of him. Just as I was finishing him off 'lightning' struck. The kid's seventeen-year old cousin, Millard Qualls, blind-sided me with a solid blow to my right temple. I fell to the ground in a stunned daze. He kicked me in the side as I struggled to get on my feet and stagger away.
>
> It was bad enough to get the hell knocked out of me, but worse yet my big sixteen-year old ox of a brother stood by and did nothing to come to my rescue. I became very defensive and approached every situation with a great deal of caution and apprehension.
>
> I managed to gain the friendship of a few students at Evening Shade. David "Pug" Kunkel was a neighbor and friend. M.A. Graddy, Carl Shaver, and Billy "Moose" Atkinson became friends.
>
> The end of the school year gave me a summer reprieve. I longed for my friend, Buford, and missed him and his folks very much. I wanted a more peaceful existence.

Things did not go well in Arkansas for the Bill Davidson Family. The farm crops were flooded out, not once, but twice. The crops were totally lost. It was a financial disaster for Gene's father and grandfather. This only added to the burden of family disunity, chaos, and problems. When the next school year rolled around, Gene refused to go back to the school at Evening Shade and all the problems. He convinced his parents it would be much better for him to go to another school.

> When school was about to start in August I was fourteen years old. I refused to go back to that school and all the problems. I told my parents there was no way I would go back to that school. I had to find a change of direction because even at my tender age I could see I was on a collision course with disaster. Someone was going to get badly hurt or worse yet, killed. I wanted no part of it.

I convinced Mom and Dad it would be much better for me to go to another school. They arranged through a relative for me to go to Thayer, Missouri, about forty miles north of Evening Shade. I was to live with an elderly couple that lived in and managed the YMCA. I was to work for my room and board and a small weekly allowance, while I went to school.

I wanted to go to school. I liked school. I wanted a good education. I saw it as a way out of poverty. But, I also knew it had to be an environment condusive to learning.

The 'YMCA' at Thayer was not a true YMCA. It was actually a large rooming house for the train crewman on the Frisco Railroad. Thayer was a railhead junction and crew changeover point.

I made the beds, cleaned the rooms and bathrooms, swept the floors, and fetched this and fetched that. I was expected to respond to every menial request regardless. I was primarily an indentured servant to the elderly couple who ran the 'YMCA.'

What little spare time I had in the evenings I went to the bowling alley across the street and set pins to make extra money. The old man and woman thought the bowling alley was a sin den because they sold beer and gambled there. When they talked to me about it I said it was on my time off and I should be able to do what I could to earn extra money. They didn't like that. The arrangement didn't last long.

The old man wrote a letter to Mom telling her the day to meet the train in Hardy. He bought a train ticket for the designated day for me to be on the train the next morning and back to Hardy and on to Evening Shade. I wanted no part of it.

That evening I used part of my earnings to buy a small ditty bag. I packed my things. Dawn the next morning I was on the highway hitchhiking to Oklahoma City. The old couple probably never knew, or cared, what happened to me. Mom probably cared, but had no idea where I was.

A farmer in a truck picked me up and took me to West Plains. A woman with two kids took me to Cabool. A salesman took me to Springfield. I stayed the night at the YMCA in Springfield.

Early the next morning I was on Highway 66 with my thumb up. A navy officer in a Ford sedan picked me up. He was being transferred from the Great Lakes Naval Station to San Diego. I rode all the way to just east of Edmond with him. He ran out of gas and we slept that night in his car.

The next morning he got a farmer to sell him a few gallons of gasoline. We drove to Oklahoma City. He dropped me off at NW 23rd and May Avenue.

I didn't know where else to go, so I caught a bus and went to the YMCA. I had a little money I had saved. I knew I could get a bed at the YMCA for very little money.

In a couple of days I got a job working at the YMCA cafeteria washing pots and pans. It was hard, hot and steamy work. However, I was fortunate. A man, Louie Stalken, that worked at the YMCA had worked for Dad when he was Ticket Agent for the Oklahoma Railway in Oklahoma City. He recognized me as one of Bill Davidson's kids. However, I did not know that at the time. I went to work for him in the gym and steam rooms picking up towels, handling the laundry, cleaning the showers, and sweeping the floors. He let me live with him at the Travelers Hotel on North Robinson. The YMCA had a bowling alley and I set pins to earn extra money.

I met a young man, Bill Schlager, who often came to the YMCA gym. He took a liking to me, probably out of pity. He showed me how to lift weights and a few pointers on wrestling. He invited me to his home one evening to meet his folks and have dinner with them. They lived in a nice brick house on NW 22nd Street. They had an aquarium with live fish. I had never seen such in a home. His parents were very nice to me. It was an atmosphere more like Buford's home life. I enjoyed it immensely.

One evening Bill took me to a party at his girl friend's house. Her name was Mona Roberts. They lived in a nice two-level house on NW 24th Street. Mona was a very good-looking blonde about nineteen years old. She had a younger sister, Marilee, about my age. She was my date for the evening, but I'm sure it was only out of deference to Bill's request.

We played the usual young peoples' games, such as spin-the-bottle. When the bottle pointed at you your date walked around the house with you. My walk around the house with Marilee was just that, a walk around the house. Mona sensed that. Later, the bottle pointed to Mona. She picked me to take a walk around the house with her. I was apprehensive about going around the house in the dark with Bill's girl friend. She planted a kiss on me unlike anything I had ever experienced.

A week or so later Bill reported for military service. I never saw him again. I've often wondered whatever happened to him. Years later I tried to locate him or his family, but unsuccessfully. I also tried to locate Mona to maybe find out about Bill, but that too was unsuccessful.

It was late August and I wanted to return to school. Since I lived with Louie on North Robinson Street I resided in the Roosevelt Junior High School District, thus I pre-enrolled at Roosevelt

In the meantime Mom and Dad left the farm in Arkansas and came to Oklahoma City where they still owned the small house at 3608 NW 13th Street. World War II was fully engaged and jobs were plentiful, though housing was scarce with rent controls. They lived with friends, Alvin and Wilma Teel, on NW First Street for a while until they got their house available to move into.

Louie somehow contacted my parents and I was reunited with them. I went to live at the Teels with Mom, Dad, Meta Lu (Ann), and Marvin (Sam). Bob came home later to live at 3608 NW 13th Street. William lived at Moore with the Morrow Family.

I went the first day of school to Roosevelt. I met with the principal and explained that though I was living in his district my family would soon move to the Taft Junior High School District. He was very understanding and wrote out a transfer slip for me which I took that day to Mr. Gilbert Robinson, principal at Taft. He eyed me with a jaundiced eye of suspicion. He thought I was up to no good. It took some amount of explaining and a phone call to the principal at Roosevelt before he reluctantly accepted my transfer. This however was not my last encounter with the ever-suspecting Mr. Gilbert Robinson.

In September I started in the ninth grade at a new school, Taft Junior High, which was a large modern educational

> facility unlike Moore or Evening Shade. I was just another kid among hundreds, so I was able to leave all my 'baggage' unnoticed at the front door. Since I was making a new start in life I quit using the name Gene and went by Don the rest of my life, though for years many of my old friends and relatives continued to call me Gene.

Don had two other unfortunate experiences with Mr Gilbert Robinson, the principal. At the time Don entertained the ambition to be an architect. He knew he had to have a foundation in math and looked forward to his upcoming algebra class.

> I was assigned to Mrs. Daughtery's algebra class. I looked forward to the class with great anticipation. Little did I know. A mere two weeks into the class I knew it was not for me. Poor Mrs. Daughtery. I think she had recently lost her husband and had just returned to teaching that semester. Two guys in the class made it their mission in life to disrupt the class. Several times they reduced Mrs. Daughtery to tears. I knew this was no environment for me to learn algebra.
>
> I went to the principal's office to request a transfer to Mr. Mathews' algebra class. I had heard he was tough and most kids dreaded his classes. Again, the ever-suspecting Mr. Robinson knew I was up to no good. He scolded me and told me to get back to class and apply myself and I would learn algebra.
>
> I decided to simply fail the class and maybe next semester I could get in Mr. Mathews' class. Not so. Mrs. Daughtery gave me a 'C' grade though I did nothing to earn it. And, wouldn't you know it. The next semester I was assigned to Mrs. Daughtery's class. Thanks, I'm sure, to the effort of 'Gilbert the Great.' I did nothing to earn the 'C' grade I received the second semester.
>
> Several years later when I was in college I drove a delivery truck for Kerr's Department Store during the summer months. I made deliveries to the residence of Mrs. Gilbert Robinson always on Thursdays. The following Monday I always had a pickup-ticket for return of merchandise. I asked the sales manager in the ladies ready-to-wear department about it. She said, "Oh, she hardly ever buys anything. She just orders

> them to wear for weekend functions and then returns them." I thought, "That figures."

It was about this time Don first really became acquainted with Patricia "Pat" Paschall. She was a neighborhood girl who lived at 3608 NW 11th Street, just a couple of blocks from where Don and his family lived. Pat and Don became good friends and ran around together though nothing very serious. They were just young kids out having a good time together. Don was three years older than Pat, and though he liked her he was romantically more interested in girls his own age, or older.

> My parents first bought the house at 3608 NW 13th Street in 1935. Pat's family lived in the neighborhood at 3813 NW 13th Street, only two blocks away. We were just kids then, but surely our paths crossed a few times.
>
> We moved to Moore in November 1937 and to Evening Shade in November 1942. I returned to Oklahoma City in August 1943. Dad, Mom, Ann and Sam returned to Oklahoma City in September 1943. They lived with Alvin and Wilma Teel on NW 1st Street. Mom and Dad knew the Teels from our days at Moore. Wilma had lived at home with her father, Mr. Stevenson, on the next farm east from where we lived on the Johnson Place. Wilma was in high school then. After she married Alvin Dad helped him get a job where he worked.
>
> I quit work at the YMCA to go to school. In the meantime I got a paper route to make a little money. My first route was Linwood Boulevard, NW 5th and NW 4th Streets between Blackwelder and Pennsylvania Avenue. It was a long route and I did not have a bicycle. It was a long walk twice a day.
>
> In November 1943 Mom and Dad were finally able to vacate the renters at 3608 NW 13th so we could move back into our house. I kept the paper route on Linwood Boulevard for a while, but it became so far for me to go to throw the route and go to school that I got a paper route close to home. I also bought a used bicycle.
>
> In those days the paperboys folded the newspapers in a three-corner fold which made it easy to ride down the street

> on a bicycle and throw the papers onto the porches. Sometime the papers ended up on the roofs, in the shrubs, and other places.
>
> Some paperboys became good at this and could hit the porches most of the time. Some never could get very good at it. I got pretty darn good. I could put the paper right where I wanted ninety-eight percent of the time. I was so good I was cocky about it. Often times the paperboys at the paper station would fool around and have newspaper-throwing contests while waiting for our paper bundles to arrive. We bet pennies on the outcome. I won most of the time.
>
> A nice warm spring day in 1944 I pedaled down NW 14th Street in the 3600 block throwing my papers. I saw Barbara Moore and Pat sitting on the Moore's porch. They were facing each other about four feet apart. They were playing 'jacks,' a girls' game played with a small rubber ball and several small metal cross pieces called 'jacks.'
>
> Cocky me! I thought, "I'll throw this paper right between them and scare 'em." I let fly. The three-fold newspaper hit Pat squarely in the side of her head. I'm sure it hurt. I turned my bicycle around and pedaled back to the porch. The Pat was fighting to keep back the tears. I felt bad. I apologized profusely. I don't think my apologies were too well received. Six years later Pat become my dear wife.

Don fit in well with his new classmates at Taft and was well liked. He didn't have to fight other kids to gain their respect and acceptance. That was a great relief for him.

He was a good student and aggressively athletic in the gym classes. The other boys recognized his athletic abilities as did the gym teachers. They recommended to the high school football coach that he be allowed to go out for spring football at the high school in lieu of gym class. Like most young teenage boys Don and his friends were not above a few occasional hi-jinks.

> Taft had an enclosed swimming pool. It was used for both boys and girls gym classes. Held separately, of course. The girls

wore swimsuits. The boys swam nude. The locker room for the boys was at one end of the pool and the girls at the other end. The door to the girls side was kept closed and locked during the boys' classes and likewise the boys side was kept closed and locked during the girls' classes. The doors were heavy and about forty inches wide. For easy maintenance and cleaning there was a crack of about two inches under each door.

The gym teacher almost always allowed about twenty minutes of free swim time where he left and the boys were on their own. When in the water at the far ends of the pool you were about eye-level with the crack under the doors between the locker rooms.

One day during free swim time one of the guys noticed three pairs of 'little eyes' peering under the opening of the door to the girls' locker room. He quietly pointed this out to several of us. We went in the water at that end of the pool and casually looked at the opening under the door. Sure enough, 'little eyes' were peering under the door. We didn't do anything about it that day. However, after school we got together and plotted our revenge.

The next day some of us secretively brought bottles of Pine-Sol disinfectant to gym class which we concealed in the locker room from the teacher. There were already two three-gallon buckets in the locker room for maintenance use. When the teacher left and we had free swim time we nonchalantly checked to see if the 'little eyes' were peering under the door. Sure enough, they were.

We mixed the entire contents of the Pine-Sol with water in two buckets out of sight from the 'little eyes.' Two of us took a bucket each of the Pine-Sol mixture and stationed ourselves on each side of the door. One guy positioned himself in the pool to where he could see when the 'little eyes' peered under the door. On his signal the two of us sloshed all six gallons of the Pine-Sol mixture under the door.

We spent the rest of the school day going around looking into the eyes of all the girls to see who had red bloodshot eyes and who smelled like Pine-Sol. We smelled so much from Pine-

> Sol ourselves we couldn't tell, or else they washed it off in the shower.
>
> This didn't stop the 'little eyes' from peering under the door though we did the Pine-Sol thing several more times to no avail. When the 'little eyes' were peering under the door we would sometimes put on a show for them. I suppose that sometime during the school year most of the girls got an eye full more than one way. I guess that was sex education the old fashioned way.

Don and Pat became more than casual friends. Her family had moved to 3608 NW 11th Street. Though not romantically involved they were good friends. After all, they were just early teenage kids. They met often at the Wes-Ten Theater on Saturdays to sit together through a movie. Pat had a pair of shoe skates and was a good skater. They sometimes went to the Uptown Skating Rink. Don liked to skate with Pat because she was good enough that she made him look better than he actually was.

Pat had a badminton set in her backyard. She played very well. Don would pedal his bicycle over to her house and park it with a kick-stand in the driveway. He and Pat would play badminton until her father came home. He always delighted in giving Don a bad time about parking his bike in the driveway.

Don and Pat well remember the first time they kissed. It was a summer evening. They and several other friends were fooling around in Dr. Coley's peach orchard near Grand Boulevard and 11th Street. Pat recorded the event in a small diary she kept at the time. She still has the diary.

In the meantime Don learned of Buford Young's address at Drumright through mutual friends at Moore. They exchanged letters several times. Buford would tell about the fun things he and some of his new friends would have and especially about riding their bicycles down a long hill in Drumright. Don missed his friend and longed for the day they could get together again.

I continued to go to school. I set pins weekends at the Plamore Bowling Alley to earn extra money. I got a job working at the Union Bus Station in Oklahoma City as a baggage checker and handler. It was a source of satisfaction. I worked from midnight until seven o'clock in the morning. I had to be in class at eight-thirty. I was making good money for a high school kid and for the times. I made the minimum wage of forty cents an hour. I had little idle time.

My cousin, Vida Roller, worked as a waitress in the coffee shop at the bus station. She started work at six o'clock in the morning. I sometimes stopped to get a cup of coffee and chat with her.

I got friendly with several of the bus drivers most of whom were older men because all the young men were in the military for the duration of the war. The MKO (Missouri, Kansas and Oklahoma) Bus Line went from Oklahoma City through Drumright to Tulsa and points beyond.

On an off day I got one of the MKO drivers to let me ride to Drumright with him. I hadn't had a letter from Buford for quite a while and I wanted to pay him a surprise visit. When I got to Drumright and found the right address, Buford no longer lived there. Mr. Young had again transferred to another location. I had no idea where they were. It was a great disappointment for me.

I stood a long time at the top of that long hill. I could visualize Buford and me having a great time bicycling down that hill. I walked all the way, and it was a long ways, down that hill and looked longingly back up the hill. Then I went to the bus station and caught the next MKO bus back to Oklahoma City.

The last two weeks of school in May Don became very ill. He had terrific headaches that reached down the back of his head into his spine and between his shoulders. The pain was excruicating for more than a week. He continued to go to school, but often sat in the cafeteria all afternoon with his head resting in his folded arms on a table.

It was war time. Don's parents worked. Don had been working but had to quit. No one seemed to have the time to be concerned about him or his illness. He didn't press the issue. He figured he could just "tough it out." In retrospect, he thinks maybe he had a slight case of polio, because afterwards his left foot was a full shoe size smaller than his right foot, and his left leg was always a little smaller than his right leg. Also, he was five feet six inches tall. He never grew any taller afterwards.

When Don was in high school he played on the football team. Pat was in junior high at Taft. It was a prestige thing for a junior high girl to be seen running around with a high school boy, especially one on the football team.

> Football was a source of fun therapy for me. I could physically take out my pent up frustrations on other guys in an acceptable manner. Though I was small I was tough as an old boot heel and the most aggressive player on the team. The coaches loved it.
>
> I played blocking back my sophomore year on the "B" Team. We played from a double-wing formation. Near the end of the season the coach moved me up to the Varsity. I got to make a road trip to play Enid though I did not get to play in the game. I mostly sat on the bench. After all, the team had a championship in the making. The team was state champions that year.
>
> Next Spring in spring football practice I was still playing blocking back and not getting much playing time. One day in a tough scrimmage George McKean, the starting guard from the year before, bloodied a guy's nose. We didn't wear nose-guards. The coach called for a guard. One of the guards jumped in and George promptly took him out. This occurred another time. Then when the coach called for a guard no one moved. He called, "Gimme a guard" again. No one moved. I ran forward from the group of backs and yelled, "I'm a guard."
>
> I knew it was now or never to show my true mettle. When the center snapped the ball I hit George with everything I had

which took him by surprise. I got past him and tackled Ray Plumb behind the line of scrimmage for a loss. For the next fifteen minutes of scrimmage George and I had at it. I beat him every time. I had three factors in my favor. First, George was tired. I wasn't. Second, I was quick and fast. Third, George was overly confident. That will get you every time.

George and I ended up in a slugfest. He was frustrated and I was determined to prove myself. The coach let us have at it for about a minute then stepped in and broke it up. He ended the practice. On my way to the locker room Coach Higbie told me, "Stop by and get a pair of cleats." A sure sign I had made the Varsity Team.

As Don grew a little older he became interested in girls more his age or older, though he still liked Pat very much. After all, she was a kid three years younger than he was. One evening Don had a date with Pat that went awry very badly.

It was the summer of 1944. World War II was in full force. Everyone able was either in the military or employed. I was fifteen and worked on the loading dock at Joe Hodges where Dad was the dock foreman.

The young eighteen and nineteen year old ladies of the neighborhood where we lived were all employed. There were no young men their age to date. They were all in the military service. Their choice was either go for a pick-up date with a serviceman in downtown Oklahoma City that was flooded on weekends with sailors from the Naval Station at Norman and airmen from Will Rogers Field southwest of the city. Or, they could date a neighborhood boy too young for military service. That was me.

I dated Joy Mae, Estelle, and Ruby. Joy Mae and Estelle were eighteen. Ruby was nineteen. Pat was thirteen. She was a nice kid and I liked her. But, nice as Pat was, I was not romantically inclined toward her. I was more interested in the older girls.

Pat was a Rainbow Girl, a youth group associated with the Eastern Stars, the ladies auxiliary of the Masonic Order. One day Pat asked me to go with her on a Rainbow Girls evening outing for a hayrack ride and wiener roast. She asked several weeks in advance of the event. I agreed and then promptly forgot about it.

I later made a date with Ruby for the same night of the hayrack ride. It was only at the last moment that mother reminded me I had a date with Pat for that evening. What to do? I reasoned, "This hay ride is for seven o'clock. It won't take more than a couple of hours. Then I can have a late date with Ruby." I called Ruby and told her something unexpected had come up and I would meet her at nine-thirty. She grumbled but was agreeable.

I went on the hay ride with Pat. Pat's friend, Betty, was also a Rainbow Girl and she was on the hay ride with a date. Betty was my age and I was interested in her, but she didn't care one whit for me. Her parents thought I was a great kid, but Betty didn't share their sentiments. The hay ride took longer than I thought it would.

At nine-thirty Ruby called the house and mother answered the phone. When Ruby asked where I was mother said, "Oh, he went on a hay ride with Patsy Paschall." That made Ruby angry.

So, here it was ten o'clock and I was still on the hay ride with Pat. At this point I decided to stand-up Ruby and make some lame excuse the next day. Well, Ruby was so angry she hit the local bar and proceeded to get boozed-up.

Wouldn't you know it? This darn horse drawn hay ride went right down the street in front of the bar at 10th and Portland where Ruby was soaking up beer. She heard the cloppity-clop of the horses' hooves and the clankity-clank of the harness chains. Here came Ruby out the barroom door like she was shot from a cannon. She bailed onto the hay wagon and laid her head in my lap. She was foaming at the mouth and reeked with the smell of beer. This made Pat angry.

I felt helpless. What to do? I tried to smooth things over with Pat to no avail. Ruby was smooching all over me. Pat turned her back, tightly folded her arms and became mum. Betty said, "If you don't get rid of her I'll never speak to you again."

Decision time. I pushed Ruby off the back of the wagon. Then, I tried to make amends with Pat and Betty to no avail.

They wouldn't even speak. I finally gave it up and jumped off the wagon and walked home.

By now it was eleven-thirty. When I got home who was sitting on the curb in front of the house? Ruby. She read me the riot act. I tried to quiet her down but she would have no part of it. Mother opened the door a crack and quietly asked, 'Don, is that you?" I replied, "Yes, Mother." She said to be quiet. Ruby finally let me walk her home. I never had another date with Ruby.

The Marconis lived next door west at 3612 NW 13th Street. Mazio was an Italian immigrant. He served during World War I and had gained citizenship. He spoke very broken English. He ran an upholstery business in the shed behind their house. Don thought Mazio was an interesting old character.

I sometimes went next door to Mazio's shop just to talk. He always had some philosophical story to tell that usually had a moral to it. He always put me to work helping him to hold this and to hold that while he hammered upholstery tacks in a piece he was finishing. He always had a mouth full of tacks that he applied to the magnetic end of his small tack-hammer from his mouth. I marveled that he could talk with a mouth full of tacks while putting the hammer in his mouth to pick up tacks and not swallow any of them.

One day I told Mazio the Haggard boy across the alley had been drafted into the army. Mazio didn't like him because he had a BB-gun and would shoot out the small glass panes in the back of his shop. Mazio said, "Good. I hope he comes back like a new moon." I thought surely Mazio had a change of heart until he added after a pause, "A quarter at a time."

Don sometimes did yard work around the neighborhood to make extra money. He had an unpleasant experience with one neighbor. He did yard work for Mr. and Mrs. Hill, Betty's parents. Mr. Hill was gone a lot working in the war effort. Don cut their grass, trimmed the hedges, and generally kept the yard looking nice while Mr. Hill was gone. He didn't ask to be paid. All this was to gain Betty's favor. Her parents thought he was a great kid. Betty didn't give a whit about him. She tolerated him only to appease her folks.

> The lady across the street had observed me working in the Hill's yard. Her husband was gone to the army. She asked me to work an entire Saturday helping her with yard work. I agreed and she paid me fifty cents an hour. We worked from sunup and until after sundown. She paid me and I went home.
>
> The next day the police knocked on our front door. They wanted to talk to me. The lady I worked for the day before called the police because her garden hose was gone. She accused me of coming back that night and stealing it.
>
> The police talked with Dad and interrogated me. I insisted that I did not take the hose. They looked around the house and garage and didn't see anything to indicate I took it, so they left. That was the last I heard from the police. I went to the lady's house and told her the police had been to see me and I did not steal her hose. She was haughty and still convinced I took it. That really irritated me.

World War II raged almost four years. Things on the battlefield went badly for the United States while the country mobilized for all out warfare. The Battle of Midway was the turning point in the Pacific. The invasion of Italy was the start of the turning point in Europe. Don's cousin, Joe Clarke, was one of the many heroic combat soldiers in Italy. The D-Day invasion of France at Normandy was the turning point in Europe. Don's friend, Bobby Greenlee, from Moore was injured on D-Day and lost his left leg but survived.

Everyone physically able and between the ages of eighteen and twenty-six was drafted into the army. Many volunteered. Others fought the war on the home front. Everyone physically able worked, mostly at defense jobs.

Alvin Teel, the friend of Don's parents, was drafted into the army. His wife, Wilma, lived alone in a small garage apartment behind the house next door to Don's parents. Wilma was a very attractive woman. She worked while Alvin was gone to the army. She loved to roller skate, but did not like to go skating alone with so many servicemen on the loose in Oklahoma City during the war. So on Saturday evenings she would take Don as her escort.

> I loved to skate with Wilma. She was so good she made me look a lot better than I actually was. Also, what fifteen year old boy wouldn't love to be seen by his friends skating with an attractive thirty-year old woman?
>
> My friends were all very curious and anxious to know about my "date" they saw me with at the roller rink. I never said very much. I let their imaginations run amuck. I silently reveled in it.
>
> Years later I saw Wilma at a Moore reunion. She was seventy-five years old but still an attractive woman. I told her about how I played my friends along about our roller skating together. Her comment was: "Oh my goodness. I hate to think what was said about me." I assured her, "Not to worry. It wasn't any thing to be concerned about."

Many women took jobs normally held by men. They became known as Rosie the Riveter. Don's Aunt Marge Weldon was a welder in the Kaiser Shipyards. His mother worked in a plant sewing army tents. During the football off-season Don worked a short time as a jig rigger and later as a spot welder making bomb racks for B-25 bombers. He went to school from eight-thirty until two-thirty, then worked the swing shift from three until eleven o'clock. He got home about eleven forty-five and had to be at school eight-thirty the next morning. He usually was late or missed homeroom. His first class was history at nine. Mrs. Gibson was the teacher.

I usually barely made class on time. I often would doze off in class. Mrs. Gibson chastised me several times about sleeping in class. She must have checked with the principal's office to see if I had some problem. Somehow she found out I was working a full eight hours on the swing shift in a war plant. She took me aside and told me it was okay if I sometimes slept in her class.

Bless her heart. She gave me a 'C' grade in history. She would be proud today to know that over the years I developed a keen interest in history, especially American History.

In the spring of 1945 the war was in its final stages. The war in Europe ended April 25, 1945. Not so many bomb racks were needed so production schedules were drastically cut back and Don was out of a job. The war with Japan raged on with the invasions of Okinawa and Iwo Jima. The B-29's bombed Japan around the clock.

When I got out of school in May 1945 I had no job. A neighbor, Otto Pemberton, had a small independent ice delivery business. I went to work for him delivering ice.

Each morning we picked up a load of four hundred pound blocks of ice at Lieberman's Ice Plant at 10th and May Avenue. The big blocks were picked into smaller blocks of one hundred pounds. These were further picked into fifty-pound blocks which was the most common size for home and apartment delivery.

Most of the people who used ice instead of refrigerators were located in the poorer area of South Oklahoma City between Western and Broadway from Grand Street south to Fourth Street including Reno, California and Washington Streets. This area was mostly cheap walk-up flats and apartments and low-income houses. They put ice cards in their windows to tell us they wanted ice and how much they wanted.

Otto drove the truck and made deliveries. He had me make the third floor deliveries. It was no easy job toting fifty pounds of ice on your back up three flights of stairs.

One day as I shouldered a fifty pound block for the third floor Otto said, "She owes me eight dollars and fifty cents. If you see her ask her to pay up."

I trudged up the steps to the landing for the door of her tiny three- room apartment. The door opened into a small living room. Believe it or not, people did not lock their doors. I turned left and went into the small kitchen. The bedroom was to my right. I placed the ice in the icebox. I turned to leave and there she stood in the living room wearing a thin loosely fitting housecoat of sorts.

I said, "Mr. Pemberton said you owe him eight dollars and fifty cents. He said for you to pay up."

She coyly replied, "Would you take it out in trade?"

I was dumbstruck. I stuttered and said, "I'll have to ask Mr. Pemberton."

She laughed as I went out the door. Back at the truck I told Otto what she said. He said, "Okay. I'll take care of it."

I worked only four weeks with Otto. It was heavy work. I was exhausted every evening when I got home. In the meantime I decided to work with Uncle Henry on the farm on Panther Creek.

Uncle Henry married Catherine Blackwood in December 1941. He was classified 4-F thus physically unfit for military service. He worked a while in a war plant in California. He and Catherine came back to Oklahoma. Grandpa and Grandma Roller had retired and moved to Maysville. Since he had no other means to support his family Henry decided to farm the Roller place on Panther Creek.

Since I had no job I decided to go to Panther Creek and help Henry raise a crop of corn, peanuts, and cotton. We spent hours tilling the soil using mules to draw the farm implements and our hands on long-handle hoes.

The farm was twenty miles west of Pauls Valley. The house was situated such that to go anywhere, even the mailbox, required crossing Panther Creek that normally flowed a small stream. There were no paved highways–just red dirt roads.

Henry and Catherine had a small tabletop radio that used a dry cell battery. We listened to it for entertainment and news about the war. But, early July the battery went dead. Batteries were difficult to get because of the war shortages. Henry had not had the time to go to town to see if he could find a new one. We were without a radio, but continued to receive the daily newspaper a day late via U. S. Mail rural route delivery by Mr. Pike Paul. There was no telephone.

August first it started raining and rained for the next three days. Panther Creek flowed bank full. The next several days it was impossible to cross the creek, even to go to the mailbox a quarter of a mile away.

By August seventh the creek was down enough that Henry and I decided to go to Davis, the nearest country store about four miles away, but on the other side of the creek. Davis was a small community with a church, a rural schoolhouse, a small country store with one gasoline pump, a blacksmith shop, and three houses. We could pick up a few items for Catherine, but most importantly we could catch up on the latest community gossip and find out the latest war news.

Henry and I saddled our horses, mounted and swam Panther Creek. We made our way cross-country about a mile to the nearest road to Davis. It was very muddy and slow going. When we finally got on the road we saw an unusual number of wheel ruts and horse hoof prints in the red mud. We sloughed along speculating why so many people were out on a muddy road making so many tracks.

As we approached Davis about a quarter of a mile away we saw several vehicles and trucks parked near the store. We also saw an unusually large number of horses and wagons with teams hitched in front of and near the store. As we slogged along in the mud we speculated about what was going on to cause so many people to be there. The only thing we could think of was that someone must have died and they were having a funeral. But, why all the activity at the store and not the church?

When we got within about a hundred yards we saw a number of people standing on the store porch and around the steps all excitedly talking. We still couldn't figure out what was going on. We rode up to a hitch and before we could dismount one of the several men standing there said, "The war is over! They dropped 'uh a-tom bomb' on Japan." I thought, "What the hell is uh a-tom bomb?" Another man said, "It wiped out a whole city in Japan." As I dismounted I thought, "These guys are nuts. They can't make an airplane big enough to carry a bomb big enough to wipe out an entire city."

Once inside the store was abuzz with everyone listening to a radio. The news announcer said something about the total destruction of a city in Japan. I thought, "They must have flown a thousand B-29's over that city." But everyone kept talking about "uh a-tom bomb." I then saw a newspaper headline in big bold letters: ATOM BOMB DESTROYS JAPAN CITY. A sub-heading read: "Hiroshima Destroyed." It finally began to sink in as I reflected: "The war really is over. But what the heck is an atom bomb? How could it destroy an entire city?"

It was several hours before we mounted up to go home. Much too long. We were gone so long Catherine was worried sick about us. She just knew we drowned in the creek.

Late August Don went home to Oklahoma City so he could return to school. He started training for football and played on the Varsity.

I played left guard and George McKean, my old rival, played right guard. During the Henryetta game in mid-season Jim Murphy, our left end, injured his knee and was out for the next several games. The coach put in the backup end. The first play he let a Henryetta back get around him for a long gain. It happened a second time. The coach yelled, "Davidson! Get in there at end! Don't let 'em around you! Turn 'em inside!!"

I played left end the next several games. Then back to guard when Jim Murphy was able to play the last regular season game. We won our district title and met Ardmore in the quarterfinals in the State Championship playoffs.

We were beset by more than our fair share of injuries. Sam Burnnel, our star fullback, was out with a broken arm. Jim Murphy, our outstanding left end was playing with a bad knee. Ray Plumb, our quarterback, was ailing with a sick stomach.

We traveled to Ardmore the day before the game and spent the night at a hotel in Ardmore. By game time (afternoon game) the next day half the team was sick with gastroenteritis symptoms (vomiting and diarrhea). We always thought it was a conspiracy to serve us bad food at the hotel restaurant.

Anyhow, near the end of the game we needed a touchdown to win. Jim Murphy gave it his best but his knee gave out. Coach Higbie moved me to left end to replace Murphy.

We were mid-field and getting a little desperate as time was running out. Ray Plumb threw a pass deep to the right side incomplete. Back in the huddle he asked me, "Weren't you open on that play?" I said, "Yeah." Ray said, "Well, get open again!," and called the same play. The quarterback called the plays in those days. The defensive back was on me like a cheap suit, but I managed to come down with the ball on the seven yard line. At this point I thought we would pull it out.

The next play Ray called for the running back, Merrel Harrel, to sweep the right end. Merrel could run like a scared deer, but had the bad habit of sometimes dropping the ball for no apparent reason. We nicknamed him "Thumbs" Harrell. True to form, Merrel dropped the ball for no apparent reason. Ardmore recovered. Even though J. C. Evans, our backup fullback, turned in a stellar performance, we lost. Our hopes for a repeat State Championship were dashed.

It was a great disappointment for me. I so much wanted our team to win State because my older brother, Bob, played the previous year on the team that won the State Championship. I knew he would never let me forget it. Coach Higbie sensed my deep disappointment. He knew I had played my heart out to win that game. He made it a special point to put his arm around me and console me.

Donald Gene Davidson - age 17

At the end of each football season it was customary for the girls pep club at Classen to hold an appreciation banquet for the team. It was also customary for individual members of the pep club to ask one of players to be her escort to the banquet. There was great competition among the most popular girls to ask and receive dates with the most prominent players on the team. There were more girls in the pep club than players on the team. Many went without a date.

I was not an outstanding star on the team. I was not a flashy player. I was an aggressive hard-hitting technician. I was a good steady reliable performer. I played in the line, part of the time as a guard and the last part of the season as an end. Coach Higbie once complimented me on my steadfastness and reliability.

I was not popular in the halls at school. I was a kid that mostly went about my own business. Only a handful of students recognized me off the playing field as a member of the team.

I dated only four girls at Classen. One was Janet Ellison. I had one date with her. I didn't have a car. Another was Esther Reno. I had two dates with her. She was more interested in my older brother, Bob. Another was Jane Harding. I had four or five dates with her. I had two dates with Betty Hill. Her folks liked me but she didn't want anything to do with me. I mostly didn't have the time or money to go out on dates. I mostly worked in my spare time. Pat, who did not go to Classen, was mostly my steady reliable date. She was still in junior high school at Taft.

The last day came for the girls to ask the players for a date. I had not been asked. I decided I would not go to the banquet. That very afternoon a young lady approached me in the hallway and embarrassingly asked me to be her escort to the banquet. I was flabbergasted. I scarcely knew her. She was in one of my classes. I didn't even think she knew who I was. I had to think hard to recall her name–Margaret Wilkens.

I sheepishly accepted. Margaret was not outstandingly popular. She was not one of the school beauties that flitted around the halls. She was rather plain and overly endowed with ample freckles. But, she was a very nice and pleasant young lady. She had that quiet inward beauty that graciously radiated outwardly.

I went home and told Mom. She went to great lengths the next few days to scrounge up some of Dad's clothes to alter and fit to me. I had a nice shirt, a jacket and a necktie to wear with my nicest pair of pants.

The afternoon of the banquet I caught the Nichols Hill bus in plenty of time to go to Margaret's house to pick her up. I'll never forget. She lived at 6608 Hillcrest in Nichols Hills, a most prestigious address. The bus driver let me off at a corner and gave me directions to the house.

I had never been in such a luxurious home–rugs all the way to the walls. Curtains hanging all the way to the floor. I later learned they were carpets and drapes. Margaret's mother was most gracious. I had a small inexpensive corsage for Margaret.

I took Margaret on the bus and streetcar to the Skirvin Tower Hotel in downtown Oklahoma City. My place setting was not even next to Margaret's. I sat at the end of one of the tables.

A man, I think it was an uncle, picked Margaret and I up at the hotel after the banquet. He dropped me off at the 17th Street Station on Classen Boulevard where I caught a late bus home.

I never had another date with Margaret, but I've always had a warm spot in my heart for her. I've always thought she asked me to be her escort because no one else had. Thank you, Margaret!

Later, I learned her father was a famous and wealthy surgeon in Oklahoma City. I think they thought I was not of proper standing for their daughter. I knew for sure I was out of my element.

Years later I saw a small notice in the Classen New-Life alumni magazine that Margaret had died. It saddened me, but I will always have that warm spot in my heart for her.

CHAPTER 13

DONALD GENE DAVIDSON

The Army and College Years

Don quit high school near the end of his junior year and joined the Army a few months before World War II officially ended. He was inducted at Camp Chaffee, Arkansas. A week later he was sent by troop-train to Accotink, Virginia, for basic training at Fort Belvoir.

The troop train made up at Camp Chaffee. It was late afternoon before we left. We had no idea where we were going. Bunks on a troop train left a lot to be desired. There was no air conditioning. Only open windows with smoke and flying soot.

The train stopped and started several times during the night. The next morning when we awoke the train was traversing a large bluff on the left side and a large river on the right side. We assumed it was the Mississippi River.

We traveled the next several days through the countryside and small towns. The train stopped a number of times and cars were added. Every time the train stopped we would shout at anyone within ear-shot, "Where are we?" They usually looked at us like we were nuts, but sometimes they would yell back the name of the town. We had a great time with the name Ashtabula, Ohio. It sounded like "Ass to Beulah" to us.

The troop train made its way in a laboriously circumventing route across Illinois, Indiana, and Ohio adding a car here and a car there, dropping off a car here and there. We wound through the Allegheny Mountains in Western Pennsylvania and finally after five days arrived at Accotink, Virginia, where we disembarked.

Don took basic training at AFSTC, 3rd Battalion, Company C, 4th Platoon, Fort Belvoir, Virginia. He was a private and was paid twenty-one dollars a month. Most of the trainees were in their late teens and had never been very far from home until now. They were quarantined to the barracks area the first three weeks except when training.

Two weeks into basic training the company commander, a captain, accompanied by the lieutenant platoon leader and the platoon sergeant conducted a standby inspection in the barracks. Everything was 'spit 'n polish' as the privates all stood at attention beside their open foot lockers for inspection. They had to have their personal dog tag serial number memorized as well as the serial number for the M-1 Garand rifle they were issued.

> I turned the serial numbers over and over in my head as I waited for the inspection team to come to my bunk. I didn't want to blow that. The captain had asked several and some stumbled on their numbers. Little did I know what was about to happen to me.
>
> The captain did a snappy left-face directly in front of me. He looked me straight in the eye. Without saying a word he glanced down at the tray in my foot locker. He did a snappy right-face and took two steps toward the next bunk.
>
> He suddenly stopped losing all military precision, turned quickly back toward me, stepped in front of my foot-locked and peered down into my tray. He sputtered demandingly, "Soldier, where did you get that?"
>
> "What, Sir?"
>
> "That straight edge razor."
>
> "My father gave it to me, sir."
>
> "What do you use it for?"
>
> "Shave, sir."

He leaned menacingly forward stared me squarely in the eye and demanded, "Is that true?"

I replied, "Yes, sir."

He apparently detected that I was so scared that I surely must be telling the truth. He turned to the sergeant and ordered, "Sergeant, see that this soldier boxes that thing up and mails it home. Then take him to the PX and make sure he buys a safety razor and blades."

I didn't have to stand the rest of the inspection.

During free time the trainees were restricted to the Company Area the first six weeks. Finally, Friday evening of the sixth week-end they were permitted to go outside the Company Area, but had to remain on base. They could go to the PX, the movie theater, the EM Club, etc. Most went to the EM Club where beer was served. Don and a few others elected to go to the PX and then the movie.

We got back to the barracks about ten o'clock and went to bed. Taps was at eleven. Everyone was supposed to be back to the barracks no later than taps, but they weren't. Starting about eleven here they came staggering back from the EM Club in a drunken stupor, vomiting all over the place, and passing out on their bunks.

The platoon sergeant, Sergeant Cohen, was quartered in a private room at the front of the barracks. He came in about midnight. When he saw all the mess he rousted me and the others that were sober out of our bunks and made us clean up the mess while the jerks that caused it all lay passed-out on their bunks. We were not very happy.

Basic training was long, hard and arduous. It was a lot of physical conditioning, manual of arms, close order drill, obstacle courses, weapons familiarization, etc. Hour on hour was spent with the M-1 Garand Rifle practicing the proper way to hold it, the proper sight picture, the trigger squeeze, etc. with hours of dry runs.

Don found this all very boring. He already knew how to shoot a rifle. He learned that as a youth roaming the reaches of Panther Creek and The Table Hills hunting game. One day Don told Sergeant Cohen he already knew how to shoot a rifle. The proper word was to "fire" a rifle. Sergeant Cohen told Don to just get busy and learn how to do it the right way.

But, Don didn't take that for a satisfactory answer and could hardly wait to get on the firing range to fire live bullets at a target. Several times he suggested to Sergeant Cohen he knew how to fire his rifle. Sergeant Cohen was from New York City and didn't believe anyone knew how to fire a rifle if they hadn't been in the army.

> It was the first day on the range. It had seventy-five targets at one hundred yards distance. My partner and I were assigned to target number seventy-two. Our platoon spent the morning under the watchful eye of Sergeant Cohen firing live ammunition for familiarization.
>
> Finally, that afternoon we fired for record. I was to fire first while my partner stood by. The targets came up. I hit the ground from a standing position to a prone position, fired one round, reloaded with a clip of nine rounds, and fired all ten rounds in the allotted time of one minute.
>
> The targets went down for scoring. Then the command "Targets up" was given. All the targets came up at the same time. The ranger officer droned over the public address system, "Looks like a possible on target seventy-two." Possible means all ten shots were in the bull's eye.
>
> Sergeant Cohen's platoon was assigned target numbers sixty to seventy-five. He knew when he heard the range officer that one of his trainees had fired a perfect score. He was standing near target sixty, but he came hustling toward number seventy-two to see who had fired the perfect score. He saw me standing there holding my rifle like a defender of The Alamo with a big smile on my face. He said, "Oh, damn, not you."

> He got even with me though. Two guys in our platoon were so scared of their rifles they closed their eyes and jerked the trigger not only missing the target but hitting the dirt a few yards in front of them. Since I had fired a perfect score and didn't need any further training Sergeant Cohen assigned me to teach these two guys how to fire a rifle.
>
> I tried and tried but with no success. I began to think they actually did not want to learn how. Sergeant Cohen came by several times asking if I had them qualified yet. Of course, I hadn't.
>
> Finally, the day was ending and Sergeant Cohen demanded that I get them qualified. I got the message. I took each of their rifles and hit the bull's eye with five shots and scattered the other five around on the target. That was sufficient to get them qualified. It also could have got me court-martialed, but I didn't know it.
>
> We later had to fire at two hundred yards, three hundred yards and six hundred yards to be fully qualified. I fired a score of 208 out of a possible 210. I qualified as an EXPERT rifleman much to Sergeant Cohen's dismay, though I think he was a little pleased that one of his trainees fired such an impressive score.

After eight weeks in basic training the trainees were permitted to get weekend passes. Don used his passes to go to Washington, D.C., and visit the Washington, Jefferson and Lincoln Monuments. He went to the National Museum of Art and Smithsonian Institute where he saw the Winne Mae, Wiley Post's airplane. He also went to some of the Washington Senators baseball games. He saw Joe DiMaggio when the Yankees played the Senators. He saw Bob Feller make a 100-mph pitch before a game with the Cleveland Indians. He also went once to Glen Echo, the local amusement park.

After hours barracks talk was mostly about girl friends, sex, drinking, and eating. A number of the trainees were from New Jersey and New York City. They talked a lot and mostly about how much they missed pizza pie and that on their first pass they were going to town and get some.

The first weekend pass Don and several of his buddies went to Washington, D.C. They wanted to go get a pizza pie. Don had never heard of a pizza pie much less taste one.

> I heard so much about pizza pie that I could hardly wait to sink my teeth into one. It sounded so good the way the guys talked about it.
>
> Soon as we got off the bus in downtown Washington, D.C. we sought out the first pizza parlor we could. We ordered a pizza pie for four. In a few minutes they brought out this big round flat piece of baked dough that had some red tomato sauce smeared around on top. I thought, "That's a strange looking pie." I took a piece and cautiously took a bite. I said, "That's not pie!"
>
> Pizza had not yet found its way from the Northeastern states to the rest of the country. Pizzas then were nothing compared to the variety of toppings that come with pizzas today. Also, they are no longer called "pizza pie."

Another weekend pass Don hitchhiked to Langley Field, Virginia, for a weekend with his older brother, Bob, who was in the Army Air Corps. Friday afternoon after retreat Don and a number of other soldiers stood by the highway south from Fort Belvoir hitchhiking.

> There were about fifteen of us with our thumbs out hoping someone would stop and pick us up. A few did, but most of us were still "thumbing it" when a passenger bus stopped. At first we didn't get on. We thought he was picking up passengers for pay. The driver finally convinced us it was a free ride and we got on. He was just discharged from the army and was ferrying a bus from Detroit to somewhere in Florida. He was picking up any and every soldier in uniform hitchhiking. I got a free ride all the way.
>
> At Langly I met Bob. He and some of his buddies were going to the NCO club for the evening. I was a private. No problem. I just sewed corporal stripes on my shirtsleeve. Again,

something for which I could have been court-martialed, but I didn't know it.

They all had dates, but me. Bob arranged a blind date for me with a WAC. He was still in rare form taunting me. She was a date from hell. This 'female' was about six feet tall and built like a matchstick. I'm only five feet six inches tall. She had a face that would stop an eight-day clock. She had the personality of a rock.

We had a few drinks and the others were dancing with their dates. Mine 'moozed' all over me. She kept trying to pour liquor down me. I guess to get me 'boozed up,' too. I kept pouring them into paper cups on the floor under the table. I didn't want to get drunk. I had already visited that scene back at my barracks.

Later Don was assigned to desert warfare testing with the Corps of Engineers, Yuma Test Branch in the desert north of Yuma, Arizona. He completed his basic training at Fort Belvoir. He and seven soldiers were transferred to the Yuma Test Branch. Don was a private. An old sergeant was in charge of their little contingent.

We were transported to Union Station in Washington, D.C. where we caught the B&O RR overnight train to Chicago. This was the first time I ever rode Pullman class on a train. We arrived early the next morning. We had to lay over in Chicago all day to catch the Rock Island late that evening for Yuma, Arizona. That gave me an opportunity to look around downtown Chicago.

We caught the night train and again we traveled Pullman class. We had meal 'chits' which entitled us to meals in the dinning car. This was the first time I had ever eaten meals in a railroad dinning car. Our Pullman car was airconditioned as was the dining car. The trip was most enjoyable.

At Tucumcari, New Mexico, we switched over to the Southern Pacific RR which went the rest of the way to Yuma. We arrived at Yuma early morning before daylight in late July. The heat was suffocating when we stepped out of our airconditioned Pullman car onto the depot platform.

We were met by an army vehicle and transported about twenty miles north of Yuma alongside the Colorado River on the California side. It was daylight when we reached the camp which was situated on a large man-made island immediately below the Imperial Dam.

Our living quarters were low one story masonry block buildings with evaporative cooling fans as were all the buildings except the special purpose buildings. We had one latrine and shower building for the troops and one mess hall. There were about two hundred personnel assigned at the time I was there. There were about ten officers permanently assigned. They lived somewhere off the island. We often had visiting officers depending on what was being tested.

I was a clerk typist in the headquarters office. My main job was to type memograph masters to 'cut' orders and directives, place the masters on the reproducing machine, print however many copies were needed and make the proper distribution thereof. Because of the 'critical' nature of my job I didn't have to pull KP. I did have to pull guard duty one time. I occasionally participated in some tests of equipment if they were shorthanded for testing personnel.

They tested all kinds of army vehicles and tanks and accessories. They also tested pontoon bridges and had something called a Bailey bridge built across one of the waterways which they were testing.

We had an air conditioned theater which showed first run movies after hours in the evenings. I learned that the guy who was the projectionist was leaving and they needed a replacement. I jumped at the chance and had a week of on-the-job training under his supervision. Then I was on my own. I was paid fifty cents an hour and got to see all the movies free.

During free time we would swim in the Colorado River or go hiking in the surrounding mountains exploring old abandoned gold mines. I thought I could make some extra money panning for gold in the sands of the river. I did this for an entire weekend, only to learn that most of what I thought was gold was actually 'fools gold.' I had only about a dollar's worth of real gold flakes. So much for my gold panning venture.

> We went to Yuma on pass. I didn't drink, but a few times I made the bars with the other guys. I found that boring. So, one Saturday I went to a matinee movie in town. I struck up a conversation with a nice young lady who was an usher at the theater. When she got off work she invited me to walk her home. Her family was very nice and invited me to stay for dinner. They were Mormans. I had never heard of Mormans. I had one other movie date with her. I wish I could remember her name.

In October Don applied for a three-day pass. It was approved. He wanted to go see Betty Hill and her folks in Phoenix. He had dated Betty a few times when they lived in Oklahoma City. Don liked Betty, but she didn't much care for him though her parents liked him. Betty went out with Don only because her parents insisted.

> I was particularly interested in Betty Hill who was my age. She had lived two blocks from our house. She was a friend of Pat Paschall who I also would go out with on occasion, but had no real romantic interest. Betty did not particularly like me.
>
> Mr. Hill was gone a lot working in the war effort. I had often cut their grass, trimmed the hedges, made minor repairs, etc. for Mrs. Hill. She thought I was such a nice boy, but Betty did not share her sentiments. Betty dated me only because of pressure from her mother. Not a way to win a girl's heart I learned.
>
> Betty's family had moved to Phoenix. After a few weeks at Yuma Test Branch I got a three-day pass. I had corresponded with Betty via her mother in Phoenix. She (the mother) invited me to Phoenix for a weekend. On a Friday afternoon after retreat I got ready as quickly as I could.
>
> I rode the camp bus to Yuma. I was soon on the highway hitchhiking to Phoenix. I caught a ride right away to Gila Bend. It was dark when we got there. Gila Bend was nothing but a junction in the highway. The right leg went to Tucson. The left leg went to Phoenix. I stood beside the road in the night desert for hours trying to hitch a ride. Very few cars came by. Most went toward Tucson.

Finally, about midnight a guy in a Ford coupe stopped and gave me a ride. He was a homosexual. I had never been around such a person. I had heard the guys talk around the barracks about 'queers,' but I discounted it as just so much barracks talk. I didn't think anyone would really be like that.

He talked and talked. He talked about women and sex. Then he talked about sex and women. Then he talked about just sex. I got a little uneasy. Soon he put his right hand on my left thigh. I pressed as close to the car door as I could to put as much distance between us as I could.

It was a long, long ride through the night far out in the desert. This guy came at me with what seemed to be six pairs of hands. I kept pushing his hands away. I hugged the car door as tightly as I could. I had heard there were men who liked to have sex with other men, but I didn't believe it. Now I knew better. Now I knew how a girl felt to be out with a guy that had six pairs of roaming hands.

I began to get desperate. I wanted to jump from the car but he was traveling about sixty miles an hour. And, when we did pass through a couple of small towns I begged him to stop and let me out. But he kept going and managed to hit the only stop lights in each town on green without slowing down.

After awhile I could tell we were coming into a larger town. I prayed that he would have to stop at a red light. We went through a couple on green, but he finally had to slow down for a red light. I was afraid the light would turn green so when he slowed down to about ten miles an hour I opened the door and bailed out.

I hit the ground rolling. Sure enough the light stayed red and he came to a full stop. I thought, "Oh, my God. He'll come back and try to get me." I jumped up and ran the other way as fast as I could. I looked back. The light had turned green. He was going on—without me, thankfully. Now, where was I? I had no idea.

It was early morning but still dark. I knew I was on the outskirts of a larger town. As it turned out I was on the outskirts of Phoenix though I didn't know it at the time. I walked about a block on a chat pathway. I came to some shrubs in someone's yard growing next to the pathway. I decided to set down next to the shrubs and wait for daylight.

In a few minutes I was asleep only to be suddenly startled awake at the break of day by a loud crunching noise. I suddenly jumped to my feet not knowing what it was.

I scared the wits out of a paperboy on his bicycle delivering the morning paper. The poor kid fell off his bicycle. He scrambled to his feet while I tried to reassure him I intended him no harm. He didn't believe me. Without uttering a word he quickly picked up his bicycle and ran away pushing it. He jumped on his bike only when he was a safe distance from me—the bad guy.

I thought, "I'd better get the hell out of here before I find myself in serious trouble." I went in the opposite direction from the paperboy putting as much distance between him and me as quickly as I could.

It was getting daylight. I dusted myself off, straightened up my clothes, and put on my most pleasant demeanor. Now to find out where I was and what to do next.

As it turned out I was only about two miles from where the Hills lived. Mrs. Hill was glad to see me. Betty wasn't very happy. She already had a sailor boy friend. Mrs. Hill let her take the family car so she could go on a couple of dates with me, once to a movie and once just out driving around.

The war was over and testing was less of a priority. The army was cutting back on testing activities and personnel. Since Don was working in the office typing orders he could see that the Yuma Test Branch was being phased out. He had been promoted to Private First Class and was making fifty dollars a month.

In December Don applied for military leave which was approved. He 'cut' his own orders to Oklahoma City for ten days leave with instructions to report to Camp Stoneman, California, afterwards for assignment to Occupation Duty in Japan.

He rode the train chair class from Yuma to Oklahoma City. Uncle Sam wasn't paying his fare this time. No one met him at Union Station where the Rock Island came in. He saw a man in uniform catching the train. It was Billy Dale Jones, a friend from Moore. They visited a brief few minutes. Don took a taxi home. No one was there when he arrived.

Don spent the next several days relaxing and visiting with friends and relatives. He had a chance meeting with Pat Paschall on the sidewalk in front of Jenkins Music Store on West Main in downtown Oklahoma City. They visited a few minutes. He told her he was soon to ship overseas.

The day after Christmas Don took the train from Oklahoma City to Los Angles. He spent the day there looking around the area nearby the train depot. He was impressed with Los Angeles and thought it was an interesting place. That evening he caught the Southern Pacific Golden State Limited from Los Angles to San Francisco, thence to Antioch, California, and Camp Stoneman, an overseas replacement depot for the Army Far East Command.

He was there three weeks. He got one weekend pass and went to San Francisco. He had never seen the trolley cars and rode one up the hill and back down. He helped push it around at the bottom of the hill. He also had another weekend pass and visited some of his mother's family at Stockton, but can't remember who they were.

Somewhere, somehow while in California Don met Patsy Fry, a second cousin to his mother. He doesn't remember when, where, or why. She was about the same age as Don. He carried her photo all the rest of the time he was in the army. He still has the photo and has since met Patsy in recent years at the Jones Family Reunions in Oklahoma. She recognized the photo but doesn't recall their meeting either. Maybe they just corresponded.

The second day of February Don along with hundreds of other soldiers was trucked from Camp Stoneman to the Pittsburg landing on Honker Bay. There they boarded an army ferry boat and were ferried to the army docks at San Francisco. There they boarded the Army Troop Transport USS Bundy.

I had never seen a boat that big. I was one of the first into our assigned compartment. It had bunk beds made of steel frames with stretched canvas looped to the frames with a small sisal rope. They were stacked five high with about eighteen inches between. I chose a bottom bunk. That turned out to be a mistake.

I was topside along with hundreds of other soldiers as the army band on the dock played patriotic music. A tugboat nudged the boat from its mooring. We glided smoothly out into the Bay, past Alcatraz Island and approached the Golden Gate Bridge. I thought, "This isn't bad." I had heard all kinds of tales about guys getting seasick. Little did I know.

We sailed under the Golden Gate and into the open Pacific Ocean. The swells were huge. The boat lunged up and crashed down listing from side to side. Before we were out of sight from land we were all heaving over the rail feeding the fish.

I was miserable the next four days. Guys puked everywhere. The guys in the bunks above me puked down on me and my bunk. I refused to eat until I thought I could keep something down. Thus, I had the dry heaves. When they stopped I tried eating a little and it stayed down.

The rest of the ocean trip was enlightening. Of course, we had to clean up all the mess, but after that things were fairly smooth and uneventful except for two days about midway when we ran into a storm. It rained and the wind howled. The boat pitched up high and crashed down with a boom. It creaked and groaned. It was all we could do just to hold on. Some of the guys got seasick again, but I didn't.

We had periods of smooth sailing and nice days, especially when we were in the tropical ocean stream. I saw flying fish I had never seen. I saw schools of porpoise leaping from the water. Sometimes they were very near the bow and seemed to be playfully going along with us. Then it turned cold.

We landed at Yokohama mid-February. It was bitterly cold. They trucked us to a place called Zuma. It used to be the old Japanese equivalent of our West Point, but was used as a processing center for replacements. We slept in tents with no heat. We had folding canvas cots. At night I wrapped myself fully clothed in my OD blanket and pancho to keep warm.

> They were recruiting volunteers for replacements in the 11th Airborne Division on Northern Honshu. I signed up. Mostly to get the heck out of that hell hole at Zuma. I wanted a warm place to sleep. Besides, I would get an extra fifty dollars a month for jump pay. Little did I know.

General MacArthur's Far East Command Headquarters were in the Dia Ichi Building in the heart of Tokyo. The Russians entered the war in the very latest stages only after Stalin learned the Americans planned to drop the atom bomb on Japan. The Russian troops invaded Korea from the north. The Americans invaded from the south. The 38th Parallel was created because that is where the Americans and Russians met.

MacArthur in his wisdom permitted the Russians to have only a minimum military attache in Tokyo under his watchful eye. The Russians began to make political and military overtures that indicated they were going to extend the 38th Parallel across the Sea of Japan and across Northern Honshu in Japan proper.

MacArthur was not about to allow that to happen, contrary to the political 'winds' from Washington, D.C., and President Truman in particular. This was the beginning of their differing views of political and military perspective that led to their bitter conflicts such that ultimately Truman fired MacArthur.

MacArthur dispatched a large part of his command to the western shores of Northern Japan in combat readiness, including elements of the 11th Airborne Division. As a new replacement in the 11th Airborne Don in very short order found his self with an M-1 rifle in hand hunched down on the beaches of western Japan wondering why it was we were preparing to fight the Russians. Weren't they our allies?

This lasted only a few weeks. The Russians backed down and stopped the diplomatic rhetoric and military sabre rattling to extend the 38th Parallel. Don was sent to Camp Schimmelphennig near Sendai. He was there only a few days.

He was sent to the Airborne Training Center at Matsushima. There the trainees were quartered in Quonset huts with heat. The airborne units got a ration and a half allotment for each soldier. They ate better than the other units. Don liked that.

The parachute training was divided into four stages. The first stage was strictly physical conditioning and hazing. Many of the volunteers quit during this phase because they couldn't take the demanding exercises, running and hazing. The second stage was learning about the parachute, how to hook up and jump from the airplane door. Hours were spent jumping from mock-ups and making PLFs (parachute landing falls). The third stage was jumping from the towers and landing. Also, learning to pack a parachute. All the time there was constant physical conditioning and running. The fourth stage was the actual jumping from an airplane. Five jumps and you were a qualified paratrooper and awarded parachute wings.

The first time Don went up in an airplane he jumped out. He went up fourteen more times and jumped out before he ever landed. The landing was no ordinary event.

> It was a normal day, early morning shortly after daylight. The weather was perfect. We strapped on our parachutes and waited for the C-46 airplanes to come down the tarmac where we were.
>
> We were to jump in two fifteen-man 'sticks' from each airplane. One 'stick' from the left side and the other from the right side. There was to be a three-airplane flight.
>
> The C-46's rolled up in a line with engines roaring. I was the first jumper from the left side in the first airplane. We lined up and sounded off our position numbers. Then climbed aboard in reverse order, sat in the jump seats and fastened our seat belts.
>
> The airplane rolled off the tarmac and onto the runway. The pilot 'revved up' the engines. We began to roll. We were airborne. Everyone shouted, "Airborne!" (a tradition) as we took off and began to climb. The landing gear did not retract.

The pilot cut back the engines and began a gradual descent in a wide circle back around toward the airfield. I thought, "Hey, what's going on? This isn't normal." The jumpmaster shouted that we were returning to land at the airfield. The airplane was losing hydraulic power. We were not high enough to jump safely. We buckled up and got ready for a rough landing.

The pilot carefully brought the airplane around on a very short final approach. In a few seconds we touched down with a hard thump and a bounce. Then began a normal roll out. Everyone cheered and unbuckled. Then it felt very rough. The pilot by landing quickly had over shot the runway. He had very little braking power, if any. We rolled off the end of the runway.

Suddenly the airplane dropped about six feet off the end of the dirt ramp and nosed over into a rice paddy. Most of the guys fell forward sliding toward the front of the airplane. The guys in the back ended up on top of the guys in the front. Some were hanging onto their seats. We scrambled out. No one was seriously hurt.

That was my first time to land in an airplane.

After parachute training Don's first assignment was personnel clerk in battalion headquarters. He didn't particularly like the 'cush' job and soon began to find ways to do other more interesting things. He quickly learned that guys who participated in sports got special duty and special privileges. His first attempt for special duty as an athlete didn't turn out very well.

I walked past the gym where the division boxing team trained. I stopped and watched. I thought, "That looks easy. I think I'll try it." I went over to the old Master Sergeant that was the trainer. I told him I wanted to get on the boxing team. He sized me up and down with a jaundiced eye. He gruffly asked, "You ever been in a ring?"

"No."

"What makes you think you can box?"

"I'm a good fighter."

"Yeah. Come back tomorrow with shorts and tennis shoes."

I was there the next day at the appointed time. A skinny Mexican kid was in the ring shadow boxing. The sergeant put gloves on me and told me to get in the ring with the kid. He said, "Spar around a little with him and warm up." The kid and I sparred around about two minutes just jabbing at one another. No serious blows were landed.

The sergeant said, "Okay. Let's see you box." I made two hard right jabs at the kid. He took the blows on his gloves. I hadn't even touched him. Then, lightning struck. I didn't even see it coming. I woke up on the canvas with the sergeant bending over peering into my eyes asking, "Are you okay?"

Boy, was I ever set up. That ended my career as a boxer.

Football season rolled around and Don tried out for the Battalion and Special Services team. He played football in high school and had better success at football than boxing. He made the second team and played guard and center.

After football season he had to go back to a training unit. They made tactical training jumps in simulated combat situations. One such mission was to simulate taking an airfield. It had been used by the Japanese in the war, but was abandoned.

The jump was uneventful until I looked down and saw we had jumped about a minute too soon, or else the wind was blowing more than we thought. Anyhow, instead of landing at the far edge of the air strip as planned it was obvious we would land in the middle of the base itself among hangers and buildings.

I hurriedly looked around to find a place to land. I saw a paved road with a small canal ditch beside it. Next to the ditch was a tall barbed-wire security fence. There were several buildings on the other side of the fence. I saw an opening across the fence and guided toward it. I sure didn't want to hit that fence. Just as I was about to safely clear the fence I saw a lone flagpole without a flag sticking straight up in the spot I had picked to land.

> Good grief! I sure didn't want to end up hanging from that flagpole. I tugged hard on my right front riser to guide me away from the pole only to see too late I was going to land on a small concrete pad several feet square. I landed with a thud smack in the middle. I think the Japanese used the pad for a small cannon to fire during flag ceremonies. Thank God! I missed that pole.

During the tactical training maneuvers Don managed to jump and land in trees and on the roof of a Japanese house. He once landed in a rice paddy in the dead of winter. It had been plowed wet. Huge clods of mud were frozen solid and were as hard as rocks. The wind was blowing harder than usual. His chute drug him about twenty yards across the frozen clods before he was able to collapse it. He got more scrapes and bruises from that jump than any of the others.

Don's friend, Buford joined the navy about the same time Don went into the army. They corresponded a few times.

> I'm vague on how it was I came to have Buford's navy address. It seems when I was home on furlough it was a chance meeting with a mutual acquaintance that gave me his address.
>
> I have a small photograph which Buford sent me of him when he was about seventeen years old standing kind of jauntily next to a jazzed up Model-A Ford with big balloon whitewall tires. He inscribed the back: "Me & my car. That's where my trouble started." I'm almost certain Buford sent this photo to me while I was in the army, because years later I found it in a group of photos I had among my old army possessions. I don't know why we quit corresponding. I guess we just drifted off in different directions.

Don was assigned to the Airborne Training Center as a drill instructor. This came about from his participation in sports. They wanted cadre with physical endurance and tenacity. He was a drill instructor in the first stage of airborne training. That consisted entirely of strenuous physical exercise, running, and hazing, though it was never admitted there was any hazing. The first stage was a process designed to 'weed' out the weak ones that didn't have 'it.'

He would start the week with a platoon of thirty-two trainees. Two weeks later at the end of the first stage he would have only ten or twelve trainees left. The airborne units were strictly made up of volunteers. They could quit any time by simply reporting to the orderly room and signing a 'Quit Slip.' They were held until they could be reassigned to a non-airborne unit. Don had an unpleasant experience with one of his trainees that quit.

> The cadre had to be in top physical shape. We had to run more and exercise more than usual. We did lots of push-ups. We did lots of running in formation. We were tough no nonsense guys with the trainees. We could get in their faces but we could not touch them. We could not use profanity and could not say anything that reflected on their ancestry. Everything else was game. Many simply could not take it and quit.
>
> I had a guy that quit. He thought I had been "too tough" on him. He was waiting to be reassigned to another unit. I had finished my first stage training the Friday before and did not have an incoming group of new trainees for Monday. It was Sunday night. Some other instructors and I were due to jump early Monday morning with trainees making their first jump. We went to bed early to rise early.
>
> The guy that quit spent Sunday evening at the EM club getting 'beered-up.' Somehow he learned which Quonset the cadre were quartered in. About midnight he burst through the door, turned on the lights, and shouted, "Where's that Sergeant Davidson?"
>
> I was in the third cot from the door. Like a dunderhead I got out of my cot and said, "I'm Sergeant Davidson." I should have hid my head under my pillow and let someone else say, "He's not here."
>
> The guy flew at me in a rage. I decked him with a right fist. One of the guys and I picked him up and threw him out the door. Someone outside must have thrown him back in. He came flying back through the door and tackled me from

behind. We went down knocking over a cot and popping the wooden brace from the end of another cot.

I got up and decked him again. Like a fool I stood there and let him get up. I must've thought the Queensbury Rules applied. He came up on his knees holding onto the loose brace in the end of the cot. He came up on his feet and at the same time pulled the brace from the cot. It made a nice club.

I barely had time to throw up my hands to protect my head as he struck a blow at my head. Again, like a fool I didn't go down. He swung back the other way again at my head. My hands took the brunt of the blow. This time I got smart. I went down. This all happened in a matter of a few seconds. Some of the guys jumped in and subdued him. They drug him off to the orderly room.

My right wrist was badly swollen. My left hand was badly bruised across the knuckles. I hurt, and I had to make a jump in about six hours. No way could I pull my emergency chute handle if need be. I decided I could pull it by hooking my left thumb in the handle and push it out instead of pull it. I made the jump okay.

I learned a few good lessons that night. Most importantly, when you have a guy down don't let him up.

After his assignment at the Airborne Training Center Don was assigned for a short time to Special Duty at Sugamo Prison near Tokyo as a minimum security guard for low level Japanese war crime criminals. He was there while they tried Tojo. It was plush duty, on 24 hours and off 48. This gave him time to look around Tokyo. Later he was reassigned to the 127th Airborne Engineer Battalion as Athletic and Recreation NCO. This was a great assignment.

My job was to handle all the athletic and recreation activities for the entire battalion. I had to make sure all the company 'day rooms' were properly equipped and maintained. Each day room had a pool table with accessories and a ping-pong table with balls and paddles. They also had lounging

> chairs, card tables, playing cards, checkers, etc., as well as reading and writing tables. I was also responsible for all the athletic equipment such as footballs, basketballs, softballs, bats, etc. to check them in and out, maintain them, and order replacements when broken or damaged beyond repair.
>
> It was an army requirement that every headquarters building have a CQ (charge of quarters) on site during off duty hours. By special arrangement I was permitted to be permanently quartered in the battalion headquarters building as a permanent CQ. That meant I had my own private room. I did not have to get up and stand reveille every morning. I did have to be up and about each workday before duty hours.

A kind of funny thing happened to Don while he was in Japan. He saw all these Japanese people running around with little rectangle frames with beads. They used them to add, subtract, multiply and divide. He thought, "How clever. I'll learn how to do that and impress all the folks when I get back home." Little did he know.

> A Japanese lady hired by the Army as timekeeper for Japanese laborers had a small office in Battalion headquarters. She spoke a little English. She undertook to teach me to use an abacus.
>
> She manipulated the beads–one, two, three, four, and carry. That never made sense to me. She tried to explain, but I was hung up on the decimal system. What I didn't know nor understand was the Japanese used the base-5 system. I had no idea what it was until years later after I got into computers and had to understand binary, hexidecimal, base-5, etc.

Don's younger brother, Sam, was in the navy. He served on several destroyers, including the USS Gerke and USS Hollister. They corresponded several times. On one such occasion Sam informed Don his ship would dock at Yokohama for several weeks. Don secured authorization from his commanding officer to provide quarters and meals for Sam. Sam applied to his ship commander and was granted a ten-day leave.

Sam spent his leave visiting with Don at Camp Schimmelpfennig near Sendai. It caused quite a lot of curiosity and interest with the paratroopers to have a sailor living amongst them. Several of them plotted with Don to figure out how they could "fake it" so Sam and Don could make a parachute jump together. But, cooler heads prevailed and it was decided it would be too "chancy."

The 11th Airborne Division was reassigned from Japan back to the United States. They traveled by train to Yokohama where they boarded an army troopship. The trip was uneventful as they sailed toward Honolulu, Hawaii. Don's father's cousin, Lorene Davidson, lived in Honolulu. Sam had given her address to Don.

> When we were several days out from Hawaii I learned I could send a radiogram from the ship. I sent one to Lorene telling her the name of the ship and the day of arrival. I had no idea what to expect, if any thing. I had never met Lorene. I didn't even know what she looked like.
>
> The ship docked in Honolulu about noontime. Everyone except those with critical duties or demerits were given shore leave. An army band played at dockside as we all crowded the railing to watch the final berthing of the ship.
>
> After a short time the gangway was lowered and we were permitted to leave the ship. I was one of a steady flow of many soldiers going down the gangway and stepping off onto the dock. As I neared the end of the gangway I saw a tall willowy good-looking blonde woman standing nearby. She held a small sign that read "Sergeant Davidson." I was flabbergasted. It was Lorene. She whisked me away in her yellow convertible as many of my buddies watched even more flabbergasted than I was. I had a very pleasant three days and two nights with Lorene.
>
> She was no ordinary person. She came to Hawaii in the 1930's looking for her sailor husband. She never found him. What she did find was success. She went to work as a seamstress in an exclusive upscale boutique catering to the tourist trade. Several years later she opened her own boutique with a clientele of wealthy tourists. She was very successful. She invested some

of her money in Hawaii real estate which skyrocketed during and after the war. She owned retail property and several four-plex apartments. She lived in one of them.

She took me in like a long lost cousin and treated me royally. She had been dating an army general but recently broke up with him so she was footloose and fancy-free. She took me sightseeing, dining at the exclusive Outrigger Club on Waikiki Beach, and dinner and dancing at the Royal Hawaiian Hotel Club.

This was a real ego booster for me. Only officers were allowed in the Royal Hawaiian Club. Enlisted personnel were allowed only if they were the invited guest of a club member. Lorene was a club member. There were a number of army and naval officers in the club with lady escorts. Several officers from my outfit were sitting at a table in the club when Lorene and I came in from the dining room. They did not have lady escorts. The maitre d' knew Lorene. With a flair of showmanship he seated us at table next to the dance floor.

We were there about an hour or so. We had a few drinks and though I was not a skilled dancer we danced. Lorene was an excellent dancer and she made it look like I could dance. All the while I could see the officers from my outfit looking me and my 'date' over. I could tell they were wondering, "Where in the hell did Davidson find that woman?" I reveled in it.

I stayed two nights with Lorene. The third night she had some kind of previous engagement she had to keep. Early that evening she dropped me off at a local 'watering hole' for enlisted men. Some guys from my outfit were there. I stayed with then until about eleven o'clock. We had to be back on board the ship no later than midnight to sail the next morning.

I never saw Lorene again. I've often wondered whatever happened to her. Thanks, Lorene, for showing me a great time.

The ship sailed from Honolulu and a few days later docked early one morning in Panama to wait its turn to make passage through the canal. Most of the guys, including Don, were permitted to leave the ship and spend the day touring Panama City. They had to be back on board early that evening.

Don got to see the ship go through the locks from the Pacific side. Passage through the canal was during the night. Thus, he didn't get to see much of the canal or the locks on the Atlantic side.

The ship docked in New Orleans. Most of guys had accumulated leave and were furloughed directly from the ship with orders to report back to Camp Campbell, Kentucky. Don's enlistment had actually expired when they were somewhere in the Pacific Ocean between Honolulu and Panama. He went by troop train directly to Camp Campbell and was discharged in a few days.

He took the train from Clarksville, Kentucky, to Memphis. He took the Rock Island from Memphis to Oklahoma City. He came home to live with his parents. No one met him at the Union Station Depot. He took a taxi home to 3608 NW 13th Street.

What to do? Don was kind of at loose ends. When he tried to call some of his old girl friends the reply (if there was one) usually went something like, "Oh, she is engaged. Oh, she is married and has two of the cutest kids. Oh, she moved to California." Etc., etc.

Don had a chance meeting with Margaret Jean Knight on Main Street in downtown Oklahoma City. She was a classmate when Don went to Moore. The Knight's were neighbors on an adjacent farm when Don's family lived on the Turk Place. They had three daughters and a son. The girls were good looking, especially Margaret Jean.

> Margaret Jean and I were about the same age. We were in the same class at school. She was the youngest of the three daughters. Jim, the son, was the youngest. The Knights were in about the same economic class as we were—poor.
>
> I had been home from the Army only a few days when I had a chance meeting with Margaret Jean on Main Street in front of Katz Drugstore. I invited her to go into Katz and have lunch with me. She accepted.

> We had a nice friendly chat about our childhood days at Moore and an enjoyable lunch. However, when I got around to ask for a date she informed me she would not date the likes of me. She said she had intentions for bigger and better things than I would ever be able to provide.
>
> A lot of guys would have taken that as an insulting put down. I didn't because I understood where she was coming from. She had been poor. She wanted more from life than that. I fully understood. I never saw Margaret Jean again. I understand that a few years later she married an older man of considerable wealth.

Don joined the '52-40 Club' (forty dollars a week for fifty-two weeks unemployment pay for returning servicemen). He signed up for the Army Ready Reserves. He decided to finish high school. He enrolled at Central High School for the summer semester in the Veterans' Accelerated Course under the tutelage of Mrs. LeBron. He intended to complete his high school requirements that summer so he could enroll in college that fall.

In the meantime, Don become re-acquainted with Pat Paschall. He had been home about two months from the military. None of the girls he dated before entering the military were around anymore. Betty Hill, Joy Mae, Ruby, Jane Harding, and Esther Reno were nowhere to be seen. He hadn't even seen Pat Paschall around.

He dated Carlene Thorne a few times. She was a neighborhood girl and only fifteen years old. Don was twenty and not seriously interested in a fifteen-year old girl. However, she was the only girl he had dated since coming home.

One day Don went to the Veterans Administration office at 10th and North Broadway to take care of some of his veteran affairs. Afterwards, he caught a bus to downtown Oklahoma City to transfer to the Linwood bus and go home.

> The bus stopped at Sixth and Broadway. Two nice looking 'chicks' got on. They came to the rear of the bus near where I

was. I kind of eyeballed them a time or two. I noticed one kept looking at me. I thought, "Gee, maybe she likes me." Then she blurted out, "I know you! You're Gene Davidson."

I was dumbstruck. I had no idea who she was. She called me "Gene." She had to be someone from my distant past. She chatted all about my family and me. She obviously knew me.

She told me she and her friend, Jeanne, were seniors at Central High School, and they had jobs through the Distributed Education Program. She wrote her phone number on a scrap of paper, gave it to me, and told me to call her. She said good-bye as they got off the bus in downtown to go to work.

I sat there dumbfounded. I had no idea who this nice looking girl was. I puzzled over the number all the way home. It was not a number I recognized. It was a CEntral exchange number which was for the downtown and nearby area. I didn't know anyone there.

My sister, Ann, was also a senior at Central High School. She was living at home but worked. When she got home from work I showed her the phone number, told her how I got it, and asked if she recognized it. She thought I was a little off my 'rocker' to think she would recognize a phone number some girl gave to me on a bus. I pleaded with Ann the next several days to call the number and find out who that girl was. She wouldn't do it. She told me to call myself if I wanted to know.

I didn't want to call because I didn't want to make a fool of myself some way. I pestered Ann so much the next several days that she finally called the number. She laughed and hooted at me. She tantalized me unmercifully. She wouldn't tell me and she said over and over, 'You'll never guess who she is." This went on for several days. I was very anxious to find out who she was but I didn't want to call until I knew for sure.

Finally, I twisted Ann's arm until she blurted out, "It's Patsy Paschall." I said, "No way. She didn't look anything like Patsy Paschall." The last time I saw Pat she was fourteen and this girl was no kid, she was a nice looking young lady. After a couple more days Ann finally convinced me it really was Pat.

I finally got up my courage and made the phone call. Sure enough. It was Pat Paschall. I was flabbergasted, but elated. We made a date and the rest is history.

It wasn't long before Pat and Don were romantically involved. Pat lived with her grandparents at 817 NW 6th Street while she finished high school and worked part-time. Don was enrolled at the school for veterans at Central. They dated steadily. Late one night after a date Don had an unfortunate experience with the police. Pat's grandparents had a large house. Pat had her own room with a private entrance near the back. Pat and Don were standing on the steps kissing and saying goodnight after a date.

> We saw a police car go down the alley behind the house flashing a spotlight around. Someone apparently had called in a prowler complaint.
>
> We said our final goodnight. Pat went in and I went down the driveway between the houses. Like any young man full of love I ran down the incline of the driveway and across the street to where my father's car was parked. I jumped in and drove half a block to Shartel and turned left to go home.
>
> Before I went another block my rear view mirror was full of bright red flashing lights. The cops pulled me over. They knew they had their prowler. They made me get out of the car. They shoved me onto the hood and cuffed me. They asked for my driver's license. I had none. They asked whose car. I told them it was my father's. They asked where I had been. I told them at my girl friend's house. I was telling her goodnight. They asked if she would vouch for me.
>
> They took me onto the front porch and rang the doorbell. Pat's grandfather answered in his night robe. There I stood with two cops. God only knows what he thought. Pat's grandfather rousted her out of bed. She came and vouched for me. The cops apologized for the intrusion, but I was not out of trouble. They wrote me up for no driver's license.
>
> The next day I appeared in Traffic Court at the Police Station. I explained I was recently discharged from the Army. The judge said that if I would get a license in the next few days he would dismiss the ticket.
>
> Pat had a driver's license. She borrowed her grandparents' car. She drove around explaining to me what to expect on

> the driving test. I then used her grandparents' car to take my driving test. Very generous of them. I passed.

Pat graduated from Central in May 1949 and worked for The Oklahoma Credit Bureau. Don continued his courses at Central with the intent to finish in time to start college that fall.

Pat's parents had sold their house in Oklahoma City several years before and moved to a resort area near Lake Murray. Pat and Don visited her folks at Lake Murray several times during the summer. They owned and operated a country grocery store, filling station, and motel. They sold all kinds of picnic items, fishing gear, bait, boating and water skiing equipment, etc.

One time Don's sister, Ann, and her new husband, Fred, drove his Mercury convertible to Lake Murray with Pat and Don for an outing. In August Don went to Lake Murray and proposed to Pat. She accepted.

Earlier that summer Don had a chance meeting on the street in downtown Oklahoma City with his former high school football coach, Leo Higbie, that changed his direction. Coach Higbie was now the Athletic Director for the entire Oklahoma City School System. After they exchanged a few pleasantries Coach Higbie sprung a surprise.

> Coach asked me how old I was. I told him I was twenty. He asked when would I turn twenty-one. I told him in December. He asked if I knew I was still eligible to play high school football until the day I turned twenty-one. I didn't know that. He suggested that if I wanted to I could enroll at Classen that fall and play football.

That appealed to Don. He finished all his courses at Central that summer except one required course for English. In September he enrolled at Classen and went out for football. That fall Pat went to all of Don's home games at Taft Stadium. Afterwards they would go to Nicolosi's, their favorite restaurant at NW 10th and May Avenue, for a late dinner date.

Coach Higbie was no longer the coach. The new coach was Mr. Conger. He was an older man. He had accepted the coaching position for two years to attain his teachers' retirement.

Coach Conger and Coach Higbie were nothing alike. Coach Higbie was a disciplined taskmaster that wanted his teams to win, but he was fair with all the players. Coach Conger had little interest in the players or in winning. He just wanted to get his time in and retire.

Don was always competitive. He wanted to win regardless of whatever it was he was doing. Thus, his objectives were at odds with Coach Conger's.

> I had no idea at first what the situation was with Coach Conger. I had not only played two seasons of high school football under Coach Higbie, but also played two seasons in the military service under some good coaches. I had quite a lot of experience and knowledge of the game.
>
> I was puzzled at the coach's actions. He never came on the practice field during calisthenics and warm-ups. He didn't take a personal interest in the individual players to instruct them in the techniques of their positions. The plays in his playbook were convoluted. The practices were short, never going more than an hour and a half. He was not a taskmaster. I didn't understand.
>
> It was a new environment for me. I didn't know any of the players. I recognized from the 'git-go' this wasn't the way to coach a team. I didn't want to be overt about my displeasure. I thought maybe things would work out.
>
> I was twenty with a little over three years in the military. Most of the other guys were sixteen and seventeen. Two players, Haskell Graves and Earl Warr, had red-shirted and were nineteen. It was no great feat to pretty well knock the others around at will on the practice field.
>
> The Daily Oklahoma high school sports reporter, Wally Wallis, wrote extensively about Oklahoma City high school

sports. His pre-season prediction was that Classen would be lucky to win two games that season.

We traveled to Little Rock to play our first game. It was a night game. I thought it unusual to have a white football. The only score of the game came on a play where the Little Rock quarterback handled the ball and then ran down field to receive a pass for a touchdown. I was almost ejected from the game for protesting.

I protested to the referee that once the quarterback handled the ball he was ineligible to receive a forward pass. The referee informed me in no uncertain terms that was true under NCAA rules (which we played under in Oklahoma) but in Arkansas the high schools played under the Southern Association of High Schools set of rules. Coach Conger hadn't bothered to tell us the rules were different and explain the differences so we could be prepared. The final score was Little Rock 6 and Classen 0.

The next Friday we played Capitol Hill, a conference team, in Taft Stadium. The final score was Capitol Hill 18 and Classen 0. Three times we were inside the opponent's ten-yard line. Three times we lost the ball on downs because Coach Conger sent in plays from the bench causing delay of game penalties. This was incredible. I was beside myself with frustration.

By then I was somewhat acquainted with most of the players and had made my determination of who were leaders and who were not. I got with Haskell and Earl. We decided the team had to turn around. We covertly took over.

Haskell, Earl and I lead pre-practice calisthenics and warm-ups. We had weekly after hours team meetings. We urged the others to take the game more seriously, and to practice harder and longer. We discussed what we did right and what we did wrong. We talked about how to make adjustments. We coached the others on the techniques of the game.

The rest of the games Haskell, Earl, and I were in charge on the field. If the coach sent in a substitution we knew would cause a delay of game penalty, or was the wrong player for the given situation, we waved him off. He knew to get off the field quick else feel the results of our ire later.

> We won all the rest of our games. The only two games we lost were to state championship teams. Little Rock won in Arkansas. Capitol Hill won our conference and went on to win the Oklahoma State Championship.
>
> Wally Wallis had to eat his words. He couldn't believe the turn-around in our team.
>
> Some of my other teammates were Bill "Beaky" Bryan, Ernie Wyatt, Bernie Thompson, Ronnie Spencer, Mike Harding, Buddy Krogstad, Tom Murphy, and Dick Pulliam. Years later Bill Bryan told me he learned more about how to play football from me than from the coach.

Don graduated from Classen in January 1950. He enrolled at Oklahoma A&M that same month taking premed courses. He also went out for spring practice football as a walk-on under another new coach, J. B. Whitworth. They would not give athletic scholarships to athletes that had the G.I. Bill. Don and a roommate lived in the basement of an off campus boarding house.

Playing football left little time for serious studying. A boarding house with about twenty young men was not the best study environment. Most of the guys in the boarding house were freshmen and away from home on their own for the first time. Some were not serious students. They were often up to some kind of hi-jinks. One evening Don was studying for an exam.

> I lived in the basement. Fortunately, I had a roommate that was a serious student and a good guy to live with. But some of the others in the house were a constant pain in the neck.
>
> I was studying for an exam the next day. One of the idiots upstairs sneaked down the hallway to the circuit breaker box in a broom closet and turned off the main switch throwing the entire house into darkness. I stomped up the stairs, turned them back on and stomped back downstairs. This happened several times over the next hour and was very disruptive.
>
> It happened again. I stomped up the stairs, turned the lights back on and stomped down the stairs. Only this time I

quietly tippy-toed back up the stairs, got in the closet, closed the door and waited. Sure enough, in a few minutes here he came. When he opened the door I threw a hard right fist squarely in his nose. Blood splattered everywhere. He ran away crying. What a baby! The lights were on the rest of the semester. Problem solved.

Several days later another idiot had too much to drink. For some strange reason he wanted in my room. He stood outside the door and beat on it. I kept trying to get him to go away. He wouldn't. I locked the door and tried to ignore the pounding.

It grew conspicuously quiet. I looked up from my study desk and his long hair shaggy head was through the transom over the door. He was trying to climb into the room. I jumped up, ran to the door, grabbed him by the hair and jerked him into the room. He hit the floor face first. I didn't give him a chance to get up. I opened the door, drug him out by his hair, jumped in the middle of him and gave him about six good punches to the head.

I went back in my room, slammed the door and locked it. I never heard another peep from him. The idiots learned I wasn't to be messed with and the rest of the time there was uneventful.

On a few weekends Don hitchhiked to Oklahoma City to see Pat and visit family. One such visit was to see his Grandma and Grandpa Roller who were visiting his Mom and Dad.

Shortly after I arrived Grandma said she had never seen me in my army uniform and asked me to put it on for her which I did. As I unbuttoned my Ike jacket to take it off she suggested I might check the pockets. I ran my hand into the inside breast pocket. I pulled out a fifty- dollar bill. I couldn't believe I had left a fifty-dollar bill in my jacket. Grandma proclaimed innocence. It was certainly money I could use. I'm sure Grandma put it there for me to find though she never admitted it.

On a few occasions Pat came to Stillwater to see Don. She worked at the Credit Bureau in Oklahoma City. One occasion in

April Pat got her grandparents to let her drive their car to see Don. Her grandparents came with her.

However, as it turned out it was a short visit. It soon became obvious a big storm was brewing and they left early to avoid it. Not soon enough. Between Stillwater and Perkins Corner they were caught in a hailstorm that knocked out the windshield and did considerable damage to their car. The hail damage in Stillwater was significant. Many of the hailstones were baseball size. The campus suffered millions of dollars in damage.

May 1950 Don completed his first semester at Oklahoma A&M. He and Pat went to Fretwell Motor Company at NW 4th and Shartel and Don used some of his savings from the military to buy a used 1947 Dodge sedan.

Pat and Don planned to get married June 1st. They drove to Marietta a week or so before their marriage. They got their marriage license at the Carter County Courthouse in Ardmore. Pat and her mother planned the wedding. They were married at ten o'clock the morning of the first day of June in 1950 at the First Baptist Church in Ardmore. They left right after the reception. They stayed their first night at a motel in Waco, Texas.

They drove to San Antonio and stayed a few days with Pat's great uncle Ledford Patrick and great aunt Gertrude. They lived near the intersection where South Saint Mary Street crossed South Alamo Street at right angles. Don never quite understood how that could be.

They drove to Houston where they rented a garage apartment. The lady landlord had twenty Pekinese dogs. This lasted two weeks.

Pat had been promised a job at the Houston Credit Bureau. The man who made the promise to her boss, Mr. J. J. Bamburger, in Oklahoma City was "gone" on vacation. No job for Pat. Don could not find temporary work. All the summer jobs had already been filled. No prospects for a much needed job in Houston. Besides, it rained every morning at ten o'clock.

Don and Pat decided to go back to Oklahoma City. They lived at Pat's grandparent's house. Pat went back to work at the Credit Bureau. Don went to work on a pipeline construction project. In a few weeks he got a job with Kerr's Department store as a vacation relief delivery driver.

The fall in 1950 they went back to Stillwater. Don returned to school at Oklahoma A&M. Pat got a job working for Stillwater Typewriter Company that had a contract to maintain all the typewriters on the A&M campus. They lived in Veterans Village at #8 Cheyenne. The 'hut' was sixteen by sixteen feet. It had a kitchen, living room, bedroom and bathroom.

> The hut was made of plywood nailed on two by two studs. It had sixteen small casement turnout type windows. The roof came to a pyramid with a vent at the peak. There was no insulation. It was furnished with a cookstove, small table, space heater, couch, and bed.
>
> We bought a refrigerator. Pat brought what few household goods she had. That included a small round table and lamp, a console radio, a few kitchen appliances and utensils, linens, bedding, and towels. She made curtains for the windows. She tried very hard to make it a cozy homey place. It cost thirty dollars a month with all utilities paid.
>
> I could sit on the couch in the living room and prop my feet on the turned down oven door in the kitchen. A regular size bed barely fit in the bedroom with a tiny closet. Taking a shower was like taking one in a shoebox.

War broke out in Korea in June 1950. The same month Don and Pat were married. It did not go well for the South Koreans. By fall the North Koreans had pushed so far into South Korea that only a small area remained under their control. The United Nations stepped in and the United States responded with troops.

In October Don was recalled to active duty and ordered to report for duty at Tinker Air Force Base near Oklahoma City. Pat's employer fired her because he thought she would leave and go with Don. She was unemployed in Stillwater and could not find another job because all the jobs had been taken for the school year. Don was in a barracks at Tinker. He had been there three days.

> The fourth morning at reveille the First Sergeant called for Sergeant Davidson to fallout for the Orderly Room. That usually meant you were in some kind of trouble. I couldn't imagine what.
>
> I reported and the Company Commander told me to report to the Adjutant General office. That usually meant you were in real serious trouble. I could not imagine what. I hadn't been there long enough to do anything wrong.
>
> I reported to a Captain Black in the Adjutant General Office. He immediately turned to a credenza behind his desk and picked up a copy of Army Regulations. He had a place marked by a piece of white paper sticking up. I thought, "My God, he is going to throw the book at me."
>
> He opened the book at the marked place and read to me. It was something to the effect that: "If a reservist with prior military service is called to active duty while enrolled at a college that offers a Reserve Officer Training Corps program then the reservist may at his request be discharged from the Army providing the reservist signs up for the Reserve Officer Training Corps program at the college." I gulped. I was dumbfounded. The captain sensed that. He asked, "Sergeant, did you understand that?"
>
> "Yes, sir. I think so."
>
> "Would you like me to read it again?"
>
> "Yes, sir."
>
> He read it again.
>
> "Do you understand, Sergeant?"
>
> "Yes, Sir."
>
> "Would you like a three-day pass?"
>
> "YES, SIR!"
>
> A week later I was discharged and back in school at A&M committed to enroll in the Army Signal Corps ROTC program starting the next semester.

Don's discharge at the convenience of the government solved only one problem. He was soon back in school, but Pat was unemployed. The G.I. Bill monthly check of only seventy-five dollars was not enough to pay the rent, make the car payment, make the refrigerator payment, and buy groceries and gasoline.

Don and Pat decided to tough it out to the end of the semester hoping Pat could get a job at the change of semesters. It didn't happen. In February Pat's Mom, Mable, came to visit. She brought groceries and a little money. It was very cold.

> A north wind was howling outside. We had the space heater going full force to keep the place warm. When bedtime came we made down the couch for Mable. She asked if I was going to turn off the space heater. I told her, "No."
>
> "But won't we get asphyxiated?"
>
> "Not a chance. See those curtains standing out from the windows. See the linoleum bowing up. There's plenty of air flowing through here."
>
> "What if the place catches fire?"
>
> "Not to worry. See that wall. I'll run right through it and you and Pat can follow me out."
>
> We got a good night's sleep. Snow the next morning.

Now the only solution was for Pat to go to Oklahoma City to live with her grandparents and work at the Credit Bureau. Don lived in the hut in Veterans Village the rest of the semester. He visited Pat on occasional weekends and Pat sometimes took the bus to Stillwater to visit him.

At the end of the Spring Semester of 1951 Don and Pat moved to Oklahoma City. They lived at Pat's grandparents' house while they spent most of the summer at their cottage near Lake Murray. Pat worked at the Credit Bureau and Don drove a delivery truck for Kerr's Department Store.

While in the army Don had expanded his interest in photography. His interest continued after he returned to civilian life. He had a 35mm Argus C-3, a Lecia 35mm, and an old 6cm x 9cm German Dresdan view camera with a roll film adapter for the back. He made a lot of good photos with it.

One day an upcoming Junior Miss fashion designer, Ann Fogarty, had a style showing at Kerr's. As a new struggling designer she was operating on a shoe string budget. At the last moment the Kerr's Junior Fashion coordinator wanted photos made of the show.

Don had the tenacity to tell her he could take the photos for a bargain price. The coordinator agreed. He bought a new Century Graphic press type camera, an enlarger, and darkroom accessories. He took the photos, developed the film in the kitchen, and printed the photos on the dining room table. He didn't make much money, but did make enough to cover the cost of all his new equipment. Thus, he launched a part-time mini-career as a photographer.

Don and Pat returned to Stillwater in the Fall of 1951. At Veterans Village they moved up to a double hut at #9 Cheyenne which provided twice the space. It had two bedrooms. Don used one for a study. They also had accumulated a few more household items to make it a more homey and comfortable place to live.

Before classes started that fall they both worked a short time for the Veterans' Administration to process G.I. Bill veterans' applications. Don dropped premed and enrolled in the School of Commerce. He decided he didn't have the financial wherewithal to see him all the way through medical school.

Pat got a job at the college infirmary. She took care of the paper work to admit students for treatment by the medical staff. Don pursued his interest in photography. He worked part-time evenings for Doc Pruitt taking hundreds of pictures each weekend of fraternity and sorority parties and dances. He later got a part-time job at the Vocational Agricultural Department as a photo lab technician. He was paid the minimum wage of seventy-five cents an hour.

Don became acquainted with Carl Wood, an outstanding wrestler on the school team. Pat and Don began to run around with Carl and his wife, Susie. Carl was also interested in photography.

> One evening we were out running around with Carl and Susie. Carl and I saw something we thought would be interesting to photograph, but didn't have our cameras.
>
> We ran by Carl and Susie's apartment to get Carl's camera. He wanted me to come up and see his new electronic flash unit. We left the girls in the car parked on the other side of a hedge about six feet high.
>
> When Carl and I came back we heard three guys on the other side of the hedge trying to pick up the girls. We heard one of them ask, "What's your name, Babe?" Carl stepped around the hedge and said, "What's it to you?" The guy replied,"Yeah, you want to make something of it?"
>
> "No, just go on and leave us alone."
>
> "Hey, Buster. I ain't going nowhere."
>
> "Look. These're our wives. We don't want any trouble. Just gone on."
>
> "Yeah. Let's see ya make me go on," as he put up his fists to fight. Carl threw a hard right fist hitting him squarely in the nose. Blood splattered. The guy and friends ran away. Carl shouted, "Hey, come back. I thought you wanted to fight." The guy shouted back over his shoulder, "If you want my ass you'll have to catch it."
>
> The first thing next morning Pat checked the guy in at the infirmary with a broken nose. She quietly snickered a little.

In the meantime Don quit football. It had ceased to be fun. He didn't like the coach and the coach didn't like him. Not a good situation. An incident on the practice field finally made Don give up football.

> I loved to play football. I was a good player in high school. I was small as football players go, especially for a guard. However, I was quick, fast, had stamina, and played smarter than most.

Nothing I loved better than to knock a bigger guy on his butt or make a hard hitting tackle.

We played without some of the protective gear used today. We did not have facemasks. We also had to be able to play offense and defense because substitutions could be made only two players at a time and only during an official time-out. We also had to know how to play several different positions. If we were on defense and recovered a fumble we often would not have a regular offense player on the field for a certain position. Someone, maybe a guard, would have to fill in as a tackle or an end until an official time-out and a substitution made to get the regular player in the game.

I went out for football at Oklahoma A&M College as a walk-on. I now was up against players who were bigger than I was, especially the linemen. I did okay in freshman football because I was going against guys just out of high school. Most of them were on athletic scholarships. The freshman coach was an okay guy. I still played guard. I would say I was at least an average or better player as a freshman.

However, my sophomore year many of the freshmen players had dropped out. Only the more promising ones were out their sophomore year. I now was under the tutorship of the head coach, J.B. Whitworth, and the line coach, Bob Johnson. I learned very quickly I not only had to go against the bigger players, but now had to go against the coaches. Whitworth had a 'win at all cost' attitude. He had a strange distorted concept of what made a good football player. His line coach reflected that same attitude. One of his strange ideas was that a walk-on player could never be good enough to make his team. That put me and the several other walk-ons at an immediate untenable disadvantage. It was several weeks before that realization sank in.

The coach constantly belittled us at every opportunity. If we made a mistake or didn't perform up to par he singled us out for severe and harsh criticism before the entire squad. If we made an exceptionally good play in scrimmage and knocked one of the scholarship boys on his butt the coach would not speak favorably of our performance. Instead, he berated the scholarship guy because he let a lowly walk-on outplay him. This occurred several times every practice session. It was disheartening but made me want even more to outplay the scholarship boys. But, a single occurrence made me change my mind and give up football for good.

In practice when a lineman missed a blocking assignment and as a result the ball carrier was tackled for a loss the coach made the offending lineman line up behind the center without blockers. He then would pick four linemen to line up on defense. When the ball was snapped to the offending lineman he had to run forward like a fullback with no blockers to protect him. Supposedly this was to teach the offending lineman what it was like to a fullback when a blocking assignment was missed. The four defensive linemen had to hit and tackle the lineman ball carrier as hard as they could else they would be put in the same ball carrying position.

Whitworth loved to pick at least one or two of the walk-on guys to be the defensive linemen to make the hard tackle. I think it was his hope to be able to make the game so dangerous and unpleasant to the walk-ons that they would quit. Well, he succeeded. I quit never to play football again.

I was one of the four defensive lineman to hit and tackle Charles, a scholarship lineman who had missed a blocking assignment on a scrimmage play. When the center snapped the ball the four of us charged Charles as hard as we could. All four hit him at the same time. I heard a loud sickening snap like a breaking broom handle.

We broke the large bone between his knee and hip. Whitworth dismissed it as an indication Charles was not tough enough to play football on his team. While the trainers worked with Charles and the ambulance was called to take him to the hospital Whitworth moved us over to another part of the practice field and continued the scrimmage. He showed absolutely no compassion, concern or sorrow for Charles.

I felt terrible. Charles was my friend. At the end of practice I checked in all my equipment, showered, and walked out the door to never return. I wanted no part of that kind of football.

The "Johnny Bright Incident" occurred the next football season after Don quit. It brought national attention to Oklahoma A&M College. Not the kind to be desired. Nevertheless, it occurred and was indicative of Coach Whitworth and his coaching style.

Prior to 1952 there were no black football players at any of the major colleges or universities. There had been Indian players but no black players. In fact Oklahoma A&M College had a Pawnee Indian, Bill Bredde, who played fullback.

Oklahoma A&M was in the Missouri Valley Conference during the 1950's which included Tulsa, Wichita, St. Louis, Detroit, and Drake University in Iowa. Johnny Bright, a Negro, was the tailback on the Drake team. He was heralded as the first black man to play football at any major college or university. The national press was giving him ample coverage.

On a Saturday afternoon in the Fall of 1953 Johnny Bright came to Stillwater, Oklahoma, with the Drake University team to play Oklahoma A&M at Lewis Field. RKO Pathe Newsreel was there to record the event as were numerous reporters and photographers. Prior to the game during the team warm ups RKO and a gaggle of reporters and photographers followed Johnny Bright around everywhere he went on the playing field.

Drake ran from the old single-wing formation. Johnny Bright was the tailback which in today's football vocabulary is the running-back. He was a good athlete and tailback with impressive statistics.

> J. B. Whitworth, the head coach at Oklahoma A&M, was what I would characterize as a Georgia 'red-neck cracker' with a win at all cost attitude. Since I went out for football at Oklahoma A&M in 1950 and 1951 as a walk-on I knew Whitworth pretty well. In 1953 I still had some good friends on the A&M team. My friends told me that Whitworth in a suggestive manner put out the word "to get that nigger."

Oklahoma A&M kicked off to Drake. Johnny Bright handled the ball several times and made some impressive gains. All this time the RKO newsreel cameras were rolling focused on Johnny Bright.

The Drake team lined up single-wing strong to the right. The ball was snapped directly back to Bright. He ran to his right and handed the ball off to the wing-back who then reversed and ran to the left. After Johnny handed off the ball he violated one of the cardinal rules of football. He came to a stop, stood erect, and looked back over his left shoulder to see how the play went.

This was the obvious opening No. 78, Willbanks Smith, left tackle for A&M, was looking for. As Bright looked back over his left shoulder Smith laid into him with a stiff right elbow upper-cut to his right jaw. Players in those days did not wear facemasks. Bright was about six feet tall and weighed about 185 pounds. Smith was six feet four inches and weighed about 220 pounds. The blow lifted Bright completely off his feet and laid him out. Bright struggled to his feet and ran two more plays then left the field of play under his own power. It was later determined he had a broken jaw and did not return to the game.

RKO Newsreel caught all this on movie film in slow motion. It was played over and over in movie theaters all over the United States. The Des Moines Press sequence camera caught the action frame by frame. The entire sequence was published nationwide. Smith was ostracized by the national press. He got hate mail from everywhere, some just addressed to "Number 78."

Poor Willbanks. He was about as dumb as Whitworth. He lost his scholarship and Whitworth lost his job.

Whitworth was at Oklahoma A&M the four years I was there. The team under his tutelage never won more than a few games, except one season when they won more than they lost. He was fired and never held another head coaching job at any college or university I know of.

A few years later I saw him on television on the sideline as an assistant of some kind for the University of Georgia football team. I had absolutely no respect for the man. I learned a few years later he died of a heart attack. I felt no remorse or sorrow.

Years later when Johnny Bright died after an impressive career in Canadian Professional football, I learned that Willlbanks Smith sent flowers to his funeral.

Don had a good relationship with his in-laws, Bert and Mable Paschall. Over the years he and Bert did a lot of things together. They went fishing in Lake Murray and Lake Texoma. They hunted ducks along Hickory Creek and along the shores of Lake Texoma. They hunted quail all over the southeastern part of Love County. Bert kept a small kennel and trained bird dogs for other people. He had a championship bird dog named Popeye.

It was a pleasure to hunt with Popeye. The only problem was he would hunt only when Bert was along. There were times Bert couldn't go hunting but would insist we take Popeye. I would tell him that Popeye wouldn't hunt for us, but to pacify Bert we would take him and two other dogs.

Popeye would jump out of the back of the truck and go right to hunting. In about two minutes he would look around and not see Bert. He would hunt another two or three minutes and not see Bert. He then would beat it back to the truck and lay there until we were ready to go home.

Once Bert and I had been hunting all day. We were returning home. There was a misty rain and it was cold. We saw a large covey of quail cross the road ahead of us. We had to get out and work that covey. Bert let only Popeye out. He kept the other dogs in the truck. Popeye pointed the covey in an open field. When the covey broke we each got a shot. The quail flew to the closest cover which was waist high grass on the other side of a barbed-wire fence.

Popeye immediately started working the singles. He had his eye on a quail that went into the tall grass. He didn't want to get in all that wet grass. He ran on the side of the fence in the short grass to point the single he saw go into the tall grass. I was about fifteen yards from Popeye looking straight at him.

> Suddenly in the middle of a leap he saw another quail a few feet away in the tall grass. So help me, I saw that dog come to point in mid-stride in mid-air. He hit the ground on point. Incredible.

Don also helped Bert with various tasks around the farm. One day they went to cut firewood. It was early morning after a heavy overnight rain.

> Bert and I decided to go cut firewood since it was too wet to do anything else. We crossed Pumpkin Creek running hubcap deep. We drove up a muddy slope and down the other side to a wire gap gate near a small creek tributary to Pumpkin Creek.
>
> I got out of the truck and opened the gate. All of a sudden I saw Bert leap out of the truck and go to his knees with his nose almost touching the ground. I thought he had gone berserk. What he saw in the early morning sunlight was a reflection from a gold coin resting on a little pedestal of mud. We surmised it must have washed downstream during the rainstorm that night from a gold stash somewhere up the creek.
>
> We spent the rest of the day intently looking up and down the full length of that little creek several times. We found a lot of things, but no gold. We didn't cut any firewood that day.
>
> The next twenty some years for the rest of Bert's life, he and I on any occasion we could spent hours looking up and down that little creek trying to find that stash of gold. We never found it.

One of the unusual places of social diversion in and around Marietta was a beer joint known as Hole-in-the-Wall. Don was not particularly fond of frequenting beer joints. However, on a few occasions after some amount of cajoling he went with his erstwhile erratic brother-in-law, Ralph Collom. Hole-in-the-Wall was located a few miles north of Marietta and east of old Highway 77 down in the Hickory Creek breaks.

> I was there only a few times in the 1950's. I have no idea who owned the place. It was always after dark when I was there so I can't really give a good description of the place. But, it was a small wood frame building with outside vertical wall planking. I'm not sure but I think it was supported on stacked flat rocks at the corners. It may have been an old early 1900's farm house converted to a beer joint.
>
> It had wood plank floors, a few tables and chairs, and a stand-up bar. No electricity. Kerosene lamps. There was a bullet hole through the wall behind the bar, thus the name Hole-in-the-Wall. I was never there when it was raining, but I'd bet a dollar to a hole in a donut the roof leaked. There were no steps. You just stepped up about fifteen inches through the front door and into the bar.
>
> I don't know if it was a daily practice or not, but the few times I was there someone always had cooked a big black pot of beans over a wood fire out in the yard. If you wanted some beans you went out and ladled them up for yourself.
>
> There was an old good size dog always laying around. One time when I went there the dog had a nasty ugly bloody wound in the top of his skull. You could faintly see a small part of his brain exposed. I asked what happened. Someone said, "He got shot." I thought, "Good grief! That poor dog must have a terrible headache."
>
> There was a lot of beer drinking, B.S. talk, and an occassional fight. Never any gun play when I was there, thank God. Pat went with me one time. That was the last time I ever went there. I have no idea what happened to Hole-in-the-Wall.

Don's younger brother, Sam, was discharged from the Navy and married Rowena Vance in January 1952. They were living in a small garage apartment on NW 10th Street in Oklahoma City. One evening Don and Pat went to visit them. Sam's friend was also visiting. He had recently been discharged from the Navy and was on his way home.

Sam, his friend, and Pat got to playing poker. Rowena and Don watched. The game went into the wee hours of the morning. Pat was the big winner. She was always good at cards. She won a goodly sum from Sam's friend. As Don and Pat were leaving she gave her winnings back to Sam and his friend. Don chastised her for it. He said, "If you would have lost they would have kept your money." Pat insisted it was all in good fun. Besides she didn't have the heart to take all that young man's money. Don finally agreed. Pat was not only good at cards but also a good sport.

Back at Stillwater for the fall semester Pat got a very good job as secretary for Walter S. Burn, an Englishman. He was the Director of the Oklahoma Power and Propulsion Laboratory on the Oklahoma A&M campus. Pat's good job eased their financial situation somewhat.

That Fall Don cast his first vote for a presidential candidate. In 1952 you had to be twenty-one years of age to vote. Don turned twenty-one in December, 1949. It was 1952 when Eisenhower was nominated by the Republican Party and Don was almost twenty-four when he first voted.

The government raised the monthly G.I. checks for all the veterans. Don now received one hundred and five dollars a month. With that and Pat's increase in salary they moved from Veterans Village to a two-unit apartment in the back at 707 Hester Street. Pat and Don lived downstairs. The apartment was owned by Mrs. Jarvis, a nice looking widow lady with a fourteen year old daughter that was 'crazy' to go with college age boys, especially if they played football.

> I had quit football but was still friends with some of the guys on the team. Bill LeClair was one such friend. He was a tall handsome guy. He sometimes came by the apartment. Judy, the landlady's fourteen-year old daughter, had seen him several times.
>
> Bill had a girl friend. She lived in St. Louis. She stayed one week with Pat and I while she and Bill went out on dates. They were very much in love and were married after Bill graduated.

One day Judy approached me to get her a date with Bill for one of her high school dances. I told her Bill already had a girl friend. She said she didn't care. She just wanted one date with him for this particular dance. Though I tried to dissuade her she persisted. She said, "I'll do anything if you will get me a date with him."

I said, "Judy, that covers a lot of things."

"I don't care. I'll do anything."

"Okay, I'll talk to Bill."

The next day I saw Bill. He thought it was preposterous. He and I discussed it. I approached Judy the next day with his answer. I said, "Judy, you said you would do anything if Bill will go as your date to the dance, right?" Judy said, "Yes."

I said, "Bill said he will go to the dance with you on one condition."

"What's that?"

"That you fix him up with your mother."

That was the last we heard from Judy about dates with any of my college football friends.

Another event while Don and Pat lived at 707 Hester Street concerned a stray dog. They went to an evening movie at a theater in downtown Stillwater. When they came out it was dark and raining.

We ran across the street, opened the car doors and jumped in. Only thing is a rain drenched half-grown bird dog jumped into the car with us before we could shut the door. I couldn't bring myself to shove him out into the pouring rain. He was shivering pitifully, so we took him home with us. We tried to find his owner but without success. By then we were fond of him and called him Bozo.

He soon grew into a full size dog. We didn't have a place for him outside so he lived inside with us. I let him out first thing each morning. He would run for about twenty minutes and come back to the door and I'd let him in.

One morning he was back in about five minutes wanting in. He was whining pitifully. I let him in. Then I saw. A car

> apparently hit him. Not hard enough to do serious damage, but it caused him to scoot on the pavement. It rubbed a hole in his scrotum and one testicle was hanging out several inches.
>
> I drove him to the college veterinary clinic with him standing in the seat next to me. I drove with one hand and held his testicle up with the other hand. You never saw a dog stand so still. They fixed him up and Pat wrote a twenty-dollar check. Bozo recovered only to run away. Never found him.
>
> Weeks went by and the veterinary clinic had not deposited the check. Pat was short on money one week and wrote a check over draft on the veterinary check. Wouldn't you know it. That was the very week they cleared the check and Pat's check bounced. That was the only 'hot' check Pat ever wrote.

Pat got a pay raise. Don made extra money as a free-lance photographer and as a photo lab technician for the Oklahoma State Vocational Agricultural Department on campus. They moved to a nicer upstairs apartment at 910 McElroy Street. It had a living room, kitchen with dining area, two bedrooms and a full bath. Don used one bedroom for a study.

Don took photographs of anything to make a little money. He sometimes took photographs just on speculation. One such occasion was when Cities Service opened a new super service station on Main Street in Stillwater. Don stopped and took two photographs on the day of the grand opening.

He took the photos by a few days later and the marketing manager was there. He purchased the two photos. A few days later Don got more orders for the two photos. Over the next several months he got more orders. Don made a nice sum on those two photos. Years later Don was looking in a book on Oklahoma Architecture. He saw one of his photos of the Cities Service station.

Don also worked on the school newspaper, The Daily O'Collegian, as Chief Photographer. He was Staff Photographer for the yearbook, Redskin. He took the feature photo of the new library building in the 1953 Redskin.

He also was Photographer for the monthly campus magazine, Aggievator. Don's good friend, James Thomas from Classen, was the editor. With James' cartoons and Don's photos of campus co-eds the magazine sold out every issue. It was one of the few times the magazine actually made money. Pat was sometimes a little irritated to come home from work and find Don with some lovely co-ed posing for photos in their living room or bedroom. But she was a good sport about it.

One hot spring day Don had been working outside. He came in hot and sweaty for lunch. Pat had made a full pitcher of ice tea. Don sat at the table and downed a full glass.

> I pushed the glass across the table at Pat and demanded, "Tea!" She said, "Ask for it right."
>
> "Give me some damn tea."
>
> "Not till you ask for it right."
>
> I threw the ice in the glass in Pat's face and demanded, "Give me some damn tea." Pat responded, "You want some damn tea," as she threw the entire pitcher in my face. Our marriage was about to hit the rocks, but was saved by the bell.
>
> An instant after she threw the tea the doorbell went ding-dong. I ran and looked out the window. There was my old maid Aunt Hazel on the porch. She had never been to visit before.
>
> Talk about teamwork. Pat and I turned to and quickly cleaned up the mess
>
> We greeted Aunt Hazel at the door with our best congenial smiles. She never knew she probably saved our marriage. We've laughed a lot about it since.

Don was in the Reserve Officer Training Corps (ROTC). By virtue of his previous military service he was Battalion Executive Officer. The summer of 1952 he had to go to Camp Gordon, Georgia, for summer camp. He drove the '47 Dodge and took several buddies to help pay for the gas. The Fourth of July weekend they got passes. Don and some buddies went to Jacksonville Beach, Florida.

> It was hot. We had just arrived in Jacksonville from Camp Gordon. There was a lot of holiday weekend traffic. My car didn't have air conditioning and the windows were down. I smelled something like an over-heated engine. I said, "Someone's car sure is hot." I very soon realized it was my car.
>
> I pulled into the first service station. The guys got out and headed for the beach. The service station guy inspected the engine and said I had a pinhole leak in the bottom tray of the radiator. It would cost forty dollars to fix. I didn't have forty dollars. I was beside myself.
>
> I went across the street to a diner and got something cold to drink. I sat there dejected. The waitress sensed it. She asked me what was the matter. I told her. She picked up a small hot sauce bottle and shook out a round toothpick. She said, "Here, put this in the hole. It will swell up and seal it." I took the toothpick and her advice. I owe that waitress. I don't think I even left her a tip.
>
> I drove that car another two years. Sold it to a guy who drove it to Oregon and back pulling a trailer. Last I knew it was still going with the toothpick intact.

The eight weeks training at Camp Gordon were fairly intensive. They had to learn about various weapons, communications equipment, and tactics. They spent a lot of time on bivouac in the pine forests of Georgia. It was hot and dusty. They had been on bivouac all week living in pup tents, eating at field kitchens, and using hand dug latrines. No shower facilities.

> One evening the cadre announced they were going to run some shuttle trucks down to a shower facility. All the guys but me and another guy, Joe Stoppy, who also had prior military service, piled into the several open army trucks stripped to their shorts. They roared away down a red dirt road in a massive swirl of red dust.

They rushed all those guys through the shower and loaded them up still wet to return to the bivouac area. They arrived with wet red dust plastered to their bodies. Joe and I had a good laugh on them.

Next day we went on tactical maneuvers to simulate a combat situation. We were divided into combat teams. Each team had a tactical objective to achieve by taking it from the 'aggressor force' made up of the cadre wearing different distinctive helmets. We studied our maps and plotted our tactics. Then we deployed over a wide area to advance on the 'aggressors.'

The 'aggressors' tactic was to let individual teams get into an isolated area. Then a single 'aggressor' would step out in front and announce, "You are surrounded by a large force. You are our prisoners. Come with me." He then took them to a compound and retained them.

When an 'aggressor' stepped out in front of my team. I said, "Yeah. Let's see your large force." He said, "You are surrounded. You have to come with me." I said, "You got it wrong, Jack. You are our prisoner and you're coming with us." He persisted, "No. You come with me." I slapped the side of his helmet right sharply with the butt of my rifle and said, "Come with us." He did.

At the group critique when the tactical maneuvers were over it was noted by the observing officers that only two teams took an 'aggressor' prisoner–Joe's and mine.

Before Don went to summer camp he and Pat got a little blonde half Cocker puppy. She was a lovable little dog. She was so small she couldn't negotiate the stairs to the apartment. She learned to scoot down. Thus, they named her 'Scooter.'

We took Scooter everywhere we went in the car. Like all dogs she loved to ride with her head hanging out the window.

We often went to the Zesto soft ice cream place similar to Dairy Queen. We always bought a small cup for Scooter. She loved her Zesto treats. She learned to recognize the Zesto sign and as we got close she would jump with excitement and put her paws on the back of the front seat panting with anticipation.

> Sometimes just to tease her I would drive past the Zesto shop. Scooter would whine and jump up with her paws on top of the back seat watching out the back window as the Zesto sign faded away. She would whine pitifully with disappointment. I would turn around and start back toward the Zesto and she would get all excited again. She always got her cup of Zesto. I just had to tease her a little.
>
> We had Scooter several years. She was a sweet loving little dog. When I graduated and we moved to Fort Worth we took her to stay with Pat's folks. She stayed with them several years until the day she died from a rattlesnake bite.
>
> Pat's grandfather swears Scooter saved his life. He was cleaning out the back of an old building full of junk. Scooter was routing out the mice. She was under his feet when suddenly a rattlesnake struck her in the face.

The rest of the summer after ROTC summer camp Don worked for the Horticultural Department landscaping parts of the A&M campus. He and several other young men did all the landscape work on the mall area from the front of the new library building to University Street passing in front of the Student Union Building, an area of about five acres.

During the fall of 1952 and spring of 1953 things were pretty much uneventful. Pat continued with her job at Oklahoma Power and Propulsion Laboratory. Don continued in school pursuing a degree in industrial management with a minor in economics. Don also completed his ROTC course requirements and was commissioned a Second Lieutenant in the Army Signal Corps. Since he had not graduated when commissioned he was granted an automatic deferment until he graduated. In the meantime he was assigned to a local army reserve unit.

The curriculum at Oklahoma A&M was not much different than most colleges and universities. Students had to take three hours credit in American History and three hours credit in American Government to graduate. Consequently, the classes were large with two hundred or more students.

Not unlike others Don had to take American History. He did not like the professor, not personally, but rather his methods. He lectured so fast it was difficult to make meaningful notes. He made frequent nuances making it difficult to understand what he meant. His exams were convoluted questions that required the ability to condense several significant historical events into a few short paragraphs.

It was the final exam. It had five, yes only five, essay questions. Each was worth twenty percent of the total. Miss one question and the final exam score was an eighty. Not the best of situations.

> The history classes were all lecture with no interaction between the professor and the students. We just listened, took notes, read the textbook assignments, took the 'pop quizzes,' and the exams. On the quizzes and exams this professor had the peculiar habit of asking, "Tell all you know. . . ." about some particular event or events in American history.
>
> First of all, I didn't particularly like Dr. Fischer. I thought he was arrogant, annoying, and overbearing. The final exam (two hours) was a five-question essay exam. That meant my final exam grade would be based on how well I answered each question worth twenty percent of my total grade.
>
> I breezed through the first four questions with no problem and felt confident I would get at least ninety percent credit for each question worth twenty percent of my final grade. But, question five had me stumped. It was one of those "Tell all you know. . . ." questions which I hated. The question was: "Tell all you know about the causes and effects of the Cuban revolutions of the 1870's on American foreign policy?"
>
> I sat there forty minutes trying my best to think of something relevant to write to get at least a few points credit. I racked my brain. I couldn't come up with anything. Finally, in dire desperation I wrote in large letters: "NOTHING" and turned in my exam book.
>
> My logic was that when the grades were posted and he graded me off twenty percent on that one question I would meet with him and insist he give me a little credit because I

> answered the question truthfully—that I knew NOTHING about the Cuban revolutions of the 1870's.
>
> Much to my surprise, when the grades were posted he gave me full credit for the question. My final grade was ninety-five. I was astounded. I couldn't believe it. I thought surely he must have made a mistake. I was not going to go tell him he made a mistake.
>
> I went to my textbook and looked up the Cuban Revolutions. There were no Cuban revolutions in the 1870's. They were in the 1890's. It was a trick question. Therefore, NOTHING was the correct answer. A lot of my classmates tried to fake their way through the question and got twenty percent taken from their final grade. Boy, did I ever luck out!
>
> I was a little disappointed though. I was prepared and psyched up to go have it out with him arguing that he asked to "tell all you know" and I told him all I knew which was "nothing," therefore he should give me some credit for my answer. It was for naught, but for the best.

All of Don's professors were not the ilk of Dr. Fischer. In fact, Don even liked some of his professors. In particular he liked Professor Baugh, his economics professor. Don had several classes with him. He also liked Professor Locke. She taught elements of speech and public speaking. He admired Professor Leftwich more than he liked him. He was a tough teacher.

> My minor was economics. I enrolled in an economics class, Pricing Theory. Typically, I would always get the book list for the courses I was taking for the semester and buy the textbooks ahead of time. I would read the Preface, Introduction, Table of Contents, and the CHAPTER summaries, if any, before the first day of class. This was so I would be familiar with what the course was to be about and give me a heads up on class content and study.
>
> I purchased the required textbook for the class, Pricing Theory, and reviewed it. The first day in class the professor, Richard Leftwich, announced we would not be using the

required textbook. He would teach strictly from his notes. I thought, "Oh, hell."

He had this massive notebook from which he taught the class. He made copious written material and graphs of all kinds on the blackboard. I worked very hard making a good set of notes because I did not have a textbook of any kind for study.

Professor Leftwich was a tough taskmaster. He went through the material rather rapidly, because there was a lot to cover, and I furiously took notes for study.

I worked harder for that three hours of 'B' than I ever did for any six hours of 'A.' In every class situation Professor Leftwich would say at least two or three times, and sometimes more often, that when he published his book he would do this or that, or say something or another. I always sat near the back of the classroom and when he would say that I often thought, "Yeah, and I'll jump over the Empire State Building some day."

Well, I graduated and went out into the business world. I worked for an oil company most of my career. I never gave much thought to Professor Leftwich during all those years–just a casual remembrance when occasionally talking about my college days.

In 1980 I worked in Dallas. I would often go across the street during the lunch hour to the Sanger-Harris Department Store. I would browse through the merchandise and occasionally buy something. They sometimes had a special sale on books. They would bring in a large number of assorted books of all kinds scattered all over the racks. I often browsed through these books and occasionally bought one if it struck my fancy. One day I saw this book, "The Price System and Resource Allocation." What really caught my attention was not the title, but the author's name, "Richard H. Leftwich."

I quickly looked inside. Sure enough it was my old professor, Richard Leftwich. He really did publish his book. I noted the first edition was published in 1955, a year after I graduated. I immediately purchased the book. It was on sale at a reduced price.

The next time I went recruiting at Oklahoma State (A&M) I took the book with me. I made it a point to see if Professor

> Leftwich was still there. Sure enough he was. It was his last year before retirement. I made it a point to go see him taking the book with me. I explained to him about my experience in his class and my doubt about him ever publishing a book. He told me he made enough from the book royalties to buy an airplane and take flying lessons.
>
> I told him I would probably never read the book, but I asked if he would autograph it for me which he graciously did: "To Don, My very best regards to a good former student. Richard H. Leftwich 10/7/80." I laid the book aside to keep just as a memento of my college days.
>
> Twenty years later, after I retired and had the time I started reading the book. I began to know how much I really learned from Professor Leftwich and how much I agreed with his theories and teachings. I was especially impressed with the very first paragraph in the Introduction. They were not the words which often characterize the usual liberal minded professor of economics at many of our universities. They were the words of a person who truly believed in individual freedom and the free enterprise system.

Near the end of the semester in the spring of 1953 Don interviewed with the Rock Island Railroad for a summer job. Pat stayed in Stillwater and worked at the Oklahoma Power and Propulsion Lab. Don went to Oklahoma City and lived with Pat's grandparents so he could work for the Rock Island. He had to work the 'extra board' and drive to El Reno to go to work. In the summer months the railroads were very busy, especially the Rock Island because it served many of the rural small town grain elevators in the wheat belt of mid-America. Also, many of the regular employees took their vacations during the summer, so there was a lot of work for temporaries such as Don.

> During the summer of 1953 I worked out of El Reno on the old Rock Island Railroad. El Reno was a railhead (main junction point) for the Rock Island in Oklahoma for its north-south (Wichita to Ft. Worth) and east-west (Memphis

to Tucumcari) lines. I was a brakeman and worked short-turn runs to the small town elevators in Northwest Oklahoma. I also worked some of the red-ball (express) freights between El Reno and Wichita and between El Reno and Amarillo.

Typically, a train consisted of three diesel units, about thirty-five to forty boxcars per diesel unit, and the caboose at the back. In those days a train crew consisted of five men–engineer, fireman, two brakemen, and the conductor. One brakeman rode up front in the diesel engine with the engineer and fireman. The other brakeman rode at the back in the caboose with the conductor. The conductor was the man in charge of the crew and took care of the paperwork.

In the 'real old' days the brakemen had to run along the tops of the boxcars hand setting the brakes on each one to stop the train. With the invention of the pneumatic air brake by Westinghouse that became unnecessary. The engineer could apply the brakes from the engine to slow or stop the train.

Afterwards the brakeman's function was to check the train in the trainyard to be sure all the hoses were connected between all the boxcars from the engine to the caboose. His job was also to pump up the brake system and test it to be sure it was functional. The 'head' (front) brakeman was responsible to throw the right switches and guide the engineer taking the train from the trainyard onto the main line. The back brakeman reset the switches as the caboose cleared them. All brakeman instructions were conveyed to the engineer by hand signals, or if night-time, by lantern signals.

While the train was enroute it was the responsibility of both brakemen to constantly observe the train on curves checking for 'hot boxes' (over heated wheel bearings) on the boxcars and the general good condition of the rolling stock. Tank cars containing flammable or hazardous materials were embedded in the middle of the train for safety reasons.

Should it become necessary to set off one or several box cars on a siding the brakeman acted as switchmen to disconnect the cars and air hoses, guide the engineer to set out the cars, and remake the air hose hook ups.

Cabooses came in all sizes and shapes depending on the individual railroads. The cupola on top with the windows had seats where the brakeman sat to watch out the windows to observe the train. On the Rock Island we called the caboose a "crummy." It had rough bunk beds for the five crewmen, a small desk area for the conductor, a potbellied stove for heat in the winter, a small coal bin, some storage, and a wood plank floor. It was our home away from home such as it was.

Pat's grandmother always packed a large lunch pail with enough food for two days. When we reached our turnaround point the caboose was set off on the caboose track. We would sleep eight hours and then be ready to reverse the process to return to El Reno.

The caboose and brakeman became the victims of modern technology with Timken bearings, heat scanners which detect over heated wheel bearings, scanners to scan the boxcar identifications, two-way radio communications with the engineer, and computers to do the paperwork.

It would have been great fun to ride up front on a big diesel engine when I was a kid, but now it was just a job.

The engineer, fireman and I often sweated out motorists trying to beat the train to grade crossings. A car or pickup can stop on a dime. It takes over a mile to stop a freight train with a hundred boxcars. We sounded the whistle full blast and hoped the drivers would stop.

Early one morning just after daybreak we were the eastbound red ball freight from Amarillo to El Reno running with three diesel units and about a hundred and twenty boxcars. We had just cleared Weatherford, Oklahoma, and were headed down grade for Hydro running about forty-five miles per hour.

About half a mile down track to our right we saw a pickup loaded with something headed toward the next grade crossing. We anticipated we would arrive about the same time as the pickup if the driver did not slow down. As we got closer we speculated whether he would slow or stop in time. We set down on the whistle blasting sound ahead to get his attention. We saw it was a three-quarter ton flat bed truck loaded with crates of live chickens.

A few seconds later we realized he was trying to beat us across the railroad crossing. We set full emergency air on the brakes. Moments later we impacted the truck at the left rear wheel. Crates, chickens, and feathers flew everywhere. It was little over a mile when we came to a complete stop. We had every grade crossing in Hydro blocked. We could not move the train until the law officers completed their investigation. That took almost two hours. It blocked all traffic in Hydro and stopped all train traffic on the line. The poor guy driving the truck was dead at the scene. Dead, crippled, and a few live chickens were scattered everywhere.

A few weeks later I was riding the Rock Island Rocket passenger train from El Reno to Kansas City to work in the Armourdale Yards in Kansas City. We went through Wichita. Just hours before a Rock Island freight train had hit a gasoline truck at a grade crossing at the south edge of Wichita. It caused a horrendous fire killing the three crewmen in the front diesel engine. My stomach became queasy when I saw it. I thought, "My God! I could have been in that engine."

In April of 1953 the family learned that Grandpa Davidson (Mord) had throat and lung cancer. He was eighty years old. It was devastating for Grandma (Meta) and Jim and Mary who they lived with in Kansas City, Kansas. Jim and Mary both worked and Grandma was alone during the days to care for Grandpa. She needed help. Jim worked for the Rock Island for years in the Armourdale Yards in Kansas City, Kansas. Through his connections it was arranged for Don to transfer from El Reno to Kansas City to work as a switchman.

I lived with Uncle Jim and Aunt Mary. Grandma and Grandpa lived in a small apartment in the basement. When I arrived in early July Grandpa looked like a healthy husky eighty year old man. I didn't realize at first how sick he was. I soon learned.

I worked the midnight to seven o'clock in the morning shift so I could be at home with Grandma during the day to help with Grandpa. Mary got home about five o'clock in the afternoon. I went to bed and slept until eleven when I got up and went to work to be on the job at midnight.

I got home about eight o'clock in the morning after Jim and Mary had gone to work. I helped Grandpa get up and get

> dressed. I helped lift him so he could sit in a chair or on a couch. Grandma fixed his meals and fed him. He had great difficulty swallowing.
>
> I took him to his doctor appointments, and sat with him while he took his treatments. I always took something to read to him. He was a baseball fan and I always had to read the morning sports page to him. He knew by memory the batting and pitching records of certain players.
>
> He talked a lot and I listened a lot, but not enough. After he died I wished I had listened more closely and made written notes about things he told me. It was this that first peaked my interest in family history and genealogy.

Don worked in Kansas City most of the summer. Pat drove up for one weekend and brought Scooter, their little half Cocker Spaniel. Don's Mom and Dad came for a few days to visit with Grandma and Grandpa. Don's cousin, Beau (James), was in the Navy. He came home on leave. Pat brought Don's camera and he took photos of Grandma and Grandpa, and Beau. Beau died a few years later in a tragic auto accident in Arkansas.

Working on the railroad was a new experience for Don. Many different and unusual situations and events occurred. One in particular occurred while he worked at Armourdale in Kansas City which was a classification yard on the Rock Island system. It had what was called a 'hump' and a 'bowl.' Trains came from points west such as California, Texas, and Colorado. The boxcars in these trains were redistributed to various eastern destinations such as Chicago, St. Louis, Memphis, etc. They were pushed over the 'hump' at a slow constant speed. A man in a tower had a 'switch list.' He called out over a loud speaker to a 'pin puller' a number that represented the number of cars to release over the 'hump.'

> I sometimes worked as a 'pin puller.' Thats a guy that runs along side the train and pulls the keeper pins at the precise moment the slack goes out between the boxcars to release the correct number over the 'hump.' Gravity rolls the boxcars

down thc 'hump' slope toward the 'bowl.' Another man in the tower actuates the proper switches to make the boxcars roll onto the right track down into the 'bowl.'

The 'bowl' had twenty long tracks to redistribute the boxcars. Each of the twenty tracks terminated at a switch onto a 'lead track.' When one of the twenty tracks was clear (empty) a 'skateman' placed a pair of heavy devices called 'skates' onto the tracks. The 'skates' weigh about forty pounds each. As the first boxcar comes down an empty track the leading wheels run up onto the 'skate' and it skids to a stop. The remaining cars bump into that car and that stops them, though the 'skate' skids a little each time.

Some of the boxcars are transfers. This means they are to be pulled out the end of the 'bowl' onto the lead track and taken to another railroad such as Santa Fe, Missouri Pacific, MKT, etc.

I was working transfers one night. Mr. Hook was the switch engine engineer. He was sixty-five and due to retire in a few weeks. We were to make two transfers–one to Santa Fe and one to Missouri Pacific.

I rode the front of the engine and used my lantern to guide Mr. Hook up the lead track to the Santa Fe track. I connected the engine to the first boxcar and signaled Mr. Hook to pull out. There were about twenty boxcars. When the last boxcar cleared the switch I threw it, climbed up on top of the boxcar and gave the signal to stop. That was the only way Mr. Hook could see my lantern light. I then gave the signal to come forward to go up the lead track to the Missouri Pacific track. As we passed I looked up the Santa Fe track we had just pulled out of.

There are several strategically placed tall light towers in the 'bowl' area. At night all you can see is the light reflection off the rails. A short break in the reflection indicates the 'skates' are in place. A bigger longer break in the reflection indicates a boxcar or boxcars are rolling toward you.

I looked. I did not see 'skates' on the tracks. I saw a distant dark break in the reflection moving down the tracks toward me. I thought, 'My, God! It's going to hit us broadside!" I quickly gave a 'wash-out' (emergency stop) signal and jumped from the

> top of the boxcar to the ground. Poor Mr. Hook saw my lantern light fly over the side and out of sight. He thought I fell off and he was running over me.
>
> I ran as fast as I could up the Santa Fe track toward the oncoming boxcar. I grabbed it on the fly and climbed up the side to the top. My lantern was hooked in the crook of my arm and as I went up the side of the boxcar Mr. Hook could see it. On top I frantically began setting the hand brakes on the boxcar. My lantern was still on my arm and making all kinds of wild motions. Poor Mr. Hook couldn't figure out what kind of signals I was giving him.
>
> When I set the brakes as tight as I could I jumped off the boxcar. I didn't want to be on it when it plowed into the side of Mr. Hook's boxcars. Mr. Hook again saw the light of my lantern fly over the side and out of sight. He was about to have a heart attack.
>
> The wild boxcar came to a stop about eight feet from the side of Mr. Hook's train of boxcars when it fouled the switch. I climbed on top of one of his boxcars and gave him a 'hold fast' signal. He still didn't know what was going on.
>
> I climbed down and went to a call box. I told the supervisor at the 'hump' tower what happened. A work crew was there in a few minutes to handle the situation. The rest of the night was uneventful. Mr. Hook later told me I scared him "half to death" with all those wild gyrations of my lantern light. I learned the next night that the 'skateman' was fired.

During the summer Don's grandfather grew progressively worse. It was obvious he was rapidly failing. He became more and more feeble and it became more and more difficult for Don to help. His grandfather was almost totally helpless.

Late August Pat came to Kansas City to get Don so he could return to Stillwater and his final year in college. Pat and Don bid his grandfather goodbye for the last time. He died August 29, 1953, five days after Pat and Don left. There was a funeral for him in Kansas City for the family there, and a funeral in Oklahoma City for the rest of the family. He was buried August 31, 1953, in Memorial Park Cemetery, Edmond, Oklahoma.

The fall of 1953 Don started his senior year. Don's younger brother, Sam, also enrolled at Oklahoma A&M that fall as a freshman. He lived with Don and Pat in their apartment on McElroy Street. He studied in the second bedroom with Don and slept on a bunk bed in the study room.

> It was a little cramped with the two of us using the same study desk. Sam or I often went to the living room to study. I was carrying a full load plus two graduate courses in economics. Sam was trying to get adjusted to the routine of studying, but with some difficulty. He just couldn't settle in and study. I didn't have the time to help him.
>
> Pat spent hours upon hours helping and drilling Sam on his course work. If it hadn't been for Pat I don't think Sam would have made the adjustment that first year. I lectured him several times about the necessity of settling down and studying, especially at exam time. One evening I told him to use the study desk to study for an exam and I would study in the living room. Pat went to bed. She had to work the next day.
>
> After about an hour I tiptoed to the door and peeked in. Sam was all bent over the desk busily working. I checked twice more. It was getting late and Sam was still studying, so I thought. I tiptoed into the room and peeked over Sam's shoulder to see what he was so intent on. "Sam!" I shouted. "What the hell are you doing?" He replied, "Designing furniture."
>
> Several sheets of paper were strewn around on the desk with hand drawn pictures of various pieces of furniture. I about had apoplexy. I read him the 'riot act' on the necessity of disciplined study habits if he ever expected to finish college. I guess it worked. He finally settled in and finished.

During January of the last semester Don got official word from the Army that he did not have to serve the obligatory two years active duty. The war in Korea was winding down. They no longer needed Second Lieutenants. He was assigned to a reserve unit.

That semester Don interviewed with numerous companies on campus. One such company, Signal Oil and Gas Company, invited him to be further interviewed at their offices. He and Pat went to Fort Worth for the interview. They offered Don a job and he accepted.

While in Fort Worth Don and Pat rented a duplex apartment on Canberra Court in southeast Fort Worth. It now was just a matter of going back to Stillwater to graduate and then move to Fort Worth and start the new job.

Don's grandmother Davidson was visiting in Oklahoma City. Pat and Don brought her back to Stillwater with them. She was there on her seventy-seventh birthday. Don took a color photo of her in a nice blue dress with a red rose in her lapel.

CHAPTER 14

DONALD GENE DAVIDSON

The Growth Years

May, 1954. Graduation day!

> I earned my B.S. degree in Industrial Management with a minor in Economics plus six graduate hours in economics. Pat worked to help put me through college. She earned her PHT (Put Hubby Through) degree.

Don's mother and father came to Oklahoma A&M at Stillwater to attend his graduation. His mother previously gave him fifty-dollars to help buy a new suit for graduation. After graduation his parents and grandmother returned to Oklahoma City.

The next few days Don and Pat set about finalizing their affairs in Stillwater and prepared to move to Fort Worth. They rented a trailer and were loading it with their household goods when the postman came. Pat went to the mailbox. There was a letter from Signal Oil and Gas Company. It was not good news. They withdrew their offer to Don citing budget cuts. What to do?

They decided that since they had already rented a place in Fort Worth they would go ahead and move there. Surely Don could find a suitable job in the Fort Worth area.

Once settled in Fort Worth Don spent the next several weeks interviewing various companies. He interviewed with General

Motors at their Arlington assembly plant. Don and Pat went through the assembly plant and watched Buicks and Oldsmobiles being assembled.

Stanolind Oil and Gas Company, a wholly owned subsidiary of Standard Oil of Indiana, offered Don a job in their management training program. Don accepted. The only problem was he was required to report to work in Pampa, Texas. Where?

Pampa was a town of about 12,000 people. It was on the Caprock in the northern part of the Texas Panhandle northeast of Amarillo. The main economic mainstay was oil and cattle. Like all small Texas towns the Friday night high school football games were the social event of the week. It was not uncommon for 5,000 people to attend the games. Most businesses closed with a sign "Gone to the Game" hanging in the front door.

The job in Pampa necessitated yet another move. Since Don and Pat did not have a place in Pampa they moved their belongings to Marietta and stored them at Pat's parents' place. Don went on to Pampa alone. He rented a room from a widow woman.

> I was to report to work on a Monday morning at the Ware Field Office somewhere northwest of Pampa. I had no idea what to look for. It took me a while to find it. I was late to work the first day.
>
> The office was a non-descript looking white frame building in an isolated area. They told me to go to the tool shed.
>
> There was no one at the tool shed. I had no idea what to do so I just waited. After a while a middle-age tall gruff looking guy in greasy coveralls and a silver metal safety hat drove up in a crew-cab pickup. He got out and asked, "You Don Davidson?"
>
> "Yes, sir."
>
> He studied me a minute looking me up and down. I was wearing a short-sleeve shirt, a pair of slacks and low-cut shoes. I was getting a little anxious. He finally grunted, "That'll never do."
>
> I thought, "Good grief. Am I fired already?"

> He reached for a broom, poked it at me and said, "Take this and clean up around here. Come back tomorrow morning in work clothes and a pair of safety toe work boots." He got in the pickup and drove away without saying another word.
>
> The next morning I showed up in new coveralls and a new pair of safety toe boots. The 'gang-pusher,' the tall guy from the day before, tossed a silver metal safety hat at me. Three other guys and I got in the crew-cab pickup and we drove away to a job. Little did I know what was in store for me.
>
> I quickly learned the "management training program" meant you started as a roustabout in the oil fields doing all kinds and manner of hard physical labor.

Don worked the first two months digging ditches, cleaning and painting tanks, building fences, cleaning out heater-treaters, cutting and threading pipe, laying oil field pipe, etc., all hard physical labor to get a couple of paychecks so he could go get Pat and bring her to Pampa.

They first rented a one-car garage that had been converted to a very small apartment. Pat dutifully prepared Don's lunch pail each day and saw him off to work with a kiss. For years she had said, "I'll be so glad when you get out of school and get a job so I don't have to work anymore."

Well, Don had a good paying job, albeit hard labor, and Pat did not have to work. That lasted three weeks. Don came home from work one day.

> Pat said, "They need a part time worker at the newspaper to run a machine punching tape for setting type. Do you think it would be okay for me to apply?"
>
> "I thought you didn't want to work."
>
> "I'm bored to death sitting around here all day waiting for you to come home."
>
> "I don't care if you want to. Just don't complain to me about having to work."

> "Okay."
>
> Pat applied and went to work that day. Several weeks went by and the first thing I knew she was Assistant Society Editor. She was spending more time at the newspaper than at home.
>
> I had to hang around the newspaper evenings just to be with my wife. It was a morning daily and they often worked late to put it to bed.
>
> Next thing I knew one evening when I was hanging around someone pushed a press camera into my hands and said, "Would you mind running over to the football game and getting some shots for the morning edition?" How could I say no?
>
> Pat was working afternoons and evenings and I was working evenings at the newspaper. Next thing I knew I not only was taking football game photos but doing special feature photos. I even did a complete full-page photo layout including the art work for a special edition on the "Top 'O Texas."

In the meantime Pat and Don moved to yet another converted garage. It however was a two-car garage that had been added on. They had much more space.

Pat became well acquainted around Pampa. She traded at a local meat market. World Series time and the guys at the market hooked her into playing in their baseball pools. She won most of them. She also began to play in their football pools. She won most of them and the guys began to refuse to let her play in their pools. She has always been tenaciously lucky.

Don soon learned that the Stanolind "management trainee" program was for all college new hires regardless of educational discipline. The idea was to give them a good basic knowledge of the oil business under the watchful eyes of seasoned old hands that knew it from bottom-hole to pipeline. They made sure trainees got the "opportunity" to work in all phases of the operation.

Don not only worked as a roustabout, but also as a relief pumper, a well service derrick crewman, a well completion crewman, a roughneck and derrickman on a drilling rig.

> I was working on a drill rig as derrickman on the 'monkey board' up in the rig. We were about twelve miles west and north of Spearman, Texas. I was sixty feet up. I could see all the way across the Oklahoma Panhandle into Western Kansas. There was nothing between us and the North Pole except five strand barbed-wire fences.
>
> It was February. The temperature was in the mid-twenties. The wind was howling out of the north. I was never so cold in all my life. I thought I would freeze to death. At the end of the tour I was almost afraid to get on the elevator to ride down to the rig floor. My fingers, hands and feet were so numb from cold I was afraid I could not hold on.

March in the Panhandle brought howling winds and devastating dust storms. Man and creatures alike suffered immensely. Several times the dust was so thick and heavy it was so dark the streetlights came on in town. Everything was covered in a pall of dust. Migrating ducks became disoriented and lost in the swirling dust storms. The glaze of dust on the streets reflected the streetlights. The flights of ducks mistook the reflections for water and hundreds tried to land on the streets of Pampa crashing onto the hard asphalt. Many were killed, others so badly injured they died.

April came and Don finished his tour of field "management trainee" training in North Texas. He was transferred from Pampa, the Top of Texas, to Brownsville, the Tip of Texas, to work with AMOCO Chemical Company, a wholly owned subsidiary of Standard Oil of Indiana, at a chemical plant located on the ship channel at the Port of Brownsville

Don and Pat packed their belongings in the old '47 Dodge and drove to Marietta to visit Pat's folks. From there they drove to Brownsville. They rented a four-room wood frame house across the road from a large tomato field. Gobs of free tomatoes at harvest time. The ripe ones were culls and left in the field for gleaners.

Don worked in the Accounting Department. The "trainees" all had to work at least six months in some phase of accounting. It was here that Don became acquainted with Leonard Holland and Tom Hill. Pat got a job with the Brownsville Credit Bureau. Life settled into a daily routine.

> Soon after we moved to Brownsville my brothers, Sam and Bob, came to visit. They were driving a convertible with the top down. Pat and I took them to Matamoros, Mexico, for dinner at the La Cucaracha, a quaint but very good little patio restaurant in the shadows of the tall twin cathedral towers next door.
>
> The restaurant served seven-course meals. The waiters were very attentive and served each course with a flair of showmanship. All during the meal Pat and I bragged about their Angel's Kiss, a wonderful dainty after dinner drink of creme de cocoa with cream.
>
> The waiter cleared the table and returned with four little bowls which he set at each place. Sam picked up his little bowl, took a sip, thoughtfully smacked his lips and said, "That's not such a good drink!"
>
> "Sam", Pat and I said in unison, "that's a finger bowl." The Angel's Kisses came later and were delightful.

A few months later Pat got a very good job at the Texas Southmost College in the administrative office. When old Fort Brown was deactivated Texas Southmost College was formed to utilize the buildings for a junior college to serve the Lower Rio Grande Valley Area. The old hospital building was converted to the college administrative offices. Some of the barracks buildings were used as classrooms. Others were available for student and faculty housing.

The campus was located at the east end of Elizabeth Street, the main street through downtown Brownsville, which also terminated at the International Bridge that crossed the Rio Grande River to Mexico. The campus was situated around a large resaca or oxbow lake that was originally a part of the Rio Grande riverbed. The campus was well kept with green lawns, tall swaying palm trees, date palms, various citrus trees, bougainvilleas, banana trees, etc.

An option for on campus housing was part of the arrangement when Pat went to work at the college, so they moved to one of the barracks buildings that had been converted to apartments. She was close enough to walk to work. It was only about a hundred yards.

While Don and Pat lived in the barracks apartment Don's parents and his grandmother Davidson came to visit. His parents took a short airplane trip on Mexicana Air Lines from Brownsville to Monterrey where they went sightseeing for a few days and returned to Brownsville. After they returned Don and Pat took them and Grandma Davidson sightseeing and deep sea fishing.

> We went to all the tourist points of interest and a visit across the Rio Grande to Matamoros. Grandma enjoyed it all very much. She always had a keen inquisitive mind.
>
> I made arrangements for us to spend the day deep sea fishing with our friends Leonard and Doris Holland and Tom and Janice Hill. We chartered a forty-two foot cabin cruiser with Captain Williams and a deckhand. He took us thirty miles offshore.
>
> We trolled with three lines from the back of the boat. We caught twenty-two king mackerel, ling, and bonita, a kind of tuna. They each weighed between fifteen and twenty-five pounds. It took a lot of effort to land one. Each of us caught several and had a great time.
>
> Grandma wanted in the worst way to land one of those fish. We finally convinced her an eighty-three-year old lady couldn't reel one in. She had a great time and often talked about her deep seafishing trip with us. She loved to fish and I remember many a time in Arkansas when she would take her line and pole, go down to South Fork and catch a mess of fish for supper.

Don completed his tenure in the Accounting Department and went to work in Chemical Plant Operations. His primary job each morning was to run a complete chemical balance on the entire plant based on chemical samples taken at specific points and times. He hand cranked it all through a Marchant calculator. Today a desktop computer could probably do in a few minutes what then took Don several hours. He also made work schedules for seven-day twenty-four hour operations. He monitored samples and made sure they were taken on schedule. He handled the paperwork for railroad tank car and ocean barge shipments.

Pat received a promotion to the college president's office. As a select faculty member she had the privilege to rent one of the campus houses that were officers' houses when old Fort Brown was active.

Don and Pat moved into a house that faced the large resaca. It had three bedrooms, a large living-dining room, a sunroom, a large kitchen, and a utility room. More room than they had ever had. The house also had a large screened front porch across most of the front. It had high ceilings and lots of large windows which made it airy and cool.

There were two grapefruit trees in the backyard, a fig tree at the back porch, and a poinsettia plant that reached to the eaves of the house. It had bougainvillea and mock bird of paradise plants. Tall coconut palm trees lined the bank of the resaca.

> It was a great place. We enjoyed it very much. Pat could walk to and from work. She lost weight and looked real nice.
>
> Pat found a Mexican woman, Sarah, who came one day a week to do housework. Pat also found Prisca, an excellent seamstress who made some very nice clothes for her. Pat needed only to take a picture of a garment to Prisca. She told Pat how much material to buy, and in a few days Pat had a nice new dress that fit.

The house was situated such that a professional golfer could tee up a golf ball in the front yard and drive it into the Rio Grande River. At night when Don laid just right in bed he could see a neon Dos XX's beer sign flashing over in Mexico.

In April 2007 Pat and Don with their son, Greg, his wife, Donna, and granddaughter, Mary Grace, visited Brownsville. They visited the college campus. It now is The University of Texas Southmost College Campus and is greatly and beautifully expanded with all the new buildings preserving the original architectural style of the old original buildings. The old hospital building is still used as the administrative offices. Much to Dons and Pat's surprise the house they lived in is the only one still standing. It has not been changed. It is used as an information center and a kind of museum piece to show how the original officers' houses looked. Greg took a photo of Don and Pat in front of the house where he was conceived.

> Pat and I often went across the river to Matamoros for dining and shopping. We became well acquainted with many of the merchants and restaurateurs. Pat loved to haggle with the merchants in the bazaar. They called her "the Jew from Monterrey."
>
> We often went dining and then to one of the several good night spots for drinking and dancing. We often met friends and would make an evening of it. We were so well known at some places that the musicians would strike up certain tunes when we came in.
>
> I could take a dollar bill, pay a nickel to walk across the bridge, pay thirty cents for a haircut, twenty-five cents for a manicure, a dime for a shoe shine, buy a sloe gin fizz for twenty cents, pay a nickel to walk back across the bridge, and have a nickel left.
>
> Sometimes at the shrimp basin Pat would take a ten-quart bucket and go 'tripping' down the pier among the shrimp boats. The guys would always give her a bucket full of fresh caught shrimp which we took home, cleaned and cooked.

Pat's grandparents, Edward and Susie Patrick, came to visit while Don and Pat lived in the house on the resaca. Her grandmother loved to sit on the big screened-porch looking out over the resaca while she ate papayas. She had never before eaten any and she loved them. Pat's grandfather had never seen tall coconut palms. He marveled that they could stand so straight and tall in the wind and not bend.

Pat's mother and father, Bert and Mable Paschall, came with their friends, the Warrs from Oklahoma City, to visit Don and Pat in Brownsville. Mr. Warr was an avid duck hunter and brought Bert hunting with him. Mable and Mrs. Warr were good friends and they mostly went shopping. One evening Mr. and Mrs. Warr had a wild duck dinner for about a dozen guests. The ducks were prepared by a local restaurant from the ones they bagged while hunting.

Things were going great for Don and Pat. They had good jobs, a good place to live. They were having the time of their lives going to the beach, fishing, and going to Matamoros shopping, dining and dancing. The Charro Days Celebration was a big annual event in Brownsville with parades and all kinds of fun activities. They enjoyed Brownsville, so much they purchased a small acreage near Boca Chica Boulevard east of town.

> This acreage was like a small jungle. We bought hoes, shovels, rakes, and a machete and set about clearing it out. We had a set of house plans drawn by a local builder. We went out evenings and on weekends to work on it.
>
> One day while clearing the land we saw a large rattlesnake slithering across the trail where we drove in. I grabbed the machete and ran toward the snake to kill it. The closer I got to that snake the bigger it got and the smaller that machete got. By the time I was in striking range that machete was the size of a dagger.
>
> That rattlesnake was every bit of eight feet long and very mean looking. I decided I did not want to chance a face-to-face confrontation. I left him to slither away into the brush.

Don and Pat felt very comfortable in their situation. They had gone in debt to buy a new car, new furniture, and a new kitchen stove. They had a circle of friends from Don's place of employment and Pat's position with the college.

Don played catcher on the company softball team in a fast-pitch league. Dale Hartz was the pitcher. Don also bowled in a company league. He went fishing in the bay and ship channel with his friend, Leonard Holland. They also went duck hunting along the Rio Grande. Doris Holland and Pat were good friends. They enjoyed shopping together and going to the beach.

Pat and Don attended various college functions and social events at the homes of the different faculty members. They socialized with the people Don worked with. They played bridge at the home of Dale and Maxine Hartz. They were instrumental in the organization of the Charro Camera Club in Brownsville. Don worked with the local Civil Air Patrol to organize, publicize and present the beauty queen contests at two of their annual air shows.

Then, Pat became pregnant. What a surprise! Don was not supposed to be able to father children. He had the mumps the worst sort of way when he was sixteen.

> After eight years of marriage and no precautions we thought we could not have children. We had kind of planned our life together that way. In fact, I was a little skeptical.
>
> A handsome bachelor friend, Hector Solis, was a co-worker. He was the 'darling' of all the ladies in our social circle. He was so polite and thoughtful. He had been coming by the house to sit on the porch and sip coffee with Pat while I went hunting or fishing.
>
> A few days after we confirmed Pat's pregnancy I kind of hinted at Pat that maybe she had been a little too friendly with Hector. Wow! Did that ever elicit a response.
>
> "Listen, Buster", she said, "If you're not the father of this child you better get ready for the Second Coming of Christ!"
>
> I never broached that topic again.
>
> Oh, and the baby looked just like me.

No problem with Pat's pregnancy. The college agreed to let her have a few weeks of maternity leave to have the baby. Pat arranged for a Mexican lady to stay with the baby during the day. And, since it was only a three-minute walk from the college office to the house Pat could check on things during breaks and be there for lunch. The perfect situation until Friday, September 13th.

> Management at the chemical plant announced the closing of the plant. There had been rumors flying for several months, but management always squelched them.
>
> Suddenly we went from a perfect situation to the worst possible situation—no job at the chemical plant, Pat pregnant and due in December, and up to our eyebrows in debt for the car and furniture.
>
> There were 1,250 employees at the plant. The company said they would place those they could in other company locations. The others would be discharged.
>
> I knew it would be impossible to find comparable employment in the Brownsville area. The economy was primarily based on agriculture, the Port of Brownsville, shrimping. trade with Mexico, and the chemical plant.
>
> The company eventually placed about 350 of the employees in other company locations. Fortunately, I was one. I was transferred to the West Edmond Field Office northwest of Oklahoma City on the west side of Lake Hefner.

Pat was seven months pregnant when she and Don moved to Oklahoma City. They lived in a motel in Putman City a couple of weeks. Don worked as a clerk processing invoices, material transfers and production run tickets. They rented a house at 5704 NW 47th Street from Tom and Marilee Ohm. Pat had to change doctors. Her new doctor was Dr. Deihl.

At six o'clock the morning of December 27, 1957, Don took Pat to the Deaconess Hospital with labor pains. About eight fifty-five o'clock that same morning their son, Gregory Scott, was born. When Pat and Greg came home Don surprised her with a new washer and dryer in the garage. Don also bought a Bolex 8mm movie camera, and thus began a long period of movie making over the next many years.

A short time later Pat's parents, Bert and Mable Paschall, came to visit and see the new grandbaby. Don's grandparents, Dill and Arlie Roller, also came to visit and see the new great grandbaby. He was a precious and much adored child by all.

Soon Don was working as a Field Material Supervisor responsible for the purchase, classification, storage, and allocation of various kinds of oil field material, equipment, and pipe. Pat worked as the dutiful wife and mother caring for Greg.

> It was February 1958. Greg was a tiny baby. I got a phone call late on a Saturday. There had been a blowout at the T.H. Williams northeast of Cement, Oklahoma. They needed a Field Material Supervisor. Now!
>
> The next morning I was on site. I was there the next six weeks. Gas was spewing everywhere. Everything for a mile around was blocked off to everyone except workers.
>
> The T.H. Williams was a deep (14,000 ft.) gas wildcat drilled in an old Skelly field among several shallow (2,500 ft.) stripper oil wells. The several stripper wells were spewing oil and gas into the air. Those old wells hadn't made gas in twenty years.
>
> The pressure gauge on the T.H. Williams 'christmas tree' was very low (300 psi) whereas the day before it was 3,000 psi. That told us right away that gas was streaming into the shallow production zone and escaping out the casings of the several nearby old wells. The pressure was so great it blew the pumps, rods and tubing out of the well casings and spewed oil and gas a hundred feet into the air. What a mess!
>
> There were tons of material and equipment to be ordered, transferred and transported to the site. Fortunately the drill rig was still on location and we didn't have to move one in. We moved a house trailer on site about a hundred yards from the wellhead. The phone company strung three private phone lines from Cement (six miles) to the trailer.
>
> I was busier than a one-arm paperhanger. Everyone wanted his "stuff" now. I sometimes was on all three phone lines at the same time. They needed tools, piping, valves, gauges, mud, cement, you name it, and they needed it now. I couldn't work fast enough.

> Though we all had motel rooms in Chickasha most of us spent the first three or four nights on site working sixteen or more hours and grabbing sleep when we could.
>
> Halliburton brought in several large mud pumps and tried for several days to kill it with mud. Not a chance. It just blew mud out the old wells all over the countryide.
>
> The engineers did a lot of head scratching and trying different things without success. Creeks were getting contaminated and ranchers were filing claims. It was always their "best" cow that drank from the creek and died.
>
> After three weeks things settled into a routine and I had to work only ten or so hours a day. I went home on a Sunday and brought Pat and Greg back to the motel in Chickasha. They stayed a week and I took them home.
>
> The rig workers finally 'snubbed' (ran in reverse) a string of special tubing with a packer past the split in the main tubing and sealed off the leak. Everything suddenly became quiet to our great relief.
>
> Twelve years later when I worked for Atlantic Richfield by chance I met the Stanolind superintendent on the T.H. Williams Well in the Petroleum Club in Denver. He told me they had just settled the last lawsuit on the T.H Williams that month.

Soon after the T.H. Williams episode Don had to make a decision about his officer reserve status with the army. He had to make a choice between either being more active in the army reserve program or his civilian job. The nature of his civilian job was such that he was often absent from army reserve drills. This did not set well with the commanding officer. Don elected to take an honorable discharge and devote his time to his civilian job.

Things pretty much returned to normal in the household. Pat was busy being the dutiful mother. After awhile she needed a free day to go shopping and do whatever she wanted to do just to be away for a few hours. Don was left to baby sit.

> Greg was about seven months old. Hc was crawling very well and starting to pull himself up on various pieces of furniture.
>
> We had a parakeet. His name was Tweetybird. He was in a tall cylinder shaped wire cage with all kinds of little bells, swings, etc. to keep him busy. He chirped a lot.
>
> I was left to baby sit while Pat went shopping. Curiosity got the best of Greg. He crawled over to the cage, reached up and grabbed hold, but as he attempted to pull himself up he pulled the cage over on top of him.
>
> I was sitting on the sofa reading. I wasn't paying a lot of attention. You can't imagine the noise and commotion. The cage crashed, Tweetybird went berserk fluttering all around and screeching. Greg screamed and cried. I about jumped out of my skin. It took several minutes to upright the cage, quiet Tweetybird and soothe Greg's hurt. He took his first steps at eight months and was walking very good at twelve months.

Don and Pat bought a new house at 5748 NW 48th Street several blocks west of the rent house. They paid extra to have the breezeway between the house and the garage enclosed to make a nice family room. Pat's grandfather helped Don frame, pour and finish a concrete patio outside the family room. They had a four-foot high chain link fence built around the backyard where Greg could play. He was a little over a year old and walking fairly good.

> I was working in the backyard. Greg was playing nearby. I was supposed to be keeping an eye on him. For some reason I went into the house for just a moment to get something.
>
> I suddenly heard a loud scream coming from the backyard. I rushed outside. Greg was dangling upside down by one foot caught in one of the links near the top of the fence.
>
> I think he must have decided to climb over the fence. When he got to the top he must have teetered and fell backwards catching his foot in the link. This was probably fortunate because otherwise he might have hit head first causing serious injury.

The house was only a six or seven minute drive from Don's place of employment. Most days he came home for lunch. Pat always had lunch ready and Greg in his crib. After lunch Don would catch a few winks before Pat woke him and he went back to work. Don and Pat had been in their new home only a few months when Grandma Davidson came to visit.

> Grandpa Davidson died in 1953. Grandma lived until age ninety-three. She lived with her daughter, Mary, and her husband, Jim Dunahoo, in Kansas City, Kansas.
>
> When Grandma was in her eighties she decided to pack her little ditty bag and spend the next few years going around and living a few days, weeks, or months with various close relatives. Kind of her farewell tour. In the summer of 1958 she lived with Pat, Greg and I most of the summer. Greg was just a baby.
>
> Grandma always loved to work crossword puzzles. She was very good at it. Just a few days after her arrival she dug into her little coin purse and handed me some money with instructions to buy her a crossword puzzle book. I told her to put her money away. I would buy her a book. I stopped at a drugstore with a large magazine rack and picked up a book with about a hundred puzzles in it. Two days later she was again digging into her little coin purse. I said, "Grandma, I just bought you a book." She replied, "Yes, they were all easy." She had worked every puzzle in the book.
>
> I went to the drugstore magazine rack and spent about an hour finding what I determined to be a book of very difficult puzzles and brought it home to her. It took only about five days for her to work all the puzzles. And, she didn't cheat and peek at the answers in the back. She considered that very unethical. I couldn't have worked that book in three months.
>
> The rest of the time she lived with us I stopped once a week and bought her a difficult book of puzzles. She was a smart and testy little old lady, yet very gentle and kind.
>
> That same summer there was a lot of talk in the news media about the Russians being ahead of the United States in space technology. They had successfully launched Sputnik, the

world's first space age satellite, in November 1957. It was only about the size of a large grapefruit.

Our good friends, Leonard and Doris Holland, also lived in Oklahoma City. They knew Grandma from the deep sea fishing adventure when we lived in Brownsville.

One evening in the summer of 1958 Leonard and Doris were visiting. We sat around the kitchen table late that night talking about the space age and discussing the possibility of sending a manned space mission to the moon and back. There had been considerable news media coverage of just such a prospect.

Doris said, "Impossible! There is no way they can send a man to the moon, much less send him there and bring him back alive." Grandma pondered that statement a few moments. Then she piped up and said, "Yes, I believe they will do it. I've seen too many impossible things come true in my lifetime to believe otherwise." Too bad she didn't live to see it come true.

One day Grandma said, "Time is getting shorter." I said, "Grandma, what do you mean? A second is a second, a minute is a minute, an hour is an hour, a day is a day, a month is a month, and a year is a year. They never change."

"Oh, yes they do. They get shorter. You just don't understand."

"So, okay please explain to me how that is."

"I will. Time is only as it relates to your existence. Remember when you were ten years old. A year seemed like forever. And, now that you are thirty a year doesn't seem to be so long. That is because a year is one-tenth of your total experience at age ten, and it is one-thirtieth at age thirty, and it is one-eightieth when you are eighty like me. And, one-eightieth is a whole lot less than one-thirtieth, or one-tenth, therefore time is getting shorter."

I couldn't argue with that logic. Now that I am eighty years old I darn well understand exactly what Grandma meant. Long after Grandma had passed on I read an account of how Einstein once described his Theory of Relativity. He said, "A young man sitting in a chair over a hot stove five minutes seems like an hour. That same young man sitting on a park bench with his sweetheart an hour seems like five minutes." I think Grandma knew something about relativity.

Don's job settled into a routine for the next several months until one day his boss asked if he would be interested in a job in New York City working in the corporate offices of Pan American International Oil Company, a wholly owned subsidiary of the parent company. It would be a promotion with a thirty-percent increase in salary. Don would be a Procedures Analyst in the Management Procedures Group.

What excitement! A new job. A big pay raise. An office on Fifth Avenue in New York City. Who could turn down such an opportunity? Don accepted.

The next several weeks were hectic. Sell the house. Prepare to move. Get ready for the movers. See everything loaded on the moving van and on its way. Close on the sale of the house. Pack the car and get on the road to New York. Don and Pat had never been to New York. They had no idea what was in store for them. They arrived a week or so later with their two-year old son, Greg.

I received instructions from the office in New York City suggesting we temporarily stay in New Jersey until such time as we could find housing.

We checked into a motel in Fort Lee about a mile from the George Washington Bridge across the Hudson River on the New Jersey side. I called the office and they gave me directions on how to get to the office. The motel employees told me I could catch a bus across the street that would take me across the bridge and into the Bronx near the 172nd Street A-Train Subway Station.

The next morning I got ready, kissed Pat and Greg good-bye, and left to walk across the street to catch the bus. Incredible! The traffic was so heavy and so fast I could not safely cross all six lanes of traffic. There was no traffic control light or crossover bridge anywhere in sight.

Twenty minutes later I was pounding on the motel door. Pat was surprised to see me. I told her to get ready and drive me across the street to the bus stop. She thought I was out of my mind, but did as I asked.

She drove me about a mile west to a crossover. Then a mile back to the other side of the street to the bus stop. Let me out. Then drove about a half-mile east to another crossover and then back to the motel. She did this every morning for the next several days.

I caught the Red and Tan bus, went across the bridge, and got off two blocks from the 172nd Street Station. As I stepped off the bus people were swarming everywhere. I was like a tourist–looking all around at everything except where I was stepping. I took several steps and suddenly realized I had stepped on something squishy that felt like a pig 'turd.' I looked down. I had stepped in a dog pile. I looked around and there were dog piles scattered all around on the sidewalk.

I learned first hand that people lived in those tall buildings and many of them had dogs they took out early each morning. There was only the street or sidewalk for them to do their daily duty. The street was out of the question because the traffic would run over them. That left only the sidewalk. Yuk!

I had never been so close to so many people all at once as when I went down into the tubes to catch the Eighth Avenue A-Train to mid-town Manhattan. People were crammed into the railroad cars so tight it was impossible to move.

The A-Train was an express. It stopped only at 168th Street in the Bronx, again at 125th Street in Harlem and then 50th Street at Columbus Circle. I was supposed to get off at Columbus Circle and catch the BB Local into Rockefeller Center Plaza.

I didn't get off at Columbus Circle. There was a rush to the door and then the push of a mob getting on. I was unable to get to the door before it closed and the train pulled away from the platform.

I stood next to the door determined to be one of the first off at the next stop. It was 42nd Street under the Port Authority Bus Terminal. I made my way to street level. I had no idea where I was. I walked a short distance. I asked the first police officer

> I saw for directions to Rockefeller Center. He told me how to get there. As an after thought I asked him where Times Square was. I had seen so many photos and movies of Times Square I knew that was the one place in New York City I would surely recognize. He looked at me kind of quizzically and matter of factly said, "You're in Times Square."
>
> After several days at the motel Pat said she wanted to change motels. I asked, "Whatever for?"
>
> "There is a constant stream of people in and out all day long. The maids clean the rooms on both sides of us every hour or so all day long. I don't want to stay here."
>
> The next day Pat located a Howard Johnson motel about eight miles further from the George Washington Bridge. The first motel people were probably glad to see us go because they were getting only one day's rent on the room from us whereas they could be renting it ten times a day for 'temporary' illicit use.

Don and Pat rented a house in Closter, Bergen County, New Jersey. It was only two blocks to the corner where Don caught the Red and Tan bus that went across the George Washington Bridge to the 172nd Street Station for the Eighth Avenue A-Train. This became a daily routine.

> My office was in the International Building in Rockefeller Center across Fifth Avenue from Saint Patrick's Cathedral. Across the Plaza was the Sinclair Building. Every time I went by there I thought about Buford and his folks. Finally, one day I went to the Sinclair personnel office. I explained to the lady I was trying to locate a long lost friend. I told her his father, Charles F. Young, worked for years with Sinclair and was possibly a retiree. She checked her retiree records. She found a Charles F. Young living at Box 303, Eldorado, Texas.
>
> I wrote a letter to Mr. and Mrs. Charles F. Young and explained who I was. I asked if they had a son, Buford. I got a letter back in a few days from Mrs. Young. Yes, Buford was their son. She gave me his address, 262 North Day Street, Powell, Wyoming. I wrote a letter to Buford, and after many long years

> we were reunited. We kept in touch from then on until the day he died.

Don liked his new job. It was different. He interfaced with many different people in the company, including the various levels of management. He had a good secretary, Pat Falco. She was very slim and ate all kinds of fattening foods trying to gain weight. Don was a little overweight. He kidded her a lot about trading some of his "fat" for some of her "slim."

Don was in the new job only a few months when his boss came to him and told he they needed someone with field experience to go to Iran. The company had started a new crash exploration program in the Persian Gulf. The people in Iran needed someone temporarily with oil field material and equipment experience to bring order out of chaos. He asked Don if he would go. Don said he would.

The next several days were hectic. Don and Pat had been looking to buy a new house. They quickly looked at a builder's model in a large development called Lawrence Brook in East Brunswick, New Jersey. They signed a contract. The house was to be finished when Don returned from Iran.

Their household goods were moved to storage. Pat's mother flew to New Jersey to drive back to Marietta, Oklahoma, with Pat and Greg. They were to live with Pat's folks until Don returned. One afternoon they stood on the Jersey shore and watched the Queen Mary ease out into the Hudson River and sail for Europe.

> Pat, her mother, and Greg took me to Idlewild Airport (now John F. Kennedy) on Long Island. We said our farewells. I boarded a TWA Boeing 707 flight for Rome via Paris. I felt somewhat lonely and guilty to be leaving my dear family behind while I went off to be half a world away.
>
> The company flew its employees first class on international flights. This was 1960 when the airlines treated their passengers like someone special. The attendant brought a menu. I saw

caviar and cognac on it along with some very choice entrees. I had never eaten caviar or drank cognac. I ordered each. Yuk! The caviar tasted like fish eggs and the cognac tasted like burnt rubber.

An hour or so into the flight I knew someone important occupied the front two seats on both sides of the aisle in front of me. They made a lot of demands on the attendants and got a lot of attention. I soon learned it was Jayne Mansfield, her then husband, Mickey Hagarity, a child with a nanny, and a Chihuahua dog in a small hand basket.

We landed in Paris at six o'clock in the morning. Most of us got off the airplane to stretch our legs in the transit lounge. Jane looked very much like an ordinary person. She had a perky nose and was slightly freckled. Her hair was swept back in a tight bun at the nape of her neck. She was wearing a long sleeve blouse with a Peter Pan collar under a sleeveless low cut jumper dress. For all intents and purposes she looked very normal and nondescript.

We were in Paris only about an hour and reboarded for Rome. About fifteen minutes out of Rome Jane went forward to the rest room. She came back without the Peter Pan blouse and her hair was long and flowing down around her shoulders. Her sleeveless low-cut jumper dress was overly revealing. Her makeup hid the freckles and showed deep red pouting lips. What a transformation!

She was determined to be the last person to deplane. I waited until I was almost the last person to deplane ahead of her. I stepped out the door onto the stairs leading down to the tarmac. I thought I was a celebrity. I paused and looked around. I saw no less than fifty photographers and three newsreel cameras all looking up pointing at me.

I hurried down the stairs. I wanted to see Miss Mansfield get off. I was not disappointed. She stepped into the door of the airplane and struck a pose. The camera flashbulbs popped and the news reel cameras whirled. She took a full ten minutes to strut down the twenty or so steps. What a show!

It was about ten o'clock in the morning when Don arrived in Rome. He checked into the Hotel Eden. His Alatalia flight to

Teheran would not depart until eight o'clock the evening of the next day. This gave him a chance to look around a little while in Rome.

Rome was interesting. I had never been to Europe. I walked around near the hotel looking in the shops, looking at the people, and looking at the sights. The streets and narrow sidewalks were a beehive of activity.

I went into several shops. I bought a few gifts for Pat and Greg. The shopkeepers boxed and shipped them to Pat's folks in Marietta. One of the lady shopkeepers was curious to know about Marietta, Oklahoma. Her name was Marietta.

I went into a restaurant for a late lunch. I sat alone at a small table. I saw a woman obviously American sitting alone at a small table. I thought how sad to travel alone and not have someone to share the experience with. I wished Pat was with me.

I left the restaurant and went out onto the sidewalk. It was siesta time. Many shops were closed. The sidewalks were crowded with people coming and going, or sitting at small round tables sipping a drink or smoking.

I passed by a group of crowded sidewalk tables under an awning. A lady daintily waving a small white kerchief caught my eye. It appeared she was looking directly at me as she smiled friendly and knowingly. I thought she saw someone directly behind me she knew and was waving to get his or her attention. Not me. I didn't know anyone in Rome.

I walked a few steps farther to the curb and stopped for a red light. I was standing on the edge of the curb with half my feet hanging over the curb. I suddenly felt someone press against my left shoulder and whisper in my ear, "You wanna make love?"

I fell off the curb into the street. I quickly stepped back onto the curb face to face with the lady that waved the white kerchief. I muttered, "What? In the middle of the afternoon?" She got a real hurt expression on her face and said, "Zee time, eet makes a deefference?"

The light turned green. I started across the street. She followed jingling keys at me saying, "I have car. I have partment. Come weeth me?" I thought, "Yeah, and you have a big brute

> boy friend who will club me when I walk through the door," and kept walking. She quickly gave up and went to look for another 'John.'

The Alatalia flight departed Rome for Teheran the next evening. It was a DC-6 overnight flight. Don was the only person in first-class. He spent most of the night playing cards with the flight attendants, a man and a woman. They landed at Damascus early in the morning before daylight. Don deplaned and went to immigration to get his passport stamped with a Syrian visa. When he saw the two immigration officials with a grim no nonsense look and guns he decided against it and reboarded the airplane.

It was early morning when he arrived in Teheran. He spent one night at the company headquarters. The next morning he boarded an Iranair Viscount turbo-prop and left for Abadan, a four-hour flight. He was met at the airport by a company car driven by an Iranian chauffeur.

It was twenty miles to Kosrovabad and another five miles to the company base of operations on the Shat-al-Arab River, the Euphrates River of biblical times, a few miles upstream from the Persian Gulf. It was desolate and the middle of nowhere. Iraq was a scant hundred and fifty yards across the river.

The Iranians and Iraqis were in constant conflict over the precise location of the boundary. The Iranians claimed it extended to the western shoreline across the river. The Iraqis claimed it extended to the eastern shoreline across the river. This dispute occasionally resulted in sporadic gunfire across the river.

The company had living quarters for employees and contract people. There was a separate building for the kitchen and dining hall. Rooms were small and everyone shared a room. Don had a small room and a roommate. He was about sixty years old and worked for a contractor. After a few days Don learned the man knew his father when he was Ticket Agent for the Oklahoma Railway Company.

It was March. The weather was mild though a little warm. Don got settled in that afternoon. Later he decided to go to the shore-base about half a mile from the living quarters.

I decided to stroll down to the shorebase that evening and just look around and check things out. Did I ever get a surprise! I found out real quick that Iran and Iraq did not like each other. In fact, they shoot at each other across the river. The Iranians had a small military detachment and several patrol boats based on their side of the river.

I had gone only about a quarter of mile on the road along the river bank when suddenly I was confronted by two serious looking guys in military uniforms pointing rifles straight at me. I came to a screeching halt with hands held high. They said something, but I couldn't understand. It sounded serious. I said, "American. Pan American Oil company."

They didn't move. I looked at the rifles. 1906 Springfields. Bolt action. My God!! Fingers on the triggers! Do they have a safety? Where? Please God, don't let them pull the trigger. What do they want? This standoff lasted a full three minutes, but seemed an eternity. I had no idea what to do.

Thankfully, a more intelligent looking man in what was very obviously an officer's uniform came strolling from a small building near where the patrol boats were docked. He said something to the two soldiers. They dropped the rifles down. Whew!

"Where you go?" he asked.

"To the Pan American shorebase," I replied.

"No go. Go next day."

"Yes, Sir." I turned around and went back toward the living quarters not looking back praying they didn't have those rifles trained on me.

The next day I went to the shorebase in a company vehicle with an Iranian chauffeur. No problem at the checkpoint. They waved us through without stopping.

I learned an important lesson. If you are white you just don't go walking around in Iran unless accompanied by an Iranian that is on the company payroll. That was my first inkling that those people flat out do not like us, the greedy arrogant Americans.

We drove through the gate to the shorebase past company paid security guards. It looked like a beachhead landing in World War II. Crates of material and all kinds of equipmet were scattered all over the place with no rhyme or reason. I saw right away I had my work cut out for me.

Don reported to the superintendent and head administrative official for the company. They were glad to see him and wasted no time giving him a brief orientation and telling him to go to work. That he did.

My offiice was at the main warehouse. There I met Hakeem, my interpreter. His English was heavily accented but reasonably acceptable, at least for the moment.

I set about getting organized. They had hired two Pakistani men for clerks. They spoke a little English. Communication was going to be a major task. I had any number of contract laborers at my disposal to do the material handling, moving, and stacking. I soon learned the contract laborers weren't really that, they actually were conscripts. The local sheik was the contractor. The laborers were working off fines and various degrees of demerits imposed by the sheik for some offense. They were not the most willing workers, especially since they didn't get paid very much or very often. The company paid the sheik and he kept most of the money doling out a little here and there to keep the "natives from getting restless."

The sheik had his several henchmen 'enforcers' or 'pushers' to make the laborers work and keep them in line. They were better fed and larger than the average laborer. They obviously curried the sheik's favor else they too would quickly become a laborer. Not desirable.

The shorebase consisted of an administrative building with a communications center that communicated via radio with the offshore drill rigs, the aircraft, the helicopters, and the main office in Teheran. There were three large warehouses, a heliport and hanger, a landing strip for a DC-3 airplane, pipe racks, and a dock on the river for the cargo tenders.

Don soon learned they actually had their own little United Nations conclave. The cooks at the mess hall were Turks assisted by Iranian mess helpers. The houseboys that did the cleaning, laundry, etc. were Iranians. The boat crews for the cargo tenders were Greeks. The boat engineers were Germans. The helicopter pilots and maintenance crews were British. The well wire-line service crews were French. The clerks were Pakistanis. The warehousemen were Armenians. Communicating was definitely a challenge.

Don set about the task of bringing order out of chaos. He worked twelve to fourteen hour days.

> I could hardly believe my eyes. What a daunting task! Tons of material, equipment, and piping scattered and stacked all over the place. All kinds of items had been purchased but no records of having been received. The company was paying large dollar invoices not knowing whether they actually had the items or not. Engineers and drillers were making emergency orders for expensive items to be shipped air freight, knowing full well they had the identical items somewhere in a crate, but unable to find it.

Not having a regular aviation servicing facility fuel was stored in 55-gallon drums stacked on their sides eight high in pyramid shaped stacks in a special area call the 'fuel dump.'

> I had been there only three days when I looked out the warehouse door and saw an Iranian laborer hunched down in the shade of the fuel dump puffing on the butt of a cigarette. The Americans and Europeans knew not to smoke anywhere near the fuel dump, but the Iranians apparently didn't. The Americans would throw a partially smoked cigarette on the ground and step on it long before they got near the fuel dump. One of the Iranian laborers would pounce on the butt and

start puffing on it to get it going again. Then looked for the closest shade to squat down and smoke the butt.

"Good grief", I thought. "That guy will blow us sky high."

"Hakeem," I shouted at my interpreter, "Get that man out of there."

"Me, no. Maybe go boom."

"Then get a pusher to get him out of there!"

I don't know what Hakeem said to the pusher, but he went over to the guy and hit him two times with a small 'billy club', grabbed him by the nape of the neck, drug him over to me and shoved him onto the ground where he cowered.

I told Hakeem to tell him not to smoke over there and to get back to work with his crew. I don't know what Hakeem said to him but it took three or four minutes of conversation between him, the pusher and the laborer.

Hakeem and I went back into the warehouse. I gave him a piece of paper and a pencil and said, "Write as clearly as possible in the local language the words No Smoking," which he did. I painted several small boards white and set them to dry. I stayed later than usual after work. I took red paint and carefully copied what Hakeem wrote on the scrap of paper. I also added in smaller words "No Smoking" in English.

It was late but I took a flashlight and posted the signs around the fuel dump knowing they would be dry by morning. I hung one on the entrances to the three warehouses. I called and a driver came to get me and take me to the living quarters.

The next morning as usual I was at the warehouse early. Hakeem as usual came sauntering in about nine o'clock. I watched to see his reaction when he saw my sign on the warehouse door. He broke out laughing. He was laughing when he came into the office. I asked, "What's the matter? Can't you read it?"

"Yes, I can read it."

"Then what's so funny?"

"I'm the only one that can read it."

I felt like a dunce. Hakeem, a few others and I were the only ones that knew what the signs meant. The Pakistanis could read a little English. The Armenians could read very little English and whatever Armenians speak. The Iranian laborers

> who the signs were meant for were all illiterates. They couldn't read anything.

Don had been there only a week or so when an old Englishman who had over forty years of living among the Arabs said to him, "The way you have to deal with these people is hobble their camel, break their sword, cut out their tongue, and speak softly to them." The longer Don was there the more he came to understand this.

Don worked long hours. He knew that as soon as he got things organized and operating he would get to go home. It was not easy. Some tasks were daunting to say the least.

Not only were the laborers illiterate but they had no concept of personal hygiene or sanitation. They went when and where they had the urge. With anywhere from twenty to fifty or more laborers on site at any given time sanitation was a problem.

The company rushed through a project to build a modern latrine for the laborers to use. It was a simple concrete block building with concrete floors, several high narrow casement windows, forced ventilation in the ceiling, three trough urinals, six flush toilets, and six lavatories. Nothing fancy, but adequate for the situation.

> The day after final inspection and checkout I instructed Hakeem to call all the pushers and laborers together for a meeting outside next to the warehouse. I told Hakeem to emphatically tell them they were no longer to relieve themselves just anywhere on the ground. I would no longer tolerate it. They were now to go to the new latrine. I had about a minute of instructions for Hakeem to relay. He had over five minutes of conversation directed at the laborers, none of which I understood.
>
> As an after thought I told Hakeem to tell them to be sure and wash their hands after using the latrine to wash the germs from their hands. Again, a long conversation. But, when I saw all the laborers turn their hands palm up and stare at them I knew he had just told them about the germs.

I had no way to know what Hakeem told the pushers and the laborers. It wasn't long before I saw a pusher grab one of the laborers and drag him to the latrine and push him through the door. In the course of the day I saw this happen several times. I decided to go take a look in the latrine. About ten laborers were cowering on the floor. Some had done their duty on the floor. Good grief!

"Hakeem," I yelled out the door, "Get over here! Now!"

He came sauntering in.

"What's the meaning of this?"

"They don't know how to use a toilet. They've never seen one."

"Well, show them!"

"Not me. I'm just the interpreter."

"Get the pushers in here! Now!"

Hakeem soon returned with the several pushers. They were just as wide-eyed as the laborers. They had never seen a modern latrine either.

I told Hakeem I would demonstrate and he would translate exactly as I did and instructed. I proceeded to slowly and exactingly go through the process of urinating in a urinal, sitting on a toilet, wiping my self, flushing the toilet and washing my hands.

I told Hakeem to tell the pushers it was their responsibility to make sure the laborers came to the latrine and they were to make sure the laborers were properly instructed on how to use the latrine facilities. Again Hakeem had a long conversation. I thought that would take care of it. Wrong.

The next day I noticed laborers going in the latrine but didn't see any coming out. I decided to check it out. When I went into the latrine I saw several laborers huddled in a corner. One was sitting on a toilet. A pusher was shouting and beating him. They thought it was some kind of punishment.

It took about two weeks to finally get everyone and everything functioning properly at the latrine. In fact, the laborers were going more than normal. It was getting into summer time. Temperatures were over a hundred degrees. It was cool in the latrine.

I noticed three laborers that seemed a little more astute than the others. Since keeping the latrine clean was a problem I decided to make them permanent 'latrine orderlies.' Their job was to make sure the others used the facilities properly and to keep the latrine clean. I soon learned they also assumed the duty of 'enforcers' exerting their authority with vigor to make the laborers clean up after themselves.

After a couple more weeks the 'orderlies' sent one of their own as an emissary to Hakeem to approach me with a request. They wanted to keep a small hibachi in the latrine so they could make tea and heat their food. I thought that a little unusual, but since they were doing such a good job and since there was some extra space in one corner I agreed.

A few days later I was in the latrine. They had painted a yellow line around their corner. It was their private space. None of the other laborers encroached without repercussions. I smiled and let it be.

I also learned Hakeem did not speak the local dialect real well. That accounted for all the conversations and misunderstandings. In all fairness Hakeem had to do a lot of explaining to get the message understood.

Don worked long hours but occasionally he had a few diversions. One such time he went to Abadan with Hakeem and an Iranian driver. They visited a shop that dealt in antiques.

I saw a large copper tray covered with a greenish dust high up on a narrow shelf. It was about thirty-two inches in diameter. The merchant climbed a ladder and removed the tray. He dusted it with an old dusty cloth. Everything in Iran is covered in dust if it doesn't move every few minutes.

He laid the tray on a bench and poured a solution over it. He took a dirty rag and scrubbed it. Then he applied another solution and used a clean cloth to polish it revealing a gleaming beautifully hand engraved copper tray with turned up fluted edges. The merchant said it was an antique about two hundred and fifty years old. He said it had gone through three periods of artistic design. He said it first was flat with a very fine delicate floral engraving around the perimeter about two inches from the edge. It had a circle of braided rope design about twelve inches in diameter enclosing a circular grouping of floral designs in the center. He said the next design transition was the ornate engraving of people figures about two hundred years ago. There were eight pairs of figures encircling three figures in the center all portraying various cultural and social aspects of Old Persia. He said the final design transition was about fifty years ago when the edge was turned up and fluted.

Sounded like a good story to me. I had no way to ascertain if it was all true or not. Anyhow, I bought if for the equivalent of about fifty-five U.S. dollars. Today it sits on the mantle over our fireplace.

The helicopter pilots and maintenance personnel were British. They worked for Bermuda, Ltd. who contracted with the company. The helicopters were Westland S-55's which were configured to haul personnel and cargo.

During off-hours Don got well acquainted with the Brits. They liked his Oklahoma drawl and asked a lot of questions about Oklahoma. Don liked to listen to their wild tales, most of which he wasn't sure were true.

One day the Chief Mechanic told me they had just finished a hundred hour engine overhaul on one of the choppers. He said they were going to take it up for a check flight and asked if I would like to go along for a fifteen-minute ride. I had never flown in a helicopter so naturally I agreed.

The pilot, mechanic and I climbed aboard. They got up front in the pilot seats above the cargo bay. I sat on a jump-seat in the cargo bay. We took off. For the next ten minutes we flew around making numerous up and down maneuvers turning one way and then another–all part of the check out.

I was enjoying the flight looking out the open door at the countryside below. It was very noisy. Suddenly, the engine quit.

It was quiet. Very quiet except for the whish, whish sound of the chopper blades. I quickly glanced out the door. We were at least a thousand feet off the ground above the heliport. My heart leaped into my throat. I thought, "We're going to crash." I don't know why I thought it would help, but I snugged my seat belt tighter.

Fifteen seconds passed. We were still airborne. I looked out the door. We were still five hundred feet from the ground. Another fifteen seconds. We were about two hundred feet from the ground. I thought, "We may survive this." Another ten seconds and we were only twenty or so feet from the ground. I began to suspect I had been had. Then, a slight jolt and we touched down.

My British friends were having a hoot. They had scared the wits out of me. They never killed the engine. They just put it into idle which made very little noise. They 'dead-stick' landed the chopper right on the pad. I didn't know you could 'dead-stick' land a helicopter.

It was not unusual for an occasional roving band of nomads to pitch their tents close by the company base. The women came to the river to wash clothes and dry them on bushes. They kept to themselves and did not bother anyone or anything.

They traveled in small bands with a small herd of sheep, a dozen or so goats, several donkeys and eight or ten camels. They pitched their several large tents about a half-mile from our base.

They did not look anything like the Iranians or Arabs. They were taller and had a more wiry look than the usual Arab. They had a hard piercing look about their face instead of the usual blank look of an Arab. The women did not cover their faces. Instead they wore bright ornate nose and ear jewelry. I think they were Bedouins.

One evening some of the guys that had been there longer than I asked if I wanted to go with them to "see the girls dance." I had no idea what that meant, but I went along. We had to chip in enough money to get together a little over thirty dollars to pay the elders.

After dark an Iranian chauffeur drove us over to the nomad tents. Two of our guys negotiated a price with a couple of the elders. They arrived at an agreeable amount.

The two dozen or so male nomads sat on the ground in a large circle in front of one of the tents. A goodly fire blazed in the center. We were told by hand signs in no uncertain terms that we had to stand about ten yards beyond the circle in the shadow of a tent. Four older men came out of the tent and sat on the ground opposite to where we were standing. Each had a crude looking instrument. One was a five-foot long three-string instrument. Another was a small drum that appeared to be a goatskin stretched over a deep wooden bowl. The others were a tambourine and a pair of hardwood sticks with a series of small notches.

They began a slow rhythmical cadence. Two young girls came into the circle with bronze castanets keeping cadence with their feet and arms. They looked to be no more than fifteen or sixteen years old. They were fully clothed from neck to ankles with full flowing colorful skirts. They were barefoot.

The cadence gradually picked up faster and faster. The girls kept with the cadence. The best way I can describe the dancing is to compare it to the Spanish Flamingo style of dancing only it wasn't the same. It was much more physical. They did not dance as a team. They danced separately. There was a lot of swirling that revealed nothing above the knee. They kept a steady cadence with the castanets that made a ringing metallic sound. This went on about fifteen minutes. I was almost exhausted just watching them. The cadence reached a pitched frenzy and suddenly stopped. The girls ran into the tent.

In a couple of minutes it started again. This time it was two different young girls. I had never seen dancing like that. It had an eeriness about it with the strange sounding musical cadence and the flickering light of the fire darting in and out among the dark shadows of the tents.

Don had another experience with the natives that he came to regret for years afterwards. The local sheik was the contractor for all the laborers. He was the one that got paid–handsomely.

He threw a feast one evening for the company employees in appreciation of the largess of the company.

> It was after dark. We were traveling in several vehicles with our Iranian chauffeurs. Every time we came to a fork in the road a man was standing there with a flame lantern to show the driver which road to take. We must have gone ten or twelve miles meandering around in the desert. We finally came to a small group of mud huts with space to park the vehicles.
>
> We were met by the sheik's emissary and several men with lanterns. They led us on foot about a quarter of a mile to a large grove of date palm trees. As we approached the grove we saw flaming torches around the area set aside for the event. The sheik greeted us at the edge of the grove.
>
> The ground was covered with numerous Persian rugs. Several tables about eighteen inches high and six feet long were strategically placed about. Several small pillows were placed at each table to sit on. A large bowl of dates, berries and other condiments I did not recognize were sitting on each table.
>
> There was some amount of small talk through an interpreter. After a bit several men came bearing an ornate pitcher and small ornate metal cups. They poured a drink of some kind for each of us. I think it may have been soured goats milk. It was not a drink to relish.
>
> In a few minutes we saw a procession of a dozen torches winding through the palm grove. As they got closer we saw they were bearing large trays of food. They set a tray on each table. We all partook of the food though we had no idea what we were eating. That was the only native food I ate while in Iran. For years and years afterwards I had an intestinal parasite that caused me a goodly amount of pain and discomfort.

The Gary Powers incident occurred while Don was in Iran. This was when the Russians shot down an American U-2 spy plane over Russia and captured the pilot, Gary Powers. It sent shock waves around the world. For the next two or three weeks the political situation was very unstable as the Americans and Russians negotiated. The world held its collective breath for fear of a major war.

This was a bad situation for many people including Don. He was half a world from Oklahoma and Pat and Greg. He worried how he would ever find his way home if war broke out. Pat worried that if war broke out would she ever again see her husband. Fortunately for all it was peacefully though precariously settled in a few weeks.

The short time Don lived and worked in that part of the world he came to an understanding of the vast cultural difference between Islam and Christianity. He experienced the Islamic mind at work and several years after he returned home he wrote the following based on his observations of Islam versus Christianity:

HATE is to Islam as LOVE is to Christianity
DECEIT is to Islam as TRUTH is to Christianity
DESPAIR is to Islam as HOPE is to Christianity
MALICE is to Islam as KINDNESS is to Christianity
GREED is to Islam as CHARITY is to Christianity
CRUELTY is to Islam as MERCY is to Christianity
DEATH is to Islam as LIFE is to Christianity
LIFE in Islam is a sacrifice to be made to Allah as a martyr.
LIFE in Christianity is a precious gift from God to be cherished.

In August 2005 Don watched a four-hour television documentary, "INSIDE 9/11," on the National Geographic Channel about events leading up to September 11, 2001, and subsequent related events. Don said, "The entire four hour documentary is a real eye-opener that everyone should see once a month just so we don't forget what happened and who our enemies are." Osama bin Laden was quoted, "We love death. Americans love life. That is the difference between us." Don said, "What Osama bin Laden really meant is they love a martyr's death by killing as many Americans as they can."

The day finally came when Don's work was winding down. A permanent Material and Warehouse Manager had been transferred from within the company for assignment to the Iranian operation at Kosrovabad. Don could soon go home.

He arranged for two weeks vacation and through the local travel agent for the company made reservations for Pat to fly to Rome and meet him there on his way home. He had tour arrangements for them to travel by bus and train through Northern Italy, Switzerland, Germany, and to Paris for a few days. Three days before Don was to depart Iran he received a telegram from Pat saying she was not meeting him in Rome. She had rather spend the money on new furniture for the new house that was to be ready when Don returned to the States. Don was disappointed but glad to be going home.

> I was packed and ready to go. My passport and papers were all in order. I was at the Abadan airport. The Pan Am Boeing 707 was on the tarmac. All the passengers had cleared customs and boarded except me. It was departure time.
>
> My luggage was still open in customs. Several Iranian customs officials and an airline representative were standing near my luggage engaged in serious conversation. Departure time had come and gone. The airplane was still on the tarmac. I was getting anxious. I wondered what could be wrong? Would I miss my flight?
>
> Suddenly, the conversations stopped. They slammed my bags closed and hustled them out the door. The representative quickly took me to a waiting luggage cart with my baggage. The driver dropped me off at the bottom of the stairs to the door of the plane.
>
> As I bolted up the steps I looked to be sure they were loading my luggage. They were. I breathlessly reached the top. A flight attendant was standing there holding the door handle. I said, "Thanks for waiting. Sorry for the hold up." She replied,

"No problem. It happens all the time. Have a seat, sir, and buckle up."

I sat down and buckled up. The plane was rolling before I could catch my breath.

After we were in flight I asked the flight attendant what was the problem. She said, "Oh, they were dickering over the banshee (bribe) so we could take off. They always pick a passenger to hold up until Pan Am agrees to pay the agreed banshee. You just happened to be the unlucky passenger."

I settled back in my seat, looked out the window and muttered to myself, "Adios, you _______ ," and ordered a whiskey. I was relieved to be leaving that part of the world far behind, and glad to be going home. I never had any desire to ever go back.

If the world had a butt-hole it would be over there. They lived in squalor unlike anything I had ever seen, even in Mexico. They are extremely devious. I made the mistake of trying to show compassion and kindness when I first arrived. I quickly learned they view compassion as a weakness to be exploited. They are not trustworthy. They are all petty thieves. They will steal anything from you if you are the least bit lax.

I got the sense they stood out there in the blazing hot desert in rags with their skinny camel looking at us, the well-heeled Americans running around in air conditioned cars stealing their oil while not understanding that it was their government (the Mullahs, Sheiks and Shah) that was receiving billions of dollars in royalty payments, but hoarding it for themselves building fine palaces and mosques while 'living it up' on the French Rivera or some other likely place.

Don returned via Rome and Paris. The Pan Am flight was in Rome only about an hour and then on to Paris. He stayed in Paris three days and two nights. He exchanged some dollars for French francs at the airport. He checked into the Plaza 'd Athene, an old but grand hotel in the heart of Paris.

The money changer gave me crisp new paper francs. I paid the taxi fare to the hotel and got old crumpled paper francs for change. I got settled in the hotel and went out to shop for a few gifts for Pat and Greg. I paid for everything with crisp new francs and always got change back in old worn wrinkled francs. I tried several times to pay with the old wrinkled francs but the shopkeepers always wanted the crisp new francs. I didn't quite understand.

I had dinner at the hotel restaurant. I couldn't read the menu. The waiter was haughty to say the least and not much help. I asked what an item was. He said, "Potatoes American style." I was curious to see what the French thought American style potatoes were. I ordered some along with the meal. He brought french fries. I don't know if it was his idea of a joke or it was for real.

I met a fellow employee who happened to be in Paris. That evening we went to several of the usual tourist places including the Moulin Rouge.

The next day I took a sightseeing bus tour. It went to the Eiffel Tower, a couple of museums, and Napoleon's tomb. I didn't like the tour bus concept. It was hurry off, hurry up, and hurry on–not my idea of sightseeing.

The next evening my fellow worker and I went to Au Petite Balcone (The Little Balcony) somewhere in the back alleys of Paris. It was an interesting nightclub with Apachee dancers.

I ran out of crisp new francs. All I had was a bunch of wrinkled francs no one wanted. I took a taxi and tried to pay with the old francs. He wouldn't take them. I told him they were all I had left. He then explained it to me.

During the month I was there France was revaluing the franc ten to one. One new franc was worth ten times an old franc. The moneychanger at the airport gave me new francs at the revalued rate. The only difference in the new francs and the old francs was the new francs had a small "NF" printed on the back in the upper left and upper right corners. Otherwise, they looked exactly alike except the new francs were new and crisp bills and the old francs were old and worn.

Everyone in France were dumping their old francs at the revalued rate on unsuspecting tourists like me. When I purchased a ten franc item and paid with a new twenty franc

> bill they gave me back ten old francs as though they had the same value. Actually, they had only one-tenth the value.
>
> I have never liked the French since. Their motto is "Fleece the ugly stupid Americans and laugh all the way to the bank." They took me for several hundred dollars.

Pat and Greg met Don at Love Field in Dallas as he arrived on a Braniff flight from New York. They spent a few days at Lake Murray with Pat's parents. Then, they drove to New Jersey.

Their new house was located at 22 Perry Road in the Lawrence Brook development, East Brunswick. It was finished and ready to move into. Don and Pat had to go to the Ninth National Bank of New York in New York City to close on the loan.

> We arrived about fifteen minutes before the appointed time. We were shown into a conference room to wait. In a few minutes the builder's representative showed up and waited with us. The appointed time came and went. Fifteen minutes passed and we still waited. The bank's representative finally came in and impatiently said, "Mr. Davidson, if your lawyer will just hurry up and get here we can get on with this."
>
> I replied, "Lawyer? I don't have a lawyer. What do I need a lawyer for?"
>
> "Why to make sure you don't sign something you shouldn't."
>
> "Sir. Are you going to give me something to sign I shouldn't?"
>
> "Uh, oh. Well. No."
>
> "Then let's get on with it."
>
> I imagine those slick New York bankers had a field day at their cocktail parties telling about those dumb hicks from Oklahoma.

The company paid to have their household goods stored while Don was in Iran and Pat and Greg were in Oklahoma. The storage company delivered the furniture and they went about setting up housekeeping in their new home. But, not without problems.

All the houses in New Jersey were built with basements. The furnace, air conditioner, and water heater were located in the basement. In a few days Don noticed water seeping into the basement. He tried to patch the walls to no avail. The builder was non-responsive.

One day Don had a chance meeting in the street with an old timer that lived nearby in a farm house before there was a development. In the course of conversation he waved his arm pointing right at Dons and Pat's house and said, "See that house there. It's built right on top of old Indian Spring." That was enlightening.

This got the builder's attention. They came and dug a trench all the way around the house. They applied a thick layer of tar material on the outer walls of the basement. That took care of the water problem except for a small amount of weeping through the floor. It surely must have diverted the water from old "Indian Spring" to someone else's house further down the hill.

Don's commute to work each day was two hours into New York City and two hours home. That is if everything went without incident. Pat drove him two miles to the commuter bus stop where he caught the bus that went onto the New Jersey Turnpike. It went through the Lincoln Tunnel into the Port Authority Bus Terminal on 42nd Street and 8th Avenue. Don usually walked the several blocks to his office.

Coming home was the reverse. Four hours out of his day to get to and from work. If there was any kind of incident like an accident on the turnpike or in the tunnel, or it rained, or it snowed, his commute time was extended anywhere from half an hour to several hours. It was not uncommon for Pat to go to the bus stop to meet Don's bus only to wait an hour or two hours for it to arrive. Sometimes she had to go home and Don had to walk the two miles to get home late at night only to get up the next morning to do it all over again.

> In the mornings Pat drove me to the bus stop without waking Greg. He was only two and a half years old. It took only about six minutes to run me to the bus stop, drop me off, and drive back home. It was so early in the morning that Greg was sound asleep. Only, for whatever reason, one morning he woke up. He looked out the upstairs window just in time to see us drive away. Poor kid. He thought we were abandoning him. He was in a panic when Pat got back. After that she always took him with her.

Shortly afterwards Greg got a serious ear infestion. He had to be hospitalized to have a myrangotomy operation on his ear. It was a delicate operation. He had to be put under with a general anesthesia.

> When Greg began to come to in the recovery room it was wild. He had crazy hallucinations. He ran from spiders, chased butterflies, ran after the ice cream truck, fought with his playmates, etc. He bounced up and down and all over the crib. It seemed to Pat and I that it went on forever. It was pitifully painful for us to see our child that way. We began to wonder if he would ever come out of it with full recovery.
>
> Thank God he did.

Most of the people who lived in Lawrence Brook were from the Bronx or Brooklyn in New York City. They had arrived. They had their own home in the suburbs and no longer had to live in a walk-up tenement in the city. They knew next to nothing about anything related to the maintenance and upkeep of a house with yard, shrubs and trees. Most had none or very minimum hand tools.

Don put in a lawn, planted shrubs and small trees. He planted a garden in the backyard with okra and black-eyed peas among other things. He became the neighborhood source of how or what to do for this or that to do with lawn work and house maintenance.

One Saturday afternoon I looked out toward my garden. I saw two men standing in it. I sauntered out and inquired what they wanted. They said they heard I had black-eyed peas growing and wanted to see what they looked like. I said, "You're standing in the middle of them." They also wanted to see okra growing. They had no idea what it looked like.

One evening I had already gone to bed but had not gone to sleep. Pat was still up. I heard the doorbell ring rapidly several times. Pat called up for me to come down.

It was a neighbor from across the street. He wanted to borrow my pipe wrenches. His wife had dropped her diamond wedding rings down the lavatory drain. I gave him two pipe wrenches and he left.

I got dressed. Took a piece of wire, a pair of needle-nose pliers, and a flashlight and went across the street. The front door was wide open. I walked in. I heard the neighbor upstairs. I quietly walked up the stairs. I saw his wife laying on the bed sobbing. He was under the sink frantically trying to undo the piping. I bent the wire to make a small hook, bent over the neighbor, and shined the flashlight down the drain.

That diamond almost leaped out at me it was so brilliant. I ran the wire down the drain, hooked it and pulled it out. The neighbor was so intent he didn't even know I was there. I took the diamond rings into the bedroom and dangled them on the wire close to her face. She was surprised. She took the rings, went into the bathroom, kicked her husband, and said, "Dummy. Don got them out for me."

Another neighbor, Marshall Frey, worked for a major advertising company in New York City. He wrote television commercials. One day I casually commented to him during the course of a conversation that television commercials are so dumb anyone could write one. He whipped out a small pad, thrust a pencil into my hand, and said, "Write me one."

"Duh, uh, duh. Gosh, maybe it isn't so easy."

He always had that little pad and pencil. Any colloquial expression I uttered he whipped out that pad and pencil and wrote it down. After a while I told him I was going to demand royalties.

The Geoseffis lived across the street. They had a bunch of kids. He worked in New York City. It had snowed all night and a major snowstorm was brewing. About noon time that day Pat got a phone call from Mrs. Geoseffi. She was about to give birth and needed a ride to the hospital. Pat was the only woman in the neighborhood that knew how to drive. Pat drove her about five miles to the hospital in a blinding snowstorm praying all the way she would not have the baby before they got there. She gave birth a few minutes after they arrived.

Don liked his job. His boss was a 'klutz' but Don liked what he was doing. What he disliked was the long commute times and the lack of quality time with Pat and Greg. It didn't take much for him think about changing jobs to get out of the New York area and go back west. An incident at work was the "straw that broke the camel's back."

> One day a young accounting trainee showed up at my office. He was working with capital equipment classifications for purposes of depreciation. He had difficulty understanding the criteria for classifying the various kinds of oil field equipment. Someone in the Accounting Department told him "Go see Don Davidson. He knows all about oil field equipment."
>
> He brought a computer listing of the field equipment installed in the recently operational Argentina properties. He asked me to look over it with him and explain why all the equipment was classified as pipeline equipment when almost all of it obviously was oil and gas gathering equipment. My eyes popped out of my head. I told him to give me the list and I would look into it.
>
> I took the list to the Comptroller and asked if he knew all the Argentine oil and gas gathering equipment was classified as pipeline equipment. He was mildly surprised but didn't really know the difference. I explained, "Oil and gas gathering equipment, because of its highly corrosive nature, receives

accelerated depreciation rates; whereas pipeline equipment which is not so highly corrosive is depreciated at a much lower standard rate."

He asked, "Then why is it classified as pipeline equipment?"

"Because someone who has worked in domestic operations mistakenly misclassfied it based on the old rule of thumb in the States that if it was no larger than four inches it was oil and gas gathering equipment. If it was six inches or larger it was pipeline equipment."

"Well, why is that?"

"Because in the States everything is small leases with one, two, or maybe three wells. Therefore, the pipe size doesn't need to be larger than four inches to accommodate all the flow."

"Oh, I see." He still didn't grasp the significance.

"In Argentine it is one very large lease with forty-five wells. The oil and gas gathering equipment has to be six inches or larger to accommodate the flow. The break point should be the flange where the oil and gas gathering lines interface with the pipeline."

"My God! We're loosing thousands." He finally saw the light.

"Yes."

I was given the project to get all the Argentine equipment properly classified. It took the accounting trainee and me about three weeks to complete. It didn't save thousands. It saved over a million dollars the first year.

We had a meeting in my boss's office for the implementation. The Vice-President of Production, the Controller, the Accounting Manager, the accounting trainee, my boss, and I were in the meeting. Congratulations were being handed out by the Vice-President and the Controller. Instead of congratulations my boss said, "Oh, that was so simple anyone could have thought of it." I wanted to choke him. He had no idea what a flange or wellhead was. His casual offhand lack of knowledge or appreciation to upper management for what the 'lowly' accounting trainee and I did helped cement my decision to change jobs.

Don came home from work late one night and said to Pat, "This isn't living. It's existing. I'm changing jobs so we can move back west." He made several inquiries and interviewed with a company in Utah. The man he interviewed with later changed jobs and sent Don a job offer to come to Salt Lake City and work at Hercules Powder Company on the Polaris, Ranger, and Minuteman Programs. Don accepted. Don and Pat set about getting prepared to move. A major item was to sell the house.

> I hand painted a 'For Sale by Owner' sign. It was still wet when I drove the stake in the ground in the front yard. Greg sat on the curb and watched.
>
> I went into the garage to clean up the brushes. In a few minutes I heard Greg call out, "Hey, Mister. You want to buy a house?" I looked out the garage door and saw a car stop. A man and woman got out. They spoke briefly to Greg. He directed them toward me in the garage.
>
> They came in and looked at the house. Before they left we signed a sales contract. I guess Greg should have gotten a real estate salesman's fee.

Don, Pat and Greg moved to Salt Lake City. They lived in a motel a week and then rented a house at 1181 Ridgedale Lane. Once again they settled into a new place and a new job. It was totally different from New York. A slower pace, a much shorter commute to work in a car pool, friendlier people, close to the mountains, and a drier climate–all very favorable and agreeable to Don and Pat.

Don's Aunt Bea lived at Price, Utah, about an hour drive from Salt Lake City. A tragic oil field accident killed her husband, Dick Riley, a few weeks before Don and Pat moved to Utah. She had stayed with Don and his brothers and sister when they were kids on NW 40th Street in Oklahoma City. She was never around them again more than a few times for no more than an hour or two on each occasion.

On one of Bea's visits with Don and Pat they reminisced about the time she stayed a year with Don's parents. When Don's mother had Sam, the youngest boy, she also had a hysterectomy. She was not well. Bea took care of the children most of the time.

> Aunt Bea was only a teenager. I was five. My oldest brother, William, was eight and Bobby Joe, was seven. She gained an insightful personal perspective of each of us that was realistically descriptive of us as adults.
>
> She said, "If I would have given each of you boys a quarter Billy would give his away. Gene would save his. Bobby would figure out how to get Billy's and Gene's quarters from them."
>
> How true! Pat and I were amazed. What she said has been so realistically true all our lives.

Don and Pat made several trips to Price to see Aunt Bea and try to be of help. Don's cousins, Evann, Walter, and David, were teenagers. It was a trying time for them as well as for Aunt Bea. Then, a few weeks later Bea's mother, Don's grandmother, died. Bea drove alone to Oklahoma. Don had just started a new job and didn't ask for time off to attend the funeral. Two years later Evann was married. Don, Pat and Greg attended the wedding.

Don took up snow skiing. He bought a Winchester Model 70 rifle and also took up deer hunting. They bought camping gear and in the summer went camping and fishing in the Unita Mountains and Yellowstone. Pat got an electronic console organ and took music lessons. Don had a lot more spare time and finished off a nice recreation room in the basement of the rent house. The landlord bought all the materials and Don did the work. It turned out very nicely.

Don worked and car pooled with Mick Cannon. He and his wife, Marion, became very good friends. Their families were old time Morman families that came to Utah with Brigham Young. Mick's family owned land with a cabin on the Upper Weber River on the western slopes of the Unita Mountains.

Don had many enjoyable days hunting with Mick in the High Unitas. They spent hours together and had lots of time to discuss many subjects of a social, religious, political, philosophical, etc. nature. Mick was easy to talk with. He had a positive and optimistic attitude toward life. Mick and Marion were salt of the earth people.

Greg attended Saint Ann's Catholic School kindergarten. He was in the Christmas pageant. The students practiced under the watchful eye of The Sister. They were to sing "Silent Night" as the finale.

> We had company. We wanted Greg to show off his singing ability by singing "Silent Night." He began to sing with the clarion clear voice that only a child has. He sang: "Silent night. Holy night. All is calm. All is bright. Round up your virgins. Mother and child."
>
> We all cracked up. Greg didn't know what was so funny.

When Greg was five years old he had his tonsils removed. At home he had to stay in bed a few days. Don and Pat gave him a lot of ice cream. After he felt better they decided to get him a small table-top television for his room.

> I took Greg to Sears to pick out a television set. We found just the right one and I purchased it. We had to go to the warehouse to pick it up. Greg wanted to know why couldn't we take the one from the store.
>
> On the way to the warehouse and while we waited to get the set I took the opportunity to explain warehousing to Greg. I explained that they couldn't keep all the televisions at the store, that people went there to pick out what they wanted and then went to the warehouse to get their set. Greg seemed to understand.
>
> A few nights later when we were saying our 'good nights' to Greg he kept talking about all manner of things. He didn't yet want to go to sleep. He was bringing up every thing he could think of to talk about. We kept encouraging him to lay down and go to sleep.

He suddenly set up bright-cycd and exclaimed, "Daddy, tell mama about that whorehouse you took me to." Wow! I did a double take. "Where have I taken this kid lately?"

"You know, Daddy, that whorehouse where we got my television." Wow! What a relief.

During the summers Don and Pat took Greg camping and fishing at Mirror Lake in the Unitas. In the wintertime Don took him skiing at Solitude and Brighton.

Greg was four years old when I started to take him skiing at Solitude. I carried him about two hundred feet up the 'bunny slope,' pointed him downhill and gave him a gentle shove. He skied all the way to the bottom, came to a stop and waited for me to come get him and carry him back up the hill. I did this over and over until I got tired carrying him up the hill.

After a few weeks I decided I was tired of carrying that kid up the hill. I took him and his mother to the chairlift at Brighton. Pat watched. She didn't much want me to take him to the top of the ski slope even though it was a 'bunny slope.'

It came our turn to get on the chairlift. We got in position to get on the chair as it came around. I looked back to catch the chair arm as it came to us. Unknown to me Greg dropped one of his ski poles. He bent over to pick it up. As I caught the chair and let it swing down for us to sit in I realized Greg was bending down and the chair would knock him over.

I grabbed him by the arm. We went off the end of the loading platform with me sitting in the chair holding Greg by his arm as he dangled over the edge of the seat. I knew I couldn't hold him like that all the way to the top. There was a big snowdrift directly below us. I dropped him about ten feet into the snow. Pat about had a heart attack. "What is that idiot husband doing to my baby?"

The operator stopped the lift. He pulled Greg out of the snow and set him in the chair behind me with another skier. The ride to the top was uneventful. We had a ball skiing down.

> Soon Greg was getting on and off the lift by himself and skiing like an experienced skier. And, I didn't have to carry him up the hill anymore.

Don loved to ski. He skied with Gary Anderson, the next door neighbor, and his friend, Phil. They were excellent skiers and Don learned a lot from them. They went skiing as often as they could at Alta.

After two years in the rent house Don and Pat bought a new house at 7102 South 1848 East in south Salt Lake City. It was a tri-level and only a mile from the mouth of Little Cottonwood Canyon that went up to the Alta ski area. Once again Don did the landscaping for a new house. Don and Pat had an exciting event while there.

> It was a pleasant Sunday morning. I was working in the front yard. Two houses away the twelve-year old daughter came running out of the house screaming, "Fire! Our house is on Fire!"
>
> I looked toward the house and saw smoke billowing out the glass sliding door that opened onto a wood deck. I ran to our front door, yelled at Pat to call the fire department, then ran across the yards to the deck.
>
> I saw a garden hose on the ground with a spray nozzle. It was connected to a faucet. I turned it on and ran up the steps of the deck and through the open door into the kitchen. There was fire and smoke everywhere. The lady of the house was trying to put out the fire. She did not realize she was on fire. I drenched her. I then began to spray the flames to extinguish them.
>
> The fire department arrived just as I was putting out the last of the flames. The lady's hands and arms were badly burned. Pat started taking her to the hospital, but met her husband on his way home. He took her to the hospital.
>
> The kitchen was a mess. The lady had made french fries the night before. She put the pot of grease on the stove to heat and went downstairs to do laundry. She forgot about it until she smelled smoke. She rushed upstairs, grabbed a towel, picked

> up the flaming pot and hurled it at the sink. That splattered flaming grease everywhere. She then began to try to put it out.
>
> Pat and I spent all the rest of the afternoon and evening cleaning up the mess in her kitchen.

Don went skiing at every opportunity. Solitude had night skiing and he would go there one or two nights a week. He went to Alta Saturdays and Sundays. He got to be a fairly good skier. He raced several times in novice races. He never won but had fun. Don's cousin, Polly, her husband Lee, and a friend came to visit for a week of skiing.

While they lived in Salt Lake City Don and Pat made several vacation trips to Oklahoma to visit their parents and other relatives. On one such trip Pat's Dad, Bert, approached Don with the proposition to buy a 120-acre farm adjacent to his. It would give him an additional eighteen acres of peanut allotment. Bert could float a ten-year Farm Home Loan in his name. He asked Don to make the yearly payments with the provision that when the loan was paid he would transfer title to Don and Pat. Don agreed.

At work Don was cleared for top secret and worked part time on an Air Force special top secret project in addition to his regular job as a supervisor in Management Systems. Hercules had a small but critical part of the overall project. It was so secret that Don had to work behind secured doors and could not work on or discuss any aspect of the project outside the secured area. The initial test by the Air Force in the South Pacific was so unstable with unexpected consequences that it was drastically scaled back. To this day Don thinks it is still a top secret project though over the years he has seen it generally described in several publications available to the general public and on the Internet. Something commonly known as the "E-Bomb."

The Air Force was cutting back on the Minuteman Program. The Navy was cutting back on the Polaris Program. The top secret program was scuttled. Hercules began laying off people. Don was laid off due to program cutbacks.

The NASA Apollo Program was ramping up in Huntsville, Alabama. The various subcontractors sent teams of recruiters to Salt Lake City recruiting excessed aerospace personnel. Don interviewed with Brown Engineering Company and accepted their offer. Thus, Don, Pat and Greg packed up and moved to Huntsville. They bought a tri-level house at 408 Cumberland Drive on a hillside facing the Marshall Space Flight Center. When they test fired the Saturn missiles it literally shook the house.

Don worked in the group responsible for testing component parts of the Lunar Excursion Module (LEM) to determine their reliability and maintainability for stress in hostile environments. This is where He first began to work directly with computers.

Greg was enrolled at Weatherly Elementary and completed the first through third grades. In Alabama they taught reading, writing and arithmetic. Pat was a stay at home Mom. She took Greg to and from school, was the Cub Scout den mother, and took care of the household. Don worked with Greg in the Cub Scout Pinewood Derby.

> It was supposed to be a father and son project. Each boy got a block of wood, a set of four wheels, two small wood cross pieces to hold the axles, and four nails for the axles. The idea, or at least as I understood it, was the son was to make the racer with the guidance of the father.
>
> Greg carved a very nice looking racing car, painted it, put on decals, added a steering wheel, and windshield. It looked very smart, classy and well done, especially for an eight-year old boy. I did very little except to suggest things he should consider and do.
>
> Day of the derby. Greg carried his car in. The other boys oohed and aahed at how nice it looked. The only thing it wasn't a beauty contest–it was a speed contest. When it came time for Greg's car to run it barely made it down the sloping course. No

attention had been given to the design for speed. His car was dead last. He was greatly disappointed.

I told him not to despair. There would be next year. I saw right away it was not a father and son project. It was a father project with the sons as spectators.

The next year I made the car. It was made for speed. The guys at work helped me design it like a flying wedge. The maximum allowed weight was scientifically distributed by a highly technical computer program. It was tested in a small wind tunnel to design it for minimum wind resistance. The nails for the axles were honed to a fine surface embedded with graphite. The wheels were honed down to a sharp razor edge to minimize resistance.

Day of the race. The Cub Scout Master's sons had won the derby every year the past several years. This was the last year for his youngest son. They had an unusually nice large trophy for the winner fully expecting the son to win.

Race time. The different heats were fast. The cars went zip. Each heat was close. Came time for Greg's car. Greg hadn't touched it except to carry it to the starting gate. His car went zoom. The other car in the heat wasn't even close. All the kids went "Oh!" The dads went "Hum." Not because of the design but because of the speed. Not one car came close to beating Greg's. He won every heat with time to spare. He took home the nice large trophy.

The next year I didn't even so much as advise Greg. I had made my point. Greg's car that year placed second. He used the wheels from the car of the previous year.

One of the men Don worked with at Brown Engineering was a pilot. He had an airplane and an instructor's license. After work hours and on weekends he made extra money giving flight lessons.

I mentioned to him one day that I would pay for him to take my son up for a short flight just so Greg would have the experience of flying. The co-worker said he had a student the

> next Saturday morning and for me to bring Greg to the airport. Saturday came and Greg and I were there early.
>
> After awhile the friend landed and discharged his student. He took Greg in tow and seated him in the student seat. They took off and were gone for what seemed a long time. Fifteen minutes passed. Thirty minutes passed. After about forty-five minutes I saw the airplane circle the airport and turn for a final approach.
>
> As the plane came in on final I noticed it was a little erratic. It bobbed up and down a little and yawed first to one side and then to the other. I thought, "Good grief. Does this guy know how to fly an airplane or not?" Just moments before touchdown the plane straightened up and made a perfect landing.
>
> I watched as they brought the plane around on the tarmac and shut down the engine. He unbuckled Greg and helped him out of the airplane. Greg calmly walked over to me and exclaimed, "He let me fly it," as though it was no big deal.
>
> My friend had not only taken Greg for a ride, but let him fly the airplane right up to a few moments before touch down. That explained the erratic approach. He would not take any money for taking Greg up. I think he had just as much fun as Greg did.

In her spare time Pat joined a group of ladies that participated in several different kinds of craft classes. She learned tole painting, miniature painting, and decoupage. She also learned cake decorating and decorated some beautiful cakes. Some looked more like dolls dressed in antebellum attire than cakes.

She sometimes bemoaned the fact she didn't have an appropriate pattern for some project. Being somewhat artistic Don would draw patterns for her. After a while they had a collection of patterns.

Pat came up with the idea to make a set of patterns, advertise them in a national craft magazine, and sell them. Don got busy and drew a set of over one hundred patterns. They had them copyrighted and printed. They called their little business "Pee-Dee Patterns." They ran several adds. They sold them for one dollar a set.

They mailed them all over the world including several sets to a lady in Africa teaching art to the natives.

It was fun and satisfying to open the mail box each day for several weeks after each ad ran and get anywhere from twenty-five to a hundred envelopes with a dollar or more in each one. The cost was twenty-seven cents per set excluding the cost of the magazine ad which was a little over a hundred dollars each issue.

The house in Huntsville had a fire-burning fireplace. It backed up to a heavily wooded area. On Saturday mornings Don insisted that Greg help perform a few chores outside the house. One such chore was helping Don cut and stack firewood.

> One Saturday morning Greg and I were in the backyard gathering, cutting and stacking firewood. Greg had difficulty understanding why we had to do this since we already had an ample supply of stacked firewood.
>
> Some of Greg's friends came by with a football. They wanted Greg to go play with them. I told them, "No, Greg has to help finish cutting and stacking this wood. Then he can go play." They left.
>
> Greg protested. I told him he had to finish what we had started before he could go. I told him that when I was a little boy we had to cut and stack firewood every day. It was good for me and it was good for him to do some of the same.
>
> A few big tears welled up in his eyes and he began to saw with a bitter vengeance. I went about stacking wood. Greg grew quiet and settled into a steady sawing motion.
>
> After a few minutes he stopped, looked up and said, "Dad, I know why you like to cut wood so much."
>
> "Yeah, why?"
>
> "Cause it makes you feel like a little boy again."
>
> I pondered that profound insightful statement a moment.
>
> "Go play football. I'll finish up."

One evening in mid-December there was a severe thunderstorm with strong variable winds. The lightening flashed and the thunder crashed. The wind howled. Don commented to Pat, "If it wasn't the middle of December I'd say we're having a tornado somewhere nearby." The next morning it was evident there had been a tornado. It flattened a number of houses a quarter of a mile south of their house. It skipped over the mountain east of them and did extensive damage to a large number of homes in Huntsville.

Another strange and unusual incident occurred while Pat and Don lived in Huntsville.

> The back of our house faced south. The area south of the house was undeveloped and heavily wooded. The master bedroom was upstairs on the south side. The bathroom for the master bedroom had a window that faced south toward the wooded area.
>
> It was February and the trees were without leaves. I had to get up about four o'clock one morning and go to the bathroom. I sleepily looked out the bathroom window. What I saw astounded me and opened my eyes wide.
>
> I saw a large florescent eerie green round ball of light through the trees. I stared at it a couple of minutes trying to determine what it possibly could be. It was either getting larger or it was getting closer. Could I be dreaming?
>
> I awakened Pat. I told her to go into the bathroom, look out the window and tell me what she saw. She was reluctant but did as I asked. She was astonished, too. By now it was even larger. It obviously was either getting larger or closer. It looked spooky through the trees.
>
> We watched it the next several minutes. The intensity began to fade. It obviously was not as bright as when I first saw it. Also, it was much larger around. We went back to bed.
>
> That morning when we got up it was all over the morning news on the local radio. Hundreds of people in Huntsville had seen it and called the police, sheriff, radio station, etc. for an explanation.
>
> It was early in the NASA space program. They didn't know what kind, if any, wind currents were in outer space. Early that morning they fired a missile from Elgin Air Force Base near Pensacola, Florida, into the outer limits of the stratosphere and exploded a container of florescent green dye so they could

observe any wind currents. That was the official explanation. Who knows?

The curvature of the earth is such that from Huntsville it appeared to be about ten degrees above the southern horizon. Since there were no winds the size of the green ball kept expanding until it completely dissipated.

The design and testing phase of the Apollo LEM Program was winding down. Don's group was scaling back on manpower. Don was given the title of "Special Projects Manager" with a box full of very nice looking business cards. Translation: "Go drum up some business for the group, or else."

The USS Thrasher was the first atomic submarine. In 1963 it suddenly and catastrophically sank while at maximum depth during a test dive during its initial shakedown cruise. All 129 aboard including a number of civilian engineering contract personnel were lost. Only a few pieces of flotsam were ever recovered.

The Navy immediately undertook an exhaustive investigation including a complete design review of all mechanical parts. Don's management made the decision to present the Navy with the capabilities of the group and the advantages of conducting reliability and maintainability studies of the various parts.

Don made numerous trips to Main Navy in Washington, D.C. to meet with various Navy personnel responsible for design integrity. He made many presentations explaining capabilities and successes of his group in the Apollo LEM program and how they could be applied to the Navy design process to assure design integrity and reliability.

At the request of the Main Navy personnel Don made a special trip to the Submarine Center at Groton, Connecticut, to make a presentation. The result was Don's group received a contract from the Navy to conduct reliability and maintainability studies and testing of the Main Blow-Down Valve System for atomic submarines. All submarines have these large critical valves plus redundant valves which enable them to submerge and return to the surface.

While Don and Pat lived in Huntsville Don's parents came to visit. Also, his Uncle Jim and Aunt Mary Dunahoo from Kansas City came to visit. Don's cousin Jim Gardner, his wife, Laquetha, and two daughters came to visit. Jim was a Lieutenant Commander and a Naval Aviator.

Pat made oatmeal for breakfast. At the breakfast table Laquetha remarked that she always had to scorch Jim's oatmeal a little because that was the way he liked it. Don about cracked up. He told the story of how he had cooked oatmeal for Jim and his brother, Robert, when they were kids. Don accidently scorched the oatmeal, but convinced Jim and Robert that was the way it tasted best.

Don was not comfortable with a career in the aerospace industry. It often meant sudden and drastic change brought on by the nature of the business where large companies constantly vied for government contracts. Workers constantly moved from one company to another at the mercy and whims of government contract letting.

Don and Pat wanted to locate in the Dallas area mostly because her parents were in failing health and they wanted to be close to help them when needed. Her folks lived at the southeast corner of Lake Murray State Park where they owned and operated a country store and tourist courts. Pat's Dad had quit farming but still raised cattle.

Don and Pat moved to Dallas in 1967. They bought a house at 7749 La Verdura Street in Far North Dallas. They lived there the next ten years. Though the house was in Dallas it was in the Richardson Independent School District. It was only an hour and a half drive to where Pat's folks lived near Marietta.

Within a few months of moving to Dallas Pat's mother became ill with a heart condition. She was in and out of hospitals a number of times over the next several years. Don and Pat made many trips to Marietta to care for Pat's mother and help her dad. Pat's parents sold their tourist court and country store business and her dad quit farming, though he continued to raise cattle. He grazed the cattle on the 120-acre property adjacent to his.

Don first worked for Forney Engineering Company in Dallas as Manager of Computer Operations. This job did not work out very well. Soon it was apparent there was constant contention between the Controller and the Chief Engineer over who actually had control of the utilization of the computer. Don was constantly caught in the middle of this internal political battle.

Don looked into the possibility of an opportunity to manage a computer service center in Guymon, Oklahoma. He made several trips to Guymon to talk with the financiers and potential customers, mostly in the cattle feedlot business. Don's longtime friend, Jack Dreessen from his days at Moore, was the president of the Guymon Chamber of Commerce. Pat and Greg flew to Guymon on one trip with Don in a Cherokee Six to look over the prospect of living in Guymon.

On another flying trip in the Cherokee Six Don and the pilot got caught up in a severe weather front with thunderstorms, heavy rain, lightening, and tornadic winds.

> The weather looked uneventful when we departed Guymon. The weather report was for a few scattered thundershowers. We soon saw a large thundercloud forming directly in our path. The pilot decided to fly around it only to be faced with yet another large thundercloud forming directly in front of us. He decided to fly around it only to be faced with yet another one directly in front. It quickly became obvious they were forming all around us.
>
> In a matter of minutes we were in heavy rain with lightening all around us. The wind buffeted the plane violently, visibility was almost zero at times. I studied the map to try to determine exactly where we were and where the nearest landing field was located.
>
> The pilot took us down to about five hundred feet for better visibility. I spotted a water tower at about eleven o'clock. I told the pilot that if that is Memphis (Texas) there is an airfield three miles northeast of town. He took it down to about two

> hundred feet and flew a tight circle around the water tower. I read "Memphis" on it. He headed northeast and we soon saw the airfield through the heavy rain. He made a low pass over the runway to check for standing water then made a tight turn and landed.
>
> We taxied to the airport office, shut down the engine, baled out and ran to the office. We were met at the door by a man who shouted, "What are you idiots doing out flying around in this? Don't you know we're having tornados?"
>
> I was relieved to be on the ground. We spent the night in Memphis and flew to Dallas the next morning.

Don decided to seek employment back in the oil business where he was more comfortable with his knowledge of the industry. Subsequently he went to work for Atlantic Richfield Company (ARCO) in downtown Dallas as a Systems Analyst in the Systems and Programming Department.

Greg was in the Fourth Grade when Don and Pat moved to Dallas. He went to Mohawk Elementary in Richardson where Mr. Malcom was principal. Pat was a stay-at-home Mom. She and Don thought it best that she be home to see Greg off to school and be there when he got home. In the sixth grade Greg attended Bowie, a newly opened school in Dallas and closer to home. Greg was the first Captain of the Bowie Student Patrol.

One hospitalization for Pat's mother was at Scott-White in Temple, Texas. She was there six weeks, three weeks in intensive care. Pat's dad had a mild heart attack while visiting his wife in the hospital. The best possible place to have one if you must.

Pat's mother recovered well enough that she was released from Scott-White to go home. Don and Pat spent many weekends and some vacation time the next several years staying with Pat's mother in and out of hospitals and helping her dad.

> Pat and I often spent our weekends with her folks. Pat cared for her mother and helped with the household. I helped her

dad with the cattle, repairing fences, cutting grass, fixing things that needed fixing, etc. It was usually a weekend full of work and we were worn out when we got home. However we did have a few fun times and I have to tell this on Pat's dad.

He bought a new Chevrolet pickup. A pack rat soon made its home in the underside of the truck. It packed all kinds of things into the crooks and crannies of the frame and engine. It often gnawed the insulation from the ignition wires necessitating replacement. Bert tried every thing he could think of to get rid of that pack rat but to no avail.

It would ride all the way to town and back. He would throw on the brakes trying to jar the rat loose, then give it the gas to run away from it if it fell off. All to no avail.

One weekend when Pat and I arrived I said the water was running across the lake spillway about four inches deep when we came across. Pat's dad had a great idea. He said he would take the truck to the edge of the spillway which was about a hundred yards across. He would give it the gas and the water splashing up would dislodge the rat and it would fall into the running water and be swept away.

He took a friend and me with him. We got out and kneeled down on the dry pavement to watch under the truck to see if the rat fell off and into the running water.

Pat's dad gave the truck the gas. Water splashed everywhere. We watched. About seven-eighths of the way across the spillway we saw the rat fall from under the truck into the water. He swam frantically toward shore. The truck went about ten yards out of the water and the engine quit. It drowned from all the water splashing up onto the engine. The rat made it to shore. It ran the short distance to the truck and jumped back up to the underneath side.

It was several months later when Bert finally got rid of that rat. He kept scattering a little corn on the ground behind the parked truck. He went out early each morning with a shotgun. Finally one morning he saw the rat eating the corn. End of rat.

CHAPTER 15

DONALD GENE DAVIDSON

The Mellow Years

Greg participated in the Spring Valley Athletic Association (SVAA) youth sports program for the Richardson and Far North Dallas area. Don volunteered to coach Greg's football team two years and his baseball team one year.

Pat was the SVAA Umpire Commissioner one year. She scheduled umpires for eight hundred games without a mix-up. First time that had ever been done. Don decided it was best that he not coach Greg's teams. So, he coached football one year and baseball two years for teams not in Greg's league. Don found it humorous when spectators accused him of favoring his son when he made team changes.

One year when Greg was twelve years old he participated in the SVAA youth wrestling program.

> As a beginner I thought Greg was becoming a fairly good wrestler. They practiced a lot and Greg held his own in a few local matches. Then the coach entered his team in a statewide tournament. Greg was matched with a blind kid. I thought, "How can a blind kid be a wrestler?"
>
> I watched the kid hold onto his coach's arm as he led him onto the mat. The kid tripped on the edge of the mat. I felt sorry for the poor little guy as the referee led him to the center of the mat where Greg stood. The only change in rules was

> Greg had to hold out both hands so the kid could lay his hands on Greg's.
>
> The referee then said, "Wrestle." That kid was all over Greg before he knew what happened–partly because Greg was taken by surprise. Any sorrow I had for the kid quickly evaporated as he soundly won the match.
>
> That was the end of Greg's wrestling career.

Greg continued to play youth baseball during the summer. He played catcher. He played one year at a summer baseball camp at Chandler, Oklahoma, while Pat had major surgery. He played baseball in youth leagues until he graduated from high school.

The summer of 1972 Pat's mother was well enough that Don and Pat took her and Pat's father on a vacation with Greg to California to visit Pat's sister, Connie, and her family at Fillmore. Enroute they visited the Painted Desert, the Petrified Forest, and the Grand Canyon.

At Fillmore Don took Greg and his cousins, Cindy and Roseanne, to the Pacific Ocean swimming. The water was cold. They did not stay long. It was Greg's first time to swim in the ocean.

Don took Pat, Pat's mother, Connie, Greg, Cindy, Roseanne and Charlotte to Disneyland. It was a full day of fun for Greg and his cousins. They stayed until after the fireworks display and the park closed at midnight. The adults were worn out. It was a long drive for Don back to Fillmore. The others slept all the way home.

From Fillmore they drove up Coastal Highway No. 1 to Monterey and San Francisco.

> It was a long drive from Fillmore near Santa Barbara to San Francisco. It was late when we finally arrived at a hotel in downtown San Francisco. We checked in and took to the rooms only what luggage we needed for the night. The parking was enclosed and we were assured an attendant was on duty twenty-four hours a day. We had to leave the car keys with the attendant.

I was flabbergasted the next morning when I went down to the car. It was completely cleaned out. They took Greg's six hundred dollar saxophone and my cameras. They took all our clothes. They even took a partial bag of dates we bought in Monterey. It looked like they ran a vacuum cleaner to pick up any loose change. All we had were the few things we took to our rooms the night before.

The car had sixty miles more on the odometer than when it was released to the parking lot attendant. I don't understand why they bothered to bring it back. Obviously, it was an inside job.

The hotel disclaimed any liability. They pointed to a small inconspicuous sign that read "The Hotel is not Responsible for Vehicles or Contents on These Premises." I had to call the cops. The hotel would not even do that. The cops were nonchalant about it. All they did was fill out a report and said, "Your insurance will take care of it." They had no interest in catching the thieves or concern that it totally ruined our vacation.

We've disliked San Francisco ever since. We've never been back since and never will. Time has proved those people are idiots.

We left and drove to Reno. We stopped along the way and bought a few clothes. We spent part of a day in Reno. Pat's dad won about fifty dollars gambling.

We drove home the most direct route and began the long tedious job of filing a claim with our insurance company and fighting them for every nickel we were able to recover.

Pat and Don went to Marietta as often as possible to help her aging parents. They usually were so busy there was little opportunity for diversion and or relaxation.

Don traveled a lot in his work at ARCO but was headquartered in Dallas. He and Pat didn't have to move around. He always came home though he often was gone anywhere from a few days to several months at a time. Don liked his job at ARCO and liked the work. He didn't like his immediate boss that much.

> He was a jerk. He was smart about a few things, but dumb as a rock about most things. He was a Yankee though he had been in Texas a long time. He was not perceptive and did not understand colloquialisms. He had no idea what a metaphor was. He was totally lacking in what we in Texas call 'horse sense.'
>
> One day he asked me to take one of his 'screw-ball' ideas to his boss, the department manager. I had a better relationship with his boss than he did. I told him, "No way, Jose. I'm not going to pluck a feather from the chief's war bonnet. That's a fast way to get tomahawked." He had no idea what I meant. He accused me of "babbling." I soon learned to talk to him like he was a semi-bright eighth grade student.
>
> I had an excellent relationship with the department manager. He had worked in the oil fields early in his career as I did. We knew the basic business of exploring for and producing oil and gas. We understood each other though we were working with large-scale computers and data communications. He often circumvented my immediate boss, the jerk, to discuss issues with me and bounce ideas off of me. He gave me special assignments without consulting my immediate boss and that irritated him. Consequently, he didn't like me. I was at odds with him a lot of the time, but I still got promotions and regular pay raises to the chagrin of my immediate boss.
>
> I was kind of a point man for the department manager on leading special state-of-the-art projects. I went to computer shows looking for leading technical innovations in computers and related equipment. I covertly brought in state of the art equipment to evaluate and determine their viability. I then designed the system and implemented it. This often necessitated that I travel to the various district offices to implement the systems and train the operators. A couple of times Pat accompanied me.

It was only an hour and a half drive from the house in Dallas to Pat's parents' place at Lake Murray near Marietta. Don and Pat had an arrangement with Pat's dad to transfer title to the 120-acre property they bought in his name but on which Don and Pat made the annual payments.

When they could Don and Greg went quail hunting on the 120-acre farm and on the farms owned by Pat's dad and his two brothers. They also went fishing in the small but deep pond located on the far backside adjacent to the Lake Texoma Game Reserve.

When Greg was ten he learned to drive using an old Chevy pickup that belonged to his grandfather. It had a gearshift on the steering column and he had to learn to use the clutch and gearshift. He drove in a pasture with several plum thickets. Don's instructions were that if anything went wrong just steer into one of the thickets.

Pat's folks were both in failing health. Her mother was in and out of hospitals a number of times with congestive heart failure. Don and Pat spent many weekends and some vacation time the next two years staying with Pat's mother in and out of hospitals and helping her dad.

Pat's mother died in February 1975. Two years later in February 1977 her father died. They are buried side by side in the Marietta City Cemetery. When Pat's mother died Don and Pat bought two adjacent eight-site burial lots. They also bought a nice headstone which they had placed at the grave site for Pat's parents.

Pat's dad did not get the title to the 120-acre farm transferred to Don and Pat before he died. It became a major item of contention in the settlement of the estate. There was no will. To settle the matter Pat finally conceded everything else, including ninety-three head of cattle, to her sister, Connie, if she would concede the 120-ace farm to Don and Pat, even though she knew Don and Pat not only paid for the farm in full but also made several annual payments on the loan for the cattle. The hard feelings were never reconciled.

ARCO was a major developer on the North Slope of Alaska and the TransAlaska Pipeline from Prudhoe Bay to the tanker terminal at Valdez on the south coast of Alaska. Over a five-year period Don made twenty-six trips to Alaska mostly to the North Slope.

These assignments usually were from a few days to a few weeks to a few months depending on the size, scope and nature of the work.

The first time Don went to the North Slope it was fairly primitive. Living conditions were much like the military. They lived in Quonset huts and kept survival gear nearby at all times just in case. In the winter it was dark all the time except for the electric lights. The temperatures were often minus 50 degrees F or colder. Don quickly learned to take short shallow breaths. Inhale deeply and his lungs ached. He had an incentive to get done what he was there for and get home as soon as he could.

The runway at the airport was ice during the winter that was from early September to late April. It took a skilled pilot to bring an airplane to a halt and not skid out of control. Also, the roads were all ice roads. One had to know or learn quickly how to drive on ice.

Each time Don returned to the North Slope things were a little better. Very little was actually built on the North Slope. Everything was fabricated at Tacoma, Washington, as modules. They were loaded on barges and towed by tugboats to the North Slope during the summer months. They were off loaded, moved to location and set in place. The several modules were fit together to make an entire building. This process was repeated over and over until all the modules were fit together and connected by corridors.

The extreme weather on the North Slope was a challenge for all manner of construction. The unions were a major obstacle to progress. They were constantly making unreasonable demands. When their demands were not met in a timely fashion they resorted to all kinds of mean tricks. They would have sit-downs in the mess halls. They would take the lens from the only 16mm movie projector and hide it for days denying them the recreation of watching movies. They would crash a crane boom through one of the connecting corridors. They would set oily rags on fire in empty trash barrels causing a lot of smoke and fire alarms to go off in the middle of the night. And, in one instance two union goons yanked the General Contractor Manager out of bed in the middle of the night and beat him up.

A favorite trick was to "time card" a non-union worker. If a non-union worker did something they perceived as a job for a union worker they could turn in a time card for four hours of work because the non-union worker had done something they were supposed to do. It was nothing but a scam in their contract.

> One day I was expecting a shipment of computer parts from the lower forty-eight. Everything was shipped to Receiving at the warehouse that was manned by union workers. I called to see if the shipment had arrived. I was told it was sitting on the back dock. I drove over to the warehouse. Sure enough it was sitting on the back dock with the paperwork. Some union guys were sitting on their butts back in the warehouse. They hollered, "Just sign the paperwork," which I did. Then I loaded it into the pickup and drove away. They filed a 'time-card' on me because a union worker was supposed to load the box onto the pickup. A union guy got four hours pay for doing nothing but hollering at me to: "Just sign the paperwork."
>
> I learned to do all my work behind closed and locked doors so union snoops couldn't see what I was doing. Some of them did nothing but walk around looking for non-union workers working at tasks they could 'time card.' Even the simple task of plugging the power cord of a piece of computer equipment into a wall receptacle could result in a 'time card' incident. I didn't want any of those nit-wits anywhere close to my computers and peripherals.

After a time the living quarters were greatly improved, especially for the ARCO and EXXON employees. They had completely separate quarters from the contractors and the union workers. It was almost like living in a college dorm. Almost everything was connected by long corridors. They didn't have to go outside to go from one building to another.

They also built a small but nice theater with 35mm projectors with continuous projection. They showed first run movies. Later they got satellite antennas for live television. The mess hall and kitchens were first class and the food was the best. So good in fact that overeating soon became a health problem. The company built a nice gym with a one-eighth mile jogging track and employed two full time physical trainers.

Once living conditions greatly improved we began to have women workers. They mostly did clerical work though a few were in the trades. The first one was a carpenter's helper. I think she may have been a 'comfort girl' for the carpenters. I never saw her do anything other than occasionally sweep floors and do minor clean up behind the carpenters.

The next two worked in the pipe shop. The guys called one Flat-Top and the other Pipe-Bender, behind their backs of course. Flat-Top had a large bosom that was flat on top. Honestly. Pipe-Bender worked in the pipe bending shop. She had large muscular arms and a no nonsense disposition.

Pipe-Bender was quartered on the same corridor I was. I was temporarily quartered in the contractor quarters due to lack of space in the ARCO quarters. She was two units away. One night in the middle of the night I heard a loud ruckus. Someone rang the emergency bell. Security guys came running down the corridor. I opened the door and looked out to see what was going on.

A guy was in the hallway near Pipe-Bender's door. He had a severely cut upper lip and a bloody nose bleeding all over the place. Security asked, "What's going on here?" A bystander said, "There was a fight in there," indicating Pipe-Bender's door. They knocked on her door. She answered in her 'nighty.'

"Yes?"

"What do you know about a fight in there?"

"Fight? What fight? There was no fight here," and she slammed the door shut.

Turns out the guy had been drinking. There was supposed to be no alcohol beverages, but some guys sometimes smuggled it in. This guy paid an uninvited middle of the night social call to Pipe-Bender's quarters with romantic overtures. She punched him out and threw him out the door. I don't think anyone else ever tried to get 'frisky' with Pipe-Bender.

What to do during free time was always a challenge. We could work, we could sleep, we could eat, we could go to the movie, we could read, or we could work out in the gym. That was about it.

One evening I heard one of the clerical ladies tell another that she wished she knew how to do macrame. I told her that my wife and I had taken classes in macrame. After some discussion about it I told them the next time I came back to The Slope I would bring supplies and teach them to do macrame.

It wasn't long before I was back to The Slope. I brought macrame supplies with me. That evening five ladies and I gathered in the lounge. I was teaching them to do macrame.

Two 'smart-aleck' guys were sitting nearby. They made fun of us, especially me. They said what a "sissy" I was and other uncomplimentary comments. Finally, one of the ladies had all of it she could take. She said to them, "Yeah, and when was the last time you guys got to spend the entire evening with five women?"

That shut them up. She later apologized to me. She said she had heard all their wisecracks she wanted to hear and she said what she said to put them down. I told her, "Not to worry. I actually enjoyed it."

Greg went to North Junior High School in the Richardson Independent School District. He was a good student. He made straight 'A' grades until his senior year when he made his first 'B.' He participated in many school activities.

He began to play the saxophone in the seventh grade. He played football and also played in the band in junior high school. It was difficult to do both. The band director was very accommodating for Greg to miss band functions to play football.

After junior high school Greg attended J. J. Pearce High School in Richardson. He played in the band and football until his senior year. He played second team guard, and center to snap the ball on point-after situations which were few and far between. The team was not the best and lost most of their games.

The football coaches were not very lenient about the players participating in other activities. The start of his senior year Greg decided he would rather concentrate on band instead of football.

> I was disappointed that Greg wanted to quit football. I played football and I thought he would play and enjoy it as much as I did. Not so. He enjoyed music and the band more. I encouraged him to stay out for football. He made the valiant attempt to please me.
>
> He came home one day from practice and told me he quit football to concentrate on band. I was disappointed. I wanted him to play football. I told him to talk it over with his coach.
>
> Greg played another week. He came home and told me, "I quit football. Period. End of discussion." I had to respect his decision. He said the coach was always in a foul mood because they lost and the band was a lot more fun.

After Greg's junior year Don and Pat bought him a 1975 Chevelle sports coupe. When he was in the seventh grade they told him that if he went all the way through junior high and high school and did not cause any problems for the teachers, for them or for the police that they would buy him a new car after his senior year. He did so well through his junior year they decided to buy the car so he would have it his senior year, and to take to college.

Greg was friends with Bobby Fackler and dated his sister, Katy. She was his date to the Senior Prom. The weekend before the prom Greg went on a weekend outing with the Fackler family to their place on the lake. Monday he came down with the chicken pox.

> His mother and I told him there was no way he could attend the prom with the pox. He was devastated. He and Katy had already coordinated their outfits and ordered corsages. All for naught. Wednesday Greg said he was well enough to attend the prom. He had bumps all over his face. We tried to discourage him but he insisted. I finally told him to call Dr. Fackler and ask if it was okay for him to take Katy to the prom. I thought surely Dr. Fackler would certainly tell him, "No way."

Not so. Dr. Fackler said that if Katy didn't mind he sure didn't care. He said Greg was past the contagious stage.

Saturday was prom day. Pat used makeup to cover up the pox as much as possible. He actually didn't look too bad. He and Katy got dressed up in their formal outfits and I took a very nice photo of them in the backyard next to the weeping willow tree. Greg and Katy went to the prom and had a wonderful time.

Greg graduated the spring of 1976. I flew home from Alaska just to attend his graduation. I went back after a few days. Greg enrolled at the University of Texas in Austin that fall.

Don traveled a lot in the course of his employment with ARCO. The nature of his work usually involved investigating and developing new computer and data communications systems to handle and process data. He traveled to all the district offices and frequently went to the corporate offices in Los Angeles. He often went to computer expositions and shows.

Wes Prince who worked in my group and I went to a computer show in Chicago. We checked into a downtown hotel and spent the next several days looking at all manner of new computers and related items. Our eyes were glazed over.

The final day we went onto Michigan Avenue to walk the several blocks to the Chicago Exposition Center. We had gone about two blocks when I saw the Chicago Museum of Art. I asked Wes, "Have you ever been to an art museum?"

"No."

"There's one right across the street. Let's go over there for a couple of hours just to see what's there."

"Okay."

We spent the entire day touring the art museum. We had never seen so many works of art. Some were huge Old Masters. Others were strange modern expressionisms. Many in between.

There was a special display of Piccaso artworks. I thought I would take a look and count the number I looked at just so I could brag, "I've seen a hundred original Piccasos." I quit

> counting at one hundred. I hadn't seen one-tenth of all the art works by Piccaso. His early works were very good and realistic. As he got older his works became more and more weird. I think he must have been on something.

Don traveled so much that Pat got a little miniature Dachshund puppy for companionship. She named her Gretchen. She was so tiny she fit comfortably into one of Don's shoes. She was a sweet delightful little dog. They had her eighteen years. It was a sad day when she died.

Ever since Don, Pat and Greg moved to Dallas Don wanted to live on an acreage as opposed to living in town. However, when they moved to Dallas from Huntsville the time to find a house was critical. They looked at a couple of rural properties near Dallas, but nothing Don was interested enough to buy. They settled on a house at 7749 La Verdura Street in Far North Dallas.

All the time they lived in Dallas it was not unusual to spend part of a weekend searching the want ads and looking at rural property when Don was not traveling in his work. They looked at one property west of Lewisville and were very tempted to buy it. However, Greg was in the eighth grade and they decided that to move at that time in his life would be too unsettling. So, they continued to look while waiting for Greg to graduate from high school and leave for college.

When Greg graduated Don and Pat began to look seriously. They looked southeast, east and northeast of Dallas because rural land was not as expensive as land north and northwest of Dallas.

> We found several places we came close to buying, but in the final analysis discovered some undesirable feature. As a last resort we contacted a real estate sales lady. She insisted on taking us northwest of Dallas to look at property. We spent the better part of two days with her. We saw several nice pieces of property but nothing that really impressed us. Finally, in desperation she asked, "Mr. Davidson, just what is it you want?" I said, "Fifty acres with a house sitting right in the middle."

"Would you object to an older two bedroom house?"

"I don't know. Where is it?"

"About a mile over here."

"Okay. Let's go see it."

She took us to a gravel road. We turned in at a large gate that said Landfall Ranch on an overhead arch. We wound around through some trees and came to a clearing with a low profile, hip-roof, white brick house inside a fenced yard. The house had four foot overhang eaves. It sat on the edge of a slight precipice that gently sloped about two hundred yards to the edge of a small lake.

My heart leaped into my throat as I swallowed hard and tried to remain nonplused. The grass was high, the shrubs scraggly, and weeds were prolific. Obviously it had not been lived in for a couple of years, or more. But, it was exactly what I had envisioned. It was about fifteen hundred feet from the road and totally secluded from view by a dense band of oak trees. There were several open meadows with a lot of trees and a small lake of about four acres.

Inside it was basically a three-room house. It had a large 32x40 living-dining room with a stone fireplace in one end. The large picture windows overlooked the lake. The kitchen was open to the dining room with an indoor barbecue oven. There were two spacious bedrooms at opposite ends with a full bath for each. There was a full-screened porch for each bedroom facing the lake. It had a full bar with sink and ice maker. It had a utility room and a large carport. There was a water well, 3,300-gallon water storage tank, and a 300-gallon pressure tank. I knew it was just what I wanted.

As it turned out it was the main house for the 256-acre Landfall Ranch that was originally owned by Fred Agnich, CEO of Texas Instruments. Later Fred told me Texas Instruments was organized in the living room of the house.

Fred Agnich sold it to a Dallas banker. He later had financial difficulties and had to divest some of his properties. He defaulted the loan and the bank repossessed it. They turned it over to a real estate man to subdivide and sell off in smaller units.

> We initially bought the house and ten acres. In the next few weeks we sold the 120-acre farm in Oklahoma and our house in Dallas. We then incrementally bought adjacent acreage amounting to an additional forty-one acres for a total of fifty-one acres.
>
> We moved from the city to the country west of Lewisville in the community of Bartonville. A few months later we sold eleven acres from the east side to Danny and Barbie Mims and the Fogels. We applied this money to the Farm Home Loan we had on the property. This reduced our loan considerably and left us with forty acres.

Don helped Danny Mims build a barn with an apartment overhead. Barbie was into horses. She stalled the horses in the lower part of the barn. She and Danny lived in the apartment over the stalls.

Danny helped Don build a 24'x48' storage shed. Don bought a 12'x32' portable barn on skids. Danny helped build a shed on the side of the barn. Over the next several months Don built over two thousand feet of field wire fence topped with double strands of barbed wire to make pastures. He bought several head of Brangus cows. He built a double corral with a shed and a chute for working the cows. Don was in his element. He had a small ranch with a few cows. Things were great.

The first year Don and Pat lived on the ranch at Bartonville they went to Fort Worth and got two puppies that were littermates. They were half Doberman, a quarter Border Collie, and a quarter Black Labrador. They were black and tan like a Doberman. Their tails were bobbed but their ears were floppy. Greg was home from the University at Austin and he went with Don and Pat to get the pups. Greg named them Ezekiel and Zechariah. Don shortened their names to Zeke and Zeb.

> When we brought Zeke and Zeb home they were puppies only six weeks old. Gretchen, the little female miniature Dachshund, was several years old. She had been queen of the

place and looked on the two pups as intruders. She bossed them around at will. As Zeke and Zeb grew they were soon larger than Gretchen. She still bossed them around.

I began to train Zeke and Zeb when they were about three months old. They were the smartest dogs I was ever around. I had no experience training dogs except to help Pat's Dad a little when he was training bird dogs.

When Zeke and Zeb were about four months old I saw Zeke take a run at the fence around the yard and try to jump over. He almost made it. The fence enclosed about an acre of yard. I strung an electric wire around the top. In a day or two Zeke tried again. This time the electric wire got him. He yelped and ran for the doghouse. He never tried again.

A few days later Zeb tried to jump the fence. The electric wire got him as he went over the top. He jumped back into the yard and it hit him again. He yelped and ran for the doghouse. He never tried again.

Within a year I had trained them to obey twelve voice commands and several hand signals. They would sit, stay, come, stop, heel, go, close, lay, okay, down, quiet, and fetch. They would not go through an open gate unless given the command "okay." They would not go through a barbed wire fence unless told to. The command "go" meant go to the house. The command "close" meant stay within ten yards of me. They had more trouble with that command than the others. They soon were fifteen or more yards from me if I did not call them back.

When they were full grown they were twenty-six inches tall at the shoulder and weighed seventy-five pounds. They were often mistaken for Rottweillers. I built a large eight by ten foot room on the carport with a swinging door which was their doghouse.

When a car came driving up the driveway from the road Zeke and Zeb would not run around and bark. They would sit near the gate and stare at whoever was driving in. People would not get out of their car until I sent the dogs to their doghouse. Everyone told me those two big dogs sitting out there staring at them was more intimidating than a barking dog running around.

> What was very funny is Zeke and Zeb were always intimidated by little Gretchen. They could have snapped her in two with one bite, but they always cowered down when she jumped on them. She would get in their face and fuss at them. If they did not cower down she jumped up and grabbed them by the ear and pulled them down to where they laid down. Then she got in their face and fussed at them.
>
> One year I bought a dozen guinea keets that I raised and kept outside the fenced yard. But the guineas soon were grown and flying. One day they flew into the yard. Zeke and Zeb delightfully chased them and caught one that they killed. I made them "go" to the doghouse. I locked the door so they couldn't get out. I took the dead guinea and beat them in the face with it until their heads hurt. They never chased another guinea.
>
> I loved to walk over the property with them to see them run through the woods, chase rabbits, and run splashing through the shallow waters at the edge of the lake. It was a sad day when they died.
>
> I had Zeke ten years. He took sick with stomach cancer and died suddenly. I had Zeb another ten months. He too died with stomach cancer despite our efforts to save him. We had little Gretchen eighteen years. She died shortly after Zeb did. I took it very hard. I dearly loved those dogs.

Don commuted one entire summer from May to September to work in Pasadena, California. He took an early Monday morning Delta flight from DFW to LAX. He then took a rent car to Pasadena. He worked all week staying at the Pasadena Hilton Hotel. He took a late Friday afternoon American flight from LAX to DFW arriving late Friday night. Pat met him at the airport. He spent the weekend at home and then did it all over again the next Monday morning.

Parsons was the General contractor for the North Slope facility development. They contracted with all manner of subcontractors both in Alaska and the lower forty-eight. Their administrative controls and accounting procedures were lax and not up to standards.

It was evident that tons of money was being expended for all manner of things with little or no controls. Property was not being properly classified for accounting and tax purposes. (Remember the same problem at Pan American in Argentina?)

Since I had oil field experience and could properly identify and classify oil field property I was sent to work in the Parsons' general offices where all the accounting records were kept. My job was to supervise a small group of guys to review all the paid invoices and determine the proper classification of the items on the invoices. Once that was accomplished we were to go to the North Slope to take an inventory and account for all the controlled property.

You can't believe the chaos. Welding supplies were capitalized and Lincoln Arc Welding machines were expensed. As I went through monthly invoice after invoice I kept thinking I had seen some of the invoices in previous months. I finally decided there was a pattern to some of them. I went back and double-checked.

Sure enough, in a number of instances the same invoices were submitted and paid over and over each month. The subcontractors month after month were simply copying previous invoices worth thousands of dollars and submitting them for payment. Parsons paid them without question and submitted their inclusive invoices plus their percentage management fee to ARCO.

When I showed this to the ARCO administrative manager in charge at the Parsons' location it hit the fan. I told him that wasn't what I was there for, but thought he should know about it. I don't know exactly what ARCO did about it, but I heard they came down on Parsons real hard with significant penalties.

Later we went to the North Slope to identify and account for all the classified equipment and property. There were a large number of items for which we could not account–such as twelve portable Lincoln Arc Welders worth about $4,800 each. The biggest item we could not find was a 65-ton Pettibone crane. How could such items just simply disappear into thin air? Ever hear the song by Johnny Cash about the automobile worker who built his Cadillac by carrying a part a day home in his lunch bucket? Only these union guys used huge trucks driven by union Teamsters.

The company built a road alongside the pipeline during construction and there was one road in and one road out to the North Slope. Big Kenworth and Peterbuilt trucks hauled lots of freight to the North Slope. They all went back empty. Or, did they?

I suggested to management that they put a checkpoint twenty-five miles down the one road to stop and check the contents of each southbound truck. They wouldn't do it. Why? They didn't want to upset the unions. Made me half-sick.

One week I stayed in California and Pat flew on my ticket from DFW to LAX. She spent the week with me and then used my ticket to fly back to DFW.

The company allowed me a rental car when I worked in Pasadena. The week before Pat came to Los Angeles I rented a car at Hertz. I couldn't find it in the Hertz parking lot. The Hertz workers were no help. The license number on the keys didn't match any car tag on the lot. Finally, one of the workers said, "Try that car over there." It was a Chevrolet Caprice. It had an Arizona tag. The keys worked. I took the car and kept it all that week, the week Pat was there, and the following week.

The car was a running 'jessy.' It seemed to be 'souped up.' It had a lot of get up and go. Pat and I did a lot of sightseeing around the Los Angeles and Pasadena Area. We visited Pat's cousin, Bert Paschall, and his family at San Diego. He was in the Navy. I took Pat to the airport late Sunday evening for a flight back to Dallas. I stayed around and watched her flight take off. I felt a deep pang of loneliness as the airplane lifted off. I turned and walked away. I have always heard it was bad luck to watch a departing person out of sight.

When I turned the car in the following weekend at Hertz they refused to take it. It didn't have a Hertz sticker. They waved me through and I had to come back through again. They waved me through again. I came through the Hertz lot again only this time I jumped out of the car with my suitcase.

> I left the keys in the ignition. The attendants yelled at me, but I kept going. I had a flight to catch for Dallas.
>
> I have often wondered what the situation was on that car. I thought maybe it may have been used to run drugs or something. It had such rapid acceleration power it was almost frightful to drive.

Neighbors, friends and others often fished in Dons and Pat's little lake. Usually they would toss back the ones they caught. However, a neighbor caught a seven pound large-mouth bass. He kept it and had it mounted. He said it was the largest fresh water fish he ever expected to catch. Two months later he caught a nine pound large-mouth bass. He had it mounted, too. Don often kidded that he had to go to his friend's house to see his fish.

One time Don's parents came to visit. Don and his Dad spent part of a day fishing. They caught a nice string of crappie and catfish.

Danny Mims liked to fish in the lake, too. It was not an unusual sight to wake up early some mornings and see him down there fishing. Friends from ARCO also came to fish. The top manager for the Dallas operation came several times to fish. He sometimes brought his teenage son.

> One morning two fellow employees from ARCO and the vice-president of the Dallas operation with his teenage son came to fish. They were there about an hour and I hadn't seen them catch a fish. I went down to give them a little advice on the best places to cast. The teenager was fishing from the dirt pier that extended out into the lake from the south bank.
>
> Pat came leisurely strolling down to the lake. She went out onto the pier and asked the boy if he had caught any fish. He said he hadn't. Pat told him to bring in his line. Then she told him to stand at the point of the pier and cast about fifteen yards toward the dam. He cast once. He cast a second time. Zap. He got a hit. He reeled in a three pound large-mouth bass. His father stood on the dam and saw it all. He shouted, "Hey,

woman. Come talk to me!" They all caught fish following Pat's advice on where to cast. Pat has always been good at catching fish, yet she herself has never been much of one to fish.

Working at a full time job and taking care of a small ranch and cattle operation was time consuming. After a particularly difficult night of helping a cow have a calf in a rainstorm, Don casually commented to a cattleman friend, "I wish there was such a thing as a maintenance free cow." The friend replied, "There is. Longhorns." Thus, began Dons and Pat's love for the Texas Longhorns.

I was doubtful, but he convinced me. I began to read about the Longhorns. I made inquiries to the Texas Longhorn Breeders Association and the local Agricultural Extension County Agent. He 'pooh-poohed' the idea that Longhorns were anything but maverick cows. I talked to a few Longhorn ranchers.

I decided to give the Longhorns a try. Pat and I went to a Longhorn sale west of Ardmore. The cow I planned to bid on sold for $24,000–too rich for my blood. We went to another sale north of McKinney. These cows sold more reasonably. We went to a sale west of Fort Worth. I bought five cows: Safari, Lady, Marquis, Victoria and Plains Classic. All had a calf at side and were bred. I bought a bull, Classic Ranger, from a local rancher, J.B. Hunn. This was my foundation herd. I had five cows, five heifer calves, and a bull.

I kept the Brangus about a year, then sold them and kept only the Longhorns. Pat and I came to love the Longhorns. Their color genes are really mixed up and you never know what color or color combinations you will get. They each have a unique personality.

My friend was right. The Longhorns are close to maintenance free. The only things I had to do were give them their vaccinations, and worm and brand them. They are great browsers and will eat things, including acorns, other cows will not. The twenty years we had Longhorns I never had to assist a calf birth. Of the over two hundred calves born I lost only one.

He was never quite right and in spite of my best efforts to save him he died after three days.

I had the mother cow, Plains Classic, and the calf in the inner corral. I penned her in the outer corral when I worked with the calf, but she kept a watchful eye on my every move. After the little guy died I carried him out to the woods and buried him. I let the mother cow out of the corral. She followed me and watched as I buried him. She hung around the grave several days before she finally joined the other cows.

She was convinced I killed her baby. She never forgot. Though she subsequently had a number of healthy calves I could never get within twenty yards of her but what she lowered her head, shook her horns, and made threatening moves at me. I had to respect her sentiments toward me.

When in Dallas Don often went browsing in the several art stores in the downtown area during his lunch hour. He always appreciated good art. One day he saw a painting in one of the galleries. It was a beautifully done scene of an old cowboy riding his horse with supplies out of an early 1920's oil boom town in the rain wearing a yellow slicker. It was by G. Harvey and titled "With No Intention of Changing" which tugged at Don's heart strings because it represented exactly how he felt. He thought, "If that painting doesn't cost more than fifteen hundred dollars I'm going to buy it." The price tag was $30,000. Don gulped, but the image stuck with him.

A few years later one of Pat's Mail Courier Express clients was going out of business. They were selling several of their nicely framed prints of paintings. One was "With No Intention of Changing." Pat bought it for a nice price. Don was thrilled. Thus, began their collection of G. Harvey prints of his paintings. They ultimately bought twelve of his prints and had them nicely framed.

Don was promoted to Manager, Computer Systems Development for Exploration and Engineering. He managed a group of forty to fifty computer systems analysts and computer programmers developing programs for the geologists, geophysicists, and petroleum engineers to aid them in the search for and finding of oil and gas deposits.

Don's group developed interactive programs that utilized well logs and seismic data to portray subsurface strata that could be rotated and selectively saturated with different colors to display various characteristics of the subsurface. His group was mostly young bright people with a lot of computer savvy and a lot of extraneous energy and vitality.

> A few of the people in my group had been out to our place to fish, picnic, tromp through the woods, or bring a group of Boy Scouts on a camp out.
>
> Most of them had been getting together on Saturdays a few times during the year at Lee Park near downtown Dallas. But it was so congested they approached me about having their picnic get togethers at our place. I said, "Fine if you guys do all the organizing, help get the place ready and clean up afterwards." They agreed.
>
> The outings were so successful that the next several years we had one or two outings a year at our place for the entire department. The gals and guys brought their boyfriends and girl friends, or spouses and kids. The guys brought all the food and drink. Pat and I made huge pots of chili. We hired professional lifeguards to be at the lake. We hired a team of horses and wagon to go on hayrides. One of guys brought several saddle horses for people to ride. We had swimming and swimming races, horseshoe pitching, washer toss, softball games, volley ball, soccer, and dancing after dark on the patio.
>
> It was great fun and the gals and guys were very good about cleaning up afterwards. We sometimes had as many as three hundred and fifty people at an outing.

Over the years when Don and Pat went to visit relatives in Oklahoma they always made it a point to stop and see Uncle Tom and Aunt Jewel at their house in the country north of Elmore City in Garvin County.

This house became a place of warm hospitality where Pat and I always stopped and visited when we could. Pat loved my Aunt Jewel and Uncle Tom just as much as I did. We had many, many pleasurable hours with them.

Shortly after we bought the small ranch at Bartonville northwest of Dallas and west of Lewisville Aunt Jewel and Norma came to visit. One of the highlights of their visit was an evening dinner at a Japanese restaurant, Beni-Hana, in Dallas. We had a mixed drink before dinner, and then we were seated at a large table where the cook prepared the meal at the table. There was a group of young women also seated at our table. I was the only male in the group. We had a rousing good time.

Since Pat and I raised Texas Longhorn cattle Aunt Jewel decided she wanted to get into the Texas Longhorn cattle business. She, Uncle Tom, Robert and Norma came to buy some of my Longhorns. We got them all loaded except for the young bull that I gave to them. I think his name was Grand Prince.

We chased him all over the place trying to get him corralled. Aunt Jewel and Norma were getting concerned about Uncle Tom over exerting himself. We finally cornered the bull in a lane near the lake and got him loaded in the trailer.

I think Aunt Jewel enjoyed her Longhorns over the next few years. We always looked at them and talked about them when Pat and I came to visit. She and I had a nostalgic family connection with the Longhorns. Aunt Jewel's grandfather, my great-grandfather, C. C. "Trick" Jones, was a drover and guard on several Longhorn cattle drives from Texas to Kansas after the Civil War.

Aunt Jewel and I often talked about the various family members and the history of the family. So much like the Roller girls, especially the older ones, she was opinionated about many things and was an engaging conversationalist.

In 1991 we had a 90th birthday celebration for Dad at the United Methodist Church in Brenham, Texas. Aunt Jewel, Norma, Robert and Jimmie came to help celebrate. I was so glad to see her. She is in some of the videos I made that day.

I thought it would be great if I could get Aunt Jewel to talk about her family, her brothers and sisters, and their life when they were growing up while I made a video tape. I had already spent a week with Aunt Marge, Aunt Jewel's older sister, in Phoenix and made some video tapes with her. Aunt Jewel agreed and I spent two different weekends with her making the videos. She was a great subject with a flair of showmanship. I got some videos that are priceless.

I also made video tapes at Aunt Jewel's 80th birthday celebration at the old Antioch Schoolhouse and at the Antioch Cemetery with her. She always had something interesting to say. One occasion she sang a little song Uncle Claud Roller used to always sing which I captured on video tape. These are all precious moments with a wonderful woman full of life.

The last video I have of Aunt Jewel is when she and Norma came to the Jones Family Reunion on the banks of the Cimarron River near Crescent, Oklahoma, in the summer of 1994. She sat next to Homer Fry, her cousin, and sang some old favorite songs with him while he strummed his guitar.

The following November I learned Aunt Jewel was seriously ill and in the hospital. I called her and talked with her. I wrote her a short letter recalling some of our earlier times together.

That December I got the sad news. Greg and his wife, Donna, went with me to the funeral. I was one of the pallbearers. I was honored to do one last gesture of love for my Aunt Jewel.

Later that day some of the family gathered at the house. Uncle Tom came to me and tearfully said, "Gene, this is the worst day of my life," and we embraced. It was a sad, sad, day of my life, too. I loved my Aunt Jewel very much. She was very special to me. A little of me died that day, too. I shall never forget her and will always cherish my fond memories of her.

Pat and I would always stop to see Uncle Tom when we traveled to and from Oklahoma and Texas. We always enjoyed visiting with him. He was a great guy and I have many fond memories of him, too. But, it never seemed the same without Aunt Jewel there. And, it was not too much longer when we also had to bid a final farewell to Uncle Tom.

My Aunt Jewel and Uncle Tom were two of the greatest people in my life. I shall be eternally grateful that they touched my life in so many wonderful and joyous ways. I truly miss them.

I started writing an account of my life with Aunt Jewel in May 1991 for her 80th birthday celebration, but I didn't finish it in time to be a part of the celebration. I regret that I never finished it in time.

It was eight years later that I finally finished it, mostly for myself, but also for Norma and Robert and any other family members. I wanted them to know the love and affection I had for my Aunt Jewel. I guess it is a form of closure for me. I am now past seventy-nine years of age and my own mortality looms not too far in the distance.

I hope I conveyed to the reader the love and affection I had for my Aunt Jewel, and my eternal gratefulness to her for the many, many happy and precious moments she shared with me in my life. Thank you, Aunt Jewel. I love you.

For years Don and Pat kept in touch with Buford Young and his wife, Georgia. They exchanged Christmas cards, an occasional letter and phone calls. Bufords and Georgia's son, Craig, and his family lived in Houston and some of Buford's relatives lived in Sherman, Texas, and Oklahoma City. When Buford and Georgia came to Texas to visit Craig and Cindy and the grandchildren, they would come by and visit Don and Pat or they would meet somewhere for lunch.

Buford grew up to be a big tall guy. I stopped growing in my early teens and am noticeably shorter than Buford. I think I had a mild case of polio when I was fourteen. My left foot is a full size smaller than my right foot, and my left leg is smaller than my right leg. We have a picture taken of Buford and I standing in front of the fireplace at our house at Bartonville. We called it our "Mutt and Jeff" picture.

Buford took a picture of Pat and I standing in front of the same fireplace. He cut a nice piece of walnut wood and finished it very nicely with the bark intact. He decoupaged the photo onto the finished wood and sent it to us as a gift. I inscribed it "Made by my Good Friend, Buford Young – 1990" on the back. It hangs in a prominent place in our study where we spend a lot of our time. We treasure it greatly.

> One time when Buford and Georgia came to visit my Longhorn bull got out during the night. Buford went with me to get him back into the pasture where he belonged. A neighbor's cow in the next pasture was in a romantic mood. My bull didn't want to go back into his pasture. I told Buford to drive my pickup and, "Don't let him get past you." I got out on foot to herd him. It was a pretty wild experience chasing that bull in the dark with Buford driving like a cowboy to corral him. Buford and I had a few good laughs about that. Two old guys chasing a bull in the dark was crazy.

Don had a good job at ARCO. He liked the work and he liked the people he worked for and with. Then one day for whatever reason ARCO under went a major organizational change at the top which permeated all the way down through the organization. Don's management was replaced by people from back East and from California who knew absolutely nothing about the basic business of oil exploration and production. Don's new immediate manager not only knew nothing about the oil business, he knew nothing about the computer business.

> It was a challenge to work for someone who knew so little about anything relating to our business. I constantly tried to inform him, but soon learned he resented my efforts and regarded them as an affront to his abilities.
>
> My group had the responsibility for the operation of a major computer system, The 4300 System, that processed 3-D seismic data to display the various characteristics of the data using selective color saturation on computer monitors, and printing specialty maps of subsurface structures for geologists and geophysicists.
>
> This was a very important part of the oil exploration process. It was frequently discussed at length in high level meetings with geophysicists and geologists. Top management illustrated the cover of the 1982 Annual Report with one of our color displays.
>
> I tried several times to get my new manager to let me give him a tour of The 4300 System which was located on a different floor. He rebuffed each of my attempts and I gave up.

A few months later he had to attend a high level meeting with some computing geophysicist and geologists. He took me along to be his technical mouthpiece since he had no idea what these people would be talking about.

After the meeting I again suggested that since The 4300 System was just a few steps away and had been a major topic in the meeting that he let me give him a tour of the computer room. He reluctantly agreed.

Since it was only a few steps I took him through the back way instead of going around to the front entrance to the controlled area.

The controlled area consisted of two separate rooms with special air conditioned environments. The peripheral devices were in the back room. The 4300 System mainframe computer was in the front room.

Two of my best programmers were in the room. I asked them to explain the various specialized peripheral devices to him and the functions they performed. They had finished explaining every device except one that set against the wall and was obviously humming away. There was a pause and I asked if he had any questions. He pointed to the large device against the wall and asked, "And, is that The 4300 System computer?"

My two programmers almost gagged. I quickly said, "No, Sir. It is in the next room," and hustled him in there. He had pointed to the air conditioner. Word of the incident spread rapidly among not only my people but throughout the entire department. He thought I had set him up to embarrass him.

I was soon transferred to another department and worked for a manager from New Jersey who knew even less than the first guy. Multiply that many times over and thus began the demise of ARCO culminating in the take over by British Petroleum.

The most important factor for the ARCO CEO in the takeover was his $43 million golden parachute. This is the same guy that came with his son to fish in our lake at Bartonville.

CHAPTER 16

DONALD GENE DAVIDSON

The Retirement Years

Don retired from ARCO in September 1986 at age fifty-eight. Pat started a small business in 1984 in North Dallas. Don retired on a Friday and went to work for Pat the following Monday. So much for retirement. He worked in the business with Pat until they sold it and the ranch in 1995 and moved to Brenham, Texas.

Pat and I knew that when an employee reaches age fifty-five in the corporate world they start making sounds for your retirement unless you are one of the top brass that has firmly entrenched your self at the top with a "golden parachute." With that in mind we set about determining what kind of small business we could start with a minimum investment. After consulting with Ann and Fred we decided on a time-sensitive specialty courier service similar to what they operated in Houston. Thus, Mail Courier Express was born.

Pat rented office space in a strip shopping center in North Dallas and set up shop. She bought a Ford van and had it painted red and white with lettering on the sides and back. She set about calling on prospective clients to get business. It was three months before she got her first customer. It was nine months before she reached break even. Afterwards each additional client was profit.

In the meantime Pat let my brother, Sam, use excess office space to try to expand his pool building business to the North Dallas area. I continued to work at ARCO until retirement.

I retired on a Friday and went to work for Pat the following Monday. I asked Pat what kind of benefits I would have. She asked, "Benefits? What kind of benefits?"

"Vacation."

"You don't get any."

"Sick leave?"

"You can't get sick."

"Well, just what benefit do I have working for you?"

"You have one benefit no one else has."

"Yeah. What's that?"

"You can tell the boss to kiss-off and not worry about getting fired."

Pat bought another van and had it painted like the first one. With me on board we were able to service more clients. We decided to expand to larger space and rented an office in an office complex on Spring Valley Road. Crystal Rowland was the leasing agent. The space was not only larger but also more professional. Sam used one of the offices a short time for his venture. He soon decided to give up on expansion into the North Dallas area.

The next couple of years the business grew to forty-two clients. Some of our clients were General Electric, Mutual of Omaha, Fox-Meyer Drugs, General Mills, Sysco, Schneider Transport, and BancTec. We had no contracts. We told our clients that if they were dissatisfied with the service and we could not resolve the dissatisfaction they could immediately terminate the service and not be tied to us with a lengthy contract. They all liked that novel approach to doing business. We also provided various small services without charge which they also liked.

We came to a time when we had to make a decision to either buy another van and hire a driver to expand the business, or level off and keep it a 'Mom and Pop' business that we could operate without help. We opted for the latter, though we later subcontracted a small part of the business to another man.

We ran the business for ten years and did very well. We never lost a client due to lack of service. Some went out of business, others moved their operation to another city, etc., but it was never from dissatisfaction with our service. In fact, one client

> fell upon bad financial times and wanted to discontinue the service. Pat told them we would continue the service without charge until they got back on their feet. It was several months but they pulled through the crisis and were again profitable. They were grateful and more than made it up to us.

While Don and Pat lived at Bartonville Don's parents came to visit. They announced they were going to South Texas to look for a place to buy so they could move to where the weather was milder. Don's mother was weary of the cold winters in Oklahoma

> After they left Pat asked, "Do you think they are really going to buy a place in South Texas?" I replied, "No. They'll go kick a few tires and go back to Oklahoma."
>
> They were back the next weekend. They announced they bought a house in Brenham. Pat and I were astounded. The next few weeks they came several times with household belongings and stayed the night. Then left the next day to take their things to their new house in Brenham.

Don's parents celebrated their 60th wedding anniversary in May of 1985. They served punch and cake at the Methodist Church in Brenham. The five children and most of their families attended. Many friends from Brenham also attended. They had a ceremony where they repeated their wedding vows.

The spring of 1988 Don and Pat with help from Sam and Rowena held a Davidson Family Reunion at Falconhead near Ardmore, Oklahoma. All the children and most of their families attended.

> The prior Christmas Mom put the 'bee' on Sam and I to organize and hold a Davidson Family Reunion. Mother was always strong on family unity and togetherness. I think she foresaw her own mortality looming in the near future. She wanted one final reunion with the family.
>
> Sam and I with Rowena and Pat organized and arranged for the reunion to be held May 29th through 31st at Falconhead,

a resort area a few miles west of Ardmore. It was a three-day event over a weekend. We sent invitations to all the family. Most attended at least on Saturday, the main day.

We were served a meal Friday evening at Falconhead and had a story telling afterwards. I was the master of ceremonies. Saturday was the main day for visiting and getting reacquainted with distant family members. Lots of photographs were taken, especially with Mom and Dad.

Saturday evening we gathered at McGehee's Catfish Restaurant for a catfish dinner. Sunday morning we held a short religious service and disbanded to go home.

I think Mom was pleased with the reunion. It was her final get together with the family. She died Christmas Day that same year. Sam and I again held a reunion at Falconhead the following year. It was not the same without Mom. Dad was promoting his desire to marry another woman showing photos of her around to all the family. My older brother, Bob, had a nasty encounter with the resort operators about use of the swimming pool. I announced that the first person to complain would get the opportunity to arrange and organize the next reunion. Bob's daughter, Paula, complained. I told her she had the responsibility for the next reunion. We didn't have any more reunions per se, just the several birthday parties for Dad that Sam and I with Rowena and Pat arranged and organized.

The 1988 Republican Convention was held August in Houston. George Bush the first was renominated for the presidency. The Union Pacific Railroad brought the Challenger to Houston to showcase the train and to be a part of the activities.

I've been interested in trains for a long time, especially the old steam locomotives. The Union Pacific Challenger is the world's largest still operating steam locomotive. It is a monster locomotive weighing in at a million pounds with twelve driver wheels. It is No. 3985 built in 1943 by the American Locomotive Company. The name Challenger was given to steam locomotives with a 4-6-6-4 wheel arrangement. This means they have four wheels in the leading pilot truck, which helps guide it into curves; two sets of six driving wheels, and finally, four trailing wheels that support the rear of the engine and its massive firebox. Each set of driving wheels has its own steam cylinder. In essence it is two engines under one boiler.

When Pat and I learned the Challenger was in Houston we checked to see if we could buy tickets to tour with the train after it left Houston. The only seats available were from San Antonio to Fort Worth.

We flew from DFW airport to San Antonio. Stayed the night at a hotel and boarded the train at eight o'clock the next morning. The train consisted of a baggage car, two pullman cars, eight passenger day cars, and a club car at the back. We got to ride in the club car. All the cars were 1930's decor.

It was one o'clock in the afternoon before we left San Antonio. The fuel supplier brought the wrong fuel. The Challenger burns bunker fuel. We waited for the supplier to find and bring bunker fuel. What he brought was not bunker fuel but adequate for the Challenger to run at half speed which was thirty miles per hour.

The Challenger tour was widely advertised and written about in local newspapers. It was amazing to see all the people gathered along the way at crossings and all kinds of places where they could sit and see the train go by. Many people brought their kids so they could see a real steam locomotive. We had great fun waving from the windows and the back platform at the crowds of people.

The train stopped in Austin for about an hour. A large crowd with many kids gathered to see the huge locomotive. Many posed their kids next to the locomotive to take photographs. One man stood a five-year old boy on the cowcatcher for a photo. The poor kid was scared to death of that big monstrous thing blowing steam and hissing.

We left Austin and went through Hutto to Taylor. The highway parallels the tracks all along there. Many people were racing along in cars and pickups with someone leaning out the window taking videos of the train. At Taylor we stopped just long enough for Mikeska's Barbecue to set up food service in the baggage car. We went through the buffet line one car at a time to get our meals and take to our seats to eat while steaming toward Waco.

It was late evening when we finally pulled into Fort Worth. Even after dark we saw many people and cars waiting to see the steam locomotive pass by. It was a fun day. Pat and I took a tape recorder/player and played old time railroad songs by Boxcar Willy for the people in the club car with us.

In September 1988 Don and Pat drove to Brenham on a Labor Day weekend to visit Don's parents.

We thought it was just a visit to see the folks. However, Mom came dragging out a Trust Agreement a local Brenham bank had drawn up for them. She asked me to read it and tell her what I thought. I read it. I told Mom and Dad they should not sign such a Trust Agreement. Mom asked, "Then what should we sign?" I said, "I'll take this and review it more closely and draw up a more acceptable Trust Agreement."

I spent the next two months consulting with lawyers and writing a Trust Agreement I thought would be more appropriate to Moms and Dad's situation. Pat and I made several trips to Brenham to discuss it with them.

Early in December Mom went into the Brenham hospital with a heart condition. Pat and I made a trip to Brenham after she was released to finalize the Trust Agreement. It was ready to be signed and we planned to bring it to Brenham Christmas Day when we came to visit Mom and Dad.

The phone rang at two o'clock in the morning Christmas Day. It was Greg. Dad had called him and said the EMS took Mom to the hospital. Pat and I hurriedly got ready and drove as quickly as we could arriving at the Brenham hospital about eight o'clock that morning. We did not see Dad's car in the parking lot and feared the worst. A check with the hospital revealed that the doctor had released Mom to go home.

Greg and Donna came from Austin. We spent Christmas Day with Mom and Dad. In our haste to leave I did not bring the Trust Agreement with me. We left about two o'clock that afternoon to go home.

When we arrived home in Bartonville the phone was ringing. It was Greg. Dad had called him and told him Mom had died about four o'clock that afternoon.

The Trust Agreement was in limbo. It later became a serious matter of contention between Dad and me as he refused to sign it. He had other considerations in mind that surfaced within two weeks after Mom was gone. There were irreconcilable differences and I withdrew from the trust effort. Much later and after considerable cajoling my sister, Ann, and an attorney convinced Dad to sign a trust agreement to protect his assets.

There came a time when Don and Pat began to think about a real retirement. They wanted to move farther south in Texas to where the weather was milder and closer to Greg and Donna in Austin. The next two years almost every weekend they traveled to Austin and spent the weekend scanning the newspaper want ads and looking at rural property within fifty miles of Austin. A number of places were interesting and they came close to placing a contract, but some negative would pop up to preclude the offer.

In the meantime in 1991 Don's Dad was approaching his 90th birthday. Pat and Don with Sam and Rowena undertook to have a birthday party for him. They arranged to use the recreation hall at the Methodist Church. They made decorations and extra large size photographs of their Dad to display. They bought a birthday cake and arranged for a caterer to provide food service. Invitations were sent to relatives and a large number of local friends in Brenham.

The party was a rousing success. About three hundred people attended. All five of Bills and Pauline's children and their spouses attended as did some of the grandchildren. Pauline's sisters Jewel, Dixie, and Blanche with some of their children attended.

In their search for property Don and Pat were told to stay away from around Brenham. The property there was too expensive. Brenham was only an hour drive from the west side of Houston. Many of the Houston people with money had weekend places in the Brenham area. Nevertheless, they decided to look around Brenham anyhow. They found a place to their liking and made an offer that after a little negotiation the sellers accepted. Thus began the process of moving from Bartonville to Brenham.

> This place was located six miles southwest of Brenham. It had a nice house with a good large barn and corrals. It had two acres of yard with a sprinkler system. It had eighty large trees which Pat liked. A Massey-Ferguson 230 tractor was included in the deal as were several household items.
>
> We closed in August 1995. We went back to Bartonville and began the process of getting ready to move. The Mims bought our Bartonville property. I cleaned out the equipment shed and barn discarding thirteen small dumpster loads.
>
> We had an eighteen-foot trailer special made. We made several round trips hauling the 8N Ford tractor and the 1962 Dodge Lancer car and other things from Bartonville to Brenham. In October professional movers moved the household goods. A month later a cattle hauler moved twenty-seven head of our Longhorns to Brenham.

The first year at Brenham was a drought year. Hay was scarce and expensive. Don and Pat spent hours scouring the countryside for fifty miles around Brenham to find hay for the cows.

Gradually Don and Pat began to settle into their new home and surroundings. They became acquainted with Charles and Joy Blake, and through them became acquainted with Frank and Ruth Kosieracki. Charles and Joy were active in local Republican Party activities. Don and Pat joined the Republican Club of Washington County and became involved in local Republican Party activities. Don became a precinct chairman and a member of the Republican Party Executive Committee. He also became an election judge. Pat became an election clerk and assisted Don at election times.

In the meantime Don's Dad continued to live at home alone. He had several lady friends that took an interest in his welfare. In 1996 as his 95th birthday approached Don and Pat arranged to have a birthday party for him at their placc. Again Sam and Rowena helped with the expense and the work. Don and Pat cooked and prepared a barbecue buffet with all the fixings. About seventy-five relatives and friends attended.

Don and Pat loved their Texas Longhorns though they required a lot of physical work. Over the twenty years they kept Longhorns they had over two hundred calf births and lost only one. Pat and Don enjoyed just watching them in the pastures. Don took many photographs of them. It was a sad day when they took the younger cows and calves to a Longhorn sale in Brenham and a few days later loaded the older cows in a trailer and hauled to the auction barn in Industry. Don kept the old steer with the big horns just so he would have a Longhorn to look at in the pasture.

Don and Pat kept in touch with Don's dear friend, Buford Young, from his childhood days at Moore. They exchanged occasional letters and called one another from time to time. A few years after Don and Pat moved to Brenham they learned Buford had cancer.

> It was a sad day when we learned Buford had prostate cancer. We called each other and had long chats. Pat and I did some intense searches on the Internet trying to find any information that might be useful in Buford's treatment. We never found anything that Buford or Georgia hadn't already told us about. We felt so helpless.
>
> Buford and Georgia had often asked Pat and I to come visit them in Wyoming. It was something we were always going to do. We had the cattle to look after, and it was so far to Wyoming. We just never seemed to be able to find the time.
>
> In the meantime we kept in touch with Buford and Georgia. Buford's condition was not getting better. Finally, early in 1997 I told Pat, "We're selling the cattle and buying a new car and going to Wyoming to see Buford and Georgia." We originally planned to go in September, but something told me to go sooner. So, in April I sold all the cattle and bought a 1995 Lincoln Town Car. We didn't think our old '88 Lincoln could

make the trip. In May we went to Wyoming and visited Buford and Georgia. I am so glad we did.

We had a nice visit. Buford and Georgia have a lovely home and we enjoyed the warm hospitality. Our last evening there Georgia prepared a very nice dinner and we ate in the bedroom with Buford. We enjoyed a good meal while we reminisced about our times together. It was nice to visit with Buford, though it saddened us to learn that his condition was much worse than we had imagined. The few people we came in contact with in Worland all knew Buford and Georgia. They all spoke very highly of them, and felt very sad about Buford's illness.

We returned home through Salt Lake City and visited my cousin, Evann (Riley) Sutton and her daughter, Monica. We also visited our friends, Mick and Marion Cannon, from our days in Salt Lake City. Then we went to Phoenix and visited Aunt Elsie. She and I had a nice long walk early one morning reminiscing about our early days on Panther Creek and current events. Also in Phoenix we visited Aunt Marge, my cousin Jimmy Weldon and his wife, Michelina, and Jimmy's daughter, Jana. We stopped in Tucson and visited my cousin, David Riley.

After we got home we went to Mammoth Spring, Arkansas, for the Clarke Family Reunion at Rose Edna French's house. We visited Old Davidsonville State Park. I sent Buford a post card from Black Rock, Arkansas.

A month later Georgia called us with the sad, sad news. I sat down and had a good cry. A little bit of me died that day, too. My greatest regret is that Buford and I did not live close enough in our adult lives to have the same level of friendship and companionship we enjoyed as young boys. There is a very special place in my heart for Buford and his Mom and Dad. They were the greatest. I will never forget them.

I have believed for a long time that God takes the good ones first so they can go ahead and prepare the way for the rest of us. I truly expect to see Buford on that fateful day standing there with that big smile and his hand out. I'll say, "Hey, Big Guy, good to see you." He will laugh real big and say, "What took you so long?" And, we will both have a good laugh together.

> Farewell for now, My Friend. Thank you for touching my life. I love you and I miss you. Take care, and I'll see you over there.

The large yard and all the trees at the new house involved much work keeping up things. Leaf management was a year round job. The post oaks shed in November. The water oaks shed in February and March. The live oaks shed in April. The magnolia trees shed all summer. Don bought a Cub Cadet lawn tractor and later a Mow-N-Vac which helped immensely to pick up the leaves. Still there was plenty of hand raking where the Mow-N-Vac could not go in and around hedges and flowerbeds.

Don had an atrial fibrillation attack June 1998 and was hospitalized for several days. He recovered but with medication. It became an affliction he had to be aware of all the time. He later had another mild attack, but has since been able to control it with medication.

Don and Pat bought a Compaq Presario computer and over several years Pat became a self-taught computer 'guru.' She collected recipes and accumulated over a million. She subscribed to recipe websites and shared recipes with people all over the world.

In 2001 Don and Pat with help from Sam and Rowena arranged and organized a 100th birthday party for Don's Dad.

> Once again it was Sam and I with Rowena and Pat that began to plan, organize and arrange for the celebration of Dad's 100th birthday. We planned to the 'Nth degree' and estimated the cost. Since we had borne all the costs of the other parties we asked each of the five children to contribute $250 each to help defray the cost. Four of us, Bill, Ann, Sam and I 'ponied up' our share. Steve and Paula paid for Bob.
>
> We thought the 90th might be Dad's last birthday. We then thought the 95th may be his last. Now it was his 100th. We wanted to make it one grand party for it may well be the last.
>
> We rented the parish hall at Saint Peter's Episcopal Church in Brenham with tables and chairs to accommodate three

> hundred people. Pat and I rented all the necessary party accessories for coffee and cake. We decorated the hall with flowers and potted palm plants. Potted flowers were set on each table. One hundred dollar bills were replicated on the computer with Dad's image on them instead of Ben Franklin. They were widely distributed to all the tables.
>
> The day of the celebration trumpets sounded. A red carpet was rolled out by great grandsons, Casey and Daryl, all the way from the entrance to a large throne like chair at the front. Dad was escorted by granddaughters, Ashley and Debbie, to his throne. Sue Johnson, a friend, sang several personal songs and sat on his lap to sing a special song. The Methodist Church choir sang a few spirituals.
>
> I was the master of ceremonies. I presented framed special greetings and proclamations from President Bush, Governor Perry, Congressman Kevin Brady, State Senator Steve Ogden, and County Judge Dorothy Morgan. Family members came forward to tell stories about Dad and to give him presents. His grandson, Steve, presented him with a nicely done plaque, "The Order of the Shoe," with a shoe attached to signify the slipper Dad used to spank him when he was a kid. Aunt Blanche gave him a very nice walking cane made from the hame of a horse harness.
>
> We hired a professional photographer and had family group photographs taken with Dad, and a large group photo of all the family that attended. Our son, Greg, made a video of all the activities. He and Donna attended with their new daughter, Mary Grace. She was only a month old.
>
> That evening we had a family dinner at the K&G Restaurant. I brought copies of the booklet I wrote, "The Life and Times of William Edmund 'Bill' Davidson–100 Years of History." I gave a copy to each of the five children and all the grandchildren in attendance.

Life resumed to a fairly normal existence for Don and Pat after the party. Don busied himself with his genealogical endeavors. He spent hours searching on the computer and found several instances of pertinent information about the Davidson Family some of which is incorporated in other chapters of this book.

About this time Don was diagnosed with glaucoma. It was caught in time and is controlled with medication.

In October 2001 Greg and Donna adopted a baby girl in an "open adoption" arrangement with the birth mother, Alicia, in Fort Worth. When the baby was two days old they brought her home to Round Rock. They named her Mary Grace. She is Dons and Pat's only grandchild. From time to time Greg and Donna take Mary Grace to visit her birth mother. Don and Pat go to Round Rock to visit as often as they can.

Don's father continued to live at home though he was getting more and more feeble. Don often helped with his needs. He took him to his doctor appointments. He kept the lawn and trimmed the hedges. He made minor maintenance and repairs around the house.

One day Don's Dad had a flair up with his heart. Don stayed with him at the hospital and when released took him of his own accord to the Gazebo Terrace, a convalescent center.. He stayed only a few weeks and came home to live with his granddaughter, Paula, and her husband, Gary. This arrangement lasted a little over a year.

The spring of 2003 Don fell from a ladder. He was cleaning leaves from the gutter on the front of the house. He landed on his right leg and fell backwards onto the sidewalk on his left hip. He already had indications of arthritis in his hip and knee. The fall exacerbated the condition to where it was painful for him to walk.

Don and Pat bought a new 2003 Mercury Marquis and that September they drove to the western part of Virginia to attend a Roller Family Reunion. Debra (Roller) Price was the coordinator. Don and Pat met Rollers they never knew.

> We drove from Brenham to Little Rock, Memphis and to Kingsport, Tennessee. Pat did all the driving. My hip and leg were not up to that much driving.

In Kingsport we called Angela, Debbie's daughter, and had a nice dinner with Angela, her husband, Brian, and little boy, Nate.

The next day we drove to the old Fairview School House near Clinchport on a tributary to the Clinch River. This is the area where the first Rollers, Johannes and Anna (Ocher) Roller, in the Colonies settled about 1750. They are the parents of Jacob Roller born 1766 who married Eve Zirkle in 1791.

This part of Virginia is in the extreme southwest corner a few miles from the Tennessee border. It is in the heart of Appalachia and very mountainous with deep narrow valleys.

As a part of the reunion activities a group of us went to the cemetery where Johannes and Anna Roller and Jacob and Eve Roller are buried on a mountaintop. It was so very steep we had to ride in 4-wheel drive vehicles to get there. And then we had to walk the last fifty yards. We had a short religious ceremony to honor the family members buried there and placed new artificial flowers on each of the graves.

From the reunion we went to Tazewell and Wyth Counties in Virginia on a genealogical safari looking for information on the early Davidsons in the Colonies. Then we went to Huntsville, Tennessee, and on to Waverly, Tennessee, searching for Davidson information. We found some interesting information but nothing conclusive.

That December Don went into Saint Joseph Hospital in Bryan, Texas, for left hip replacement surgery by Dr. Joseph Iero. He recovered very nicely.

Don's Dad passed out one morning at breakfast. The EMS was called and they revived him and transported him to the hospital. Don stayed with him to assist in whatever manner needed. This episode scared Paula. In a few weeks she and Gary went back to Oklahoma after checking her grandfather into Gazebo.

November 2004 Don again went into Saint Joseph for right knee replacement surgery. The next day after surgery Don received a pleasant surprise visit from two former classmates from his days at Classen. Bernie Thompson, who played football with Don, and his wife, Martha (Goode) who also went to Classen, popped into his room. They had a nice visit reminiscencing about their days at Classen.

Don was in therapy three days a week and worked very diligently. He recuperated very nicely. Pat was a champion 'Nurse Jane' to care for him during his convalescence.

Don decided over two years ago to lose weight to relieve the pressure on his hip and knee joints. He went on what he called a "half diet." He ate just half of what was placed in front of him. He went from 224 pounds to 168 pounds in two and a half years following this method. He also worked out vigorously and religiously at home and at the gym.

Don's Dad continued to live at Gazebo. Don ran errands and took care of his needs. Ann was the trustee of his Trust Fund. Don handled all his financial matters. Don's Dad died December 7, 2005, Don's birthday.

> The phone rang at 1:45 a.m. It was the night nurse at Gazebo. She told me Dad died at 1:40 a.m. Pat and I were unable to sleep the rest of the night. Early that morning we began the sad task of calling relatives and friends to give the sad news.
>
> We had a funeral in Brenham officiated by Rev. Calvin Beckendorf, and then one at Memorial Park Cemetery in Oklahoma City officiated by Greg and Steve. Dad is buried next to Mom with his mother and father.

Don and Pat continued to live at their place near Brenham. They were active in the local Republican Club and Republican Party activities. Pat served one year as club treasurer, and as chairperson for special projects. Don served as the chairman of the bylaws committee and chairman of the scholarship committee. Don usually goes to the gym three days a week for a two-hour workout each time.

Don took a strong liking and keen interest in two neighbor boys, Cameron and Austin Wehmeyer. Since they had no grandfathers and he had no grandsons he took a grandfatherly interest in the boys. He enjoys going to their baseball games and talks with them about their interests and school activities. He gives them grandfatherly advice.

Don and Pat often go to Round Rock to visit Greg, Donna, and Mary Grace. She is a joy in their lives. They go to watch her play soccer and to her ballet recitals. She also is in gymnastics and swimming. Greg and Donna own twenty acres at Blue, a small community half way between Elgin and Lexington, Texas. We sometimes meet there for country outings.

In March 2005 Don and Pat went to Liberal, Kansas, to celebrate the eightieth birthday of Don's brother, Bill, at Debbie's house in Turpin, Oklahoma. On the way to Liberal Don and Pat received a cell phone call from Steve that Bob had a serious stroke at the racetrack in Houston and was in Hermann Memorial Hospital in Houston.

After they returned from Liberal Don and Pat went to visit Bob in the hospital. He was very much out of it. The prognosis was not good. Bob was later moved to Oklahoma City and Don and Pat went to visit him there. He was not much improved, though he seemed to kind of recognize people and understand what they said.

September 23, 2006 Bill's wife, Mary, died in Liberal, Kansas. Pat and Don attended the funeral.

Bob was later moved to a facility at Catoosa near Tulsa where he died June 24, 2007. He is buried at Antioch Cemetery in Garvin County.

July 2007 Pat and Don went to Moore, Oklahoma, to attend Don's 60th Class of '47 Reunion. It is the class he would have graduated with had his family stayed at Moore. Don always felt closer to that group and kept in touch with several of them over the years.

Don and Pat occasionally visit his sister, Ann, and her husband, Fred, at their country place near Flatonia, Texas.

January 29, 2008 Pat had a regular scheduled visit with her primary care physician. She had been complaining about shortness of breath and weakness. He had been treating her for asthma. Pat insisted there was more to it than asthma. He ordered a chest x-ray (for asthma) and an EKG. Her chest x-ray did not reveal asthma, but the EKG showed her heart rate to be 160. He immediately sent her to the Trinity Medical Center ICU in Brenham. They tried a procedure that was ineffective. The next morning the doctor had Don take her to Dr. Schwartz, a cardiologist in Bryan. They did an echocardiogram. She was diagnosed with atrial flutter. They immediately took her to St. Joseph's Hospital. There they performed a transesophageal echocardiography and then a catheter ablation. That is where a long wire is inserted into the main vein in the right groin and run into the upper right chamber of the heart to create a scar blockage. That interrupts the run away circular electrical impulse creating the fast, but weak, heart beat. The next day she felt fine. They did another echocardiogram. Dr. Schwartz said she had very slight signs of congestive heart failure and minimal valve leakage. Nothing to be overly concerned about. She was discharged to come home.

March 24, 2008, Pat had knee replacement surgery for her right knee. Dr. Iero performed the surgery. He is the doctor that did my hip and knee replacement surgery. Greg and Mary Grace came to St. Joseph's Hospital to be with me during her surgery. She was in the hospital three days and then cleared to come home. Don was her caregiver. Her stitches were removed April 24 and her incision is healing nicely. She is able to flex her knee 95 degrees. Dr. Iero said she was in the upper 2% of people able to do that so soon after surgery. Only six weeks after surgery she was walking without assistance.

> When Pat complained, which was infrequently, I reminded her, "This hospital is run by an amateur." We ate a lot of bacon, scrambled eggs, oatmeal, and canned soups for a couple of

weeks. I can open cans and heat the contents, I can cook oatmeal, and I can fry bacon and eggs. That is the extent of my culinary prowess.

Six weeks and four days after surgery Pat and I attended the St. Joseph Joint University Alumni Luncheon at the hospital. Fifty-three former joint surgery patients attended. Pat walked the best without assistance or a limp. I was proud of her.

CHAPTER 17

ANN LUVIDA DAVIDSON

ANN (Meta) LUVIDA DAVIDSON, fourth child and only daughter of William "Bill" Edmund Davidson and Mary Pauline (Roller) Davidson, was born 1 July 1931 in Wesley Hospital at Oklahoma City, Oklahoma County, Oklahoma.[1]

Ann married Carl Fredrick "Fred" Melton 31 December 1948 at Gainesville, Cooke County, Texas. Fred was born 6 July 1930 in his parent's home at Southeast 48th Street, Oklahoma City, Oklahoma County, Oklahoma. Fred's father was Eugene James Melton, born 1898 in Indian Territory at what is now Wynnewood, Garvin County, Oklahoma. His mother was Velma Jewel (Stapp) Melton, born in 1899 at Box, Oklahoma Territory.

Ann and Fred have three children. They are:

(1) Sheril Kay, born 27 March 1951, in Wesley Hospital, Oklahoma City, Oklahoma County, Oklahoma. She married Christopher Allen Vaughn 16 February 1970, in Joplin, Jasper County, Missouri. They have four children, Honey Ann, Roman Christopher, Heather Lee and Julie Lynn. Sheril Kay divorced Chris 23 January 1984 and later married Charles Lynn Gant 12 December 1987 in Tomball, Harris County, Texas.

---

1 (Ann's given name was Meta Luvida. She did not like the name Meta and began to go by Ann. When she was fifteen years old she had her name legally changed to Ann Luvida.)

(2) Randy Gene, born 12 January 1953, in Wesley Hospital, Oklahoma City, Oklahoma County, Oklahoma. He married Donna Jean Shelton. They have a son, Culley Brant (Melton) Turner. Randy and Donna divorced. She remarried and her husband adopted Culley. Randy later married Pamela Gwinn Gorden. They have a son, Shane.

(3) Bonny Len, born 3 February 1960, in Baptist Hospital, Nashville, Davidson County, Tennessee. He married Angela Yvetta Hutchison 15 December 1979 in Nashville, Davidson County, Tennessee. They have three children, Xanthea Leigh, Zane Pierce and Zara Jill.

After three rambunctious boys Bill and Pauline were very happy to have a daughter with the arrival of Meta Luvida. They named her for Bill's mother, Meta, and Pauline's mother Arlie Luvida. Ann's earliest memories are when the family lived at 2709 NW 40th Street in Oklahoma City.

> My first memory is of a girl about eight or ten years old that lived next door. She had a broken arm in a cast. She also had brothers and I remember baseball games between the two families. We had a gentle milk cow named Bossy.
>
> I don't remember this myself, but was told that Dad lost his job as ticket agent with the Oklahoma Railway Company. Our house was foreclosed and we had to move.
>
> We moved to a smaller house at 3608 NW 13th Street. This was during the Great Depression years of the 1930's. Dad tried several jobs. One was selling insurance but people were not buying insurance during the depression.
>
> He finally got a job as a milkman delivering milk for Meadow Gold Dairy to homes from a horse drawn milk wagon. His regular route was several blocks north of our home. One morning I was not feeling well. I looked out the window and saw Dad stop his milk wagon in front of our house. He brought me some orange juice.

Our house on 13th Street was fairly small, but part of the backyard was fenced for Bossy. The rest was mostly garden. One day I was privileged to see Bossy give birth to a calf. I was in kindergarten at Linwood Elementary School and told my teacher about our cute little calf. A few days later my entire class came to our house to see the baby calf. Mom served lemonade and cookies.

Since there was no grass in the backyard for Bossy to eat, my brothers each day led her to a grassy area along a creek about two blocks away so she could graze.

When I was six years old we moved to a farm near Moore, Oklahoma. It was called the Johnson Place. We used wood for heating. One day I was "helping" Dad saw logs with a crosscut saw. My First Grade teacher happened to drive by and saw me. The next day at school she mentioned it to me. I felt very proud that I was able to help my Dad.

This time was during the Dust Bowl days of the 1930's. We had terrible dust storms. Mom stuffed rags around the windows and doors trying to keep the dust out of the house, but a dustpan full of dust came through the keyhole in the door.

One of the most traumatizing events to occur while we lived there was when a friend of my brother, Gene, drowned in a pond near our house. His name was Arbry Lee Davis.

Later we moved to a farm two miles south of the Johnson Place. It was called the Turk Place. It had a two-story house with a large porch on the front and part of the south side.

One evening Mom saw a tornado coming our way. She herded all us children into the stairway. After it was over we surveyed the damage. I especially noticed that the plaster had fallen from the dining room ceiling.

We did not have a storm cellar, so another time when Mom saw a storm brewing we all began to run down the highway to a neighbor's house that had a storm cellar. The wind blew so hard it seemed all I had to do was move my feet up and down and the wind blew me the rest of the way.

Another time I was visiting my Aunt Hazel Roller in Garvin County. She was a rural school teacher and lived in a house next to the school building. She saw a tornado coming and hurried us into a cellar next to her house. After the storm passed we came out and discovered the schoolhouse was moved a foot from its foundation, but the house was totally missed.

I dearly loved my Grandmother Roller. When I was ten years old I spent several weeks with her one summer. My Uncle Henry and Aunt Catherine had a baby girl, Beverly, old enough to sit in a highchair. I felt very proud that Catherine let me feed the baby.

Grandma and Catherine canned vegetables from their garden. They put me to washing the jars. Sometimes there were spiders in the jars. I just knew one was going to bite me and I would die. I told Grandma this with tears in my eyes, but I still had to wash the jars.

Grandma sold eggs for her spending money. She let me gather the eggs. We would carefully place them in a box to take to town. She cautioned me to always look in the nest before I put my hand in because there might be a chicken snake in the nest. One day I saw one in a nest. I ran for Grandma to deal with the snake.

It was an exciting time for me when the work crew came to Grandpa's to thrash his broomcorn. This was during August which was the hottest part of the summer. Grandma had her wood burning cook stove going full blast as she turned out heaping platters of fried chicken, potatoes, gravy, garden vegetables, home made bread and several pies to feed the work crew. I helped with the dishes after the meal. It seemed I had never seen so many dishes.

One day I was raking leaves in the yard and tidying it up. My Aunt Hazel came by to view my handiwork. As I raked away I suddenly saw a bright shiny nickel among the leaves. I exclaimed over the nickel. Aunt Hazel said it must be payment for a good job. Looking back I feel certain she put it there for me to find.

Later we moved a mile east and a quarter mile south of the Turk Place to a farm called the Sullivan Place. It was a mile west of the interurban that ran from Oklahoma City to Norman. One day Mom and I rode it to Oklahoma City to go shopping. When we boarded to come home it was full of sailors returning to their base at Norman. World War II was in full force.

We had several cows that my brothers milked. My job was to turn the handle on the separator that divided the cream from the milk. We put the cream in big cans to take to town and sell. The skim milk was mixed with bran feed and given to the hogs.

Dad changed jobs. He worked for a trucking company loading and unloading truck trailers at night.

We had a big garden, pear trees, chickens for eggs, hogs for pork, and milk from the cows. I helped Mom can vegetables from the garden for use during the winter. Although we didn't have much money it seems we always had food to eat.

When I was in the second grade at Moore our class was going to put on a play for the school. I really wanted a part in the play. When I came home I told my brother, Gene, about the part I would be auditioning the next day. He spent most of that evening coaching me. The next day when I tried out for the part I was selected. I'm sure it was due to the excellent coaching I received.

I especially remember my Fourth Grade teacher, Mrs. Varndell. I told her something one day and used the word "jist." She began to correct me and would say "just" to which I replied "jist." She persevered until finally I said "just." To this day I am careful to pronounce this word correctly as she instructed.

Beverly and Phyllis Kitchen were friends. They were twins. One Friday afternoon at school Phyllis told me that when she went home for lunch she saw my Dad at the store. She said she asked him if I could spend the night with her. She said he told her I could so I went home with her. The next day Dad came to their door looking for me. It seems this all was a figment of

> Phyllis' imagination. Mom was worried to death when I didn't come home. Needless to say I was also in big trouble.
>
> Another friend was Marilyn Reichert. Her father was the local doctor. I was invited to their home several times. Marilyn was an only child and liked to have someone to play with. They had a lovely two story home beautifully furnished. I was duly impressed and think that was when I first began to appreciate nice things.

When Ann was in the sixth grade the family moved to Evening Shade, Arkansas. The change from the school at Moore to Evening Shade was a cultural shock for Ann and her brothers. The school at Evening Shade was not the same quality as the one at Moore. The students were far behind at the same grade level as the students at Moore. This caused problems for Ann and her brothers. They were looked on as "those smart aleck new kids" by the general student body. There is a detailed account of this in the CHAPTER on Ann's brother, Gene (Don).

Two successive floods a month apart wrecked havoc on Ann's Dad and his attempt to succeed at river bottomland farming in Arkansas.

> Our family moved to Evening Shade, Arkansas, which turned out to be a disaster. Strawberry River ran through the place. Every time we planted crops it rained, the river flooded and washed it all away.
>
> The Kunkels were our neighbors. They had a riding horse. My brother, Marvin, and I went to visit one day. They offered to let us ride the horse. I was thrilled. Their son, Pug, wanted to ride behind me. They didn't have a saddle so we were riding bareback. We rode up a hill a ways and turned the horse to ride back to the house. Just before we got to the house the horse jumped a ditch. I held onto the horse's mane for dear life. Pug held me around the waist. He started to fall dragging me off

with him. My arms were around the horse's neck. As I fell I swung down under its neck. I landed in a pile of rocks beside the road. The horse jumped over me. It felt as if the hoofs were pounding all over my body. I ended up with a concussion and was out of my head most of the night. Luckily I had no broken bones.

During the winter my brother, Gene, and Pug fell into the river. Pug caught pneumonia and had an extremely high fever. I believe it was 107 degrees. I was told it made medical history. Mom went to their home to help care for him. Later I heard an ambulance taking Pug to the hospital in Batesville. I remember kneeling beside my bed and praying that Pug would get well. God must have heard my prayers. Today Pug is very much alive and in his seventies.

In the summer we walked barefoot to town on Saturdays. It was three miles. I would have a piano lesson. Then I would meet a friend in town. I would use my ten cents allowance to buy each of us an ice cream cone for five cents. We would walk around town looking in all the stores. Just before it was time to go home she would spend her ten cents allowance to buy each of us an ice cream cone.

One time I was walking home from town. There was a spring a ways back from the road. I was thirsty so I went to get a drink. I heard our truck coming. I began to run for the road so I could ride home but alas, I was too late. I trudged the rest of the way home.

At Evening Shade school started in July. This was strange to me. I learned later school was dismissed in September and October so the kids could pick cotton. Classes resumed in November.

In September Ann, her little brother, Marvin, and her parents moved back to Oklahoma City. They lived a short time with friends, Alvin and Wilma Teel, until they were able to move into their house at 3608 NW 13th Street. They were soon joined by Ann's two older brothers, Bob and Gene. Her oldest brother, Bill, lived with the Morrow Family at Moore while he went to school there.

Ann was in the seventh grade and enrolled at Taft Junior High on northwest 23rd Street at May Avenue. Her brother, Gene, enrolled at Taft in the ninth grade. He started using his first name, Don, instead of Gene. Her other brother, Bob, enrolled in the eleventh grade at Classen High School.

> When we moved back to Oklahoma City I was to attend Taft Junior High School. It was several miles and I didn't know the way. Mom asked a neighbor boy, Perry Bennett, to let me walk to school with him. My brother, Gene, couldn't show me the way because he had a paper route. He got up early to throw his papers and then rode his bike directly to school. Perry must have been embarrassed to have a girl walking with him because he stayed about twenty steps in front of me the entire way.

When Ann was fourteen years old she got a job working after school hours at the fountain for Veazey's Drug Store. They had several stores around town where she worked. She soon became adept getting around town by herself. She was paid forty cents an hour, the minimum wage.

When Ann graduated from Taft she attended Central High School near downtown Oklahoma City. She took typing, shorthand and a business course in addition to a regular curriculum. She worked part time at the Oklahoma Audit Bureau after school hours.

Ann's older brother, Bill, was in the Navy during World War II serving in the Pacific. Her brother, Bob, served stateside in the Army Air Corps. Her brother, Don (Gene), quit high school and volunteered for the Army a few months before the war ended. He served on occupation duty in Japan with the 11th Airborne Division.

Ann Luvida Davidson - age 15

While in high school at Central Ann became acquainted with Fred Melton, a fellow student. One of Fred's main attractions was his flashy Ford convertible, a rarity for a high schooler in those days. Fred's Dad owned and operated the drug store at 14th and

Portland Avenue just two blocks from where Ann lived with her parents and younger brother, Marvin.

> I had a friend, Mildred Randolph. We sometimes played tennis at Reed Park at 12th Street and Drexel. Usually after we finished our game we went across the street to the soda fountain in the drugstore at 12th Street and May Avenue.
>
> One day after our game Mildred suggested we go to the new drugstore at 14th Street and Portland Avenue as there was a cute new boy working there. We entered the store and sat at a booth to order our cokes. The boy came over and sat down with us. He said, "My name is Freddie. What is yours?" During our conversation he said he also went to Central High School. Before long I found myself going steady with Freddie. His Mom and Dad owned the drugstore. Fred was expected to work until 10:00 p.m. So, I went there and we did our homework together between customers. Fred also worked after school from 1:00 to 5:00 p.m. at a sign company downtown near my work. He would pick me up and take me home.

Ann began to attend the Church of Christ with Fred. October 1948 Ann was baptized and became a member of the Church of Christ. December of Ann and Fred's senior year they decided to get married.

> I spoke to Mom about getting married and told her I wanted to be married in the Church of Christ. She was very much against this. She wanted us to marry in the Methodist Church where she was a member. She had some firm ideas about our wedding which were not as Fred and I wanted.

December 31, 1948, Ann and Fred eloped to Gainesville, Texas, where they were married in the home of a local Church of Christ minister. They returned to Oklahoma City keeping their marriage a secret. They each continued to live at home with their individual parents while they completed high school. They graduated the following June from Central High School.

In the meantime Ann's brother, Don, received an honorable discharge from the Army. He was completing his high school requirements in an accelerated course for veterans at Central High School so he could enter college. Though Ann and Fred were keeping their marriage a secret Don surreptitiously learned their secret. He was dating Pat Paschall and agreed to keep their secret a secret.

Don and Pat ran around with Ann and Fred. On two occasions Ann and Fred took Don and Pat in Fred's convertible on an outing to Lake Murray where Pat's folks owned and operated a tourist court and convenience store. Once when dining at a restaurant in downtown Oklahoma City they were talking about the unusual things in life they would like to do. Don said he had been jumping out of airplanes and decided that was unusual enough. Fred said he would like to "go bear hunting with a knife." That caused a great deal of laughter.

Ann did secretarial work and Fred worked at Katz Drug Store in downtown Oklahoma City as a window trimmer. This job didn't last long. Fred was much too creative and artistic to suit the whims of the store manager. Fred then worked a while as a silk screen artist and painter.

Then Ann and Fred moved to Dallas and lived there for over a year. New Years Eve 1949 Don and Pat went to Dallas to visit Ann and Fred to help celebrate their first wedding anniversary. Fred's brother, Jack, and his wife, Wanda, were also visiting. They all had dinner at Sammy's Restaurant and then went to White Rock Lake. They made a bonfire to snuggle around.

A few months later Ann and Fred moved back to Oklahoma City. Fred's father wanted him to go to Oklahoma University to study pharmacy. Shortly afterwards Ann was expecting their first child. Sheril Kay was born March 27, 1951. Fred dropped out of school and took jobs with Steffens Ice Cream Company and DeCoursey Milk Company. Later Ann worked in the membership department of the YMCA in downtown Oklahoma City.

Ann and Fred bought a home at 3550 Garden Avenue and lived there several years. Their son, Randy Gene, was born January 12, 1953, while living there. Fred again changed jobs and worked for Eastern Electric Company as a field representative which required him to travel extensively. This soon became old and Fred decided to quit.

Ann and Fred bought a small vending business in Carthage, Missouri and moved there. They later moved to Joplin, Missouri. Ann took a temporary job with the law firm Burden & Shortridge where she learned to be a legal secretary. Fred worked in a local foundry while also running the vending business.

Fred began to preach at a small church in Webb City. He felt he needed more Bible training. He left the foundry, sold the vending business, and took a job with a tower company in Fort Meyers, Florida. He attended Florida College in Tampa. Ann got a job with the law firm Cooper & Cooper in Tampa.

A year later Ann went to work for the law firm Gibbons, Gibbons & Tucker. During this time Mr. Sam Gibbons ran for Congress and was elected. He served in Congress until 1996.

While Fred attended Bible classes at Florida College he also preached for the 40th Street Congregation, and later the Castle Heights Congregation in Tampa.

After three years of Bible study Fred accepted a position as minister of the Church of Christ in White House, Tennessee. While at White House Ann and Fred's son, Bonny Len, was born February 3, 1960, at Baptist Hospital in Nashville, Tennessee.

Ann and Fred moved from Tennessee to Alvin, Texas, near Houston. Fred helped establish the Park Lane Church of Christ Congregation in south Houston.

One day while Ann and Fred were at work their house caught on fire. Neighbors saw smoke coming from the roof upstairs. They moved everything out of the downstairs before the fire trucks arrived. They had very little water damage.

> It looked like rain so we moved everything into a vacant house a mile away. We lived in this house when hurricane Carla hit. This was our first hurricane. It was a very traumatic experience.
>
> We decided to buy a home with some land. After looking for about a year we bought five acres with a house northwest of Houston located on West Montgomery Road. It was hardly more than a trail. Years later it became a fourteen-lane highway. We owned this property forty-four years and saw many changes in that part of Harris County.

Ann went to work for the law firm, Crouch, Cole and Pacetti, in Houston. Mr. Cole was blind. He was not only a lawyer but also a Texas State Representative. Her responsibilities were greater than for most secretaries because Mr. Cole relied on her to read and be sure the papers he prepared were correct. He also wanted to know her impression of clients. He later ran for the State Senate and won. Ann helped with the campaign along with her other office duties. It became quite a heavy workload.

Ann decided to change to a larger law firm where she would have fewer responsibilities. She became legal secretary to Wiley Caldwell, a lobbyist and senior member of Fulbright, Crooker, Freeman, Bates & Jaworski, a very prestigious law firm. She learned politics from a very different perspective working for a lobbyist. During this time Fred worked at the Houston Public Library, attended school at South Texas University, and helped establish the Cy-Fair and Lang Road Church of Christ churches.

> Our son, Randy Gene, had a difficult time in the junior high school that had over two thousand students. One teacher in particular often embarrassed him in front of the class. He would leave the classroom and go sit in the principal's office. This ultimately resulted in him being expelled.
>
> We made arrangements for Randy to live with my Aunt Blanche on a farm near Elmore City, Oklahoma. There he attended a small rural school that seemed to suit him better.

> When our daughter, Kay, was nineteen she met and married Chris Vaughn. In 1970 they had a daughter, Honey Ann. Kay became seriously ill and was hospitalized. She had an infected kidney removed.

In 1970 Fred received a church letter asking for someone to help with church work in Europe. Fred answered the call. He, Ann and Bonny moved to Tonbridge, England, a quaint, picturesque village. It was an exciting and broadening experience with Fred preaching for Church of Christ churches in England, Germany, and Switzerland. It was also a great opportunity for them to travel throughout Europe, the Eastern Communist countries, and parts of Asia. Four years later Fred began work with Saint John's Lane Church of Christ in Bristol located in the West Country of England.

While Ann and Fred lived in England, their daughter, Kay, had two children, Julie Lynn and Roman Christopher. Kay had separated from her husband and was having problems. Fred came to Oklahoma City and brought Honey, age four, and Julie, age two, back to live with them in England.

When Bonny was fourteen he traveled alone from London to Bern, Switzerland to visit friends. They loaned him a motor bike and he spent his two-week stay exploring Bern and the surrounding area. He returned by train to Paris, then to London and home to Bristol.

Randy Gene continued to live with Ann's Aunt Blanche at Elmore City, Oklahoma, and finished high school. He married Donna Shelton and they had a son, Culley. The marriage soon ended in divorce. Later Randy Gene married a local girl, Pamela Gwinn Gorden. They had a son, Shane. But, that marriage too ended in divorce. However, Randy Gene and Pam have since twice remarried and divorced each other.

Elementary schooling ends at age fifteen in England so Ann and Fred returned to the States so Bonny could finish his education and be eligible for college. They moved to Waller, Texas. Fred worked as a Church of Christ minister. Ann worked for Computer Sales, Inc. as Executive Assistant to the Senior Vice President of Marketing. This was the most fun job she ever had as she was constantly planning parties, fishing trips, golf tournaments, and other exciting outings for customers.

Ann worked a number of years with the international computer company. They awarded her canal boat tickets for two plus airfare to England for her years of meritorious service. She and Fred chose the Llangollen Canal because of its picturesque mountain setting, the attraction of a tunnel and an aqueduct spanning the beautiful Dee River and Valley. They however had not reckoned on the infamous five stair locks near Wrenbury, the unusually low level of the canal because of drought, and a music festival that was in full swing at Llangollen. Following is an account (condensed and edited) of this trip written by Fred:

> We checked in at the British Waterways Station and had a fifteen- minute instruction on how to operate and maintain the canal boat. It is shaped like a cigar with an outside tiller at the rear. We loaded our baggage and supplies and set out on the Grand Union Canal.
>
> Shortly, we encountered our first lock. You are on your own when negotiating a lock. Ann hopped off and tucked into the first lock-arm, a six by eight timber six feet long. It didn't budge. A boatload of young toughs had entered the lock with us. They waved Ann aside and triumphantly opened the gate while shouting about their strength and ability. We held back and let them get far ahead.
>
> A slight drizzle of rain began. I donned a slicker and captain's hat and stationed myself at the helm. As we glided up the canal Ann ducked down into the galley to prepare tea and scones. In a few minutes I shouted, "Lock ahead!" Ann scampered up from below and exclaimed, "I haven't even started fixing tea." I retorted, "I can't help these locks." Ann said, "Well, I'll have a hand at the tiller myself after the next lock and you can open and close the gates."

Ann was less than adequate as captain. Canal boats respond slowly to the helm. Turn the helm sharply and hold it too long and the boat over reacts. After struggling at the helm Ann reluctantly said, "You are going to have to steer this boat." I replied, "It is settled. I shall be captain and you can be first mate." Ann said, "Evidently I'm to be second and third mate, plus cook and bottle washer, as well as, maid and washer woman. Some holiday this is turning out to be!"

After several locks Ann began to tire. We had gotten only a cup of tea and a few cookies to eat. We moored for the night at Wrenby Mill. I walked a short distance to a stone bridge over the canal. I looked back and Ann was washing clothes and hanging them to dry. An approaching boat veered too far to the other bank to miss our boat. A man on the boat chastised Ann for mooring where the canal was too narrow. Ann shouted, "If you had been watching where you were going you wouldn't have ended up in the mud." After extracting themselves from the mud-bar they floated downstream muttering, "Stupid woman." Ann shouted, "I'm not the one that got stuck in the mud." I was determined to give Ann a "cook's night out", so we went to the Dusty Miller, an exquisite little canal side pub for an evening meal.

Next day there was a lot of boat traffic on the canal. By the time we got to the stair lock at Whitchurch there was a traffic jam. Ann was busy running from gate to gate as we negotiated one lock after another. I tried to help as best I could, but I had to control the boat, didn't I? The lockmaster watched Ann as she struggled with one of the gate arms. "You have the wrong kind of gloves," he observed. "Here let me exchange gloves with you so your hands slide off the gate better." He was happy as we took his picture while chugging upstream.

The next night we moored at Ellesmere, an interesting village that was a busy commercial center when freight moved in England by way of the canals. A few miles from Ellesmere Ann got off onto the bank to run and lift a cattle bridge. I cleared the bridge and turned to the bank so Ann could get on. She was running to catch up. She reached out and grabbed the boat railing just as the boat drifted away from the bank. I shouted, "Hang on! No, turn loose!" Too late. Her toes were spiked in the bank and her fingers clutching the boat railing. She was perpendicular spanning the water between the boat and the bank. Down she went into the canal. In my effort to help her I swung the boat toward the bank just as she fell. That banged her pretty good. "Back off," she shouted, "I can't take much more of this." She dragged herself on board and we stopped for tea. I hugged and kissed her and said, "You'll feel better after a good night's rest."

I was impressed with Ann's stamina and durability. Permit me to digress, perchance a young man perusing these pages who is searching for a wife would be advised to seek a bride, having not only spiritual traits, but physical ones as well. Broad shoulders, sturdy back, strong legs that are pleasantly utilitarian so that in her autumn years she might travel to distant and exciting places with ease.

The next morning our boat would not start. I noticed we spent the night slightly tilted against the bank. I walked two miles to a village, called for a company mechanic. In about an hour two chaps arrived, drained the diesel, primed the fuel system and sent us on our way.

The canal became increasingly narrow and shallow. At length we entered a narrow tunnel about four hundred feet through a mountain. It was black as pitch. All we could see was the small light at the other end. Ann thought it was spooky. Beyond the tunnel the boat bumped rock bottom. The helm had become hard to handle and the boat difficult to steer. After supper, I dove into the canal and wrestled the rudder back into its harness.

At last we reached the aqueduct with the village of Llangollen six miles beyond. The aqueduct and valley were impressive, but the number of boats on the canal caused pandemonium. We turned around and started back.

The weather was nice, except for a little rain. The scenery was superb. The night moorings were pleasant. Meadows and steams divided by hedge rows and rock fences made a patchwork of pastoral charm. These framed a beautiful scene of grazing sheep and cattle perfectly in tune with nature, yet hidden from the eyes of the common tourist. Though Ann did most of the cooking and washing we occasionally ate at quaint pubs and chatted with the locals. Canal travel is wonderful and allows travelers to observe the rural country, life at its finest.

Near disaster struck at the last lock as we were about to enter the Grand Union Canal. One of the poles on the boat is equipped with a hook on one end to hold the boat back to keep it from hitting the gate as the water rushes in from the high end of the lock. I was manning the gate and was positioned on top of the lock. Ann was holding the boat back with the long pole. I was at the gate when I saw Ann dive headfirst into the water in the lock. She bounced off the hull of the boat and became wedged between the boat and the lock wall. I realized this could be serious. Ann was a pitiful sight hanging there whimpering, glasses askew, hair plastered to her head, and about to be crushed between the boat and lock wall waiting for the other shoe to drop, which it did. Her new $300 pair of glasses slipped from her face and sank to the bottom of the lock. I jumped down and pulled Ann onto the boat. The lockmaster saw what happened and rushed out of his little house with a rake. I had already slipped into the lock and feeling for the glasses. I finally found them with the rake. "The pole slipped," mumbled Ann, "it happened so fast."

The next day Ann was black and blue. "There isn't any place on my body that doesn't hurt," she moaned. Two days later I called British Airways to confirm our flight to Houston. The voice on the other end said, "Your flight left thirty minutes ago, Sir." We had miscalculated our return date by one day.

Finally arriving home, Ann downed several aspirins and fell into bed. "Ann," I said, "Our next trip should be more structured. Perhaps one of those planned African safaris. What do you think? Ann, Ann, ANN!"

Property taxes on their Houston property increased to the extent that Ann and Fred decided to build storage units to generate income to pay the taxes.

We weren't sure how well they would rent. To our amazement people rented them faster than we could build. They actually

> would move in as we were constructing the walls between the units. Initially, we built six storage buildings and three boat stall buildings which more than paid the taxes.

Bonny took flying lessons shortly after he returned to the States from England. He soon soloed and became a private pilot and then went on to become an instructor. He attended Florida College where he met Angela Hutchison from Dickson, Tennessee. They married the following year and moved to Waller. Later they had a daughter, Xanthea Leigh.

Ann and Fred leased a small airport near Waller. Bonny became a Cessna dealer and gave flying lessons. In the 1980's a recession set in and flying lessons were one of the first cut backs people made. In the meantime Kay had reconciled with her husband, Chris, and moved into a mobile home on the property and managed the storage units.

Ann and Fred saw the need for a mail delivery service in the northwest Houston area. They soon had three separate routes. One each for Fred, Kay, and Bonny delivering incoming mail and picking up outgoing mail for banks and other companies.

Bonny felt the need to work for the Church of Christ. He left and became the minister at a church in Wayne, Michigan. Ann and Fred hired a young man, Charles Gant, to take Bonny's place as a driver.

While in Michigan a son, Zane Pierce, was born to Bonny and Angela. Two years later they moved to Lyndhurst, England, and began work with the church in Brighton. Their daughter, Zara Jill, was born in England, but they registered her as a citizen of the United States. They lived in England three years and then returned to Columbus, Texas, and later to Houston where Bonny preached at the Pinehurst Church.

In the meantime Kay was again having marital problems with her husband, Chris. They soon divorced. Kay began to date Charles Gant and two years later they were married. Kay drove one of the mail routes and Ann quit her job at Computer Sales to manage the storage units. Charles took another better paying job and Ann also drove one of the mail routes. The company Charles worked for transferred him to Dayton, Ohio. They reorganized the routes and sold the one Ann was running.

Later Kay and Charles became missionaries for the church. They spent eight years in Russia. They moved to Nizhny Novgorod (previously Gorky) just a year after the famous wall came down. In 1994 Ann and Fred visited Kay and Charles while in Russia. Following is Fred's account (condensed and edited) of their experience:

> I don't think I shall ever be quite the same again after my trip to Russia. My first impressions began at St. Petersburg as we descended through an ever-darkening layer of clouds into a doleful and forbidding place. Ancient Aeroplot jets with a stark and deserted look lined the airfield. On arrival passengers from the British Airways flight were bussed to a small terminal building and into a Spartan hall with four immigration booths. The expression "Russians never smile" took on a new meaning when faced with these immigration officials. They finally released us to pick up our baggage. We had to snatch it quickly from a conveyer belt else it would go outside into the rain for another trip around.
>
> After negotiating customs we stood in the lobby waiting for Reta, our Christian contact. Shortly a small plain woman with straight hair and sad countenance appeared. Managing a smile she said in perfect English, "Have you been waiting long?" Without another word we followed her through the terminal to a row of waiting taxis. Although we stood waiting on the curb none of the waiting cab drivers approached us. Reta was looking beyond the cabs. At length she approached a tall better dressed man with a lapel clip that said "TAXI." After a bit of bargaining we settled on fifteen pounds sterling (about $22). Reta said it was too much but we assured her it was okay. She said, "These people are sharks." She meant mafia. For about ten minutes we rode in silence except for an occasional direction by Reta to the driver.

On arrival at Reta's flat, a tenement building thirteen floors high, we entered via a keypad through a steel door that when shut reminded one of the unforgiving slam of a jail cell door. We went down a dark hallway to an elevator that had the same kind of forbidding door. After ascending ten uncertain floors we stood in front of Reta's flat. The first door was of the aforesaid steel emplacement, the second a heavy wood door with four large dead bolts.

Once inside we took off our shoes according to Russian custom and settled in. At that moment the real Reta emerged. One who has a heart of fine and pure gold. In one of her two small rooms she had prepared her own bed for Ann and a chair unfolded beside for me. She would retire to a cot in the kitchen. In her tiny apartment Reta became transformed into an "old mother hen" anticipating and supplying our every need. Never had we witnessed such kindness and love among strangers as she showed us.

The next morning we set out with Reta for the train station in downtown St. Petersburg to buy a next day ticket for an eighteen hour train ride to Nizhny Novgorod, where Kay and Charles lived. We made our way past decaying buildings, down dirty streets and past unkempt areas of grass and shrubs to the underground Metro line. Street vendors were everywhere. Sellers were mostly women and children with perhaps a single item to sell–a shirt, or a blouse. Beggars were at intervals along the corridors of the underground. We got on the appropriate subway train. I stood near the door. Ann and Reta sat but it began to get crowded. After a few stops it was wall to wall people. I thought not one more small person can get on. At the next station at least twenty-five more got on. At the next stop, to my relief, we all got off–you had no choice. We were swept en mass to the other side of the platform and into a waiting train with passengers already pressing their faces against the doors. We swayed to and fro in one nauseous mass for two more stops. I could barely see Reta pinned beneath shoulders and arms.

Disembarking we walked to the train station where Reta asked for a very nice two place sleeping compartment for us on the train to Nizhny. The clerk said to Reta, "It's very expensive." (63,000 rubles, about $31.50.) It seemed to please Reta to reply, "I'll take it anyway." We took Reta to a nice restaurant for lunch. Then we went on a sightseeing boat tour that charged foreigners three times the rate for a Russian.

The next day we insisted Reta call a taxi to take us to the station. An old beat-up Russian Lada (automobile) arrived in due time. When the driver saw our bags he snapped open the trunk with a screwdriver. It had enough "stuff" to start a respectable junkyard. Reta turned away embarrassed. A small bag went in the trunk–the rest in the back seat with us. Weaving, screeching, and honking (he had a good horn) we made our way through the streets of Saint Petersburg to the station. Reta paid him 10,000 rubles ($5 American) a fourth the price from the airport for twice the distance. She saw us onto the train and approved our compartment. She said, "Only deputy ministers, movie stars and certain businessmen travel in this kind of compartment." Others make do with board seats at the back of the train. With the sound of Russian music on the intercom we sped into the night headed deep into the hinterland.

The next morning Kay, Charles and a Russian named Oleg met us at the station in Nizhny Novgorod. After negotiating another Russian bus ride we arrived at their flat. It was a dismal place. The only redeeming feature was the Volga River flowing within a hundred yards. Nizhny Novgorod is the third largest city in Russia.

The next several days I lectured through an interpreter at church meetings. A number returned to the nightly meetings. One person was Natasha, a Jewess who taught English with a German accent. She insisted I be interviewed by a newly formed trading company in Nizhny that wanted to import goods from the United States.

After the meetings Kay and Charles decided to accompany us as far as Moscow on our return trip to St. Petersburg. We gathered at Natasha's apartment for a last meal of chicken and unleavened bread. It was wonderfully done and we took some with us to eat the next day. Natasha arranged for us to stay with kinsmen near Moscow. On arrival we found they moved out of their two room flat so we would have a place to stay. A sister-in-law (another Natasha) came from across the city to attend to our needs. She prepared meals in a communal kitchen and tended to Ann who was very ill from eating the day old chicken. Our every need was met.

Natasha is a scientist teaching at a local institute. Her husband, Uri, is a technician at a paint company. They took us on a sightseeing tour of a famous monastery at Zagorsk which is a Russian Orthodox religious center. When we came out the door of the monastery an old woman had a boy about eight years old by the hair violently shaking him. I commented that the old woman was sure disciplining her little boy. I was promptly informed the boy was not her son. He was a beggar encroaching on her territory. He was crying in a pitiful way. Kay and Charles went to a kiosk and bought food for him. When they got back he was rummaging in a trash bin.

Before we left we all gathered for a group photo. Natasha and Uri showered us with candy and gifts. They with a neighbor, Luba, accompanied us on the long walk to the train station carrying our luggage. Uri insisted he purchase our train tickets to Moscow. We embraced each warmly and took our leave. Never had we received such devoted attention by absolute strangers. Most Russians we met didn't have many worldly goods but they gave their utmost expecting nothing in return.

Moscow was the low point of our trip. I recall an old Englishman years ago said, "I had just as soon live in a coal mine as Moscow in the winter." It wasn't even winter and I couldn't agree more. I have seldom witnessed such filth and degradation as in the train station near Lenin Square. I've never seen so many drunks–men and women. The public toilet was like something out of Dicken–holes in the floor for both men and women. It cost 100 rubles (5 cents) for entry. The stench was so bad people staggered out holding kerchiefs over their faces. Wouldn't you know? Ann had to avail herself to the facility. Red Square and the Kremlin were anti-climatic. I just wanted to get out of there.

On the train back to St. Petersburgh a rough looking Chinese and his Russian interpreter joined us in our overnight cabin. Kay and Charlie were fit to be tied. The cabin was supposed to be for two, but as Charlie said, "This is normal for Russia." Actually, the Chinese was very courteous and the Russian quite intelligent and affable. He spoke three languages including English. We talked several hours. He said, "I can't believe I'm traveling with Americans." Ann replied, "I can't believe I'm traveling across Russia on a train."

We arrived in St. Petersburg at 5:00 a.m. Vladimir, the Russian, was determined to see us through the terminal until Reta arrived. The Chinese insisted he carry our luggage. After an hour Reta arrived. She led us through a gang of mafia cab drivers to the street. There she approached a regular checker cab.

Back at Reta's flat we relaxed. Reta fussed over Ann who was still somewhat ill. Reta fixed a murky "brew" of herbs and told Ann to "drink it right down" which she did. Her eyes teared and her head spun as it burned a path to her stomach. With quivering lips Ann exclaimed, "What was that?" The "remedy" had been heavily laced with cognac. Ann took some other pills provided by Reta's sister, Nadia, and began to mend.

Nadia was a younger copy of Reta. She stayed for dinner. Tears came easily when she spoke of the government and unjust Russian laws. After a while her fears and anxieties waned. She even smiled and laughed a couple of times. Someone said, "I like to be with Americans. They are so happy."

We waved goodbye to Reta and Nadia and negotiated customs and immigration without a problem. As our British Airways Boeing 737 rose over the Baltic Sea through a layer of clouds to where the sun always shines, I could scarcely restrain my tears as I pondered, "Will Russia ever smile again?"

A few years later Ann and Fred again went to Russia to visit Kay and Charles. Following are excerpts (condensed and edited) from Fred's account of that trip:

We were welcomed by another dreary day as we arrived in Nizhyy Novgorod. The ubiquitous "militia" guard stood by as we funnelled into a single door constructed according to Communist specifications. We were met by the ominous immigration. These unsmiling Russians spend ten to fifteen minutes perusing your papers. Customs inspected our bags and asked how much money we were bringing into the country. They released us through swinging doors to be greeted by a small group of wellwishers, including Kay and Charles. They presented Ann with a bouquet of flowers and warmly greeted Tara Lynn, an American friend of Kay's. We proceeded to the curb. An old tarp covered Russian truck came smoking out of the parking lot and stopped in front of us. Ann and I were given the seat of "honor" in the cab with the Russian driver. He could speak no English. The Russians waiting in front of the terminal recognized us as Americans expecting a limousine to collect us. They watched in amazement when we all jumped into the old truck. An old Russian woman looked horrified. I loved every minute of it.

There is a new class of people beginning to arise in Russia called "new Russians." They are usually entrepreneurs who are very wealthy either by honest or dishonest means since the fall of the Communist regime. All the way across town we were surrounded by old rusty buses belching smoke and spitting fire, laden with passengers peering through dirty windows. A pedestrian doesn't stand a chance in Russia. Even on a crosswalk. If a car or bus hits you it is your fault. You shouldn't have been there.

We made our way directly to a hotel where Ann, Tara and I had to have our visas stamped. Entry rules now require you must have your visa stamped at a hotel within three hours of arrival. Charles advised we take a shower at the hotel, a primitive affair that at least had hot water. Kay and Charles' flat was devoid of hot water that had been shut off to their section of town. It remained off throughout our stay. Water is heated at a central plant and piped underground to outlying flats.

Disembarking from the old truck the women and I squeezed into a four by four elevator with our baggage while Charles and Tara ran up the stairway to open the flat door. We pushed the ninth floor button because someone had destroyed the eighth floor button which gave access to Kay and Charles' flat. We got off at the ninth floor and walked down to the eighth floor. The apartment was guarded by two large doors, a steel implement replete with sliding steel deadbolt and a second wood door with deadbolt. We settled into quite a comfortable little flat.

We noticed right away the people looked healthier, dressed better and smelled quite a bit better. A commotion drew us the window. It was a funeral procession for an old man in an open wooden coffin followed by a small band of several horns. He was surrounded by family and friends.

In the countryside I was impressed that the country looked a lot like Texas just west of Houston only instead of pine trees there were tall slender white birch trees. I was surprised to learn Russia is filled with both small and large lakes and rivers. Potato fields were everywhere. Wheat, strawberries and other fruits and vegetables were abundant but I did not see corn. Vodka is made from potatoes that are subsidized by the State. It is cheap and adds to the woes of an already problematic society.

We visited one of the many crowded markets in town. Food and clothing were abundant. People still "hawked" their wares along the walkways but the quantity and quality are much better since our previous visit in 1994. The scent from the meat and fish stalls was disagreeable but the vegetable and flower stalls were quite pleasant.

We visited a Russian Orthodox Church surrounded by a large graveyard. I was struck by the density of the graves. A great many died in 1947. I asked our Russian friends why. They gave several explanations such as deaths from WW II, that Stalin purged the country killing more Russians than the war, and a great famine raged across Russia then.

Don't get sick in Russia. If you have to go to a dentist you must first go to an unknown pharmacy and pick up your own anesthetic and needle. If you are in the hospital you must provide your own food and linens.

A very pleasant highlight of the trip was having front row center seats for a piano performance by Vladimir Viardo, an extremely talented Russian living and teaching in America. After the concert we joined the crowd strolling along the promenade beside the Volga River. We sipped tea in a little

> cafe on the banks of the river as the evening sun slipped below the horizon.
>
> All our exit papers were in order due to Charles' experience and diligence. A rather anxious but amusing moment occurred as we passed through customs. A nervous customs man asked in broken English, "Do you speak Russian?" I replied, "Nyet." One of the three Russian words I learned while there. He began to inspect Ann's tote bag. He seized on a half-used roll of Cert mints. He turned it around and around in his hand evidently inquiring in Russian what it was. Ann tried to show him it was mints intended for your breath.
>
> All and all our trip was most enjoyable. However, I would not recommend Russia for a vacation unless you have someone in the country that knows the language and can "walk" you through. Our Russian friends insisted on giving Ann and I a party at Kay's flat. Although they can't afford much, they insist on bringing a small gift every time they come to visit. Several gifts were hand made and of excellent beauty. We now have a special section for Russian gifts in our home near Flatonia.

Over the years Ann, Fred and Bonny gradually built and expanded the storage facility as they continued to operate the specialty mail delivery service. They also built and operated a private mail boxes facility. As their business grew and became more successful Ann worked in the office.

Looking toward retirement Ann and Fred began to look for property within two hours of Houston. They found ten acres a few miles southwest of Flatonia, Texas, with a house and purchased it. The house was an old 1890's style farmhouse. It had been used for hay storage and was in terrible condition. Over the years it became a weekend refuge as they gradually restored and improved the old farmhouse. Fred wanted to give it a definite Old English cottage appearance. Ann's brother, Don, wanted them to restore it as a Texas farmhouse on the prairie. He said he would "puke in the yard" if they made it into an English cottage.

Nevertheless they restored it as an English cottage and Don didn't puke. In fact, he and his wife, Pat, helped with some of the labor to build an extension dining room to the "cottage."

One day Fred and Don went to the lumberyard to buy lumber for the rafters. Fred went into the office to buy some small items needed for the job. Don busied himself pulling pieces of lumber from the rack for the rafters. He carefully 'eye-balled' each and every piece to be sure there was no warp and they were straight. He rejected several pieces that failed his inspection. He had carefully chosen about two dozen pieces. When Fred came back he said, "Oh, no. I want the warped and crooked pieces. They give it character." Don shrugged.

Ann, Pat and Don helped Fred frame the roof. It was no easy job framing an open roof with warped and crooked pieces of lumber, but they managed it to Fred's satisfaction. The room does have a quaint 'character' with an arched ceiling and large exposed cross beams.

For a time Fred preached at the Pinehurst Church in Houston. After a while he decided he didn't want to work full time. Ann and Fred became members of the Yoakum Congregation in Yoakum, Texas. Fred preaches part time at various churches as they need him.

Deciding the mail route was too confining Ann and Fred sold it. Bonny became manager of the storage business. Ann and Fred were able to spend more time living and working at the Flatonia cottage.

Ann and Fred decided one day it would be a nice vacation to have all the family go to England on a canal trip. They contacted Kay and Charles in Russia, but only Kay was able to make the trip with them. Following are excerpts (condensed and edited) from their account of their canal vacation in England:

> We had talked for months about a "family outing" to visit England and go on a canal trip. Bonny went to England a few weeks before on business. He met the rest of us at Gatwick Airport with a rented van. We loaded up in the van and went

straight to Dolly's Pantry for a noon meal and the proverbial cup of tea. Next day we met Kay at Heathrow Airport. She flew in from Moscow. There would be five adults and three children on a fifty-six foot narrow canal boat for fourteen days. We remained berthed at the marina three days while Kay sorted out her visa situation.

Early Tuesday morning we ventured out into the River Severn, the first leg of the Avon Ring up the Stourport Canal to Birmingham, then back down the River Avon on the Grand Union Canal to Bill Shakespeare's home town of Stratford-on-Avon, thence to Evesham, Tewkesbury, and back to port at Upton on Severn. We were going to have to 'hump it' to make 150 miles at a flank speed of six miles per hour and negotiating over 100 locks.

British Waterways Board provides water points along the canals and rivers where boats can replenish their supply of fresh water. We could take on only a limited amount of water at a time. The women were constantly looking for water points. They took turns preparing aromatic meals that would waft up through the hatch to the helmsman. This aroma with the sights and sounds of the canal and pastoral countryside tended to create delusions of grandeur not easily forgotten.

On the River Severn leg all the kids were disgruntled because the locks were power operated by an attendant. "When do we get to open a lock ourselves?" they complained. The kids were all over the boat like ants. If they were on the front they wanted on the back. When on the back they wanted on the front. It was the same with the locks, back and forth from lock to boat and boat to lock. Zane lost his footing and went into the lock water. I grabbed him by the seat of his pants and pulled him on board. After twenty consecutive hand operated locks on the Stourport Canal the kids were complaining, "Do we have to open another lock?"

Since the Avon Ring stretch would take most of a day we decided to moor for the night between two locks. The lower locks were leaky and the upper locks held fast, thus the entire area between the locks drained overnight. We awoke the next morning grounded on a muddy bottom. We had to open three locks above to get enough water to float the boat.

> Birmingham awaited us on the other side of a long tunnel through the mountain. A very small light shone at the end of the two-mile tunnel. Half way through Bonny killed the engine and lights amid screams of anguish from the rest of us. Birmingham is a murky and grim industrial area with many derelict factories. A huge wharf rat scurried along a brick ledge just in front of our wake. He turned and gave us an angry stare before scurrying into an empty warehouse. In Birmingham we visited the Black Country Museum, a self-contained village of shopkeepers dressed in dated costumes of the Industrial Revolution. It was like a step back in history two hundred years. We passed through the industrial area and were soon overlooking a huge shopping mall with a monorail connected to modern office flats. We soon came to Cadbury's chocolate plant. The kids went to look but came back disillusioned because they wanted five pounds for a tour and a "free" sample.
>
> We dined the next night at a local pub. We now were dining out most evenings. We took an open upper deck bus tour of Stratford-on-Avon and visited Shakespeare's home and Ann Hathaway's cottage.
>
> We made our way downstream to Eversham, a beautiful little Cotswold village where Kay took the train to London to catch her flight to Moscow. We arrived back at our marina at Upton on Severn in time for Angela to tidy up the boat one more time. Bonny went by train to Haywards Heath in Sussex to pick up a van to take us to Tunbridge Wells for the weekend, and then to Gatwick Airport Monday. We took a less traveled road to Gatwick down leafy country byways and quiet villages as golden autumn colors bid us a grand farewell.

Ann and Fred have always had a wanderlust about them for travel. They like to visit offbeat and out of the way places. They seldom ever take the usual tourist treks to the usual tourist spots. They love the experience of meeting and getting to know people in their social and cultural environment. One such trip was to Malta in 1996. Ann and Fred made contact with a couple on the island through a mutual English friend in Tunbridge Wells. Following is Fred's account (condensed and edited) of their trip:

The Mediterranean Sea has always been a charismatic ancient center of civilization holding many mystical secrets in its memory yet to be discovered by those who venture into the soul of this wonderful world of days gone by.

As the gentle dusk of evening slowly extended its arms around this ancient sea, our flight from London descended into a ring of shimmering lights along the shoreline of the timeless island of Malta. This jewel of the Mediterranean has a long and interesting history involving many ancient people including important events in the life of the Apostle Paul.

A narrow cobblestone street led us to the home of George and Carmen, Malta natives. They had invited us to visit and stay with them in their five-story flat. It was two rooms wide with a winding stairway to the roof. They had lived there "forever", and no wonder. George said their rent was the equivalent of seventeen American dollars per month. It was located within the ruined walls of a bastion built around the 17th Century by the Knights of Malta. It reeked with Mediterranean flavor.

We were shown to our bedroom on the third floor. It was a marvelous little room with a balcony overlooking the rooftops and old church steeples of the inner city and waterfront cove. Lace curtains flowed through an open window with a gentle breeze bring-ing in the sounds and smells of this island life in this strange world.

Malta's history extends almost as far back as written records. It was a key trading port for the Phoenicians about 1000 B.C. It has been occupied by the Romans, Arabs, Turks, Spanish, French and English. Much of the Western World remembers Malta as the island upon which the Apostle Paul was shipwrecked in about 60 A.D. and he was shown "no little kindness by the barbarians" living there. St. Paul's Bay has been marked by a cross and is promoted as a tourist attraction.

George is of Greek extraction while Carmen is Maltese. I'm not sure what races are involved in the term Maltese. They showed us all hundred and twenty-two square miles of the island in an old Russian Lada automobile. It was exciting to ride with George. He approached every intersection roundabout at breakneck speed. He said that whoever got there first had the

> right of way. The only roads that got maintenance were the ones traveled by visiting celebrities.
>
> Carmen was a wonderful cook. We always drank Coca-Cola at meals which suggested the water supply wasn't the best. George teaches welding and crafts at a local polytechnical school and preaches for the church.
>
> While George was at school for the day we accompanied Carmen by bus to the Capitol City of Valletta across the bay. The bus plummeted down narrow streets at white-knuckle speed. Wiping sweat from our brows we finally disembarked at our destination. We wandered through quaint shops and stopped for tea at an outdoor cafe listening to church bells across the square. The port looked no larger than ten football fields yet an American aircraft carrier was there for several days.
>
> It still remains that the real joy of traveling is much more than just sight-seeing. If it were not, I probably would never leave home. To me, it is participation in the lives of others whom you have never met but can identify with for a short time. It is always rewarding to find those who are completely honest and open and who will not take any recompense, even for their expenses.

Ann and Fred have a passion for things English, thus they have taken several trips to visit Merry Old England and its environs. In 1998 one such trip was the result of an ill-fated plan to visit the Emerald Isle that went awry, so instead they spent a few days reminiscencing in some of their old haunts of Devon and Cornwall. They then went to Bristol where they borrowed a car from a friend and drove to Glasgow, Scotland. From there they decided to visit the Hebrides. Following is Fred's account (condensed and edited):

> We decided to visit the Hebrides, a place that has held a fascination for me ever since reading Robert Louis Stevenson's Kidnapped. I longed to witness those fabled desolate realms inhabited by the MacDonald, MacLeod, Stuart, and Campbell clans.
>
> After an enjoyable farm bed and breakfast on a hillside overlooking Loch Lomond, we left the car at the airport and

hopped a flight to Stornaway, a remote village on Lewes Island in the Outer Hebrides.

We rented a small car and ventured to the far side of the island. Black heather and stunted broom dominated the desolate moorland. Occasionally we caught a glimpse of a lonely cottage high upon the moors. None of the cottages had paint, very little brick and virtually no wood, just dull stone construction. Constant wind and rain wore the paint off unprotected buildings. The few trees were stubby, bent and gnarled.

As dusk approached we chanced to find a quaint village overlooking a quiet bay and rugged stretch of shore. We found a bed and breakfast that happened to be the home of none other than Angus MacDonald, retired seaman and more recently constable of that district. His wife, Arlene, was a sturdy and friendly woman of considerable talent. She was also a sometime constable in Stornaway. They both spoke fluent Gaelic.

After an excellent evening meal of crab cakes, vegetables and trifle we retired with Angus to a room with a great window overlooking the bay and ocean beyond. We watched the evening shadow edge its way along the rocky cliffs while each wave died among the myriad of pebbles along the beach. The sharp but pleasant scent of peat wafted through the room as it smoldered in the fireplace. Angus reminisced about the days when he was at sea. He had been around the world a number of times and had been to Houston several times. Presently, Arlene served tea with biscuits. She joked about her family being the honorable ones on the island while Angus washed up on shore after a life of crime at sea. As I gazed around this warm room filled with family remembrances of their life on this island I wouldn't trade these rare moments for a palatial suite at a posh hotel–not for a moment.

The next day, being the Lord's Day, we asked Angus where we might attend church. We attended an orthodox Church of Scotland a few miles distant as observers. That evening we went to church with Angus and his son who is a steward on a mainland ferry that docks at Stornaway.

We awoke the next morning to a steel gray sky laden with low dark billowing storm clouds amid a stiff wind. Midmorning found us at a remote tip of the island at a stone fenced graveyard. Angus directed us there to see the MacDonald family gravestones, as well as those of ancient clansmen and the occasional body washed ashore by an unforgiving sea. The gravesites were sheltered in a tiny cove amid huge cliffs overlooking the Atlantic Ocean. I pulled my heavy overcoat around my shoulders and climbed some awesome cliffs by way of an ancient pathway high above the angry waves lashing large stone islands near the shore. The cold wind tore at my coat as I gazed spellbound out to sea toward America.

That evening Angus invited us to join his family in a community sheep shearing the next day. Sheep roamed at will around the island and fences were rare. The women of each family held and sheared the sheep after the men identified and caught the ones with their mark. I had on a sweater and coat. I was cold. Angus' daughter wore a light sweater and shorts. Her legs were beet red as she kept shearing without a complaint.

As it was we stayed with Angus and Arlene the entire four days of our visit. The Hebrides, cloaked as they are by that "brooding Scottish sky" constantly purified by wind and rain, are hauntingly beautiful. I can quite understand how someone could seek spiritual solace and freedom from the riggers of modern humanity and feel they have discovered spiritual fulfillment in a place such as the Hebrides.

After nine years in Russia Kay and Charles moved to Almaty, Kazakhstan to continue work for the church. Ann and Fred had never heard of the place and did not even know where it was located on the planet. In a few months Kay and Charles invited Ann and Fred to visit, so they set about making plans and arrangements.

Kay and Charles invited us to visit, so of course Fred and I made our plans. We were to leave on September 18th. We had our tickets in hand and bags nearly packed when September 11th happened. Most of the family begged us not to go. I was in a quandary of indecision, but Fred was adamant not to be deterred by the terrorists. We set off on the appointed day and arrived in Almaty without incident.

> We were pleasantly surprised to see how progressive Almaty is. The nearby mountains are beautiful. We made several trips into the mountains and played in the snow. We seldom ever see snow where we live. We spent one day at the Grand Canyon of Kazakhstan and were within eyesight of China.
>
> A few days after we arrived the war in Afghanistan began and we were a little nervous about our return trip to the States. Charles mapped out a train route for us to take across Russia and Europe in the event we were unable to get a flight from Kazakhstan. As it turned out our flight was still operating and we arrived home safely.

After a few years with Ann's help the place in the country near Flatonia looked more and more like a little bit of the English Countryside sitting in the middle of the South Texas plains. They spent many weekends relaxing in the country and working to improve their 'get-away' in the country. Fred did all the considerable brick work and became quite an accomplished brick mason. He built an elaborate fishpond with a small Dutch-like windmill. He made a rampart sort of like one on an old English castle. It became known as "Fred's Folly." It has minimum living quarters and an upper deck where to sit and gaze across the Texas plains at the setting sun. The most recent project was a rather large aviary with live plants and places for birds to nest. The latest report is a pair of canaries hatched off at least two offsprings.

When Fred isn't busy building something he is usually busy thinking and planning what to build next. Only God and Fred knows.

In their seventies Ann and Fred retired and moved permanently to their English cottage near Flatonia. They set aside a small plot for a family cemetery. Planning ahead Fred set their headstone for their exact burial plot. Two years later they sold their storage business and property in Houston. Their only connection to Houston is now Bonny and his family.

CHAPTER 18

SAMUEL MARVIN DAVIDSON

SAMUEL "Sam" MARVIN DAVIDSON, fifth child, son of William Edmund and Mary Pauline (Roller) Davidson, was born 20 January 1932 at Oklahoma City, Oklahoma County, Oklahoma. He married Martha Rowena Vance 26 January 1952 at Bernalillo, San Doval County, New Mexico. She was born 18 December 1932 at Cogar, Caddo County, Oklahoma. Her parents were Charles and Charleen (Varney) Vance. Sam and Rowena have two children. They are:

(1) Samuel Marcus born 15 July 1953 at Oklahoma City, Oklahoma County, Oklahoma, married Cynthia Gail Gibson 21 July 1972. They have two children: Samuel Myles, born 12 March 1975; and Daryl Denton, born 25 August 1981. Myles married Marilyn McDow 18 November 2005 at the Oklahoma State Capitol.

(2) Charles Edmond born 11 March 1956 at Oklahoma City, Oklahoma County, Oklahoma; married Beverly Lanor Ingram 23 February 1980. They have two children: Ashley Elizabeth, born 9 February 1981; and Casey Edmund, born 16 October 1983. Ashley married Allen Stephenson 12 June 2004 at Wickline Methodist Church in Midwest City, Oklahoma. Casey married Laura Alice Smith 10 June 2006 at the home of his grandparents, Sam and Rowena Davidson, in Norman, Oklahoma. Casey and Laura have one child, Liam Edmund, born 26 March 2007.

Marvin was the youngest child. His parents lived at 2709 NW 40th Street, Oklahoma City, Oklahoma, when he was born. They lived there until 1935 when they moved to 3608 NW 13th Street. In 1937 they moved to the Johnson Place northwest of Moore, Oklahoma. Marvin attended the first grade at Moore. He tells about one of his earliest recollections:

> I have only a vague memory of this, but my brother, Gene, tells that one day we were all going somewhere in the old Windsor car on a sandy country road. Mom and Dad were in the front seat and the five kids were in the back seat. I was six years old.
>
> As usual there was a lot of noise and commotion in the back seat which Mom and Dad usually tuned out. All of a sudden the back door flew open and I fell out. I got a face full of sand, but even worse I saw through the swirling dust the car going away. I was terrified they would never stop and come back for me.
>
> I jumped to my feet and ran through the swirling dust toward the car that was getting farther and farther away.
>
> Gene told me that the kids were all screaming to stop, that I fell out. It was a full fifteen seconds before the realization filtered through the noise into Mom's head what had happened. Dad slammed on the brakes. Dust swirled everywhere. Dad put the car in reverse to back up. Mom screamed, "No, you'll back over him." They all jumped out of the car to go back and look for me expecting to find the worse.
>
> Gene told me that suddenly through the swirling dust they saw this little figure of me frantically running toward them crying out, "Don't leave. Come back. Don't leave. Come back."

Life at the Johnson Place was not easy. It was a small wood-frame two-room house with a lean-to on the back. The three older boys slept in the lean-to. One room was the kitchen and dining room. The other room was the bedroom for the parents, Bill and Pauline. Marvin slept in the room with his parents. Meta Lu (Ann), the only girl, slept in a small closet between the two rooms.

The state required that school age children be vaccinated prior to the start of the school year. Marvin and his siblings experienced an unusual incident on the way to get their vaccinations.

When we lived on the Johnson Place Mom was taking us five kids and the three Lagali kids in the old Windsor to Norman for our vaccination shots. As usual there was a lot of noise and commotion, especially my two older brothers who argued and fought a lot.

We had gone about five miles south on old Highway 74 when we came to a sharp ninety-degree turn to the left. Mom steered the car too close to the outer edge that had a lot of gravel. The car began to slip over the edge toward the bar ditch. She turned the steering wheel sharply to the left. This caused the car to gently slip into the bar ditch and turn over onto its side against the embankment.

Poor Mom. Here she was with eight kids in a car turned on its side in the ditch. Thankfully, a truck with four workmen stopped and helped get all us kids out. Then they did a heave ho and righted the car. One of the men drove it out of the ditch for Mom.

The rest of the trip was subdued and uneventful.

Two years later the family moved two miles south to the Turk Place. It was a larger and much nicer house though it did not have any of the modern amenities like running water or indoor bathrooms. Marvin was just a tyke. The fierce competitiveness of his older brothers was so beyond him that Marvin would often seek solace in his own small way.

When we lived on the Turk Place I was seven years old. I had three older brothers and an older sister. I had a hard time trying to keep up with them. They always seemed to take the limelight. I was just the "baby" and often teased by the others.

One day our old cat came dragging a baby ground squirrel to the house. She laid it down on the front porch as though she wanted to show off her trophy. She waited for it to move so she could play with it. I made her get away and picked up the little guy. As I held him in my hands he opened one eye and peeked at me. That melted my heart.

> I took him in the house. Mom helped me revive him and clean him up. We fed him a little milk with an eyedropper. He rallied and became a household pet.
>
> He was a cute little guy and was my special pet. He climbed around over me and ate from my hand. When the cat came in the house he would make a dash for the foot treadle on Mom's old sewing machine. He would hide under it. She had a footpad on the treadle. The cat would stand on top looking down at him but couldn't get its paws through the pad over the holes of the treadle.
>
> He was my favorite little pet all that summer, but he met a sad ending. He had learned to jump up on the buckets of skimmed milk on the back porch. We placed them there to take to the barn and mix with ground corn and wheat bran to feed the hogs. He would hang on the side of the bucket and drink the skimmed milk.
>
> One day we found him floating in a partial bucket of milk. He had leaned too far to reach the milk and fell in. He drowned. I was heart broken. Mom and I put him in an empty matchbox and buried him near the garden. I missed my little pet.

After a year at the Turk place the family moved a mile east and a quarter of a mile south to the Sullivan Place. The house wasn't an improvement over the Turk house, but it had a better barn and the entire hundred and sixty acres. It also had an old croquet set in the front yard. The older boys usually played croquet and Marvin was mostly left to be very much the spectator most of the time, except for one day.

> One day when we lived on the Sullivan Place my brother, Gene, and I were playing croquet. Being several years older than me he was able to "roquet" my ball just about any place he chose. Did he bother to "stake out" and win the game? No, he wanted to tantalize me. Every time I got set to where I could make a wicket he would "roquet" my ball out of position. He did this over and over. I became very vexed with him.
>
> The next time he bent over to "roquet" my ball I swung my mallet like a golf club and smacked him squarely in the

nose. Blood splattered. He ran to the house screaming bloody murder to tell Mom on me.

I was severely scolded and made to sit in the kitchen with Mom the rest of the day. Gene went upstairs to lay on the bed and nurse his sore nose. I had the keen satisfaction I had settled an unfair score.

Marvin was in the fifth grade when his family moved from Moore to Evening Shade, Arkansas. Marvin's older brothers did the chores and worked with their Dad on the farm. Marvin and his sister mostly stayed around the house and helped their mother as they could. Marvin had a harrowing experience while living in Arkansas.

I was about nine or ten years old when we lived in Arkansas. Grandma Davidson lived across the river from our house. She liked fish and often fished in the river to catch a few for a meal.

I heard some older boys talk about dynamiting fish. I thought I would give it a try only on a smaller scale. I twisted the fuses of four T-bomb firecrackers together and filled a large fruit jar about half full with small gravel.

My plan was to light the T-bomb fuses, drop them in the fruit jar, rapidly screw on the lid for a water-tight seal, throw the jar as far out into the river as I could and wait for it to sink a few feet under the water and explode. I would dive into the river, get the stunned fish and surprise Grandma with a mess of fish for supper.

Needless to say, my timing was off. I successfully lit the fuses, dropped the T-bombs into the jar, and tightened the lid to make it waterproof. With a hefty heave I threw it high into the air for a successful trajectory toward the water.

BOOM!! The glass jar exploded with a deafening clap of thunder nearly bursting my eardrums. Suddenly pieces of glass and gravel exploded in all directions with the speed of light about five feet in front of my face.

Both arms were still extended outward and took the first onslaught of the shattered glass and gravel. This gave me an automatic reaction to close my eyes thereby preventing

> blindness, though today I still have several tiny pieces of glass embedded in my face near my eyes.
>
> My entire frontal body took the explosive onslaught with numerous cuts and bruises. I went screaming toward the house over a hundred yards away. I was bleeding from head to toe. Grandma came tearing off the porch. She heard the explosion and my terrifying screams. When she saw me covered in blood she just knew I was dying.
>
> She got me to lay down on the porch and poured ice cold spring water over me and started the hours long process of picking the many slithers of glass and small pieces of grave from my tattered body.
>
> Fortunately, I had no real serious injuries. In those days a doctor or hospital was not anywhere within a reasonable distance. Grandma soaked me down in kerosene until the bleeding stopped. She ripped strips from clean flour sacks she was saving to make shirts and dresses. She individually bandaged my more intense cuts. Then she bound my head, arms, legs and torso with these strips.
>
> I never again tried to dynamite fish.

Marvin was in the sixth grade when the family moved back to Oklahoma City from Arkansas. He went to school at Linwood. World War II was in full force. His older brothers went to school and worked after school hours. His oldest brother, Bill, was drafted into the Navy. When Marvin was a little older he got a paper route. Gene sometimes helped with the route.

One weekend Gene took his little brother, Marvin, on an outing to Turner Falls in the Arbuckle Mountains. They swam in the pool under the falls and climbed the rocks beside the falls to dive into the clear cool water of Honey Creek. The last day they climbed to the top of the tallest peak downstream from the falls. The view was magnificent with an unobstructed view of old Highway 77 winding through the mountains next to Honey Creek. Gene and Sam decided to build a monument atop the peak. They worked all afternoon stacking a rock pyramid about six feet high. For years afterwards their rock pyramid was visible from the highway far below.

In 1946 Marvin's three older brothers were in the military. Marvin and his sister, Meta Lu (Ann), were the only ones at home with their Mom and Dad. They and Meta Lu (Ann) worked. Marvin was fourteen years old and had much too much unsupervised idle time on his hands. He fell in with a group of boys that resulted in him getting into trouble. He was sent to a training school for errant boys.

Samuel Marvin Davidson - age 15

It wasn't long before Marvin realized the training school was not the best of environments and he had trouble adjusting. His solution was to get away and join the Navy at age fifteen. He took basic training at San Diego. Afterwards he was assigned to the destroyer USS-Hollister. He also served on the destroyers USS-Orlick and USS-Gerke.

Marvin occasionally corresponded with his brother, Gene, while he was in the Army serving on Occupation Duty in Japan with the 11th Airborne Division. By then Gene was going by his first name, Don. This was according to military protocol (last name, first name, middle initial). Marvin also was going by his first name, Sam.

Sam's ship put in to Yokahoma for a couple of weeks. Don arranged with his commanding officer to write a letter to Sam's ship captain stating that his unit would provide quarters and meals for Sam to take leave and visit Don at Camp Schimmelpfennig near Sendai where he was stationed.

Don was a buck sergeant and the battalion Recreation NCO. He was in charge of all the company day rooms, recreational facilities, and organizer of sports and competitive events such as ping-pong and table pool tournaments for the troops. He was also permanent CQ (charge of quarters) for the battalion headquarters and was allowed to have his own private quarters in the headquarters building. Don moved a bunk bed into his room and Sam lived there for the week. They took their meals in the Headquarters Company mess hall. Sam in his Navy outfit caused quite a sensation in the mess hall and around the general camp area.

It was around Christmas time when Sam visited Don. In keeping with the holiday spirit they both decided that since neither had ever been drunk to do so. Don paid fifty dollars for a fifth of bootleg whiskey from the Officers' Club. They both got sick and threw up before they got drunk. They decided that wasn't a fun thing to do.

Sam returned to Yokahoma and his ship. Early in 1949 the 11th Airborne Division was ordered back to the states. Shortly thereafter Don was discharged and took up civilian life while Sam continued in the Navy.

In the summer of 1950 the Korean Conflict broke out. Sam was serving on the USS Gerke. The Americans entered the conflict in the fall of 1950 and pushed the North Koreans back to the Yalu River. At this point China entered the fray and thousands of Chinese troops came pouring across the Yalu River. Many American troops were cut off from escape to the south. Their only chance was to retreat and be rescued from the beaches of North Korea.

The USS Gerke was one of many Navy ships covering this retreat with naval bombardment. Sam was working near one of the gun mounts when it prematurely exploded killing the gunners inside the mount and severely injuring several, including Sam, outside the mount. He was treated and transported to the hospital at San Diego.

Sam's Mom went to San Diego to visit him in the hospital. It was then revealed that he had fraudulently entered the Navy, but by then he was eighteen and of legal age for military service. He received an honorable medical discharge.

Shortly after Sam got out of the Navy he bought a Harley-Davidson motorcycle. He got a job with a drugstore delivering prescriptions and anything else they had to be delivered.

> Don, was in college at Oklahoma A&M. He was out of school for the summer and working part-time in Oklahoma City. One day after work I went by to see him. I badgered him into taking a ride with me on my Harley. He finally got on behind me. I took off going kind of fast. I took corners so fast we had to lean in sharply to go around the corners. Don was yelling to get off. I had a great time putting a little fear into him.
>
> When we got back Don got off and said, "I'm never getting on one of those things again, especially behind you."

> My Harley was not in the best of condition. I was having a problem with the gearshift. It would not shift smoothly and I had to jiggle it to make it shift. One day I was west bound on NW 23rd Street. I stopped for a red light at Classen Boulevard. The light turned green and I took off. The gearshift handle stuck. I looked down to jiggle it to make it shift. It shifted and I looked up to see a sedan automobile crossing the street right in front of me. I did not have time to react. I smashed into the left rear of the car. The impact catapulted me over the back of the car landing me on the pavement on the other side. This occurred right in front of the Smith-Kernke Funeral Home. Some of the guys I knew worked there. They came rushing out to see what happened only to see me laying unconscious in the middle of the street. They thought I was dead.
>
> An ambulance was summoned and I was taken to the hospital. When I finally came around the first thing I said was, "Get rid of that motorcycle." I never got on one again.

In January 1952 Sam and Rowena Vance were married. They have differing accounts of how it was they first met. This is Sam's version:

> I first saw Rowena when I was home on leave in 1950 at the Melton Drug Store at 14th and Portland. This was a block from my parent's home. She worked part-time as a soda-jerk while finishing high school.

This is Rowena's account of their first meeting and consequent romance:

> Sam's father frequently visited the store for cigarettes, ice cream or a cup of coffee. He would tell me of his sons that were not married. One day he told me he had only one son left unmarried.
>
> I first saw Sam when he and his sister came into the drug store. Sam's sister was dating Fred, the son of the storeowner. Sam walked up to me, placed his arm around my shoulders,

and told his sister, "This is the girl I am going to marry." I was surprised because I had never seen him before.

I had heard a lot about Sammy from Mr. and Mrs. Melton, his sister, and his father. He was a very good looking fellow; however I was not particularly impressed or excited because he had a mustache, and I had heard about SAILORS.

It was the following year in May before I saw Sam again. He was working on a car with his now brother-in-law, Fred, in front of the drug store when I walked by to go to work. I had on a special dress I had worn to my senior high school graduation luncheon. He came into the store and asked me for a date, which I accepted. The date is an old argument between Sam and me. I say it was May 9th, and he says it was May 11th. We went to a drive-in movie at the Northwest Drive-In and saw a double feature. We don't remember the first movie, but the second movie was "Ma and Pa Kettle on the Farm." During the movie we saw a large fire several miles away. It was later we learned it was the Baptist Church a block away on the street where Sam lived.

January of 1952 over a weekend Sam and I eloped to Albuquerque, New Mexico. We had planned to elope the weekend before, however Sam informed me that we had to wait another week because he was not of age. This really surprised me because he had served three years in the Navy, and you had to be seventeen years old to join. I had never asked him how old he was, but figured he was nineteen or twenty years old.

Sam explained:

Actually I had never told Rowena I joined the Navy right after my fifteenth birthday. The minimum age to join the Navy was seventeen with your parents' approval. My father and mother falsified a birth date in a family bible which was acceptable at that time in the Navy recruiting office. So, at age fifteen I became seventeen and after three years in the Navy I was still only twenty years old by any acceptable legal document. Every document left me a year short. Rowena was nineteen and of legal age, but I was still one year short. In Oklahoma a male had to be twenty-one years of age to get married.

Rowena continued:

> We wanted a small church wedding. However, there were several things that made us reconsider. First, my parents were divorced and both remarried. I could not begin to think of their meeting at my wedding. There were still very bad feelings between my stepmother and mother, and between my stepfather and father. There also was the financial factor. We knew our parents were not in a position to assist us. We made the decision to visit my favorite uncle in Albuquerque, and get married there. New Mexico did not require a blood test or the three-day waiting period.
>
> The courthouse was closed on Saturday so my Uncle Floyd telephoned a neighboring county (Bernilio) to find an open courthouse. We obtained our license, and inquired about a Justice of the Peace to marry us. The clerk informed us he was a J.P. and could marry us. He was Hispanic, could speak very little English, had a bandage over one eye, and several bruises over most of his visible body. We understood very little of the ceremony, but when he finished he asked for sixteen dollars. Sam asked him if he meant pesos. He answered, "Dollars." We left Oklahoma City with only sixty dollars so this left a big hole in our pocket.
>
> My aunt was a Seventh Day Adventist and would not prepare or eat meat. Uncle Floyd took us to a diner for a fried chicken dinner. When we returned to their house we had a small cake and fruit punch for the four of us.
>
> Early Sunday morning we started back to Oklahoma City. There were times on long hills when Sam would coast for as long as he could to save gas. There were times we were sure we would not make it back home. We returned home with only sixty cents in our pockets.

While Sam and Rowena were dating and during their early marriage Rowena dreaded going to Sam's parent's house for family gatherings. When everyone was there with their spouses the house was overflowing with about twelve people. Sooner or later an argument would start.

> It didn't have to be about anything serious. In fact, most of the time it was about which was the best–Fords or Chevys. I don't think it made much difference. The two older brothers were always on the opposite sides of the argument. The others would enter just to keep the argument going. I never told Sam my feelings until after we were married.
>
> Today at our house when a discussion becomes an argument I likely will say I personally like Fords. Everyone laughs because the discussion was about something completely different. They have all heard my stories.

After a few months of marriage Sam and Rowena began to discuss the building of a house. They liked the idea of building their own home. Rowena's mother gave them an acre of land that faced the street and was adjacent to her five acres. They started very slowly paying for materials as they could. Rowena helped with this endeavor.

> We dug the foundation and poured the floor. Sam finished the concrete. We poured the floor in sections so we could pay for it after each payday, and the sections were easier for Sam to finish. The walls were concrete blocks. They were very heavy weighing forty-eight pounds each. My job was to hand the blocks up to Sam and mix the mortar to keep Sam supplied as he laid the blocks. I was pregnant with our first child at the time. We have joked that was why our son looked like a football player when he was born.
>
> As soon as we had enough of an apartment finished we moved in. We didn't have running water so we ran a garden hose from mother's house. After dark we went behind the house to take a shower in cold water. It was our plan to build a double garage with an apartment behind, and when we finished that phase we would build a house.
>
> While we were building our garage apartment Sam's grandfather Davidson visited for several days. He helped with the block walls. He told us stories about his life. This was shortly after Sputnik. His feeling was, "If God meant for us to fly he would have made us with wings."

> Sam worked the late shift that ended at ten o'clock at night. Pay days he went by the concrete block company and bought enough blocks to fill the trunk of the car. That made the back of the car ride very low. This was during probation in Oklahoma. One night the cops thought they had a bootlegger. They stopped Sam and made him unload all the blocks so they were satisfied there was no moonshine or illegal alcohol. They drove away and left Sam in the dark to re-load all the blocks.

When Sam and Rowena were first married they had limited funds for recreation. One of their favorite getaways was to camp out for the weekend in the Wichita Wild Life Refuge. They would leave home as soon as they could after work. It was usually after dark when they arrived at the park. Rowena fixed sandwiches which they ate on the way and did not need to prepare supper. They set up the army style cots and quickly settled down for the night. On one such occasion they awoke in the night to strange noises.

> There stood the biggest buffalo I ever saw. He was very close to the front of the car. I quickly woke Sam. He used the flashlight to shine in the buffalo's eyes. He slowly ambled away and we went back to sleep only to awaken again by the strange noise. This time we were surrounded by a herd of buffalo. I definitely was afraid though the buffalo were not making threatening moves. Sam shined the flashlight on them and they ambled away to another nearby campsite. The campers threw fire sticks from their campfire at the buffalo. It was sort of amusing as we imagined what was happening.
>
> The next day we drove to the top of Mount Scott and had a picnic. We left the car doors open to listen to music on the radio. We ran the battery down and engaged the help of some other campers to give us a push downhill to start the car.
>
> The last time we went to the park we saw a herd of elk about a quarter of a mile away near some trees. Sam set out with his camera. A short distance and Sam realized there was a swamp area between him and the elk. He waded in sinking to his knees but that did not deter him. As he approached the elk made threatening moves and Sam ran for the trees.

Sam went to Classen to finish his high school education. He played football and was a member of the 1953 graduating class. That fall he enrolled at Oklahoma A&M in Stillwater, Oklahoma. The first semester he lived with Don and his wife, Pat, in their apartment at 910 McElroy Street. The next spring semester Rowena and their newborn son, Marc, joined Sam at Stillwater. Rowena enrolled at Oklahoma A&M and later obtained a degree in Dietary Science. They rented a house north of the campus. It was a real struggle to just get by with both in school the same time.

> Professor Baugh was my economics teacher. Don had several under graduate courses under his tutelage and had spoke highly of him. One evening Rowena and I invited Professor Baugh to have dinner with us and Don. It was an interesting evening. Professor Baugh and Don had a great time reminiscing about their teacher-student relationship.

The first job Sam had when he finished college was with Wilson meat packing company in Oklahoma City. He had taken some courses in time and motion study and was hired as a junior time and motion study engineer. Only in the meat packing business time and motion studies functioned in reverse as the animal is disassembled.

> One day I got permission from management to take my brother, Don, on a tour of the plant. I took him to the Hog Kill. The hogs were herded into a pen about twenty feet square. There was a big 'bull wheel' on one side of the pen. It was about fifteen feet in diameter. It had evenly spaced hooks about every four feet.
>
> Two black men were in the pen with the hogs. They were Shankers. They shanked (snared) the hogs by the right hind leg with a hook that had a chain and O-ring attached. As the bull wheel turned around they slipped the O-rings onto one of the hooks. This yanked the squealing hogs up as it rotated to the top. There the hooked O-rings automatically transferred to a

> hook on a double wheel transport mechanism on a downward sloping rail.
>
> The hogs were hanging head down over a trough slowly rolling down the line to the Stickers. They were workers with long sharp knives. They stuck the hogs and severed the main artery in the neck. The hogs bled to death draining blood into the trough to be used for commercial purposes. The saying, "They use everything but the squeal," was never more true.

Sam always had a creative spirit. The job at the meat packing company was mundane and the company culture had little room for creativity. One day Sam suggested to one of the supervisors a way to try an innovation to improve the efficiency of the operation. The supervisor asked, "What for?" Sam replied to make the operation easier and more efficient. The supervisor's caustic reply was that the workers had already found the easiest way to do their jobs. Sam soon left after that.

Sam then went to work for Brown Optical Company as a traveling salesman. He thought that would lend itself to a form of individual creativity with sales presentations and without pre-conceived notions of what was effective and what was not.

After a year selling optics Sam decided that was not his "cup of tea." The company sales manual left little room for innovation and the supervision was overly "hawkish." He wanted to use his creative bent to make things. So, he started a swimming pool construction business. This way he could do it his way. If he succeeded or failed it was his own doing. One of his early experiences building pools was a real shocker.

> I was just getting started in the business of building swimming pools. It was 1960 and backyard swimming pools were a rare novelty in Oklahoma City. Only the most prestigious and expensive homes in Nichols Hills had backyard swimming pools. It was a struggle just to get started and build a few pools so I had some to show to prospective buyers.

> One day I was giving a man my best sales pitch. He asked if we could go look at a pool I had built. I told him we could. There was one not far away.
>
> We jumped in my car and drove to an address about a mile where I had built my second pool. No one answered when I rang the doorbell. I told the prospective customer that I was sure they would not care if we looked at the pool in the backyard.
>
> The yard had a high stockade fence. I opened the gate and we walked in. There was no pool. I was astonished. I thought, "Good grief. I've gone to the wrong address." I double-checked the address. It was correct. All this time the customer was looking more and more suspicious of me and my motives. I assured him I had built a pool in that backyard. I did not know what happened. He looked at me with a suspiciously jaundiced eye that said, "Yeah, sure. And I'm Superman." Needless to say, I did not make the sale.
>
> I could not wait to find out what happened. I went back to the house and waited until the man came home. He said he had the pool filled in and grass turf laid over it. I asked, "Why?" He said, "Because my life was no longer my life. All kinds of people at all hours of the day showed up to swim in the pool. One Sunday morning I was sitting in the family room in my underwear reading the paper when four people I did not know paraded through the room and out to the pool. That was it. The next morning I called a dirt contractor."

Sam continued in the swimming pool construction business and at one time was the largest builder in the Oklahoma City area. Sons, Marc and Chuck, and Chuck's wife, Beverly, also worked in the business for several years.

Sam was very good with creative design and state-of-the-art construction techniques for swimming pools, but lacked a little in business acumen. His brother, Don, on two different occasions spent several days doing business audits of Sam's business. The result of one such audit revealed that Sam's superintendent of construction was taking inventory from the warehouse to build pools on the side in competition with Sam, his employer.

Rowena worked awhile at the Anna Maude Cafeteria in downtown Oklahoma City as manager. She later became the managing dietician at the Midwest City Hospital and later the Head Dietician. She worked there until her retirement in 2001. Over the years she visited China and Australia as a member of a delegation of visiting dieticians.

In 1959 Sam and Rowena took their first family vacation with the two boys, Marc and Chuck. Their destination was Yellowstone National Park. They had two weeks and a budget of two hundred dollars. They had a 1959 Edsel station wagon. Since they had most of the camping equipment the plan was to sleep in the station wagon.

The first night they spent at the home of Sam's oldest brother, Bill, in Liberal, Kansas. The next night they camped in San Isabell National Forest west of Pueblo, Colorado, as described by Rowena.

> We found a pavilion with two tables and a campsite, primitive and very isolated. There were no other campers. We were completely surrounded by tall pine trees. When the wind blew through them it made such a wonderful sound. As darkness set in it got a little scary. As the years passed that sound became very special to us and we planted thirty pine trees at our home in Norman.
>
> The next morning Marc and Chuck ran around and helped Sam gather firewood. We cooked a large breakfast. Perhaps it was the mountain air but one item became a favorite every time we camped. I heated oil in a small pan. The boys poked their fingers through store bought canned biscuits. We dropped the doughnut looking biscuits into the hot oil. When done the boys rolled them in sugar and cinnamon. They were great when hot, but not so tasty when cold.
>
> After breakfast Sam and the boys built a rock dam in a small stream next to our campsite. This became another tradition at our camp outings. We always looked for campsites near small streams.

Next Sam and family went to Colorado Springs. After seeing all the attractions there they camped at the Garden of the Gods campgrounds that night. The boys fed crackers to the chipmunks.

The next day they went to Yellowstone. They stopped at West Thumb for a break. The facilities were rather primitive. When Marc opened the door to leave a bear was sitting near the door.

> We had been watching the bear waiting for Marc to open the door. His eyes were as big as silver dollars. He looked at the bear and the bear looked at him. Marc didn't know what to do. He just stood there frozen. After a few minutes the bear ambled away and Marc ran for the car keeping a sharp eye on the bear all the way.

They found a more modern camp ground with pine trees for the night. They slept in the station wagon. They covered air mattresses with blankets. Marc slept in the front seat, Sam and Rowena slept behind the front seat with Chuck at their feet. Sleeper, the dog, slept on the front floorboard. It snowed that night, the Fourth of July.

While driving in the park they saw two cub bears beside the road and stopped to look and take pictures. They didn't see the mother bear. Sam started the car slowly forward only to have the mother bear rear up and place her paws on the open window on Sam's side. Her nose was about twelve inches from his face. He was very concerned. Rowena continued to take pictures of Sam and the bear. They slowly rolled forward as the bear held on and walked beside the car. Finally some cars from the other direction honked and the mother bear turned loose and walked away with her cubs.

The next afternoon a fellow camper gave Rowena some trout to cook for supper. Sam and the boys went to service the car while Rowena cooked supper. She rolled the trout in corn meal and put the trout in a skillet of hot oil. This almost immediately attracted a bear. It wanted the fish. Rowena was determined not to let it have the fish. They circled the table several times with Rowena carrying the skillet but the bear was gaining on her. A fellow camper saw Rowena's dilemma and came running with a bucket and broom.

He beat the bucket and hollered. Several other campers joined in to make noise. The bear finally ran away. The fellow that gave them the fish angrily said to Rowena, "Lady, give the damn fish to the bear. I have more I can give you." Sleeper, the dog, was tied to a tree. He didn't even bark. He just peeked around the tree.

They decided to store the ice chest with food items on top of the station wagon to keep it from the bears. They slept in the car to be safe from the bears. During the night they woke up. The station wagon was shaking violently. Sam thought it was an earthquake. He opened the car door only to jump back into the car and slam the door shut. A bear was on top of the car helping itself to the contents of the ice chest. Sam beat on the window and the top of the car. The bear finally left.

Sam and Rowena's boys, Marc and Chuck, attended the Midwest City Schools. They played youth sports. Marc played football in highschool while Chuck was on the high school wrestling team.

Sam has a great flair and taste for fine art and collectibles. He and Rowena have collected several pieces of fine art. He particularly likes eagles. He bought a number of prints of eagles by Ted Blalock, a noted painter of eagles in action. He also collected fine statuettes of eagles in bronze, crystal, and gemstone. They also collected original paintings and scrimshaw. Rowena did quilting and made some beautiful quilts.

Sam also has a penchant for writing tidbits of insightful wisdom. In June 1975 he wrote:

> Knowledge is a servant to those...to those, who seek it... and serves them well, who understand how to judiciously, with solicitude, apply it.

July 1980 he wrote:

> That's What Life is All About: You are deserving of the best possible life that you can achieve for yourself. Do it! Learn patience, dedication to purpose, a positive attitude, the skill of

achieving, the fortitude to never give up, the energy to prevail, the knowledge to seek knowledge, the ability to accept life's little gifts graciously, the warm feeling and the joy of happiness in giving the gifts of knowledge.

To which his brother, Don, replied in December 1995: "The only problem is it takes sixty years of living to learn all this." In October 1995 Sam wrote this to his Aunt Elsie Runyon:

> Ecstatic Love: This love I dream about...
> A lovely woman dreams of
> Promises...possibilities...fantasies.
> Ardently entwined in love, now is the time...
> This is our moment into eternity.
> Inamorata, intenerate, fervent, intense desire.
> Ecstatic Love together my darling at last.
> We are much more ardor
> Than we were ever, ever before.
> Love's reward is love itself !
> Never let it go...Love...without saying so...Love.
> Love reassured is love everlasting...Love.
> Rhythm of Love sings its song...Love

April 4, 2006, Sam wrote: "I am amazing. January 20, 2040, at midnight I shall leave this worldly earth to join the Universe at 107 years of age. After a trillion times a trillion times a trillion there shall never be another person exactly like me. Now, that's AMAZING!!"

Sam wrote this epistle of worry in 2005:

> I worry about all my family, my darling wife and her family, my two very great sons and my two wonderful daughters-in-laws and their families, and all my lovely grandchildren. I worry about my health and my family's health. I worry about the medical profession being able to take care of us as individual persons. I worry about clean air because I have asthma. I worry that the government doesn't see fit to build a medical

research facility on the order of the National Space Agency. I worry about whether the national health system is capable to provide adequate health for everyone. I worry about the Social Security and Medicare systems running out of money. I worry about lawyers getting super rich with multi-million dollar verdicts. I worry about we, the people, who end up paying for these lawyers' windfalls with higher prices on our products. I worry about my banker approving my next loan. I worry about how high taxes are going to go. I worry about the economy, and who will control inflation and/or deflation. I worry about all the fees being tacked onto all of our bills. I worry about the stock market as I depend on it for my living. I worry about my dogs running off and not coming home. I worry about the honesty and capability of our business and government leaders. I worry about who is setting the proper examples for our future leaders. I worry about what kind of leaders we will have for our future. I worry that they will be willing and capable to accomplish the necessary tasks. I worry about computers and cell phones taking away the human to human touch and contact. I worry about becoming a nation of unemotional robots. I worry about solar energy. I worry about will solar energy be in abundant supply before the earth runs out of energy? I worry about the progress of education that never seems to make the grade. I worry about professors not teaching both sides of the whole subject. I worry about the political parties and whether they can set aside their egos and differences to pass laws for the true benefit of the people. I worry about Congress giving away so much money on frivolous waste and programs. I worry about the security of our borders. I worry about illegal immigration. I worry about who we allow into this country. I worry about how our forefathers went to great pains to select the finest from around the world to build this into a great nation. I worry that this nation of people is being rapidly downgraded. I worry about my grandchildren and great-grandchildren being a minority. I worry about the children no longer being able to enjoy a United States of America that I have been able to enjoy for seventy-three years. I worry about being able to live the next thirty years in the home I built for my wife, myself and my family. I worry about

> the weather, the extreme hot and cold, dry and wet. I worry about living in Oklahoma that has one hundred miles per hour straight winds and over three hundred miles per hour tornadoes. I worry about staying alive during a tornado. I worry about the Oklahoma Sooners football team wining another national championship. I worry about road rage and the effect it has on people. I worry about the dangers of automobiles and the indifference of people to the thousands of lives lost every year in accidents. I worry that the next automobile I see will send me to my Maker. I worry that our leaders no longer value our lives. I worry about gangs that run rampant, kill and destroy everything in their path. I worry that this is the future for America. I worry that the news media no longer takes the time and effort to inform the people of the true story. I worry that we are misled on important subjects that affect our individual lives. I worry about the world being capable of ample amative relationships. I worry that hate is overcoming love of fellow man. I worry that the United States of America and the world are being overrun with hate. I worry that our leaders and governments no longer have the best interest of the people. I worry that the people no longer have the interest or desire to take the time and effort to direct our leaders and governments in the right and proper directions to benefit the people. I worry that this nation, the United States of America, will fall into and become a third world nation. I worry that I, Samuel M. Davidson, only hope that I am not here on this earth to see it happen.

Sam's brother, Don, replied, "Wow, Sam, you sure have a lot to worry about. When you worry about something over which you have no control, you have assumed a heavy burden God never intended for you to have."

APPENDIXES

APPENDIX I

WILLIAM EDMUND "Bill"

DAVIDSON Family Lineage - 2007

WILLIAM EDMUND DAVIDSON (1901 - 2005)
Mary Pauline Roller (1905 - 1988)
1.0. WILLIAM LEE DAVIDSON
•Mary Elizabeth Grisham
1.1. Johnny Lee Davidson
+Margaret Rosemary Brewer
1.1.1. Isabella ELizabeth Faye Davidson
1.2. Jimmy Lynn Davidson
®Ruth Elaine Frederick (1st spouse)
1.2.1. Brandie Dawn Davidson
+Eldon Dewayne Reynolds
1.2.l. 1. Katherine Rachelle Reynolds
1.2.1.2. Felicity Nicole Reynolds
1.2.1.3. Sydney Deanna Reynolds
1.2.1.4. Mattie-Bell Elain Reynolds
1.2.2. Joshua Dean Davidson
+Mindy Holbrook
+ Pat Crittenden (2nd spouse - no issue)
1.3 •Joseph Allen Davidson (no issue)
1.4. Deborah Jean Davidson
®Don Horton (1st spouse)
1.4.1. Angela Marie Horton
+Brian Chad Whitley
1.4.1.1. Nathanial W. Whitley
1.4.1.2. Anna-Kate Carsyn Whitley
®Kevin Holt (2nd spouse)

1.4.2. Julian Carl Holt
• Amy Renee Lynn Cunningham (1st spouse)
1.4.2.1. Aspen Jacob Holt
1.4.2.2. Ashland Kai Holt
+Amy Holliday (2nd spouse - no issue)
*Regan Holliday (stepchild)
+Randy Schmitzer (3rd spouse - no issue)

2.0. •ROBERT JOE DAVIDSON
®•Dorothy Jean White (1st spouse)
2.1. Paula Jean Davidson
®John Luther Ford (1st spouse)
2.1.1. John Jason Ford
+Margaret Elizabeth Walmer
2.1.1.1. Taylor Cole Ford
2.1.1.2. Brittany Layne Ford
2.1.2. Nicole Jean Ford
®Christopher Even Michael Brown
2.1.2.1. •Jamie Christopher Brown (infant)
®Gary Lynch (2nd spouse - no issue)
2.2. Steven Joe Davidson
®Shelia Rosaline (Husinka) Gallant (1st spouse)
2.2.1. Stefanie J. Davidson
+Kenneth Nicky Malone
2.2.1.1. Madelyn Jean Malone
2.2.1.2. Conner Jet Malone
®Terri Gay Gilbreath (2nd spouse)
2.2.2. Scott Joseph Davidson
#Brandy Mann
2.2.2.1. Sylar Jacoby Davidson
+Janet Jessalie Redman (3rd spouse)
2.2.3. Sara Jessalie Davidson
2.2.4. Shannon Joy Davidson
Bonnie Mae Craddock (2nd spouse - no issue)
2.3 David Eldon (Fleshman) Davidson (Bonnie's son by previous marriage. Adopted by Robert Joe Davidson.)
®Sherry (unknown)
2.3.1. Michael Davidson (adopted)
2.3.2. Amanda Davidson

3.0. DONALD GENE DAVIDSON
+ Patricia Sue Paschall
3.1. Gregory Scott Davidson
+Donna Elva Garcia
3.3.4. Mary Grace Davidson (adopted)

4.0. ANN LUVIDA DAVIDSON
+Carl Frederick Melton
4.1. Sheril Kay Melton
® Christopher Allen Vaughn (1st spouse)
4.1.1. Honey Ann Vaughn
®William Howell
4.1.1.1. Lacey Howell
4.1.1.2. William Howell III
4.1.2. Julie Lynn Vaughn
+Jonathan Cliffton Blair
4.1.2.1. Leigh Ann Blair
4.1.2.2. Lyndsey Nicole Blair
4.1.2.3. Savannah Grace Blair
4.1.2.4. Vaughn Cliffton Blair
4.1.3. Roman Christopher Vaughn
+Shannon Nicole Agee
4.1.3.1. Kayla Marie Vaughn
4.1.3.2. Ryleigh Christine Vaughn
4.1.4. Heather Lee Vaughn
+Michael Gary Smith
4.1.4.1. Michael Gabriel Smith
4.1.4.2. Shepard Lee Smith
4.1.4.3. Melody Grace Smith
+Charles Lynn Gant (2nd spouse - no issue)
4.2. Randy Gene Melton
®Donna Jean Shelton (1st spouse)
4.2.1. Culley Brant (Melton) Turner **
+Aimee Renee Campbell
4.2.1.1. Braden Culley Turner
4.2.1.2. Chanden Brant Turner
+Pamela Gwinn Gorden (2nd spouse)
4.2.2. Randy Shane Melton
®Felicia Ann Kemp
*Kimberly (Felicia's by previous marriage.)
*Tricia (Felicia's by previous marriage.)

4.2.3. Shanna Gwinn Melton
4.3. Bonny Len Melton
+Angela Yvetta Hutchison
4.3.1. Xanthea Leigh Melton
+Steven Wesley Camp
4.3.1.1. Xayda Elaine Camp
4.3.2. Zane Pierce Melton
+Julie Christine Phelps
3.3.3. Zara Jill Melton
+Christopher Cecil

5.0. SAMUEL MARVIN DAVIDSON
+Martha Rowena Vance
5.1. Samuel Marc Davidson
+Cynthia Gail Gibson
5.1.1. Samuel Myles Davidson
+Marilyn McDow
5.1.2. Daryl Denton Davidson
5.2. Charles Edmund Davidson
+ Beverly Lanor Ingram
5.2.1. Ashley Elizabeth Davidson
+Allen Wayne Stephenson
5.2.1.1. Isaac Allen Stephenson
5.2.2. Casey Edmund Davidson
+Laura Alice Smith
5.2.2.1. Liam Edmund Davidson

• Deceased
+ Current Spouse
® Divorced
* Stepchild
**Adopted by Stepfather
Significant Other

APPENDIX 2

META PAULINE CLARKE'S JOURNAL

Farina, Illinois to Hardy, Arkansas

Following is a transcription of the original handwritten journal kept by Meta Pauline Clarke when the Edmund Stillman Clarke Family moved by covered wagon from Farina, Illinois, to Hardy, Arkansas, in the Fall of 1897–a distance of about 350 miles. She was twenty years old. The journal was transcribed as nearly as possible as it was written, including misspelled words, misuse of grammar, abbreviations, etc.

Meta's grandson, Donald Gene "Don" Davidson, transcribed her journal years ago from the original. For years Don and his wife, Pat, kept Meta's original handwritten journal readily available on a coffee table in their home for anyone who wanted to read it trusting it would be treated with respect and kept in its proper place. Unfortunately, not so.

In 1996 Pat and Don hosted a 95th birthday party for William Edmund "Bill" Davidson, Meta's son, at their home for friends and family members. All five of Bill's children attended with their spouses, as did numerous grandchildren with their spouses, and great grandchildren.

The Journal was in its usual place on the coffee table in the family room. A few days after the party Pat and Don missed the Journal. They turned their house upside down over the next several days searching for it. They never found it. Paula (Davidson)

Lynch, Bill's granddaughter, said she read part of it the day of the birthday party. That is the last we know of it. Thankfully, years ago Don made a Xerox copy and had previously transcribed it.

JOURNAL OF TRIP FROM ILL. TO ARK.

Oct. 20, 1897. Left Farina, Ill. at 7:30 o'clock, this Wednesday morning just 16 years from the time of entering that place from Westerly, R.I. We had such a time starting, the horses were young and not used to pulling. They jumped around, and threw themselves, breaking their harnesses, but soon got started; at nine o'clock passed through Kinmandy, and waited on hill south of there for John Metzger, wife and little Eva to join us. Just before reaching Alma, went off a bridge into a chuck hole, and broke the feed box off and had to stop to patch up. Passed through Alma, went four miles and stopped for dinner. Reached Salem at half past three. Stopped a while to buy a few things, then went south about four miles and by half past four camped for the night in a pasture full of cows. (Morning) Last night Rubie set a bucket of water in back part of tent. Father did not know it and about half past eleven thought he heard cows around the tent. Went to raise the corner to look out and tipped water all in his bed. He hates cold water and such a laugh as we had.

Oct. 21. Left camp at 7:20 o'clock and by 11:15 o'clock reached Dix, a small pretty town build on rolling ground. Soon after passing through Dix came to, and passed under, a large stone railroad bridge, just being built. Went a mile and stopped for dinner. By half after three reached Mt. Vernon, where we waited an hour to buy corn and hay. Then drove one mile south of Mt. V. and camped for the night in a grove of gum trees. Had music and such a noisy crowd camped a little below us. To day have driven over hills and through woods.

Oct. 22. Left camping ground, went south for eight miles, came to a small town called Pleasant Hill. Such a delapidated town. So many houses with no one to inhabit them. Went a mile south, and camped for dinner. Then went seven miles, and came to Old Ewing, only a small place, store buildings used as dwelling houses. Near was a field of a hundred and twenty acres in which was about seventy-five head of mules. About a half a mile farther south came to New Ewing, a good sized place with two school houses (boys and girls), a large church, and several very good stores. A couple girls in front of school house said “How do you Do”. I guess they thought we would be glad to have some one speak to us, but they got no answer. We stopped at a harness shop to get a straight bit for horse, were just opposite to a blacksmith shop, and I heard some one say “Those are darn pretty horses”, so I put my head out the back of wagon to see what he looked like, when I met the eyes of a good looking young man with two small children (boy 4 and girl 3). When he saw me he said, “Well, that’s a darn pretty girl”, and I said I thought he was a darn married man. Tonight we are camped in woods seven miles south of New Ewing.

Oct. 23. We were up early and about five o’clock. While I was getting breakfast, a young fellow from New Ewing drove up with a load of apples, and asked if we were a going to light a fire yet–said his feet were cold and he wanted to warm. We had a tent stove up and he came in to warm, said he was looking for a out door camp fire, not such a cozy stove. Asked where we were from and when told, said he knew the band boys at Farina, (he was an Ewing band boy), but when told that father was one of the boys said he never would have known him without his uniform on. Gave us lot of apples. Had breakfast and left camp by 7:30. Went seven miles and reached Benton at 9:05 o’clock. Stopped in center of the town to get water, but such hard puckery water. It was a large city, but so dirty, perhaps caused by the fire they had Monday which burned out several blocks, a saddle and harness factory and several stores. To night, we are camped about a half mile off of the road, back in the woods, where we found a mud hole in which to water the horses. There are marks on the trees eight feet high, for (200 300) two or three hundred feet back from the stream where the water rose last spring during the rainy flood time. Oh! the woods are just full of hoot owls and such a noise. To day saw people using and drinking water out of a muddy pond that I would not think of washing dishes in, well gone dry. To night we are having music. We have plenty of musical instruments, as father has his flute, three fifes, piccalo, while Mr. Metzger has his fife, violin, guatar, banjo and clarinet with him, and we have all kinds of books.

Oct. 24. Father and Mr Metzgar are out hunting. I dreamed of Neil Stephens all night, thought I was there (at Loogootee, Ill.) and we were just driving home. Left camp went about three miles and came to Buckhorn, a small place of a store and three dwelling houses, a black and white goat. Got some water and went about seven miles when we came to a coal shaft and village, about fourty houses all built and painted alike, painted green. I said it aught to have been call Greenville, but it was a part of Carterville which was about a half a mile farther south, a very nice city, having three coal shafts, three churches, school house, store, six saloons on main street, and no knowing how many more. The town on the north side had been burned and new one that is brick buildings being built. To night, we camped near a creek of water, but such a dirty place, a regular camping ground. It has been such a hot dusty day.

Oct. 25. Left caming ground by 7:30 and reached Carbondale about 8:10 (went two miles). It is not such a nice place, has a good high school, college, church and stores, very nice houses, but such a lot of colored people everywhere. Left here and traveled over such a rough, stony road, went ten miles came to a steep jump off. We were on level ground when all at once we came to a place where the road lead down for a mile then up for a mile and a half when we were up on level ground again. Stopped and ate dinner, could look down and see tall trees way below us and such a rough road. I do not see how a wagon ever got over it. Yet men were hauling large loads of hay over it. Went four miles came to Cobden, about five o'clock. Got water and hay. Cobden is not a very neat town, but has plenty good stores, houses and large box factory and mill for fixing lumber for boxes. About a mile south of Cobden we camped for the night in a roadway near the Illinois Central railroad. Norman found a good spring in field on the other side of railroad. To day land has been rich and is a great small fruit country.

Oct. 26. At 8:15 left camping ground for Anna, which is not such a grand place as I have heard it said it was, although it has some richly made houses of frame work, brick and stone. It has good well kept streets. Anna and Jonesboro is so near one can hardly tell where one begins and the other ends except Anna is built on low land while Jonesboro is built up on a bluff and I think is a much prettier town. If it did not have its large billiard hall and saloons. I never saw so many saloons as there is here in the south. The road from Jonesboro to our camping was a rough one, although the scenery has been grand. It was a rough, hilly, rocky bluff road with high rock bluff on one side and valley on the other side. For dinner we stopped on the road way where the rock bluff was twenty five feet high on one side and valley way below us on the other side. Had a rocky shelf for a table and rocks rolled up to it for chairs. Rubie, Edmund and I climbed up it to see what was on top. Found only rocks, then we all played "Duck to rock" and had plenty of fun. Found all kind, and all colors of stones, but of course we never saved any, because if we tried to save one there were twenty others just as pretty. After dinner we passed on up the bluff road, pass rock bluffs from twenty to two hundred feet high. The rocks in places looked as if they were laid in layers and thee were great oak, beach, hickory, and gum trees growing out of the cracks to rocks, roots running down nearly two hundred feet along the rocks to find the ground. We have passed by several springs flowing from the rock bluff, and to night we are camped on the bluff road after passing, by about, a mile of rocks over two hundred feet high, and where we are camped the bluff rises a hundred feet high strait up and down, but Norman found a place where by hanging to roots and in snake holes he managed to reach the top. We have plenty company to night, as two other tenters are camped near, and a house each side of us. One of the tenters is a Mrs. Martin, son (about twenty five), two daughters (about nine and eleven) and a Mr. Miller (about twenty) who is driving them through with his team. The other tenter is a photographer, with a horse and a little wooden house on wheels. He (the photographer) is a large man, bout fifty years old and weighs two hundred and fourty five pounds. He has a possium he is cooking for his supper on Mrs. Martin's camp fire. It is dark and John Metzger and Norman have gone over to call on the other campers. Lillie Metzger helped to dress up in Mother's motherhubbard and my sun-bonnet and then he went over to the other camp to call John and make him believe it was his wife a calling him, but he could not, but one of the boys thought something was up and said he thought there was a woman a wanting something. Then father tried to go back to our tent, but Lillie and I pushed him back and told him to go on over. The old photographer thought something funny was up so he gave chase. Met Mother and the rest of us women and asked mother if it was the governor. She told him yes, so he gave chase and how funny they looked both so large and fleshy (father weighed two hundred and thirty pounds) and father was not used to having a dress on and did not know how to run in one so of course he got caught and such a hug as the old photographer gave father. T'was a good thing it was not a woman. Such fun we had.

Oct. 27. This morning Ruby, Edmund, Lillie and I climbed up the bluff, but how slippery, and only a root or snake hole to hold to keep from falling. We would never climb it again although the top was pretty with moss and snail shells. The people here says the rocks are just full of timber rattle snakes, but we did not happen to find only the holes. But, Oh! If there had a been one of those nine foot rattlers where would we have been? We had the picture of our and selves taken this morning and at ten o'clock was on our way going pass such a bluff. Part all rock and then a place with dirt bottom and large pyramid top rising higher than the great beach trees at their sides. Then under the swinging rock a rock that swung out over the road far enough for two large caravan wagons to stand sheltred under it. Went about half a mile along this bluff, then turned off, went a half mile and came to McClure, a small town where every thing was high. Near it was a field of about five acres in pumpkins. The field was yellow and the pumpkins so thick any one could have walked all over the field on pumpkins with out stepping on the ground. Some would not go in a bushel basket, and our boys guessed some of them would weigh a hundred pounds. Saw some castor beans that was as tall as peach trees (old ones) which stood near them. About twenty minutes to one came to the Mississippi River, and about half past one camped for dinner on bank of Mississippi River, where it is nearly a mile wide. Horses are tired so we are to stay her until sometime tomorrow. Now it is nearly dark and I sit writing on the bank of the river. I have watched a steam tug boat plow up the river on it way from Cape Girardeau to St. Louis. Watched some row boats coming in from fishing. The photographer just passed by. Has a proof of the pictures. It is good, but not half as pretty as the real. Tonight I sat on the bank and watched the sun set and it was such a pretty sight. It cast a shadow on the water that looked like a golden ladder reaching from the river to the sky. This morning before we left camp the young fellow at other camp Mr. Miller, he is about five feet four inches, weight about a hundred and fifty pounds. He was dressed in black, had dark eyes, dark complexion. He came over to our tent was talking to Mr. Metzger. Said, "Say that is a pretty girl over here hain't it."

Oct. 28. When we woke this morning it was raining and we did not leave camp until nearly ten o'clock. Then we went over some rough road, in great chuck holes, and the road was so near the river it looked as if the wagon would go over and down the bank. Went about a mile, came to the eastern side of Cape Girardeau, where is a small town with pecan trees for shade. Here we stopped to get the feed box fixed, which the horses broke last night. The old photographer finished the pictures and at two o'clock drove down to the landing and by twenty minutes past two had landed on the Missouri side of the river. Where we were ferried across, the river was nearly a mile and a half across. The horses were driven on the ferry boat, but they did not seem to be afraid. On the river was a train ferry, steamer, boat houses, tug and several row boats. Cape Girardeau is a very nice town with very good streets, nice houses, beautiful churches, a nice high school, college and a Ladies Academy. So far the roads in Missouri have been good gravel roads, houses set far back in rolling green lawns surrounded by tall trees. To night we are camped on the road way near a ledge of whetstone nearly twenty feet high and on top of it are large beach trees full of beachnuts. We have met one team three times on the road. They are a Sink Family, a man wife and daughter and two brothers of Mr. Sink from Clay Co. Indiana headed for Izard Co. Ark.

In crossing the ferry, Mother was afraid the horses would get scared and run off. She always was afraid of horses, but they were as gentle as little lambs.

Oct. 29. Left camp about quarter to ten and reached Dutchtown, a dirty little town of about a dozen houses on a branch of Little River. Stopped to water the horses, so asked which was the nearest road to Delta, and a man directed us over a road along the river (instead of across it on the closed bridge) which he said was the shortest way. And as we were driving off he got down and looked under our wagons and laughed. I told Mother I bet he directed us wrong and we would never reach there (but we did). Oh! Such a road along the river bank, over cypress knees, through woods, along a new railroad, down deep revenes, or creeks. Some of the revenes so deep and the bank so steep the boys had to shovel them down and then it seemed as if the wagons would tip over. In one of the creeks were some longs laid across and such holes between them a horse could not go across without breaking its leg, so the horses had to be unhitched, drove around and wagons pushed across by hand, then re-hitched. Soon reached a small lumber town on the railroad side called Sparksboro. Went two miles, then came to Delta, but such a rough town, but could spot five railroads, a large rail road hotel, a dozen one story houses, a store where nothing any one wanted could be got. Best of anything was a talking, swearing parrot swinging in a barrel hoop. (before reaching Delta we went through a cyprus swamp with great cyprus knees sticking up.) To night we are camped on the Little River about three mils from Delta. Camped at half past one. The water of the river is so clear can see the bottom and plenty of fish. The boys have caught a good sized bass and channel cat. Have squirrels and quails. At supper had lots of fun Mother and Mrs. Metzger swaped (changed) men and Mr. Metzger ate with us and father ate with Mrs. Metzger. Mr. and Mrs. Metzger are such jolly people and little Eva (two years old) is so sweet and michevious.

Oct. 30. Nothing of note today. Had black bass, channel cat, squirrels and quails for breakfast, and squirrels for dinner. Now night and just finished supper. Mrs. Metzger was drinking a cup of hot cocoa, tipped it over in her lap and said she had scalded herself clear through. We are all a laughing so about it that I can hardly write, and father has had to sit down his cup of coco for fear of spilling his while he laughs.

This morning father row Mrs. Metzger and I across the river on two logs nailed together so we could get a few nuts as they were on the other side of the river. Found hickory, hazel and black walnuts, also a few beech nuts.

Oct. 31. Today has been such a rainy day, that every thing out and indoor are wet and muddy. Have had to stay in the tent all day, as well as to have a hot fire in the camp stove and a large camp fire out of doors. Had two callers this morning. Men looking for their cattle that went astray.

Nov. 1. Rained all day. Such a bad day. Grew colder. Had a large camp fire and I rubbed out what cloths that had to be done, but cannot hang them out until morning. We have had music most of the day. I started a book we brought with us titled Earth Born. Such a silly story.

Nov. 2. First thing hung out the cloths and got breakfast and by nine o'clock had pulled up camp and started on our way. Such a muddy road. First came to Allenville, a small town of about a half dozen houses, one store, two saloons, a blacksmith's shop and a depot. Went about two miles over a stoney rutty road and reached Sneedtown, a small place of about half a dozen houses, one store and blacksmith shop. About a mile and half from Sneedtown came to woods and hills. On top of one of the hills was a church (which reminded me of Chicken Foot Church). Here we camped for dinner and to rest the horses. Oh, such roads clayey up and down hills. After dinner did nothing but go up and down hills. Such rough hills. Came to one we had to couple up the teams to pull the wagons up. And up one hill Norman did not follow Mr. Metzger's wagon, so got stuck in the clay and Mr. Metzger had to bring his horses to help pull our wagon out. Then father got on the seat and drove up several hills while Mrs. Metzger and us girls walked up. Our dog, Fido, would get out to walk with us and as father was driving down the last hill Fido ran under the wagon wheel and got his head and fore foot run over. Such a banged up head and foot. We thought he would die (but he did not). About four o'clock reached Advanc town, a very pretty little town about the size of Farina, Ill. (900) and such a lovely brick school house (4 rooms). Looked like a new one. It was the prettiest common school I ever saw in so small a place. To night we are camped in a lovely piece of woods on rolling ground. The only dry place we could find to pitch our tent about two miles from Advanc. And now father and Mr. Metzger are seeing which can tell the largest bed bug story.

Nov. 3. Left camp this morning at quarter to eight. Found the woods where we camped were mostly sasfras. We have traveled over some rough roads, through Missouri swamp land, composed of marshy land and cypress trees with great knees, over Missouri plank road which is as bad as the Illinois cordaroy roads. For dinner we camped on the Castor River, about a quarter mile before reaching Leora. The river was clear and full of fish which would come to the top to get crumbs we threw in to them. There were several wagons camped on the river bank for dinner. Three of them were going the same way we were, but they were going to Izard County, Arkansas. About two miles before we camped for dinner we passed an old country road fort built in war time. Left and crossed the river on an iron bridge and soon came to Leora, a small town built in the low land with the houses built up on under pinions five or eight feet high to keep them from being washed away in the rainy seasons. To night we are camped in one of the Missouri swamps. Got on as dry land as we could find in the dark by the aid of the lantern. Just before we reached our camping round we passed a ditch full of water, by the road side, there was a young girl and fellow watering some horses. As they left she went off up one hill and he another. When they reached the place where a turn shut off the sight, he and she turned and threw each other a kiss. Oh! Yes, I forgot to say that after dinner as we were coming up a hill, father was out walking, we passed a field of cotton and as Edmund had never saw a cotton ball and wanted one, father went and picked him one and then ran up the hill so as to throw it in the wagon, but just before he reached the wagon tho caught his foot in a snag and fell flat and rolled over like a ball. Got up laughing so we all had to laugh. He looked so funny. Have seen several pretty farm houses, school houses and country churches today.

Nov. 4. Left camp at twenty minutes past eight this morning and traveled over some hills. Found plenty hickory nuts. Passed a field of such corn as I had never before seen. Must have been sixteen feet tall and the ears so high up that a medium sized man could not reach it standing on tip toe. Soon came to a small place called Asherville. Had a few very good stores, about fifteen good houses and more being built. After passing through there in about five miles came to the St. Francis swamps. Went through about three miles of swamps and came to the St. Francis Rver which was about a hundred and fifty feet wide and quite deep. Here we were ferried across on a Polland Ferry boat (pole and hand ferry). Here we stopped to eat dinner, then traveled about five more miles of swamp. Saw plenty springs, and such rough rocky roads. Some of the roads tipped up on one side so that it seemed as if the wagons would tip over. To night we are camped on Black River about two miles before reaching Poplar Bluff. There are three movers' wagons camped below us. (Just before reaching camping ground we passed a dray wagon full of girls and boys. One of the boys in the back threw me a kiss. I turned my back on him and told Mother. She said she had a notion to thumb her nose at him. I told her to and she did and such a bow as he gave her and how he laughed. I guess he was not much from his actions.

The camping ground is damp from the rain not long ago. Such high trees some over a hundred feet high.

Nov. 5. It began to rain in the night about eleven o'clock, and about one o'clock father and I had to get up and go out to fix the tent for a storm (Norman always slept in the covered wagon) and not much sleep for us. About seven o'clock it cleared off and turned cold. At about half past nine we were ready to start on our trip. Went about two miles along the river, over a long bridge and up a high bluff and came to the city, a pretty and a hustling city. Had a fine court house, school houses, churches, and fine brick store buildings. As we were leaving the city, passed a large lumber factory where pork barrels were made. In the last building a darkey, who thought he was awful smart, threw me a kiss. About half past two reached Cain River which we crossed on a long iron bridge, pushed on over such clayey roads, and by evening reached the East Fork of Little Black River. Here we camped on the river bank just below a long bridge. Just above the bridge was a grist mill ran by water power. There was a water fall of six or eight feet.

Nov. 6. Today it has sprinkled most of the time and is now raining. To night a gang of three moving wagons came to camp opposite to us. They seem rather quiet. One of the men asked me if it was not hard to bring water up the bank it was so steep and slippery. I told him it was pretty hard. I at least thought so as once in going down I slipped and slid to the bottom where I ended at the water edge against a fallen tree. Mr. Metzger laughed and said he called such a slide a "Otto Slide". Soon after he went to come up with a pail of water in each hand, and when about half way up, slipped and sent pails, water and himself a sailing down to the water he looked so funny a turning a hand spring down a slippery bank. Mother was so sick she laid in bed all day yesterday in bottom of the wagon and to day she has been in bed and had such a hot fire in the camp stove although it is not cold.

Nov. 7. Today it has rained off and on most of the time. I put out a small wash and then went out in the woods to find all kind of leaves and berries for Mother to see as she could not walk out to see them herself. We have had five men callers today. One of them John Metzger asked if apple trees did well here. He said they did that he had an apple orchard of two tree and one of them was most dead. They all think this is just the place, but I do not think they looked as if they knew very much. I went out to try and fish. Got my hook caught in a fallen tree in the middle of the stream and thought it would have to stay there, but it soon came loose and I went back to the tent giving fishing up as a bad occupation. I just had a good laugh at a young boy (about fifteen years old and just came in with a caravan crowd to camp for the night). He came down to the river to get water and did not know the bank was slippery so he slipped and slid until he was knee deep in water. He looked so scared just as if he thought he was a going to drown, but I knew the water was not more than waist deep and could not help laughing. Soon after Mr. Metzger went down after a pail of water, but went a tumbling down with the pail a coming after him, just like Jack and Jill. I asked him if he called mine an Otto Slide what he called his. He said his was a Bargain Slide and he would not have cared if he had not have swallowed his cud of tobacco.

Nov. 8. Rained the latter part of the night but was not raining this morning although it was cloudy. Had breakfast and father went out to fix the wagon ready for starting. Was oiling the wheel when it slipped off and let the wagon bed down on his head, and sit him on an old burnt log. Hurt his head so it swelled quite a bit but he would not own it hurt much. Left camp by half past eight and over such clayey roads, up and down hills. The horses could not stand it to go up a hill very far with out stopping to rest from ten to twenty minutes and we had several hard steep hills to climb.

Once in a while we would strike a clay road full of stones and my then how things would shake around and how you had to hang on if you kept your seats. One of the farms we passed had had about an acre of land on it plowed and there was so many small stones about the size and shape of good sized potatoes that it looked just as though there had been a great crop of potatoes plowed up and left in the sun. We did not stop for dinner, but by twenty minutes to three crossed a small branch of Current River and soon reached Donaphan, a nice clean city with plenty nice pretty houses, well kept door yards, nice brick stores, beautiful churches and school houses, but such a delapidated court house, so old and looked as if it was not much used and s if there was not much need of it. There was such a pretty Y.P.S.C.E. Church set back on such a pretty green and rolling lawn. After leaving Donaphan we came to and forded Current River. Such a pretty, clear, pebbled bottom river about a quarter of a mile wide, and water up to the wagon bed. Now we are camped on the bank of the river for the night. Just below us is an island on which part of the lumber mill stands in a small stream of water between the main land and island and the mill stand across this. Then above us is a log boom which is used to push the logs down to the mill.

I have just came in from the boat that is near our camp. We have had lots of fun. Lost one of our poles. Norman dipped the boat with water and Mr. Metzger gave it such a shove that he like to have thrown Norman overboard. They say the water is so clear that when it is sixteen feet deep the bottom can be seen. Have two men callers out side talking to our men. All Missourians seem friendly and kind and willing to help you find a good farm if you want to settle among them. We have seen a good many Illinoisans here and they are glad to see people from Old Illinois, but they say they would not go back for anything as thing there is no place like Missouri. They say they have never had so much to live on and so least sickness as since they have been here.

Nov. 9. The wind blew hard all night although it was a lovely moonlight evening. It was to pretty to stay in the tent so we sat out on the river bank. Saw five teams of cotton, two bails to each team, and each bail weighed five hundred pounds, and each team had to ford the river, and horse back riders crossed each way all night long.

They say last spring when the water was up and the current swifter, a man went to cross with his team they got frightened and ran away down stream, threw the man out and the current was so strong he drowned before he could reach the shore or bank. This morning father went out to shoot ducks. Saw some mallards and wood ducks swimming around. Shot at them and killed one. As he supposed it to be a mallard duck he came hurrying back to the tent to send Norman out on horse back at the ford to catch it as it went floating by. But the duck got lodged in the log boom down near the mill. Norman did not know the river and thought it all like the ford so started out toward the boom on horse back, but went down in a deep hole so the horse had to swim back to the ford with just her head out of the water and Norman had to hold on by her main. Then he drove out to the island, hitched the horse and walked out on the boom and got the duck and found he had taken his ducking for a wood duck. Then came back across the river just as six load of cotton from two to three bail each crowded the ford. After breakfast Norman had to cross the river to Donaphan to get an iron to fix the axle to the wagon which was craked by going down into a chuck hole. Mr. Metzger went up to a house, hired a boat, oars, and fish gigs, then he and father took their guns and went up the river to fish and hunt while Mrs. Metzger and I walked out on the log boom to fish. We saw only small minnoes that were so tame they would come up and bite our fingers, but we were not quick enough to catch any. When Mr. Metzger and father came back, Mr. Metzger took his wife, Rubie, Eva, Edmund and I for a boat ride along the log boom and we had lots of fun. Then we let the children out and Mr. Metzger, wife and I went across the river and when we came back Norman was back from town and wanted to tow us along the boom. He was running on the boom and before us girls knew what he was up to he banged the boat against the boom and we like to have went overboard. Then he tried it again but we were watching for him to do it so we were only thrown off the seats. Had our dinner and then started on the road to Pocahontus. Hilly but good gravel roads and such lovely scenery forest on one side and rolling ground covered with green grass. As we were going through a revene, Mr. Metzger's wagon went down in a chuck hole and cracked his reach pole. To night we are camped on the top of a hill where there is a plenty of stones if nothing else. We had to clear the stones off of the tent ground before we could make the beds. Had duck and fish for supper.

Nov. 10. This morning it was cold and frosty. Had a late breakfast as the boys went out to hunt. By nine o'clock we had started on the road and such a day of accidents as we have had. Such bumps over rough stoney hilly roads. First, we came to a long hill which took until after dinner to climb. Such large rocks raised anywhere from a half foot to two feet out of the road. Jump up a stone, go a short ways and jump up a stone, go a short ways and jump up another and so to the top. Some of the stones were large enough to make a floor to a good sized bed room (about twelve by fourteen). In one of the jumps Mr. Metzger broke one of the back springs to his wagon and Oh! how everything would shake around in the wagons. Saw peach trees with peaches on them just getting ripe. Soon came to a little level place and found a country accomidation town called Poyner. Went a short ways and came to another called Middle Brook. Here we got on the wrong way or road which landed up in a door yard. Had to back out and go over a hill covered with wood and such stones and down this hill through an old lane where was just room enough for the wagon to go without running in the fence, and this road brought us up to the door of a house. Here we found the people at home and they showed us a way out through the field which would bring us to another door yard and here we could find the right road, which we found and here we stopped to eat dinner. Then went over such a rocky road where the trees were so low some of the limbs had to be cut off before the wagons could go through. Soon came to a nice large country school house with about sixty or seventy scholars. Soon got off on the wrong road. Got on the right road again and now tonight we are camped near a coffin makers house where there is a good spring of water. He says we are within nine miles of Pocahonitus, but they have the yellow fever there so we can not cross the river (Pontus), but will have to go another way. About two miles from where we camped last night we crossed from Missouri into Arkansas. Tonight we have five callers—one man and four young men sitting around the camp fire. The young men likes to see Norman run and to have the dog, Fido, run after them. They say Norman looks as if he was flying he went so fast. I do not wonder at it, they go so slow. Now they are out racing their horses. But Oh! such poor horses. Father asked the man if it was not a healthful country around. He said, "Oh, no. I have made five coffins since Sunday a week", and this was Wednesday when we came to find out they were all old people over sixty years old, except one which was his wife's sister's baby. Today we have seen all kind, color and shaped stones. Some sparkled like diamonds, some were dull.

Nov. 11. Left camp a little before nine o'clock and traveled over a new cut road on the way to Elm Store. About a mile and a half from camping ground Mr. Metzgers reach pole broke in to and the boys had to stop to make a new one out of a young tree.

Mrs. Metzger and I went and got hickory nuts to crack to pass away the time. Soon after we again started, we forded the Portia River and in a mile or so reached Elm Store, a small country store so named from the elm tree which stood in front of it. Went over a rocky hill road and ate dinner on one of the large rocks. Out of its cracks grew the Prickly Pear Catus. The pears were just ripe and tasted and looked like a little long red tomato with seeds almost like a tomato seed. Found a spring coming out from a rock at the foot of a large oak tree. After dinner we kept on up the hill jumping up great rocks or stone ledges. It was just like going up a pair of stairs. Jump up one, go a little ways, jump up another, and so on until the top as reached. It is or was an old military road and is now little used, but is call the Devils Stair Steps. Mr. Metzger's horse fell down trying to pull up over one of the ledges. We all walked up the steepest part of the hill so it would be easier for the horses. Up the steepest place, Mother walked. She is short and fat, weighs near two hundred pounds. Could not walk as fast as the rest, so when we got to the top Father and Mr. Metzger began to roll small stones down at her calling out "Werk on the rock", and Mother said she would not budge if one was to hit her. But when one rolled pretty close to her foot she did jump, and we all had a good laugh at her. It was easier going down hill and by three we had reached the foot and got on the wrong road. They say the county roads are all marked by three gashes cut in a tree, but the roads all seemed to be marked and the roads leading to the houses are as well traveled as the county roads. So we ran up to a farm house and had to turn around and go back to find the right road. The trees in the woods are too low for a covered wagon to pass under, and we broke our bows more than once. We have had some bad accidents but lots of fun mixed in. To night we are camped about five miles from Eleven Point river, on the side of the road near a good spring coming out of the side of a large hill, coming out of a rock and empties in a large rock basin. The spring is about as large as a bowl. It was so full of old dead leaves. The woman just above said the doctors had said it was a medical spring. (I guess it was, for it made us all sick.) On the road saw two of the prettiest goats, one a fawn color with a black streak down its back. The other was a spotted black and white goat.

Nov. 12. Left camp about nine o'clock and retraced half a mile to get on county road, and most of the day we have had pretty good roads. ate dinner under hickory trees on top of a hill using stones as table and chairs. Before dinner we forded Eleven Point River just below a cotton gin, and about four o'clock crossed Spring River on a long iron bridge nearly a quarter (mile) long and entered Imboden, a small town built on hills. Has a railroad and cotton gin. We stopped to do some trading. The boys all went off and left our teams standing, ours just behind Mr. Metzger's. Ours took a notion to go up hill for once on their own accord, so started off. Mother hollered, "Whoa!" at them but they would not stop, so I tried to reach the seat from the back of the wagon. Had to squeeze between Mother and the bows, jump over bedding, seat and reach to the foot board or dash board for the lines, but the horses ran into a large rock and stopped just as I reached the lines. But, such a sight as I was for I had torn my dress skirt off in trying to jump over the bedding. Just then some men came up and wanted to know if I could hold the horses. I know I was not very civil to them for their kindness for I only said, "I don't know whether I can or not." They are young, and just think of any man asking a young girl not more than five feet high, weighs a hundred and two and not quite twenty-one if she could hold two young horses that a man would not want to hold if they took a notion to run away. After leaving Imboden, we forded Spring River so as to water the horses. Then retraced a mile. Then came through woods until tonight we are camped near a creek about five miles from Kingsville. At Imboden we saw no church. This morning Edmund, who is not quite five years old, took the hatchet and cut down a four inch tree to get a piece of mistletoe that was in the top of it.

Nov. 13. This morning had to leave camp at half after eight as it looked so much like rain we wanted to get out of the clay hills or we could not for some time, and no good drinking water. Just as we were taking up the tent a young married man came up on horse back to talk with the men. He was a going the same way we were for a mile or so. About ten o'clock we reach Spring Creek fed by several different creeks. For dinner we camped on a foot hill of the Ozark Mountains. It was on a rock road and had dinner on rocks with rocks for chairs. I never saw such roads for county roads. We broke bows to our wagon and had to stop to patch up. About three o'clock we reached Martin Creek, a clear stream with no cattle around it so we stopped to camp for the evening. In helping to get supper, Mrs. Metzger ran into the table, up set it, dishes, vituals and all, all over the carpet and bedding. Such a laugh as we had at her. She looked so funny sitting the midst of it all as though she did not know what had happened. It has been such a sultry day and looks like a heavy rain. The woods are full of Blue Asters all in bloom. Seen houses to day which looked like barns except for the chimney (stove pipe) and children were playing around the shed-like house. It had cracks in it large enough to put your hand side ways through, and small double doors, but no windows as we could see. Father saw an old Judge at Imboden yesterday that wanted to know where he was from. When father told him he said "Well, you came from one of the sickliest places on the whole face of God's earth." I guess he did not know as much as he thought he did.

Nov. 14. This morning we left camp at nine o'clock. It looked bright for a while and then clouded up. For some miles we traveled over good roads for this country with foot hills of Ozark Mountains on one side and Martin Creek on the other. We crossed Martin Creek again, passed through forest, then up and down short foot hills and crossed Forty Island Creek. Watered our horses, saw some fine corn. Soon reached and crossed Fourty Island Creek on a bridge near a railroad and in half a mile reached Hardy by two o'clock and stopped for a time. Some men wanted to talk with our men. It is a small town of about four hundred and fifty people. A large court house, large brick bank (Now changed into a saloon), jail, very good stores and a five room school house. After leaving Hardy crossed Spring River on a long bridge and camped on the west side of town. The bridge was about two or three hundred feet long and the water in the river eighteen feet deep. Near us is a stoney hill, also, a very good spring which our boys found coming out from under a large rock which they pried out with the crow-bar leaving a large mouth to the spring. We expect to camp here a few days while the boys look around to see the land. A man about three miles west or south west of town wants to sell us his farm. We have had fourteen callers (men callers) this evening. Some came before we had our tent put up. It seems odd to see how quick everybody knows when a mover is near and flock around to find where you are from and where you are a going. Father and Mother thought the man said he was a bachelor why he wanted to sell out (but he was not—had a wife and three children) so Mother asked father why he did not tell him he would trade his daughter for the land. She did not say which one so I guess it must be Rubie as she would probably suit best. Have seen blue asters, white and blue daisies, golden rod, some small blue clusters which looked like heiletrope in the woods and how pretty it looked. We broke our front bow and tore the canvas on the wagon to day. I never saw such luck as we have had. It has now began to rain and such a dark night.

Nov. 15. This morning was cloudy but the sun soon came out but it did not stay long. Have had company all day long. So many men around and one with a white felt hat, Joe Walla, a married man, so homely. Says such silly funny things and how he can lie. A regular Arkansas professional. The boys went out on horse back to look at some land. The men got tired riding so came down the steep hill a foot, leading their horses. How we codded them. Got dinner, then Mrs. Metzger and I left the dishes and went over in town. Every fellow we met had to stop, take off his hat and say "How do you do" to us, and smiled so sweet that Mrs. Metzger and

I codded each other about it. We went to the post office to mail some letters and get some paist board to fix some pictures, but the stores seemed to be scarce of it. We went even down to the Spring River bank. I guess they thought we were greenies. We did not get home until dark and so many around the tent. Oh! Such fun as we have had laughing at each other at what the people said of us and at the way they acted here. Some thought Mrs. Metzger and I were sisters, some asked if Mr. Metzger was father's son-in-law, some asked if Norman was his brother, some thought father was Mother's son, and some thought Rubie and I belonged to Mr. Metzger's family. And such fun we had about it for Mr. Metzger's family is no relation to us, only a friend of father's.

Nov. 16. Rained and wind blew hard most of the night, and Mother got up and tied a chair to the tent door. We all laughed and wanted to know if she thought that it would keep the tent from blowing away. Along toward morning it cleared off. The wind changed and it turned colder and this morning the sun came out so Mrs. Metzger and I put out a large wash. Have had callers all day. Such a number of land agents to sell land and Dr. Durham for a long talk and smoked his rotten old cob pipe. The men here smoke, swear, and drink while the women dip and take snuff.

Nov. 17. This morning was cold and frosty. Everything white and ice froze about a quarter of an inch thick. The boys caught a two and a half foot eel (silver eel). Lillie had a nervous chill last night. Got up and built up such a hot fire in the tent stove. Mrs. Metzger and I went to town to day to get Eva some shoes and the children some candy. We have had such fun to day telling stories about making and baking bread in a tent oven. Have had callers all day. As we were eating breakfast this morning some one came up and hollered, "Hello, Ed. Are you in there?" Father jumped up, grabbed his hat, said, "I know that is Willis", and sure enough there was Willis Burdick of Farina. Said he left home yesterday morning. Got here this morning and was eating breakfast at the Hardy Hotel when Mr. Clayton told him there were some folks from Farina camped on the other side of the river and when had describe us out he knew who it was and came right over.

Nov. 18. To day not done much. Lillie and I went in town to do some trading. This morning father and John took a boat and went fishing. Caught a large buffalo fish and this evening Willis Burdick came in as we were eating supper and ate supper with us. After supper the men went over in town and Mrs. Metzger and I took Eva and Edmund to walk up the hill. Have had callers all day. This morning was a wreck on the Kansas City, Fort Smith and Memphis Railroad a short distance below Hardy. The morning Passenger was thrown off the track and three of the coaches rolled down an embankment of thirty feet into the Spring River. The coaches were full of people, several killed and bruised and coaches burning. No knowing how many yet in the wreck.

Nov. 19. A pleasant day. Mr. Burdick staid all night with us and this morning father, Mr. Burdick, Mr. Metzger, wife, Eva, Norman, Edmund and I took our covered wagon and drove three miles east (or northeast) of town to Mr. Ed Jackson's place which Mr. Burdick has bought. It is a farm with a poor small log house on it. Contains a hundred and sixty acres and he sold it for a hundred and fifty dollars. Lillie and I took Eva and Edmund and went in the house while the boys looked around. Mr. Jackson is a widorer with five sons with him. He has a daughter married and living in Ohio. He is going back there to live while there son, George (about 22 or 23 years old) came in with a large wild turkey he had shot. They had a girl about 26 or 28 working for them. I believe her name is Carrie Craig. Mr. Burdick came back with us and will stay all night.

Nov. 20. To day is Edmund's 5th birthday. It has been a quiet day. Have had music and this afternoon three young girls called. They seemed quiet and pleasant. Two of them were a Mr. White's daughters. The other Mr. Hale's daughter. Mr. Hale has just come here from Kentucky. This evening have had men callers. I never saw such a place or such folks. No one knows a stranger here, though most of them seem to be very pleasant people. This evening father and mother went for a walk up a long steep hill. Went about two mile and it did not seem to tire mother very much. Now, tonight Mr. Hale, a blacksmith, Mr. Raby and several others are here talking with our men folks.

Nov. 21. It has been a pleasant warm day. Had callers before breakfast and after breakfast father and Mr. Hale went off on horse back to look at the country. Since there have been about a dozen callers Geo. Jackson was here and invited our boys out to their farm to camp and look around and we intend to go tomorrow. Tonight Lillie and Mother is out calling on Mrs. Hale. Father and John are playing, Father on his flute—John on his guatar, and such a crowd around—from town men to town boys.

Nov. 22. It has been a cloudy day but we left camp to move out east of Hardy about three miles near Mr. Jackson's place. We crossed Spring River on the bridge, passed through Hardy and then through woods to Spring River which we forded at Humphrey's Ford. Mr. Ed Jackson and Willis Burdick rode out with us. Tonight we are camped near Humphrey's Ford on rolling ground in the woods. In the river are several natural water falls which makes it look so pretty with a high rock and dirt bluff across the way. Have had several callers and they say the woods around us are full of quails, squirrels, wild turkey, ducks and deer. I am glad we are out of town so we will not be bothered with so many callers.

Nov. 23. A clear day. The boys went out to hunt. Our boys got squirrels and quails. Mr. Burkick and Geo. Jackson each got a turkey. Geo. sold his in Hardy for Thanksgiving. Mr. Burdick brought his to the tent to have it roasted.

Nov. 24. Had turkey for dinner, so we had Thanksgiving the day before hand. We have had several callers—one a Doctor Schank. Geo. Jackson cut down a tree and pulled up some under brush from under a grape vine that looked down from two trees so we now have a swing at the tent door. Six men came in to night. A lady, Mrs. Henry, came in yesterday, and last night Geo. Jackson took my journal and read part of it. the funny parts. Mr. John Metzger, wife, Mr. Burdick, Rubie, Eva, and I went to Mr. Jackson's this afternoon and had peanuts to eat.

Nov. 25. Thanksgiving Day and such a stormy day. The boys went out to hunt a deer that was seen to go to the river for water, but did not get it. George Jackson got a piece of mistletoe with the white berries on it and gave it to me. I went up to Mrs. Henry's after dinner to get some milk and eggs. Never got home until after dark. Lost my path through the woods. It was stormy, but we had a few callers.

Nov. 26. Was cloudy most of the day. Such a damp chilly day. Had a few callers and in the evening Mr. Jackson's two young boys called with the work girl, and we had music.

Nov. 27. Had callers and land agents today and music this evening. I have had a sore throat, lungs and a lame shoulder all day, but is better now.

Nov. 28. Had hack berries. We went down to the river to watch some young fellows get a horse out of the river. It was in a hole near a ripple near the ford. After dinner Geo. Jackson came over and took Lillie and I for a boat ride. Went up to the second waterfall and walked in the middle of the river on stepping stones until we came to what is called the bottomless basin because they could never sound a bottom to it. We walked all around it on a stone, as it seemed to be as water in a great basin, and we walked on the rim. In some places we did not have a half a foot of stone to stand on and again it would be three feet wide. Norman, two of Jackson's boys and a Henry boy ran away with our boat and tried to tease us. In walking around the bank of the river Geo. said we aught to be able to step where he could, but he and Lillie is taller and can take a longer step than I can but I thought I would not be beat so I tried to step where they did, and in stepping over a fallen tree onto a rock as they did, down I sit but jumped up about as quick. I felt so cheap. (John and George was down to the rock soon after and it was cracked in to. They said I was so heavy, the reaction cracked it.) Geo. and Lillie laughed so at me. So I had a laugh when walking back the same path Geo. slipped on the same rock but caught himself by a limb to a tree. He rowed us back on the opposite side from which we went on, so we went under a tree with a hornets nest in it and he would have got it for me if I had only a said so. And we also went under two trees just full of mistletoe. Such a pretty day for a boat ride, and Geo. was so good. I bet it will be a long day before Lillie or I forget what a time we had. Tonight we are having a concert of flute and guitar music.

Nov. 29. Early this morning father went out to hunt and shot a large wild turkey. Mr. Metzger has rented one of the houses on the Jackson place and moved today so now we are all by ourselves. George Jackson and Mr. Burdick went out to hunt turkey. Mr. Burdick soon got tired and came back to the tent but Geo had more pluck. He staid out until noon when he came back with two nice looking turkies. (He said I was not to forget to put it in my book, so of course I could not forget it.) It is colder tonight. Waters freezing.

Nov. 30. Such a lonesome day although in the afternoon I went up to Lillies' little log hut.

Dec. 1. It has been a lovely day. I went up to see Lillie an soon after I came back Charlie and Jim Raby came to see father about taking their place of 320 acres for 240 dollars (but Jim now is to keep 40 acres to prove up and give father a deed of the rest.) They are to take our camping outfit. About half past eleven o'clock Geo. Jackson came by and wanted father to go a turkey hunting with him. He had company so could not go. Norman said he would go. Then Geo. wanted to know if Rubie and I did not want to go too and see the old distill about two and a half miles down the Spring River. So we went and such a splendid time as we had walking over bluffs, stones, hills, up high bluff, then down to the river. Saw the distill, an old burnt building in a hidden revene between high hills surrounded by underbrush to hide it. Then we went over the hill to the river along the river bank with the river on one side and a high stone bluff on the other. The bluff was about seventy five feet up and down and no climbing it except at one edge where was a zigzag path led up to a cave like hole called Wildcat Hollow, and such a wild looking place. Geo. filled the nest of the hole with stones then we went home. It has been a day to be long remembered. Geo. found a tree with mistletoe in it hanging out over the water. He climbed out and got it, and we all went back decked in mistletoe and such a time as we had. This evening Mr. Burdick, Mr. Ed Jackson and Son Geo., Mr. and Mrs. Metzger with Eva are here and such colds as we all have.

Dec. 2. Began to rain the later part of the evening and still raining and freezing this morning. Ice all over everything. Father and Edmund was sick all night. Edmund is all right now but father has been in bed all day and the noise hurt his head, so I took Edmund and went up to Lillies' to spend the day. Geo. Jackson was there most of the day, and Willis Burdick was there for a time. Norman and John made a "fox and geese" board, a twelve men Morris, and also a Waterloo board and played games. Such a rainy day, but what fun we had playing stick pin and watching the children romping and holloring and laughing so hard. We had a talking and a story telling time and we all laughed until we thought our heads would split open. Came back to the tent about dark and so muddy.

Dec. 3. Rained most of the day and froze as it fell. Norman and John went to town so Lillie and Eva came down to spend the day. Willis Burdick went in with the boys to leave on the morning train for Farina.

Dec. 4. Mother sick in bed. And so cold, quit raining about eight o'clock last night. Moon came out and it turned cold. Froze up and this morning it was snowing. But no snow staid on the ground long. I took Rubie and Edmund up to Lillies' and staid all day. Lillie made ginger cookies and such a time as we had. Geo. Jackson was there part of the time and what a fuss over pins. Mr. Henry, wife and little boy came down to the tent after dinner, or rather in the evening.

Dec. 5. A quiet day. Mother sick and father not well. Mr. Ed Jackson and Geo. called in the afternoon.

Dec. 6. Mother up. Father and Norman went to town to buy a stove, windows, and some groceries. While they were gone Geo. Jackson came to the tent and talked with mother. Afterwards when Rubie was ready and we had every thing ready to move out on our farm, the Raby places. Geo., Rubie and I went down to the river and out on a sycamore tree that lay down over the water, and cut our names and I drew my hand and then as boys had not yet got back, I went up to bid Lillie goodby. (She was washing.) Then when I reached the tent father, Jim, and Charlie Raby was there to take us out to the farm which is four miles over hills through vallies, or two and a half miles over high hills southwest of Hardy. I rode out with Jim Raby and I asked him if he called it only three miles, and if so, they were the longest ones I had ever seen. I guess it was like the old saying "measured with a bob sled with tongue thrown in." Reached the farm about five o'clock and found a little box house of one room twelve by fourteen with a log leanto eight by fourteen. Cooked supper on our new stove which we put up in the kitchen.

Dec. 7. Norman's nineteenth birthday and we have been busy fixing up the house fit to stay in. Norman has went to tent to take some of Charlie Raby's things which he left here. Father nearly sick. Sitting over the fire place.

Dec. 8. Nothing of note but work, work and fix, fix. I will now close my Journal as we are now settled in our new home and all seem to like it well here among the hills and forest.

Meta P. Clarke

Though Meta closed her Journal, she afterwards from time to time made short entries in the back of the same notebook. These are those entries:

March 25, 1900. S. M. Davidson I first saw. Went to see his Mother on Herron Place on South Fork.

April 22, 1900. Mord Davidson first came to our house. (Apr. 15 Rubie, Wilbur Weaver, Leo Theis and I went to South Fork to boat ride. There I was first introduced to Mord Davidson.)

June 2, 1900. I went to Many Island 1 mile south of Afton. Stayed till June 16 with Mr. and Mrs. Metzger. Met Mr. Jim Sherwood and Dr. Hamlin of Chicago. Also, little Willie Rote of Their. (9 years old)

June 21. I was taken sick with the Malaria Typhoid fever. First that I set up was July 15. Mord Davidson came by.

July 22. Mord Davidson asked if he could come to see me. I said "Certainly you can, if you want to."

Aug. 18. Mord took me to Hardy to hear Wild Bill Evans preach. At the spring below our house after we came home, Mord told me he loved me, asked if I loved him. I told him I was sorry for him. I was although I loved him. Went up the road to the corner of fence to find horse, but did not. We kissed at the spring, again at fence corner at fence by the gate. Kissed him and told him yes I loved him, so I could not let him go.

Sept. 9. Had a talk with Mord at night. Told him but he loves me. And if it could be I love him more and more every time I see him. He is so good.

Oct. 7. Mord asked father for his consent which father gave. They all like Mord and how could they help it he is so good, and if he only knew how I loved him.

Oct. 21. Mord staid all night at our house. It rained. I pinned Mida's picture on his coat. (Mildred Lacey's picture age 2 yrs.)

Nov. 18. Mord and I went to Cedar Springs. At home by bed he pulled me down on his knee. My, how my heart beat. My Love, My Darling Mord.

Nov. 28. Mord took me to a dance at Cab Armstrong's.

Dec. 2. Mord and I went to Cornelius. Got his violin. Had a spat about whole hear and jealousy. How I love him. In kitchen at table Edmund pulled my chair away from me and Mord sit me on his knee.

Dec. 17. Mon. Mord came home stopped here to see me. Ate supper and I and he sat in kitchen and talked. He took me on his knee. Oh, how I love him. It does not seem as if I could live without him. He has my whole heart if he but knew it. I don't see how I ever thought I cared for anyone else when such a man as My Mord lived, but I am glad I found out my mistake before it was too late for how could I have lived as another man's wife when Mord was living. I believe if I had a met him at any time my heart would have left me for him and how sad and misable I would have been without My Mord, My Love, My Darling.

Jan. 2nd. 1901

Married at home of E .S. Clarke's. His daughter, Meta P. Clarke (age 23) to Sam M. Davidson, age 26, by Esquire H. D. Dark on Wednesday, January 2, 1901 at 3:15 o'clock. Dinner at 4:00 o'clock.

Meta Clarke no more, but Meta Davidson, stayed with her sweet dear husband at E. S. Clarke's & Wife's the first night.

Hardy, Sharp Co., Ark.

William Edmund Davidson born Sunday morning at half past two o'clock on Nov. 10, 1901.

Mary Arabella Davidson born Tuesday morning at half past three o'clock on Sept. 29, 1903.

APPENDIX 3

POEMS by WILLIAM E. "Bill" DAVIDSON

UNNANED

By the window this morning
I stood and watched the sun
Trying to poke through the fog.

It was a wonderful thing to behold,
The geraniums holding their
Beautiful red blooms high
And the prettiest rose peering at me.

Below was the pretty green asparagus
With a white blanket of dew.
Farther up was the broccoli
Shedding a quilt of green
Against the fence.

I thought as I stood there
How beautiful God can paint things,
And how wonderful it is to have
Eyes to drink in this beauty,
And a mind to enjoy it.

TONIC

When grieved with problems and woes and ills
I take my way to the friendly hills.

On old compassionate roads that wind
Through field and forest and there I find
That still the valleys are rich and green,
The air is good and the sky is clean.

The corn still marches in crested ranks,
The woods still wave on the mountain flanks.
The squirrel knows where his nuts are hid,
The river flows as it always did.

And the cows still graze in their old content
In spite of human mismanagement.

LIVING ON THE LEFTOVERS

A little retirement cottage with
A guest room for visiting grandchildren.

Though they own it free and clear,
A modest savings account for a rainy day,
It took some doing to add to it month by month.

Memories, the kind that grow
Warmer and deeper with every passing year.
Affections, it reaches across the miles,
From more than scores of loving hearts.

And faith, the firm courageous ever
Celebration faith that has made life
To granny and grandpa a confident.

Walk with God.
No, they don't have much as many people
Count riches.
But, they do have certain treasures
That can never be lost, stolen or foreclosed

Priceless things whose value reaches
Beyond time and eternity
They are living on the leftovers
Of a Life of Giving.

THAT LITTLE CHAP

A careful man I ought to be
A little fellow follows me.

I do not dare to go astray
For fear he'll go the selfsame way.

Not once can I escape his eyes
What'ere he sees me do he tries.

Like me he say's he going to be
That little chap who follows me.

I must remember as I go
Through summer sun and winter snow,

I'm molding for the years to be
That little chap who follows me.

A GIRL

A sixteen year old girl,
A kiss good night.

I climbed the door
And shut the stairs.
I said my shoes and
Took off my teeth.

I pulled down my alarm
And set my sheets.
I shut off the bed
And climbed into the light.

And, all because he kissed me goodnight.

SNOW

You look out at the lawn
Was dried brown and ugly.
Now as smooth as a child's face
And a beautiful white.

Cars are a beauty
Cannot tell the new cars
From the old rusty and dented.
White, white everywhere.

Streets a dirty black
Now a pretty white blanket
White, white everywhere.

So nice and restful
To cast your eyes upon.

WIND

May the wind blow
With a gently breeze
At your back,
And, no rocks in your path
Of happiness.

ACHE

After the spat they had
The girl said, "I am leaving you"
He said, "It's like having a
Tooth pulled to get rid of the ache."

APPENDIX 4

WILLIAM E. "Bill" DAVIDSON'S FINAL DAYS

Excerpts from Don's diary.

Nov. 21: Dad was sitting in his chair with his head in his hands and in severe pain. I'm almost at my wit's end as to what to do to help him. I've taken him to three different doctors, two neurologists. Nothing seems to help. Checked with Ann, the charge nurse, about the Tegretol prescription Dad was supposed to start today. They let it fall through the crack. Got her to call Norman's Rx. I went and picked it up and brought it back. Ann gave him a Tegretol pill. I helped him eat. He can't hardly hold a spoon or pick up a small glass of milk. I pushed him to his room and got him situated in his recliner chair.

Nov. 22: Shirley from Gazebo called. She wants me to sign a DNR on Dad. Told her I didn't want to. She said he says he is dying. Called Dr. Maraist's office. Talked with Kristy. Told her about Dad so she could talk to Dr. Maraist. She said she would have the doctor call back. Pat and I had intended to go to Mary Catherine Wehmeyer's funeral this afternoon, but stayed home to receive any phone call from Dr. Maraist. Called Ann. Charley answered. Left message for Ann to call. A lady called for Dr. Maraist. She said he said to double the Tegretol dosage. I asked her to call the nurse at Gazebo and tell her. She got the message from Dr. Maraist's office to double Dad's dosage of Tegretol. Ann returned my call. She couldn't understand why I called her because there is nothing she can do. She has a house full of company for the Thanksgiving holiday. Told her I just wanted someone to vent on. Valerie from Gazebo called. Talked with her about Dad. She is understanding. Went to Gazebo to see Dad. Valerie was with him when I got there. He is not doing very well. He mumbles and hallucinates at times. He complains over and over how much he hurts. I helped Norma, a Gazebo aid, feed him a little chicken noodle soup, ice cream, and milk. I stayed with him for a while until I thought he was asleep.

Nov. 23: Pat called me on the cellphone and said Ann from Gazebo called and said Dad fell this morning. Went to Gazebo. Dad is not any better. He had a scuff on the left side of his head from the fall. He will not eat. I had to really coax him to just eat a small amount of chicken noodle soup and three sips of milk. He said his head is not hurting. But kept saying over and over, "It hurts. It hurts." He keeps his eyes closed. I finally coaxed him to open his eyes and look at me. Then he closed them. Talked with Ann (Gazebo) and Shirley. Ann will get a restraint strap to put on him to keep him in his chair. He would not even talk with his good friend, Gus, who is also a client at Gazebo. It really tears at my heart to see Dad like this.

Nov. 24: THANKSGIVING DAY. A day to be thankful for God's bounty. To bed at 0130. Awake at 0330. Layed in bed thinking about Dad, and Gus, Cleo, Hannah, Gerri, Alice, and other old people at Gazebo. I've become acquainted with some of them, as well as members of the staff. It made me so heartsick thinking about Dad and how much he has deteriorated just the past week that I was fighting back tears. I sat on the edge of the bed for a while. I finely quieted down and was able to go back to sleep. Greg, Donna, and Mary Grace came to spend the day with Pat and I.

Nov. 25: Greg, Donna, Mary Grace and I went to Gazebo to visit Dad. Mary Grace gave him some pictures she drew for him. We tried to talk with Dad but he doesn't talk much nor very well. He has a fairly firm grip in his hands for a man his age. His left eye is really bruised from the fall. He has a bad black-eye that looks like someone socked him in the eye very hard. Donna asked him questions and asked him to squeeze her hand once for "yes" and twice for "no." He responded to that fairly well. Dad's good friend, Gus, at Gazebo told me he thinks Dad may have had a stroke and that is the reason he can't talk very well. Introduced Greg, Donna, and Mary Grace to Alice, Dad's lady-friend at Gazebo that can hear but can't talk because of a stroke. Greg said a prayer for Dad when we left.

Nov. 26: Went to Gazebo to see Dad. A little change from yesterday but not much. Sobrina was shaving him when I came in. I'm not sure he recognized me at first. Helped Sobrina help Dad to the bathroom. She changed his diaper. Got him back in his wheelchair and I pushed him to the dining room to his usual place. He did not acknowledge Alice which is very unusual. I fed him what little he ate. He had five small bites of baked potato, three small bites of green beans, three small pieces of meat. He had a bad sneezing spell so I took him back to his room. Sobrina brought his tray. He ate four bites of pumpkin pie and drank about a third of a small glass of milk. He asked for a drink of water and drank about a third of a small glass. When I say he asked he said, "Waaaer." He talks very little and then doesn't talk very well. We have to guess a lot at what little he says. I think I finally got him to recognize me and say, "Don." I asked if he remembered who came to see him yesterday. He didn't answer. I asked several times. No answer. I finally asked, "Greg?" No answer. I asked him what 2+2 was and he said, "Four" which was the best response I got from him. When I asked who his mother was I got no answer. I asked several times. No answer. I asked him to grip each of my hands. His grip in each hand is fairly firm. I taped two of the drawings Mary Grace made for him to his closet door. Sobrina came and helped me get him from his wheelchair to his recliner and strap him in so he doesn't fall out. He still has a nasty looking black eye but it doesn't look as bad as it did yesterday.

Nov. 27: Got ready and went to Gazebo to see Dad. He did not recognize me. He was non-responsive. He would not talk or open his eyes. He would not grip my hand. He would not eat. I helped the aids put him back in bed. He was as limp as an old rag. Called Ann from Dad's phone but got the answering machine. Left a message for her to call. I finally decided to sign a DNR on Dad. A man by the name of Doug Basgal signed as a witness. He and his wife, Ann, had visited Dad when they came to visit Doug's mother. They live between Navasota and Hempstead. Ann called. Told her I signed a DNR on Dad. She approved. Sent an "Update on Dad" email to members of the family. Spent most of the rest of the day going through all of Dad's business papers to get everything in order. I need to go to the safety deposit box and find the Teamsters Death Benefit Certificate and Bob's note. About 4:30 p.m. Ann called from Dad's room. She said she thought he recognized her, but was not sure. Pat and I could hear Dad groaning over the phone. Ann said Dad was in pain. I called Valerie. She gave Dad his second Tegretol for the day at 3:00 p.m. Later called Ann on her cellphone. They were at Applebee's Restaurant. She called me when she got back to Dad's room. She said Dad was asleep. She said Kay and Charley would come by about 11:00 p.m. on their way from Houston to San Antonio. Pat called Greg. They got the email. We talked a while about family matters. Bill called. Told him about Dad. Bill doesn't have email. Bill said Mary is not doing very well. She has trouble keeping food down. Monday they will find out when and where she will go for the shunt surgery on her head. Debbie called. She wanted to know about Dad. Told her what we could. She is worried about her mother going in for brain surgery. She is also worried about her dad, my brother, Bill. It has been a stressful day.

Nov. 28: Called Dr. Maraist's office and asked the nurse to have the doctor reduce the Tegrenol dosage for Dad to one dose twice a day. Went to Medi-Care Specialities and got diapers for Dad. Went to post office sub-station and mailed email letter to Bill. Went to Wells-Fargo Bank. Went through the safety deposit box and took out items relating to Dad. Went to Gazebo. This is the email I sent to the Family to update them on Dad's condition:

> I visited Dad twice today. This morning at 11:00 for two hours and this afternoon at 4:30 for an hour and a half. He is somewhat better.
>
> This morning when I first got there he was somewhat lucid. He recognized me. He was responsive to most of my questions. His handgrip was firm. I asked if he wanted me to push him around outside since it was a nice day. He said "Yes." By the time I got him out of his recliner and secured in his wheelchair and the nurse took his temperature (97.9 °F) and blood pressure (100/60) he was totally zonked out. I took him back to his room and lifted him onto his bed. He did not have lunch.
>
> This afternoon when I first got there he was in his recliner alternatively lifting his legs. I asked him if he was doing exercises. He said, "Yes." He also did a few arm exercises just lifting his arms up and down. His grip was firm. I asked him what 2+2 was and he said, "Four." I asked what 4+4 was and he said, "Eight." I asked what 4+2 was and he said, "Don't you know?" He answers with "Yes" and "No" most of the time. Sometimes with an emphatic "No." He ate about six bites of a chicken casserole, two bites of green beans, 7/8ths of a glass of milk, 1/2 a glass of water, and four banana slices. He also had two sips of a Sprite. The aid gave him his medication (Tegretol-100mg) crushed and mixed with applesauce. He took it, but said, "That's terrible." He drifted off before I left.
>
> I now think the Tegretol is causing him to go totally out of it. He was taking two 100-mg twice a day. Afterwards he was just totally zonking out. A few hours later as the effect wore off he would gradually come around. I called the doctor this morning and he cut the dosage back to one 100-mg twice a day.
>
> Glad to have a little better news to pass on.

Came home about 1:30 p.m. Called Ann and told her about Dad. Went to Gazebo. Dad was better. Sam called. Bill called. Updated them on Dad.

Nov. 29: Went to Gazebo. Dad was sleeping. I didn't want to wake him. Talked with Ann, the charge nurse. She said he ate a little breakfast and talked to them. She said he is taking all his vitamins. Went by the Banner-Press to check on how obituaries are handled. They said the funeral home takes care of it and tacks it onto their bill. They said the average cost is about $80. Talked with Bud Chambers. He was interested to hear about Dad because he did a feature article on Dad for the newspaper when Dad was 100 years old. Ann called and wanted to know about Dad. Told her he was about the same.

Nov. 30: Called Kristy at Dr. Maraist's office. Told her to relay a message to the doctor that I wanted him to review Dad's medication and circumstance to see what can be done to get him back to his normal self like he was two weeks ago. Looked up the Teamsters Policy on death benefits for union member retirees. Aunt Blanche called. She wanted to know about Dad. Went to Gazebo to see Dad. He recognized me. When I asked if his head hurt he said, "Some." He is not very talkative. He mostly answers "Yes" or "No", though he did tell me he wanted to roll over onto his left side. Donna and Sobrina helped me reposition him. Talked briefly with Shirley, Director of Nursing. She said they would cut back on the Tegrenol dosage some more to see if Dad rallies a little more.

Dec. 1: Went to Gazebo to see Dad. He seems to be a little better. He recognized me. He doesn't talk much. The TV was on and he said he could see the TV. His grip was pretty good. Talked with Margie, the charge nurse, about Dad's new Tegredol regimen. He takes half a 100 mg pill three times a day at 9:00 a.m., 1:00 p.m., and 5:00 p.m. I hope this is better for him. Aunt Elsie called from Phoenix and left a message. She wants to know about Dad.

Dec. 2: Went to Gazebo to see Dad. He was asleep in the recliner. Did not wake him.

Dec 3: Met Steve and Janet at Gazebo to see Dad. I don't know if he recognized Steve and Janet or not. I'm not sure he recognized me. Norma fed him a little. I also managed to get him to eat a little, but not enough. He would moan at times like he was in pain, but when I asked if his head hurt he would shake his head "No." He would not grip our hands, though he would reach up and hold hands with Janet and me. We left and came home. Had a nice visit with Steve and Janet. We went to the Steak and Seafood Restaurant for supper. Then went to Gazebo. Could not tell if Dad was asleep or not. He opened his eyes and looked at us. Could not get him to respond. I left Steve and Janet with Dad so they could have a few moments of private time with him. Pat and I came home. Steve and Janet said they would drive part way home and spend the night somewhere on the road, then drive home to Oklahoma City tomorrow.

Dec. 4: Went to Gazebo to see Dad. He was awake. I had to really "badger" him to get him to say my name. I got him to drink about 3/4's of a small glass of orange juice. He probably was thirsty. He took only a sip of water. The aid took him to the dining room for supper. I tried to feed him. He would not eat. I took him back to his room and tried to get him to eat. Norma Tarango came in and was able to get him to eat a little. As I left I talked briefly with Sherel, the charge nurse. She said Dad did not eat breakfast and did not eat lunch. Got Dr. Maraist's FAX number from Sherel. Wrote a FAX memo to Dr. Maraist. Pat tried three times to send it to Dr. Maraist's FAX number but each time it replied, "Transmission not completed." Pat and I called Josephine. She got back from Temple about 6:30 this evening. She went to see Dad, but he was asleep. She will go see him tomorrow and see if he recognizes her. Ann called earlier today to check on Dad. Pat told her I was at Gazebo. She said she would call back after she got home from church. Ann called about 11:00 p.m. Told her about Dad.

Dec. 5: Went to Round Rock for Mary Grace's ballet class recital. Got home about 7:00 p.m. Called Josephine. No answer. Left message. She returned the call an hour later. Talked about an hour mostly about Dad and his condition. He is not doing very well. He could not or would not recognize Josephine. That's significant because he likes her so much I thought surely he would recognize her and respond to her. Not so. I'm thinking maybe Dad had a stroke or this Tegretol has dumbed his faculties like a stroke.

Dec. 6: Cold this morning. Frost on the grass in the pasture. Went to Gazebo. Talked with Billie and Gene Cooper about what to expect when Dad expires and how they handle the situation. Went to see Dad. About the same. He did not recognize me. Went to the nurse station to talk with Ann, the charge nurse. She was on the phone. While I waited I felt someone poke me in the back. It was Bob. He took some horses to Houston and came to Brenham to see Dad. Took Bob to Dad's room. Dad did not recognize Bob. I tried to get Dad to drink but he refused. Talked with Bob about Dad and what has happened the last few weeks. Left Bob with Dad. Went to the Nurse Station and talked with Ann, the charge nurse. She said they took blood from Dad yesterday and she had lab results. Dad's white blood cell count is over 18,000. Extremely high. All the test results were poor. Went to Brenham Memorial funeral home and talked with Troy Arndt. He gave me some literature to read and a form to complete. Dr. Marek called. He said he did not know Dad was in the condition he is. Dr. Urbina that had been treating Dad left the clinic suddenly day before yesterday. Dr. Marek took over his patients and hadn't had a chance to examine Dad until today. He said that at this point we have two options: 1) to hospitalize Dad and hook him up for dialysis and life support, or 2) make him as comfortable and pain free as possible until he dies. I opted for the second choice though it breaks my heart. Until a few months ago I just always felt that Dad was invincible, that he would live on and on. Dad told me months ago he did not want to be hooked up on life-support and live like a vegetable. Tried to call Ann. Line busy. Sent an email "Update on Dad" to the family members. The prognosis is not good. Cold. Slight north wind.

Dec. 7: TODAY IS MY BIRTHDAY. To bed at 1:00 a.m. Phone rang at 1:40 a.m. It was the charge nurse at Gazebo. She said Dad had just died. Pat and I were up the rest of the night trying to make phone calls. Could not get through to Ann. Finally called on her cellphone about 0700. Fred answered. Told Ann about Dad. They took Dad to Brenham Memorial Funeral Home. The rest of the day was hectic. Making phone calls, getting papers together, and working on Dad's obituary. Went to Gazebo and gave Billie a check for $978 and she returned the $4,260 check I gave them yesterday. Took everything from Dad's room, except the recliner, wheelchair, walker, and bookcase. Brought his things home and put in the barn apartment. Called James to borrow his truck. Mine won't start. Drove James' truck to Gazebo and got the other items and brought them to the garage. Met Ann, Fred, and Kay at Brenham Memorial. Ann and I met with Wayne Roberson to make all the arrangements and select a casket for Dad. We will have a funeral Friday at ten o'clock at the Brenham Memorial Chapel. Then will have a graveside service Monday at 10:30 a.m. at the Memorial Park Cemetery. Blustery north wind with a driving rain as we left Brenham Memorial. Came home. Made phone calls to everyone. Got photos together and spent most of the evening sending them via email to Wayne so he can use them in a powerpoint presentation during Dad's funeral. It is midnight and I am dog-tired. Blustery cold rain.

Dec. 8: Got Dad's suit, white shirt and tie ready and took to the funeral home. The wind was howling out of the north when I went outside. Bitter cold. Went to the Brenham Memorial funeral home and gave Dad's things to Wayne. He said I needed socks and under clothing for Dad. Went to Penny's and bought T-shirt, briefs, and socks. Took to Wayne. Called Sue Johnston to see if she would sing at Dad's funeral. She is going out of town this evening. She suggested I call Charles Otto. He was out of his office. Came home. I did not have time to winterize things before the cold blast from the north. Outside faucets are frozen. Called Charles Otto. He agreed to sing at Dad's funeral. Dad had requested "The Old Rugged Cross" and "How Great Thou Art." Called Rev. Calvin Beckendorf and told him Charles Otto would sing. Called Wayne and told him Charles would not need an accompanist. Called Ann to brief her. Had several emails and phone calls from Sam and Steve coordinating what it is they need at Smith-Kernke in OKC and the obituary for the Daily Oklahoman. The Flower Market from Brenham delivered a bouquet from Evann Sutton and David Riley. Pretty flowers for Dad. Too bad he can't see them. I will miss him. Pat made motel reservations in Oklahoma City for us and Ann and Fred. Emailed Dad's obituary to Sam and to Steve. Sent an email to Steve about Dad's story telling and the bear. Cloudy overcast all day. Blustery bitterly cold north wind all day.

Dec 9: A SAD DAY. WE HAD DAD's FUNERAL THIS MORNING. I'll miss him. We developed a unique relationship during his final months. We talked about a lot of things. Sometimes we just sat together and enjoyed the sunshine and fresh air. For some reason I always thought my father was invincible, that he would always be here. It was only the last few weeks that I came to realize that he would not always be here. Pat and I got ready and went to the Brenham Memorial Chapel. We were met by Wayne Roberson. The floral arrangement on Dad's casket looked very nice. Wayne let me preview the DVD program they put together on Dad's life with the photos I sent them. It was very nice and touching. Greg, Donna and Mary Grace came. Anns and Fred's family was represented by Kay, Julie and John with Savannah and the week old baby; Bonny and Angela, Xanthea, Zane and his new wife, Julie. Bob came over from Houston. Anns and Fred's friends and the minister from Yoakum attended. Pat Elliott, Charles and Joy Blake, James and Sharon Wehmeyer, Rhonda Wehmeyer, Mike and Joyce Brown, and Bill Keels, all friends of ours, attended. Ron and Barbara Pohlmeyer from Gazebo also attended. There were others I can't recall that were also there. Rev. Calvin Beckendorf delivered a nice service and Charles Otto sang "The Old Rugged Cross" and "How Great Thou Art" beautifully. The DVD pictorial presentation of Dad's life was beautifully done. All the family met at Casa Ole Restaurant for lunch afterwards. Pat and I went to the Banner-Press and got ten copies of yesterday's newspaper with

Dad's obituary in it. Greg, Donna and Mary Grace came to our house so they could change clothes and rest a little before they went to Lexington to see friends and witness the lighting of the town Christmas Tree. I napped a little. Went out and tried to start the pickup. Battery dead. Got my pills together to take with us tomorrow when we go to Oklahoma. Also, got my suit on a hanger and in the suit bag ready to go in the morning. We will leave as soon as we can and drive all the way to Oklahoma City tomorrow. Cloudy overcast all day. Off to Oklahoma in the morning to attend the graveside burial service for Dad. He will be buried next to Mom and with his Mother and Father.

APPENDIX 5
CLARKE ELEVEN GENERATIONS CHART

John Clarke, b. ca 1503, Westhorpe, Suffolk, England, d. March 3, 1559, Finningham, Suffolk, England, m. ca 1535, Suffolk, England, to Margaret ____ (?), b. ca 1515, Finningham, Suffolk, England, d. aft. 1565. Issue: John Clarke.

John Clarke, b. unk., d. April 4, 1598, Finningham, Suffolk, England, m. October 12, 1567, Westhorpe, Suffolk, England, to Katharine Cooke, b. unk., d. March 27, 1598, Finningham, Suffolk, England. Issue: Thomas Clarke.

Thomas Clarke, b. November 1, 1570, Westhorpe, Suffolk, England, d. July 29, 1627; m. May 13, 1600, Saxsted, Suffok, England, to Rose Kerrich, b. unk., d. September 19, 1627, Westhorpe, Suffolk, England. Issue: Joseph Clarke. (Rose Kerrich's parents were William Kerrich, b. ca 1540, Saxsted, Suffolk, England, d. March 30, 1593; Saxsted, Suffolk, England; and Margery ____ (?), b. ca 1545 Saxsted, Suffolk, England, d. April 23, 1610, Saxsted, Suffolk, England.)

Joseph Clarke, b. December 9, 1618, Westhorpe, Suffolk, England; d. June 1, 1694, Westerly, Rhode Island (USA); m. ____ (?). Issue two sons: Joseph Clarke, Jr., and Joshua Clarke. (2nd marriage: Margaret _____ (?), 1658, issue Sarah, January 29, 1663.) (Joseph's brother was Rev. Dr. John Clarke who with Roger Williams founded the colony of Rhode Island.)

Joseph Clarke, Jr., b. February 11, 1642, Newport, Rhode Island, d. January 11, 1726, Westerly, Rhode Island, m. November 16, 1664, Westerly, Rhode Island, to Bethiah Hubbard, b. December 19, 1646, Springdfield, Massachusetts, d. April 17, 1707, Newport, Rhode Island. Issue: Nine children. Seventh child was Thomas Clarke. (Joseph was one of the three first settlers of Westerly, Rhode Island, in 1661. He was one of the first of the Clarke Family to become identified with the Seventh Day Baptists. He transferred his membership from John Clarke's church to the Newport Seventh Day Baptist Church soon after its organization in 1671 where he served as clerk until the Westerly Church was organized in 1708. In this service he gave evidence of business ability and made his entries in a very legible hand. He was elected ten times to the Rhode Island Colonial Assembly. The church frequently sent him on missions to New London and elsewhere to visit and encourage other Seventh Day Baptists who lived at some distance from the home church.)

Thomas Clarke, Rev., b. March 17, 1686, Westerly, Rhode Island, d. November 26, 1767, Hopkinton, Rhode Island, m. 1710, Westerly, Rhode Island to Mary Elizabeth Babcock, b. Feb 18, 1691, probably Westerly, Rhode Island., d. unk. Issue: Five children. Third child was Joshua Clarke. (Will of Thomas Clarke of Westerly, dated August 10, 1766, proved January 25, 1768, at Westerly, Rhode Island. Mary Elizabeth was the daughter of Captain James Babcock and Elizabeth Saunders of Westerly, Rhode Island.)

Joshua Clarke, Rev., b. April 26, 1717, Westerly, Rhode Island; d. March 8, 1793 Westerly, Washington County, Rhode Island, m.1738, Rhode Island, to Hannah Cottrell, b, 1719 probably in Rhode Island, d. November 4, 1808. Issue: Eleven children. Eleventh child was Job Bennet Clarke. (Joshua Clarke was a Revolutionary Veteran #124809. In the early part of his life he was Justice of the Peace. He represented Westerly in the Colonial Legislature in 1753, 1754 and 1756. He was elected deacon of the Sabbatarian Church in 1756, but declined the office. He represented Hopkinton at its incorporation in 1757. He was one of the original incorporators of Brown University and a trustee. He was ordained an elder of what is now the First S.D.B. Church of Hopkinton in May 1768. The last twenty-five years of his life he was pastor of that church. He appears in the 1774 Census as resident of Hopkinton. He participated in the early colonial wars and also the Revolution. Will dated July 31, 1792, proved Hopkinton April 7, 1793, 3:20 Hopkinton vr. Washington County, RI.)

Job Bennet Clarke, b. May 13, 1765, d. 1860; m. January 1, 1787 to Mary Rogers Wells. Issue: Twelve children. Seventh child was Paul Rogers Clarke.

Paul Roger Clarke, b. August 7, 1802; d. 2 April 1877; m. December 29, 1827 to Polly Barton Rogers b. 1800; d. 30 July 1869. Issue: Eight children. Eighth child was Edmund Stillman Clarke.

Edmund Stillman Clarke, b. June 23, 1852, d. July. 27, 1930; m. August 12, 1876 to Arabella Taylor Champlain Stillman, b. August 2, 1852; d. July. 2 1934. Issue: Five children (2nd marriage). First child was Meta Pauline Clarke. (Arabella Taylor Champlain's parents were Charles Champlain, b. February 10, 1824; m. Hannah Maria Taylor June. 29, 1850. They had four children. The second child was Arabella Taylor Champlain. She first married Edmund Russell Stillman September. 15, 1870. They had two children. Edmund Russell Stillman was born April 6, 1828. He died an accidental death March 19,1876. Arabella then married Edmund Stillman Clarke. Edmund Russell Stillman and Edmund Stillman Clarke were first cousins.)

Meta Pauline Clarke, b. May 1, 1877; d. 6 July. 1970; m. January. 2, 1901 to Samuel Mordecai Davidson. Issue: Two children: William Edmund Davidson and Mary Arabella Davidson.

APPENDIX 6

ROLLER SIX GENERATIONS CHART

John (Johannes) Roller, b. 1725 Germany, d. 1816 Rockingham Co., VA; m. Anna Ocher/Archer b. 1730, d. 1786

Jacob Roller, b. 1763 VA, d. 1861 Scott Co., VA; m. Eve Zirkle, b. 1773 Shenandoah Co., VA, d. 1858 Scott Co., VA

Elias Roller, b. 1812, Lee Co., VA, d. 1887 Douglas Co., MO; m. Elizabeth Payne, b. 1817 Scott Co., VA, d.1882, Douglas Co., MO, Issue:

Enoch Roller and Margaret Johnson
Art Roller and unknown Stubbs
Henry Harrison Roller and Mary Ann Osborn
Harm Roller
Eve Roller and Antha Bunyard
Bill Roller
Jake Roller
Ebby Roller and John Osborn

Henry Harrison Roller, b. 1848 Hawkins Co., TN, d. 1915 Antioch, OK; m. Mary Ann Osborn, b. 1851 Virginia, d. 1935 Antioch, OK
Issue:

Willis H. Roller, m. Lizzie unknown

Cory Ellen Roller, m. Dennis Brown
John Alvin Roller, m. Lula unknown
Dillmus Elias Roller, m. Arlie Luvida Jones
Robert Etcyl Roller, m. Maud Luther
Lloyd Thomas Roller, m. Mattie Cooksey
George Walter Roller, m. Bessie Daniels
Lilley Azalea Roller, m. George Harrell
Donnel Otis Roller, m. Dovie Roberts
Claud Elmer Roller, m. Gertrude Smith

Dillmus Elias Roller. b. 1877 Douglas Co., MO, d. 1965 Maysville, OK; m. Arlie Luvida Jones, b. 1881 Parker Co., TX, d. 1961 Maysville, OK

Issue:

Loyce Elmer Roller, m. Jessie Mae Gardner
Mary Pauline Roller, m. William Edmund Davidson
Margaret Ellen Roller, m. James Thomas Weldon
Hazel Pearl Roller (never married)
Cora Jewel Roller, m. Thomas Gardner
Edna Blanche Roller, m. Walter Bryan Gardenhire
Emma Beatrice Roller, m. Walter Kent Riley
Henry Cornelous Roller, m. Katherine Blackwood
Naomi Elizabeth "Dixie" Roller, m. Edgar Huffman
Elsie Alice Roller, m. Ollie E. Runyon

Mary Pauline Roller, b. 1905 Antioch, OK, d. 1988 Brenham, TX; m.

William E. Davidson, b. 1901, Hardy, AR, d. 2005, Brenham, TX

Issue:

William Lee Davidson, m. Mary Elizabeth Grisham

Robert Joe Davidson, m. (1) Dorothy Jean White, (2) Bonnie Mae Craddock

Donald Gene Davidson, m. Patricia Sue Paschall

Ann Luvida Davidson, m. Carl Fredrick Melton

Samuel Marvin Davidson, m. Martha Rowena Vance

APPENDIX 7
EXCERPTS FROM HENRY HARRISON ROLLER LETTERS

The following was copied from "The Roller Family Papers, 1866 - 1871 (Part II)" by Dr. Mark C. Stauter:

In December 1868 General R. Johnson had just moved to Douglas County, Missouri, from Scott County, Virginia. He wrote to his mother, Sarah Bowen Johnson, that the trip took 32 days. He bought 160 acres of land, ". . . about half of hit perrerrey (prairie). . . me and Enoc Roller is a carren onn a steam distilrey." Pleased with the new land Johnson wrote, "Mother if yew will com out hear i wil giv yew a home on my land as long as yew live. . . yew may think hard of me for moveing off ann leaving yew behind but yew considder tha i hav a gang of little chilldren to tak ceare of and I think i have got in a cntery that I can take cear of them and hav them all a home besides."

In January 1869 Henry (Henry Harrison Roller) now situated in Douglas County wrote, ". . . general jonson has com. him ande Enoch.. James Bunyard has boughte the lead (?) still ande are making littil things hapen. . . this Country is a settel up a greate deal sinc laste fall and still a coming in." Still upset about their mother's estate, Henry wrote, ". . . she wants to no if that Bank nots has be come good yete or note. She donte much think thate her father wild her thate sothern money nor she dont think hite was righte to pute hite all off on her."

He concluded by once again entreating Jacob to return, claiming, ". . . this is the county for you for hit is free for all that wants." In an undated fragment of a letter Henry gave instructions on how to find their father"s farm, ". . . you can com to march field and from ther to Samuell Turners Store on Cow Skinn and father livs six miles South of that on Spring Creek."

In late spring James Bunyard wrote, ". . .lives is very good her. i am a miller in this sumer. i have bin holling from the railroad this spring. i will start to fort scot in the morn with a load of flour in cans." It was a good time for Bunyard to leave the county, for, ". . . i got in trubel with that old still. tha com and tuck me a prisoner. i got away from them. tha hant got me yet. i dont want them to git me. you bet i dont. they sold the old still. i bot it back. you bet. i was not at the sale. it brot 16 dollars. that was not much. if they will let me alone i will let them alone."

In July 1869 Henry again wrote, ". . . i am workin at the saw mill 13 miles from home. i am giting $262 Dollars per month. times is hard in this country at present. money scarse her. no sale for stock at present. prospect for crops is betar than they have bin sinc i hav bin to the stat. this country is fast improving up. in sixty six ther wer no over 500 inhabitanc an now there is the rise 5,000 at this time. ther hav bin a working on the railroad from the first of January 1869 from rolley to Springfield. the will hav hit compleet agains the first of march next. Springfield is as large again as hit were when you left her."

Jacob favored his Missouri relations with a letter in August, prompting a reply from Henry on September twentieth. He reported that, ". . . times is a good her among the peopl. ther ha bina big meeting a going on her last week. there has bin a grat many confessions mad." On an old and sore subject Henry wrote, ". . . mother said she wanted to now how much you had colected on her estat," and he passed along condolences to Andrew on the death of his wife. Then he added, ". . .a few line mor about that not (note) that Enoch has got on you." It seems Jacob had carelessly endorsed an I.O.U for a man called Faling, who lived up to his surname, and the note was now held by Jacob's brother, Enoch. This unfortunate circumstance did nothing to ease family tensions over monetary matters.

Henry wrote to Jacob again in April 1870. He described conditions as, ". . . hard her. eve thing scerse." Salt by the barrel had fallen to four dollars, coffee was four pounds to the dollar, shoes two dollars a pair, and shirting 12.5 to 18 cents per yard. He predicted, ". . . eve thing will soon com down mor. now the cars is a running from Rolla to Springfield. now hit will go on to fort Scott. ther is a nother road vewed out from memphis Tennisee threw this co to ozark and from ther to Springfield an from ther to cansas sity. ther has bin one rought viewed in six miles of her. ther ar surviying the roads and at work on boath ends of the road. Ther has bin so many new comers her hit has mad provisions scerse." In October Henry wrote again to report, ". . . no money in sirculation in this part. Crops light of all kinds. Ther is a heap of wheat sowing in part." Henry told Jacob that James Bunyard had bought Jacob's note from Enoch, and that Jacob's assets left behind in Missouri, most particularly his horses and cattle, were still in good hands. "This co is fat (fast) settling up. all the valuabel land is taken up. Ther is stil talk of the ralil road threw this Co. Ther is a right smart excitement a bout the election and politik, but that is comon. This Co by majority is Radical."

In Henry's next letter, dated May seventh 1871, he reported that, ". . .the country has improved more in the last 2 years than all the balanc sinc i com her. We hav a nic Sabbath School a going on her in hour destrict and a ever day school. Ther is a good many mills and machinery coming in the co. I hav quit work at the saw mills." Henry also wrote that he, ". . . had giv you out bringing me that Tennisee girl, but think i hav found me one that suit me bettar. I am maried to a girl by the name of Mary A. Osborn. her parants is both living. they are nise respctful popel. They came from Georga sinc the War. her father is a mishionary Babtic Preacher and a good mill wright." Jacob's mother added a page to the letter expressing her concern about the spiritual health of the family, ". . . i want you to write to me how you ar all getting along with yore Christain and church bisness, whether you hav any good meeteings or not. yore Paw has entirely quit tending church. he takes no entrust in going or trying to get his childrin to go. thar is non of the children liveing in the Church. i am the only won of the famly that has there name on the church book."

> Henry wrote again in August 1871, noting, ". . .time is hard in this part. The thrash machine is in this neighborhood now. The people ar improving all they can and ther ar just a compleeting the cort house and ther ar a building several store houses ande other machinery at the County Seat. At this fall ther will open puple roads threw the county seat is about 8 miles north of me. there is a post office [Forfest Store] in 5 hundred yards of me just opend. We hav a three month free school started the 7th of this month and a Sunday schol ever Sunday and preeching there twis time a month. i think the people has set the resolution to be somebody & to school ther children after so long a Strugill. ther is som horse steeling parts of this county & theavs her. ther ar tryin to rue the Bibel out of schols. som thinks that will be hour next fight. This Co holds to the Republican ticket. there is a right smart toung clashing in the nuse pape. the rebels will hang to the Democratick."
>
> The last dated letter in the collection was written by Henry on October first 1871. "I have bad nuse to you. Elias is ded." Elias was Henry's and Jacob's eighteen year old brother. "He had the infamation of the boweels & bladder. he was in his wright mind all the time and a whil before he dide he said he was willing to dye. his funeral will be preched this day week." Elizabeth's estate remained uncollected, and "father & mother says they want your & ther business to come to a settelment. So I will close. wright soon & a littel oftener."

Henry Roller eventually left Missouri in 1892 and was living in Indian Territory. He died in 1915 and is buried in Antioch Cemetery in Garvin County, Oklahoma. Mary Ann died in 1937. She is buried in Antioch Cemetery next to Henry. Jacob Roller remained in Virginia. At the time of his death, in 1934, it was accepted that he was over 100 years old, but Census Records and Civil War pension applications suggest he was only 95. He is buried beside his wife in back of the family homestead overlooking the Clinch River in Scott County, Virginia.

APPENDIX 8

ROLLER ANCESTORS

Johannes Roller was born in Germany. He arrived in Philadelphia August 11, 1750. He came on the ship, Patience, Hugh Steele, Captain from Rotterdam, last from Cowes. He was a soldier in the Revolutionary Army from Virginia. He married Anna Ocher/Archer. He was married three times and fathered sixteen children. His will was signed 6 June 1806 and admitted to probate April 1816 in Rockingham County, Virginia.

Jacob Roller was born ca 1762-63 in Rockingham County, Virginia. He was the first born child of Johannes and Anna Roller. He married Eve Zirkle 20 March 1791 in Rockingham County, Virginia. Eve was the daughter of Lewis (Loudowick) and Mary Magdalene Roush Zirkle. Jacob and Eve later lived in Lee County, Virginia, in that part that later became Scott County when it was formed in 1814. Scott County borders Hancock County, Tennessee. Here they lived, raised their family, died and are buried there in the family cemetery. Eve died 21 April 1858. Jacob died December 1860 or January 1861 as his estate was entered into probate 21 January 1861 in Scott County. He died intestate and there were nine children living at the time of his death.

Elias Roller was born 12 September 1812 in Lee County, Virginia. He died 3 March 1887 in Douglas County, Missouri. He is buried with his wife, Elizabeth, and son, Elias, in Walnut Grove Cemetery near Rome, Douglas County, Missouri. He married

Elizabeth Payne about 1831. She was the daughter of Enoch and Sarah (England) Payne. They all lived near each other in Scott County, Virginia, and Hancock County, Tennessee.

The Englands owned England Valley, Enoch Payne owned land in Scott County and Hancock County. The old log house where Elias and Elizabeth first lived is still standing. The log house was built in two parts connected by a 'dog-trot' (breezeway). They slept in one side and the kitchen and dining were in the other sidet. The state line runs through the 'dog-trot.' They always joked that they slept in Tennessee and had breakfast in Virginia.

The house the Paynes lived in is still lived in. The state marker between Virginia and Tennessee is in the yard. Elias and Elizabeth with their children and their families, except for Andrew, migrated from Virginia in 1859 to Christian County, Missouri, near Ozark and Linden, but by 1870 they had moved to Douglas County, Missouri, and settled along Spring Creek near Smallette southeast of Ava. Elias was called "Grey Dad." Elizabeth was almost blind from having had scarlet fever but she functioned very well and was a mid-wife. These people were "mountain people" and their speech and writing shows that; however, they were very savvy in business affairs.

Henry Harrison Roller was born January 1848 in Hancock County, Tennessee. He was the seventh born child of Elias and Elizabeth (Payne) Roller. He married Mary Ann Osborn 15 January 1870 in Douglas County, Missouri. She was the daughter of Etcyl and Cyntha (Nelson) Osborn. Henry died 17 October 1915 at Antioch, Garvin County, Oklahoma, and is buried in the Antioch Cemetery. Mary Ann died 5 May 1935 near Antioch and is buried next to Henry. In 1892 Henry and Mary Ann with their ten children left Douglas County, Missouri, and moved to Indian Territory near what is now Byars in southeast McClain County, Oklahoma. Their eleventh and youngest child, Claude, was born September 1893 in Indian Territory. Henry's grave marker is a Woodsman of the World headstone. He probably held some political office in Douglas County.

Dillmus "Dill" Elias Roller was born 15 October 1877 in Douglas County, Missouri. He was the third born child of Henry and Elizabeth Roller. He married Arlie Luvida Jones 10 February 1901 at Old Johnsonville in Indian Territory near what is now Byars in southeast McClain County, Oklahoma. Arlie was the daughter of Cornelous Coats (C.C. "Trick") and Sarah Luganie (Jones) Jones. Dillmus died 28 December 1965 at Maysville, Garvin County, Oklahoma. Arlie died 14 October 1961 at Maysville. They are buried together in the Antioch Cemetery. Dillmus and Arlie had ten children, two sons and eight daughters. They are: Loyce Elmer, Mary Pauline, Margaret Ellen, Hazel Pearl, Cora Jewel, Edna Blanche, Emma Beatrice, Henry Cornelous, Naomi Elizabeth ("Dixie"), and Elsie Alice Two years after marriage Dillmus and Arlie moved to a farm near Antioch on Rush Creek in Garvin County. They later moved to two different farms on Panther Creek in western Garvin County. The last place was on the upper reaches of Panther Creek near the foot of The Table Hills where they lived until they retired in 1942 and moved to Maysville, Oklahoma.

Mary Pauline Roller was born 1 March 1905 near Antioch in Indian Territory in what is now Garvin County, Oklahoma. She was the second born child and oldest daughter of Dillmus Elias and Arlie Luvida (Jones) Roller. She married William "Bill" Edmund Davidson 8 May 1925 at Pauls Valley, Garvin County, Oklahoma. Bill was the son of Samuel Mordecai and Meta Pauline (Clarke) Davidson. Bill and Pauline had five children. They are: William Lee, Robert Joe, Donald Gene, Meta Luvida "Ann", and Samuel Marvin. Pauline died 25 December 1988 at Brenham, Washington County, Texas. She is buried at Memorial Park Cemetery, Section 12, Lot 114, Space 2, in Edmond, Oklahoma County, Oklahoma. Bill died 7 December 2005 in Brenham, Washington County, Texas. He is buried next to Pauline.

Pauline grew up on the farm on Panther Creek in western Garvin County. She attended grade school at Bell School in Garvin County and attended Edmond Normal School, Edmond, Oklahoma. She taught elementary grades at Parks School in Garvin County. She worked as a sewing machine operator during World War II, cafeteria worker, and ladies apparel saleslady. She was a devout member of the Methodist Church most of her life. She was a member of the Methodist Women's Service Organization, and a member of the League of Women Voters.

APPENDIX 9

DEBT OF THANKS

There are several people to whom I owe a great debt of thanks for the development of my life and character.

MOM was a considerable influence. Though she had two older boys she spent many hours with me as I helped her with household chores which I mostly resented. However, during these times she taught me how to do many things to be self-sufficient. She taught me to have a healthy respect for hard work. She taught me to honor the goodness in people. She listened to my many tales of woe and consoled me.

GRANDMA ROLLER was a kindly woman. She too spent many hours with me. She taught me how to do many different things. We talked endlessly while shelling peas or snapping beans. She encouraged me to read. We spent many hours reading to each other. She was a great storyteller. I loved her stories. She was part Cherokee. She had that Indian serenity of peace with her surroundings.

MRS. KENDELL, my second grade teacher at Linwood, was a sweet loving kindly grandmotherly woman. She reminded me a lot of my Grandmother Roller. For whatever reason I will never know she took it on herself to make sure I learned to read and read well. She kept me after school each day for about an hour. Just the two of us. I remember sitting in the little chairs in the classroom and Mrs Kendall sitting in her chair right next to me as she had me read aloud to her. I became a very good reader.

MRS. VARNDELL was my fourth grade teacher at Moore. She was strict but in a kind and understanding way. She insisted that I read and read and read. She insisted that I comprehend what I read. I had to make book reports for her.

MR. and MRS. CHARLES F. YOUNG were Buford's parents. They 'adopted' me as the brother Buford did not have. Buford was the 'brother' I wished I had. They took me into their home on many occasions. They took me many places with Buford. They showed me that peace, harmony and kindness can be a meaningful part of family life.

MISS RUTH WOMACK was my sixth grade teacher at Moore. She let me freely expand my thoughts to greater heights. She let me soar like an eagle but always brought me gently back to earth. She taught me logic and reason, and how to diagram sentences with the various parts of speech.

COACH LEO HIGBIE was my football coach at Classen High School. He taught me the rewards of hard work. He taught me discipline and team effort. He was a strict taskmaster and insisted I be my very best, yet in the moment of my greatest disappointment after we lost in the state play-offs he showed me compassion and comfort. I visited him years later when he was a frail ninety-year old man. I told him he was "tough but fair." He said that was the greatest complement he could have, that he was fair.

PROFESSOR BAUGH was my economics professor at Oklahoma A&M. I took several of his classes. He, too, was a taskmaster, yet he was a very good teacher. He knew how to make the complex simplistic and understandable. He taught me there is more to life than "guns and butter" to quote Samuelson. He taught me to seek the true underlying causes that influence a given situation. He taught me the value of evaluation.

PROFESSOR VIVIAN LOCKE was my speech and drama teacher at Oklahoma A&M. She was a very interesting person. She spoke fluent French and served on General Eisenhower's staff during WW II. She taught me the value of being a good speaker. She insisted that I properly pronounce and enunciate words, and learn to speak without all the "uhs." Her principles of speech, which I have always remembered, were: "Be prepared. Be prompt. Be concise. Be brief. And, for goodness sake. Be seated."

MILTON "Mick" CANNON was a co-worker when we lived in Salt Lake City. He is a Mormon. We had an excellent relationship. I learned the true value of good wholesome male companionship. We hunted and fished on the Upper Weber River in the Western Uinta Mountains where his family owned property. We talked about many things religious, philosophical, sociological, and political. He helped me to see the world in a more meaningful light with a tolerance and respect for other viewpoints.

JACK DREESSEN. No particular reason. He has just been a long-time true and loyal friend from my childhood days at Moore. I have to tell this little story. Jack had recently retired as President of the First National Bank of Moore. He had a keen interest in the preservation of the old Moore School Building. Our Fourth Grade room had been restored the way it was when we were kids. When I was about sixty-eight years old I visited the room. Jack was acting as my docent. I saw a goodly number of the names of some of our classmates posted on a bulletin board. I didn't see my name. I asked Jack how come my name wasn't on the list. Jack said, "Because you're not qualified." I said, "What do you mean? I'm just as qualified as any of them." Jack smiled slyly and said, "No, not yet. That is the list of our classmates that have died." Yiiipes!! Talk about egg on my face!

PATRICIA. And, finally, my wife. She worked hard to help us have a good life together. She worked to help put me through college. She has always been very supportive of all my endeavors. She has been more often than not tolerant of my misgivings for which I am eternally thankful. She surely must love me to put up with so much of my nonsense.

INDEX

C

D

P

S

T

U

XYZ

PATNDON 7 @ATT.Net

grandranch.blogspot.com

Davidsonbio.com

2252807

Made in the USA